THE HANDBOOK OF

Dream Analysis

by

EMIL A. GUTHEIL, M.D.

Director of Education, Postgraduate Center for Phychotherapy; Author of *Psychotherapy for the General Practitioner* and *The Language of the Dream;* Editor-in-chief of the *American Journal of Psychotherapy;* Diplomate, American Board of Neurology and Psychiatry.

LIVERIGHT

NEW YORK

ISBN 0 87140 019 7 **Paper Edition**
ISBN 0 87140 920 8 **Cloth Edition**

MOTTO

Night is the true democracy. When day
Like some great monarch with his train has passed,
In regal pomp and splendor to the last,
The stars troop forth along the Milky Way,
A jostling crowd, in radiant disarray,
On heaven's broad boulevard in pageants vast.
And things of earth, the hunted and outcast,
Come from their haunts and hiding places; yea,
Even from the nooks and crannies of the mind
Visions uncouth and vagrant fancies start,
And specters of dead joy, that shun the light,
And impotent regrets and terrors blind,
Each one, in form grotesque, playing its part
In the fantastic Mardi Gras of Night.

— EDWARD J. WHEELER

TABLE OF CONTENTS

LIST OF ILLUSTRATIONS

Chapter One

DREAM ELEMENTS

A dream is an intermediary product of the thinking process. It is a phenomenon occurring at the threshold of consciousness in the process of awakening or falling asleep. It appears when the lights of consciousness are dimmed or when they are in the process of flickering up and it is characteristic of this state of mind.

Dreams reflect intra-psychic processes, which are ever-recurrent in each individual. The study of dreams is the study of the devious trails over which unconscious human instincts[1] often with clandestine bearing, come to a rendezvous with the waking thoughts on the borders of consciousness. They come like the Osirian legend laden with all the truths of the past, present, and future, but they vanish before the cock's crow of our consciousness, or, rather, they change their appearance. But they are real and their messages are real. With adequate investigation we can understand them.

To make the concepts of "conscious" and "unconscious" clear, and to introduce the basic terminology of psychoanalysis which will be employed throughout this book, we shall discuss briefly what Freud calls the "Anatomy of the Mental Personality."

[1] For definitions of technical and psychological terms see the glossary.

Through careful studies of post-hypnotic behavior, dreams, slips of memory and action, and some types of hysterical reactions, Freud proved that our mental life extends beyond the borders of consciousness. His work in this sphere is one of the milestones of psychology and is the foundation of psychoanalysis. He called that part of our mental life of which we are unaware, the *unconscious*. He observed that the unconscious possesses dynamic qualities and exerts influence upon the other "strata" of personality, the *conscious* and the intermediate stratum, the *preconscious*.

Unconscious material is barred from consciousness when it is not needed or is unacceptable. Dream analysis offers a way to penetrate into the unconscious and to discover the forces that are opposing the acceptance of the unconscious material. Part of the material had once been conscious, but it has been repressed. Other parts have never been conscious.

It is primarily from the study of repressed material that psychoanalysts have obtained their knowledge of the dynamics of the unconscious. The influence of the unconscious on psyche and soma is stronger than that exerted by the conscious.

As early as 1892, Breuer and Freud discovered that hysterical symptoms are products of unconscious memories, of experiences which were repressed from consciousness. Later, particularly under the influence of his studies of dreams, Freud concluded that the unconscious harbors infantile instinctual material with all its inherent amorality.

The "layer" of our mind which we described as being located between the unconscious and the conscious is called the preconscious. It contains material which, while not a constant part of our conscious, can be rendered conscious by an act of our will. It is capable of becoming conscious (*"bewusstseinsfähig"*) as it is not kept down by repressing forces. It can also be lifted by associations. Parts of the preconscious material which are more closely connected with the unconscious than with the conscious are the more difficult to lift.

Freud also found that the preconscious harbors censoring forces which act as a protective and regulative authority. The censorship determines which parts of the unconscious material are acceptable to the conscious and which parts are to be rejected.

It was predominantly in connection with the investigation of the repressing forces that Freud was able to formulate his "Anatomy of the Mental Personality" which is, in effect, the Anatomy of the Ego.

According to Freud, our mental personality can be divided into two parts, one of which functions under the observation of the other. He called the observing and criticizing part of our personality, the *superego*. The latter takes over functions originally fulfilled by our parents. It is as though parental influence had been assimilated and incorporated so as to become an integral part of our personality.

One of the main tasks of the superego is that of upholding of ideals which education, custom and morals have set before us. It is for the sake of these ideals that most of our primordial cravings have to be sacrificed ("repressed"). Freud calls that part of our mental personality which harbors all primitive cravings and instincts, the *id*.[1] It contains all the energy we have inherited from our ancestors by way of our constitution.

Rooted in man's somatic organization, the id expresses itself mentally as the quest for absolute and total gratification, a trend not without danger to the individual and the world in which he lives. And so the id's dynamic expressions are forced to undergo a gradual but steady modification which continues as long as the individual maintains his contact with

[1] The originator of this name is Nietzsche. The psychoanalyst George Groddeck, author of *The Book on the Id*, introduced this term into psychoanalysis, and Freud adopted it.

the outside world. That part of the id which is exposed to the influence of the outside world adapts gradually to it and ultimately becomes what is known as the *ego*. Its relation to the id then corresponds to the relation of the external, cortical part of an organ to its internal or medullary part. The cortical layer of the organ is endowed with specially structured cells designed, on the one hand, to protect the interior of the organ from external stimuli, and on the other, to mediate the external world to the organ's interior. Similar is the double task which the ego has to accomplish when it gradually develops into an intermediary between the id and the external world.

The ego controls all voluntary motion through sensory perception and muscular action. By its sensory organs it mediates perception of stimuli coming from outside and from inside and stores these stimuli as memories. It can perform its task of self-preservation more efficiently by utilizing these accumulations of memory and by modifying both the impact coming from external sources and the pressure for instinct gratification stemming from the id. The latter can be gratified, attenuated, shifted from their original goals to others, or suppressed altogether.

The ego's two main goals are "pursuit of pleasure" and "avoidance of displeasure." The ego learns to anticipate displeasure by the reactions of anxiety.

In its task of self-preservation, the ego has to withstand three types of pressure that lead to the development of anxiety: (1) the pressure of the *outer world* with all its demands for adaptation; (2) the pressure of the *id* which craves gratification regardless of the conditions of reality; and (3) the pressure of the *superego* which forces the ego to comply with moral codes, tribal and group precepts, and demands curtailment or suppression of all that does not conform to the accepted ideals. The individual's feelings of inferiority and of guilt are the morbid products of this influence.

The following sketch will illustrate the conditions described.

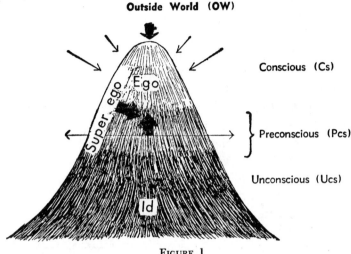

FIGURE 1

On this sketch we see that the id reaches into an impenetrable depth of mental life. It reminds one of an iceberg whose peak is clearly visible while its lower part is obscure. On our sketch we also see the id exposed to the influences of the outer world (OW) to which it has to adapt. We notice that the transition from the id to the ego proper is indistinct and that there is an area of overlapping. The preconscious (Pcs) is thought to be located in that area. The sketch makes clear our supposition that, on the one hand, parts of the ego are beyond the realm of consciousness (Cs), and on the other, parts of the id extend beyond the boundaries of the unconscious (Ucs). The superego is not entirely conscious either; parts of it represent an unconscious factor which can be termed "unconscious morals." The illustration graphically explains why it would be incorrect to identify "ego" with "consciousness" and "id" with "unconscious."

In this work we are using the word "unconscious" in a somewhat inexact way, inasmuch as we consider it to be that part of the intellectual and emotional material of which we are not aware and which exerts a dynamic pressure to be admitted to awareness. It is much more part of the preconscious than of the unconscious; the latter, like the blackest sea, buries an as yet unpenetrated, and perhaps impenetrable realm.[1]

When Jung, e.g., speaks of the "collective unconscious," he refers to deep layers of the preconscious of the human mind in which all humanity participates. The awakening consciousness appears to duplicate the awakening of humanity's thought. At the dawn of human "cerebration" the human mind passed through a stage of development similar to that found in the awakening of the sleeping ego. Some of the characteristics of this stage of awakening of the human mind are detectable today in the images of our dreams, in religious concepts, in myths and legends which hark back to mankind's infancy. Ontogenesis here, too, repeats phylogenesis.

THE MATERIAL

> *Science is nothing more or less than a well-tested method. If one follows this method, the results may be regarded as scientific.*
>
> ISRAEL WECHSLER
> *("The Neurologist's Point of View")*

Dream interpretation is based on psychoanalytic findings and is, as a rule, used in conjunction with the psychoanalytic method.

Psychoanalysis as an interpretative procedure attempts to bridge the gaps of knowledge we encounter when dealing with phenomena that are inaccessible to direct observation and objective scrutiny. Here lies its strength and its weakness. However, this is also true of all psychology, a realm so replete with "symbols of human agreement" (Korzybski). Its most elementary and basic concepts are vague, the very object of its research is obscure. What is Psyche? What is Thought? What is the *reality* behind all these accepted linguistic constructs?

---

[1] Rado uses the term of "non-reporting level" for experiences which are not lucid enough for us to be aware of them. Froeschels uses the term "not speech-ripe".

In the field of dream interpretation we are confronted with still another difficulty. Most of the material with which we are dealing is derived not from objective observation and experiment but from the subject's self-observation and self-evaluation. To make matters worse, the dreamer himself must completely rely on his faculties of recollection which are limited and often defective. If he is honest and sincere, this impediment is not too weighty and, besides, we are compensated by the "first-hand experience" for any loss of recalled substance.

However, between experience and recollection there is always a gap which, in most cases, is filled by a certain amount of confabulation and secondary elaboration. Fortunately, we are able to observe some of the rules of the distortion which takes place in the process of recalling. Thus the scientific value of the procedure is not curtailed too much. Careful self-observations conducted by scientists of high moral integrity (including Freud, himself) have provided us with additional data and copious confirmations of our patient's reports so that in many areas of our research valid generalization can be established.

Day Residues

> *You eat, in dreams, the custard of the day.*
>
> Alexander Pope
> (*"The Dunciad"*)

Our dream life is, in the main, autonomic. Most dream material is selected from recent experiences, but the experiences influence the dream plot only to the degree that they cause in it an echo of deep-seated personal complexes.

Real experiences are only the frame, the occasion, for the expression of conflicts which have long existed in our mind. If someone attends the opera *Carmen*, and on the following night dreams of the performance, the dream is not a simple repetition of the drama; its emotional content is personal and is inspired by specific associations precipitated by the opera.

Only some of the impressions of recent events such as unfulfilled desires and incompletely repressed thoughts enter the dream. These "day residues," as Freud termed them, are handled in various ways. Some remain in the preconscious until they are discharged in daydreams as moods, symptoms, symptomatic acts, or otherwise. Or they may combine, and be seen in the dream in distorted form: important facts may be mixed with unimportant ones; psychic accents may be displaced, material from infancy may be associated with material from recent times and may further distort and disguise the dream.

The following is a dream of a physician in training for psychoanalysis. It runs as follows:

[1] *"I see a large truck. I go up to it to get a ride somewhere. The wife and little girl of the driver are sitting in the front seat, so there is no room for a hitch-hiker, so I decide to walk."*

The doctor was treating a very attractive married woman, mother of a little girl. In one of her sessions, the patient described to her doctor her family life and complained about her husband's lack of understanding for her child. While listening to the woman's story, the doctor permitted himself to indulge, for a passing moment, in a little daydream of his own in which he [1a] *saw himself as the patient's husband.* He showed her that he could be a better father to the little girl, than her real father.

At this point the doctor realized that "counter-transference" had carried him too far and he stopped this "unprofessional" trend of thought. The sexual daydream then vanished from his conscious awareness, but it remained in the fringes of his consciousness, sufficiently active and expansive to form the nucleus of the dream. Its latent content represents the warning: "Don't meddle in a married woman's affairs; there is no room for a hitch-hiker on your patient's family truck."

This case confirms the findings of Freud and the tachystoscopic experiments made by Pötzl that it is primarily the "unfinished business" of the day (day residues), the peripheral impressions, the events taking place in the fringes of our visual fields, that are used as building material for the dream plot. (See page 68.)

When Do We Dream

No satisfactory answer as to *the time of the dream appearance* has yet been found. Some investigators believe that we dream during all the time that we are asleep, but there is no reliable proof for this postulate. We can suppose rather

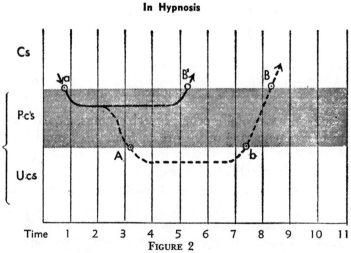

In Hypnosis

FIGURE 2

The "Partial Sleep" in Hypnosis (a-B'). Can turn into real sleep (a-A-b-B).

that dreams occur each time we are awakening, when our mind is passing from unconsciousness (as maintained in sleep) into consciousness and this transition finds itself on a preconscious level. This can be substantiated particularly in dreams influenced by external stimuli, noises and odors, for example, which initiate the awakening. (Fig. 9, p. 34.)

Since the dream is experienced on a level of thinking on which the thought processes take place not in words but in images, the dream may last an unimaginably short time,

In Somnambulism

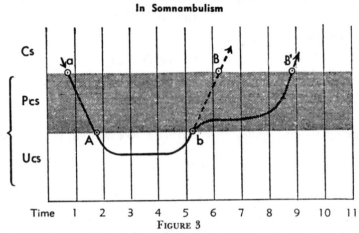

FIGURE 3

Incomplete and Delayed Awakening in Somnambulism. (Instead b-B, we find b-B'). The subject is fully asleep between A and b.

even though it contains events covering hours, days, and even years. The rendering of the dream from this figurative state into the state of a logical conscious thought, as is done when we attempt to recollect the dream, takes time.

Somnambulic actions, such as walking or talking in one's sleep, are not dreams in the strict sense of the word. They are actions performed in a "hyponoic" condition and are comparable to states of hypnosis and to epileptic and other deliriums. (See Figs. 2 and 3, and the text on pp. 333 and 385.)

Maury's famous report on one of his own dreams may serve as evidence of the speed with which dream pictures are perceived:

[2] *He dreamed about the horrors of the French Revolution. He witnessed a large number of terrible scenes of murder and then found himself in front of the revolutionary*

tribunal. He saw Robespierre, Marat, Fouquier-Tinville, and other despots; he answered their questions; and finally, after all kinds of adventures, he was sentenced to death. He was led to the place of execution while large crowds followed. When he arrived at the guillotine he was tied to a board, pushed under the suspended blade and beheaded. As he felt his head being chopped off, he awoke in panic.

He found that the top bar of his bed had fallen on his neck in a manner similar to the fall of a guillotine blade in the act of decapitation. All the colorful and exciting events of this dream were nothing other than the fantastic elaboration of the physical irritation caused by the blow of the bar, and were produced and perceived at the moment when Maury was struck.

The next dream is a similar example from our own collection. A twenty-five-year-old woman employed in a factory had serious conflicts emanating from her relationship with her manager, a middle-aged man, whose offensive advances she dared not openly repulse for fear of losing her job. One day as she was lying on the couch in her home listening to her sister read, she dozed off for only a moment during which she had the following dream:

[3] *"It was three o'clock. A girl came to me in my office and told me that the manager was locked up in his room upstairs and was going to commit suicide. I ran upstairs and begged him to open the door. The man answered: 'I'm sorry, but I am going to shoot myself at three-thirty.' Highly terrified I watched the minute hand of the clock turning. As I saw the time coming nearer and nearer, my fear turned into despair. Finally, I heard the detonation of a shot and knew it was all over."*

She awoke with a scream as the book which had fallen from her sister's hands thudded against the floor. While the entire dream lasted but a split second, the dream content spread over a period of half an hour (from three o'clock to three-thirty).

There is no doubt that this dream was precipitated by the noise. We cannot assume that an originally indifferent dream content was deflected into a suicide episode because of the auditory impression created by the noise of the falling book. The idea of suicide had dominated the dream from the onset.

It is necessary to emphasize that this finding does not explain the dream. It merely indicates the conditions under which the dream originated. Dreams have contents which are closely related to the dreamer's personal problems. They express these problems in a specific way no matter what external or internal stimuli may have given rise to the dreams. In dream [3] the patient attempts to solve her personal conflict. By the death of her chief she is made free. Her unsuccessful attempt to save the man is a hypocritical effort to placate her superego.

Summarizing, we may say that the duration of a dream is dependent on the condition of the ego and not on the question of whether or not we are asleep. If a functioning ego exists during sleep, it has not been detected. Jung maintains that such proof is provided by the fact that the human race has dreamed certain dreams since time immemorial. In my opinion, Jung owes proof that it is the unconscious of a sleeping ego and not the preconscious of the awakening ego where the buried treasures of the collective human psyche are to be detected.

The Purpose of Dreaming

> Freud regards dreaming as fiction that helps us to sleep; thinking we may regard as fiction that helps us to live. Man lives by imagination.
>
> HAVELOCK ELLIS
> ("Dance of Life")

As everything in our biological experience has a purpose, so does the dream. In fact, it has three main purposes: (A) protection of the sleep, (B) regulation of the affect metabolism, and (C) protection of the integrity of the ego.

THE DREAM IS THE GUARDIAN OF THE SLEEP

Dreams have the function of protecting our sleep. External and internal stimulation, which normally would cause us to awaken, give rise to dreams which stave off complete awakening, even if only for a short time. Freud considered this as the foremost function of dreams.

In the chapter on "Physical Conditions" (page 70), and elsewhere in this book, a large number of dreams are quoted in which this characteristic can be observed. However, it has also been emphasized repeatedly that a number of other concurrent functions of the dream must be taken into consideration to do justice to the polymorphous structure of the dream.

THE DREAM REGULATES THE AFFECT METABOLISM

(a) Because dreams are *discharging emotional energy,* they are relieving emotional pressure. If we feel like attacking our adversaries, we may refrain from taking the action because we might expose ourselves to the danger of injury or destruction. But, in dreams, we can discharge these emotions without risking these dangers.

During the day we are exposed to various internal and external pressures, coming from our instinctual life and from the outside world. We also endure various physiologic stimuli, reactions and conditions which exist, or take place, within ourselves. Because of the manifold changes of emotional tension to which we are subjected, changes which may be gradual, prolonged, or sudden, we would undoubtedly suffer mental or physical harm if we did not have, in the dream, a regulator and a safety valve which helps us to maintain emotional equilibrium. In this respect, the process of dreaming is comparable to the processes of thermo-regulation of our body.

(b) *The dream can prevent shocks* which might injure our ego. Certain events and experiences which could seriously upset us if they occurred suddenly (death of a beloved person, etc.) are weakened and attenuated by their repeated appearance in dreams. If a girl has a strong fixation to her father and dreams that he has died, she experiences the

FIGURE 4
DREAM OF THE DOCTOR
Engraved by Albert Dürer (1596). Courtesy
of the Metropolitan Museum of Art, New
York.

An elderly man (doctor?) enjoys a comfortable nap while a demon instills licentious wishes into his mind. A nude woman appears and points deprecatingly toward the stove, as though she wished to demonstrate that there are other—and better—ways of warming one's blood than the use of the old stove.

Meanwhile, little Cupid gets ready for an enjoyable play on stilts.

This drawing has been interpreted by art critics in many ways. To this author it appears most probable that it represents a wish-fulfillment.

whole range of emotion, anxiety, excitement, worry, grief, as if the scene were real. In this way she gradually becomes immunized, as it were, for the actual death experience. Ultimately, she will accept the experience of losing her father.

(c) *Dreams also serve as warnings.* One dream may say, "Be careful, you are not fully prepared for the test" (cf. page 46); the other may convey the warning, "Control yourself when dealing with strange women or you'll lose your wife and your children."

Of a more serious character are dream warnings generated by physiological stimuli indicating that the dreamer's health is in jeopardy (see page 74). They impel awakening so that the physical danger can be eliminated.

(d) *The dream fulfills wishes.* One of the first discoveries of Freud was that the dream fulfills our wishes. He had the impression that *all* dreams were wish-fulfillments. Later, he and others found that other tendencies also are gratified in the dream. In general, we call the material containing the tabooed, the repressed, the thwarted tendencies, "catagogic." (The Greek prefix *cata* means "downward.") Incestuous cravings, criminal, tabooed homosexual cravings, and similar tendencies belong to the catagogic material. *Anagogic* tendencies, on the other hand, are those which lead "upward," toward the high, the sublime, the ideal. Both tendencies can be found in dreams. Jung has devoted a great deal of his study to the problem of anagogic dreams. A "catagogic" type of dream is portrayed by Fig. 4.

How often in the dream "wish is father to the thought," poets and philosophers of all times know well. Interesting in this respect is the following little story about Nasr-ed-din, the famous Turkish poet and wit, told by Müllendorf:

When Nasr-ed-din was five or six years old, he once approached his father and said:

"Father, last night I dreamed of wonderful cookies."

His father replied:

"My son, this dream has a good meaning. If you give me 10 paras (small coin) I shall interpret the dream for you."

Whereupon the boy exclaimed:

"Do you think I would be *dreaming* of cookies if I had 10 paras?"

THE DREAM OFFERS SOLUTIONS TO OUR PROBLEMS

A series of dreams may present many solutions—not all very realistic—for the same problem. In one dream, a marriage problem may be solved by the death of the wife; in another dream, the patient may not be married at all; in a third dream, he is married to another woman, etc. (A good example of this type can be found on page 271.)

Some famous scientists have found the solutions to their problems in their dreams. The story of Kekulé, the inventor of the graphic representation of the benzene ring, is well-known. After many years of fruitless attempts to express the

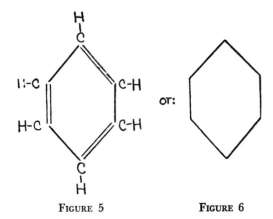

FIGURE 5   FIGURE 6

specific configuration of atoms in a graphic formula, he dreamed of a snake biting its own tail. (See page 127.) He awakened and drew the formula on paper.[1] (Figs. 5 and 6.)

[1] A benzene molecule (trimethyl-benzene) can be seen by the new electronic microscope which enlarges an object to one hundred million times its size. A photo made by Dr. Maurice L. Huggins of the Eastman Kodak Research Laboratories reveals exactly the structure foreseen in a dream by the German scientist, Kekulé, seventy years ago. (According to *Time*, of January 22, 1945.)

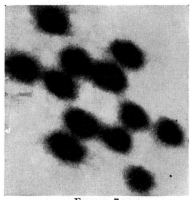

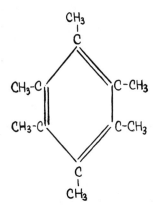

FIGURE 7
Dr. Huggins' miscroscopic photo of Trimethyl Benzene (Only the C-atoms showed on this photo. The H-atoms are invisible).

FIGURE 8
Trimethyl Benzene

Kekulé's vision of the benzene ring has been called "the most brilliant piece of prediction to be found in the whole range of organic chemistry." Kekulé wrote about his dream as follows: "One of the snakes seized its own tail and the image whirled scornfully before my eyes. As though from a flash of lightning I awoke . . . occupied the rest of the night working out the consequences of the hypothesis."

Playwrights may sometimes find in their dreams important dramatic solutions. Composers may visualize pictures of fugues which failed to materialize in their conscious work. Hermann Swoboda tells a story of a mathematician who once had to solve a difficult algebraic problem. Month after month he tried without success to find the desired solution. He had many dreams in which he saw himself working at this problem. In the course of years he entirely forgot this mathematical problem. Seven years later he dreamed once again of working on the problem and, behold! he visualized with perfect clarity the long-desired result.

Tartini who was laboring at the composition of his sonata fell asleep, exhausted, and had a dream [4] in which *he saw the devil playing the sonata* which had been giving him so much difficulty. He awoke and reproduced what the devil had played for him in the dream. This is the famous "Sonata with the Devil's Trill."

THE DREAM PROTECTS THE INTEGRITY OF THE EGO

When we are falling asleep, our mind passes from the state of consciousness through the layer of preconsciousness and into unconsciousness. During this evolution we produce rudimentary, immature, and archaic forms of thinking which have been recorded. We observe similar thought formations also when, in the process of awakening, our mind passes from the unconsciousness to consciousness. In the preconscious layer we are capable of producing thoughts of a special type which we discussed before (page 26).

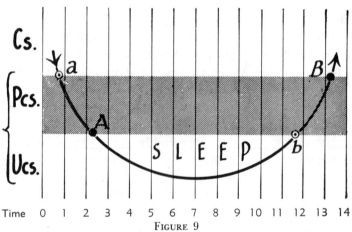

FIGURE 9

A = Onset of sleep; B = Moment of complete awakening
a-A = Falling asleep; b-B = Awakening

In falling asleep the individual's relation toward the outside world disintegrates and so does his ego. Only a few published papers refer to the psychodynamics of this phase. The available sources (Silberer, Federn, Jekels, Froeschels, Isakower), all attest to the fact that the ego "fades out" after passing through several stages, some of which resemble those found in amnesic aphasia and in schizophrenia. As is well-known, the end-of-the-world fantasy, in particular, has been connected with the process of ego disintegration (Freud, Schilder, Kurt Schneider and others).

As an individual gets drowsy, he finds it increasingly difficult to retain contact with his own self and to cope adequately with the outside world. Thinking becomes burdensome; action becomes impossible. Thoughts, at this point, appear to replace actions.

Jekels thinks that the loss of ego feeling may be experienced by the individual as dying. Jekels sees no reason to shrink from identifying the pattern of sleep and wakefulness "with the pattern of almost incomprehensible cosmic processes which produced life out of lifeless matter."

Jekels, unlike Freud, believes that he did not learn of the nature of sleep through his studies of dreams but from studies of individuals who, although awake, are found in various states of ego disintegration. He refers here specifically to the fact that during sleep the autistic retreat from the outside world is the same as that found prevalent in schizophrenia.

Loomis, Harvey, and Hobart, basing their theory on an extensive study of electroencephalograms, describe five stages called A, B, C, D, and E, of brain activity which occur as a cycle during the interval between falling asleep and awakening. The EEG demonstrates this impressively (Fig. 10).

Sleep deprives the individual of the feeling of being "himself," of being different from everybody else. In sleep, Kronfeld says, "the ego sinks to the stage of the id." Jekels supports this concept. He reminds us of the close relation between the concepts of sleep and death in Greek mythology. Hermes is the representative of sleep and dream as well as of quick death. He is lover of Persephone, the nether world's bringer of slow death. From Homer to Grimm, sleep and death have been considered as closely related—and, often, as twin

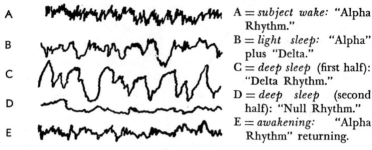

A = *subject wake:* "Alpha Rhythm."

B = *light sleep:* "Alpha" plus "Delta."

C = *deep sleep* (first half): "Delta Rhythm."

D = *deep sleep* (second half): "Null Rhythm."

E = *awakening:* "Alpha Rhythm" returning.

FIGURE 10

brothers.

In senile individuals, in conditions of abnormal fatigue, and in some cases of brain injuries, there is a resemblance to the phenomena manifested by the ego as it disintegrates in the normal process of going to sleep. Thoughts, formation of concepts, ability to unify concepts with higher concepts, and speech are involved. With the gradual depletion of sources of energy, various phenomena of lowered function appear such as automatisms, perseverations, and recrudescence of concepts with antithetic meanings. The ability of abstract conceptual thinking is impaired, and with it, there is a growing tendency for thinking in concrete forms. Stereotypes of all kinds appear.

The more the conscious thought disintegrates, the more images come to the front and become experiences. All these "primitivisms" of thinking are carried into the dream formation.

It is at this stage that thought processes undergo a change. A shift takes place from one conceptual sphere to another; from the general to the specific. Two objects become identical. And it is at this point that "symbolization" occurs.

Jung points out that the tendency to fuse perceived objects increases as our power of apperception decreases. Whenever the lucidity of our perceptions is lowered, the differences between the individual objects become indistinct, and "condensations" occur more easily. In this connection Freud speaks of images which appear "overdetermined." (More about this on p. 111.)

The shifts in ideas stem from the individual's changed attitude toward the outer world. The low integration of the dream processes accounts for the low critical analysis of the dream events and persons. This is also the reason for a general decline of surprise and shame reactions which make unexpected situations appear as everyday experiences, e.g., walking in the nude, etc. Since the highest critical levels connected with analyzing, interpreting, and inhibiting the incoming (afferent) stimuli are the first to be affected in the process of falling asleep, the censorship is reduced and uncritical attitudes increase.

Hartmann emphasizes the *creative potential of our unconscious.* He calls the consciousness a denying, criticizing, contrasting, correcting, measuring force which is never creatively productive and never inventive. He thinks that for creativity man is entirely dependent on the unconscious.

The process of awakening is the reverse of that of falling asleep. In a way resembling the restitution of aphasias, the ego is reconstructed. As the ego-consciousness is restored, the ego is coordinated with the outside world and with itself.

The awakening—apart from the fact that it is regulated by the sleep center—is prepared by some physiological processes. The distention of a urine-filled bladder, the hunger contractions of an empty stomach, the increase of noises, the rise in the body temperature, the retinal reactions to increased influx of light stimulation—all these factors contribute to the conditioning of the cortex for the task of adaptation to the wakeful life.

In awakening, the ego, which has been prepared by the dream to accept reality, rallies to establish normal relations with the outside world. It enters these relations as a well-adjusted agent. The dream has conditioned the ego for such a function by hallucinating a functioning, adaptable, and efficient ego.

The dream protects the ego by preventing sudden changes in object and subject cathexes; it thus preserves the continuity, cohesion, and unity of our mental processes.

As we see, the dream is a function of the ego. We have reason to assume (Federn) that the ego does not exist during sleep. I should be inclined to deny any function of an ego which does not exist.

In deep sleep we are unconscious. There is no ego, no thought, no dream. In awakening, we are at first not fully conscious, but the conscious is flickering up gradually. The ego is awakening. And it is then that the thought-dream is awakening; at first, passing through a pre-logical archaic layer, and then becoming more conscious and recallable. The closer to awakening a dream is perceived, the less distorted is its content.

Various attempts have been made to explore thought activities which allegedly take place during deep sleep. Some workers employed hypnosis; others roused the patient several times at night asking him each time what he was dreaming. However, experiments of this type prove nothing. Hypnosis does not penetrate deeper than the preconscious, i.e., it does not reach the layer characteristic for the state of sleep, and in the other experiment, each time the patient awakens, his thought process runs its usual course and his dreams represent products of the preconscious. (See Fig. 2, p. 25.)

From the above material we may assume that consciousness is but a quantitative factor. Instead of asking whether or not an individual is conscious, we should ask, "How conscious is he?" In other words, we are interested in the degree of lucidity of consciousness, a figure which varies between zero (as maintained during sleep) and much higher values (as maintained in the preconscious and conscious states). A lowering of lucidity can be noticed particularly often in states of depression. When reality becomes unpleasant the individual shows an increased tendency to withdraw from it, to be "less conscious of it," and to regress to primitive forms of thinking (daydreams, repetitive thoughts, etc.).

During the moments of falling asleep and of awakening, the dream forestalls a sudden disintegration of the ego and facilitates its restitution. This function of the ego is particularly important as all rapid transitions entail a danger of a sudden flush of panic and of shock to the individual. We see similar explosions of anxiety in connection with other sudden losses of ego cathexis, as, e.g., in depersonalization (see page 422).

The study of the dream gives us information not only concerning the processes that go on between conscious and unconscious, but also casts a light on a number of other psychological phenomena taking place in the borderlands. I am referring to the so-called *hyponoic* conditions. Hyponoic is a condition of lowered lucidity, of lowered acuity of consciousness. It comprises states such as found in amnesia or in somnambulism. In investigating amnesias, fugues, and somnambulic conditions, dream research offers us an instrument to penetrate into the sphere of lowered lucidity.

(Q) "You have stated that we dream while we are going to sleep and while we are awakening. But from the body of the material you have presented so far one would gather that we recall only those dreams which we have while awakening. Is this so? And if it is, why?"

(A) It is true that we have presented here almost exclusively dreams produced on awakening. The reason for so doing is that dreams occurring in the phase of falling asleep are more likely to be forgotten, since a phase of total unconsciousness follows their appearance. Some material from this segment has been collected under the name of "hypnagogic hallucinations," i.e., hallucinations preceding the total dissolution of the ego. (See page 34.) But the vast majority of images used in dream research are derived from that phase of the preconscious which is followed by the complete lucidity of wakefulness.

INTELLECT AND DREAMS

> *Whatever theory you adopt, whatever vain efforts you make to prove that your memory moves your brain, and that your brain moves your soul, you must admit that all your ideas come to you in sleep, independently of you, and in spite of you.*
>
> VOLTAIRE
> *Dictionnaire Philosophique*
> ("*Somnambuler et Songer*")

The content of the dream corresponds to the mentality of the dreamer. Simple people have simple dreams. However, the intellect affects only the external form, the environmental trappings; the substance of the dream which lies within it like the seed in a fruit is not affected at all. If you compare dreams of olden times with those of our time, you will note that the basic problems have remained the same, although objects pictured are often peculiar to the immediate environment. The automobile, the radio, the airplane, the television set, and all the new inventions have come into dreams of mankind as they have into the hallucinations and delusions of psychotics. New political parties and recent scientific movements have also become the building material for the dream world of modern man. But the nature of man's dreams has not changed.

One of my patients, a mason, expressed his sexual difficulties by dreaming [5] that *he had to wind up a hanging scaffold and found it very heavy.* A physician, an X-ray specialist, expressed a similar conflict by dreaming of [6] *exhausted X-ray tubes.* We see that both patients speak about the same problem (impotence), using different language. But it is the nucleus of the dream that matters.

EMOTIONS IN THE DREAM

> *Believe me, man's truest fancy is revealed in his dream.*
> RICHARD WAGNER
> (*H.* Sachs in "*Die Meistersinger*")

Stekel said, "The dream is not a play of thought, but a struggle of affects." And Havelock Ellis has maintained that "sleep is especially favorable to the production of emotion because, while it allows a considerable amount of activity to sensory processes, and a very wide freedom to the imagery founded on sensory activities, it largely, and in many directions, inhibits motor activity." The action suggested by sensory excitation cannot, therefore, be carried out. As soon as the impulse enters motor channels it is impeded, broken up, and scattered in a vain struggle for expression. This process is transmitted to the brain as a wave of emotion. According to Ellis, the thwarted motor discharges account for the affect tone of the dream.

THE INTENSITY OF EMOTIONS

In general, for purposes of interpretation, the emotions displayed in the dream are its most reliable elements. The emotion usually corresponds to the latent, but not always to the manifest content of the dream. The secret censorship which brings the antimoral and antisocial segments of the dream into consciousness in a more or less disfigured state proceeds to exert influence even in the dream's emotional phases. We have to face the fact that all psychic values in dreams are re-evaluated (Freud). The intensity of the single elements and pictures is not indicative of the true importance of the elements of the dream material. Sometimes the most intensive dream qualities may be found in dream pictures which are lacking in tone.

Freud stated that, in general, dreams are less emotional than the incidents (the psychic material) which gave rise to them. In presenting the dream events, we are exposed to various contradictory psychic forces, impulses and counter-impulses, which thwart and partly extinguish each other.

Sometimes emotions appear to be absent altogether, as in the following case of a clerk, aged twenty-eight, who complained of a complete lack of emotion and a pronounced apathy.

Contrary to his conscious state of mind, this patient offers dreams full of activity, dreams carrying strong emotions. This is to be expected. The reason for the apparent lack of emotion lies in the fact that the patient's emotions are strongly antisocial in their character. It was his sibling rivalry, his intolerance toward some members of his family, along with his emotional fixation to his family, which gave rise to the symptom of an apparent emotionlessness.

Here are some fragments from his dreams:

[7] *"I was in the playground of the school to which I went when I was a small boy. My brother Danny was the pilot of an airplane and refused to take me up for a ride. I was very angry."*

[8] *"My father shot himself."*

[9] *"There were many wild bulls running loose. . . . One bull was shot, but the shot did not kill him."*

[10] *"I was working with my sister Ann on some job, and she bossed and domineered me, and unfairly took most of the money that we got."*

[11] *"I was at a party with a girl who in the course of the dream turned out to be my sister, Bessie. I kissed her—a long, sweet kiss that felt very pleasant, although I expected no passion."* (Inhibition because of the incest!)

In dream [7] the patient shows his sibling rivalry. He was angry at his brother. His hostility toward his father is shown in dream number [8], a wish-fulfillment dream. The "bulls" in dream [9] symbolize the patient's impulses; "shooting" represents his criminal and suicidal tendencies. In dream [10] the patient behaves as though his sister Ann had taken advantage of him. His fear of women is shown by the "domineering" woman. Dream [11] expresses his sister fixation. We understand the patient's sensation of emotional dullness. He is repressing criminal tendencies, incestuous desires, and other specific antimoral and antisocial emotions, and the sum total of these repressions is a virtual emotional apathy. We found through the study of his dreams that beneath the schizophrenic-like callousness of this neurotic man surged a storm of emotion.

This was one of those cases where the necessity of repressing one particular emotion (murder impulse toward his brother) led to repression of all emotion.

With the aid of his dreams, the individual determining factors of his illness were elicited to make the picture complete. His father had been an invalid confined to a wheel chair. The patient, as a boy, had been disciplined by his older brother (who acted upon the orders of his father) with thoroughness, with the inexorable vigor of a pet bulldog. The boy would try to hide under chairs and tables, but he would be dragged forth and the punishment meted out without mercy. The boy consciously swore that when he grew up he would take revenge on his brother. Indeed, this desire for revenge, this stubborn conviction that he would and must account for each wrong inflicted upon him, played a great part in his daydreams. He indulged in fantasies in which he employed cruel violence against his enemy. But when he grew up he did not carry out his plans. Nothing happened, except a gradual and general diminishing of emotional responses. All potential aggression seemed to seep into the patient's unconscious.

Now let us look at his dream material. In one dream [7] he says, "I was in a playground." That is, he was in the past. "I went to school as a small boy. My brother was an airplane pilot, and when he refused to take me up for a ride I was very angry." The words "very angry" are an understatement. Their meaning becomes clear when we consider the revenge fantasies which the patient reported in analysis. He remembered that at first these fantasies had been concerned with his brother, and that later they became concerned with anonymous people; for example, a large group of individuals whom he would attempt to kill with a machine gun. His fantasies had become generalized; the original target was more and more disguised.

"My father shot himself." This phrase from the patient's dream is a clear wish-fulfillment. The father is on the same emotional level as the brother who was the father's deputy.

"One bull was shot, but the shot did not kill him." We may presume that still another shot will have to be fired to finish the pending business of his past. In analysis the patient was able to recognize that he was constantly toying with the idea of killing his brother (the "bully").

Dreams of impulsive and temperamental people sometimes show a striking lack of emotional coloring. This is usually caused by the patient's tendency to conceal his real personality. In such dreams, nothing happens and nobody experiences any sensation. Closer analysis is able, in most cases, to bring the hidden emotions to the surface. Here are some examples of colorless dreams:

[12] *"In the streetcar I meet my friend Charlie."*

[13] *"I see a long row of pine trees."*

[14] *"The doctor says, 'That's appendicitis.' He tells me about the necessity of an operation."*

[15] *"I dreamed of the work of enzymes and the saponification of fats by $NaHCO_2$ and the bile acids."*

Dreams of this sort are also had by people who are completely ruled by their intellect, who make believe that they do not love and do not hate, who know everything, who understand everything, who are experts in psychology, and, who are, alas, neurotics. Their dreams are purely intellectual constructions and disguise the true personality just as the sophisticated cleverness of these people disguises their real self in everyday life. Dreams of this type are difficult to interpret.

The following are a few dreams of a doctor; they are strikingly monotonous:

[16] *"Talking about cases to one or two of my colleagues."*

"Talking" was the most frequent happening in his dreams. But in some, he reduced the entire dream plot to one or two sentences containing an observation:

[17] *"I walked into church. My wife sat in the pew behind me."*

[18] *"Met Dr. F. on the street. Talked to him for a while."*

This patient was suffering from claustrophobia. He was afraid to go to church because there he felt hemmed in. He also suffered from inferiority feelings. He compared himself with his fellow physicians and was inclined to consider them superior in skill and training. Often, he became anxious when he was to report a case at a clinical conference or to talk to a group of people.

The patient led a "double life"; he had a mistress and a wife. To be "found out" had a double meaning.

"Talking to colleagues," in the above dream, was wish-fulfillment; it showed the patient as the equal of his colleagues.

In dream [17] in which his wife sits behind him, he is, of course, under her scrutiny and cannot engage in illicit interests.

The information revealed by these dreams is scant and has to be augmented by the patient's conscious revelations.

In 1899, Freud published his *Interpretation of Dreams* which, to a large extent, is based on self-analysis. He stated that it took him a full year to break down his resistance to publication of the material. His feelings about this reluctance were expressed in a dream which, strange as it may seem, carried no appreciable affect:

[19] *Freud saw himself having the task of dissecting his own pelvis and was aware of the absence of the awe that should be commensurate to the situation.*

The lack of affect was explained by Freud in the following way: The dissection represented his auto-analysis. His wish to be indifferent to the printing of the intimate material expressed itself as absence of awe.

EMOTIONAL ECONOMY

As stated on page 29, dreams serve as emotional valves when they anticipate and reduce the impact of shocking experiences. Emotions which we discharge within the dream are real and are not different from those of wakeful reality. A person who has dreamed repeatedly, or even once, of a tragedy that later does actually occur, has lowered the intensity of his emotional reaction to the anticipated tragedy.

This is an important function of the dream: affect economy. Guilt feelings, however, sometimes come from this influence of the dream on our real life.

The dreamer who experiences in his dream the death of a beloved person may blame himself both for having had a dream of this kind and for not having been sufficiently grieved on this occasion.

As emotional valves, dreams also permit us to express our urges and desires, even those which are morally and socially prohibited. The dreamer can commit adultery, destroy his mate, his siblings, his children—any or all without responsibility to his conscience or to society. He can remove competitors and scale the highest peaks of success.

WARNING

In this connection we must also consider the phenomenon of the warning dream, mentioned on page 31. When we dream that our automobile has crashed against a truck, we are likely to drive more carefully thereafter just as though we had really had an accident. A mother who dreams that, because of her neglect, her child had a bone-breaking fall is prone to exercise better attention to her youngster after this dream.

ANXIETY IN DREAMS

The primitive quality of the neurotic's emotional experience is particularly obvious in his unconscious belief in the omnipotence of his thought and in his readiness to confuse reality with fancy. The dream shows us these and other expressions of the neurotic psyche and informs us also of the extent of the patient's emotional regression.

In the dream, some pairs of contradictory emotions seem to have a fixed relation to each other in accordance with the principle of bipolarity. We shall discuss this principle later. *Desire and fear, love and hate* are such units. K. Abel emphasized that the oldest languages, for instance, Old Egyptian or Old Aramaic, had expressions such as "strong-weak," "far-near," "clean-unclean," "to bind-dissolve," etc. And Freud spoke of "the contradictory meaning of primal words" (*Gegensinn der Urworte*).

One of Freud's first discoveries concerned with analytical dream interpretation was that *anxiety,* as symptom or as dream reaction, may represent a precipitation of a repressed, tabooed, libidinous *desire.* As soon as this desire seriously endangers our peace of mind, logical thinking tends to be swamped with emotion. Anxiety is the endopsychic perception of this danger.

A Yugoslavian lady suffering from agoraphobia had the following stereotyped dream:

[20] She saw *a soldier standing in front of the window and shooting his gun through the pane at her.* Each time she awoke with excitement and fear. One of her symptoms was that she could not stay at home alone. The only person whose presence was sufficient to give her complete mental peace was her husband, particularly if he held her hand.

A careful analysis elicited the fact that this woman's agoraphobia started a short time after the following incident: she was walking on the street of her home town when she suddenly saw a detachment of soldiers. She recognized the lieutenant as her cousin whom she had not seen for fifteen years. It was during the time of military maneuvers, and during the operations her cousin's detachment passed through town. The patient was joyfully surprised to see her relative. When he called to her that he would not be able to visit her because of his orders, she was severely disappointed. She had a spell of physical weakness and almost fainted.

This account indicated the advisability of studying the patient's relation toward her cousin. The investigation uncovered the fact that this relative was the first man with whom the patient had been intimate. She was sixteen at that time. We found that her frigidity which prevailed during her married life was associated with this early sexual experience.

The dream is a symbolic reproduction of the sexual relation with the cousin. To understand this dream we must know that a "gun" is a common symbol for the male organ (see page 136), and that a "window" is a common symbol for the female organ (see page 149).

And now let us consider the emotion of fear in this dream. Is the fear a real one? If we view the manifest dream content, we find the fear of a gun credible. But what about the fear of the male organ? We see in this fear a defense reaction of a woman who wants to remain a morally firm and faithful wife. She is frightened by the unconscious immoral impulse. Sexual desires, unsatisfied in her marriage, make her revive the only pleasant sexual experience she ever had. Year after year she had unconsciously waited for her first lover to come and rescue her from her emotional frustration. And then, when she suddenly saw him, the accumulated and once-more thwarted desire threatened to overwhelm her; she almost fainted. Soon she began to develop symptoms of agoraphobia, a condition which protected her from leaving her husband to join her first lover. We can understand the "therapeutic effect" she derived from holding hands with her husband when she displayed anxiety. In this close contact with her lawfully wedded mate, she received added protection and was better able to maintain her mental equilibrium.

In some dreams fear has roots other than those of repressed sexual desires. *Fear of death* and *fear of one's own criminal tendencies* are observed often also.

In general, we can say: *the most reliable part of the dream content is the emotion contained therein.*

(a) If a dreamer expresses disgust or fear of a certain thing, and if this emotion has no understandable (manifest) reason in the dream, then we may postulate that the thing in question symbolizes something else which *is* capable of creating this reaction in our patient.

(b) If, in the dream, we are not afraid of, or disgusted by a thing which usually does cause such a negative reaction, we may postulate that the object in question is a *symbol* of something else.

HYPOCRISY IN DREAMS

In addition to these rules, we have to consider the possibility of a *distortion of affects* in the dream, the dreamer's unconscious hypocrisy.

A frigid woman dreams [21] that *she has intercourse with her husband and experiences a strong orgasm.* She wakes up with a numbed head, has neuralgic pains, and walks all day in a sort of daze. This dream contains hypocrisy. Stekel states that if a frigid woman dreams of an orgasm obtained with her husband, then the husband of the dream stands for another person whom she wishes to be her husband. The patient's reaction after she experienced her dream expresses her inner disappointment rather than her sexual gratification. We can explain this as the somatic expression of her conscience reaction which has been caused by the act of infidelity in the dream.

If a man who has an attitude of rivalry toward his brother dreams that his brother has obtained success and that he is glad about it; or if a husband who exhibits neurotic symptoms as a result of repressed death wishes toward his wife, dreams of her death and adds that he is deeply grieved by it, we may assume that these dream reactions are hypocritical and may be able to confirm this view by other dreams and other analytic material.

EMOTIONS OFTEN APPEAR DISPLACED IN THE DREAM

A man whose hatred against his father was evidenced by several dreams, came to the analytic session one day with the following dream:

[22] *"Our neighbor was ill. I wanted to call a doctor, but he objected. His son said, 'If he should die, my only joy in life would be gone.'"*

The patient suffered from depressions. The dream was interpreted as a wish by the patient ("neighbor's son") that his father ("neighbor") should die. (In the dream, the neighbor refused to see a doctor.) The patient's joy in life is "gone," even in reality. Through his depressions the patient anticipates atonement for the wished-for and expected death of his father. The depression here is a "rehearsal reaction"; the patient rehearses an attitude of mourning.

Another hypocritical dream of a patient who is strongly attached to his family and finds difficulty in mixing with girls is the following:

[23] *"I say to a girl, 'Now we are through with our relatives.' I kiss her passionately."*

In reality, the patient's difficulties stem from his failure to be "through" with his relatives.

Dreams show us both sides of a mental conflict, the id and the superego, from either side of which the emotion may be derived.

Sometimes the dream informs us of the true emotional state of the patient who complains of guilt feelings, and we may find that the patient's reaction is altogether displaced. The following analysis will demonstrate this point.

A thirty-year-old engineer, suffering from depressions, anxiety and hypochondriacal ideas, reports that in his opinion his whole trouble is due to the fact that a few years ago he had broken off relationship with a divorced woman. The thought of this woman—let us call her Mrs. Black—is now a kind of obsession. Our patient is engaged to a girl named Elsa, but he thinks incessantly of Mrs. Black. When he walks down the street he seems to recognize Mrs. Black in many women. When he reads the newspaper, his eyes are always in search of the name "Black." Day and night he must fight down the idea of visiting Mrs. Black in her home. His main self-reproach is, "I shouldn't have broken with Mrs. Black."

If our patient is still so much in love with Mrs. Black, why did he stop seeing her? On closer study the following was brought to the surface: Mrs. Black was schizophrenic. Our patient had wanted to end his relationship with her for a long time. There were many reasons for this. He was a Catholic and she was a Protestant. She was older than he. She was a homely woman, and the patient was so conscious of this fact that when he was out with her he tried to avoid main boulevards so that few people would see him with her. And yet he claimed that it was his feeling of guilt that was driving him toward getting in touch with her. He doubted that he would ever be happy in a marriage to Elsa.

"Didn't you tell me that the woman is a psychotic?" he was asked during analysis. "How can you think of marrying a woman who is in such a condition?"

"I know all that," he replied. "Nevertheless, the idea persists that she needs me, and that God will punish me because I deserted her."

The patient, whose illness prevented him from working and who, therefore, always stayed at home with his mother, was upsetting his whole family by his self-accusations. In his hypochondriacal ideas, he revealed many features which he described as similar to the symptoms shown by his former sweetheart. He was generally inclined, as is common with patients of this type, to assume all the symptoms he had ever heard mentioned (will to illness), and the problem for the analyst was to determine what the real reason was for the patient's self-punishing tendency.

The obvious nonsense in the patient's interpretation of his feeling of guilt toward Mrs. Black made us suspect that the real cause lay in another direction. Dreams served as a source of information and means of control. The first dream seemed very insignificant.

[24] *"I saw a man in my bed."*

As you see, this dream is distinguished by its remarkable

brevity. But if we simplify it, we can extract the following fruitful idea: "Somebody took my place." Or perhaps: "Another man took my place." We examined this problem and discovered that the patient was in general an extremely jealous person. But the analysis made no further progress until subsequent dreams gave more productive material:

[25] *"I dreamed that I became emaciated, that I shrunk away until I was nothing but bones."*

[26] *"I dreamed that I was crazy."*

[27] *"I dreamed that I wanted to have intercourse with a lady in whose apartment I have been sleeping for the past week. In this dream I had an emission. I had this dream, or one similar to it, two or three times."*

The patient, in associating to his first dream, said that someone had told him that insane people "shrink away to bones." Hence this dream was, as was the next, a picture of insanity. It must be emphasized that the main fear of our patient was that he might become insane. Such a fear has nothing in common with actual insanity. It is merely the result of the patient's perception that he is harboring some unusual idea which he considers "insane." The next deduction of the patient is that if one has "insane" ideas, one must be insane.

The third dream brought us the explanation for the patient's "insane" thoughts. The lady in whose apartment he had been sleeping for the past week lived in the apartment below that of the patient's mother. The lady who let him use her apartment was an elderly woman, mother of many children, a familiar "mother image." (See page 133.) The intercourse he had in his dream was, therefore, incestuous.

As the analysis turned in this direction, we discovered facts which gave us a proper explanation of the patient's feeling of guilt. The interpretation of the last-quoted dream broke through the wall of the neurosis and uncovered the real feeling of guilt. The patient related that a short time after his father's death, his mother began an affair with a man named Charles. When the patient first discovered this relationship he was so shocked that he thought of committing suicide. He had always been his mother's favorite child, jealous of his other brothers. Now, seeing another man enter his mother's life (the man in the patient's bed in the first dream), his despair was boundless. Thenceforth, he would sit near his mother and watch her. His attitude toward her changed entirely. He was embittered, irritated, and "grouchy," yet he never directly reproached her. Unconsciously, he considered himself the guardian of the honor of the family. He confessed to me that the man, Charles, played an important part in his daydreams, and whenever he happened to see him on the street he immediately became excited and filled with criminal intentions against the violator of the peace and honor of his family.

But, most important, these disturbances took place a few weeks before our patient first met Mrs. Black. In answer to my question as to his feelings at that time, the patient replied, "My mother's affair was a terrible insult to me. I thought if she could do a thing like that, I was justified in going with Mrs. Black. *I should never have begun going with this woman had I not been so embittered by my mother's behavior. . . .* I first met Mrs. Black in a restaurant. I should never have taken my meals in a restaurant if my mother had been at home."

The patient's "love" for Mrs. Black was nothing but revenge and defiance against his mother. His feeling toward Mrs. Black was not one of guilt, but it was an expression of his inner conviction that because of his infantile fixation he could not offer love to any woman but his mother. This was his "insane" idea.

The conflict of this patient would never have been resolved had not his first two dreams led our analysis in the right direction, namely, the patient's attitude toward his mother. In our investigation we refused to pay much attention to the "problem" of Mrs. Black, which the patient again and again attempted to present as his main conflict. We were faced with the problem of the patient's mother, and the patient's shattered ideals of womanhood and love. In analysis we did our best to convince the patient that it was time to detach himself from his mother, to give up his infantile love for her, and to adopt a more mature and responsible pattern of living, no matter how his relatives might act.

WISH-FULFILLMENT

> *I dreamt that I dwelt in marble halls*
> *With vassals and serfs at my side.*
> ALFRED BUNN
> ("*The Bohemian Girl*")

There is an enormous amount of material to prove Freud's statement that dreams contain a fulfillment of the dreamer's repressed (unconscious) wishes.

A wish is expressed openly or appears in the language of symbols in which, as stated before, the emotions may be changed, displaced, or transfigured. Almost all dreams quoted in this book contain wish-fulfillment with regard to various phases of human life—sex, will-to-power, all sorts of antimoral and antisocial impulses. The wish-fulfillment idea may also concern itself with the innumerable little commonplace details of our daily life, such as the desire to take a trip, to satisfy hunger, thirst, and to eliminate our many routine frustrations. In our dream we may indulge in taking petty revenge, attracting attention, and the like.[1]

Special attention should be given to dreams in which the fulfillment of a wish is supported by the so-called "coefficient of reality." The dreamer offers himself a sort of alibi for his wish by granting to himself—in the dream—another wish which is equally difficult to attain. He thus creates a precedent in his favor.

A thirty-two-year-old business man who was going through a severe spell of depression worried about his future reputa-

[1] It is necessary to emphasize here that the dream is not the only way the unconscious expresses its wishes.

tion among his business friends and creditors. He was afraid that they might lose confidence in him and consider him insane, mentally defective, or the like. Toward the end of his depressive period his dreams began to show more optimistic trends, and one of them sounded highly encouraging:

[28] *"A young man, named Herman, had one leg amputated. (He is all right in reality.) I asked him how this had happened to him, and he told me that it was amputated because he used to knock playfully on his thigh with his key ring. I left then with my friend Sidney and said, 'It requires great courage to live in a condition like that! He must be happy that he at least has a job. What would he do if he should lose his job?' Sidney said, 'With all his gifts he could easily find another job.'"*

This dream is in its core greatly consoling. It says that if it is possible for a man with an amputated leg, a cripple, to go on and to "make good," it will also be possible for *him* to succeed.

Several other ideas expressed in the dream contribute to the patient's satisfaction. One of his business competitors has the habit of hitting a thigh with a key ring. In the dream, this habit leads to an appalling denouement. If we consider the person of Herman in the dream as a substitute for the dreamer, the habit described above suggests a masturbation complex. The amputated leg would then suggest an undesirable consequence of the habit (castration fear). In his dream, the patient consoles himself also in this respect: "Even if I have damaged myself, don't worry, everything will be all right again."

PAIN

Let us now present a dream in which the patient remarks on the absence of pain and thus shows that the pain-instigating phenomenon has a symbolic meaning to him.

[29] *"I stamp out a fire in a paper box. Then, I notice that several of my toes are anesthesized, and I break off the*

first phalanx with my fingers. My family is present, but they do not pay attention to this. I wonder how this could happen when I did not feel myself being burned at all."

The patient was about to break off his relationship with a girl because his parents disapproved of her. He had to "stamp out a fire," in a metaphorical sense. In his dream he reproaches his family ("they do not pay attention") for their lack of understanding of the sacrifice (breaking off toes) he is making for their sake. His symptoms for a long time were emotional dullness and general lack of initiative. They resulted from his suppression of an emotional fixation to his family. When he had made an attempt to free himself from this attachment (by falling in love with the girl) it was his family who interfered. Thus he was thrown back into his infantile position and had to deal with his fixation again. He suppressed all emotional responses, and the result was his apathy.

ANGER

The emotion of anger in the dream usually corresponds to the dreamer's real attitude. In some dreams, however, as in the following, the real emotion is not anger but its opposite. The patient is *angry at himself* that he cannot overcome an infantile attitude.

[30] *"I give a young girl a thousand dollars. My father takes the money for himself and, in addition, accuses my girl of having stolen it from me. I get into a violent rage and knock my father down."*

At the time of this dream, the patient had but recently partially overcome symptoms of self-consciousness and had made an attempt to enter upon an affair with a girl. In the dream, his father seems to interfere with his affair, while in reality the father does not know the girl at all.

Interpreting the large amount of money as "love" we find, without difficulty, the patient's fixation toward his father in the picture of the father appropriating the money which was destined for the girl. The father takes the love which the patient had ready for a girl. The patient seems to feel his emotional dependence on his father, and he tries to free himself by developing a violent hatred against him, as if he were to say, "It is your fault that I have remained infantile and am not able to offer love to a real object. *I hate you because I feel compelled to love you even if it means my ruin.*"

The mechanism we see here is important and makes understandable not only dream reactions but also some of the impulsive criminal acts, such as killing a beloved person (Wertham). We call this process *transformation of an emotion into the opposite.*

WORRY

Can worry create a dream? Freud is of the opinion that in such a case another propelling power must be activated by the worry, and this propelling power must be a wish, as in this case:

A father had been keeping watch at the bed of his sick child day and night. After the child's death, an old man was engaged to watch over the child's body which was laid out and surrounded by candles. Meanwhile, the father retired to an adjoining room, leaving the door to the death chamber open.

During the same night, the father dreamed [31] that *his child came to his bedside, touched his arm, and whispered reproachfully, "Father, don't you see that I am burning?"* He awakened and noticed a bright light coming from the adjoining room. He rushed into the room, where he found the old man asleep and the child's body burning, apparently set afire by a fallen candle.

Freud assumes that the light of the fire stimulated the sleeping father's eye, since the door to the death chamber was open. In his dream he came to the conclusion that a candle must have been upset and caused the fire. Before going to sleep the father may have harbored a worry that this might happen. In his dream, a trace of alertness to reality must have been present.

Freud finds that this interpretation has other determinants also. He believes that these determinants can be found in the words spoken by the child in the dream. For instance, "I am burning" could be understood to mean "I have fever"; "Don't you see, Father?" could have another meaning, e.g., that of a reference to an unknown situation.

At the same time, Freud considers it surprising that the dreamer takes the time to create a dream under circumstances in which awakening and quick action are so urgent. He ascribes this delay to a wish-fulfilling idea. The dream becomes more important than reality. By awakening too soon he would have shortened, so to speak, the life of the child— for the duration of the dream.

SURPRISE

If the patient expresses his wonder or surprise at something in his dream, we may assume that he had noticed in his mind an area which he considers strange. He wonders at himself.

One of Stekel's patients dreamed:

[32] *"I am riding in a street car. A man throws stones at me from a window of a nearby building. The wife of my colleague is there and I wonder why she is not afraid that her child might be hurt."*

In her dream, the patient displaces her feeling of guilt to the wife of her colleague. If people knew the truth, they would "throw stones" at her. The woman, who is self-respecting and devoted to her husband, is surprised at finding thoughts of another man in her mind. The symbol "throwing stones" is taken from the Bible. It refers to the passage John 8:7, and the words, "He that is without sin among you, let him first cast a stone at her." In the dream, this picture is condensed. It signifies the prohibited contact with men, the "crime," and, at the same time, the moral self-condemnation and self-punishment for the objectionable contact.

COMICAL DREAMS

When a patient considers a dream situation as comical, we have the right to presume that an important conflict has been portrayed in the dream. *The patient attempts to belittle his tragic conflict by making fun of it.*[1] In reality, such a conflict seldom offers anything worthy of laughter.

The following is an instructive example of a "comical dream":

[33] *"In preparing myself for a trip, I pack my belongings. Among other things, I put a little bronze statue into my suitcase. It is a figure of a running soldier. I say to my wife, 'Here is Mr. Pinkenstein making an endurance run. When you call "Pinke!" he comes to you immediately. He is being pursued by a woman called Marie. She is always on his heels.' It seems that at this moment I see 'Marie' mounted on a white horse. My wife and I laugh at the peculiar situation."*

In order to understand the comical dream, it is necessary to know that "Pinke" and "Marie" are German synonyms and that, in a humorous sense, they mean "money." The joke is that Pinkenstein, whose nickname is Pinke (money), is pursued by Marie (money), that is, Pinke (money) again.

Here is the story of the patient. He is thirty-two and has been married for two years. He had had intimate relations with his brother's wife years ago, but had stopped seeing her a short time before he married. Her name was Marie.

Deeper analysis revealed a tragic conflict in the patient's mind. His sweetheart Marie committed suicide on the day of the patient's wedding. Nobody knew the real cause of this suicide except our patient. He married his wife because of

[1] Freud found a similar mechanism in the psychology of wit. (*"Der Witz und seine Beziehung zum Unbewussten,"* Psychoan. Verlag, Vienna, 1925, Fourth Edition.)

her money ("Pinke"), and the picture of his deserted sweetheart haunted him day and night. "Mr. Pinkenstein" is the patient himself; he is the "soldier making the endurance run" (fortune hunter); but, behind his back, on his heels, we see the haunting recollection of the deserted woman, the only person he ever loved. In the dream, the statue, as usual, symbolizes recollection. (Cf. page 140.)

M. Grotjahn found that *laughter in dreams* is the result of the dreamer's comprehension of a repressed situation, particularly an aggressive one. He quotes Freud who proved that laughter is a discharge of stored energy; and he cites Freud's example of an impotent, arteriosclerotic old man who, through his laughter in a *dream* [34] *about the unavailing efforts of his wife and an acquaintance to help him turn on the lights in his dark room,* transformed his embarrassing and miserable condition into something light and funny.

A dream of our own observation follows:

[35] *"Bert and I are straightening up the living room before leaving. Rearranging pillows, etc. Butterflies are in the room like moths from a closet; some get in my hair and one stings me. Bert and I are fanning at them with pillows. We are laughing."*

The dreamer is a thirty-three-year-old divorced woman, mother of a small child. She was engaged to marry another man, Bert. She had the habit of fixing up her apartment before Bert came to see her. In the dream, the word "rearranging" refers to the emotional rearrangements which have become necessary after her divorce. The resistance of her family had to be overcome (Bert was of a different faith), the child's friendliness towards the "new man" had to be awakened, and, above all, she had to detach herself from a dominating mother who was poisoning her mind with aggressive remarks.

In this dream she is stung by a butterfly or moth. Apparent nonsense, for butterflies do not sting. It was, in fact, the *thought* of a moth that "stung" the patient so deeply that she awoke with a headache. This thought refers to her previous husband who once made a scene about a suit that was moth-eaten. She resented that outbreak at that time, but now she is inclined to consider this as a masculine act while Bert impresses her as lacking in masculine determination. She tries to fan this thought away—but it is obtrusive. The dream ends with laughter. This laughter covers up her *sadness* over the fact that she suspects her mother (who warned her against marrying Bert) might be right, after all.

Telepathy and Prophecy in Dreams

. . . they speak
Like sybils of the future.
BYRON
("The Dream")

We are short of scientifically observed facts as to whether or not we know more in the dream than we ever know in reality; in other words, whether or not a dream reveals a so-called sixth sense. As judicious observers we have to consider the inclination of many neurotics to believe that they have a mystic power of presentiment, and that they can establish a connection between real events and their preceding dreams. This is one of the various primitive reactions of neurotics. It is similar to their belief in the omnipotence of thought. In general, science rejects the idea of prophecy in dreams, although this idea plays a conspicuous role in the lives of many laymen. To know what the future holds for us has been a long-standing wish of mankind.

The question as to whether or not the dream has telepathic qualities can be answered only in connection with the question as to whether or not there is telepathy. Stekel answers this question in the affirmative; and Freud is of the same opinion. Freud maintains that telepathy is not a problem of the dream, and that we must not base our opinion about its existence or non-existence on dream studies. However, he admits that even if we submit the reports on telepathic experiences to the same criticism which we apply to other statements concerning the occult, we still retain a great number of facts which cannot be easily disregarded. While this observation permits a more friendly attitude toward the entire problem of telepathy, it is not sufficient for coming to a definite conclusion. All we can say at present is that it *may be possible* that telepathy does exist, but in acknowledging this we must defend our skepticism, and we should retreat only before the overwhelming might of evidence. If messages can be transmitted telepathically they may also reach the mind of a sleeping individual and be perceived by him in his dream.

The problem of telepathy in dreams has been discussed by scientific writers again and again. Most authors were concerned primarily with the recording of observations they considered as bearing some evidence of the existence or non-existence of telepathy.

Recently, research in the question of telepathy has been resumed. Eisenbud and Ehrenwald have made serious contributions in this respect. Eisenbud maintains that under some circumstances the repressed wish-fulfillment of one person may be found in the dreams of another person. He submits: "We are no longer at liberty to assume that a given dream is exclusively the private concern of the dreamer who had it, since analysis is capable of demonstrating that one dream may be the vehicle for the latent material of two, three, and more individuals. . . ."

Ehrenwald maintains that telepathic experiences "are confined to the fringes of conscious mental functioning. They show all the characteristics of unconscious material such as a tendency to symbolic representation, secondary elaboration, displacement and condensation, peculiar to the dream or the neurotic symptom."

Ehrenwald believes that telepathic dreams may throw some light upon the psychodynamics of the case and the therapeutic situation. In more cases, however, they are reflections of the doctor-patient relationship ("transference").

The work of Eisenbud and Ehrenwald was subject to criticism. Albert Ellis has re-analyzed one of the dreams Eisenbud had published. He denies that there is any specific relation between the dream material reported by Eisenbud and Eisenbud's own innermost thoughts and emotions. To prove his point, Ellis proceeds to illustrate how the findings reported by Eisenbud are applicable to the lives of at least three other individuals "who are hardly intimately related to Eisenbud or his patients." The three individuals are Ellis, a female analysand, and a fictional hero of a recent novel. Ellis then takes each segment of the reported dream and concludes that it is just as applicable to the lives of these three unrelated individuals as to Eisenbud. The inescapable conclusion of these findings, says Ellis, is that either Eisenbud's patient was telepathic not only to his analyst but also to these three unrelated individuals, which would be a miracle of miracles, or that there was no telepathy involved. Let us hope that the future of dream research will throw more light upon this problem.

Meanwhile, in the following cases we shall see how easily our criticism can be biased by coincidences.

A forty-six-year-old artist had to give his daughter a hundred dollars for a trip. He put a one hundred dollar bill into his pocket and intended to offer it to his daughter before she left. The girl, however, postponed her journey for one day. When the artist looked for the bill in the evening, he found, to his great shock, that the bill was missing. He went to bed in a very depressed state of mind. That night he had this dream:

[35a] *"My mother (now dead) says, 'Don't worry, the money is in your brown trousers.'"*

The artist jumped out of bed immediately, and lo! he found the bill just where his mother had predicted in the dream.

Telepathy? Not at all. The artist loved his daughter and

was not very willing to allow her to leave for the trip. Besides, the sum of one hundred dollars was large to him as, at the time, he was not earning much money. Thus he repressed the fact that he changed his trousers in the course of the day. In his dream, the recollection rose into consciousness driven by the distress over the presumptive loss of the money. The situation of mother-son which appears in the dream is a substitute for the real situation of father-daughter. The dream shows what we could term "pseudotelepathy."

The next dream is also pseudotelepathic. The patient is a thirty-two-year-old physician. He reports:

[36] *"I dreamed that I was in a store where Persian rugs were sold. My mother and my fiancée were also present. We were buying a very large Persian rug."*

Upon awakening, the patient was asked by his mother whether he had seen anything in the next room when he came home from the clinic the night before. When the patient answered in the negative, his mother revealed to him that the day before, as a surprise, she had bought a Persian rug.

The patient had not entered the room where the rug was spread, nor had he heard anything said about buying a rug. He remembered his dream about the rug only when his mother questioned him. And, so it would seem to all intents and purposes, that the dream was freely conceived and deserving of the appellation "telepathic."

We had to investigate the possibility that the Persian rug was mentioned at a time when the patient was in a state of decreased consciousness; for example, if he were falling asleep or just awakening, the feeling of reappearing consciousness could have absorbed the words, yet not to such a degree that they could be remembered. This supposition rested on the fact that the patient seemed especially given to such states of decreased consciousness, and, among other things, exhibited tendencies toward sleep-walking. The patient was requested to ask his parents, who slept in the next room, if they had used the words "Persian rug" late that night or early the next morning. The affirmative answer corroborated our supposition. There was nothing telepathic, therefore, in his dream. The possibility that the characteristic smell of a new Persian rug might have caused the patient to dream this dream was discussed with him, but his answers indicated that such had not been the case.

Do dreams contain *prophetic messages?* While science has, so far, hesitated to accept such a proposition, the mind of uneducated, superstitious people has continued to accept the age-old belief that dreams contain prophetic or guiding messages, or even that they have curative value.

The Bible is replete with such examples. Many of them contain simple messages of divine origin such as the dreams Joseph interpreted to Pharaoh's cup-bearer and baker, while others represent general prophecies, such as those about the seven cows dreamed by Pharaoh.

FIGURE 11

THE STORY OF JOSEPH. Cassone Panel, Florence. Courtesy of the Mettropolitan Museum of Art, New York.

But the ancients were not satisfied with the irregularity of such messages and prophecies. They took the initiative and appealed to the divinities to *send* them "favorable dreams." Such dreams were expected to cure disease, or bring good luck. This process of directing man's fate through the medium of dreams was called "incubation." In Egypt and Greece, incubation was a part of the religious practices, and priests were busy interpreting the prophetic messages of the dreams. Some gods, e.g., Aesculap, the "father of medicine," were considered as especially competent to send curative dreams down upon the sleeping worshipers. Temples were built in Aesculap's honor, the most famous of these in Epidaurus, Greece. Later, the Christian church took over some of these practices. The ancient gods were superseded by saints, although in the new theological theory the latter were not worshiped. Some of these customs have survived until today. Instead of dreams, some of the pious experienced visions of saints, a phenomenon which later laid the foundation for the reputation of a particular place as a miraculous healing site. The Archangel Michael, the Virgin Mary, and other holy figures have been considered, at various times and places, as carriers of curative forces.

Similar customs can be observed in many parts of the world. In a forest near the Vienna suburb of Salmansdorf, there is a part called "Waldandacht" (Forest Prayer). Superstitious people sleep there on St. Agnes' Day in the hope that they will be favored with a dream which will change their luck. (This luck refers predominantly to the lottery.) The trees at this spot are decorated with holy pictures, bronzes, statuettes and other religious paraphernalia.

If we look over the "prophetic" dream books, we find in them one feature which stands out; they offer the believer a welcome means of dispelling his most pressing worries and of bringing him closer to happiness—the goal he shares with all mankind.

THE RECOLLECTIVE POWER OF THE DREAM

Hunt half a day for a forgotten dream.
WILLIAM WORDSWORTH
(*"Hart-Leap Well"*)

Freud was able to prove that from a patient's dreams it is possible to learn more about his personality, the background of his illness, and his main attitudes, than we can learn from his direct reports. Dreams retain more recollections than consciousness.[1]

Dreams cannot, however, as a rule, reveal information which the patient has never possessed. Many details we elicit from dreams but cannot elicit from straight confession point toward the early, the formative period of our ego, chiefly before the age of three. At that inchoate stage of the patient's ego, he may undergo experiences which are to be decisive in establishing his subsequent patterns of response. The patient may not be able to recall consciously what had taken place at that early stage.

One reason for the hypermnesia of the dream is that the unconscious lacks the category of time; there the past and the present exist simultaneously. Old impressions are coupled with new ones. Often, new experiences accentuate old experiences, just as in Pavlov's experiments a neutral new stimulus superimposed upon an ineffective original conditioning stimulus may lead to a telling reaction. Subliminal stimuli may thus become activated. Old and new mnesic material, repressed, rejected, or simply forgotten, is stored together and may reappear in the dream together. Thus, dreams often introduce persons long forgotten or events barely remembered. The only difference between the repressed and the forgotten material is the extent of preconscious resistance toward recalling it.

Some dreams seem to have no relation to real experiences. However, closer examination may elicit hitherto repressed facts which can be recognized as the underlying, the *cryptomnesic* material.[2]

Freud reports the following informative case in connection

1 In some cases the individual is in doubt as to whether a specific recollection was real or transmitted by a vivid dream. Experience teaches us that such doubts should be decided in favor of the dream.

2 Many composers and poets have submitted artistic productions as "originals" which, in reality, were involuntary reproductions of works they had seen or heard.

with cryptmnesia. One of his students told him a dream [37] in which *he saw his former tutor in bed with the nurse who had been in his home until he was eleven years of age.* The student was of the opinion that this dream was in all its parts a deliberate invention. When he described it to his brother, the latter declared laughingly that the dream reproduced a real scene which occurred when the dreamer was three years of age. At that period the tutor and the nurse made the older brother, who was then six, drunk with beer whenever they wished to have intimate relations. The three-year-old, who also slept in the same room, was unmolested because he was considered too young to be suspicious.

Real experiences which are sources of the dream content may be recent (*day residues*) or old (*childhood impressions*). They may consist of one fact or of a number of facts which may be condensed into a single dream picture or may appear separately. They may be portrayed in their own shapes or in the shapes of other experiences which are of the same validity and are suitable as substitutes. They may be actual facts or mere thoughts, important or unimportant. In reality, no dream is unimportant; each dream carries a significant emotional and intellectual cargo.

As stated on page 25, the material which is offered by the day residues stems from the fringes of the perceptual field. A good example of this type is furnished by a dream of a thirty-nine-year-old gynecologist. The following is the doctor's report:

"Before falling asleep I was thinking about a patient. In the dream [37a] *I was implanting a 3¢ stamp into her thigh.*"

—In what way have you been thinking about this patient?

—"The patient, who was referred to me by an out-of-town physician, was complaining of pains and tenderness in her right lower abdominal quadrant. An acute appendicitis and a possible operation had to be taken into consideration. I had the necessary laboratory tests made and they were negative. When I was ready to let the patient know that an operation was not necessary, she failed to keep her appointment with me. Before falling asleep, I was thinking of the possibility that another physician, whom she might have consulted and who was ignorant of the negative laboratory findings, might submit her to an unnecessary operation. This is what comes to my mind in connection with the implantation."[1]

—What about the stamp?

—"I think of it as of something cheap."

—Don't you place a 3¢ stamp if you want to mail a letter?

—"Yes, indeed. Your question reminds me that I had also other thoughts regarding this patient,—peripherally, so to speak—but I pushed them aside right away. I was thinking that this patient was a cheap-skate. She was causing me trouble and expense, and it did not appear to me as though I could collect a fee in this case. When she did not keep her appointment with me, I thought it could not be a great loss if she decided to discontinue treatment. As a matter of fact, I was even thinking of a pretext to *send her on* to another doctor."

We see that it was not the main worry of the dream but a peripheral thought (dealing with the referral of the patient to somebody else) that was the day residue to be elaborated in the dream.[2]

Because several experiences may be condensed into one dream picture we sometimes have to put several cross sections through a dream. We find single details in dreams to be foci of several intersecting lines of thoughts and ideas. That is the reason why, when reconstructing thoughts and ideas, we often get more than one interpretation for a dream.

(Q) "Can the content of the dream be influenced, or steered if necessary, by the use of hypnosis?"

[1] Pellets of glandular substance are often implanted under a patient's skin to stimulate the function of the particular gland (usually the sexual).

[2] Other references of this dream, particularly details of counter-transference are omitted here.

(A) Experiments with this objective in view have been made. We must not forget that hypnosis preceded chronologically the psychoanalytic method of obtaining from the patient relevant pathogenic material. Hypnosis has been used to improve the recollective power of patients by Ericson and Hill; some work along these lines also has been done at the Menninger Clinic; and Kanzer published an article on the therapeutic use of dreams induced by suggestion; also Farber and Fisher and others have explored the possibility of steering the treatment by properly suggesting dreams.

The problem is not yet sufficiently clarified, and one must be careful in evaluating the results. The conscious ego reacts to the therapist differently than the hypnotized ego; insight, therefore, must be secured by confronting *in all cases* the hypnotic findings with the patient's conscious ego.

At the early stage of psychoanalysis, suggestion was frequently used in eliciting the material and the patient was often asked (while under hypnosis) to relate important data in his next dream. The results of this suggestion were never impressive, however. In most cases the analyst was forced to rely upon the material produced by the patient consciously and voluntarily. Incidentally, the same holds true for narcosynthetic efforts regarding dream material.

There is an undeniable advantage in collecting essential pathogenic material by analyzing night dreams. We do our work amidst all the resistances the patient mobilizes to protect his complexes. Hypnosis and narcosynthesis deprive us of this important object of study, even if it does stimulate the production of the material.

PHYSICAL CONDITIONS AND DREAMS

The widespread idea that the dream is created by a physical condition such as a full stomach or a particular food we are digesting is only partially correct. The desire to evacuate the bladder may lead to awakening, and in the process of awakening we may have a dream, but, as stated above, (see page 23), the content of the dream will always be strictly personal.

Rank has proved that dreams leading to awakening (micturition dreams, emission dreams, etc.) often show several strata. On the lowest level, the patient may experience his urge by some archaic image; the symbol may become more and more transparent; and finally, the urge may break through in an unconcealed way. We can also say that, in the process of awakening, the character of the dream image may change from a general to a specific one.

A woman patient, aged twenty-eight, dreams:

[38] *"I am taking a bath. Suddenly I notice that it is not water I am in but blood. Then I am in bed. I see my body covered with blood, and the linen and the pillows are also filled with blood. My friend's little boy is sitting in a chair. He, too, is covered with blood. I am frightened. I awaken and notice that I am menstruating."*

This dream gives us diverse information. At first the "menstruation" is expressed generally as "bathing"[1]; then, after the water changes into blood, as "bathing in blood"; then the dream refers to the possibility of being covered with blood. This part sounds definitely as a warning: "Do something about it, or your bed will be full of blood."

There is no doubt that the stimulus for this dream came from the onset of the menstrual hemorrhage, but a certain personal problem can be found in the background. The patient reports that her friend's boy always arouses envy in her and a desire to have a baby. Unfortunately, her husband is not in favor of having a child at this time because the couple's economic condition is unsettled. She secretly hopes that she will become gravid by "chance," so that she and her husband would have to accept a *fait accompli*. In her dream she sees not only herself, but also her friend's boy, covered with blood, that is, her hopes for her "own son" have gone down with the hemorrhage, at least for this month.

We said that the unconscious lacks the category of time. Our sense of duty, however, a function of the superego (see page 163), can induce awakening at a given time. It is as though we were endowed with a "brain clock." (Similar experiences were made by the use of hypnosis.) Many of us may lie down at night with the idea that we must wake up at a specific time next morning. We do. It is as though

1 Compare the symbols of menstruation, p. 152.

throughout our own sleep a clock were running with the alarm set to go off at the exact moment when we wish to be awakened. It is clear that this is not a function of the unconscious, although its performance does not take place in the spotlight of our consciousness.

Of course, personal problems are to be found in this connection as they are attached to any form of dream activity. One patient was awakened by his alarm clock early one morning. He looked at the clock, noticed that he could spare another half hour, and fell asleep. The following dream awakened him—at the right time:

[39] *"I was in Europe and was to take my violin lessons. The teacher was waiting for me, but I had difficulty in unpacking my instrument. When I finally succeeded in opening my violin case, I saw other instruments in it, a ukulele and some other exotic instruments. My teacher became indignant at my delay and shouted: 'How long do you expect me to wait? It is getting late.'"* The words "It is getting late" sounded in the dreamer's ear as he awoke.

During the few months immediately preceding his departure from Europe, the patient, who was a good violinist, had not practiced. He was worried by the possibility that his skill might be impaired or lost by this long absence from the violin, and he thought, in particular, of a friend who had forgotten how to play the piano when he stopped taking lessons. The patient felt the passing of time and the decrease of his musical skill. In his dream, he saw himself back in Europe taking lessons (wish-fulfillment), at the same time he expressed apprehension that it might be too late to go on with music. After awakening, he resolved to resume his practice regardless of difficulties. Thus, the dream exerted a beneficial influence by acting as a warning.

The combination or superimposition of two contents is apparent in his dream. He is warned: "It is getting late! See that you don't lose your contact with music," says the dream.

"It is getting late! See that you don't oversleep," says the patient's "head-clock."

The following dream was experienced under the stimulation of a full bladder which caused the sleeper to awaken:

[40] *"There is a kind of meeting in a yard. Many people are gathered and are standing about, waiting for somebody or something to come. The yard seems too small for the crowd. Then somebody distributes burdens to all waiting persons and orders them to carry these burdens (boxes, lumber, and so on) to some destination. The people line up and leave the yard through a narrow passageway. One member of the crowd says, 'It isn't far!'—as if to encourage his fellows."*

As all the carriers passed through the narrow passageway, the dreamer awoke. He was forced by the strong urge to urinate to get up and go to the toilet ("It isn't far"). In his dream, he had experienced the congestion of urine in his bladder as an accumulation of people in a small yard, and he symbolically anticipated the discharge of the "burden" (See Fig. 12) instead of urinating in reality. The dream postponed his awakening, a substantiation of Freud's theory that the dream acts as a guardian of the sleep.

FIGURE 12

In the state of half-sleep, the wish to continue sleeping sometimes creates a dream about awakening and thus overcomes the tendency to awaken. Freud reported that when he ate anchovies or olives or other salted food before going to bed, he usually got thirsty during the night and awakened with a stereotyped dream, [40a], namely, that *he was drink-*

ing; he was sipping water in full draughts. Then he would wake up and have to drink in reality. According to Freud, this dream has the following explanation: The dreamer perceives thirst while he is asleep; the thirst causes a desire to drink and the dream fulfills this desire. A sound sleeper, Freud was not used to being awakened by physical urges. If he succeeded in satisfying his thirst by a dream about drinking, he did not have to disturb his sleep. The dream guarded his sleep.

Although finally we do fully awaken, the dream, which has come and gone as a flash, has given us the sensation of having forestalled any actual physical fulfillment and of having had protracted sleep.

Not all irritations become a part or a source of the dream content. Some of them pass by, others cause awakening, and the dreamer can remove the irritation.

Various observations have proved that a *rapid pulse* is often responsible for dream pictures of running, driving, or moving, and is usually connected with the emotion of anxiety.

One of my patients, a young doctor aged twenty-nine, awoke suddenly and found his head resting on his forearm. This position interfered with the circulation of blood in his arm. In awakening, he felt the numbness of his forearm and the blood throbbing toward the obstruction. However, what caused him to awaken, and, in so doing, probably saved his arm from injury, was a dream.[1]

[41] *"I was chasing somebody in order to deliver a scrap of paper to him. It was some kind of warning, a matter of life and death. I ran under a terrible strain. My legs were heavy; I could hardly move. I was afraid I should never get close enough to the man to deliver the warning message. I wanted to call him back, but my voice failed. . . . I awoke in anxiety."*

---

1 Obstructions of circulatory passages, respiratory and vascular alike, are frequently accompanied by dreams in which the affect of anxiety prevails. It is usually this anxiety that leads to awakening.

We notice a close connection between the idea of warning and the awakening. The man running into disaster was the dreamer himself. It was he who was to be warned so as to prevent injury to himself.

The same patient had another dream when he was again lying on his forearm:

[42] *"I am taking the State Board examination. One of the officers interrupts me as I write the test and says, 'You are not permitted to take this examination; the credentials you submitted for evaluation are not sufficient.' I go into a terrible rage and tell him that this is by no means my fault, that I have sent over all that was requested, and that since I received the official admission card I was sure that everything was all right. The man smiles maliciously, and I have the impression that probably he is right and my examination will be declared void. . . . Then I see an older woman, apparently one of the supervisors at the examination, sitting near by in a chair. Her legs are swollen. She interrupts me again and says something about being unable to walk.[1] She asks, 'Are you in good health? Are your limbs all right?' I say, 'Yes, I think so.' But at this moment I feel that I am not entirely well, that my arms are aching—or is it one arm?* I awaken and find myself in the usual position, my head resting on my forearm, and I experience considerable pain."

The first part of the dream uses recent material (examination) in order to show a general symbol of difficulty and danger (invalid examination). The excitement of the dreamer might have been caused by the change in the pulse rate following the blocking of the circulation. The second part shows where the difficulty or danger lies—at first, in a general way, "difficulty to walk," "limbs," then "arms," then specifically, "one arm." The dreamer's attention is turned

[1] In this scene, the young doctor demonstrates to the supervisor his medical superiority, as if he wanted to prove that the examination is out of place. He would rather see the supervisor as a patient than as a representative of the university.

toward the exposed part, and the patient awakens and removes the irritation by changing his position.

One patient who was tightly wrapped in his blanket dreamed [42a] *of being held up by robbers who forced him to do various things at gun-point.* As his body was forced into an unpleasant position by the binding blanket, his mind was forced into an unpleasant situation (hold-up). The dream transferred a compulsory state of the body into a mental compulsion.

Another dream of this type is the following, dreamed by a forty-two-year-old lawyer who a short time prior to his analysis had suffered a coronary occlusion:

[43] *"I am in Cleveland. I enter a room of a large hotel. I am surprised that I am not accompanied by my wife, for usually in such a setting she would be with me. I seem to be slightly worried about what could happen in case of another heart attack. I am not feeling my best physically. To a hotel maid passing by, I mention rather nervously the name of a friend, Mr. Beta, a man of high standing who resides in Cleveland, and also give his address to make sure that in case something should happen to me, he would be notified. This announcement is made in a loud voice as it is also meant to be a sort of introduction to the hotel manager.*

"Suddenly the door on the right side opens and in walks a man who seems to be a hunchback or a person suffering from a stiff neck. I stop him and ask him what he wants, but he silently points to the door on the opposite side of the room and walks out.

"At this moment I awaken. I have been lying on my right shoulder in a clumsy and painful condition. I change my position and go to sleep again."

The "hunchback" entering the room from the "right side" and pointing silently to "the opposite side" reflects the dreamer's unconscious perception of physical discomfort.

We may repeat here in passing that the wish not to disturb

the sleep prevents the uncomfortably situated patient from awakening for the duration of the dream. But important personal problems avail themselves of the opportunity of hitching themselves onto this vehicle. The dream is illustrative because of the multitude of problems involved.

First, "Cleveland." The dreamer, a married man, was told by an attractive, married lady-friend, Mrs. Alpha, that he may stay in their home whenever he happens to be in Cleveland. Although consciously determined to maintain the not-more-than-friendly relations with Mrs. Alpha, he apparently had an antimoral wish which was evoked by the lady-friend's invitation, only to be rejected. In his dream, however, he saw himself in Cleveland, and without his wife, who, following his heart attack, usually accompanied him on all his strenuous trips. The dreamer's complaint, "I am not feeling my best physically," acquires also a psychic connotation, and the sentence can be understood as "I have a bad conscience." The name of Mr. Beta, which the dreamer mentions with gusto, serves as a rationalization: "I don't have to sleep in the home of Mrs. Alpha; I can sleep in the home of my friend Beta." This is a concession to the superego ("the man in high standing"). The dreamer tries to outshout the voice of his superego and to justify himself (the "loud voice").

Fear of punishment by the superego ("in case something should happen to me") fuses here with the fear of physical injury.

Then, in the dream, the door on the right side suddenly opens. Many observers have noted that "left side" in a dream usually represents the "wrong" side. This appears to be one of the symbols of the collective unconscious, the real meaning of which is not concerned with immediate questions of handedness. We shall treat this problem at length, later.

The patient's uncomfortable position appears projected into the hunchback. He comes from the right side and points to the left, the side to which the sleeper should have turned.

The sleeper awakens and turns to the left side.

To weave into its plot the physiological stimuli which cause the disturbance of sleep is a typical property of the dream. Dreams assimilate, elaborate, and regulate continuously all stimuli coming from the organs. All organ sensations, those charged with affect, and those which remain on a purely vegetative level, continuously influence the dream as they influence our mood during the day even though most of them are subliminal and thus escape our conscious awareness. Among such subliminal influences are those of our *glandular activity*. The role of the sexual cycle in women in the production of dream imagery has recently been studied by Benedek and Rubenstein. We shall discuss this problem on page 378.

The psychosomatic sources of the dream often lead to a specific emotional coloring of the dream content. The *circulatory* and *respiratory systems* account for some types of anxiety dreams in which the material is of diagnostic importance in the incipient stages of angina pectoris, in the threat of coronary occlusion, or in the beginning of serious infectious diseases of the respiratory tract. Of course, the anxiety is spun into the dream plot in which the dreamer's specific conflicts are precipitated.

Gastro-intestinal disorders, too, lead to and are indicated by dreams in which the symptom itself (Silberer's "autosymbolism") plus the psychological factors in the patient's given life situation are expressed. Such dreams prove S. Lowy correct when he states that the dreamer's total personality in all its psychosomatic inter-relations is unified and expressed in his dream.

G. R. Heyer pointed out that the gastro-intestinal system is that physio-biological part of the human body which is charged with the preservation and protection of the individual. Heterogeneous material is rendered body-specific, and assimilated. Heyer emphasized that in such processes there is a constant inter-relation between the organic system and specific mental forces. The circulatory system, according to Heyer, serves the preservation and stabilization of the body ego.

Let us summarize the remarks about physical conditions and dreams. The stimuli coming from the organs, those charged with affect as well as those occurring on a vegetative level, are assimilated, elaborated, and regulated in the dream. Such stimuli are to a definite, but varying and inexactly known, degree responsible for the dreamer's mood when he awakens. Daydreams, too, are engaged in metabolizing subliminal physiological stimuli which are partly responsible for changes of mood occurring during our waking hours and also for some acute symptoms, such as anxiety, depression, or headache. We also mentioned the subliminal character of endocrine influences.

TIME AND SPACE IN THE DREAM

> *A slumbering thought is capable of years,*
> *And curdles a long life into one hour.*
> BYRON
> (*"The Dream"*)

In dreams, Einstein's Theory of Relativity appears realized. Time and space have a close relation to each other, and one is often expressed by the other. Rhythms pervading our biologic existence fuse with the man-established chronometric rhythm to which the individual has been conditioned. All values of time such as speed, duration, and sequence of events, appear distorted in the dream.

Certain pathological conditions, particularly diseases of the inner ear, dizziness, migraine, and other disturbances, may influence the speed of the dream events. Some of them remind us of the "fast motion" in the movies (Schilder, Hoff, Allers).

Pathological changes in the vestibular apparatus of the ear distort the rhythm of the patient's perceptions and the special concepts as they appear in his dreams. Schilder and

Hoff studied this problem in a large amount of material. Schilder treated a case of a labyrinthine fistula in which he observed that peculiar spatial transformations were taking place in the patient's dreams.

The patient, in her dream [43a], *was skating with many people on a very large rink. Two children were among the crowd. When she wanted to get nearer to them, she saw herself in front of a glittering screen.* (The skating rink turned apparently into a vertical plane.)

Schilder also observed that vestibular disorders produce irregular and broken up movements in the patient's real conduct as well as in his dreams.

One of his patients in her dream [43b] *saw a scarf lying on the ground. When she wanted to pick it up, it turned into a group of guinea pigs, and soon scattered in all directions; some of them ran up her legs.*

Another patient dreamed [43c] *of a funeral at which the music played very fast and people were moving very fast. Then she saw herself climbing a pole and sliding down very fast. The crowd moved in an irregular way. The hearse became as big as a room and the carriage moved very slowly.*

We see that in these vestibular dreams, movement and speed are affected. The type and speed of movement in the dream are changeable. There is also a peculiarity about size. In vestibular dreams many objects appear to be small, distant, and rapidly moving. (Allers has shown a close relationship between micropsia and disturbances of the vestibular apparatus.)

High fever, intoxications, and some brain disturbances can lead to contrary dream phenomena and cause an exceedingly *slow dream action* similar to "slow motion" in a movie.

A pneumonia patient, while in a 105° fever shortly before his crisis, dreamt:

[44] *"I was dozing. The door opened very slowly. Somebody approached my bed, as slowly as if it were a slow-motion*

picture. I felt strange. This somebody walked or moved around my bed and placed his hand on my heart. The hand was ice-cold. . . . I woke up bathed in sweat. I had the impression of having seen Death and I was afraid to fall asleep again."

We sometimes awaken after seeming to dream for a virtually endless time, and, in glancing at a real clock, note that no more than five minutes have passed since we last observed the time.

The anatomical centers of the "sense of time" seem to lie in the thalamus, the cortex, and the center for sleep regulation. In Korsakoff's psychosis, the time perception appears disturbed.[1]

Our emotional tone also determines whether the action is perceived as slow or fast. If we are impatient, all motion may seem slow. A specific secret "life plan," or an abnormal fear of death and damnation may make the patient think of time as moving dreadfully fast.

In the following dream the patient's attitude toward time is clearly depicted:

[45] *"I am teaching a little girl while I am tired. I fall asleep during the lesson. I look at the watch. It is five-thirty. I fall asleep again and seem to sleep a long time. I look at the watch and see that the time is still five-thirty."*

To the neurotic mind, time means nothing. Entangled in fantasies of his childhood, this man does not perceive the passage of time.

According to Freud, in the dream the time of day may signify the time of the dreamer's life. Thus, "five-thirty" may represent the age of five-and-a-half years. The above dream contained an important reference to this age in the patient's life, a time when his development seemed to come to a halt. His fantasies and his dreams remained in that early period.

[1] For disturbances of time perception as found in states of intoxication, see p. 473.

Sometimes we see in the dream an anticipation of time as an expression of wish-fulfillment. A boy of sixteen had the following dream:

[46] *"I was fifty years old and had had a position for about forty years. I had done my job efficiently, and my mother thought I was a hero. There were a lot of girls who worshiped me. Then I had to resign my position and get a job in another city, and everybody was sorry to see me go and said that they could never forget me."*

At the time of the dream a conflict existed in the boy's home because he was neglecting his school work. The boy was attached to his mother, who, a long time ago, had divorced his father. For eight years the woman had been married to another man. After a quarrel over the boy's indifference toward school work, he solemnly promised his mother to pay more attention to his studies. He is in reality not a hero, and does not feel like one; on the contrary, he has strong feelings of inferiority whenever he compares himself with others. His dream is a wish-fulfillment with regard to his school and social situation.

And yet, the dream also contains an important complex based on the patient's past experiences. This interpretation is more fully appreciated when we learn that the boy's real father was about fifty when he was divorced. The patient could never forgive his mother for not having prevented the collapse of the original family setting. His mind was constantly preoccupied with daydreams regarding his father. He perused obsessively the address books of his schoolmates in order to study the first names of the other children's fathers. He walked the streets with the fancy that he would meet his father. He could scarcely remember his father's face, but he was certain that if he should meet him on the street something from within would enable him to identify him.

He tried to imitate his father's walking and writing as he remembered them. In the dream he *was* his father; fifty years old, having had a position for a long time and having done his job well, he now had to leave his job (divorce) and go somewhere else. The dreamer expressed the tragedy of his young life in the words, *"Everybody was sorry to see me go and said that they could never forget me."*

A time problem in the dream is sometimes a reproduction of a real time problem. People who in youth failed to find satisfaction are sometimes impatient and restless, eager to fill their emotionally empty lives with experiences, thrills, excitements. Their lives seem to run fast, with the picture of inescapable death in front of their eyes; and they hasten even more. In dreams, they vainly try to prevent the hands of the eternal clock from turning; in vain, they try to stop the motion of the wheel of time.

A fifty-five-year-old lady dreams:

[47] *"I awake late and see on my dresser a wonderful bunch of roses. I look at the clock on the wall—it is a quarter to twelve. I jump out of my bed as I am filled with fear that I have forgotten to give food to my canary. I prepare to dress, but instead of my everyday gown I see a silk dancing dress on my chair. I dress quickly—but soon feel somehow disturbed, and I really awake. . . . The picture on the wall was gloomy and mysterious."*

The elderly lady realizes in her dream that the hour of her life is late, "a quarter to twelve." She is surrounded by symbols of youth and pleasure—roses and a dress for ballroom dancing. "One more fling before it's too late!" The giving of food to the bird is a sex symbol which will be treated more explicitly later (page 135). It is not by chance that our patient complains of swallowing disturbances of the type known as "globus hystericus" which have close connection with repressed sexual impulses.

The time problem is also expressed in dreams containing the *fear of coming too late to a train,* or to school, for example. (See page 226.) The dreamer feels an inner retarding tendency in his way of living. A strong desire for the past, which may have given richer satisfaction than the present, is the main reason for this retardation. The trains which he fears to miss are often headed homeward, that is, into the past, into his childhood.

Annulment of time is seen in dreams of people who are disappointed in their present life situation. Married people sometimes see themselves in a premarital state, young and single again, ready to choose a partner.

A thirty-year-old business man, married nine years, dreamed [48] that *he was in his home town with his girl friend, Mary. It was Saturday night and he was at a dance, then at a show. He saw no harm in being with his girl friend. He said in the dream, "I am single and do not understand why anything should keep me from Mary."*

The various connections between sex and time and their expression in dreams will be discussed together with the sex problem.

A stereotyped dream had by a teacher, who came for analysis because of his psychosexual infantilism, shows victory over time and space:

[49] *"I am running to the station in great fear of missing my train. In spite of my hurry I fail to catch the train, and I see it roll away just after I reach the platform. I would run after the train and try to jump into one of the cars, but a railroad officer prevents me by holding my sleeve. I become angry but realize that it is senseless to quarrel now that the train has departed. In despair I remain where I am and watch another me who rushes at tremendous speed after the train and jumps skillfully into the car."*

When we learn that the train was going in the direction of the dreamer's home town, we understand the picture of neurosis which the dream portrays. The conscious part of the patient's personality lives in the present, that is, he functions as a serious-minded teacher. Another part of his ego is reflected by his fantasy which enables him to regress to childhood, to revive old sources of pleasure.

"Running after a train," "fear of missing a train," and the like are often pictures of a difference in age between the patient and one of his relatives (sibling rivalry), a difference which, of course, cannot be overcome.

Persons who in the dream appear to be *far away* often signify persons of the patient's childhood. Space then represents time. If the dream persons are strikingly *tall* they, too, may represent persons from the dreamer's childhood. Their abnormal size results from the childhood perspective maintained in the particular dream.

"Tall" and "short" are often used in the sense of "important" and "unimportant" respectively. An example of this is in the paintings on old Egyptian vases where the King is the tallest figure present and the slave is the shortest. (Fig. 13.)

FIGURE 13
THE JUDGMENT OF THE SOUL
(The Tribunal of Death)

In general, persons of enlarged size in the dream are carriers of stress. The dreamer's minimizing tendency can be seen in his presenting a person in an extremely diminished size.

The following is the case of a forty-one-year-old business man who throughout his life showed the tendency to rely upon the counsel of others, particularly elderly men (father images). His business difficulties were in part due to this dependent attitude. At the time of treatment he was associated with a Mr. Smith, whose decisions the patient always accepted without questioning. In analysis, this relationship was submitted to a prolonged discussion, whereupon the patient produced the following dream:

[50] *"Outdoor scene. People at café tables. Mr. Smith serious, in miniature size—as though seen through the small end of telescope—appears in middle ground and walks rapidly, diagonally, from left to right and disappears."*

The patient conveys to us here the idea that he considers it the right thing to view his relationship with Mr. Smith in a long-range perspective, and to have him disappear altogether as a factor in the patient's life. His quest for emotional freedom and independence is portrayed in the dream as a tranquil open-air scene.

Jaensch emphasized that size and depth of visual perceptions are often influenced by the factor of attention, that is, by the tonus of our eye musculature. In dreams, also, we sometimes see objects to which less attention is paid portrayed in diminished size.

A twenty-six-year-old woman patient had a dream in which we see the decrease of size as indicative of diminished importance and regression to the past:

[51] *"I see Alfred, the boy with whom I was in love when I was fifteen. (He is married now, and I hadn't seen him for years.) In the dream he is not feeling well and looks as if he were close to fainting. Then he shrinks, becomes smaller and smaller, and finally looks as if he were a small boy. This frightens me, and I awake with heart palpitation and my symptom of depersonalization."*

The patient suffered from spells of depersonalization during which she had the confusing and frightening feeling of not being herself (loss of the ego feeling). In the dream, her first lover is not feeling well (projection of her own discomfort), and finally, he shrinks to the size of a small boy. Closer investigation proved that her feelings of depersonalization were caused by interference of thoughts and feelings from her past. In her spells, she felt as though she were a baby. She daydreamed herself into early childhood, and each time this daydream occurred she was frightened and doubted that she was herself. The shrinking of Alfred reveals the regressive tendency of the patient. The film of her life is run backward. She revives the scenes with Alfred who seems to represent all her early emotional cravings. In the dream she vainly strives to minimize his importance and to present her affair with him as an insignificant childhood experience. (For more on depersonalization see page 422.)

Ferenczi, in his "Gulliver Phantasies," studied the so-called Lilliputian hallucinations by analyzing dreams in which patients saw persons and objects enlarged or minimized. Ferenczi, as well as Freud, attributes these changes to the dreamer's desire to express the relations of an infantile world, where children look up to adults. He also says that the unusual reduction in the size of objects and persons is to be attributed to the compensatory wish-fulfillment fantasies of the child who wants to reduce the proportions of the frightening objects in his environment to a less menacing size.

Lorand gives several interesting examples of Lilliputian dreams in his article, "Fairy Tales, Lilliputian Dreams and Neurosis." The following are a few of the dreams he describes.

A male patient in his twenties had many dreams in which he saw himself as a dwarf and his parents as giants. One of his dreams ran as follows:

[52] *"I was in the mouth examining the back of the teeth."*

Associations to this led back to early years when he used to climb all over his mother's bed in the morning, opening her mouth and looking in, pulling open her eyelids, blowing into her ears and nose, and, as he said, being quite a nuisance.

Another dream: [53] *"An enormous nose. I was climbing up and sliding down it. I wanted to climb into it, but the breath coming out of it nearly blew me away."*

[54] *"Mother had an enormous breast, and I was sucking it."*

Lorand says about these dreams: "I believe that they are rooted in an exceedingly active period of childhood. At that period, when fairy tales are abundantly told, the environmental situation is such that more than the usual amount of attention and time is spent by the child in fantasy and elaboration on the stories he hears. At the same time his emotional attachment to the parents, notably the mother, is also more strongly determined than is usual. This should explain why certain patients have such a great number of these dreams. It should also explain why they elect to recall their whole repressed infantile past in this type of dream."

It is important also to discover in these characteristic dreams the child's desire to investigate his parents' secrets, to break into their well-guarded intimacies, a problem which is found in fairy tales about prohibited rooms, in stories about the *Tarnkappe,* in "Tom Thumb" and in "Rumpelstiltskin."

But sexual curiosity is only one aspect. We must remember that in these stories and disguises it is the small, weak child, the Lilliputian who conquers the giants, that is, the parents. The ultimate triumph is reserved for the small; that is one of the foremost reasons why these dreams and fantasies are produced.

Space perception is highly dependent on the general affective tone. All our perceptions and sensations occur in relation to space (Schilder), and the space is perceived only in relation to the human body. Space perceptions of and about our body finally lead to the concept of a "body image," a reflection of our body on our cortex.

Under organ-pathological circumstances (brain lesions, certain intoxications, some forms of schizophrenia) the human space concept can become distorted. In some cases of schizophrenia, space itself may appear to be sexualized. "Before" may then refer to the genitals; "behind" to the rectum. The organs can also appear projected outside of the body.

In cases of depersonalization, people may appear "distant,"

or "separated," or the patient's own ego may appear to be "absent," "distant," "smaller," or "larger."

Anxiety in cases of hysteria may also lead to changes in space perception dependent on the patient's changing attitudes; love decreases distance, hate increases it.

When in the dream the patient looks or walks backward he is looking or walking backward in time, to the past. When he passes a series of rooms, he is really passing through various phases of his life or through stages of his development. The following is a dream[1] which shows this rather clearly:

[55] *"I dreamed of death.* (The patient, a young social worker, is afraid of dying.) *I was lying in bed and I was dying. I had to get certain records before I died. So I returned to my old office for these records which referred to a man living in a dilapidated house. I return to the office and I am embarrassed because I am wearing my old red dress which is torn in front. I run to the locker and put on my smock which covers the torn dress, and I go to the ladies' room and wet and comb my hair, put on lipstick, and then go to the supervisor to ask for the case records. I am told that the records are confidential, even though I had written them myself, and that they are now city property. I say casually, 'O.K. I will take them, copy them, and return them to the files.'* "

This patient is concerned with some records to which she wishes to attend before she dies. There are some matters to be straightened out before she can die in peace—an "unfinished business."

The records she associates here are social service records of a man who lived in a dilapidated house. As a social worker she deals with records (case histories). But what she tells us here is not the record of her social case. She is dreaming about herself, just as we all are dreaming exclusively about ourselves.

She says that when she returned to her old office she felt

[1] Contributed by Dr. Helen Papanek of New York.

embarrassed because she was wearing her old red dress. (The color "red" indicates sex, excitement, emotion. The "old" dress refers to the patient's past.) Her dress is "torn in front." She must hide this embarrassing fact, and that is what she is doing in front of her analyst. She goes out of her way to compensate for her defect. She combs her hair, puts on lipstick. In other words, she creates a masterpiece of masquerade. However, this dream shows us not only how she behaves in order to hide her shame, but also *what* she is trying to hide. And, as though we did not know, her supervisor in her dream implies that these things are confidential, one must not carry them about. "Even though I have written them myself."

We are dealing here with a woman who is in the state of resistance and determined to hide something. I am speaking from my experience when I assume that this patient has been deflorated (red dress torn in front), and that this must have happened early in her life. It is not a wish fantasy. It is something that has happened in the past ("I *returned* to my *old* office"), an experience to which her fantasy eagerly regresses. You can imagine the importance of such a finding, if it can be confirmed, through the investigation of the material.

(Q) "If the defloration was traumatic and unpleasant, why should the patient dream about it?"

(A) A psychic trauma which, we presume, the patient has experienced, has not been traumatic *per se,* i.e., because of what really happened. An intimate act, even an illicit one, may have been pleasurable. What makes a sexual experience traumatic is the unconscious wish for a repetition of the experience. Here repressive forces are mobilized and the constant clash with the superego censorship fixes the experience neurotically, turning it into a trauma. The patient may be married now and eager to ward off antimoral desires; or there may be other logical reasons why she would not indulge in this recollection. Repetition of a traumatic experience in dreams serves the purpose of attenuating the impact of it. Re-experiencing it lowers its painfulness (law of diminishing returns).

As a rule, all anticipations of displeasure in dreams and daydreams have this auto-immunizing effect. Anxiety in general is in the service of the ego, protecting it from sudden experiences of displeasure. If such occurrences, however, do take place without proper preparation by anxiety—such as we have observed in the battles of the war—these usually shocking experiences have to be dealt with by repetitive fantasies and recurrent catastrophic dreams. (More about this on page 389.)

In the following dream we have the symbol of "looking back" to the past. It was dreamed by a twenty-nine-year-old actress, suffering from headaches:

[56] *"I was in a sailboat with my brother Frank and his wife* (with whom I do not get along. When I last saw them, they were talking about a sailboat trip they made together). *We were enjoying a nice sail. The sun was shining right on us. I looked over my shoulder at the ocean and was very frightened to see how high the waves were. I looked away from them quickly."*

Just as in the biblical story about Lot's wife, there is danger in looking back. The patient identifies herself with her brother's wife whom she wishes to replace. Her brother fixation was found to be based upon overt sexual experiences the patient and her brother had had in their childhood. She must not look at her sinful past (a "Sodom-and-Gomorrah" motive). In her dream she says to herself that if she concentrates upon the present and keeps looking forward instead of backward she will enjoy smooth sailing.

Chapter *Two*

DREAM MECHANISMS

> *"The affairs of man are conducted by our own, man-made rules and according to man-made theories. Man's achievements rest upon the use of symbols."*
>
> A. KORZYBSKI
> *("Science and Sanity")*

"DREAM CENSORSHIP" AND "DREAM WORK"

What we recall as "dream" is the end product of an evolutionary thought process which begins in the unfathomable depths of the unconscious and ends with complete wakefulness and consciousness. As stated before, under the influence of growing lucidity, the prelogical, amorphous thought material gradually obtains shape and content, until it conforms to the rules of logic, becomes fully intelligible and relates to situations which are thinkable. It reaches our consciousness in the form of a dream. We speak of its content as of the "manifest dream content." Analytic experience has taught us, however, that this "manifest" dream content is a product of compromise with our superego, i.e., the principle of law and order in our mental affairs, which acts as "dream censor." Behind the facade of the manifest dream content lies another content, the "latent dream content," which expresses all the cravings and anxieties of the individual kept down by the repressive forces of the ego. These unconscious trends of the id avail themselves of the relaxation of repression during sleep, in order to push its way into consciousness. But the resistance offered by the ego never completely disappears; parts of it remain awake and express themselves in form of dream censorship. Through their influence, the language of the id becomes distorted until it is gradually translated into the language of the manifest content.

The process of transformation of the latent content into the manifest one, a function of the dream itself, is called "dream work." Interpretation is the reversed procedure; by interpreting a dream we retranslate the manifest dream content into its original language.

Summarizing, we may say that we distinguish between the manifest dream content which the patient is able to report, and the latent dream content which is shut out from the patient's range of awareness and becomes intelligible only through a psychological exploration of the dream.

According to Freud, the task of the dream interpreter is not only to "change the manifest dream content into the latent," but also "to explain how the latent dream content had turned into the manifest." Freud, in fact, compares the manifest dream content to a picture puzzle, a rebus, and points out the error of earlier dream investigators who judged this picture puzzle as an artistic drawing. The rebus derives its value not from the drawing, which may be senseless, but from the idea hidden behind the pictures.

The task of the dream censorship is to ward off antimoral and antisocial thoughts which seek to enter our consciousness. This action lessens the moral tension in our personality caused by the run of these primitive impulses on the barrier of our consciousness. The primitive thoughts to which we are subjected in the course of the day are warded off by the same authority. The dream censorship takes place in our preconsciousness.[1]

[1] In reality, there are, according to Freud, two censorships. One prevents unconscious desires from entering the sphere of preconsciousness; the other separates the preconscious from the conscious.

Freud also pointed out that it is sometimes advisable that the patient report dreams twice and that the analyst then compare the reports. Details which appear changed in the second rendition are, as a rule, the more vulnerable ones.

"Dream work" comprises the following processes:

(1) Distortion and Displacement; (2) Symbolization; (3) Condensation; (4) Secondary Elaboration.

All these processes are predicated upon the fact that dreams are experienced on a prelogical level. Their logic is that of a delusion, their mechanisms duplicate ancient (paleologic) forms of thinking.

In a very important contribution, Arieti quotes von Domarus who had this to say regarding the thinking of schizophrenics: "Whereas the normal person accepts identity only upon the basis of identical subjects, the paleologician accepts identity based upon identical predicates." Arieti offers the following instructive example: "If the following information is given to a normal person, 'All men are mortal; Socrates is a man,' this normal person will be able to conclude, 'Socrates is mortal.' A schizophrenic woman, on the other hand, who happens to think 'The Virgin Mary is a virgin. I am a virgin,' may conclude, 'I am the Virgin Mary.'" Her logic corresponds to that which dominates the dream.

In addition to this shift in the identification process which leads to distortion, other psychological thought mechanisms found in schizophrenic thinking are revived in the dream. Arieti enumerates the *representation of the "general" by the "special."* (A "wheel" will not necessarily mean "a circular body capable of turning on a central axis," but a specific wheel, or its pure verbalization which lacks any conceptual connotation). Causality laws are deprived of their general validity and rendered exclusively "anthropomorphous." Everything happens "because of" or "to suit" the individual. As in delusions, so also in dreams, wishes conjure up realities regardless of their causal or logical correlations. The prevalence of the present tense over the future tense is emphasized.

A person does not have to develop or to strive far to become a millionaire, he *is* a millionaire (magic thinking).

The ability to abstract is greatly reduced. This defect increases the tendency toward fusion of concepts, particularly those which show common characteristics, such as are found in the mechanism of condensation or in neologisms.

DISTORTION AND DISPLACEMENT

The recollection of the dream is, in general, defective. As in all our thinking processes, all kinds of inner psychic resistances make themselves felt at our attempt to recall our dreams. We, therefore, take the incompleteness of the recalled dreams as a matter of course and try to analyze the fragments saved from oblivion.

Some dreams are so inconsistent that it is almost impossible to place them in a logical context. S. Lowy is probably right when he postulates that in such cases "non-conceptual, affect-energetic processes" are present, that is, that the dream thoughts have not yet attained the stage of being "thinkable," have not yet left their "embryonic," affective level. Lowy believes that the dream is not primarily destined for conscious memory "but for intrapsychic affect-energetic purposes."

The effects of dream censorship can be seen in the following excellent example of distortion and omission given by Hug-Hellmuth:

"The patient, aged fifty, a refined lady, the widow of an officer, dreams that [57] *she goes to the military hospital and says to the guard that she must see the chief physician (and she mentions an unknown name) because she wishes to do service in the hospital. She emphasizes the word 'service' so much that the guard notices at once that she means 'love service' (Liebesdienst). The guard admits her with some hesitation, for she is an old lady. However, instead of coming to the chief physician she enters a large, gloomy room crowded with officers and military physicians standing and sitting at a long table. She presents her proposition to a staff surgeon, who understands her after just a few words. Her words are: 'I and many other women and young girls of Vienna are ready to—(a murmuring ensues) to the common soldiers and officers without preference.' The partly embarrassed, partly malicious faces of the officers show that the murmuring has been understood correctly. The lady continues: 'I know that our decision sounds strange, but we are absolutely serious about it. They don't ask the soldier in the trenches whether he does or does not want to die.' A silence lasting for a few minutes follows. The staff surgeon puts his arm around her waist and says, 'Madam, suppose it would really happen—(murmuring).' She removes his arm with the thought, 'All men are alike,' and replies, 'My Lord, I am an old woman and shall never be in the position. By the way, there is one condition that would have to be considered—age. To prevent an older lady from—(murmuring) to a very young boy, that would be horrible!' The staff surgeon replies, 'I understand perfectly.' A few officers, among them one who courted her in her youth, roar with laughter. The lady wishes to be shown to the chief physician in order to get everything straight. At this moment it strikes her that she doesn't know his name. Despite that, the staff surgeon asks her politely and respectfully to go to the second floor up a narrow, winding, iron staircase leading from his room. As she mounts the stairs, she hears an officer say, 'That must be a great decision, no matter whether one is young or old.' She walks up an endless flight of stairs with the feeling of simply fulfilling a duty."*

We see that in this dream all important names and events have been changed or eliminated from the patient's recollection.

Some dreams, however, reveal the repressed antimoral and antisocial forces more openly.

The recalled dream content is different from the original one, not only because of the incompleteness of our memory, but also because of the mechanisms of distortion which operate simultaneously with our efforts to recall the dream. As smaller or larger parts of the dream plot are lost in this attempt, we are in general inclined to substitute creations of our fantasy for the missing parts of our recollections.

Now we shall examine the mechanism of *disguise and displacement* in the following dream [58] of a twenty-nine-year-old man suffering from impotence:

"My friend S. was pregnant which caused him to suffer great pain. No physician could help him so I decided to see a magician who received his patients on the same floor where I was located. I entered his office feeling uneasy and self-conscious. There I saw an old man with a white beard. He had me sit down and asked me some questions concerning my friend. At first, I didn't have enough confidence in him, but he explained my friend's condition to me so exactly that my doubts disappeared and I described to him my friend's disease in detail. I told him that my friend had a very sick stomach and a weak bladder, that he had to get up during the night to urinate, and so on. The magician answered that this report was not sufficient and that I had to tell more about my friend. I promised to do this and went away."

This dream is a good example of distortion. If we know that the patient's friend not only is not "pregnant" but is healthy and athletic, and we know that our patient is weak and impotent, we shall realize that the "friend" in this dream means the patient himself. In the dream the patient "displaces" his personal conflict to another person—a very important defensive mechanism of the dream. The "magician" is but the mask of a "physician." This immediately becomes apparent when we learn that he is "receiving patients." Our patient, who is seeking help for his pitiable friend, enters the room feeling self-conscious. There is no reason for this feeling if it is the friend, and not the patient, who is sick; but there *is* a reason to feel uneasy if the disease in question is his own and, above all, if this disease is as embarrassing as sexual impotence. We see in this dream not only the physician and the patient disguised, but we also see the disease changed into several diseases. This is common in dreams.

We summarize: *Instead of a picture which is painful, we see another picture (or a chain of other pictures) of a less disagreeable character.*

Sometimes an apparently insignificant detail of the manifest dream content covers, as a result of this change in the evaluation, a very important detail of the latent dream content. The value of the single dream element is, in general, changed by means of displacement and disguise. In the above dream we see "pregnancy," "pains," "sick stomach," and "weak bladder"—all that instead of impotence. The other details of the session with the "magician" are the exact reproduction of the patient's real experience during his first session with his analyst, especially so far as the emotional part is concerned (self-consciousness).'

There is a reason why the dream magician saw his patients on the same floor. In the house where the analyst lived the patient had met one of his friends, and each time he entered the doctor's house he did so with trepidation lest his friend see him walking into a psychiatrist's office. As a secondary factor, this detail of the dream fulfilled a concurrent wish of the patient. "I wish nobody would see me when I enter the office of the doctor."

From such a detail we can surmise how economically a dream operates. The dream as a biological phenomenon has all the characteristics of all other biological phenomena, namely, that of greatest functional economy. In this connection, one may think of the function of the diaphragm. When we breathe, the diaphragm moves up and down. During this motion a great number of functions are performed simultaneously. An exchange of gases takes place in the lungs; the liver is squeezed out and filled with blood by the negative pressure thus created; blood is pumped from the abdomen up into the thorax; the entire body circulation receives a powerful propulsion.

The same functional economy is operating behind the dream. I once heard the anecdote about a visitor who came to see Thomas A. Edison and expressed surprise that it was so hard to open the gate leading to the garden of the great inventor. The inventor smiled and said, "You may be right; but each time you open this gate you automatically water my vegetable garden."

In displacement, one idea surrenders to another idea the entire volume of its emotional charge (cathexis). Consequently, an idea which was not endowed with this special type of cathexis receives this endowment from an idea which apparently was not deemed acceptable by the dreamer's consciousness. *The cathexis is shifted from the forbidden to the acceptable, from the more embarrassing to the less embarrassing.*

We might note here that sexual desires often appear in the dream as criminal desires. It is as though the antisocial element in our culture is more tolerable than the antimoral one.

Symbolization

"The language of the dream is the language of primordial man. For man's aboriginal ancestor also expressed himself in symbolic writings," says Stekel. We see in the writings of the Chinese and in the picture writings of the primitive Indians an abundance of symbols.

The Egyptian writings consist of pictures signifying single letters. The word KLEOPATRA (Fig. 14), for instance,

K L E O P A T R A Divine
Feminine gender

FIGURE 14

shows an ideo-symbolism only in the determinants "divinity" and "feminine gender." See extreme right figure 14 below. In the semicircle "divinity" we recognize our "aureola," and also the "egg" as expression of the "feminine gender" can be accepted as a female symbol today as well as at any previous time.

The Chinese writings come closer to the ideographic system. The Chinese thinks of a *tree* and draws a tree:

FIGURE 15

He thinks of *the sun,* and writes it in his way:

FIGURE 16

And when he looks over the landscape and sees the sun rising behind the trees, he calls this part of his world "tung"—meaning East—and fixes this natural phenomenon in his writing.

Tree   Sun   East

FIGURE 17

The writing of the primitive Indians is almost purely ideographic. Figure 18 consists almost exclusively of symbols and contains pictures which can be understood only by means of interpretation.

The drawing represents a *Petition to Congress*[1] which was sent to the United States Government by a delegation of the Chippewa Indians. It refers to certain fishing privileges in small lakes near Lake Superior and was written in 1849. It consists of ideographs which denote that all tribes represented

[1] From *Pre-Alphabet Days,* by Otto F. Ege. Norman T. A. Munder, Baltimore, Md.

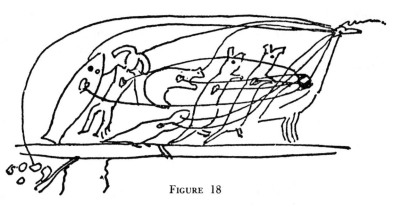

FIGURE 18

by their respective totems (crane, marten, bear, man, catfish) are united in their views and feelings (lines drawn from eye to eye and from heart to heart) and are looking forward toward Congress (line leading forward from the crane) regarding the lakes (line leading back toward the "lakes").

A "symbol" is an idea which substitutes for another idea from which it derives its significance. "Symbol" is derived from the Greek "symbállein" meaning "to throw together." Symbolization is a process in which one object is represented by another. We assume that symbols are products of condensation of several ideas. The latter are of the metaphorical, allegorical, and allusive kind. As in displacement, the object which is embarrassing, painful, or forbidden is replaced, i.e., symbolized, by another that is less embarrassing or forbidden. The dynamics of symbolization represent one of the most fascinating problems in dream interpretation.

We know much about symbols and yet we do not know enough about the deeper processes leading to symbolization. There are certain points of contact between the psychological, etymological, anthropological, and semantic approaches to symbolization. Symbolism appears in dreams under the same conditions as any other distortion appears, and the basic laws of symbolization appear to be uniform in all parts of the globe. Symbols have been retained for generations by various ethnic groups of the past and present. They emanate from what C. G. Jung has called the "collective unconscious" of mankind. There is a layer of our mind from which our pre-logical thoughts are derived.

In folklore, fairy tales, old writings, ideograms, we find a great deal of symbolization. Religions operate with symbols. The famous picture of Madonna treading on a snake is not called "Madonna Treading on a Snake," but "The Immacu-late Conception." The meaning of the picture can be under-

FIGURE 19
THE IMMACULATE CONCEPTION

stood only by accepting the meaning of symbols. The snake equals primal sin. Treading on the snake equals the con-quest of primal sin.

Even the average person of today has a good understanding of symbolic expression. There are pictures of fixed symbolic value. *The snake,* for instance, has been used as a picture of sin since the earliest stage of Hebraic-Christian culture. (The Legend of Paradise.) We understand pictures like "The

FIGURE 20

Immaculate Conception" or "St. George Killing the Dragon," which are age-old portrayals of Man conquering Evil. (See Figs. 20, 21 and 22.)

FIGURE 21

ST. GEORGE KILLING THE DRAGON (After Vittore Carpaccio, Venice)

Rank has pointed out that the basic concept of the composition of a dragon killer is derived from the universal and omnipresent Oedipus situation. The "rescuer of the maiden" in most cases represents symbolically a patricide, while the "maiden" is a mother image. (Cf. Figs. 21 and 22.)

We must admit, however, that no symbol is generally valid

FIGURE 22

After Raphael's St. George and the Dragon (Original at the National Gallery of Art, Washington, D. C.)

and that under certain circumstances every symbol may contain a meaning other than its usual one.

In our endeavor to understand symbols we find the concept of "spheres" (Bleuler, Schilder) very useful. According to this concept, ideas and perceptions which are related to the original one and to each other conceptually or emotionally may serve as symbols.

We can think of them as concentric circles, spheres, which show a relation to the factual objects and their meanings for the individual. Some of their properties overlap. (See Fig.

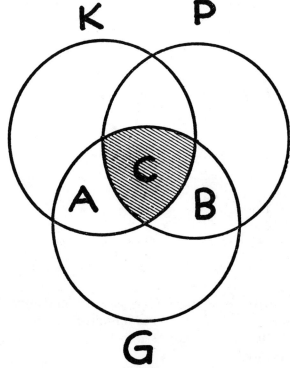

FIGURE 23

CONCEPTUAL SPHERE   A = Common to K and G (Weapon)
K = Knife   B = Common to G and P (Emitting Content)
G = Gun   C = Common to K, P, and G (Oblong in Form
P = Penis   and Potentially Dangerous)

23.) The qualities they have in common form the matrix for symbolic shifts from sphere to sphere. The concept of the "male genital," for example, has the following properties in common with the concept "gun": it is oblong, can be used as an object of aggression, and it can emit contents.

The three spheres and their common properties may be brought into a symbolic relationship and shifts from one sphere to the other may occur. The reason for such a process has been mentioned before: it is the necessity to represent a prohibited desire in a disguised form because of the interference by the superego.

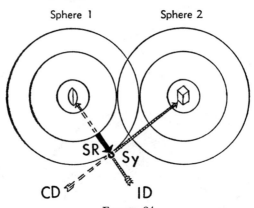

FIGURE 24

SR = Superego   Resistance;   Sy = Point   of Symbolization; CD = Concurrent Desire (for possession); ID = Id Desire (for illicit sexual gratification).

When drives reach their objectives without interference, we have action. When action is inhibited by counterforces, the desire for imagery comes into being. Such drives then express themselves in symbols.

Symbols appear through a clash of contradictory trends. We may have to repress an overstrong desire for an illicit gratification. The less tolerable desire then gives way to a more tolerable one. Thus the symbol is, as a rule, a compromise of two (or more) tendencies. It appears at focal points of two (or more) spheres. A person who suppresses his over-strong desire for possession of jewelry and also his desire for an illicit sexual gratification may experience a dream in which [59] *he opens a precious jewelry box.*

In his dream the antimoral desire remains unconscious, and the less embarrassing desire becomes the manifest dream content. The "opening of the box with a key" then represents the symbolic representation of the original (sexual) impulse.

In the dreamer's mind a shift has occurred from the sphere of the "female genital" to that of the "jewelry box," since both concepts have many properties in common (desirability, the quality of being a container, of representing a thing of value to the woman, etc.).

From the preceding we can see that symbolization is a displacement from one sphere to another. The symbol acquires qualities of two or more spheres. Condensations occur on the basis of attributes which are common to two or more spheres. A similar process takes place in the representation of the whole by a part (*pars pro toto*) and of a part by the whole (*totum pro parte*). In this manner, to the fetishist a

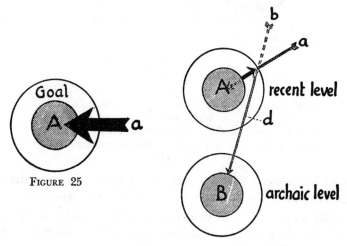

FIGURE 25

FIGURE 26

woman's apron, e.g., may symbolize the woman. Counterforces and inhibitions are responsible for such shifts of
cathexis within the conceptual realm.

A goal-directed desire leads to action designed to satisfy
it. If no interference occurs, the desire finds its gratification.
The interference which a desire may encounter stems from
the superego. Figure 25 illustrates this: a desire *a* is directed
toward a goal *A*. It reaches this goal because there is no
superego resistance.

If, however, the desire *a* meets a superego resistance, the
desire tends to be repressed and deflected. The following
sketch illustrates this deflection. It follows the rule that an
accessory, less prominent, less inhibited affect-laden desire

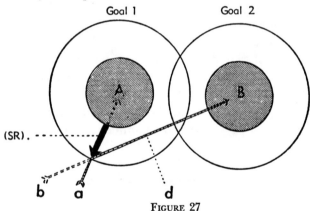

FIGURE 27

a = goal directed thought (desire).

b = accessory, less prominent, less inhibited, less
affect-laden thought (desire) which has existed simultaneously.

d = deviation of the original thought *a* in the direction of the accessory goal *B* due to superego resistance (SR).

b which has existed simultaneously with the desire *a* determines the ultimate direction of the deflected energy. (Fig. 27.)

With Schilder we can distinguish between shifts occurring
on the level of two coordinated spheres, i.e., spheres of the

between two subordinated spheres or spheres belonging to
two spheres of different categorical level (*vertical shift*). In
the latter case, we may be dealing with one sphere of recent
genesis and another sphere of archaic character.[1]

Distortions in the dream occur in both ways. (Fig. 26, p.
107.)

Generalized "sphere reactions" often substitute for specific "concept reactions." They occur in normal thinking,
too, but as a rule are suppressed. When we have difficulty in
finding the correct word, we tend to react with generalized
concepts or spheres (undirected thinking). A substitute word
of the same sphere is then used. This is particularly the case
when the desired word represents an abstract. "Church" may
be used instead of "religion"; "soldier" instead of "courage."
Under pathological circumstances, a person may develop a
peculiar "sphere consciousness" (Stengel). That which was
the background of our thoughts may become the foreground
and influence the formation of images.

In this respect, there is a close resemblance between
aphasia and agnosia on the one hand, and symbolization on
the other (Schilder). In these organic diseases it is the affected
organ rather than the superego which inhibits the emerging
affect-charged material. As far as the thought processes are
concerned, they resemble, during sleep, those found in organic brain injury.

Just as words are in themselves not symbols of objects and
events, but symbols of concepts and attitudes, "figures"
shaped against their "background," so also the dream pictures
must not be considered as fixed characters but as expressions
of attitudes. The time is past when the mere appearance of a
telephone pole in a dream induced the analyst to regard the
phenomenon as a phallic representation. It is the dreamer's
internal emotional attitude that gives the symbol its specific
meaning.

Our thinking is not a smooth process in which one con-

[1] Cf. the "layer symbolism," page 70.

cept ranks with another; our thought, in developing, forces its way through various resistances. In selecting the most suitable expressions of thought we reject inadequate synonyms and other related ideas. We have to render thoughts from their formless, embryonic state into formed, conscious ideas. We have to observe rules of grammar and syntax. And, above all, as a sacrifice to our superego, we have to suppress the tendency to enact thoughts in their uncontrolled way.

All this takes place unconsciously and in an unthinkably short time. The integrity of our mental function is closely connected with the ability to select and arrange thoughts. Certain intoxications and brain disturbances impair the efficiency of this psychic task. Then the patient's thoughts and speech become primitive and unrestrained, as is often seen in cases of sensory aphasia and in schizophrenia. We then see a confusion between categories and spheres and an astonishingly frequent use of symbols (see page 458).

Schroetter and Silberer have made very valuable experimental contributions to the study of symbolization. Schroetter hypnotized a woman and suggested an idea which was repulsive to her, namely, that in her dream two women would have sexual intercourse with each other. The patient then produced a dream in which the sexual part was disguised by the use of symbols. In her dream, [60] *she saw her friend carrying a bag which bore the label, "For Ladies Only."* A bag is a female symbol. (See page 149.)

Silberer proved that abstract ideas sometimes turn into visual pictures (visions), particularly if the person is extremely tired or sleepy. He described one of his own hypnagogic visions. He thought of a particular passage in one of his articles that was to be corrected. His symbolic vision was [61] *planing a piece of wood.* Silberer in his extensive experimental work also proved that not only thoughts but also the dreamer's attitude toward thoughts sometimes turns into symbolic visions when the individual is struggling against obtruding ideas.

CONDENSATION

In the process of symbolization similar objects or ideas frequently become condensed and fused into unities. Condensation often occurs on the basis of an emotion which is common to all constituents.

Suppose we have three persons: *Mr. A, Mrs. B,* and *Professor C,* of a certain equal quality, *Q,* (for example, they are all widows and widowers). The product of condensation (*P*) may be found according to the formula:

$$P = (A + B + C) Q$$

All three persons show specific relations toward the environment:

Aa = generous;
$B\beta$ = living in a foreign country;
$C\gamma$ = famous teacher.

In the dream the persons *A, B,* and *C* may become unified in the picture of, let us say, *B* (in which *A* and *C* are rejected and invisible). The end product of condensation would represent the formula:

$$B\ (a + \beta + \gamma).$$

The fictitious dream may have the following text:

[62] *I see Mrs. B* (B) *in Alaska* (β) *in a mourning dress* (Q) *teaching children* (γ) *of the poor* (a).

The reason for the condensation of the three different persons, *A, B,* and *C,* may lie in the fact that all three have the equal quality, *Q,* which in itself may be insignificant. *B* in the above dream is a "composite person" synthesizing the characters (a, β, and γ) from three personalities.

Sometimes the product of condensation in a dream may have the appearance *A* and the name *B*. Or the figure *A* may have the traits β (from *B*) and γ (from C).

The reasons for condensation in dreams are (1) functional economy, (2) apperceptive deficiency, and (3) evasion of censorship.

Condensation is a process by which an idea appropriates the emotional cathexis of one or many other ideas. Condensation of contrasting ideas is based on a primeval trait of human thinking (see also "Bipolarity," p. 229). Primitive language abounded in words of double meaning. Even Latin has preserved some of these concepts: *altus* means "high" as well as "deep"; *sacer* means "holy" as well as "accursed"; and we also know the ambivalent meaning of the word *taboo,* as "holy" and "unclean."

Condensation, displacement, and projection can be observed in the following dream of a forty-two-year-old businessman:

[63] *"I was in bed and woke up seeing Martha (a twenty-year-old girl, very attractive) washing my wall. At the same time, I had the feeling that a woman (Mary?) was looking in through the window from outside. I felt upset about the fact that somebody was eavesdropping on me."*

The patient has had trouble with his wife recently because of his extramarital interests. His wife threatened to divorce him. He maintains that while he loves her, he is obsessively attracted to other women. He tried to "whitewash" himself by telling his wife (and his analyst) that his infidelity was of obsessive-compulsive nature. In the dream, the girl who is the object of his interest (and not he) does the whitewashing. The patient is a Catholic, and we see the conscience reaction in the image of (Virgin) "Mary" looking through the window.

The picture of Martha washing the wall while the patient is in bed represents a scene in which the dreamer's sexual object is brought into his immediate proximity. We can recognize without difficulty that Martha's activity is guilt-provoking. But the choice of the symbol "washing" reveals a condensation of two contrasts: the illicit act and its annulment.

Neurotic symptoms have a similar structure. The innervation absorbs the entire cathexis and represents a means of motor discharge of energy which had been accumulated (dammed up) by repression; but, at the same time, it affords the patient a means of secret gratification and of self-punishment.[1]

Neologisms, new word formations, should be mentioned in connection with condensation. They are characteristic not only for the speech of schizophrenics, but also for the language of the dream. The following dream series will be especially illustrative:

[64] *"I see a man in kneeling position. There is an air of tragedy. The room is in darkness. I go to the phone to call the police. When I return the body has disappeared. Out of the darkness I see a hand pointing in the general direction of where the body was. I hear a voice saying, 'That was Oylemani or Ale-a-mani!'"*

The dreamer has coined a new word. Before we proceed to the interpretation of this dream, here are three more of this patient's dreams to make the point more comprehensive.

[65] *"A barren field like Mexican desert. I am all alone. In the far distance a bright shine like sunrise. Air of mystery and suspense."*

[66] *"I woke up and was told by my mother that I had been crying in my sleep. Then with tears I kept repeating, 'Please, God! Make me a good person.'"*

[67] *"A steep hill. I am walking uphill carrying a stack of books. The road seems endless and I don't seem to make any progress. Awake tired and depressed."*

The patient had discovered in himself a talent for sculpture. Here is one of his favorite sketches for a statue. He called it "The Fettered Man."

The patient was thirty-one-years-old, slim, tall, with a history of tuberculosis. His religious background was Protestant.

---

1 In mucous colitis, e.g., we can see a clear demonstration of this principle: the motor excitement leads to the evacuation of diarrheic stools, the stimulations of an erogenous zone (rectum) and the accompanying sexual fantasies. Unconscious gratification proceeds simultaneously with the pain and the discomfort of the self-inflicted punishment.

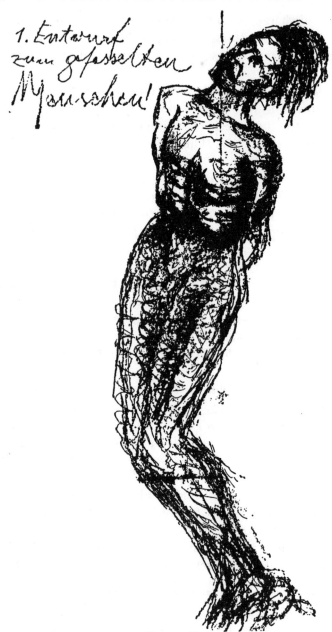

FIGURE 28

His parents were divorced when he was six or seven, and he lost track of his father. He never saw or heard from him during all the ensuing years. His mother remained unmarried. At first, the boy was placed in a boarding school where he remained until he was fourteen. Then he rejoined his mother. The boarding school had been very strict and strongly accented its religious training which included, in particular, the reading of the Bible.

When first seen, the patient presented himself as a homosexual masochist whose specific fantasy was to be ill-treated by a woman. In the course of analysis it became imperative to reconstruct the patient's secret life plan which appeared to represent the core of his neurosis.

Alfred Adler emphasized that all neurotics strive toward a secret goal; but Adler considered this striving to be exclusively a quest for power. We agree that every neurotic has an unconscious neurotic goal. Sometimes, it is fantastic and fictitious. The patient's actions, his conduct in his neurosis as well as in life in general, serve the achievement of this goal. In our case it was possible to discover the specific life plan: it was the patient's *reunion with his father*. He had last seen him in early boyhood. But in fantasy he cherished a picture of the missing parent, and the fantasy father, subsequently, received almost divine characteristics.

We do not maintain that the dreams recorded here should serve as a paradigma of how dreams in general should be interpreted. We offer the above dream series only as an illustration of the importance of neologisms for the understanding of dreams. In dreams, words or ideas congeal, and sometimes, a seemingly nonsensical word may prove to be of the utmost importance for the understanding of the case.

First, in these dreams we detect a contrast, an "antithesis," between *darkness* (dream 64) and *light* (dream 65). In dream 64 the patient has a general impression of darkness. Out of this darkness and gloom, as it were, emerges a figure, a victim of tragedy, against a background of light.

Consider some of the sentences in the dreams: "I am alone in a barren field." "I am in a dark room." "I am walking uphill, carrying a stack of books" (compare: "stack of Bibles"). In such sentences, we see repeated motives which are of diagnostic importance. His lonesomeness, his desire to please his father ("make me a good person"), his carrying of a burden, his sense of having a great historic mission,—all participate in his unconscious life plan, the "central idea" of which is identification with Jesus Christ, who, after all His suffering on this earth, was also reunited with His Father.

The neologism "Oilemani" (or "Ale-a-mani") was found to be a condensation of several words used in the New Testament. The complete text is "Eli, Eli, lama sabachtani?" ("Oh Lord, why hast Thou forsaken me?"—Matthew 27:46.)

The dreams contain precipitates of the patient's many years of religious training during which he had become well-versed in the New Testament. Under the influence of his personal experiences, a masochistic *ideal of suffering* was born with the view of gratification in the hereafter. In his unconscious mind this gratification was equivalent to a reunion with his father.

Here is another example of neologism:

[68] *"With Dr. G. on a bus. He introduces me to a nice-looking, shy girl. Her brother is with her. We all sit on the top deck as the bus proceeds. The girl is in the center, the brother on the right. I sit on the left, and Dr. G. is opposite me. The girl and I talk with much interest. It is as if we were*

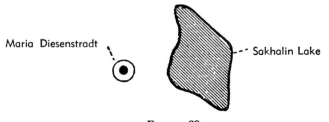

Maria Diesenstradt   Sakhalin Lake

FIGURE 29

*a little naïve, but we like each other very much. She tells me
she is from Siberia, from a place called 'Maria Diesenstradt'
or 'Deenstradt,' just to the left of Sakhalin Lake.''*

The patient elaborated on the dream as follows:

"This dream reminds me of many strange places on the
globe. General feeling of strangeness. I associate 'decency'
with 'Diesenstradt,' and 'Mary' and 'to marry' with 'Maria.'"

The patient had the obsession that, in order to be acceptable to a girl and to be successful with women in general, one
had to abandon decency. In his neurosis he vacillated between
acceptance of the superego demands and renunciation of
them. He wanted a girl he could love and wed, but the deep
distrust of women ("if you are decent they will cheat you")
restrained him for many years from establishing normal relations with them.

His compliance and the dependency on parental protection
are expressed in the dream when a girl is introduced to him
by the analyst rather than by his selecting her himself. The
problem of whether he should have a decent (complying)
girl who is unattractive but faithful, or an indecent, un-
dependable girl who is sexually appealing is expressed in this
neologism. "Where can I find such a girl? Will she offer me
the warmth I am craving, or will she be cold like the Siberian
winter?" Although he is drawing a geographic location, in
reality he sketches a symbol of the female genital (cf. page
149). We have reason to believe that an important latent
homosexual trend expresses itself in the dream in the person
of the girl's brother. Here lies one of the roots of the patient's
ambivalent attitude toward women.

The next dream contains an interesting example of new
word creation.

The patient sees in his dream [69] *a telegram and on it
the words "Operation Quilty." While he is inwardly shaking
with emotion, he controls himself outwardly and says, showing off his sophistication: "This means the Atomic Bomb."*

According to the patient's associations, the word "Quilty" is condensed and contains the words "Quilt" and "Guilty." "Quilt" refers to forbidden sexual pleasures he had enjoyed in bed and for which he feels "guilty."

The patient masks his concern with these experiences and shows off his superior insight by giving an explanation. The explanation is nonsense; but it reveals to the investigator the "atomic" importance of the guilt factor in the patient's neurosis.

Condensations serve as disguises. The patient does not simply shift his personal conflicts to another person in the dream, but, on the contrary, takes over the shape or character of the other person in order to camouflage his real character.

The following dream contains a large number of scenes in which we can see products of condensations. The dream was reported by a girl, aged twenty-two. At the time, she was worried because the man for whom she had cared very much spiritually showed a strong physical desire for her. She refused him, to be sure, but not without an intense emotional conflict as the dream indicates:

[70] *"A nun is visiting us. She takes off her clothes, and I see that under her cowl she wears an up-to-date silk dress. I also notice that instead of having her hair cut, as all nuns do, she wears it plaited. Her face is pretty and she has a nice, almost coquettish smile. She has come with the intention of stealing some jewels.*

"A young man enters. He is tall, blond, and handsome. He says something and then takes a jewel out of his brief-case. Apparently he has received it from somebody, and now he feels that he has no right to keep it. I take the jewel, but at the same time the nun jumps at me and tries to take it away from me. We are fighting hard at the door. I succeed in pushing the jewel through a slit under the door into the other room. I am glad because I have thus saved the jewel. I then go to the other room in order to get the jewel but, to my great surprise and horror, it seems to have disappeared. I go back,

and the nun tells me that she has taken the jewel from the other room. Then she leaves."

In this dream we see the patient's conflict between her moral and her instinctive tendencies as she struggles with the nun. The patient's moral ego, which is represented by the nun, is condensed in the dream symbol. The nun is also an up-to-date lady in the dream. This fact alone would suffice for our interpretation of the nun as a representation of the patient's ambivalence and of the whole scene as a picture of her main conflict: *physical or mental love?* The jewel symbolizes a treasure, a thing of great value; it is the patient's chastity. It represents something which she is afraid to lose. It is a bipolar symbol which represents both her virginity and the physical love of which she is fearful.

The patient saves the jewel from the nun, that is, she follows her instinctive desires and permits the physical approach by her male friend. But in the end the nun retains the jewel, that is, the moral tendencies prevail and temptation is conquered.

The young and handsome man does not take the jewel, the virginity, from the patient, but he offers it to her. This shows another idea intertwined with the previous ones, namely, the idea of a man who helps her to preserve her chastity, and offers her his respect (wish-fulfillment). The young man "has no right to have the jewel" unless he is the patient's husband. The struggle with the nun at the door also contains other roots, the discussion of which would lead us far from our present issue.

Because of the fact that dreams in general are products of multiplied condensation, there may be several explanations of any given dream event; and all may be true, but at different levels and from different angles. It is often difficult to decide which of the possible explanations are essential and which are contributory.

A form of condensation of infantile and current guilt feelings must be also considered because we meet it frequently:

[71] *"I had an old Packard car. I parked it somewhere but didn't remember where.*

"Then I met my wife on the street. She said something to me, but I was still very much worried about where the car was. I was angry at my wife's interference and I shook her.

"A tough fellow attacked my wife. I went for him, and he threatened to gouge out my eyes."

The contrast here is the worry about the "old Packard" and the attention he is to pay to his wife. The "old Packard" represents the patient's mother, an object of strong incestuous fixation, who was against his marriage. In this dream the patient's wife is attacked by someone else, but this happens immediately after the patient "shakes" her. We recognize here his own aggressive designs toward his wife who "interferes" with his thought of the "old Packard."

The Oedipal situation expressed in this dream contains the element of gouging out the patient's eyes as a form of retaliation. It reminds one of the fate of the mythical Oedipus. In this dream, the self-punishment idea occurring as a result of the patient's inner hostility toward his wife is surcharged with the punitive ideas derived from the basic oedipal situation.

Incomplete condensation in dreams can be seen in the picture of changing objects or persons. The following dream of a twenty-three-year-old woman is a typical example of this mechanism.

[72] *"My father tries to murder me. My daughter is with me. My father becomes my husband. I'm finally shoved into a closet. Then it is my sister, and I am watching her. Police catch my husband who again is my father. My brother is another alternative. My father is getting married. I say he should be analyzed."*

The dream will become intelligible if we realize that the patient has a strong father fixation. The father's attempt to "murder" the patient, in our interpretation, is his attempt to get married.[1] He is divorced from the patient's mother and the patient is constantly afraid that he might get married again. (That would "kill" her.) Her remark, "he should be analyzed," has a double meaning. It indicates the importance of the father complex; it is as though by means of this phrase the patient admonished her analyst to take up the father (complex) in analysis. On the other hand, she also doubts her father's sanity if he can look for another woman's love while "disregarding" (shoving into a closet) his daughter's affections. These affections are represented by the shifts in the cast of the dream's psychodrama: from the patient's brother (with whom she was connected by common intimacies), her husband, her sister (who did marry a short time ago), and her father, whose many expressions of genuine love were responsible for the patient's emotional attachment. In her dream, the patient indulges in a naïve expectation that some superior force (the police) would stop her father from committing his "crime."

SECONDARY ELABORATION

We call secondary elaboration those changes of the dream content the patient makes when, in the process of recalling the dream, questions of intelligibility and logic are taken into consideration. This is a concession the ego makes to the superego. But there are also other difficulties present. The resistance of the ego against the presence of unconscious material is so strong that it lasts to the very last moment, and, before the dream is fully recalled, in the last fraction of the second, as it were, additional changes in the dream contents still are taking place.

[1] Jung and Silberer emphasize that in the dream "killing" may have the meaning of "overcoming." If a man dreams [73] *that he killed his father*, this does not necessarily express his Oedipus complex, but his desire to outdistance, outdo and overcome his father.

(Q) "Why do we sometimes dream in symbolic disguise and sometimes without?"

(A) The dream contains, as a rule, manifestations of both forces—the instinctual and the inhibitional, the latter governed by the super-ego. Either or both representatives may be found in an individual dream. However, there seems to exist also a connection between the ego lucidity and the dream distortion; the closer to the full awakening, the less distorted is the manifest dream content.

Chapter Three

DREAM SYMBOLS

> *True symbolism is the representation*
> *of the general by the specific, not as*
> *dream or shadow, but as the living*
> *momentary revelation of the Unex-*
> *plorable.*
>
> GOETHE

SYMBOLIC PARALLELISM

According to Freud, Scherner was the first to discover that dream symbolism is a suitable material for scientific use. Scherner's findings were foreign to our way of thinking and appeared to be beyond what we call science. But the use of dream symbolism in scientific investigations became a fact, and today it seems impossible to understand a dream without accepting the phenomenon of symbolization.

To interpret a dream is not a simple matter of translation according to universal rules. The interpretation of each dream requires some knowledge of the patient and the assistance by the patient which he provides with his confessions and associations. The doctor's intimate knowledge of the psychodynamics of disease is a safeguard against misinterpretation. Therefore, any dictionary of the science of dream interpretation would be unreliable if its offerings were applied without respect to the given practical situation. This applies also to all our definitions.

123

Their validity is limited by the characteristics of the individual case. Symbols discussed here have to be considered only as general schemes; they represent the most frequent and average meanings. Any new case may bring about a new meaning of the most common symbol.

However, in spite of all mental reservations we are to observe in regard to symbolism, we must emphasize that symbols used by dreams are not at all arbitrary constructions of the dreaming mind. Symbolization proceeds along certain lines which we call "symbolic parallelism." In accordance with a previous statement (page 101), symbols occur as an effect of amalgamation of two or more ideas. At least one of them, usually a wish, is opposed by other forces within the ego.

Because of her moral training, a woman's inner sexual cravings may lead to the fear of being sexually overpowered by a man. Through suppression of the sexual character of this idea, this fear in the dream may be shifted to a parallel, and less embarrassing, socially accepted situation, and may appear as fear of being, for instance, shot by a man. "Sexual intercourse" then appears in the symbolic picture of "shooting." This symbol stands for danger; on its manifest level it is danger to life, on the latent level it is danger to morals. Ideas and concepts related to one another logically or emotionally are usually expressed in this symbolic parallelism. Disguise, displacement, distortion, condensation, etc., are products of this process.[1]

In the symbol of "shooting" sometimes both tendencies, the sexual and the criminal, can be detected.

The following is a dream in which this can be observed. It was dreamed by a twenty-eight-year-old salesman whose latent sadistic tendencies toward women accounted for most

[1] It would lead too far if we wanted to give the complete associative background for all its symbols in each case. Let me state that the interpretations of symbols quoted here have, in the main, been arrived at through dreamers' revelations and associations as well as the author's extensive experience with dream symbolism.

of his difficulties in maintaining normal heterosexual relations.

[74] *"Mother has two or more little dogs and girls. She encourages me to take them out, and I have success.*

"Then there is a plot to shoot at women (murder them?) for sport. It seems very cruel to me after we get close enough to see them. The whole town assembles to watch the ambushes.

"We shoot. I don't at first, then I shoot at a woman's hip instead of her head or heart to avoid killing her. She laughs and sneers, however, and so I shoot at her head in anger."

The patient's mother is what we call a "phallic woman," i.e., a woman who runs the lives of all members of the family, including that of the father. Her exaggerated concern for the patient's girl friends, whom she selected for him according to her own taste, led him at an early age to hate her and to become enraged at the slightest provocation. He protested against this infringement of his personal rights all the more as he felt a very strong sexual attraction toward his mother which he tried to overcome. His first sadistic aggressions thus were directed toward his mother. Killing her (in his fantasy) meant overcoming her influence, asserting his masculinity and independence.

The patient carried this latent grudge against his mother into his relations with women in general. He hated them because he was dependent on their love; judging in a way of clichés, he suspected dominating tendencies in all of them ("she laughs and sneers"). He was determined not to yield but rather to "beat them to the punch"; hence his sadistic attitude towards women.

In the act of shooting, as portrayed in the dream, we may detect a symbol of that sexual contact which had to be repressed as far as the patient's mother was concerned. In the dream he can let himself go—everybody else is doing it ("sport," "the whole town watches"). But his initial statement, "Mother has two or more little *dogs and girls*" (he has no sisters) shows his low consideration for girls. The words "I have success" contain a hypocrisy. It is this success in taking out the girls on mother's terms that drove him into his bitter, anti-feministic attitude.

"Archetypes"

Some symbols have been used by mankind for millennia and have appeared again and again in myths, rituals, legends, fairy tales, and religious images. It appears that if we penetrate to the deep layers of the human psyche we find that mankind has much more in common than many of us have been inclined to believe. On that level, we all seem to have the same religion, but we call it by different names and express it in different symbols and metaphors. On that level, our holidays are the same whether we call them Christmas, Chanukah, or Feast of Light; our initiation ceremonies are the same whether we call them confirmation, Barmizvah, Baptism, hazing, cornerstone ceremony, inauguration, or the like. We all believe in the supreme idealism of sacrifice. Throughout the history of mankind, the idea of sacrifice was expressed in all sorts of dramatic imagery, varying according to the cultural level and the spiritual objectives involved. We read in the Bible of Abraham, who is called upon by God to sacrifice his son; of the Son whom God, the Father, himself sacrifices; we read about crude and primitive religious concepts of savage tribes, subscribing to human sacrifice as a supreme service to their divinity; we are ready to sacrifice life and fortune for ideas or for country.

Jung, Silberer, Roheim, Frazer, and others have done meritorious work in tracing some of the common symbols back to their sources. Jung refers to these symbols as "archetypes," that is, symbols which are derived from universal mental qualities of mankind. Jung calls them "organs of the soul." They are formally determined without regard to their contents. To describe their deepest meaning is impossible, for knowledge of them consists only of approximations. Their meaning and importance has been molded by influences of time and space. Jacobi, in her excellent introduction to Jung's theory, compares the archetypes with the axial system of a crystal. The system's framework determines which habitus of crystallization are *possible;* the environment determines which possibility can be *realized.*

Jung claims that some images are pre-formed and are deposited in the "collective unconscious" of humanity in which every individual emotionally participates. These images may, under certain circumstances, rise into individual consciousness. The creative process, according to Jung, is based on the ability of the individual to raise such dormant images into his consciousness.

An archetype is, e.g., the *idea of rebirth,* which can be found in ancient rites, in dreams, in alchemy, in ceremonies of baptism and of initiation. Another archetypal concept is that of *conservation of energy,* which received its scientific formulation by Robert Mayer (1814-1878). Whether this energy is described by psychoanalysts as "libido" which undergoes various vicissitudes; or whether it is regarded, as in ancient times, as a "magic force" which directs our fate; or as a "soul" which lives immortally through all transfigurations, transmigrations, and transubstantiations; it is still the same universal force, and the universal mind of all humanity

FIGURE 30

FIGURE 31

sees in it an *eternal principle.* Some symbols, such as that of the snake biting its own tail (Fig. 30) have been used to represent this principle.

A few of the other archetypes described by Jung are: the "Old Wise Man," the embodiment of the lofty spiritual and creative principle; the "Magna Mater," the personification of the realistic, down-to-earth principle. Here we may also mention the eternal, life-giving principle represented by the archetype of the *uterus*. Its most primitive form is a geometrical concept representing a circle with a dark center. (Fig. 31.)

Courts with a fountain in the center which we find commonly designed in human dwellings through the millennia are unconscious reproductions of this principle. They represent the "font of life," the eternal "mother principle."

The following is a sketch after V. van Gogh reproducing a scene from the courtyard of the hospital at St. Remy where he was temporarily confined. (Fig. 32.)

FIGURE 32

This motive can also be found in old Moslem mosques, in Persian regal courts or in medieval German castles. (Fig. 33.)

Another ancient archetype is that of the "double" which Jung calls "the shadow." It is the "alter ego," our dark complement, the faithful companion who never leaves our side; our polar antagonist who has survived thousands of years

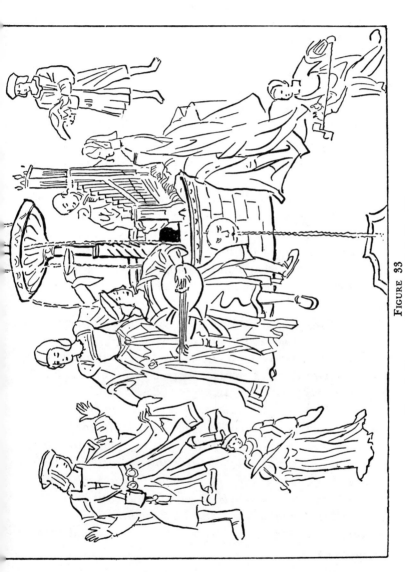

FIGURE 33

After a Concert. From the Gobelins Museum.

under many names. (See also page 191.) Rank has devoted a book to this subject.

"Mirror dreams," i.e., dreams in which the dreamer sees in a mirror his own image (frequently a distorted one) belong here. (See also Roheim.)

Psychologically speaking, "the shadow" is that part of us which we want to reject on moral and esthetic grounds—the Devil. We usually project it.[1] With an unsurpassed mastery, Dostoevsky described Ivan Karamasov's encounter with his "double." Ivan attacks his counterpart with the words: "Not for one minute shall I accept you as a reality. You are a lie, a disease, a phantom. I don't as yet know how to destroy you. You are my hallucination. You are the embodiment of myself —incidentally, only of a part of myself, of my thoughts and feelings—but only of the most ugly and stupid ones. All that is bygone—about what I have changed my mind long ago— you drag up to me as though it was news. . . . You say what I think."

Dostoevsky's genius thus reproduced the endopsychic perception of approaching insanity in his hero.

The following dream of one of my patients portrays a similar mechanism. The patient perceives in his dream the repressed complex.

[75] *"I was at school, apparently still a student. A young, emaciated, tall boy with long black hair coming down to his shoulders was permitted by the man in charge to use the toilet for the purpose of constructing an artificial urinary device. The construction would enable him to have an outlet for waste products. I believe it was to replace his penis. I sort of feared this man, considered him something to be avoided, maybe because he carried an infectious disease and because he looked so hideous."*

The patient sees in the hideous creature Shakespeare's Caliban, Stevenson's Mr. Hyde, Shelley's Frankenstein, all in one.

---

[1] Some clues to the understanding of race hatred are contained in this mechanism.

It is his own counterpart. In our case, we see in the picture of a "boy with long hair coming down to his shoulders," the dreamer's feminine (homosexual) component. It is not a coincidence that this strange individual is interested in replacing his penis by some artefacts. The patient's endopsychic perception of his feminine trends makes him frightened. One can fall victim to homosexuality as a consequence of an interpersonal relationship ("infectious disease"). The dream conjures up the image of homosexuality and also shows the patient's dread of it.

Other symbols of "the shadow" are "the fellow-traveler," and "the companion."

In the following dream it is "the hitch-hiker."

[76] *"I am driving along on a dark foggy, rainy night, road very bad and covered with snow and ice. A hitch-hiker stops me and I let him in. He starts to tell me that without him I am lost and I feel frightened. He tells me that I am going crazy. I shout, 'You get out!'*

"He is then out on the road behind me, looking very sorry, and I see that he is a little replica of myself, only shabbier.

"I gather all my courage and drive on. To my great elation, I now can see much better and awake with the feeling that I will get rid of my neurosis."

(Compare this dream with the dreams presented on page 189.)

Among ancients, the shadow was considered to have a close relation to the problem of *fertility*. An expression of this connotation is to be found in Hoffmannsthal's "Woman without Shadow" which was set to music by Richard Strauss.[1] Also in the Bible (Luke, 1:35), the angel prophesies to Mary that "the power of the Highest" will *"overshadow"* her, and that she will bear the Son of God.

Primitives often fear to cast a shadow on other people or things and also dread other people's shadows. To them, shadow, soul, and conscience appear identical. A shadow that

[1] Most symbols of good luck are originally symbols of fertility (Rank).

falls on a person may also be a "shadow of death." It may bring death or ill fate to that person.

The idea of resurrection also is expressed in the symbol of the shadow: the father is reborn in his son. The shadow of the father lives in the son. Often the shadow becomes identical with the "name." Thus, Mr. John Smith, in the hope of carrying on his own name through his son, calls his boy "John Smith, *Junior*." The ancients considered a name to be a part of the person.

Jung emphasizes that "archetypes have always belonged to the contents and treasures of religions." He mentions, e.g., the "Mandala symbolism," the symbolism of the protective "magic circle" which reaches back to paleolithic times.

All religions based on the image of immortality are based on the archetype of a magic force which directs the events of the world.

THE FAMILY IN DREAM SYMBOLS

(a) FATHER

According to the parallelism described above, the dreamer's father often appears in the dream as king,[1] emperor, master, conductor, chairman, teacher, father of someone else, pope, the "old man," God, engineer, chief, policeman, or other representative of authority. We use Freud's term in calling these masks "images" or "imagos."

Freud, Jung, Jones, Rank, Reik, Roheim, and other psychoanalytic investigators found that in myths, legends, and primitive religions, the *Sun* symbolizes the father. Freud's Schreber analysis offers a good example of this symbolism.

---

1 Jones points out that "king" derives from the Sanskrit *"gan"* which means "to beget." *"Ganaka"* means "father." Similar creations are "Pope," Latin: *"Papa,"* "Holy Father"; "Czar" was called "Little Father" (*Batyushka*); "Attila" comes from *"Atta,"* the father; the German King was a *"Landesvater"* and George Washington was "the father of his country."

Let us explore a few dreams in which the father is represented symbolically. A clerk, aged twenty-eight, dreamed:

[77] *"I am sitting in a street car. An elderly gentleman enters the compartment and speaks to me in a rough manner, saying, 'Can't you get up when I come in?' I resent his manner of speech and say, 'I am an adult and have the same right to this seat as you. If it had not been for your rudeness, I should have offered you my seat voluntarily.'"*

A short time prior to this dream, the patient's father (the "elderly gentleman") had complained of his son's practice of eating dinner without awaiting his arrival from work. To the father, such conduct was offensive. The parent also complained to the patient about the independence of the youth of today. The son reacted to this criticism with obstinacy, and this is also what we find expressed in his dream.

(b) MOTHER

The dreamer's mother may be represented by the image of a queen, an empress, a woman teacher, a nurse, the mother of someone else, a servant, a housekeeper, an old lady, the Virgin Mary (God's Mother), or, occasionally, by impersonal symbols such as the earth, a city (metro-polis = Mother City), an island,[1] the patient's birthplace, the font. (Compare what was said about the respective archetypes.)

Other symbols of mother are "Mother Church" or "Alma Mater."

One patient felt intensely that his *university* "does not care enough" for its students. He was an illegitimate child whose *mother* deserted him when he was an infant.

Symbolization in the dream occurs as the result of a prohibited, tabooed involvement of the person in question.

Rare but not unusual is the following symbol of the mother presented by a forty-one-year-old tailor. The patient

[1] As, for instance, Orin's dream in Eugene O'Neill's "Mourning Becomes Electra."

was engaged but he encountered unexpected difficulties in making the final decision regarding marriage. His analysis[1] revealed that a strong mother fixation was at the bottom of his neurotic indecision. In the terminal stage of his analysis he brought the following dream:

[77a] *"I was showing a guest through our new house and pointed to an upper floor where, through an opening, we could see a huge shaggy beast resembling a bear standing on its haunches. 'The family ghost,' I explained. Later the beast, which had fallen asleep with its paws clinging to a pole, had slid slowly down to our level, still asleep. I started to scream at it angrily in order to chase it away, but Ethel put her hand on my arm to restrain me. To my surprise she suggested I treat the bear kindly. I did, even putting out a saucer of milk for it. The response was amazing. It acted like a little kitten, gentle and friendly. It was a mother and had a cute little cub. They became our pets. One day the bear escaped through an open door. It never returned. We were sorry to see it go."*

"The family ghost" is the patient's overprotective and dominating mother. It is represented as a bear, a symbol not infrequently used to portray this type of parent. Here we think of the verbs "to *bear*" (in connection with "children") and "to be *born*." The patient's mother complex which was brought "down" to his conscious awareness, is not dead yet; it is "asleep." The patient wants to eliminate it ("chase it away") by force, but his fiancée, Ethel, suggests a more psychological approach. The patient feels that the hour of parting is at hand. . . . (For more about dreams occurring in the last phase of analysis see page 529.)

(c) SISTER

The dreamer's sister may appear in the disguise of a nurse (in England called "Sister"), a nun (the sister is "taboo" as is the nun), someone else's sister, etc.

---

[1] Carried out by Dr. J. O. S. Jaeger of New York.

(d) BROTHER

The dreamer's brother may be symbolized by a fraternity brother, someone else's brother, the "second ego," a clergyman (who addresses his audience as "Brothers and Sisters"), and may appear in many other disguises suitable for association.

SEX SYMBOLS

GENERAL VIEW

The sex instinct, as one which cannot be indulged fully, has a formidable part in our unconscious. If the instinct of self-preservation were subjected to as many taboos as is the instinct of propagation of the species, many conflicts would spring from it. Dreams, symptoms and delusions would then disclose a repression of hunger.

In our dreams, sex appears either openly or disguised, and we, therefore, find it necessary to become acquainted with its symbolic expressions.

It is important to note that in the early era of psychoanalysis, dream interpretation was concerned primarily with deciphering sexual symbols. Adler, Stekel, and Jung enlarged the scope of dream interpretation considerably. Today, only inexperienced or old-fashioned analysts are still hunting exclusively sexual equations in dreams.

In symbolic parallelism, the satisfactions of all human urges and desires are equal. Sex, hunger, thirst, desire to defecate, and to urinate—all are on the same plane. Symbols of the sex desire often appear displaced, which is in accord with the general tendency to replace more embarrassing by less embarrassing desires. The dream *"My child is starving"* or *"I will give some food to my bird"* may thus have a sexual meaning.

Stekel said: *"According to the symbolic parallelism, all bodily openings are equal to each other and may substitute for each other in the dream."* Mouth, eyes, ears, nasal openings, female sex organs, anus, urethra, and navel are symbolically equal.

Symbols of the Genitals in the Dream

MALE SEX SYMBOLS

1. *Inanimate Objects:* The phallus is symbolized by umbrella (opening represents erection), hat,[1] necktie, sail, flagpole, key, fishing pole, fountain pen, pencil, brush, rifle, gun, sword, knife, arrow, baseball bat, pipe, syringe, golf club, tail, rope.

As an example, let us look at the dream which a twenty-three-year-old bride had just after her wedding night:

[78] *"A young man in our office used his pencil so awkwardly that he pushed it into my eye which immediately began to swell. I was frightened and upset and ran crying to my mother."*

2. *Persons:* Common male names like John, Dick, Henry; my friend, the little one, little man, my boy, my brother, servant, janitor, burglar, soldier, dwarf.

3. *Animals:* Snake, rat, squirrel, mouse, horse, bull,[2] other animals with a tail, cow's udder, bird.

This might be the place to say a few words about the *snake symbolism.* In some dreams the snake symbolizes "the woman," or "the sin." Occasionally, it is connected with a patient's poison complex.

The snake worshippers attributed to the snake divine powers, but the connection between phallic concepts and serpent worship in many epochs of human history is unmistakable. It is particularly the *paternal* phallus which finds its symbolization in the serpent cult. In the disguise of a snake, Apollo seduces Atys, Zeus seduces Persephone, and Odin se-

1 Jung stresses the significance of *the hat* as an image of power. Hat, crown and halo are in the same category. "To bring everything under one hat" corresponds with the unifying intellectual power of logos.

2 See Figure 39A.

FIGURE 34
Ancient Serpent Worship

duces Gunnlodh. Snakes were held sacred in the temple of Aesculapius, son of Apollo, where they represented the God himself. (Figs. 34, 35 and 36.)

The snake has been considered a healing force and also a demon. It was closely connected with the tree of life where it represented evil lust. Snake worship was closely related to ancestor worship (China) as souls of the ancestors were believed to be living in snakes.[1]

FIGURE 35

[1] For more on the subject see page 144.

FIGURE 36

After an Ancient Seal Impression. God, Fire Altar, and Caduceus. (Iraq Excavations of the Oriental Institute).

Other symbols of the phallus are:

4. *Fruit:* Banana, pear, and other elongated kinds.

5. *Plants:* Particularly the stalks of flowers, the flowers themselves, trees, roots, trunks, the latter signifying erection.

6. *Other parts of the body:* finger, nose, hair, arm, tooth, female breast, and many more.

7. *Geometric figures:*

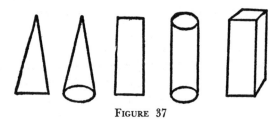

FIGURE 37

8. *Numbers:* 1 and 3 are the most frequent ones. The *tertium comparationis* in the choice of these symbols is: (a) the oblong shape; (b) the ability to emit contents as in the case of a rifle, gun, or fountain pen; (c) the penetrating tendency, that is, the intruder, burglar, or like symbol; (d) the element of service, as the servant typifies; (e) it may also represent as a *totum pro parte*, a whole person instead of its part. The

numeral "3" represents the three constituent parts of the male genital, the two testicles and the penis.

A patient dreams:

[79] *"A nickel-plated instrument of some kind, triangular in shape, from five to six inches long, was held in an erect position by someone."* Figure 38 is the patient's drawing of the instrument. The longitudinal triangle held in erect position is undoubtedly a penis.

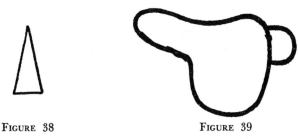

FIGURE 38   FIGURE 39

A woman who complained that her husband never spoke a word to her while being intimate dreamed:

[80] *"My husband kept handing me pitchers of food without speaking."* Her drawing of the pitcher, figure 39, indicates a distinct phallic symbol.

A forty-year-old woman physician dreams:

[81] *"I saw my sisters Eileen and Helen as young girls. We were packing our suitcases preparing for a journey. I had in my hand three golden keys tied together. I said to Eileen, 'Look, I have the keys to our rooms.' Eileen seemed to take it for granted that I should have the keys, but I felt it was some kind of magic that was bestowed upon me. I had a feeling of power. I was a plenipotentiary. (When, during the first war my father was serving his country, I had the key to the safe.) In the dream I had a wonderful feeling of fulfillment and gratification."*

The patient displayed what is called in psychopathology, "penis envy." The latter has not, necessarily, a sexual determination. The analysis of this case showed a masculine identification as a function of the patient's quest for power. The "key" which consists of *three keys* represents the phallus. (See "Numeral Symbolism," page 202.) It offers the patient a feeling of power and omnipotence ("plenipotentiary") such as (she thinks) the possession of the male attributes would offer. It is also the "key" to the psychology of her case, and a fantasy that fills the patient with a "wonderful feeling of fulfillment and gratification."

Let us now shed some light upon the significance of *monuments*. As memorial structures, monuments, as a rule, represent memories (see page 159). Their oblong shape (obelisk) may in some dreams be the reason for their being used as sexual (phallic) symbols. *Totem poles* and *tombstones* are known to have such significance (see page 142). Also the use in dreams of monuments in association with the cemetery and death is plausible. The dreams quoted below have none of these meanings. Let us hear them first:

[82] *"With my friend, Lieutenant Brown, I was in a field at home. We saw a statue, a deformed figure in the garden at the spot where my mother was standing. Brown referred to mother as Janice (my girl friend's name) and said: 'You don't want her. She is all used up. I told you before that she calls a guy in Bristol, England . . . (we are also in England just now,* Janice used to be there during the war) *. . . whenever she is depressed and wants to have intercourse with him.' He made it sound very tough to show how promiscuous Janice was."*

The dreamer, a twenty-year-old navy officer, sees here a "deformed figure" of his mother who, at the same time, is also Janice, his girl friend. The patient's mother who used to be his idol when he was a child, later became the object of his hate and distrust because she was domineering and always treated him like a baby. In his mind, *his mother idol became deformed* (statue = idol), a fact that has greatly affected the patient's attitude toward women in general. That is why in his dream the image of mother appears fused with that of Janice. Lieutenant Brown is the patient's "alter ego."

The patient doubts his ability to keep his girl interested in him; he suspects all women of being promiscuous. "Mother" and "Prostitute" appear to be the alternatives of womanhood in his mind. He wants to be free from mother, but his distrust in women ("all women are prostitutes") throws him back to his infantile position.

The second "monument dream" was dreamed by a thirty-two-year-old dentist of Russian descent who lived in a very clannish New England community. He tried to hide his foreign descent from his clients. Having embarked on this policy of playing the part of a native American he felt very uncomfortable, insecure, and self-conscious.

His dream ran as follows:

[83] *"We had a meeting at which various emblems were presented to designate the club. They were to be used in front of the house in the form of a post. I believe each could choose which they desired. There was one representing, I believe, Catherine or Peter the Great of Russia. I thought that would be a striking one but did not announce it as my choice inasmuch as I did not wish to let people associate my Russian background with my choice. I believe I chose one with male and female Indian heads."*

The "totem pole" to be placed in front of the dreamer's home, represents here, as it does under real circumstances, the *family tree,* the string of ancestors. The dream distinctly portrays the patient's reluctance to admit publicly his foreign descent—to place a statue of Russian monarchs right on his front lawn for anyone to see. He decides to put up Indian heads, instead, to impress others with his American origin. A slight irony lies in his choice, however; he taunts his New England community by demonstrating to it that its members, too, are "foreigners." The real natives are the Indians.

Phallic symbolism is inherent in the picture of a *tree* (Tree of Life). It signifies fertility and also the creative prin-

FIGURE 39A
The Egyptian Sacred Bull, Zor-Aster. (After an
illustration of the London Magazine of October
1776.)

FIGURE 40
Totem Pole Rep-
resenting the Ra-
ven Post (Yehlh-
Gars). Tsimshian
Indians.

ciple. However, as will be shown in the chapter on Bipolarity
(page 229), the "tree" may also symbolize the "family tree,"
in which case it is the equivalent of the symbol of a *totem
pole*. Its inherent phallic importance remains even if used
as a symbol of ancestry. A particularly instructive example
of this type is seen in the painting "The Stem of Jesse," by
Jan Mostaert of Harlem (1500). The "Stem" seems to grow
from the pelvic region of the old man lying on the ground.
In his thought-provoking book, *The Painter in History*,
Ernest H. Short comments on the unusual composition of the
painting. He mentions the "sleeping old man" at the base

FIGURE 41
After THE STEM OF JESSE by Jan Mostaert (Part of the
composition omitted.) M. C. von Pannwitz Collection.

and the tree in the center. In the branches of the tree he identifies David, the harpist, and other ancestors of the Virgin. The figures on the side branch of the tree following David are two of the prophets who predicted the coming of Messiah. The Virgin and Child are seen on the uppermost branch of the tree. (Fig. 41.)

In the author's reference to the "ancestors of the Virgin" we see an indication that the tree stem has been conceived as a "family tree" in the sense of a "totem pole."

The phallic significance of the tree used (consciously or unconsciously) in the painter's composition does not contradict the inherent religious character of the painting, inasmuch as the ancients considered the phallus primarily as the source of fertility and did not attach any immoral meaning to it. In all primitive religions, we find traces of the primeval "phallus cult." Procreation was considered by the ancients as that sphere of human activity that made man a holy, god-like creature; through his phallus man believed he participated in the divine process of creation. He placed his hand "under the thigh" of the man to whom he swore an oath (Gen. 24:2 and 47:29). By placing one's hand at the genital region of the other man, he accentuated the solemn character of the ceremony. (Cf. "testis" and "testimony"; in German *"zeugen"* for "creating" and *"Zeuge"* for "witness.") Most commentators agree that the words "under the thigh" are not an euphemism. (In Gen. 9:22, no such euphemism can be observed regarding Noah), but the result of the hesitation of the ancients to call a holy object by its name. (The holy name "Jehovah" is equally taboo and unmentionable; it is usually circumscribed by the word "Lord.")

According to Dulaure, the early beginnings of the phallus cult coincide with the worship of stars. The advent of the Spring, in particular, as a season following the cold and rough months of Winter, has been associated in many parts of the globe with celebrations in which the awakening of Nature to a new life and fertility were the outstanding motives. The time of vernal equinox, astronomically speaking, is a time when the Sun enters the Taurus (Bull) constellation. The Taurus of the heavens thus became a symbol of the rejuvenating power of the Sun (see Fig. 39A) and, in further consequence, the bull on our own planet became the originator of all the blessings of Spring. For similar reasons, and in a similar way, the buck (Capricorn) has been associated with rejuvenating forces of the resurrecting Nature of Spring. Faun, Pan and other semigods endowed with buck's feet and horns bear testimony to this fact.

In the course of time, a reduction took place in the symbolic imagery to the effect that it was not the whole animal (bull) but its procreative power that was the object of veneration. The rest of the divinity was, as a rule, represented by a human figure. We mentioned Pan and Faun and could add here Silen, Satyr, and others. All these figures had a close relation to sexual activity and were also often portrayed as carriers of powerful phalli. Gradually, the association with the animal was lost altogether, and the cult of the phallus remained alone as a cult of fertility.

The phallus cult was known the world over; it was practiced by the people of Asia Minor as well as by the Greeks, the Romans, the aborigines of Australia, Africa, Asia, and America. Originally it was connected with the Sun worship in a way similar to that of the bull or buck cults; later this connection became more and more obsolete. The phallus cult survived until the conquest of the pagan world by Christianity, and then it was gradually eliminated.

PICTURES OF CASTRATION

The dreaming human mind preserves recollections from primeval days of mankind, days when the phallus had the divine significance mentioned above and coitus had a religious or magic importance. Everything pertaining to procreation was holy and venerated. Consequently, castration was prominent in thoughts and rites of primitive peoples.

From the psychological analysis of primitive peoples we have to take for granted the existence of a *castration wish* as a hostile impulse, and of a *castration fear* as a reaction to it; that is, we find in the human unconscious what is called an "active" and a "passive castration complex." Castration complexes are also found in the unconscious material of many of our patients; they have significance in the general psychodynamic constellation.

It is probably an atavistic effect of this primitive wish when some parents use the threat of castration in their educational endeavors, particularly when they employ it in efforts to prevent their children from masturbating. The same seems to apply to the castration fear in which the child sees God or his parents as castrators, a fear which is sometimes developed in connection with sexual activity.

An example of "castration fear" as guilt reaction is revealed in the following dream had by a nine-year-old boy who suffered from enuresis:

[84] *"I had done something, was a little naughty or so, and was locked somewhere in a cabin. Then some terrible men came in and wanted to do something to me. I made friends with one of them and we chased away Death. But Death came back again with double strength and killed me. And do you know how? He did something to my penis that made me die. Such an ugly dream, isn't it?"*

"Cutting off," "blinding" (compare Samson), "wounding," "hurting," etc., are common symbols of castration. A mute person can also be used sometimes as a symbol of a castrated person (compare the resemblance between "mute" and "mutilation").

The following is an example of a castration dream:

[85] *"I am fighting against another man who is trying to shoot. I am afraid lest he shoot into my eye and blind me."*

"Fighting" often has a sexual meaning. The dreamer was a man who was struggling against his latent homosexuality. His unconscious sexual attitude was distinctly feminine. In the above dream he wishes—and is afraid—that the other man may castrate him, that is, turn him into a woman ("emasculated man" means "woman").

A very masculine woman who hated the intimate relations with her mate and felt aversion to his physical approach dreamed:

[86] *"I touch my husband's genital and find it is bleeding."*

We see here the patient's active castration wish. "Bleeding" in this dream has undoubtedly been caused by the patient's action. Yet this action has been obliterated in the dream. We call this omission of the most important segment of the plot an "ellipsis." It is often seen in dreams, and in the structure of many jokes it represents a direct stimulus of laughter.

The following dream portrays another example of the "active" castration complex:

[87] *"I am fighting with a man, grab his necktie and tear it to pieces. The single parts are bleeding."*

Necktie is a phallic symbol.

The following is an active castration wish expressed in the dream of a "phallic" woman. In her case, the castration wish was based upon "penis envy" which the patient displayed in her childhood in relation to her brother.

The patient states: "When I was twelve I had the following nightmare:

[88] *"I saw my brother standing in front of a mirror and combing his hair, as he used to do every day. He was undressed. A tiger came suddenly and tore the lower part of his body away (from the waist down). The upper part somehow remained suspended in the air. I awoke with trepidation."*

People who dream of having lost a limb or parts of their bodies, in most cases refer to their castration complexes.

Often, however, the "loss" portrayed in the dream does not concern the whole genital but the prepuce ("circumcision complex") or the hymen ("virginity complex").

One of Stekel's patients complained in his dream [89], that *he lost an eyelid and because of this his career is in jeopardy.*

The dreamer expressed his "Jewish complex" in this way. He lived in an anti-Semitic locality and was afraid that because he was Jewish (circumcised) he would not get the job for which he had applied.

EMISSION DREAMS

A good example of an emission dream was offered by a twenty-one-year-old student:

[90] *"I see an auto speeding by and suddenly I see a bomb breaking. Then I see another bomb in the process of exploding. I run home. In my house I see people and the help walking around nude. Then I go upstairs and see the sister of my friend Joe in the kitchen all nude. I have intercourse with her, whereupon I ejaculate."*

This dream contains an ejaculation and at the same time its symbolic picture, the explosion of bombs. Notice also the "Layer Symbolism" of this dream (Rank). The intercourse and the emission first appear in symbolic disguise, that is, as a speeding auto and an exploding bomb. In the course of the dreamer's awakening, the symbols disappear and the sexual desire becomes manifest.

The "auto" symbolizes the patient's sexual urge. The female partner is seen here with increasing distinctness; first, the dreamer sees "people," then the "help," the latter an allusion to the "house," then he sees the friend's sister (read: "patient's sister") in the "nude." The tabooed character of the sexual scene causes its symbolization, and even the act of emission is expressed symbolically (as an explosion).

A spinster, aged forty, suffering from a neurotic stomach disorder, delivered the following series of dreams, all of which contained her repressed sexual desire in symbolic expression:

[91] *"An Indian poked with a pointed bone toward my*

stomach." (The "pointed bone" is a phallic symbol. The dreamer shows the connection between her repressed sexual desires and her stomach trouble.)

[92] *"I fall out of an automobile."*

She is a "fallen" woman. One who does not take care "falls out of the car."

[93] *"I am lying under the wheels of a train that is passing over my body. I feel the rhythmic shaking of the train."*

[94] *"A house collapses and buries me under its ruins."*

SYMBOLS FOR MASTURBATION

Riding a bicycle, picking flowers, riding in an automobile, pouring liquids, squeezing fruits, swimming, washing with soap, shaving, pumping water, etc. Masturbation dreams are important for they show also the *specific love fantasy* of the dreamer. (See also page 368.)

FEMALE SEX SYMBOLS

1. *Inanimate objects:* bag, pocket, wound, nest, cavern, ring, target, muff, front door, room, window,[1] pot, box, cage, stove, pool of water, lake, boat, drawer, and other similar things.

2. *Persons:* my girl, my girl friend, my little one, maid, servant girl, my daughter, several common female names.

3. *Animals:* shell, oyster, kitten, mouse, and others.

4. *Fruits:* Fig, peach, etc.

5. *Plants:* Cabbage, leaves, rose, etc.

6. *Geometric figures:* See Fig. 42.

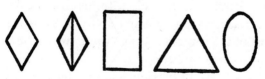

FIGURE 42

[1] "Opening a window" sometimes symbolizes "giving an outlet to one's urges"; "looking through a window" may represent the "world outlook."

7. *Other parts of the body:* Openings, mouth, eyes, ears.

The *tertium comparationis* is: (a) the shape, (b) the character of a container, and (c) the object of an attack (target, etc.).

A woman patient brought her analyst the following dream:

[95] *"I was in a barn. From a wall a bag was suspended. I noticed movements in the bag. I thought: 'If it is a squirrel it will run up the wall. If it is a rat it will run toward me.' When I saw a rat coming out of the bag, I became terrified, and rising about three feet off the floor, remained suspended there while the rat ran under my feet."*

We know the symbolic significance of the "squirrel," the "rat," and the "bag," and we understand that the scene in which the patient observes "movements in the bag" is a coitus fantasy which has been repressed from the patient's consciousness. The patient in her married relationship is frigid. In this dream, she reproduces certain experiences of her past in a disguised form; she turns them, however, into the opposite; that is, pleasant sensations become unpleasant and repulsive—like rats. (Dream elements like the patient's rising up into the air have "functional" significance.)

In the following dream the female genital is symbolized as a "box or vault."

[96] *"I went to the post office to see whether I had any mail. I opened the box (or vault) and noticed the contents were partly damaged and some apparently had been pilfered. I decided to postpone the claim I wished to make against the post office."*

Here is a young man who does not know that, unconsciously, he cannot forgive his wife for not having told him before marriage that she was not a virgin. Someone has "pilfered" part of the contents of the "vault" which he felt he was entitled to receive intact.

An unusual symbolization of the female genital was claimed by Bertram D. Lewin:

"Well, doctor, I've been thinking of nothing all day," said

the patient. The analyst concludes that by "nothing" the patient was referring to the female genital.

He even goes on to say that this interpretation is in agreement with the usual association with "nothing." Lewin's patient continues:

"I have never faced reality. I haven't faced reality since the day I was born." The analyst concludes that "reality" also represents the female genital, the real one, in contradistinction to some illusionary female genital.

"Vagueness" and "confusion" are also associated with the female structure, according to Lewin. And "concentration" represents the urinary flow which is unconcentrated in the female and the incontinent male. A girl who complains that she cannot concentrate may have a urethral situation to relate.

This interpretation is a sample of arbitrariness in deciphering symbolism which proves the analyst's conscious views rather than the patient's unconscious reactions.

One of my patients had a remarkably similar dream and there was *"nothing"* in it to support Lewin's views. The dream ran as follows:

[97] *"Brenda was looking around and I thought to myself, she was looking for nothing (or at nothing)."*

The dream derives its light from the fact that the patient, a thirty-two-year-old banker, displayed strong jealousy reactions whenever he saw his friend Brenda looking around in a restaurant or theater. He tried to control himself in this respect and the dream helped him to deprecate the objects of Brenda's interest. In reality, the patient's jealousy was based upon his own latent homosexuality. It was he who was interested in the reaction other men would show when flirting with Brenda. This abnormal interest in other men was suppressed in the dream by means of deprecation: "It is nothing," he said to himself, "nothing to worry about."

This dream in which the most important part has been condemned by dream censorship reminds us of the dream quoted by Hug-Hellmuth on page 95 in which mumbling replaces the embarrassing parts of the dream plot.

UTERUS

The "mother" may appear as a symbol of the "uterus" (mother's womb). We are thinking here of the dream the young lady had after her wedding night. She said (page 136) "I ran crying to my mother." Her thoughts are directed toward her womb and the possibility of conception. (Cf. page 154.)

Water, particularly when it is a circumscribed body, such as a pond or a lake, may also represent the uterus.

MENSTRUATION

Menstruation may be represented in the dream as "flowing," "bathing," as experiencing a congestion, as seeing the red color, as a visit by a particular person (in accordance with popular expressions for menstruation such as "I expect to have guests tomorrow," or the like). Another popular code for menstruation, "Falling off the roof," can be dramatized as an actual falling from the roof. (For other references to menstruation consult the index.)

One of my patients, a forty-five-year-old lady, whose menstrual periods were connected with a great deal of physical discomfort, dreamed as follows:

[98] *"I was in the kitchen of a large apartment. I must have been eighteen or nineteen years old. My grandmother, who looked like the Queen in 'Alice in Wonderland' came in. I noticed that her eyes were circled in black and felt that mine were too. She looked down upon me and said: 'Poor child, you are going to be sick tomorrow.'*

"When I woke up I was thinking that I have never associated her with any kindness. When I was about to get up I realized that I had my menstruation."

The patient would like to get into menopause to stop

worrying about menstrual discomfort; on the other hand, she still enjoys being "young." Her dream exaggerates this desire. The grandmother's visit represents here the onset of menstruation which must have announced itself along psycho-physiological channels, so that the patient's unconscious could utilize them in the dream.

BREASTS

Frequent symbols of the female breasts are: mountains, (the "foothills of Nebraska" in *Rain* by Somerset Maugham), apples,[1] a spring, source, well, fountain, balcony, etc.

Rather unusual is the following symbolization of breasts:

[99] *"Frances played all kinds of roles. In one she showed me that she had colostrum in her nose."*

The patient, a young physician, is afraid his girl friend Frances may be pregnant. In his dream, "breast" is symbolically replaced by the "nose." The displacement is designed to deprecate the affair and thus to allay the dreamer's fears.

COITUS SYMBOLS

Some coitus symbols express *contact*. We find them in the pictures of telephoning, dancing, writing a letter, eating a meal with, traveling or walking with a member of the opposite sex, giving a party, heating a stove, sewing, weaving, rescuing a person,[2] riding in a car, or on a horse.

---

[1] Goethe's *Faust*:
"*Der Aepflein begehrt Ihr sehr*
Und schon vom Paradiese her . . ."

[2] The rescuing idea plays a large part in the dreams of mankind. Fairy tales, legends, myths, religions, all make use of this idea. As Freud and Rank proved, this idea expresses basically the Oedipus situation. It represents killing the father (dragon) and taking possession of the mother (maid). This interpretation is, of course, one-sided. Other problems connected with religion, lust for power, and ambition are also represented by this concept; but the sexual content of the hero fantasy is beyond doubt. (Cf. page 103.)

Other symbols of sexual intercourse are scenes of *increasing excitement*. In the dream, having intercourse may mean climbing a mountain or a staircase. Figure 43 shows a diagram of physiological excitement in intercourse leading to orgasm.

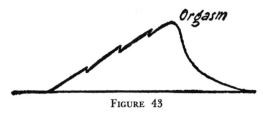

FIGURE 43

A *man* may express the act of intercourse by the picture of fishing, plowing, bowling, riding, shooting, etc. Erection may be represented by "rising," "flying," or the like. A *woman* may express the sex act by images of earthquakes, burdens on her chest, trains passing over her body, or the like. *Defloration* is symbolized by wounds, things which are torn in front, soiled, broken, lost, destroyed, canceled or used. One of Stekel's patients dreamed:

[100] *"My windshield was broken and I was desperate about it."*

The *orgasm* is often expressed by the words: "to arrive at the terminal," "to come," "to die," "come to the top," and the like.

Pregnancy may appear in the symbolic disguise of an infection (germ = sperm), or intoxication (poisoning = fertilization), and also as pushing a baby carriage, or bearing burdens.

It must be emphasized that the above-mentioned objects and actions are symbols of our sexual thoughts only occasionally in the dream. No dream interpreter will, as one of our critics asserted, "see phalli in all telegraph poles." We have stated before that painful and, therefore, repressed sexual notions *can* be recognized behind these symbolic pictures. But we shall also see cases in which, for example, "climbing" shall be interpreted as a symbol of the patient's ambition or his idealistic strivings rather than as a sexual manifestation.

Bettelheim and Hartmann made interesting experiments in which they demonstrated the distortive influences of the superego even in cases of organic defects of memory (Korsakoff psychosis). The distortion proceeded according to the freudian mechanisms of repression. The authors presented to their patients all kinds of indecent texts. The patients whose recollective abilities were more or less disturbed by their disease, changed indecent texts, in the retelling, into decent ones. In doing this they made abundant use of symbols.

The fictitious story presented by Bettelheim and Hartmann was as follows:

[101] *"A young girl took a walk alone in a field. Suddenly a man came along and attacked her and threw her down. The girl struggled hard against him, but in vain. The man lifted her skirts and inserted his membrum into her vagina. After the intercourse, he left the girl alone lying on the field and weeping loudly."*

One of the patients reproduced the story in this manner:

"Two girls walked upstairs. Two boys followed them. Then they married the girls because one of them was pregnant; the other went home."

Another patient reproduced the sexual scene by the words: "and put the knife into the sheath."

Another patient substituted "cigarette" for "membrum."

The change of the material toward decency is evident. We also observe the symbolization in the patient's reproductions: sexual intercourse is presented as the act of walking upstairs; the male genital as a knife and cigarette; the female genital as a sheath.

Similar conditions are to be found in other organic disturbances of the brain, for example, in the old-age Korsakoff and "Presbyophrenia."

Secretions and Excretions

In the symbolic parallelism all secretions and excretions, indeed, all liquid contents of our body are equal to each other and may be substituted for each other. Of interchangeable value are: blood, urine, pus, water, semen, milk, tears, vomitings.

A woman who was intimate with a married man dreamed [102] that *she was urinating in a toilet which belonged to another woman.*

Symbols of the *anus* include: ring, eye ("the brown eye"), circle, the rear door, furnace, exit, etc.

Feces are frequently symbolized by "money." Freud emphasized the connection between the tendency to accumulate money and to suffer from constipation. (For other meanings of money see page 203.)

The *urine* is symbolized by water, river, flood, fountain, rain, bath.

Defecation is often the symbol of another activity considered by the patient as unclean, as, for example, sex. In many instances defecation represents a symbol for the analytic treatment. The object of comparison is the cleansing process such as takes place in analytic psychotherapy.

Abstract Ideas in the Dream

PERSONIFICATION

"Personification" in the dream means that a thought is symbolized by a person. A mechanism of this type can be seen in a dream reported by a twenty-eight-year-old patient who suffered from the fear of insanity:

[103] *"I saw an old silly-looking man, apparently a half-wit, who followed us and insisted upon joining us. I ordered him away, but he still persisted in following us. Finally, I lost patience and hit him on the head with a stick and pushed him off the sidewalk and into the gutter."*

The "silly old man" symbolizes the *thought* of insanity. The patient's father was a gambler and a man of weak character. The patient identified himself with his father, but, at the same time, resented this idea and tried to suppress it. His dream expresses this conflict.

Another man, who had entertained an intimate relationship with a widow, suffered from an annoying lack of libido. He also had inferiority feelings as a result of comparing his own male qualities with those of the widow's former husband. He dreamed:

[104] *"I am sitting at a desk telephoning to a woman. I am conscious of the presence of another person, a man. To change the subject of the conversation, to make it innocent, I say over the phone, 'To return to—'"*

The "presence" of the "man" signifies the *thought* of the presence of the man, the latter being the woman's former husband.

In the above dreams we see the important fact that abstract ideas cannot be represented in the dream without being put into concrete symbols. Instead of saying, "The thought of my father comes to my mind," we may say, "My father enters the room."

The patient, who felt the presence of a man while telephoning to a woman, was in the habit of making appointments with her by telephone. The thought of the man interfered with the dreamer's contact with his partner. The interfering thought may be concerned with a comparison of himself with the dead husband and may lead, as it did in this case, to inferiority feelings. The dreamer changes the subject of conversation in order to make it innocent; he desexualizes his attitude.

The next dream is that of a man who had difficulties in trying to establish a business:

[105] *"I meet my friend G. again and again and finally laugh about this peculiar 'law of series.'"*

"Friend G." in this dream means the frequently occurring,

annoying thought of the friend who, in contrast to the patient, is successful in business.

Opposition may be portrayed in the dream as "sitting opposite to somebody."

An interesting dream is the following in which a principle has been "personified." The dreamer, a twenty-eight-year-old divorced woman suffered from spells of anxiety. One of her phobias was that some day she might want to awaken and would not be able to.

[106] *"I was dreaming that I was asleep, when suddenly I was awakened (in the dream) by a person near my bed. At first, I thought it was our housekeeper. She seemed to have taken hold of both my hands to help me get up and out of bed—then suddenly she was my grandmother. She was holding on to my hands as I struggled to wake myself up, twisting and turning. She was trying to help me get up. . . .*

"This struggle became so real (along with the fear of not being able to wake up) that when I first woke up I felt relieved."

The housekeeper who is an old-fashioned but very efficient woman, and the grandmother who is a realistic though also a domineering person, represent here the principle of reality. The patient's desire to sleep and to indulge in pleasurable fantasies clashes here with her everyday obligations (symbolized by the two women). The patient's fear of not being able to exert her will-power in brushing aside her dreams corresponded to the patient's general feeling that her instinctual demands were pressing and that they might some day overpower her more realistic considerations. Her "fear of sleep" in reality was a "fear of herself," a fear lest the "pleasure principle" overwhelm the "reality principle."

All figurative expressions can be found in the dream in their literal meanings, as, for instance: "to put all one's eggs into one basket," "to give a person a lift in life," "to be in the dumps," "to be up in the air about something," "to have one's hands full," etc.

Rosenbaum reports the following instructive dream:

[107] *"I am sitting at a dinner table eating meat. Suddenly I notice that it is the dead body of a man that I eat."*

The dreamer lives on the money his deceased father left. In spite of all the advantages this kind of life offers to him he is unhappy because he wants to prove to himself and to his family that he is a useful member of society and is able to make his own living. In his dream, he literally lives off his dead father.

When describing the characteristics of the dream language, we mentioned that in dreams the individual's capacity for abstraction is greatly reduced. Abstract ideas are, therefore, as a rule represented by concrete things. We can hardly dream of religion; but we may dream of a church, a symbol of religion. Old and unforgettable recollections are represented by *monuments, museums, etc.* (See also page 140.) The concrete statement, *"My husband left the living room,"* may represent the abstract idea of his death.

Freud first considered the *coat* as a symbol of man and later as that of a phallus. He pointed to the resemblance between *"Mann"* (male, man) and *"Man-tel"* (coat). If this interpretation has a general value at all, it is applicable only in German. Stekel emphasized the frequent use of a coat as a symbol of love. Jones doubts if Stekel is right and believes that his interpretation is too general. To support his view, Stekel reports the following dream of a woman patient:

[108] *"I was sitting on a bench in the open air and felt cold. My father came and laid his coat around my shoulders, his warm, soft coat made me feel warm."*

Jones is of the opinion that this dream is to be interpreted by inversion. Instead of being "wrapped in a thing," it should be understood as "receiving," "wrapping up a thing" (the phallus).

Other frequent concrete symbols of abstract "love" are: "fire," "flood," "money," some birds, for instance, pigeons (doves), etc. Many other symbols can be found in popular expressions, folk songs, fairy tales, myths, etc. As they live in the imagination of the human race, so also do they live in the unconscious of the individual, and occasionally transgress the borders of consciousness through the medium of the dream.

Depicting the General by the Specific

We interpret the phrase in a girl's dream:

[109] *"Three men refused me"* as an expression of her inferiority feeling and of her opinion that she is unattractive. Instead of a generalized statement such as "men refuse me," the patient makes the statement: "Two (or three, or four, or X) men refuse me."

Depicting a General Opinion by Specific Symbols

The dreamer often expresses his general opinion on important problems of life by the use of several examples which substantiate this opinion. For instance, a young man sees in the course of the events in his dream three different men. On closer examination, we discover that two of these men are unhappily married and that the third is divorced. We then say: In this dream the dreamer has represented his idea that "marriage is a danger" by giving the illustration of several unhappily married persons.

The Id in Dream Symbols

The dreamer's impulses may take the form of pictures of animals (Fig. 44), fire, automobiles, streetcars, a flood, prisoners, criminals, railroad engines, skittish horses, pupils in a classroom, soldiers, and so on. These pictures are significant because of their reference to the problem of controlled and uncontrolled powers.

Sometimes *the inhibition* of annoying impulses can be seen in the dream as the inability to move, or as other pictures of inhibited movements. One intends to walk and feels fixed to the ground; one wants to do something and cannot find his belongings. These frustrations are usually accompanied by an annoying discomfort, nervous turmoil, and tension. In these pictures the conflict of our will is portrayed. One part of ourselves desires what another part abhors. The result is an inhibited movement of contradictory tendencies: *Impulse A* is arrested by the *Impulse Counter-A*.

The Spanish painter sees his dream thoughts as beasts of prey that fly and hunt by night, the owls, the bats, and the

FIGURE 44

THE SLEEP OF REASON PRODUCES MONSTERS. Etching by Francisco Goya (1746-1828). Courtesy of the Metropolitan Museum of Art, New York.

cat. The flying creatures descend upon him "when reason sleeps." The painting is an impressive reproduction of a nightmare (cf. page 163) and also an expression of the painter's pangs of conscience (cf. page 171) which appear under the cover of darkness.

A thirty-five-year-old physician dreams:

[110] *"A man was involved as a careless driver in an automobile collision. I saw him go out. A policeman came and pressed me up against a telephone booth."*

We see here a displacement: The careless driver is the dreamer himself. This is verified by the fact that not the "careless driver," but our patient, is pressed to the wall by a policeman. "Careless driving" means to be careless of one's drives (motor), to lose control over one's instinctual cravings.

Inhibitions may appear in dreams as pictures of obstacles, fences, road blocks and the like.

[111] *"I am following a beautiful girl on the street. I am already very near to her when suddenly a turnpike jumps like a spring from the other side of the street and bars my way."*

The "turnpike" which obstructs the dreamer's progress is his fear of women. In this particular case it represents also his fiancée's virginity which prevents him from making a direct sexual advance.

The inhibitions sometimes fail to prevent the dreamer from carrying out his impulses. Tabooed desires may break through and drive the dreamer out of his bed (somnambulism) or stimulate him to commit or to attempt actions he would normally abhor. One of my patients, a kleptomaniac, carried out his incestuous impulse by walking in his sleep onto his mother's bed. There he stopped, however. Another patient used to leave his bed while in a somnambulic state and walk toward his brother's bed with his fists clenched as if he wanted to choke him.

What applies to dreams is true also of other hyponoic states, that is, states of decreased consciousness, such as somnambulism, epileptic deliriums (equivalents), and, with limitations, of criminal hypnosis.

To a certain degree the consciousness and the unconsciousness are complementary functions. If consciousness loses its cathexis, the energy that virtually is lost in reality floods back to unconscious positions, and renders the unconscious dynamically more potent and active. Its pressure toward expressing itself in its own way increases.

The *unconscious* itself sometimes appears in symbolic disguise. We shall see (page 209) that it may be symbolized, e.g., by deep water. Often it is also represented by a person whose features are indistinguishable, by "a stranger," a Negro, a "person behind" or "below"; also by the depths of a shaft, a mine, a volcano, basement of a house, or a closet ("skeleton in the closet"). Some figures from mythology may also appear as symbols of the unconscious, e.g., Hermes, Poseidon, and others, particularly those associated with the nether world.

Very often the unconscious is represented by sinister animals; this is particularly true in cases where unconscious pressures make the patient doubt the efficacy of his repressions. In such cases we see nightmares containing pictures of the uncanny, such as cats, bats, dwarfs, imps, and other inhabitants of the realm of ghosts. A dream of this type is presented in the famous painting of Fuseli (Fig. 45).

THE SUPEREGO IN THE DREAM

In the entire ancient dream literature the dream has been considered as the medium through which the supernatural world communicated with man. Hints received in dreams were heeded by man as divine messages.

In the course of time, mankind's views on dreams have changed, and today we know that dreams are "messages from within" rather than "from without." Today we also know

FIGURE 45
THE NIGHTMARE. (After J. H. Fuseli, 1782).

more about the origin of religions and the remarkably close
relation which exists between humanity's dreams and humanity's religions.

When we have recognized the fact that all religions are
projections of the dreams of fear and hope, it may be inter-

esting to observe how *religion* as an active force in an individual's mind expresses itself in his dream.

Freud, at first, did not realize the importance of religion (the moral ego) in our unconscious. Later, he acknowledged it and named this part of our personality the "superego." It was found that not only antimoral and antisocial tendencies but also religious feelings can be repressed. Many people live in the self-deception of being "atheistic" when, in reality, their infantile, religious feelings still live in their unconscious.

The introjection of the ideal "Father" into the ego survives all liberalizing efforts and becomes a moral authority, supervising all emotional activities. We know various neurotic and psychotic symptoms which are the direct consequence of the superego activity. The analyst knows women who suffer from severe diarrhea attacks whenever they attempt to have a date with a man; men who become impotent whenever they attempt to commit adultery. In all these cases the symptom is in the service of moral tendencies which are enforced against the will and conscious intentions of the patient. An exact study of these mechanisms can be conducted by the use of dreams.

The symbol of the superego is the same as the symbol of morality and religion. We usually see pictures of persons in authority: father, mother, teachers, guides, doctors, old friends. Inanimate objects may also serve as symbols of the superego, e.g., churches, synagogues, crosses, candlesticks (menorah), monuments, etc.

In the following dream the superego appears in the picture of a statue. (For other symbolic meanings of statues see page 140.)

The patient sees in his dream [112] an *Aztec procession. He climbs into the statue portraying the Aztec God.* And then he adds:

"There was something highly ceremonial about the dream.

I became the incarnation of the God. I gave life to the statue. I became part of the whole thing.[1]

With this dream he associated the sacrificial altars of the Aztecs on which young men were sacrificed, and added that through his identification with the God he felt protected and sure that he would not be sacrificed.

The patient felt that his family demanded the sacrifice of his private life and the adaptation to the family's rigid traditions. His neurosis was a compromise between tendencies to rebel against the strict rules laid down by the patient's family, and his unconscious desire to comply and conform (to be the sacrificial object of his family).

Certain persons who offer the dreamer an example of an extremely moral life may also be used as symbols of the superego.

The next two dreams are of this kind. They are produced by a twenty-two-year-old woman:

[113] *"I come home and find a young fellow whom I had met at a summer resort. He kisses me, but at this moment, Kay, our maid, opens the door. I feel ashamed."*

Kay is the patient's maid, a very old and religious spinster.

[114] *"Our maid Kay has been taken ill and is in a hospital. She is replaced by the grocer's maid. When Kay comes back the other girl does not want to leave. She is an actress."*

The patient wants to replace her moral principles by a more liberal outlook. She plays with the idea of taking life easier and following her old ambition of becoming an actress. The "grocer's maid" represents this part of the patient's personality.

The most frequent symbols of *God* in dreams are: the sun, father, engineer, master, the man above, commander, chief, judge, etc.

---

1 This scene reminds one of the religious concepts of redemption which can be traced back to the early stages of civilization. The myths of Osiris, Orpheus, Dionysus, and some of the messianic concepts belong here.

Christ is symbolized by the child, a child in a niche, a child with a peculiar hat (hat = halo), the little monument, son, savior, teacher, a wounded person, and the like.

Symbols of *Virgin Mary* include: mother, woman with a child, picture in a frame, a person named "Mary," etc.

A twenty-nine-year-old teacher, whose mother had vowed that he would become a Catholic priest, was forced to give up the idea of becoming a priest because he was not able to control his sexual desires. His mother never forgave him for the disappointment. After her death the patient several times made an attempt to establish relationships with women, but he always failed. In the course of his treatment (for sexual impotence) he brought the following dream:

[115] *"I am in a church, and a priest fits me with a suit as though he were a tailor."*

The "suit" which the priest fits on the patient is, of course, a priest's suit, and our patient is a "masked priest." It is small wonder that he was unable to have relations with women and thus violate his unconscious determination to adhere to his celibacy. Among other reports the patient made in the course of his treatment was a statement that since his mother's death he had had the peculiar compulsion to bless, in his mind, the streets upon which he walked every day. In so doing, he used, as clergymen would, the Latin words: *"In nomine Patris, Filii et Spiritus Sancti, Amen."* It was not surprising to hear that this patient considered himself to be a free-thinker and did not realize the degree of his unconscious religiousness.

A picture of the inner moral attitude is seen in the following dream by a forty-two-year-old physician:

[116] *"I was acting as a messenger boy. I was asked to carry some flowers to a man who was very wealthy. I stopped by a lunchroom. I was in a great hurry to deliver the package, but at the same time I was very hungry. I had lunch and then delivered the package to the man. In giving it to him, I noticed that the flowers were pressed as if they were in a*

book. I was much worried when I saw the flowers in that condition. The place where I met him looked like a graveyard, and I saw tombstones."

In this dream we see the patient's conflict between duty (delivery of the package) and desire to gratify his physical wants (hunger). While he is satisfying his physical desires, the flowers become spoiled. We understand this dream if we interpret the "wealthy man" who receives the flowers in the graveyard as God. It is as if the patient were worried that at the end of his days, God would ask him, "What did you do with the flowers you had to deliver to me fresh and intact?" The flowers here are a symbol of the patient's innocence. In the dream the flowers are spoiled and faded and we see in the patient's emotional reaction a distinct feeling of guilt.

A lawyer, aged forty-two, who considered himself non-religious had a dream in which he expressed his inner feelings as follows:

[117] *"I saw a church which at the same time seemed to be a kind of zoo, because when I came closer I saw bulls, monkeys, and other animals in it. Some strange looking fellows seemed to be guards at the zoo. I was shocked at this sight and thought of taking steps in order to stop this scandal."*

In this dream the patient identifies himself with Jesus Christ, who once drove the usurers and moneychangers from the temple. In a similar way he wants to remove all sinful thoughts from his mind.

Another example of moral tendencies working from the unconscious is the dream of an unlicensed bookmaker:

[118] *"I was coming home by subway from New York when I sensed that I was going in the wrong direction. I just sat still but started to get a little upset. Then I finally couldn't wait any longer and I asked someone and he told me I was going wrong. I got off and went on the right train and felt much better."*

The patient suffers from globus-like symptoms of throat constriction. It is as though a noose were thrown around his neck. His first symptoms occurred two years earlier when he was threatened with a police action. Many secret "bookie" dens were raided and the patient expected a similar fate at any moment. His throat was organically conditioned for such a reaction when three years prior to the outbreak of his neurosis he suffered from acute streptococcus infection.

The patient did not like the illegal type of "work" in which he was engaged. He explained that he would have been glad to "give it up" if it were not for the "suckers" who were always calling on him, offering him money for bets. He had tried again and again to switch to another occupation, but his patrons would not let him go. Judging from his dream, he definitely is not the "bookie" type. His dream expresses the trends of his superego as well as those of his id. He says in his dreams, "I was going in the *wrong* direction." Now, this man sometimes *did* "go in the wrong direction" (to other women, instead of going home to his wife). That was another problem he had to cope with. But he always felt that what he was doing was wrong.

In the dream he tells us that he "started to get a little upset," and that finally he asked someone (analyst, superego) who told him that he was going wrong. Apparently he wants to be told by the analyst, authoritatively, that he should give up his illegal work. He even tells us under what conditions he would feel better: "I got off and *went on the right train* and felt much better."

The following is an interesting case of a thirty-two-year-old Viennese lawyer who suffered from digestive disturbances. His main complaint was the fear that he might suffocate while swallowing food. On the first day of treatment he presented a dream:

[119] *"I am in a hallway. It is open on one side so that I can see down a terrible precipice. I pass through a narrow door and find myself on the roof of a house, in danger of falling down. Then I see a small, very pale, thin boy walking up and down on this roof. I am surprised that he is not afraid,*

and I ask him about it. He says, 'Oh, that's nothing. My mother made an angel of me.' I notice at this moment that the boy has wings on his shoulders. He rises suddenly, looks at me in a very stern and gloomy way, and then flies off. I feel as if I were lost and awake with anxiety and heart palpitation."

The hallway reminds him of a hallway in the court. Feelings of guilt express themselves in the patient's fear of falling down a precipice.

The central figure of this dream is the boy. The patient reports that he had an affair with a dressmaker when he was eighteen. This relationship lasted for about six years. They had three children, two of whom died of malnutrition. The last child was adopted by the man who afterwards married the dressmaker.

The death of the children was not entirely accidental. The babies were secretly placed in the home of a woman who was called (sardonically) an *"Engelmacherin"* (angel-maker). Her criminal profession was to let illegitimate children starve to death, thus offering mothers a way of getting rid of unwanted infants.

The dream becomes clear. It was his own child he saw on the roof, the child made into an "angel" by his parents. The patient's whole life was like walking at the edge of a precipice. He felt like a criminal who had murdered his own children. The digestive disturbance began in a restaurant, at a time when he was unusually hungry. He had the idea, "This is the way our children also must have suffered from hunger," and he almost choked on a piece of bread. Since that day he had not been able to eat anything without the fear of choking. His fear was a distinct conscience reaction. His disease was self-punishment exacted by an inwardly religious person.

The analysis of the other dreams offered further evidence of the correctness of this view. In his dreams, children appeared again and again. In one dream [120] *he saw the living child clad in rags, selling newspapers on the street.* He could not get used to the idea that his own flesh and blood had to live under such miserable circumstances. He moaned in his dream and was sleepless for the greater part of the night.

After successful treatment he gave up his erotic escapades, married, and provided sufficient allowance to take care of the last child, thus paying his moral debt for the ruthless negligence of his younger years.[1]

According to the symbolic parallelism *crimes* may substitute for each other. Thus, *"I have committed a theft"* may signify, "I have done something else that was wrong." The "wrong" may refer to sexual, criminal, or other tabooed actions.

Pangs of conscience are often represented in the dream as animals, bugs, and insects biting and stinging. (Compare the German translation of "pangs of conscience," *Gewissensbisse,* literally "bites of conscience.") Insects may be also interpreted as obsessive thoughts. In conscience reactions such thoughts are directed against the patient's own ego, as are the bites of animals directed against his body. Bugs also, at times, signify "dirty" (sexual) thoughts, particularly in those cases where the dreamer is persistently fighting against them and they keep on oppressing him.

Lorand maintains that vermin or lice are "usually interpreted as representing children." Although we can doubt the word "usually" in this statement, he quotes a dream of a female patient which seems to prove his point.

[121] *"I had lice in my head; nice, big ones. Something is growing on my body and I am nursing it on my own flesh and blood."*

Knowing how often parents use the words "my own flesh and blood" with regard to their children, and also how much women are aware of the fact that their children are growing

1 This case was analyzed by W. Stekel.

of their body, we are ready to accept this interpretation—at least for the dream quoted.

But alas, the analyst does not pursue this path further; indeed, he follows the patient's associations here and concludes that "the something growing on her body" is "her own penis."

A forty-two-year-old lawyer suffered from a strong conflict. He was married, the father of a child, but he met a young lady and fell in love with her. He knew, though, that he would probably never be able to have sexual relations with her. He dreamed:

[122] *"I am at home and suddenly there apears a swarm of very dangerous insects of the firefly variety which in some way seem to threaten the very existence of men. I am an entomologist (in the dream) and undertake to study the insects and to find a remedy. I work all night and all the next day and finally find a way to keep the second crop of insects from hatching that evening (which is the time they are scheduled to hatch). But there is still a group of eggs that I know will hatch despite the knowledge I have gained, and these are going to be worse than the first because, while the first have not had the power of luminescence, the new insects will have that power. I determine to work again that night, but my fiancée wishes me to go out with her. If I do not go, she threatens to go out with another man. I say I must work. She goes off with the arm of the other man about her shoulders, and I turn away to resume my work."*

The "firefly variety" is the self-reproach of the patient. The dream was dreamed while the patient was in the state of resistance, and thought that analytical insight into his conflict situation ("power of luminescence") might do him some harm. (It might make him realize the futility of his sexual situation.) He sees his wife (fiancée) being unfaithful—a projection of his own unfaithful thoughts. We see here, also, another wish-fulfillment idea in the patient's statement that his wife is a fiancée, that is, he is not yet married; theoretically, therefore, he is still able to marry someone else.

It is not generally known that pangs of conscience in dreams and symptoms may have a hidden libidinous root and serve the patient as a particular form of recalling and reliving a past experience.

This mechanism can be found in cases of disconsolate worries, of persistent mournings, of depressions with self-accusation after the death of close relatives, and in similar situations. According to analytical theory, the impulse to inflict pain on one's self is derived from a libidinization of the suffering. The libidinous charge originally belonged to a tabooed craving from which it has subsequently been withdrawn. The tabooed craving then appears bare of any libidinous cathexis (and may even be charged with anxiety), while the sufferings of the patient show an invisible libido quality which renders them valuable to him (will to illness).

There is a clear difference between the neurotic feeling of guilt and the conscience reaction of a normal person. The neurotic feeling of guilt demands self-punishment, the degree of which corresponds to the primitivity and cruelty of the given neurotic personality. Most striking is the fact that the unconscious does not distinguish fancied from real guilt and that, in most cases, fancied guilt is punished by the patient's superego as if it were real.

In hysteria, visible symptoms may appear as a result of this self-punishment. Patients who feel that their eyes are constantly committing sins may become "blind"; others may render themselves "anesthetic," "dumb," or "paralyzed."

The problem of neurotic self-punishment, the "poena talionis," finds a remarkable illustration in the dream of a forty-two-year-old man who suffered from nervous asthma:

[123] *"My bed neighbor (in hospital) has been murdered (choked?). The police search for the murderer in all countries. Somebody constructs a doll in the exact shape of the victim in order to make the identification of the murderer*

easier. I say, 'The one who has reconstructed the victim so exactly must be the murderer.' And it was true."

In this dream we see the patient identifying himself with his wife (bed neighbor), who had been murdered by the patient himself through the medium of his death wishes. The patient's criminal idea was that of choking his wife to death. This idea was repressed. The criminal wish then boomeranged against the patient's own ego. In his asthmatic choking symptom, he experiences on his own body both the criminal aggression and the punishment for it at the same time. The identification mechanism is alluded to in the dream where the patient says, "The one who *reconstructed* the victim so exactly must be the murderer."

A similar neurotic construction is seen in dreams containing the so-called "Christ-identification." A patient dreams:

[124] *"I am forced to stand erect and to raise my arms as high as possible. My hands are then tied to a horizontal bar overhead and I am left thus for some time. All the blood flows away from my arms, which become numb and lose all sense of feeling."*

The Christ-identification is clear. The patient nailed himself to the cross of his neurosis and lost his normal feelings. Originally, he was exposed to the pressure of strong sadistic and criminal impulses which he succeeded in suppressing by constructing his pseudo-sexual condition. He withdrew from normal life in order to save the objects of his violent and "bloody" impulses from destruction. In his neurosis his arms are "bloodless," and if there is any cruelty to be noted, it is one that is turned against his own ego.

In some dreams the patient affords himself permission to commit antimoral acts. One of my patients was on the verge of a divorce because of his frequent extra-marital relations. He dreamt as follows:

[125] *"I am in a room with Mr. S. and Mrs. S. who is in bed. Mr. S. says, 'See what you can do for her.' I go with her to a couch and try to have intercourse with her in a posterior*

position. After a long time, I fail to have orgasm. I go out and get into my car and I begin to think, 'I wonder if my wife knows about this.' "

The dreamer, at first, attempts to circumvent his guilt reaction by stating that Mr. S. himself has invited him to commit infidelity. But the last phrase together with the indication of inhibiting forces (lack of orgasm) reveal the patient's strong unconscious moral attitude.

One of the unconscious motives of the patient's sexual promiscuity is his latent homosexuality. The above dream indicates this complex in the scene where a man invites the dreamer to share his wife with him. (The "triangle pattern" of latent homosexuality.)

Of special interest here is the "posterior position." Apart from the fact that it is suggestive of latent homosexuality, it depicts one of the patient's major frustrations. He is particularly potent in the posterior position; but his wife, a puritanic woman, does not permit any other approach but the one she considers normal, the frontal position. Much friction exists between the two marital partners because of this problem. As a rule, details of this sort tend to become "vital issues" in marriages only when there is a deep-seated feeling of incompatibility; trivialities then assume undue proportions. (In such cases, we must expose the deeper problems involved, rather than assume the role of arbiter.)

A female patient, aged thirty, had during adolescence the stereotyped, anxiety-laden dream [126] that *sheep were separated from the wolves and that she was on the "wrong" side (i.e., among wolves).*

The patient who was well-versed in the Bible recognized in the dream scene the modification of the Bible passage Gen. 30:35. The "wolves" appear in the dream (instead of the goats of the Bible passage) to emphasize the antithesis. The dream portrays the patient's unconscious tendencies to abandon her god-fearing attitude of the passive sheep and to join the "wolves," i.e., those who lead a less restricted and less sheltered life. The affect of anxiety, however, betrays the patient's fear of letting her barriers down.

A Catholic dentist, aged thirty-seven, dreamed [127] that *he was in a ferry ship and saw a wagon bearing a casket. The casket was on fire. He wanted to call the fire department but could not find any fire alarm box.*

He associated the "fire"—"hell-fire," and to the "ferry," the mythological river "Styx," across which dead bodies were carried to the underworld by the boatsman Charon. The dream thus depicts the patient's concept of Hell and contains a warning (the fire alarm box) against his antimoral conduct; for although he is married, he maintains a relationship with his assistant.

We cannot cover the problem of religion in dreams without saying a few words about *neurotic clauses,* as we detect them in the dream material. Some of the neuroses are locked by certain clauses which the patient has unconsciously established. We profit a great deal by discovering the character of these clauses, and by determining their function and extent.

A female patient who suffered from depressions reported that she was brought up by a very religious mother. According to this mother, to live properly one had to suffer. (The woman, by the way, later died in an insane asylum.) Throughought my patient's childhood, she was prepared and conditioned for suffering which would be rewarded in the hereafter.

The patient came from Germany and presented her dreams in the German language. One of her dreams ran as follows:

[128] *"A black-haired girl with a fine pale face draws back her loosely hanging hair so that her fine suffering features are emphasized, and she says, 'I am Jesus; so holy, and noble, and godlike as He is.' Then she shakes her head emphatically and says in English, 'No, no!' She does not want to be Jesus who suffered for the whole of humanity."*

It is not difficult to realize that the girl in the dream is the patient herself. The "No, no!" she says in English has an interesting connotation.

The dream occurred about two days after the patient had become an American citizen. In this connection she had studied the American Constitution. What perplexed and shocked her was the phrase of the Bill of Rights which deals with the right of the individual to *"life, liberty, and the pursuit of happiness."* That there should be one nation in this world that makes the pursuit of happiness a constitutional right affected the patient deeply. She reacted to it with anxiety. The "pursuit of happiness" entailed a frightening prospect which we were able to understand after extracting the following formula *(death clause)*: The patient felt that she must never be happy; for if *to live* means *to suffer, to be happy* means *to die.* She was determined to remain unhappy to preserve her very life.

If we find a clause of this type in the background of the depression, we have something tangible and therapeutically useful to deal with. The patient cannot tell us the cause spontaneously. She does not know it exists. She will tell us all she knows, namely, that she was brought up in a puritanic home where she heard that people were born to suffer and to get a reward in the hereafter. But she did not know that while in her conscious activities she rebelled against this ascetic ideal, unconsciously she perpetuated it by means of her neurosis.

The *chastity clause* is psychodynamically just as important as the death clause. The case of the impotent man has already been reported, the frustrated priest who maintained an unconscious celibacy. Having given up his aspirations as a clergyman, he became a teacher. As such he met a female colleague whom he wanted to marry. There was some premarital contact and he found on this occasion that he was impotent. He did not realize that through his impotence he showed the phenomenon of "belated obedience" to his mother. He remained "faithful" to her, and to her vow, and thus he fulfilled symbolically her promise to deliver him to the service of his Church.

SPLITTING OF THE SYMBOL

Freud has proved that our dreams are not simple fantasies but rather complicated, polymorphous formations of emotionally charged ideas. They are of a truly stereometric structure. Just as we may put cross sections through a globe from many directions, so can we interpret a dream from many different angles. As a matter of fact, most dream pictures are the result of condensation and can be used in several senses, according to the method of interpretation.

Carefully made studies of dreams have proved that the scenes are constructed, like everything in nature, according to the principle of "the simplest possible solution for the most complicated problem" (functional economy). The symbol is the focus of several ideas of the dreamer.

Less known are the following possibilities of symbolization which can be considered exceptions to the above statement. The dream may split the symbol of a person into two persons who indicate the role the person is playing in the dreamer's life. The reason for this transfiguration is once again the tendency to conceal the dreamer's real attitude. Because it is an opposite tendency to the well-known mechanism of condensation, we call the above-mentioned mechanism the "splitting of the symbol," an example of which is given in a dream of a twenty-four-year-old woman patient:

[129] *"I arrive at your office for my first session. You tell me to take off my clothes. I take off some of them. You tell me to take off more and I remove the rest of them. . . . Shortly after I have removed my clothes, two women enter and stand before you. One is about thirty-five years old, the other gives the impression of being her mother and is dressed conservatively in dark clothes. The younger woman removes her*

clothes also and, while standing in the nude, she converses with you."

The situation in the doctor's office is symbolized in this dream. The "undressing" is the mental "undressing," the analytic confession. At the same time, we see the transference situation. We interpret "mother-and-daughter" as "mother" and consider the appearance of the daughter, who behaves in the dream as the patient does in reality, only as an accentuation of the fact that it is a "mother" who is present. The patient showed a strong mother fixation with an increased homosexual component, and the dream revealed that she is now transferring her mother fixation toward the doctor.

Such split-off symbols are common in mythology. The "father-and-son" principle, e.g., as a symbol of creativity has found expression in several religions.

Doubling

The picture of *twins* or of two similar persons is called "doubling." It sometimes expresses the patient's double personality. We find this mechanism particularly in cases of bisexuality, where the patient has identified himself with a person of the opposite sex whom he loved in his childhood.

A homosexual woman whose analysis uncovered her identification with her brother and the projection of her own personality into the female sex partner dreams:

[130] *"My brother and I are going into the woods to build a cabin. I am to select two girls to come along and help us. A long procession of girls is passing by in single file. I ask my brother if he wishes to choose one of our companions. He tells me to select a certain blonde. In doing so, I notice there are two blondes who are exactly alike, apparently twins. I take both of them."*

The dream shows the identification of our patient with her brother (the brother tells her to select a partner for him). She sees twins; that is to say, the identification with a heterogeneous object, brother, leads to a splitting of the patient's personality; the brother-sister relationship changes into a woman-woman relationship.

In the doubling of *things* usually a condensation takes place as in the dream of one of Stekel's patients:

[131] *"I am swimming with a girl who wears two bathing suits, a black one which is loose and a light green one which is beneath and fits tightly. I think that she wears two suits because after she had reduced her weight the black suit became too wide."*

According to the patient's associations the figure of the girl is a condensation of two persons, his dead mother and his fiancée, Erna. "Black," symbol of death; "green," symbol of life. Past and future are united in his mind.

Compare here also the symbolism of the "shadow," described on page 128.

CHANGING SITUATIONS

The problems of "splitting of the symbol" and "depicting the general by the specific" lead directly to another important mechanism which is seen in the changing situations of the dream. (Cf. page 178.) A woman patient, aged thirty-one, dreamed:

[132] *"I was in the house of a friend (woman). Later on in the dream this friend seemed to turn into another friend, but remained in the same house. Then this second friend was my friend Virginia. She was going to undress. She did. All of a sudden she seemed to turn around, and at this moment she was a friend of mine named Ethel, from St. Louis. She took off her dress and I saw that she had on that type of band which they put on a woman's abdomen after childbirth and which I used to wear."*

If, in a dream, one person changes into another, the first person is only a symbol and a carrier of a certain quality of the second person (or the one for whom the second person substitutes). Here the pictures run through several stages:

friend → another friend → Virginia → Ethel. We do not know details about the first two persons (the patient's associations fail us here); therefore, we consider this change wherein a friend turns into another friend, as only an indication that the symbols of the dream are going to be changed.

From the patient's associations with the persons of the dream we learn: (a) that Virginia once advised our patient to divorce her husband; (b) that Ethel is a smart woman who talks very much, is independent, and takes pleasure in undressing in front of other people. (We must also realize that "undressing" is a symbol of "analysis.") The "band" supplied the connection between Ethel, the last link in the chain, and our patient who has the same band. The undressing friend thus signifies our patient "undressing" in front of the doctor, and the dream itself is classified as a so-called transference dream.

The analysis of the above dream reveals the following wish-fulfillment idea as the latent content: (1) a divorce from the husband as Virginia advised, and (2) social independence as it was exhibited by Ethel. Taking certain qualities from both friends out, the dreamer produces an oscillating and confusing chain of pictures.

The same patient reports:

[133] "I dreamed last night that *I was at the home of the same friend* (see dream 132). *A man kissed me and said he wanted to see me next day. This made me very angry. After I had left and told the story to a friend, I realized that the man had been not a man but a woman. This aroused in me even greater indignation.*"

We see here an unreasonably strong negative reaction. The latent homosexuality flashes through the dream and frightens the unsuspecting dreamer.[1] The patient shows in

---

[1] In reality there is no reason for this fear. Flashes of homosexual desires may be found in the dreams of anyone. The importance of the latent homosexual component for the mental conflict and its position among other repressed instincts are the only significant factors.

her general manner strong polyandrous tendencies (in the dream she is unfaithful to her husband), and we can see here that the root of her neurotic behavior lies in her latent homosexuality.

Emphasis should be placed on those dreams which in a concrete form present the problem of inhibition. They are important for the study of impotence, frigidity, stuttering, and some occupational diseases. Whenever the patient experiences a *symptom* of this type in his dream, you can also observe the *inhibition* in a dramatized form.

A typical inhibition dream is the impotence dream where a man attempts to have intercourse and another person or an unforeseen event interferes. These are dreams in which the patient tells us *what* his main inhibition is. A typical example would run as follows:

[134] *"I try to have intercourse with my wife. I make preparations while my mother (or friend X) enters the room."*

Now, why should his mother or friend enter the room at such an inopportune moment? The patient is the author of his dream. It would be easy for him to treat himself to an undisturbed pleasure. But the dream portrays the antithetic forces, both very much parts of his personality. The above dream would have to be understood as follows: "While my desire turns to my wife, my unconscious thoughts turn to my mother. She enters my mind, as, in the dream, she enters the room. This is the cause of my disturbance."

The "friend X" may be a lady who had experienced an undesired pregnancy a short time before and may, therefore, express the patient's fear of making his wife pregnant by accident. "Friend X enters the room," would then signify that *the thought* of "friend X's mishap" enters the patient's mind when he approaches his wife sexually.

One patient, who was frigid, dreamed [135] that *while she was intimate with an elderly man* (a father image) *her sister came into the room and disturbed her.*

The reader can easily suspect that a sibling rivalry exists between the two sisters. The incestuous act, on the other hand, does not necessarily indicate that incestuous relations have occurred in reality. Unconscious *wishes* often appear in the dream as over-dramatized *fulfillments*. "Love" easily becomes an extreme physical embrace. The patient's feelings toward her father may be ambivalent. Attachment and sexual attraction may coexist with rivalry, homosexuality, and aggression.

The dream also offers clues regarding the symptom of frigidity. It shows two pathogenic fixations: the father complex and the sister complex. The first may interfere with the patient's sexual enjoyment inasmuch as it gives rise to defenses against the sexual partner who unconsciously is identified with the incest object. The second leads to the same result because it mobilizes homosexual energies which detract the interest from the heterosexual object.

[136] *"It seemed as if I were lying in bed with Dorothy W., and Joan M. was suddenly seen lying there. And she seemed to have wedged herself between us and turned over— that is, she turned her back to me and flopped over to another area of the bed carrying me with her—or something like that."*

In this dream another woman "wedges herself" between the patient and his sweetheart and carries him with her. The patient is *carried away* by the thought of Joan M., a thought which interferes with his sexual relations. Of importance is the fact that Joan is very active and takes the initiative in the dream, a behavior which was deplorably absent in Dorothy's sexual approach. The dream thus shows us why the patient, who in his relations with women is rather passive, is attracted by Joan.

THE PERSONS AND THE DREAMER HIMSELF IN THE DREAM

One of the most perplexing problems of dream interpretation is the identification of "persons" who comprise the *Dramatis Personae* of the dream. They may appear in the dream as symbols, as an expression of the dreamer's split personality, as a crowd hiding individuals, or as an expression of some of the dreamer's opinions.

Persons as Symbols

We have discussed the significance of a single person in a dream as a family image, and as a symbol of sex and death. The transfiguration of persons sometimes shows several stages. We often find ourselves faced with the fact that the transfiguration is two or more times removed from the person the dream symbol represents.

Freud analyzed an informative dream of his own [137] in which *old Bruecke,* (Freud's teacher in physiology), *gives him a problem to solve, makes a microscopic slide, and picks out something that looks like tin foil.*

Freud's associations with "tin foil" were "Staniol" and "Stannius." The first association was a Vienna expression for "tin foil" and the second referred to Stannius, the famous psychologist who wrote a pioneer article on the nervous system of fish. One of the first research problems Freud received from Bruecke was concerned with the nervous system of a fish—"ammocoetes."

The chain of associations was from "Bruecke" to "ammocoetes" to "fish," to "Stannius," to "Staniol," and finally to "tin foil."

In this dream Freud attempted to solve one of his personal problems. The dream took him back to the days when he was a student of the physiologist, Bruecke, when he used the "physical microscope" for examining organisms instead of using the "psychic microscope," as in psychoanalysis. Maybe at the time of his dream he was in doubt as to whether he should alienate himself so much from organic medicine, as he did by his devotion to psychotherapy, or whether he should leave a bridge (*"Bruecke"* in German) between general medicine and psychology. In his dream book, Freud does not analyze this dream so far, but the above supposition has an element of probability.

SPLIT OF THE EGO

> *I think of my ego as though I saw it*
> *through a multiplying prism; all forms*
> *moving about me are egos, and I am*
> *annoyed with their actions.*
> E. T. A. HOFFMANN

Now we shall briefly discuss the fact that in the dream other persons may play the role of the repressed part of our personality. This displacement is called "projection." The cause of projection is the desire to eject from our mind the embarrassing contents of our thoughts. The pattern of this mechanism is set early in our life. The infant's two main reactions to the outside world are (a) acceptance and incorporation (by mouth) of all that is pleasurable, and (b) rejection and spitting out of all that is found unpleasurable. The act of spitting out the undesirable is an early pattern of the projective mechanism. It is only the unacceptable that is projected. In psychoses it may reappear in the hallucination of a hostile voice. In dreams, it is the other person, or persons, who "do the dirty work" for us.

In some dreams we appear represented by several other characters, perhaps even antagonistic to each other, each representing a certain component of our personality. The split of the personality as a problem has attracted the writers of many countries and times. Oscar Wilde's *Picture of Dorian Gray*, Stevenson's *Dr. Jekyll and Mr. Hyde*, Edgar Allan Poe's *William Wilson*, and many others, describe the split of the human personality into two antagonistic personalities.

Oberndorf quotes Oliver Wendell Holmes as saying:

"Dr. Johnson dreamed [138] *he had a contest of wit with an opponent, and got the worst of it;* of course, he furnished the wit for both."

Freud says in connection with this problem: "It is an experience to which I know no exception, that every dream represents the dreamer himself. Dreams are absolutely egoistic. When some other person than myself appears in the dream I must assume that my personality is portrayed, through identification, in that person."

Interesting in this respect is the dream of a young man who had to leave Germany when Hitler came to power.

[139] *"Herman Goering's son, a tall, good looking fellow, came from Germany to visit my dad's house. We all sat around the family table. I was conversing with Goering junior and asked him many things. Suddenly my mother butted in and I got exceedingly angry at her. I said, 'I'll split your skull.' "*

Herman Goering's son is the young man's own "alter ego." The matricidal impulse portrayed in this dream (expressed also in many other dreams of this patient) was a reaction to an overstrong incestuous fixation to the patient's mother. We have found that criminal tendencies toward one's mother very often are aroused by the conviction that the love fixation toward this person transcends normal standards and that it incapacitates the bearer for any other love adjustment. Oscar Wilde's thought that "each man kills the thing he loves"[1] is particularly true in cases of this type. In the above dream "Herman Goering, junior" is the dreamer's own matricidal impulse. He attempts to sit down with it "around the family table," to deal with it intelligently, but the thought of his mother interferes and stirs up the dormant criminal tendencies.

An interesting example of the split in the ego is reported by Stekel in the dream by a judge:

[140] *"I had a cottage next to a prison, and it appeared that a room of that cottage became a sort of veranda which led to the roof of that prison. Next, I knew that an inmate had escaped and there was some talk about it. It seemed to be an uncomfortable situation, as the escaped prisoner might break in on us. In fact as I sat alone in my room looking through the veranda, I saw on the roof a miserable looking, thin, emaciated, pale-faced prisoner with sunken eyes. At*

---

[1] *The Ballad of Reading Gaol.*

once I had the impression that this prisoner would break away. Next, I had the impression that he might attack me. I seized a knife lying on the table, went into a little room separated by a glass door from the first, locked myself up there, and watched through the glass door. Great God! I thought to myself, he may perhaps break through the glass door and I should have to drive him off with a knife."

A peculiar dream for a judge! Stekel describes the patient as an adventurous character, a man who had committed adulteries so many times that he sometimes feared a scandal in his family which would endanger both his marital and his social position. In his office there was an attractive woman, separated from him only by a glass door. The patient was fighting against his inner impulse to make advances to this woman.

In the dream we see his divided emotions. The judge's cottage and the prison are close together. The "prisoner" is that part of the patient's personality which has to be kept in custody because it is antimoral. It is the patient's sexual impulse toward the girl. We see here also an example of a "transformation into the opposite." The good-looking girl seated behind the glass door is here transposed into a "miserable-looking, emaciated, pale-faced, unshaven prisoner."

The girl in the next room is as dangerous to our patient as a criminal would be. The dream shows us the reaction of the patient's conscience to the thought of a reckless sexual approach to the young girl. "Great God!" he exclaims. "He may break through the glass door" (defloration).

The personality split is occasionally made evident in the form of a warning, of which the following dream may serve as an example:

[141] *"I see my friend John riding in a car. I say to him: 'Don't go this way (the patient points with his hand to the left), for you will find there a very steep incline. You will not be able to use your brakes effectively.' He laughed and said, 'My car is accustomed to going over rocks and marshes.'*

I see him later lying dead on the ground with a broken neck. I am terrified."

Friend John is the patient himself. The dream contains a warning against the steep inclines of life, on which one's self-control can easily be lost. The patient was fighting against his gambling impulse. He feared that unless he could control himself he would ruin his health by staying up late at night and would upset his family life by spending money.

The following dream was produced by a physician, aged forty-two, who had fallen in love with a nurse, a Catholic nun in his home town in Italy, and who realized that his love had no chance of fulfillment:

[142] *"I am in the hospital. I hear the nurse coming into the room, but cannot see her. I only hear the rustle of her skirts. I call out to her, but she does not answer. I try to think why I cannot see her and decide that I must have developed a central scotoma, and try looking out of my eyes using the lateral fields. It seems that I can see everything in the room but cannot see the nurse."*

This dream portrays the patient's struggle against his "sinful" thoughts. He finally succeeds in repressing the picture of the nurse ("central scotoma"). He does not see her any more. What he is doing in his dream is done by most patients who are suffering from so-called "psychogenic blindness." We know today that the so-called "concentric constriction of the visual field," which we find with the perimeter in examining certain types of hysteria, is not caused by a disturbance of anatomic centers but by "narrowing" of the patient's emotional scope and by a fixation of the patient's mind on particular ideas (Janet).

We may find in dreams the image of the dreamer's body divided into two parts as a symbol of the split in his ego. Following the analogy of *above* and *below,* we interpret the upper and lower part of the body as symbols of the spiritual, platonic tendencies, and of the baser instincts respectively.

The *longitudinal division* separating the left side of the body from the right side has been discussed in connection with the problem of the "left and right" in the dream on page 76.

The split in personality can be observed clearly in cases of *depersonalization*. As the patient's ego or his environment can lose its emotional cathexis, an organ of the body can also lose its cathexis. This can be seen in some cases of hysteria. We then can observe psychogenic blindness, deafness, paralysis, analgesia, and anesthesia.

It is worth mentioning that in the perception of our organs it is not only the mental interest we have in them, an interest which under pathological conditions may be withdrawn, but also the physical interest that matters. There is a definite physical relation between the ego and the body ("body image"). Schilder, Hoff, Kogerer, and others even proved that this interest is not equally distributed over the body, and that in our perception, single parts are represented more strongly than others. Thus patients who have suffered the amputation of an arm often preserve the feeling of this arm for a long time. This "phantom limb" usually is shorter than the real one, or has an infantile character, which proves that the most impressive experiences (childhood) influence the shape of the preserved images of the organ in our brain.

A situation in which the patient has lost her feeling of being identical with herself is illustrated by dreams published in the *Psychoanalytic Review*:

[143] *"I am in a hospital. The nurse shows me my bed. It is the bed of another patient and is very dirty."*

Another dream by the same patient:

[144] *"I enter a room and sit down. Suddenly I see myself seated opposite me.[1] I become very anxious. A conflict arises between my real and my strange ego. I make my other self certain concessions and run out."*

---

[1] "Sitting opposite someone" often represents opposition to that person (cf. 158).

One patient who suffered from depersonalization had a dream [145] which began with the words, *"I see myself in a coffin."*

All of these dreams contain the estrangement of one part of the patient's emotional personality as a special form of repression. This estrangement may go so far that the patient, as in the above example, may feel as if his ego were dead or as if he had lost his ego. We can understand the close connection of this state with depressions.

A religious Catholic patient said:

[146] *"I dreamed that in the moving picture which I had seen the night before, the villain, who was the main character, had also played the part of the hero. This was announced, to my amazement, at the end of the picture. It proved that one actor could take two parts and not be detected while doing it."*

In this dream the patient himself perceives the split in his emotions. He combines in his personality Christ and Anti-Christ, the religious and the sacrilegious ego.

The displacement from the dreamer to another person usually proceeds according to the rule of substituting representatives of the same sex for the dreamer. The opposite is found especially in persons who have a contrasexual identification.

The *theatrical performance* a patient sees in his dream is, as a rule, the play of his own life.[1] It is the projection of his main conflicts and emotions, a mechanism very similar to the one of writing a play. ("Every artistic work is a confession" —Stekel.)

The following dream is illustrative of this feature:

[147] *"I am in a movie theater. There is a wild hunt for two persons. The end of the performance seems to be tragic, and I have the impression that after the death of one of the*

[1] In fewer cases it is a repetition of an impressive scene which the patient has previously experienced.

*actors I shall get an auto as my inheritance. I have driven
this car before."*

The "nonsense" in this dream is the fact that the patient
who is watching the performance has played a part in it
before and is now obviously participating in its action.
Doubtless, the "performance" is a part of his own life history. The dream contains the patient's "secret, life plan." He
really intends after the death of his wife to marry another
woman with whom he has already had relations. The "two
persons" are the two women. The "auto" is a symbol of his
antimoral urges; the phrase "I have driven before" has reference to his previous experience with other women.

THE NEGRO IN THE DREAM

In the United States, the "Negro" appears in dreams of
white people as a symbol of repressed desires, or as a symbol
of white, but otherwise tabooed persons. It is the "second
ego" or the "person in the dark." (Compare this with the
symbolism of "the Shadow," described on page 128.)

The following dream is an example of such symbolization:

[148] *"My friend Jack and I explore underground caves
where we see Monroe White, a Negro prize fighter. I think
he has escaped from prison."*

"Monroe White" (the real name has been changed) was
in prison because he committed a rape-murder. In this dream
he represents the patient's own violent instinctual cravings
which he tries to control (prison). The picture of the "underground caves" represents the patient's "unconscious."
(For other symbols of the unconscious, see page 160.)

The distinguishing feature of the Negro, his dark skin,
makes him also suitable for the portrayal of "death." Religious (white) people also associate the figure of the devil
with the "black man."

In many dreams we find the symbol "Negro" associated

with concepts of "another race," with "the different," "the (sexually) abnormal," and the like.

In the following dream the Negro represents the symbol of repressed homosexuality. The dreamer is a twenty-four-year-old clerk:

[148] *"I was walking along the street with a colored boy. He had just come from a bank where he got some money in an unlawful way. He split with me some of this stolen money. I believe there were quarters.*

"When I left him I had the feeling that the police had some knowledge of this and were after us.

"I started to run and noticed that a policeman started after me. I put all the quarters into my mouth and was trying desperately to gulp them down. I was thinking of the possible ill effects on my health of all the dirty money I was swallowing. The policeman caught up with me and took my footprints to keep a record and bring me to justice."

The dream will become intelligible if we know that when the patient was twelve years old, he was lured into the men's room by a homosexual man who asked the boy to perform fellatio on him. He promised to give him a quarter—a promise he did not keep.

In his dream, the patient shares the guilt with a "colored boy" (projection of his own latent homosexuality). He gets his quarter (compensation for the disappointment he experienced in reality), and not only one but many of them. The fellatio experience is revived in the scene where the patient puts all the quarters into his mouth.

At the same time, this scene reproduces a disorder from which the patient was suffering during adolescence: *stuttering*. His repressed homosexuality played a part in the disorder which, incidentally, the patient succeeded in overcoming by conscious effort.

The latent homosexual trends, however, based primarily upon the patient's brother fixation, remained an active force in his neurosis. He refers to it when he speaks of "possible ill effects" to his health and of "dirty money." His moral component (police) is ever watchful and will ultimately deliver him to justice (although in the dream it was the "colored boy" who had committed the unlawful act).

In some dreams the picture of a Negro substitutes for a repressed picture of a (white) person with dark complexion or dark hair.

A forty-year-old man suffering from migraine dreams:

[149] *"I am trying hard to drive a wagon up a steep hill. A short distance from the top of the hill I am in danger of losing my equilibrium and falling down the hill. Suddenly a Negro appears at the top and pulls me over the dangerous spot. I awake with a headache."*

This dream is a picture of the migraine attack. The psychological background of the acute attack of migraine is a prohibited (homosexual) fantasy of the patient. The presence of such a fantasy causes an inner struggle and brings the patient into a state of tension (driving up a steep hill). Finally, the tabooed ideas become victorious and are discharged, while the lights of consciousness are dimmed. The "Negro" at the climax symbolizes the attack of migraine, which in this case also awakened the patient.

As stated before (in connection with the symbolism of the "shadow") in the dreams of whites, the "colored" person often represents the uncanny, the unknown, the thing that is different in itself. He symbolizes everything in the ego which is opposed by the superego. Could we draw from this fact our conclusions as to what anti-Negro spirit, in general, expresses? We said that it is the mysterious part of our own psyche. Because we do not comprehend it directly, we are afraid of it. When anti-Negro people say, "We don't want them to become too strong," they are talking about their own id drives. What is outside of us can be attacked and destroyed, while forces which we harbor internally cannot be dealt with effectively. This is an intolerable situation. Therefore, people who suffer from this type of anxiety create an external object, a target; they attack it and, in so doing, have the satisfaction of having attacked the "cause" of their own discomfort. They believe that their cause is just. However, such a projection is always futile; it can lead only to repetitive patterns, since it is operating on a purely symbolic level. It does not offer real solutions. It is this, among other things, that makes a person who is sick with prejudice inclined to consider the object of his attack as abnormally sensual, criminal, and cunning.

What I have said of racial prejudices applies to all forms of xenophobia. The fear of the foreigner is the fear of the foreign in ourselves. We do not want to face it. Recognition of and insight into one's own unconscious make projections of this type unnecessary. Here, as in so many other forms of living, knowledge is the best way of eliminating morbid fears and hatreds.

A CROWD OF PEOPLE

In the dream this may signify secretiveness or a particular person hidden in the crowd. The following dream belongs to the first type:

[150] *"I was at a place which seemed to be at first a golf course and then a bowling alley. There was a girl whom I had previously seen in a restaurant and who was very homely, but well-built and seemingly pleasant. I dreamed that I was lying beside her and soon I embraced her in anticipation of an intimate act. There were many people present. I knew then, and I was bashful, but the girl said that if they were broadminded, they would not mind. Then we seemed to talk of sexual intercourse in terms of golfing and bowling."*

We interpret the words: "There were many people present" as "There was no one present." (This is an example of an "interpretation by the opposite," see page 244). The girl whom the patient had previously seen in a restaurant is his sister; the "restaurant" he previously saw was his "first restaurant," his home. A place where physical hunger can be appeased is a symbol of a place where sex hunger can be satisfied. This on the principle that physical urges may substitute for each other. (The deduction that the restaurant represented the patient's home was based upon the patient's associations.) The entire dream content was built on the patient's early experiences which consisted of intimacies with his sister, leading to a strong fixation.

We see a similar meaning in the following dream:

[151] *"I dreamed that I was in my room with Mrs. B. and that her behavior was gay and playful. I next remember that I had noticed some men working in a building opposite our window. I felt certain that if they turned around they would see us, so I moved away from their view."*

The people who can look into the dreamer's room represent "public opinion." The dreamer seems to ask: "What would people say if they noticed that you were having relations with Mrs. B.?" He had been divorced from Mrs. B. for some time. The dream is a wish-fulfillment. While, in reality, she was frigid and unresponsive to him in the sexual act, in his dream she becomes gay and active. Their marriage is restored and everything is all right.

The second type is represented in a dream by a thirty-seven-year-old physician:

[152] *"I am running down a hill on skis. I pass Peggy, then Mitzi, but have no time to talk to them. Then I pass a crowd of physicians from our department in the hospital. I am sliding at a tremendous speed."*

In this dream we see "Peggy," "Mitzi," and a "crowd." The dreamer had never been to ski parties with any one he recognized in the dream, but he had gone with *Erna,* his former fiancée, whom he lost and whom he thought he had forgotten. The dream shows that he did not cease loving her and thinking of her, and that he wished to ski with her again. His present difficulties proved to be based on a "chastity complex." He was preserving the ardor of his emotion for his former love object.

Another dream of the same type is the following:

[153] *"I dreamed that I was at my grandfather's house. All my relatives on my father's side were there also. I was very grouchy and nobody noticed me."*

The patient, a twenty-six-year-old woman, felt badly because her father did not care so much for her after she married ("nobody noticed me"). In her dream she sees "all my relatives" instead of only her father. The reason for this disguise is that the patient first attempted to conceal her dissatisfaction with her father's cool attitude.

One of the tricks frequently used by the patient's dream censorship in order to disguise an important person in the dream is the constant replacement of persons acting in the dream plot. This mechanism sometimes seriously obstructs the therapeutic work. Again and again the patient introduces new persons into his dreams, and the recognition and identification of them take a great deal of the available time. It is often a single dream or a little detail of the dream which enables us to get behind the dreamer's secret. This is exceedingly difficult, however, and has often caused serious misinterpretations of the case, particularly when persons of both sexes are used interchangeably.

VISUAL AND AUDITORY FLASHES IN THE DREAM

A fragment of a phrase which is perceived in a dream as an auditory flash can contain a complete thought, or a part of a thought, which is suitable for interpretation. However, it can seldom be understood without the patient's associations. A twenty-four-year-old woman reports the following dream:

[154] *"I just heard the words, 'Go through his pockets.' I think it was about my father. I am reminded that those same words also came to me yesterday when I was too tired to write them down."*

The patient related that she often thought of the inheritance she would receive when her father died. Once she examined his pockets and found the draft of his will. She saw in the will that her father planned to leave to her sister five thousand dollars more than to her. She felt hurt, particularly because she had always wanted to be her father's favorite child and had always suffered because of a lack of attention from him.

A twenty-four-year-old male laboratory technician dreams:

[155] *"Dr. Gutheil and I are walking through an old school house. There is something on the blackboard I have written as a school child that goes like this:*

'I to my perils . . .' etc. We are searching."

The incomplete phrase refers to a poem by A. E. Housman which begins with these words. The poem, in essence, expresses the author's feeling that because his life had been hard and his resistance strong, he was able to withstand the blows of fate better than many others.[1]

The dream reproduces the analytic situation. In the company of his analyst, the patient goes through recollections of his past (old school house). There they find a rudiment of an inscription which was preserved from the patient's childhood days. And what does this inscription convey?

It shows the patient's conviction that the strict training he has received from his parents (school house) has its advantages, that it lowers his sensitiveness to life's demands upon him, that it serves him as an "armor" against the potential aggressions by the outside world. At the same time, this armor indicates that he is not ready to accept the op-

[1]   I to my perils
        Of cheat and charmer
        Came clad in armor
        By stars benign.

      Hope lies to mortals
        And most believe her;
        But man's deceiver
        Was never mine.

      The thoughts of others
        Were light and fleeting,
        Of lovers' meeting
        Or luck or fame.

      Mine were of trouble,
        And mine were steady,
        So I was ready
        When trouble came.

timistic viewpoint represented by his analyst because "hope" is a "cheat and charmer," and a "deceiver"; it brings about "perils" to those who "believe her."

A fragment of a sentence—and yet it reveals a great deal about the patient's attitude (a) toward his parents, (b) toward life, and (c) toward analysis.

CONVERSATION IN THE DREAM

Freud found that the sentences spoken in the dream are recollections of sentences which actually have been spoken in real life. This statement seems to have many exceptions, because we often cannot find any echo of the dreamer's real life in the conversation represented in the dream. At any rate, we can consider an opinion uttered in a dream as one of the mental components of the dream. Word condensations and neologisms appear frequently in dream conversations. (Cf. page 113.)

A minister, aged fifty-nine, who in his neurosis showed a high degree of infantilism and whose various disturbances could be traced back to an early stage of his development, dreamed the following:

[156] *"Playing baseball 'against the rules' and someone saying to me, 'early dearl.'"*

"Early day" and "early girl" were associated with "early dearl." The patient thus expressed his disturbed attitude toward women, and his interest in very young girls which was caused by his infantilism ("early day," "early girl," represent "young girl").

A musician, aged thirty-one, who suffered from impotence, dreamed:

[157] *"I am in a doctor's office where I meet my friend Joe. I ask what is the matter with him and he tells me the name of his sickness, which sounds like 'retrocitive.' It means 'flowing back.' I understand that his urine, instead of flowing out, flows back into the urethra because of some obstacle."*

Our patient (friend Joe) is at the doctor's office; he has a "retrocitive" disturbance of urination. On closer scrutiny the patient finds an association with our conversation about "retrospective tendencies" discussed in the preceding session. The other word that comes to his mind is "recidive," the recurrence of a sickness. He associates "recidive" with the gonorrhea he had several years previously. In the dream he was still suffering from the consequences of the gonorrhea which (in reality) had created a partial stricture of his urethra. This disease was, as was found in analysis, an important mental trauma for the patient. It greatly impaired his sex life, for he developed a neurotic fear of venereal disease, leading to psychogenic impotence. In the dream this infection complex is portrayed by the obstacle in the urethra. The man's experience with gonorrhea and the fear of its recurrence ("recidive") were the causes of his neurosis. (The urine "flowing back" represented emotional regression.)

Mutilated words may be hard to decipher. A patient dreams:

[158] *"I am about to kill a man. Name: something like 'Wrather' or 'Werther'; the name was not clear and definite in the dream."*

The "Wrather" or "Werther" proved to be—"brother."

In the dream, *advice* given to the dreamer is usually hypocritical. It serves unconscious tendencies and contains a wish-fulfillment. A forty-one-year-old teacher dreams:

[159] *"I went to see a doctor about my deformity. It seemed to be my hip. After a thorough and complete examination the doctor said he was sorry he could not help me. He advised me to take a vacation."*

The patient has no deformity. One of her colleagues, Miss P., of whom the patient believes that she is more successful professionally than she, has a congenital dislocation of the hip. Our patient is very ambitious, and in this dream identifies herself with the more successful teacher. The dream-doctor's advice is hypocritical. It corresponds to the patient's feeling of physical superiority and her inner satisfaction that her competitor has an irreparable deformity. "Taking vacation," in this dream, means leaving for good, dying.

Advice given to others by the dreamer usually reveals an important attitude of the dreamer. A forty-two-year-old lawyer dreams:

[160] *"Two friends of mine got into trouble. Somebody (a woman?) was killed. The friends were arrested. I suggested that they should tell the judge a false story."*

The lawyer had trouble with his wife. He often displayed violent rage which was followed by attacks of dizziness. In analysis the symptom proved to be a neurotic reaction due to the suppression of an impulse to commit murder. In his dream the patient suggests misleading the doctor ("tell the judge a false story"). The advice given to his clients reveals the patient's unconscious resistance to treatment.

A *quarrel* or a *battle* in the dream often signifies a mental conflict, the contrast of two antagonistic ideas or impulses. The quarreling persons represent individual contradictory tendencies. A quarrel with a particular person may, of course, portray a real conflict with this person.

Reproaches are mostly self-reproaches of the dreamer and usually express his feeling of guilt.

"Artificial" Dreams

We often hear the reproach that the dreams presented by patients are changed and disfigured arbitrarily or by chance. The patient may even attempt to mislead the analyst by purposely giving wrong information. So far as this is concerned, there is little danger.

Freud has proved that our associations are never entirely arbitrary, but are always colored by the patient's particular complexes. The same is true of artificial dreams. Freud has emphasized, for example, that in W. Jensen's "Gradiva" there are "artificial" dreams which, however, can be correctly interpreted as though they were real ones.[1]

Sometimes we ask patients to invent dreams when they have not reported them for some time and we analyze them just as if they were real dreams. A woman musician, aged thirty-two, suffering from frigidity based on active castration wishes, once brought to me what she called a "fake dream." The dream was remarkable because it was not wholly invented. The patient took a book on animal psychology and opened various pages. She used the first line of each page as material for the "dream." Nevertheless, her personal complexes seeped into the presentation, and we could see that it was not as "artificial" as she seemed to believe. We think here of Jung's statement that "one does not dream; one is dreamed." According to him, we "undergo" the dream, we are its objects.

BOOK MATERIAL	FAKE DREAM [161]
1. "not go in the right direction if more than 25 seconds"	1. *"I walked in the right direction for 25 seconds."*
2. "animal moved once"	2. *"When I came upon an animal, it moved once, then remained quiet."*
3. "fect of colored rays was independent of their intensity and"	3. *"Rays of multicolored light began to flash . . .*
4. "onds a fairly high degree of readiness; this is shown by the"	4. . . . *"and a loud voice cried out, 'Ready.'"*
5. "sight and do not perceive their prey until they touch it"	5. *"I sought out the animal but could not perceive it except through the sense of touch. Finally I seized the animal and sank my teeth into it."*

Any analyst would discover without difficulty that the "animal" which moved once and then remained quiet, and which was perceivable only "through the sense of touch" was a phallic symbol. We see here distinctly the patient's

---

[1] Ferenczi calls the artificial dreams "forced fantasies."

sadistic (castrating) attitude in the biting scene, almost entirely a free invention of the patient.

NUMBERS IN THE DREAM (NUMERAL SYMBOLISM)

Numeral symbolism, which plays a great part in the dream books of the superstitious, is also of some importance for the scientist, but in a different sense. Numbers very often have a close relation to certain important data of the patient's life. Birthday, age, number of relatives, etc., can find expression in this way in the dream.

Sometimes the dreamer reveals through a numeral symbolism a "secret calendar" in which important experiences of his life are registered. In it we may find a key to the interpretation of other parts of the dream.

Numbers used in the dream are, of course, also disguised at times, so that in most cases the dreamer himself is not able to understand their deeper significance. Sometimes we find a religious meaning in the number, for instance, a reference to the Ten Commandments, a specific Commandment, e.g., one that concerns parents, or chastity, or the like. The word "six" may be used as a substitute for "sex" because of the phonetic resemblance. (The same applies, by the way, also to the word "sox.") Like other symbols, numbers reveal their significance best through the patient's associations, but "three" seems to have a fixed relation to the male genital.

An impotent salesman, aged forty-three, dreamed:

[162] *"There is one thing that can cure you—twenty-one."*

To the question, "Who is now twenty-one years old?" he promptly replied, "My daughter." The patient thus revealed his daughter fixation as the deepest root of his impotence.

In dreams we sometimes see a displacement of amounts when amounts are charged emotionally. One of my patients in Vienna had to pay a fee amounting to one hundred (Austrian) *schilling*. He paid fifty and promised to pay the balance another time. In the meantime he dreamed:

[163] *"Somebody helps me to take a trunk down from the roof of my car and asks fifty groschen for this job. After I have given him this amount he looks at me as if it were too little money for him. I think: 'Other people work an hour for one schilling and he complains about half a schilling for a little service like that.' "*

"Fifty *groschen*" stands for "fifty *schilling*," and refers to the patient's debt. The man who helps the patient is his doctor; in his dream the patient accuses his analyst of overcharging him.

In dreams in which we find numbers indicating certain amounts of money the interpretation emphasizes more the importance of "money" than that of the quantity. However, knowing in general, that "money" symbolizes "love" (in addition to its anal meaning) we can often draw our conclusions from that point as to the dreamer's love life. We are interested particularly in that passage of the dream which reveals whether the amount in question is relatively high or low. But even in such cases we must also analyze the particular number (the amount) as to its possible references to a birthday, a "secret calendar," the number of members of the family, some important dates, etc.

A good example of "money" signifying "love" is found in the dream of a frigid woman (see page 377) who "wished to buy pickles" (phallic symbol) and found that she "did not have enough money."

To *pay* is sometimes used in dreams in its religious meaning, as "to atone." ("You will pay for this!")

Dropping coins may signify squandering valuable things. As "dropping semen," it may refer to masturbation.

Spending money may mean spending love, and may refer to promiscuity (harlot-fantasy in women).

Picking up coins shows, as a symbol, close relation to the collecting tendencies of the anal-erotic type of neurotic who exhibits also in other ways his "money complex." We see in the dream of "picking up coins" the dreamer's ambition to accumulate money.

Counting in the dream, often used illogically, may signify "counting" also in our interpretation; for example, anticipated counting of an expected inheritance sum, or counting the family members before they die, etc.

COLORS IN THE DREAM

Colors are also of some interest to us. *Brown* may cause in our minds conscious associative connections with defecation; *black* with death; *white* with innocence; *red* with blood and love. *Yellow* may be identified with cowardice, *green* may be associated with jealousy (the "green-eyed monster"—Othello).

A "lady in black" may appear as a symbol of death. *Rose-colored* things may have an association with a person named Rose.

Among uneducated people specific superstitions concerning colors may be discovered. It is, therefore, necessary to inquire as to whether the dreamer has any special associations with the color he dreamed about.

Blue played an important part in the dream of Lisa in Moss Hart's "Lady in the Dark." In one of her dreams, everybody was dressed in blue and every object was blue. In a masterly presented analysis of the case, the blue color was introduced in connection with a blue dress the patient's mother used to wear. One of the early traumas in the patient's life occurred when her father once remarked that even if she wore her mother's blue dress, she could never be as beautiful as her mother. This trauma was followed by several others, leading ultimately to a refusal by the patient to compete with other women.

Let us quote here from several dreams about color:

[164] *"I was intimate with Mrs. W. We were lying in a bed on top of my wife. My wife was covered with a black cloth and did not seem to object to our doings."*

The "black cloth" symbolizes death. The dream contains a death wish against the dreamer's wife.

A young unmarried woman dreams:

[165] *"I had on a white dress. Suddenly, I noticed that it was soiled in front."*

This dream reveals the patient's self-reproaches because of a sexual experience ("soiled in front"). The "white dress" is a symbol of chastity. The patient made the attempt to conceal this fact in her report. The above dream betrayed her, however.

The same patient had also the following dream:

[166] *"I have done something wrong (stealing?). I saw two girls. Both were myself. One of them was dressed in a red, the other in a white toga. It seemed that the white Annie (name of the patient) was ashamed of the red one."*

A clear example of the split of the patient's mental attitude into a moral (white) and an immoral (red) ego. "Stealing" is a substitute for sexual misbehavior.

In the next dream, "black" signifies the patient's dark outlook on life. In his dream [167] *he saw that everything was black. Then he realized that he was being fitted for eyeglasses. They were not the usual kind, but like polaroids, rotating two lenses until striations were parallel. Just as the right adjustment was reached to his satisfaction,* he awoke.

In this dream the patient was trying to find a compromise solution to two of his contradictory trends (the two lenses) which, he hoped, would eliminate the gloomy, neurotic outlook he had on life.

An unusual meaning of the color Blue was found in the case of a forty-nine-year-old man who suffered from ejaculatio praecox. In his dreams, the color Blue appeared very frequently and it was, at first, unintelligible. Strong sadistic and necrophilic trends were uncovered in analysis. It became more and more obvious that the main reason for the patient's sexual disturbance was his latent hostility toward women, until a dream [168] in which *he saw a castle and a man with a long beard,* revealed the presence of a "Bluebeard complex." His impotence represented a defense against his criminal impulses toward women.

The following dream deals with the color Red:

[169] *"I see big, red, fleshy ants crawling about. I had them in my pocket and they broke through. I am scared."*

The (male) patient attended a lecture on "Art in Schizophrenia." The instructor presented to the audience a painting called "The Ant." The artist made it look like an overdimensional phallus. In the patient's mind a synthesis occurred between "red ant," a "bug" (slang for "insane"), and "schizophrenia." But the phallic appearance of the painted insect stimulated in the patient's unconscious a strain of homosexual fantasies which, however, were quickly repressed. Repression created tension, and fear ("I am scared") lest the repressed material break into consciousness ("they broke through"). This break-through, in our patient's mind, was equivalent to "insanity." In his opinion, only an insane person ("a bug") could entertain a craving for a "red, fleshy ant."

Some patients see bright and cheerful colors in their dreams, while others experience the dream events in more drab shades. Some parallels exist between the color responses in the Rorschach test and the awareness of color in dreams.

Depressive moods account for drab and gloomy colors, while elated states are accompanied by colorful dreams. A conspicuous plethora of colors with low visualization of objects bespeaks lability of affect. (Colors in dreams of the blind are described on page 208.)

INDIVIDUAL SYMBOLS

One who has had an opportunity to analyze many dreams usually makes the observation that most patients use their own specific symbols. A young man, for example, used to dream about motorcycles and automobiles when he tried to express his impulse to leave his home. Other people may have "political dreams," "school dreams," "traveling dreams," "water dreams," and so on. But that is only a matter of external form.

As stated previously, the more embarrassing situations are usually represented by less embarrassing ones, their specific meaning has to be discovered by interpretation.

A married patient expressed his desire to commit infidelity by the following dream, produced during the era of prohibition:

[170] *"I walked up to the bar, ordered a glass of beer, and jokingly said that I was going to drink water."*

The dreamer tries to convince himself that he is not doing wrong (beer was a prohibited drink at that time). In Europe or in the United States today, this special interpretation of "drinking beer" would be invalid.

If an orthodox Jew eats pork in his dream, we are correct in interpreting it as a prohibited enjoyment, an interpretation which is without value if a non-orthodox Jew or a Gentile is the dreamer.

A student, aged twenty-two, who suffered from impotence, dreamed:

[171] *"I have a quarrel with my father. Then I meet a girl and we eat something. I think it was meat and butter."*

In order to understand this simple dream, it is necessary to know that the patient is a son of a very religious Jew. He was brought up in a strictly religious atmosphere, and was accustomed to fulfilling all the requirements of the Jewish ritual. When he was twenty-one years old he gave up his orthodox way of living and became "progressive." So he believed; but in his dreams and symptoms, his unconscious religiosity remained. His impotence was one of its consequences. He once promised his father to have intercourse only after his marriage. His impotence forced him to keep his promise.

In the dream we see his inner conflict with his father (and all he represented) in the picture of the "quarrel." The patient is aware of his intention to disobey his father and to go out with girls without the intention of marrying them. We see the portrayal of the sin in the words "meat and butter." An orthodox Jew is not allowed to eat meat and milk products at the same time. In the patient's dream, we see him do this while he meets a girl.

Among many of the advantages offered by the interpretation of dream series there is one which has a connection with the individual symbolism. If we encounter an individual symbol, the meaning of which is obscure, other dreams may offer us a clue. It is one of the peculiarities of the dreams produced in the course of a treatment that the uninterpretable symbol tends to appear again and again until its correct meaning has been recognized.

DREAMS BY DEAF PERSONS

Dreams by people who are deaf on one side require a different interpretation of "right" and "left." The most important dream events usually take place on the side of the healthy ear. Exceptions are rare. People who have become deaf on both sides often dream about hearing music, conversation, sounds, explosions, and so on (wish-fulfillment).

They are usually drawing heavily upon the visual experiences of their past, and visual images determine the contents of their dreams. Kinesthetic dreams are rare (labyrinth involvement?). All kinds of compensatory features can be noted in dreams of the deaf. Inferiority feelings are countered by strong narcissistic and magic dream concepts emphasizing omnipotence.

DREAMS BY BLIND PERSONS

Blind people whose defect is congenital or acquired at an early age, dream of their environment, using symbols perceived predominantly by the sense of touch. They often say, to be sure, "I see," but what they express in this way are qualities such as "roundness," "softness," "heaviness," "warmth," "roughness," and so on. Naturally they are lacking in a sense of perspective or in the effects of light. If their blindness developed at a later age they often dream of wonderful colors, flowers, and lights (wish-fulfillment).

As is to be expected, dream images of congenitally blind persons are poor in visual content. Wish-fulfillment ideas are shifted to the auditory field; the patients dream of music, conversation, etc. Anxieties are frequent and refer predominantly to fire. The fire perception in dreams is almost entirely based on tactile sensation, such as heat, burning, destruction.

Kinesthetic dreams do occur. Self-hero dreams are less frequent. Kimmins maintains that a child who has become blind before the age of five does not see in dreams, and that children who become blind after seven do "see" in their dreams.

WATER SYMBOLISM

With Freud, we usually consider water as a symbol of birth.[1] Yet we know that it is also a symbol of life (the ancient symbol of the concentric circles mentioned on page 127 belongs here). We speak of a "stormy life," a "smooth sailing," a "shipwrecked individual," etc. Water is also a symbol of the psyche of instinctual cravings (which sometimes can, like a flood, break through moral barriers), a symbol of the treatment, particularly if bathing or cleansing is involved. It is also an ancient symbol of the unconscious. We speak of deep, turbid waters. Particularly the dark, mystery-bearing waters are understandable symbols of the unconscious.

We see water as a symbol for the treatment in a dream of a thirty-one-year-old physician:

[172] *"I was following a man who was swimming. The*

---

[1] Birth of Venus from the ocean (Fig. 46); the stork brings children from the pond; Moses was found in the watery rushes by the river; etc. See also Rank's *Myth of the Birth of the Hero* and Ferenczi's *Thalassa, A Theory of Genitality.*

FIGURE 46

After Boticelli's BIRTH OF VENUS. (*Original in Florence*)

water was rough and muddy. I thought that the man's attempt to swim from the place where I was born to the place where I lived was an unusual feat inasmuch as the distance was about a hundred and fifty miles. But I had confidence in the swimmer and I was not worried about the outcome. The swimmer was probably you."

The dreamer has his analyst swim from his birthplace to his present place. This is a reference to the treatment which deals with his whole life from birth to the present. The dream shows us the confidence the patient has in his doctor, but, at the same time, indicates his passivity and the desire to let the doctor do all of the work. The passage, "I was following a man," is especially important. The dreamer who was in training for work in analysis really intended to "follow" his analyst.

The following is a fine example of a dream in which water is used in connection with the birth problem:

[173] "*I see bears jumping into a pool of water. A female bear is dancing in the water. I see my sister dancing among the bears. She says, 'The bear is going to have a baby.' And really, the bear lifts its hind leg and delivers little embryos.*"

The birth problem in such cases is charged with disturbing emotions. The patient may be jealous of possible new brothers and sisters, may be envious or merely curious; or may have had impressive experiences connected with a delivery, either as the person giving birth or as a witness. All these factors are able to charge dreams with pathological affects.

One of these patients dreamed [174] *about a party for which not enough preparation has been made and about herself rushing around in fear of being late for the arrival of the guests.* The words "party," "preparation," and "arrival" have definite sexual connotations.

Very often women who are in the *premenstrual state* see themselves wading in water or exposed to waves. They may, in this way, experience psychosomatically the congestion and engorgement of the genital apparatus indicating the impending hemorrhage. Water, as something that flows, associates itself easily with the expected flow.

Many water dreams are generated by a *full bladder* and the urge to urinate. The dream usually fulfills this wish in an open or disguised manner. A few examples were given in connection with the discussion of physical stimuli as dream influences. It was stated at that occasion that although the physical stimulus finds its representation in the dream, the specific conflicts of the dreamer may also be shown in symbolic disguise.

The following dream is illustrative in this respect. It was dreamed by a thirty-nine-year-old public accountant who was temporarily unemployed and dependent on the economic assistance of his wife, a school teacher:

[175] *"I see myself stroking the nose of a horse who is standing up. The horse shows almost human reactions to my stroking and almost quivers with satisfaction. I then see the horse cuddled up in bed and I play a stream of water on the bed so that it reaches the horse. The water is warm and the horse seems to enjoy it tremendously."*

Playing the warm stream of water at first glance suggests urination. The patient awakened from this dream with an urge to urinate which he satisfied. The dream horse expressed this emotional tone. The scene with the horse, which in the dream is treated as a human being, would immediately suggest a homosexual scene. Playing the warm stream of water on the bed in which the horse lies would in this cross section represent a seminal discharge. In this context we may add that the patient was found to have had a definite feminine identification with strong feelings of dependency and craving for guidance and domination by a masculine woman. We are, therefore, not surprised to find that the patient's associations to the horse ran as follows:

"I, too, would like to be stroked and caressed. I need warmth and comfort. I need sympathy. Throughout the dream I felt that the horse should be doing things, should be working and not crouching on the bed. He is losing his function as a beast of burden. . . . " Then he came to the conclusion that it was his wife who was the "beast of burden" of the family.

In still another cross section of the dream, the horse symbolizes the dreamer's sexual organ. The dream represents a masturbation scene terminating in an emission. The first masturbatory impression was quite unusual in this case. The patient saw one of his male teachers masturbate and soon imitated him. In analysis we had reason to believe that the patient's unconscious accompanying fantasy during this act was the scene he had observed.

You can see from this example, on the one hand, that the discovery of a physiological dream stimulation is insufficient and that we must find the dreamer's emotional affects expressed simultaneously.

Fire Symbolization

Fire is an old symbol of love. We find it in the ancient Hindu Vedas where creating fire by rubbing two pieces of wood together represented copulation. The underlying sexual character in *pyromania* belongs to the same category of symbols. (See page 471 and figure 83.)

There is a close relation between *Fire* and *Water* which, in dreams, often obtains symbolic expression. Freud emphasizes this relation in his article on "The Acquisition of Fire" (1932). Fire which Prometheus brings to man significantly in a hollow fennel stalk, has many properties which human passion also betrays: it warms, it "devours" (in German: *"verzehrt"*). Its phallic significance becomes even more obvious if we think of it as "licking", or as sending fiery tongues up (in German: *"züngeln"* and *"Feuerzungen"*). Mythology also contributes references to the ambivalence of the fire symbol, specifically, with regard to its counter-part, water. For the phallic container in which the promethean fire is carried (against the will of Father Zeus) is also closely related to an organ which contains "water" (urine). Because of the functional structure of the human bladder, the sexual and urinary functions are mutually exclusive, as are fire and water. Some primitive people (Mongols) who were concerned with the preservation of fire more than with its causation, prohibited by law the extinguishing of fire by urinating upon it. Freud also refers in this connection to Hercules' struggle against the water serpent, Hydra, and its innumerable heads which, when chopped off, grew always anew. Hercules had to *burn* the immortal head of the serpent to destroy the water monster. This fire, then, has to be extinguished with—water.

THE SYMBOLISM OF THE EYE

The *eye* carries a special symbolic significance. It is an organ of pleasure, primarily used to perceive afferent stimuli, i.e., it has a female, receptive, vulvar quality. But *the gaze* is, as a rule, in the service of efferent tendencies; the eye is then emitting energy. You flirt with your eye, you challenge another individual with it, you can use it to annoy another, to disarm him, to plead with him, and—in hypnosis—to subdue him. Under pathological circumstances the gaze represents aggression, and the eye then has a purely phallic significance.

This is particularly conspicuous in cases of gazing compulsion. "Looking" in such cases represents an act of aggression. It signifies symbolically an attempt to undress the other person, to touch his (or her) genital, or even to destroy him.

The following dream is very instructive in this respect. It was dreamed by a thirty-two-year-old mechanic who suffered from a compulsive habit of gazing at other people's physical defects. A scar on a person's face, a disfigured finger, a mis-

FIGURE 47
Buddha Temple in Nepal

shapen nose, a bald head, or heavy legs—these were the preferred targets for the patient's uncontrollable and embarrassing compulsion. (Several other dreams of this patient are reported in the chapter on compulsions, page 429.)

[176] *"I dream that a heavy-set man is attacking my sister. I plunge two daggers into his rib."*

The "two daggers" represent the patient's two eyes which he uses as instruments of aggression. The connection between his staring compulsion and his sister fixation is quite obvious. The patient's sister has an operation scar on her face. He has displaced his interest in her sexual organ to her scar.

It is important to know that the patient's first impression of the female organ was that it was a "wound."

The "evil eye" belongs to this category. We find the gaze involved in many superstitions. Also many obsessive-compulsive rituals belong here. To "look again," to "look into a person's face," and "not to look at anything that has black color" (symbol of death), are some of the more commonly observed symptoms, all based on the patient's secret belief in the magic of his eye. Ancients were not allowed to see certain tabooed objects and the divinities of many religions are not to be faced with one's eyes open. Fig. 47 represents the opposite: the ever-watchful eyes of Buddha.

The phallic significance of the eye was mentioned in connection with the symbols of castration. "Loss of eye-sight" is considered by some individuals unconsciously as "loss of sexual power."[1] Some of the post-operative psychoses in ophthalmology (e.g., those following cataract operations) have this psychological background.

TYPICAL DREAMS

Typical dreams are dreams which occur with only few variations to most people. There are several groups of typical dreams: (1) tooth dreams; (2) kinesthetic dreams; (a) flying

[1] Oedipus blinded himself after having discovered that he had committed incest.

dreams; (b) falling dreams; (3) exhibition dreams; (4) examination dreams; and (5) coming-too-late dreams.

TOOTH DREAMS

These dreams attracted the attention of men for thousands of years. The first attempts to give them a significance based on scientific interpretation were made by the Greek Artemidoros of Daldos, one of the first writers of a scientific dream book. Because of the time in which he lived he was not yet free from the tendency to consider the dream as a prophetic expression and so he interpreted tooth dreams as having a relation to death.[1]

Even today primitive people are inclined to believe that a dream of teeth falling out is an omen indicating that a relative shall die.

The analysts see the patient's *death wishes* toward his relatives expressed in this way. The appropriateness of this symbolic representation is made clear to us when we consider the fact that a tooth falling out from its place among other teeth leaves an empty place in its group, just as a dying person leaves an empty place in the midst of his family. In both cases a preceding illness is the usual cause of the disappearance.

Other interpretations of a tooth dream are dependent upon the accompanying emotion which has to be reported with the dream by the patient. If extraction of teeth means removal of something rotten and putrid (well-known symbols of the *treatment* and the overcoming of difficulties), then we shall find in the dream a feeling of relief or at least an indifferent reaction by the dreamer.

A tooth dream which shows a connection with the treatment is the following:

[178] *"The doctor has pulled out one of my teeth. I am*

[1] In the Talmud (Berakoth 56 a), Bar Hadia, a contemporary of Artemidoros, interprets a tooth dream: [177] *"I saw my premolar and incisor teeth falling out."* Interpretation: death of the dreamer's sons and daughters.

holding it in my hand and I am thinking: 'The tooth is re-moved, but the root is still here.' "

The patient, a compulsion neurotic, is alluding to the fact that, thus far, the treatment has not uncovered the root of his illness.

Masturbation problems, as well as, occasionally, the "castration complex" may be represented by teeth falling out, or being pulled out (in which case the "tooth" symbolizes the genital) and may have an attendant feeling of anxiety.

Lorand reports a dream by a woman in which she saw [179] *a pus sac which was clinging to the root of an abscessed tooth.*

Lorand states that the dreamer thought at this point of a penis in a contraceptive which was filled with the seminal fluid. Lorand explains that the patient wished to be a tooth-less, helpless infant again in order to be free from sexual troubles, and she also had castrative tendencies toward her husband.

Her other characteristic associations were: self-castration, self-deprivation by fellatio and biting off her husband's penis, guilt and self-mutilation as punishment, becoming unattrac-tive and thus less likely to get emotionally involved with men, etc.

We see that the patient's associations—and the analyst's deductions—move dogmatically along the established freudian lines.

We find anxiety in dreams of losing teeth, when the sym-bolism represents the idea of *getting old*. The anxiety in this case is equivalent to the fear of death, or of becoming im-potent, ugly, undesirable.

An example of a simple tooth dream follows:

[180] *"I dreamed that I broke off one of my upper front teeth. I put my hand into my mouth and pulled the tooth out. I woke up. Emotion indifferent."*

The dreamer was a forty-year-old woman who was unhap-pily married. The "upper front tooth" was her husband. To interpret this dream as a fear of growing old is out of the question because of the indifferent reaction of the patient. The loss of a front tooth means very much to a woman; it is a disfigurement and is fraught with pain. We would have found something of this reaction in the dream. It means less to her to get rid of her husband.

In some cases the problem of "teeth" has a traumatic character because of troubles with teeth which the patient had at some time in the past. People who suffered much with their teeth, or had to endure many extractions, resections, and so on, may dream of their teeth falling out without pain. This type of dream has to be considered as wish-fulfillment and consolation.

We also sometimes find dreams in which the tooth symbolizes the *female genital* or another opening of the human body, as, for example, the mouth or the anus, particularly in connection with dental operations. In these cases it is not the tooth which matters as a symbol but rather the cavity of the tooth as the object of the therapeutic efforts (boring and drilling).

A male patient whose high degree of latent homosexuality was discovered in analysis and who had a rather feminine attitude toward men, dreamed:

[181] *"I was at the dentist's. He put an oblong instrument into my hollow tooth. I felt a strong pain."*

The patient drew the following picture of the scene:

FIGURE 48

The oblong instrument is a phallic symbol; the hollow tooth stands for another opening of the dreamer's body.

The physical stimulus of a *toothache* can lead to its psychological elaboration by a tooth dream, which either impels awakening or attempts to allay the pain.

KINESTHETIC DREAMS

FLYING DREAMS

Almost all modern psychologists have made contributions to the interpretation of this type of dream. Freud has emphasized that the impressions which we retain in our early life of such things as swinging and rocking arouse in us the desire to revive the pleasure of these sensations. He thinks, therefore, that flying dreams help us to re-experience this pleasure. Freud also has emphasized the close connection of the flying dream to the erection in men and coitus fantasies in women.

Stekel saw symbols of death in some flying dreams. According to him, flying means being suspended in the air like angels and ghosts.

Jung is inclined to see in flying dreams the tendency to overcome the difficulties of life, to overcome all gravity pulling us down to the ground.

According to his general conception of the neurosis, Adler considers flying as an expression of our will to dominate, to elevate our own personality over that of others.

People standing under a compulsion, people who are forced to endure certain unhappy circumstances, unhappy marriage, unpleasant job, or the like, experience their desire for freedom in their flying dreams.

To a certain extent each of the above-mentioned interpretations may be correct. For the investigator, it is necessary to be acquainted with all of them and to apply individual interpretations to individual dreams.

The next dream was dreamt by a thirty-six-year-old auto mechanic who prior to analysis was very dependent on an overprotective motherly woman. The dream is as follows:

[182] *"Helen said, 'Let's go for a walk.' We started down the steps. Suddenly, I didn't want to walk with her. I said, 'I'm going to fly.' So I forced my wings out and I took off over the fence. I was sort of scared because I wasn't sure my wings would work and if I was too heavy because I couldn't fly as*

high as I wanted. Below me there was a haunted-looking place with animals roaming about. Suddenly, I came upon a most beautiful garden. It looked idyllic, the grass was plush green and the landscape continued to the heavens. I was so happy. It looked like peace I always yearned for."

Here we see the patient's desire to emancipate himself from the dominating influence of his woman-friend, Helen, who surrounded his world with a narrow spiritual fence and isolated him from others for selfish reasons. All of a sudden he feels himself in possession of wings which will help him fly over the "fence" into freedom.

Ambitions awaken, and with them idealism and the hope for fulfillment. The "garden" in his dream is an archetype of paradise, the Garden of Eden.

FALLING DREAMS

These dreams occur frequently, and usually are attended by strong anxiety. Falling is a losing of the equilibrium. (To sink slowly and to float, in the dream, usually is to be considered among the flying dreams.) The analyst regards the equilibrium as mental. Thus the "falling" may be interpreted as "loss of temper," "loss of self-control," "yielding," "falling down from the accepted moral standard," etc. Persons who fear the loss of self-control frequently suffer fits of anxiety after dreams of falling.

The loss of the ego consciousness which occurs during the moment of falling asleep may sometimes create such a feeling of fear in the dreamer that he awakens after having had a dream flash similar to the following:

[183] *"I am falling down a precipice into an endless depth."*

One of my patients perceived the moment of falling asleep (losing the ego consciousness) in his dream [184] as *a candle going out.*

"Falling" in dreams of women may signify intercourse. We speak of "fallen women" meaning "morally fallen."

Dreams in which we see other persons falling are usually the result of unconscious death wishes.

An interesting dream in which we see a combination of flying and falling is the following:

[185] *"A dog jumps on me. I cannot defend myself otherwise than by rising in the air. Then I am flying in the air but am still within the reach of the dog which constantly snaps at me. I continue flying until I am suspended over a precipice. Then I fall down and lose consciousness. The falling down was a pleasant sensation which became intensified after I hit upon a rock on the ground."*

The dreamer is a woman aged forty. She is forced to live in a very unhappy and sexually unsatisfactory marriage. For financial reasons she cannot get a divorce. In her dream she feels "attacked" by the urges of her "animal ego" (the dog). Her desire to attain freedom is expressed by her rising in the air. She sees the dangers and difficulties of free love (the precipice), but she "falls" successfully; the pleasant sensation accompanying this falling is due to its sexual content (hitting the ground = orgasm). The attacking dog may also represent the dreamer's wish to be attacked by a strong man (masochistic component).

The following two dreams were dreamed by a thirty-five-year-old unmarried woman, who was struggling inwardly with strong sexual temptations. She was brought up very strictly and later blamed this hypermoral training for her difficulties in finding a proper mate. She was inclined to believe that girls who do not take virtue so seriously are more successful.

The following was the first of her dreams:

[186] *"I am leaning from a window which seems to be high above the ground and call to someone above me, also leaning from a window, not to try to recover something falling from her window. She does, however, and in reaching too far after it, falls. I am horrified."*

In this dream—whatever the object is that she is after

(husband?)—"reaching *too far* after it" causes the woman to fall. She is a "fallen" woman. We see that in the patient's unconscious strong moral forces are guarding her conduct.

The next dream is even more outspoken:

[187] *"I was grasping a turret on the pinnacle of a building. There was a large spike at the top. I had my fingers around it. There was something in my other hand which I did not want to fall down. In attempting to re-arrange it, I lost my grasp and fell down."*

The patient's associations to the "pinnacle" go back to Matthew, Chapter 4, which deals with Jesus' temptation. Verse 5 of this chapter reads as follows:

"Then the devil taketh him up into the holy city, and sitteth him on a pinnacle of the temple," and then suggests to Jesus that he should hurl himself down as a test of his divine protection.

Verse 7 says then that "Jesus said unto him, It is written again, thou shalt not tempt the Lord thy God."

This dream shows more distinctly than the previous one the patient's inner struggle. The scene where she is clutching her fingers around the "long spike" (a phallic symbol) reconstructs a sexual experience the patient had some time prior to this dream, an experience which excited her, but at the same time caused her to suffer inner conflicts.

She should like to hold on to this memory, and at the same time, she also wants to hold on to the principles which had guided her life heretofore (the object in the other hand). Her wavering is expressed in the dream literally as "on the one hand" and "on the other hand." When she attempts to change the balance of power, she loses her grip and "falls" down.

In the following dream, "falling" refers to the patient's emotional insecurity. It was dreamed by a thirty-seven-year-old male patient who suffered from anxiety states. The dream ran as follows:

[188] *"I was in a room with my mother. I seemed to be*

annoyed and angry with her about her making the two beds
which were in the room. I climbed into one of them which
seemed to be slanting toward a window. As I got on it I slid
off and down into space. It was night and I was scared. At
first I thought I would land about six feet below the window
on the stony ground. But the slant caused me to slide to the
other side of a stone wall such as the one we used to have
when I was a child. I continued to descend, getting more and
more frightened, for I thought the end was here. When I
landed, I found that the soil was soft and muddy and I went
in half-way up to my thighs. What a relief that was!"

The patient had left his parents' home a long time ago
because of their overprotectiveness. Particularly, his mother's
pampering attitude annoyed him. His parents were foreign-
born and illiterate while the patient was born in the United
States and was well-educated. The patient thought that his
parents' old-fashioned pattern of living hampered his development. He blamed them for making him self-centered
and insecure.

In his dream, the bed his mother has made for him gives
him no stability. It makes him lose his balance and slide
down. He is afraid of the knocks and bruises that are in
store for him in his social and his business life if he continues to maintain too close a contact with his family. But
the dream consoles him: "Don't be afraid, the danger is not
too great."

EXHIBITION DREAMS

Freud has observed how often we dream of walking naked
in the streets. In his opinion these dreams contain a wish-
fulfillment idea based on the infantile exhibitionist tendency. Everyone represses the infantile exhibitionist desire.
Therefore, everyone is inclined to indulge in this desire
through the medium of the dream.

Another interpretation of this type of dream is that it
expresses the dreamer's feeling of guilt or feeling of inferi-

ority. Being naked, he shows his "shortcomings" freely; he can be criticized by people, he has reason to be ashamed of himself, etc. A dream of this kind is the following, dreamed by a twenty-four-year-old student:

[189] *"I was on the way to the university. Suddenly I noticed that I was naked. I felt terribly embarrassed and thought of hiding somewhere. Minnie came and gave me her cape."*

The patient has a reason to be ashamed. He is suffering from an infantile paraphilia, masochism, in which he craves being humiliated by a woman. If people knew that his serious manner is but a mask hiding a ridiculous infantile fantasy life, they would despise him. Minnie is a friend who plays a great role in his fantasies.

(Q) "Do real exhibitionists dream the same way?"

(A) No. Dreams of real exhibitionists have entirely different contents. Exhibitionism is, as experience teaches, based on the patient's unsatisfied desire to see some tabooed person undressed (scoptophilia). Because of this unsatisfied desire, the patient feels compelled to take active part. In his fantasy he identifies himself with the person who has refused to fulfill his desires. He attempts to do by himself what he really wants to be done to him by the tabooed person. In other words, exhibitionists are, in reality, unconscious "voyeurs." It is this situation and not the exhibition that we find in their dreams.

An exhibitionist whose analysis revealed a very serious sister fixation brought the following dreams:

[190] *"I see a nun who suddenly loses her clothes and stands nude and white before my eyes. Emission."*

The "nun" is the patient's sister who is unapproachable like a nun.

[191] *"I am sitting in a bathtub washing myself when suddenly my sister comes in and says something about her friend."*

[191a] *"I am a very powerful man. In a hospital or a similar place I see many patients, all girls, all nude. I order a princess to sew up the genitals of all the girls."*

The patient showed a striking dullness in his emotions, particularly in his attitude toward girls. His lack of interest in extra-family objects (he orders a princess "to sew up the genitals of all the girls") was overcompensated by the extraordinary attention he paid to his family, particularly to his sister.

In dream 191a we see the reversed situation: the nude (exhibiting) girls are "patients." Their normal sex (genitals) is sewed up; their nudity is all they have to offer sexually. The "princess" is again the patient's sister.

EXAMINATION DREAMS

These are frequently had by persons who have already passed the concerned examinations. Freud interprets this type of dream in the following way: "Don't be afraid of tomorrow. Think of the fear you suffered before the examination and, in view of the fact that everything turned out well, see how senseless it was to be afraid."

An examination can also signify the "final" examination as to one's "good" and "bad" deeds, the examination before the Highest Examiner:

[193] *"I had to take the final examination in Church Law. I did not know anything and was very much excited."*

This dream expresses the patient's feeling of guilt. Since it is the first dream in the treatment, it also shows the patient's resistance toward the examiner, the doctor.

The dreamer is usually unprepared and unsuccessful. He goes through a turmoil of tension and excitement. He has to repeat an examination but has forgotten all the information he had when he first took his examination. He becomes frightened and upset, and sometimes his distress can be relieved only by awakening. And what is his reaction immediately after he awakens? "Am I glad this is over!" "Am I glad that I don't have to take this exam again!"

Examination dreams often occur at the threshold of important decisions, when the dreamer's self-confidence is at stake. For instance, there is the young man who is about to marry and who doubts his success during the wedding night; or someone who has to undertake new responsibilities (a new job), and is uncertain of passing the "test" which life imposes upon him.

In our mental ledger, as a rule, there are items which, as time goes on, we can check off as successes and achievements. Following an examination nightmare one can say to oneself, "The problems with which you are now confronted may be difficult; but don't worry, during your lifetime you have also achieved success." In this way it is possible for the patient to counter his anxieties; the dream "rallies the assets" for the individual to bolster his morale.

COMING-TOO-LATE DREAMS

The train is about to leave. The dreamer is afraid he may not make it. The train leads toward a goal. The dreamer is afraid he may not reach it. However, since it is usually a neurotic goal he is trying to attain, his effort is doomed in advance. We are dealing here mostly with neurotic life plans such as incestuous or other antimoral schemes. For instance, a man may develop the idea that some day he will join his sister in an incestuous relationship. Such a life plan may be maintained for many years, although its "coefficient of reality," that is, its chance of fulfillment, is rather low. Neurotic goals of this sort can be found expressed in coming-too-late dreams. The patient always has the feeling that he must be there "before it is too late." Why? Because he secretly realizes that it *is already too late,* that his life plan is futile.

In dreams of this type we sometimes see also signs of resistance to analysis. They are often followed by tardiness at sessions, or sometimes the patients arrive far too early for their appointments and, in this manner, compensate for the original desire not to come at all.

Coming-too-late dreams belong to the category of *frustra-*

tion dreams. The latter occur in people who harbor such contrasting desires which neutralize each other and produce zero as a result. The "wish to go" and the "wish not to go" may lead to the dream picture of "not being able" to get there. The goal in such cases is a neurotic one.

In addition to the above, we find coming-too-late dreams in conditions of extreme *fatigue*. They contain a warning that the vital resources of the individual are getting low, and that the effort to find a proper adaptation to the outside world is frustrated by physical exhaustion. This condition, as you know, has been called the "effort syndrome." The dreams of this type are usually accompanied by other frustration dreams, by repetitive patterns and other manifestations of disturbed adaptation. The following dream is an example:

[194] *"I had been in the city and I wanted to go back home. My home was in a suburban residential district. I had been out all night and wanted to catch the 'morning connection.' I started to walk. I walked and walked and I reached a great round place. Here I wanted to call a taxi, though I thought that this would be expensive. There had been several taxis going my way earlier, but the taxis that came (and there were only a few of them) were taken. Finally a bus came, and, it seemed, another bus came. Each was overcrowded. I first went to a 'wrong' stop and was told that I had to go to another bus stop. I ran over the road to the 'right' stop—but had to board the bus from the 'wrong,' the traffic side. I didn't know if this was the right bus. Finally, people helped me. One, I think, even wanted to look up my home or destination on a map. The front of the bus was crowded. I had to go to the rear to board it. Here the map incident occurred. The rear was also filled and I wanted to climb up to the top of the bus. I don't think, however, that I ever boarded the bus, but I awakened."*

If you study this dream you see that the dreamer cannot get any place. There are troubles and complications. It is not even certain whether he ever got under way. The dream produced while the patient was in a state of exhaustion reminds him to pull himself together otherwise he will get bogged down.

Dreams in which one is rooted to the ground also belong to typical dreams. A dream of this type is that of [195] *the woman who is pursued by a man. She would like to run away but she is rooted to the ground and cannot help herself except by awakening.*

Two conflicting tendencies are responsible for this reaction. One is to remain and face the forbidden sexual experience, the other is to withdraw. The conflict cannot be solved and, as a last resort, awakening occurs.

Typical dreams, on the whole, do not enlighten us much unless they are connected with other more specific images or with an outspoken emotional reaction.

Freud's pupils emphasize the connection of coming-too-late dreams with physical urges such as micturition or defecation. They see in them recollections of past experiences when the patients were afraid of reaching the bathroom too late. One rarely observed aspect of the coming-too-late dream in women is the patient's fear that she might not have her orgasm when her sexual partner has his ejaculation.

A special kind of a typical dream has been reported by S. Feldman. He refers to the dream in which something or somebody interferes with the analytic session. The interference as a sign of resistance may also bespeak conflicts of transference.

Feldman enumerates the following circumstances which prove disturbing: (1) A member of the analyst's family is present; (2) the patient's relatives are present; (3) strangers disturb the session; (4) two analysts are present; (5) the real analyst is replaced by a substitute; (6) there has been a change in the arrangement or in the location of the analyst's office.

THE DREAM WITHIN A DREAM

The *dream within a dream* is an intriguing problem. Analytical experience indicates that this device reveals the dreamer's wish to turn a specific real experience or emotional situation into a dream, that is, into an unreality.

A woman patient suffering from frigidity states:

[196] *"I dreamed that I dreamed that my daughter had died. I awoke in my dream and told you this dream in our session. You said to me in a calm voice 'Don't worry.'"*

In this dream the patient tries to nullify her neurosis by transforming it into a dream. Her frigidity is symbolized by the dead daughter.[1] The patient has no daughter in reality.

BIPOLARITY IN DREAMS

> But Oh, my two troubles,
> they reave me of rest,
> The brains in my head,
> and the heart in my breast.
> A. E. HOUSMAN

GENERAL VIEW

The dream symbols are influenced by our mental bipolarity. The contradictory meanings complement rather than exclude each other. The dream's quality of condensation accounts for this result.

Bipolarity is an expression of primitive thinking rather than a specific characteristic of dreams. It belongs to the primitive expressions of quality, expressions which are found in old languages and old traditions.

In the Old Testament we read, in the laws about meat offerings (Lev. 6:15, etc.), that meat may be eaten only "in the holy places." One who touches meat (Lev. 6:27) "shall be holy: And when there is sprinkled of the blood thereof upon any garment, thou shalt wash that whereon it was

---

1 For other symbols of frigidity see page 376.

sprinkled, in the holy place. (28) But the earthen vessel wherein it is sodden shall be broken: And if it be sodden in a brasen pot, it shall be both scoured and rinsed with water." According to Leviticus 11, 33, and 35, the same or similar procedure is followed in case the dead body of an animal touches a person or his belongings, while Leviticus 15:12 requests the same ordeal on touching a person suffering from a venereal discharge.

The use of contrasting words by children and people using certain types of "slang" is also an indication of the primitivism of their verbal expression. At an early stage in their development the human language "yes" and "no," "down and up," "cold and warm," and other pairs of opposites are not clearly differentiated.

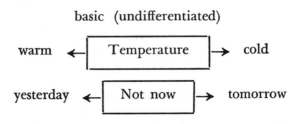

We observe this phenomenon occasionally in adults who suffer from aphasia. Their concepts do not represent *per se* definite categories, but basic undifferentiated experiences which can deviate in either direction (K. Goldstein).

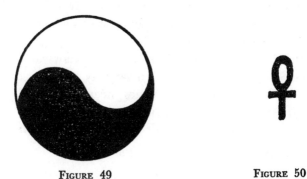

FIGURE 49   FIGURE 50

Bipolarity is a characteristic of undirected thinking. The ancient Chinese sign "Taigitu" shows that we are dealing here with an archetypal form in the jungian sense. (Fig. 49.)

The Taigitu is probably one of the most ancient symbols. It represents "light" and "dark," "masculine" and "feminine," "above" and "below," "right" and "left," "uneven" and "even,"[1] "before" and "behind."

Dreams revive such prelogical, undirected forms of thinking, and, in so doing, prove that the influence from the deepest strata of our souls is in evidence.

BISEXUALITY

In a similar way, the sex expressed in our dreams is freed from the barriers of convention. It corresponds with our innate, pan-sexual predisposition. In our unconscious, in psychogenic symptoms, and in dream images we all employ these primitive cravings. They are understandable to those who understand prelogical types of thinking. Many primordial drives reappear in dreams. With them, bisexuality, cruelty, and cannibalism.

Bisexual motives can be observed in myths and religions as well as in dreams. Ancient divinities were often represented as bisexual beings (the statue of a male had female breasts, for example). And Egyptian kings carried a bisexual symbol of their power. (Figs. 50 and 51.)

Most of our patients provide us with homosexual dreams, as for instance, a dream in which a man is pregnant (Dream 58, page 97). One of my patients, a twenty-eight-year-old druggist, dreamed [197] that *he was a married woman "trying to get a divorce."*

A forty-two-year-old teacher, a woman whose analysis disclosed strong masculine identification, and revealed that during her girlhood she had envied boys for their possession of a penis, dreamed:

[1] Compare this with the uneven number of chromosomes in the male and the even number in the female gametes.

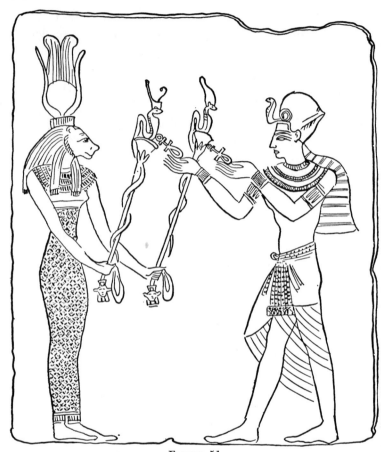

FIGURE 51

[198] *"I am pregnant. My abdomen is not very large, but I carefully count back over the months and decide that the time of delivery is at hand. I collect my belongings and prepare to go home from school.*

"I wait in a large room for the baby to be born, but labor does not occur. Various pupils come in to see if I am really going to have a baby. When they do, I pull in my abdomen tightly. They look around to see if a baby has already been born, then, puzzled, look at me and ask if I am going to have a baby? Standing with my abdomen well-pulled in, I laugh

and ask, 'Do I look as if I were going to have a baby?' They finally decide that I am not, and go away. During at least one of the interviews, I am wearing white sailor pants and a male shirt."

"I don't know whether the child was really born," she commented. "I only recall that the embryo was in my abdomen in a kind of bag which was connected to my genitals by a narrow tube filled with mucus." She then drew the picture which is reproduced below.

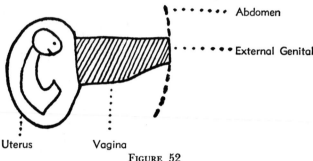

Uterus   Vagina

Abdomen

External Genital

FIGURE 52

We see in the dream the patient's main conflict; her struggle between masculinity and femininity. She wants to be a woman and an efficient wife; but her inferiority feelings about her feminine role and her fears (pregnancy) as well as her masculinity complex are driving her away from her husband toward homosexuality.

In general, what we have stated about bipolarity holds true for bisexuality. The psychosexual development follows a path similar to that of the somato-sexual development. At an early period of the child's intrauterine existence the two sexual systems are one. Later, a separation and differentiation take place. One apparatus attains full development; the other remains rudimentary. The psychic development duplicates this process. From bisexual beginnings, monosexuality emerges; the opposite trend remains latent. It can be released by overt traumatic experience, or by accumulated anxiety regarding the contrasexual partner, but it can always be detected in the dream, where, as the common saying goes, "Every Adam carries his Eve within him." Plato's concept of love as halves which once were a whole and have been forced to search for each other is also well-fitting in this connection.

LIFE AND DEATH

Naïve people, in their superstitions, betray a peculiar attitude toward life and death. For example, the idea is prevalent among many of them that a dream in which there is a funeral forecasts a wedding or another pleasant event, and vice versa. In the dream, we indeed often find birth and death, fortune and misfortune, wedding and mourning, representing each other.

Stekel reports the following dream, dreamed by a woman painter:

[199] *"In a primitive forest there stands a tall, spreading tree. From a far-spreading branch of the tree there hangs a long, sharp sword. Before me stands a man whom I am unable to distinguish clearly. The sword hangs between us, and therefore we cannot see and recognize one another. Stronger and warmer grows our mutual longing for each other; with a powerful grip the man seizes the sword with the determination to bring it down. I shout exultantly, and throw both*

FIGURE 53
"TREE OF LIFE" WORSHIP (Assyrian)

arms into the air. He has seized the sword too hastily, and it slips from his hand and pierces my heart. I sink to the ground with the sword sticking in my breast. The figure of the man dissolves like a shadow and I am alone, lying on the ground, mortally wounded."

Stekel says: "Does this dream really portray nothing more than death caused by an accident resulting from a man's lack of adroitness? Not at all; this is not a death-dream—*this is a dream of life.* The 'tall, spreading tree' in the primitive forest is the phallus. The erection is represented as a long, sharp sword."

FIGURE 54
The "Tree of Life" Motif in Assyrian Art (Seventh Century B. C.)

"Stronger and warmer grows our longing," says the dreamer, and then comes the congressus which is portrayed as an act of being pierced by a sword. ("Heart" and "breast" are selected by displacement from below upward.) We see here a tree symbolizing life and procreation as it does in the Bible where it is a sexual symbol ("Tree of Knowledge," "Tree of Life"). We find the tree, like the serpent, among the oldest symbols of life. As such it appears in myths, primitive art, and religions. (Figs. 53, 54, and 55. Fig. 54 portrays also the bull, a symbol of creative power. Cf. p. 145.)

A tree in a dream may also symbolize the parents (family tree, see Fig. 41 on page 143). According to an old and widespread conception human life is often portrayed as a journey, a voyage; so also in dreams. "A ship on the ocean" is a common dream scene, depicting the journey of life. The various

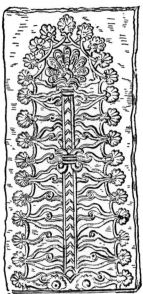

FIGURE 55
The Sacred Tree of the
Assyrians

obstacles, such as storms and accidents, are symbolic of the difficulties of life. (They sometimes endanger also the "ship of state.")

The *death idea* can be disguised in the dream if it is a carrier of repressed feelings connected with death wishes. People who in reality are dead, but who appear in the dream as alive, intruding into the dreamer's life at times with a tendency to damage him, are usually symbols of death. Sleeping or blind persons, statues, wooden figures, motionless persons, pieces of ice, the old man, the stranger, the farmer with a scythe, an old friend, "dead body," and the like, are also symbolic of death. A box is often the symbol of a coffin.

A death wish against his wife is clearly seen in the following dream produced by a thirty-two-year-old man:

[200] *"I dreamed of buying flowers, almost dead ones, for twenty-five cents and giving them to my wife."*

Sometimes, criminal thoughts can hardly be recognized. A simple dream expression such as [201] *"He went to the drug store"* may have an association with poison and death. In general, *chemistry* in the dream (as also in certain phobias) is to be suspected of having a reference to poison and death. The associations of the patient may bring forth this context.

Let us consider the next dream which sounds rather innocent:

[202] *"Mother served dinner. I saw Dad eating hamburgers. Later Mrs. Smith came to talk business with Dad."*

This simple dream was found to have a criminal background. A few associations brought this to light. The patient mentioned that he ate hamburgers two days ago and they did not agree with him (ptomaine poisoning). The picture becomes even clearer when we learn that Mrs. Smith, who comes "to talk business with Dad" has been dead for years. Death thus is calling on the patient's father, an idea which was found active within the patient's Oedipus complex.

"Dying" is often represented in the dream by "arriving" or "leaving." (See page 154 for the resemblance to orgasm dreams.) "Terminal" can symbolize "death" (and "orgasm" as well); likewise, a "long trip," "going across the bridge," or "across the river." Also open to suspicion are all dreams concerning journeys and trips in the direction of a cemetery.

A woman patient, aged twenty-four, had the following interesting dream:

[203] *"My uncle, who is really dead, came into my house and told me he went next door to my neighbor but could not talk business with her. She insisted on sending him into the living room, but wasn't able to give him any satisfaction."*

The "uncle who is really dead" visits the patient's neighbor. "The dead (that is, *death*) visits her neighbor." This expresses a death wish. The neighbor does not play any part in our patient's life and, therefore, must be considered a symbolic figure. The uncle was the patient's stepfather. The patient's mother lived with him ("living room") for a long time before she married him. This was a source of considerable distress to the patient at the time. The patient's mother now lives in an adjoining room ("the neighbor").

The dream is a death wish against the patient's mother. Of clarifying importance for our interpretation was the additional information that one of our patient's most disturbing symptoms was the compulsive idea to kill her mother. This idea made her fear of becoming insane. The patient accused her mother of being very selfish, but although she suffered from her mother's moods, she decided to let the woman spend the rest of her life with her. The dream expressed the wish that the mother should join the dead uncle. The use of the word "satisfaction" is a reference to a statement made by the mother shortly before the dream, that "the uncle" never satisfied her. Our patient felt this confidential remark to be out of place and resented it; the dream picked up the episode.

In one's childhood, the death of a close relative may activate death wishes toward another relative. Children do not fully comprehend the state of death, and often regard it as a mere absence. They are, therefore, inclined to develop death wishes at the slightest provocation.

The popular dream books based on superstition give much space to dreams in which an admonishing, threatening, or warning voice or gesture of a dead person is interpreted as an intermediary between the dead and the living. In reality, in most of these dreams we can discover only the phenomenon of increased recollection (hypermnesia) and recognize in the admonition, threat, or warning, the dreamer's own conscience reaction.

One of my patients dreamed [204] that *he was on his way home when he saw an elderly lady in mourning dress coming from the opposite direction. There was something peculiar and sinister about the woman. She seemed to know him, for as she passed she glared at him with ghastly countenance. He* turned back and noticed that the woman also had turned back and was approaching him. At first, he wanted to run away, but he could not move his feet. He wanted to ask her, "What is the matter?" but his mouth remained shut. With difficulty he finally succeeded in passing through his teeth the words "What is—what is—" as he awoke.

His first idea was that the woman in black was his mother. He then remembered that he had received a letter from his sister a few weeks ago calling to his attention the exact date of his mother's death which had occurred one year ago. He looked up the particular passage in the letter, only to discover that he had the dream on the exact anniversary of his mother's death, a day he had been about to forget.

We see that the appearance of the mother in the dream was not a communication from another world. The patient's unconscious memory apparently was more efficient than his conscious one. It protested his failure to remember the anniversary.

With another dream[1] we will illustrate the fact that if a person who is dead appears in the dream as alive, then this person is spiritually alive in the patient's mind.

[205] *"I want to turn on the light. There are many electric bulbs in the room. I try to turn them on but they do not work. I call the electrician. He explains that I have a very strong bulb in the room and that it must be removed before the lights will go on. He removes the bulb which had consumed the whole current and, behold, all bulbs are alight. Queen Victoria is also in the room. The electrician and the queen leave, and I am glad that now I can switch on any bulb I want."*

The patient had had affairs with numerous young ladies, but he terminated each affair after a short while as he feared marriage. He was strongly attached to his mother, and in the dream she is symbolized by the powerful bulb and by Queen Victoria. The mother has been dead for a long time, but his

[1] Stekel's analysis.

love for her still gleams alive in his mind. She attracts his interest (current) so much that no other woman can replace her. The electrician symbolizes the doctor.

From time immemorial it has been accepted as a fact that there is a close relation between Eros and Thanatos. Celsius[1] maintained that a part of the human soul is shed in every seminal emission (*"Seminis emissio est partis animae jactura."*) And Euripides asked: "Who knows whether to live does not mean to succumb, and to succumb does not mean to live?"

THE INTRA-UTERINE FANTASY

Birth, as well as death, is often symbolized in dreams. In the regressions of our dreaming mind, we sometimes re-experience our intra-uterine life (mother's womb fantasy). A male college student, twenty-three, dreamed:

[206] *"I am in the place where I was born. I am sitting in a room which is overheated. I am glad to be in safety, for out of doors there is a snowstorm, and the weather is severe. I think, 'To live in solitude like this is wonderful and not without consequences for one's further development.'"*

This dream was a beautiful picture of the patient's tendency to give up his struggles and to look for protection from storms by enjoying the warmth and security of the mother's womb. The expression "the place where I was born," the contrast between the warm "inside" and the cold "outside," his philosophical considerations concerning the value of this condition for his "further development," all are highly significant when viewed from this standpoint.

The dreamer's desire to repeat his life is shown in the mother's womb fantasies and in dreams of rebirth and of the birth process.[2] We should not be surprised when we find

---

[1] Quoted from H. Swoboda's *Die Periode im menschlichen Organismus*, Deuticke, Vienna, 1904.

[2] Nandor Fodor treats the intra-uterine fantasy from many aspects in his book *The Search for the Beloved*.

such ideas occurring in dreams of people who are pessimists by habit, people who are disappointed with their achievements, and whose only pleasures lie in the forgotten past.

Dreams of this type are clinically important inasmuch as they are connected with symptoms of respiratory embarrassment (see page 336) and various anxiety states. These symptoms are caused by the patient's idea that he is still unborn, is in an uncomfortable place, and lacks air.

The following is an example of a birth dream:

[207] *"I am crawling through a long, narrow, muddy, dark tube which has in it a large number of curves. Whenever I think I am approaching the end, I discover that what I believed to be the exit was in reality another curve. I am uncomfortable and anxious. After much strain, I come to a narrow opening on the upper part of the tube and am free. I feel relieved and breathe freely. I have had this dream repeatedly."*[1]

A girl, aged nineteen, envied her younger brother because he attracted more parental attention than she. The girl wished to be as young as her brother, and dreamed herself back into her mother's womb:

[208] *"I am in a bed with my brother. We have rolled ourselves up like embryos."*

Frequently people who are gravely ill or dying produce dreams in which the wish to continue life is expressed. When Benvenuto Cellini was seriously ill he dreamed [209] that *an old man with white hair called for him from a boat.* Cellini opened his eyes and continued the dream as a daydream in which *he implored his young servant Felice to hold him tight. He felt that this was the only way to make the old man disappear.* Cellini clung to a representative of youth and in this way tried to dispel the idea of death, represented by the old man (Charon) in the boat.

The intra-uterine fantasy is ancient in origin and is based

---

[1] This dream also contains the fulfillment of the wish to get out of his difficulties, to become free.

on archetypes. Ideas of rebirth, transfiguration, transubstantiation, reincarnation, resurrection, and the like are all derived from our eternal desire to elevate our lives to a higher, more spiritual, more idealistic level. This desire may continue its upward direction, its drive towards improvement (birth symbols), or, in the face of difficulties, it may be turned toward a protective setting (withdrawal symbols). In either case the intra-uterine fantasy appears, regardless of whether or not the dreamers know the anatomy of pregnancy.

Jung has pointed out that every time an idea rises from an individual's unconscious to his conscious, or a symbol ascends from his latent archetype to its manifest position in a dream, a vision, or in artistic creaton, the process involved is like that of the expulsion into light of an infant from the dark repository of its mother's womb. In the beginning, the two are one. There is a static equilibrium between the seed and its repository. Then this balance is upset, a factor which gives rise to an impulse for creation of a new form. A similar mechanism is observed when contents of the unconscious (womb—"mother principle") rise and become conscious (creation—"father principle").

ABOVE AND BELOW

> Man is like a tree; the more he strives
> upwards and toward the light, the
> stronger his roots grow earthwards,
> downwards, into the dark, the depth,
> —into the evil.
>
> NIETZSCHE

The transformation evident in the dream of the sword piercing the breast (page 235), or the swollen eye as symbol of pregnancy (page 136) may be called (with Freud) *displacement from below upward*. The reason for this transformation, as for all other transformations in the dream, are moral considerations.

(Q) "Does this shifting from below upward also apply to hysterical symptoms?"

(A) Yes, it does. We shall refer to this in connection with the discussion of clinical symptoms and dreams (page 300).

In addition to their sexual connotations, the symbols "above" and "below" have also another significance. We find in them the contrast between "spiritual" and "carnal," "intellectual" and "sensual." Freudian analysts have often neglected this aspect of interpretation. "Above" (upper apartments, etc.) also represents ambition (Adler). "Below" (basement, etc.) can be used as a functional symbol of the unconscious (cf. page 163).

On the sexual level, the "lower stories" of buildings may symbolize the genital zone. A thirty-two-year-old student dreams:

[210] *"I am at a lecture. From the lower floor where there is a dance hall I hear music and such a noise that I can hardly understand a word of the lecture."*

The implied "above" in this dream, the upper floor on which the lecture is held, represents the patient's morals, conscience, his superego. The dreamer wants to follow the call of duty, but the sensual drive for pleasure (noise from downstairs) calls and disturbs him.

A woman patient who suffered from fear of committing an exhibitionistic act had the following dream:

[211] *"I am talking to a friend. A girl is passing, and when she is close she sticks out her tongue. My friend explains to me that she is only doing this 'because of her sexual inhibitions.'"*

"Sticking out the tongue" in this case means a genital exhibition. The patient, a forty-five-year-old widow, is afraid that she may lose control and by exposing her genitalia will demonstrate her sexual frustration. It should be added that in her unconscious the patient saw herself in a male role, the tongue being a phallic symbol.

In neurotic and psychotic symptoms, displacement from

below upward plays an important part. Occasionally we can also observe *displacements from above downward* or *from the front to the rear.* In some cases amputations of eyes and breasts are followed by psychotic episodes which can be interpreted as castration reactions, the removed organ being the symbol of the genital. "Blinding," as in the Oedipus story, may stand for castration (see page 146).

A young man who used to avoid contact with women because of his syphilophobia dreamed:

[212] *"Mary G. is sick and the diagnosis is a tuberculosis in the armpit. I wonder how she received it in such a strange part of the body."*

"Tuberculosis in the armpit" symbolizes the dreaded genital disease.

Under pathological circumstances, other forms of displacement can be observed. In obsessive-compulsive diseases, we often observe a shift from *important problems* to *unimportant problems* (shift of cathexis); in fetishism, the shift is from *the tabooed genital* to *another object* (e.g., handkerchief); in melancholic conditions, the guilt complex may be shifted (see page 49); in paranoia, projective mechanisms show the shift *from ones self* (moral self-reproaches) *to the outside* (voices), from *ideas* to *sensations;* in homosexuality, the partner may be the symbolic representative of the patient himself.

The *reversal of cathexis* is a special form of displacement. We see it particularly in those cases of exhibitionism where, as stated on page 244, a repressed scoptophilia (desire to peep) has been reversed into the desire to expose one's self.

AFFIRMATIVE AND NEGATIVE

In dreams we frequently find a transformation from the affirmative to the negative. Freud proved in his book on dream interpretation that there is practically no negation in the dream. A sentence such as, *"My husband was not there,"* may be interpreted as *"My husband was there,* but his presence was painful to me. I wished he were not there."

Religious significance can be found in the symbols "left" and "right," "even" and "uneven," "straight" and "crooked," and the like. In general, the "left" symbolizes the tabooed impulses like incest, criminality, homosexuality, and paraphilias (perversions). "The right" is usually representative of the just, legal, good, and accepted principle. As such it is also a symbol of marriage and heterosexuality.[1]

An instructive dream produced by a tailor aged thirty-nine, married, illustrates this phenomenon:

[213] *"I was walking on a road. On my right hand there were large apartment houses, on my left were small farmhouses. At the windows of these farmhouses, I saw, from time to time, women who were apparently prostitutes. The sun had set and the darkness had increased. The road became more and more impassable. I was afraid of the precipices I passed. Finally, it was absolutely dark. I could not recognize the path. I came up from the main road and fell into a deep shaft.* At this moment I awoke with a scream."

The patient suffered from attacks of dizziness. The dream shows a connection between the patient's thoughts of infidelity ("prostitutes") and his symptom of dizziness ("darkness increased").

A student, aged twenty-four, dreamed:

[214] *"I see my friend who is having intercourse. He uses therein his left penis. He can do it only with his left penis and not with his right penis."*

The patient had promised his parents that he would not

---

[1] The general inclination of hysterics and neurotics to *display their functional symptoms* (paralyses, tics, pains, etc.) *on the left side of their bodies* has been emphasized by numerous observers. This "choice" of the organ has probably the same psychopathological background as the dream symbolism.

have sexual intercourse before he got married. In the dream, the patient's friend stands for the patient himself, the "right penis" means the penis used under "right" conditions, that is, in a legitimate relationship, the "left penis" is a penis which commits sin.

Chapter Four

ACTIVE ANALYTICAL
INTERPRETATION

DREAM ASSOCIATIONS

Following the supposition that our thoughts, even those without any conscious purpose, always have inner coherence, Freud asks the patient to associate ideas and recollections freely with individual passages of the dream and tries to find in these associations the unconscious "intermediate" ideas of the dream. He asks the dreamer to disregard the manifest dream content and to turn his attention away from the dream as a whole and toward its individual parts. The dreamer is encouraged to tell (to associate) whatever comes to his mind in connection with each of these parts.

Freud took the patient's associations in the following ways: (a) by proceeding chronologically, that is, by having the patient associate with the individual consecutive elements of his dreams; (b) by securing the interpretation of the dream from one particular element picked out of the dream, perhaps the most striking one or the one that has the most distinct sensual intensity; discussing a dream conversation may lead to a recollection of another conversation from the patient's real life; (c) by renouncing first the analysis of the manifest dream content and asking the dreamer questions concerning his recollections of the preceding day that may be associated in his mind with the contents of the reported dream; or, (d) by leaving to the patient, after he has become acquainted with the technique of interpretation, the type of associations.

We ordinarily speak of "free associations" as being the chain of ideas called to mind by the patient when in response to the doctor's suggestion he lets his mind drift. The assumption is that the patient expresses his ideas without censoring them with regard to their importance. Actually, there is no such thing as a "free" association. The form and content of the association are influenced by particular emotionally charged unconscious ideas called "complexes." It is these complexes which are the objects of our interest.

In the technique of analysis as used by Freud, the analyst is dependent upon the associations of the patient to a very high degree. The collection of the material in this way consumes a great part of the time devoted to the treatment.

The method of interpretation described in this chapter represents, in part, a deviation from the standard technique as it is practiced by Freud and his school. In order to render the analytic method more efficient and to reduce the duration of the average treatment, a reformed technique of interpreting the analytic material has been introduced by Stekel and his school. We shall deal with details of this method in the following chapters.

Now we wish to analyze dreams as far as possible without any associational aid from the patient, but by applying the rules of "active analysis."

SIMPLIFICATION

Our first rule is that of simplification of the manifest dream contents.

To "simplify" a dream means to reduce its whole content to an outline, to a few words. Let us do this with the following dream of the sixteen-year-old boy of whom we have spoken (see page 82).

[215] *"I dreamed that I was back at high school and lived in the same boarding-house. I saw my schoolmate Douglas with a pipe in his mouth. I was surprised at this, for he had never smoked before.*

"Then I was in Elizabeth's house and all her other boy friends were there, too. I felt irritated and jealous—I wanted to have her to myself.

"Then I dreamed that I was with my mother and the assistant principal of my high school. The latter asked me some question about Canada and I answered in the negative."

Conclusions: (1) The dreamer sees himself in the past, in his high school days. Simplification: *return to the past.* (2) He is surprised at seeing his former schoolmate smoking, inasmuch as he had never done so before. Simplification: *people have changed.* (3) He is then in his friend's (Elizabeth's) house and feels jealous—"I wanted to have her to myself." We simplify: *rivalry, jealousy, and desire for possession.* (4) He sees his mother with the assistant principal (father image). To the latter's question about "Canada" the dreamer answers in the negative. (The dreamer's stepfather lives with the patient's mother in Canada.) We simplify: *opposition to the parents.*

We summarize: The patient's thoughts spin round his childhood. He notices a change in the circumstances in his house ("people changed"). The patient has the feeling that he has lost his love object and, therefore, he develops an opposition toward his parents. The lost love object is the patient's mother who, by chance, also has the name Elizabeth. And indeed, the dreamer's thoughts jump from his friend Elizabeth and his jealousy of her to his mother Elizabeth and Canada.

In this dream we are able to study the patient's principal relation toward his parents. We see the boy's disappointment in his mother ("people changed") and his profound denial of his stepfather ("disappointment and opposition").

The simplification of this dream gives us considerable insight into the patient's complaints without any assistance from him. No matter what we explain to the patient at this stage of the analysis, no matter how far at this moment we make him conscious of his complexes, after hearing such a dream we know the patient's conflict situation. At the proper time we shall utilize his associations and additional reports in order to give him an opportunity for discharging his complexes.

In the following dream we shall see how far the active method enables us to interpret without the patient's associations and to what extent we must ask questions in order to clarify the background of the dream.

A thirty-five-year-old lawyer dreams:

[216] *"I was with my sister Peggy. She said that her sister-in-law was going to kill her on the 12th of March, which was the following Sunday. She did not seem to be afraid in the slightest degree, which caused me to admire her courage. The reason that her sister-in-law wanted to kill her was that she (the sister-in-law) loved the brother so much and she knew that his marriage with Peggy was unhappy."*

In the dream the patient's sister Peggy is strikingly calm despite the dangerous situation in which she finds herself (namely, that her sister-in-law intends to kill her). The patient notices and admires this calmness. This point is the only fact to hold to in our analysis. Furthermore, we see here a great love as the motive for the intended murder. Simplifying, we say: "The sister is going to commit a murder in order to avenge her brother's unhappy marriage with Peggy." Absolutely unintelligible is the date "12th of March" which happened to be "Sunday." By looking at the calendar I could see that the 12th of March was a Thursday.

We summarize the facts: (1) The hostile attitude of a sister toward her sister-in-law; (2) an indifferent reaction by this sister-in-law toward the prospect of being killed; (3) unintelligible date in the dream.

Now we ask the patient to render associations with the date, hoping in this way to increase our understanding of the dream. The patient's first idea was: the Ides of March, the time in which Caesar was killed. The next association was another 12th, the 12th of October, Columbus Day, which reminded him of a crossword puzzle he had attempted to solve on the last Sunday he had met his sweetheart Lucy. We notice with much satisfaction the relevant association with Sunday.

His associations now lead to his sweetheart's room, some details about the crossword puzzle, his disparaging attitude toward his sweetheart, who did not possess certain facts of common knowledge, one of which had to do with answering a question in the puzzle that involved Columbus Day. The discovery of the significance of the date of the 12th of March is thus seen to lie in the direction of the patient's sweetheart whom he was soon to marry.

The patient, whose strong fixation toward his sister Peggy had been proved before by many dreams, shows us the conflict which has resulted in his neurosis. His sweetheart Lucy was the future sister-in-law of Peggy. This fact enables us to understand the meaning of "killing." Lucy will figuratively "kill" the patient's sister; she will kill the love he feels toward his sister by occupying his full interest and by replacing her as the object of his passion.

In this dream the chain of associations leads along this line: from "12th of March" to "Ides of March" to "Caesar" to "Columbus Day" to "crossword puzzle" to "Lucy."

This finally brought us to the root of the neurotic conflict, the love toward his actual object Lucy versus his pathological love toward his sister Peggy. He is afraid of losing his sister; hence the difficulties in his real life.

The dream and its successful interpretation give a clear idea of just what part the associations play in assisting the analyst's work. It is to be utilized only after the independent rules of interpretation have been applied and there are still elements in the dream lacking explanation.

A woman patient dreams [217] *that she wishes to depart by train. She comes to the clerk at the ticket office and asks for a ticket. Strangely, she hands him a cancelled postage stamp, damaged at one edge, instead of money. The clerk, however, a man whom she has known as a restorer of old paintings, exhibits no surprise and gives her change as though the stamp were a one-hundred-schilling bill. The patient then calls a porter and, although she knows that her luggage is already in the train compartment, asks the porter to bring her luggage into the car, and he complies.*

Let us simplify this dream. It consists of two parts. The first one concerns the ticket, the second the luggage. The simplified ticket scene: The patient acts in the presence of men as if something is to be done, in spite of the fact that it has already been done. In both cases the men take her actions for granted. "To stamp" and "to seal" are well-known sex symbols, as is "luggage."[1]

Summarizing the interpretation of this dream, we may say the dreamer acts as if she were an inexperienced girl, but this is not true. The reason for such behavior can be nothing other than the wish to deceive the partner. This interpretation was verified when, upon questioning, the patient admitted that she desired to conceal her experience previous to her marriage.[2]

NONSENSE IN THE DREAM

We shall hear many more dreams which will amply illuminate the problem of simplification. Therefore, we discontinue quoting them here. With reference to dream 217 we

---

[1] Luggage may represent a burden, pangs of conscience; if it is something that must be put into a vehicle, it may have a sexual meaning.

[2] This interpretation was done by Stekel.

take the opportunity of emphasizing the importance of the nonsense in the dream. It was, of course, nonsensical to allow the porter to take luggage that was already in the car. Equally illogical was the behavior of the clerk. It must be noted that nonsense is often the carrier of the most important idea of the dream. In this instance it is the wish to deceive the partner.

In passing it may be mentioned that the "as-if" motive is connected with the main problem of the dream, namely, that the patient wants to appear to her partner as if she were inexperienced. The clerk is a "restorer of old paintings."

Another dream shows again that the apparent nonsense is the carrier of the main problem:

[218] *"I am climbing up a mountain. I see two parallel paths leading up. My path is partly boggy and slippery. A fence blocks the way. A young man in a topcoat with a trunk in his hand swings himself easily and gracefully over the fence, while I, though I carry neither trunk nor coat, can take this hurdle awkwardly and with much difficulty."*

The nonsense here lies in the fact that a burdened man can take the hurdle more easily than an unburdened man. The analysis reveals that the trunk and coat symbolize the dreamer's marriage. In his dream the patient says to himself: "Life as such is full of dangers, pitfalls and difficulties (boggy and slippery ways); married men are much better protected against these dangers than are unmarried men."

Succession and Coexistence—The "Optative" and the "Indicative" in the Dream

We often see in the dream that "near" and "far," "today" and "tomorrow," etc., are mixed up or used in a logical connection other than the usual one. But the most striking distortion concerning the logic of the dream construction may be found in the fact that two thoughts of the dreamer which originally had a causal connection appear in the dream as following each other independently (succession).

An example: [219] *"I am standing in front of a synagogue. My father is inside. A lawyer passes by."*

The dream expresses an important conflict. The patient wishes to study medicine or law. His father, a rabbi and a very pious man, opposes this idea, for he considers any profession except that of a rabbi, profane and undesirable.

The interpretation of the dream: The patient has a conflict as to whether he should become a lawyer or a rabbi ("I am standing in front of a synagogue"). He sees that in the meantime he is doing nothing and that the chance of his life is passing ("the lawyer passes by"). The repressed emotion here is his hatred of his father who is "inside," who lives in his old-fashioned world and knows nothing about modern life (the "outside").[1]

Let us refer to the sentence "I am standing, etc.," as "A"; "My father is, etc.," as "B"; and "A lawyer, etc.," as "C." Then we can say that in the dream we see "A + B + C" instead of "C because of A + B" (*"post hoc"* instead of *"propter hoc"*).

[220] *"An actor is on his way to the theater. On the way, being hungry, he steals an apple and eats it. Farther on he eats a hamburger, and while eating he becomes the center of a street fight and is nearly shot. He saves a girl from an automobile wreck and then goes to the theater and plays his part. After the play he again meets the girl. . . . I am in a play as an actor."*

A development as the above, leading from the words "An actor is" to "I am an actor" may be found quite frequently in dream series. At first, the dreamer uses the mechanism of displacement ("An actor is"), then he changes this method of disguising his own personality and declares himself openly ("I am . . . an actor").

In the above dream the dreamer does several things: (A) he steals; (B) he eats; (C) he saves a girl; (D) he plays; (E) he meets the girl again. In the meantime he becomes

1 "Inside" and "outside" are an antithesis. See more about this on page 256.

the center of a battle (A + B + C + D + E). This "succes-
cession" of events in reality represents a "coincidence" in
time and has an inner causal connection.

Simplifying the dream we may say: (A) The dreamer does
a prohibited thing (stealing). (B) He satisfies a natural desire (hunger). (C) He has intercourse with a girl ("saving"
is a symbol of the intimate act, as indicated by Freud, Rank,
and others). (D) He is deceiving his environment (theater
play). (E) He hopes to become reunited with the girl. The
battle is a symbol of a mental conflict.

We summarize: The patient has a grave mental conflict.
(In his dream he is the "center of a street fight.") He is
driven to his former sweetheart (the patient is married) and
realizes that this desire is futile. The consequence is: (a) suicide idea ("nearly shot") as an expression of his hopelessness; (b) a criminal idea against his wife, because he wants
to return to the girl after his wife's death (after the play he
again meets the girl). In his fancy he satisfies his prohibited
desire. The patient sometimes receives letters from his former
sweetheart, a fact of which his wife is not aware. Hence the
symbol "stealing." His behavior at home is a "theater,"[1] is
artificial; he is not sincere toward his wife.

Examining a *series of dream pictures* and events in succession (A + B + C, etc.) or changing into each other (A to
B to C, etc.) we must answer the following questions: (1) Is
A, B, C, etc., a simple stringing together of events or pictures,
or is there an inner connection between these events or pictures (intermediary thoughts)? (2) If there is a connection,
is it (a) causal or (b) alternative? The coincidental events
and pictures may be expressed as a succession of events and
pictures through several dreams during the same night or,
rarely, during several nights. We, therefore, advise the examination of dreams in series. (See page 267.)

A twenty-seven-year-old man, a school teacher, dreamed:

---

[1] In a dream, "performance" usually means the performance of the
dreamer's life, the projection of his own conflicts.

[221] *"I kissed Mary in the presence of my father"* (A). *"Then I saw my father poisoned"* (B).

Note: The patient's father objected to his relations with Mary. He once said that his son's marriage with Mary would hurt him grievously. In his dream the patient sees himself (A) disobeying his father, then (B) sees his father poisoned (dead). The construction of this dream shows the formula "A *and* B." Our interpretation: To our patient, kissing (marrying) Mary means killing his father" ("B *because of* A").

We frequently find the alternative *"Either* A *or* B" expressed in the dream as "A *and* B." Then "A *and* B" as an expression of *"Either* A *or* B." Doubt is mostly expressed by the alternative "either-or."

THE REDUCTION OF THE AFFECTS

The reduction of affects is the reduction of the different emotional reactions within the dream down to a single basic emotion. In some cases this part of dream interpretation is the only method of securing access into the patient's unconscious. Patients are not always clear about their deeper emotional condition. We know of many cases in which the most important attitudes were repressed and entirely eliminated from the patient's consciousness. Repressed jealousy, hatred, and love are in many cases the inner emotional conditions of neurosis as many of the dreams reported here illustrate. Dreams, therefore, must be simplified to the basic emotion.

THE ANTITHESIS

The neurosis is the result of a polar tension between the superego and the instincts. The patient's difficulties in adjusting himself to the necessities of real life show a distinct parallelism with this polar tension.

An instructive antithesis can be seen in the dream of a thirty-year-old man who became a teacher instead of a Catholic priest (see page 167).

[222] *"I was in my home town and there was going to be a wedding. I had quite a bit of money with me and I was going to the wedding. At the church I met a priest who impressed me very favorably. I did not seem to care to go to the wedding."*

We see here the antithesis between "wedding" and "priest." The wedding is our patient's own. The dream shows that the "priest" in him is not entirely silenced. (We also found this complex in his dream [115] about the suit with which a priest was fitting him. We recognized our patient's desire to develop a "belated obedience" toward his mother who had always wanted him to be a priest.)

"I did not care to go to the wedding," he says. We recognize here his resistance to an attachment to a woman and consider it an important task to help him find a possible compromise.

Another antithesis is revealed in the dream of a manufacturer:

[223] *"Several couples are dancing. In the kitchen, women are preparing meat, cake, and other food. I note that the persons dancing, particularly the women, are ugly, and I think of them as being intellectual but ugly."*

In this dream we see the antithesis "kitchen" and "dancing." The dreamer says that the women who are dancing are intellectual but ugly. He does not give us his opinion about the kitchen women, but it is not difficult to see from the contrast he expressed in his dreams that he prefers the simple woman. The dreamer is a man about forty years of age who has not succeeded in creating an independent home because of his strong fixation to his family. His sister was his housekeeper, a "kitchen woman," so to speak.

The dream has an infantile or retrospective component and also a prospective component. A widow of his acquaintance would always emphasize how much she liked to be a housewife. He, however, fears that this widow's disposition would make his life one-sided and unattractive. As a result, he tries to make contacts with other women by participating in dancing parties and other social functions. He seems, however, to prefer home life as expressed in marriage.

THE ANAGOGIC AND CATAGOGIC TENDENCIES

Anagogic or constructive tendencies are, according to Jung, the desire for everything that is high and ideal. They comprise the patient's religion, morals, and often a desire to fulfill a "historic mission." Jung considers this tendency, in contrast to Freud's "causal" and Adler's "programmatic" approach, the only subject for analysis. We are of the opinion that the knowledge of the anagogic components of our inner life is indispensable to an accurate analysis; but we believe that this knowledge is only one phase of what we must learn. We must know the various contrasting forces peculiar to each individual in order to estimate the degree of his inner mental tension.

Let us analyze the following dream brought by a man aged thirty-five who lost a good deal of money on horse races. We must remark here that our therapy helped him to overcome his unfortunate passion.

[224] *"A jockey threatens to do me bodily harm. There are some policemen around, and I call them to arrest him."*

The "jockey" here means the patient's gambling tendencies. As stated before (page 156), the dream personifies abstract things by concrete pictures; hence "jockey" instead of a "passion concerning jockeys." The "policemen" represent the patient's healthy mind, his inhibiting tendencies— that is, all anagogic trends. ("Policemen" are symbols, too, of the analyst who also is attempting to help the patient by stressing and supporting his "anagogic" tendencies.) Thus interpreted, the dream shows the patient's serious desire to get rid of his weakness.

Besides the "anagogic" tendency, we attempt to reconstruct the patient's "catagogic" or destructive ideas, that is to say, his tendencies which lead downward, in the direction of the primitive, the aggressively selfish, the blasphemous, and the antisocial.

A dream brought by a forty-three-year-old Catholic lawyer may serve as an example. This dream consists of only one sentence, but it shows the catagogic tendency distinctly:

[225] *"I dreamed that I participated in some debauchery with nuns."*

The patient was a religious man and after awakening felt terrified at having had these thoughts. He did not realize that his inner personality was split and that he was also a rebel against God and against everything that is high and holy.

There are some people who, stimulated by an irresponsible press, consider antisocial acts as heroic.[1] Such instincts also can be found in dreams.

FUNCTIONAL AND MATERIAL DREAM CONTENTS

Freud's analytical interpretation was for the most part "material"; that is to say, symbols replaced the repressed emotional cravings. Silberer was the first analyst to point out the reflected image of intrapsychic processes which lead to symbolization. According to him, dreams show us not only symbols, but also the way in which symbols come into existence. The interpretation which takes these mechanisms into consideration may be called "functional." Using this method of interpretation enables us to recognize not only the repressed impulses but also the repressing forces.

The process of thinking often finds a functional symbolic expression in the dream. We see it in pictures of a crowd of people, of a meeting; we see one man pushing his way through the crowd (obtrusive idea); another man standing in the first row (leading idea); the leader gets up; a public speaker delivers a talk; one person pursues another (persecution idea); an orchestra is being conducted ("polyphony of

[1] The catagogic "historic mission" is anarchism (Stekel).

thoughts"—Stekel); the low voices in a symphony (unconscious trends) get the upper hand; a confusion in the orchestra; and so on.

"Being oppressed by unpleasant thoughts" appears often in the dream in the picture of *a swarm of insects swarming around the dreamer's head,* or of *animals attacking him.*"

"Thinking" may be portrayed also by "visiting a museum" (museum = brain); the process of recalling may appear in the picture of walking through a suite of rooms.[1]

Most dreams can be analyzed materially as well as functionally, as the following interesting dream from Stekel's collection demonstrates:

[226]) *"I am breaking through a locked door; in doing so I destroy the lock, and the door cannot be locked again."*

We may interpret this dream "materially" as concern about the possible consequences of a sexual act which the dreamer is hoping to experience with his virginal girl friend. "Functionally" speaking, an idea is breaking into his mind, that is, he is gaining insight. He must destroy something valuable, (a precious recollection, a treasured complex) in order to obtain insight. After this introspection he will never be able to lock himself out from the external world again (improvement dream.)

A thirty-eight-year-old lawyer suffered from a grave disturbance of his sex life. Since his seventh year he had used a sadistic fantasy in order to attain orgasm. In this fantasy he saw himself spanking his cousin Mary. He had great difficulty in getting acquainted with girls, was isolated socially, and the sadistic fantasy kept his mind in a continuous tension.

The analysis found that the patient's sex deviation started a few years after the birth of his younger brother John. The patient developed a strong hatred of this brother whom he considered a competitor for the love of his parents. However,

---

[1] Freud's interpretation of "room" (German: *"Zimmer"*) as "woman" (that is, *"Frauenzimmer"*) seems to be applicable only in particular cases even in the German language. "Room" may, however, represent the female genital, as many rituals based upon "threshold symbolism" seem to indicate.

he soon repressed this hatred. When John grew older his father used to spank him, and it was at that time that the patient developed the fantasy of spanking. But John was not the object of the punishment in the patient's fantasy. First, it was a girl at school and then his cousin Mary. It is clear that the girls were only objects of "displacement." In one of his dreams we see the merging of the patient's brother John and his cousin Mary expressed in the following way:

[227] *"As I go into a house (not our house) I see that Mary and John have just been married. I am a little surprised that John should do this, but there is no feeling of jealousy on my part, merely wonder. They walk to the door arm in arm."*

According to our knowledge of negation in the dream we interpret the phrase "not our house" as meaning "our house." The "marriage of John and Mary" (which did not really take place) is the functional expression of the patient's symbol meaning that "John" and "Mary" are fused, married, in his mind. The words "there is no feeling of jealousy" must be considered as having reference to the fact that by the shift from "John" to "Mary," the patient succeeds in overcoming his jealousy and turning the original hatred into a neurotic enjoyment. Wonderment in a dream represents a reaction to a piece of insight which was obtained through the dream.

The copulation of the patient's brother with his cousin which he portrayed in his dream was a reflex of a real thinking process. It was a process of symbolization which took place each time the fantasy of the patient turned to the past. He thought of his brother and his fantasy turned this figure, immediately after repression, into that of his cousin.

The next dream displays the function of emotions that have led to the patient's neurosis. A twenty-nine-year-old patient, a musician, still clinging to his mother, had not succeeded in establishing a normal social life nor in choosing a proper profession.

[228] *"I am living in a room facing the yard of my mother's home. I am to go to school but realize that I have*

forgotten my school schedule. Af first I am terrified but immediately I think that I shall tell the teacher I was sick and could not study anything."

The dream leads the patient back to his past. The school schedule here means the life schedule, the life plan which, in this case, is a desire to stay with his mother and pretend sickness (neurosis) which should free him of all obligations and responsibility. Here the patient says, "I could not study (adjust myself to real life) because I was sick (neurotic)." But we interpret: he did not study because of his mother fixation and his desire to be supported by his family.

A young man has a conflict concerning a love affair. He is in love with a married woman, and although he knows that he will have to give up this relationship sooner or later, he continues meeting his sweetheart.

In his dream this attitude appears in a peculiar symbolic disguise. He shows the function of his thinking, the separation between his rational and his emotional ego.

[229] *"On board an ocean liner with other people. Suddenly the upper part of the boat is separated from the lower part. I remained on the upper part with two other people, and the two different parts, one being a large boat and the other, part of the original steamer, being a smaller boat, began to sail away from each other. Then one of my companions begins talking to me, the essence of what he has said I do not understand. This talking of my companion changes into talking of two people. . . ."*

The upper part means his rational ego; the lower part represents his emotional ego. We see the patient remaining on the upper boat, that is, following his rational thinking. He realizes apparently that he is to give up his relationship. The patient's companion is his doctor; the patient does not understand the "essence of what he has said," namely, to get rid of his sweetheart. The doctor's reproaches are introjected into the patient's mind. This is a picture of the mental conflict the patient was having at the time of treatment. The opposite mechanism, the projection of self-reproaches, can be seen in paranoia. The patient perceives his self-criticism as coming from outside.

Well-known picture representations of *mental conflicts* are: wrestling, battles, quarrels between two or more parties, and the like. But we find also other pictures which represent the conflict in the patient's mind, as the following example illustrates. A man who continued loving a woman unconsciously after he had broken with her dreamed:

[230] *"I saw the form of a woman being pressed out through shutters of a window or the like and then withdrawn."*

The dream shows the patient's thought of the woman forcing its way into the dreamer's mind. We here interpret "woman" as the "thought of a woman."

REPEATED DREAM MOTIVES

The young boy whose tragic home situation has been discussed on page 82, repeatedly had the following dream:

[231] *"I dreamed that everyone had changed his style of dress. I also dreamed that the game of bridge had been changed and that I was playing with my family and found that they all played in some new manner which I did not know. I dreamed further that I saw the pastor of the church and that even he had on a new type of religious clothing."*

The principal emotional reaction of the patient in his dream is his perception of the change in his environment. These many changes are representative of the one, the principal change of the boy's life, namely, the divorce and remarriage of his mother, which, as we had occasion to point out by other examples, was the trauma of our patient's childhood. (See, e.g., dream 215 on page 249.)

In general, the repetition of motives serves to emphasize the importance of individual ideas.

A forty-eight-year-old man dreams:

[232] *"I am intimate with a woman and see myself giving*

the woman three dollars and having difficulty in finding the third dollar in my pocketbook; or there is some hesitancy in giving the money. I see in my pocketbook only a five-dollar bill, an old one."

[233] *"Then I see the same woman. There is an additional intimacy, but in the act I have some difficulty."*

In the above dreams, the motive of "difficulty" is present. It pictures the patient's difficulty in establishing normal relations with the opposite sex because of his strong family fixation (the old bill). "Money" (love) preserved in his "pocketbook" (mind) apparently represents a higher value to him than every other available realistic love (five dollars is more than three dollars). We also see here the patient's low opinion of women in general. They are prostitutes in his estimation. (He pays them three dollars for sexual relations.)

[234] *"I am in the bank. I must get the mail. There are two boxes, one of them containing my private mail, the other the mail of the bank. I see a letter from Mary that has been opened. Is it possible that the bank authorities have opened it? Then I am in a movie with Mary. She is very talkative which gets on my nerves. Other people in the audience notice it also. Finally she gets up and talks again. I say, 'This is already a public lecture!' The audience laughs."*

The motive "private" vs. "public" appears in this dream twice, the first time in connection with the mail, the second in connection with Mary's talk. Both the opened mail and the public conversation can be easily simplified in our interpretation as "a privacy that has been exposed."

Our patient has the pathological habit of asking girls about their past experiences and of talking about his own. This exhibitionist tendency, together with his pathological curiosity, is expressed distinctly in his dream.

The following dream is that of the lady whose dreams we discussed on pages 179 (dream 139) and 232 (dream 198).

[235] *"My brother and I are sitting at a table. He has been playing the part of a ne'er-do-well youth in a play. He*

urges me to take over his role so that he may take another part in the same play. I want to do this very much but raise two questions: First, can I impersonate the youth well enough? Second, shall I be able to learn the lines quickly enough? My brother assures me that I can do the part and tells me to begin learning the lines at once. I begin searching for a copy of the play in the basement of an old house. In a sort of cabin I come upon a toilet bowl which is filled up with gin bottles, therefore unfit for use. I remove the bottles from the toilet, but it still seems to be out of order. A girl offers to sell me a tattered copy of the play. I take it to my brother. He says that it is no good because the third act is missing and most of my lines are in the third act. The girl takes the play and reads it aloud, showing that my part in Acts One and Two is not so inconsiderable after all."

We observe the patient's tendency to identify herself with her brother. In this dream she takes over his role. Her pathological fantasy is a "lingam," a bisexual organ, as expressed in Figure 50 on page 231. In the dream, the same idea is expressed once more by the "bowl" (female symbol) filled up with "bottles" (male symbol).[1] The patient realizes that her imaginary organ is "unfit for use," a statement which appears twice in her dream—proof that it is important. In her analysis she once expressed the notion that if she could have her clitoris enlarged, perhaps she would have greater sexual satisfaction.

The "Third Act" in the copy is missing; the copy is therefore "no good." The "Third Act" is the symbolic expression of the "third sex" to which our patient belongs: She is a woman with an imaginary penis.

A girl whose homosexual promiscuity was the result of repression and over-compensation of her incestuous (though heterosexual) brother fixation dreams:

[236] *"Six Jeannettes are in bed around me. All six have*

[1] On closer consideration, the "bottle" also shows bisexual symbolism: it an open container (female) and at the same time a thing of an oblong ape (male).

black veils. I first grab one Jeannette and kiss her. I can't take all, they move around. Finally I solve the problem by taking the nearest Jeannette and holding her tight in my arms."

Behind the multitude of female persons (Jeannettes) there is one person hidden—a tabooed person, the patient's brother. In her dream she re-experiences a childhood scene with her brother. This dream was dreamed several times. It was her stereotyped dream.

Stereotyped dreams as well as stereotyped motives, point toward important problems. The repetition is, on the one hand, the consequence of the patient's unconscious desire to solve the problem, and, on the other hand, his lack of means of accomplishing this task.

The dreamer's unsuccessful attempt to resolve a conflict can be seen often in the dream as repetition of certain actions. The following dream is a good example of such a repetitive pattern. The patient, a young woman of twenty-four, had fallen in love with a fifty-six-year-old married man.

[237] *"Jeannette MacDonald and Maurice Chevalier are again and again on the stage, although (in the dream) they are very old. It is annoying that they still want to play their parts. I know that they feel it themselves, and I suffer with them. Then I am in a bathing place with an older gentleman. I have been writing letters to my father for years and years, and I continue doing so in this place. I know it is nonsense. I put the letter into a special mailbox made for this purpose. It has a baby picture on it. I know that perhaps this box will never be emptied. I want to go swimming again and again. The gentleman who is with me does not know how to swim. All the other people are already through swimming and are engaged in some game. I am still making attempts to go into the water. Then I have some toy for my sister's baby. It consists of pictures—innumerable pictures. I am busy putting them in order and that keeps me from swimming."*

In this dream we see the patient's efforts to extricate herself from her love for the "older gentleman." She sees the old age problem in the first part of her dream. She criticizes old people who want to behave as though they were young (for instance, to make love to young girls). She "suffers with them." She tries to suppress this idea, but, as we see, in vain. "Again and again" it comes into her mind.

This dream also has other aspects. The second part shows a distinct father fixation of our patient ("I have been writing letters for years and years"). These "letters" have been put into the patient's unconscious ("a special mailbox"). It is the storage place for the patient's unforgettable childhood recollections ("a baby picture on it"). It is this father fixation which keeps her tied to the older man. She knows that her fixation will last forever ("the box will never be emptied"), and, at the same time, she knows that time is passing (time complex). All other girls have their partners, husbands, sweethearts (are "engaged in some game"), while she is entangled in a hopeless affair. She then identifies herself with her sister's baby. The "pictures" of her childhood (third part of the dream) have such fascinating power that she cannot get through with them; she cannot put an end to her childhood fantasies.

ANALYSIS OF DREAM SERIES

In order to augment our knowledge of the inner mental mechanisms of our patients we must examine chains of dreams and look for their "central ideas." Very frequently, dreams produced at a later time give us data for the interpretation of preceding dreams (Freud). In many dreams, we can also follow a logical development. Consecutive dreams sometimes give the impression of being continuations of the preceding topic, or, as Stekel puts it, they are comparable to the installments of a serial story in a newspaper.

Jung believes that in examining dreams in series one finds that they have a common significance which forms the focal point of all these dreams. He thinks that the real arrangement of a series according to its contents is radial, grouped around a "center of significance." (Fig. 56.)

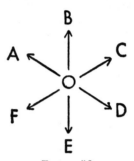

FIGURE 56
Drawn after J. Jacobi's sketch in *The Psychology of Jung.*

Jung attributes to the dream series a great practical importance. Its main advantage is that in investigating a series of dreams, one can detect and correct errors committed in preceding interpretations. This observation is correct.

An artist, aged thirty, suffering from stammering, dreams:

[238] *"I am seated near an attractive young lady and I caress her. Suddenly, I become aware that she is old and ugly."*

[239] *"A very well-dressed and attractive lady enters a jewelry store and looks at several pieces of jewelry. Suddenly she walks out of the store, and the owner notices that one of the pieces is missing. He suspects that she is a thief."*

[240] *"I am in a room. The mother of a friend of mine is lying in bed. I am standing near the bed and want to embrace and kiss her but she turns into an elderly woman with hanging breasts."*

[241] *"I am in a square among many people. In the middle of the square I see a woman apparently insane. I throw her a card with derisive remarks."*

Looking over this series of dreams, we can see deprecation as the common motive. A young and attractive woman turns into an old and ugly one; a well-dressed lady proves to be a thief. Furthermore, we see the mother of our patient. She appears here once as the "mother of a friend," another time as an "insane person." (Our patient's mother suffered from epilepsy with postepileptic deliriums.) In dream number 241 the patient derides her.

Summarizing this dream series, we consider the patient's distrust of his mother as the most important factor of his neurosis. The situation is made clearer by an examination of the next three dreams:

[242] *"I dreamed about Hamlet. I was identical with him, or I had the feeling that I had met him somewhere."*

The patient is thoroughly familiar with Hamlet. He knows of the incest of Hamlet's mother with her brother-in-law and that she also induced her brother-in-law to poison her husband. The following dream develops this motive further:

[243] *"My father eats soup and says that he is poisoned, as has happened once before. I drink his soup immediately."*

[244] *"My father talks to a prostitute in my presence. I am astonished."*

The dreams clearly point in one direction. The patient accuses his mother of adultery (the prostitute). We see this also in the deprecation of the female figures in the dreams, and we also recognize here an identification with Hamlet (the Hamlet complex appears as the "central idea" of the dream series). It is important to know that the patient's mother confessed that once, while in a state of post-epileptic delirium, she had committed incest with her brother. This confession made a shocking impression on our patient.

We know that in many instances a secret plays a great part in the psychology of stammering. The patient is afraid lest some elements of his secret thoughts be expressed in uncontrolled moments. Hence the pathological control of the speaking process. In this case, the confession of the patient's mother was the secret which had a close connection with the patient's symptoms. It showed the patient how embarrassing the loss of self-control may be if one has to maintain a secret. The analysis further proved a criminal attitude toward his father with the self-punishing tendency to sacrifice his life for his father. This is shown in the last sentence of the dream: "I drink his soup immediately."

The following series of dreams provided the clue to the understanding of a complicated doubt and compulsion neurosis. The case is that of a thirty-one-year-old manager of a factory.[1] His first few dreams dealing with fire could not be fully comprehended. They ran as follows:

[245] "*Two gentlemen are arguing with each other. One of them makes a 'dig' at the other by saying: 'You have erected a pyre, haven't you?' The other says, 'It was only a few empty boxes.'*"

[246] "*On my way to the factory I see smoke rising. I ask my mother what the matter is, and she says indifferently: 'I am burning the garbage.' I see various papers in the garbage and dare not put my hands into the fire as I fear that I will burn my fingers.*"

The patient's associations gave some information about his fire insurance and his thought that a fire in his factory would cause his worries about business to disappear. But the next two dreams afforded a deep insight into his conflicts.

[247] "*My dead father comes back and asks me if all his orders have been carried out. He says: 'I have ordered that you support the family G. Did you do it?'*"

[248] "*I am at a meeting and am supposed to deliver a speech. . . . I am talking about the Catholic Church and Christ.*"

The patient is a Catholic but he does not go to church and does not care particularly for ceremonies. But he sometimes reads the Lutheran text of the Bible. The discussion about the Old and New Testament led to this question: "Did your father leave a testament (will)?"

Under a very strong emotional reaction the patient re-

1 Analyzed by W. Stekel.

ported that after his father's death no will could be found and that his mother, therefore, took over the whole property.

"Weren't you surprised that your father did not leave a will?"

"Yes, I was very much surprised. Before my father died we visited the family G. Their father died without having left a written will. My father remarked: 'It is incomprehensible that any man should leave his family without a will. . . .'" The patient thought at this moment that his father had certainly made his will. Being his favorite son, he had expected him to will to him the ownership of the factory.

Now the dreams about fire become intelligible. The patient suspects that his mother burned the "old testament" (the old will) and thus destroyed his hopes of becoming the owner of the factory. The quarrel between the two gentlemen expressed his own doubts. In dream 246 we see clearly that he accuses his mother of having destroyed the will. He does not dare think of it clearly ("to put my hands into the fire"), in order not to violate his relations with his mother and in order to keep her person and his family honor free of suspicion ("in order not to burn my fingers"). But in dream 247 his father comes back and inquires if his "orders have been carried out," namely his last order, his last will. The passage about the family G. refers to the conversation mentioned above. It is supposed to furnish the evidence that his father must have left a will.

We see that in this case a deep-seated doubt causes a doubt neurosis. A series of dreams and an interpretation which employed intuition brought about the resolution of this doubt.[1]

A marital conflict and its background can be studied in the following dream series of a thirty-five-year-old teacher:

[249] *"I am making a boat trip with my husband. After one day we stop over in New York (to see my mother?). He*

---

[1] Note the deprecating remarks: "It was only empty boxes," "burning garbage," etc., covering a vitally important problem.

stays on board, I go home by subway. Next day I am at the harbor again. After another day of travel we stop over in New York again and I go home again (to say good-bye?).

"Next morning the boat leaves at dawn. I am late, I get into a state of panic, I scream, rant, am uncontrollable. There are men at the dock, rather natty looking, who want to console me. I avoid them. A lady tells me there is another boat leaving soon. I say, 'But my husband will think I'm dead.' "

The conflict "husband vs. mother" is clearly depicted. We know from the dream that the patient has difficulties in maintaining her marital relations on a satisfactory level because she is attached to her mother (who, according to the patient's report, was always planning her life for her and otherwise interfering with her personal affairs).

The dream makes mention of the "natty" men who are eager to "console" her once she has been separated from her husband. "You won't 'miss the boat'," for "there are more boats sailing," says the wise lady. ("There are more pebbles on the beach," she won't have to "miss the boat.") The exaggerated reaction of panic and hysteria betrays the importance of the separation complex.

(Q) "Has the last sentence, 'my husband will think I'm dead,' any special meaning?"

(A) The words have an important meaning. In discussing death symbolism we mentioned the symbol of "leaving." In the patient's dream her husband's boat "leaves at dawn." This part of the dream contains a wish-fulfillment. The last sentence is a reflection of the active death wish: The patient conjectures that her husband would think about her the same way as she has been thinking about him.

While the above dream tells us primarily about the patient's "mother complex" as a cause of her mental difficulties, the next dream contains another component of her psychosexual infantilism.

[250] *"A gathering of gay people. It is somehow arranged for me to marry a girl friend's brother. (She has none in reality.) In the dream, he is a young attractive boy. I am*

vaguely disturbed about impending marriage. (It is not clear in the dream whether I am married to my husband or not, although his face appears in the dream often.) *I decide finally to break up our engagement, explaining to friends that even though he is very wealthy, he is not grown-up enough. I say to them, 'I made that mistake before.'"*

The patient, in this dream, is either not yet married or is already divorced. Her unconscious has been toying with such plans for a long time. In dream 250 she is to marry a brother, *her* brother. As a child she used to bathe with him and later she developed a strong attachment to him. He is happy in his marriage and she envies him. She blames her husband for not being "grown-up enough," the phrase she uses in regard to her dream suitor. She is not going to make this mistake again; the next man she marries will be mature.

We see that in her fantasy she is trying to annul the fact that she is married, although her husband's face appears in the dream often—to remind her of her legal status.

The patient's "brother complex" is even clearer in the next dream:

[251] *"My brother tells me he is going to divorce his wife. This seems incredible as they have always been a model couple. He says he's found some one else. Suddenly it is my husband who is asking me for a divorce. I think he is joking but he is adamant. I am crushed, feel I cannot go on living.*

"My mother arranges for me to marry Patrick B., a movie actor. I tell her I don't love him, but he says he'll give me everything I need. At the ceremony I back out."

In this dream we see the "brother vs. husband" constellation. In the last dream she first has her brother divorce his wife (wish-fulfillment). In doing this she consoles herself with the idea that even good marriages can break down. Then she has her husband ask her for a divorce. This is a favor he is doing for her. By asking her for a divorce he takes away from his wife the feeling of responsibility and spares her the social disgrace of having to ask him for a divorce.

Of course, her ever-helpful mother immediately supplies her with another husband (wish-fulfillment), a much better one, a movie actor who is ready to provide for her. (In her dreams her future husbands are wealthy and influential.) At the last moment she backs out, however.

In the patient's marital relationship there is no talk about divorce. While she is sexually not able to respond properly, her marriage, to all appearances, is a good one. We see, however, that her dreams, without considering any reality factor, are constantly spinning a yarn of sexual adventure and are concerned primarily with obtaining a better marital adjustment for her.

The next dream series demonstrates how much we can learn by following the common motives contained therein. If you study a neurotic and find that in one of his dreams the symptom is connected with a particular family constellation, and you find a number of symptom dreams depicting the same constellation, you will be able to draw the necessary conclusions.

The following is a dream by a homosexual who was treated two years ago and who meanwhile recovered and married:

[252] *"In bed with sister Betty. She was pregnant. I had my hand on her stomach. I could feel the tenseness of her stomach and also the rapid beat of the heart of the foetus. Betty told me that the foetus was asleep."*

It is important to know that Betty was about five years younger than the patient, and that when the patient's mother was pregnant with Betty, the little boy was permitted to touch the mother's abdomen to "get acquainted with the baby." This may have been a mistake, although you will find books where such behavior is endorsed. In this dream the patient is in bed with his sister Betty. In the dream she is pregnant (in reality she was not). He identifies her with his mother and so this dream represents an incestuous Oedipus desire.

What makes this dream significant, however, is the fact that this patient sees himself in it in a heterosexual situation. This heterosexual wish is such that it cannot be tolerated by his superego. Homosexuality can be defined as heterosexuality in which the two homosexual partners are playing both sexual roles; where, as was customary in old Shakespearean dramas, men played the female roles. The reason for this transformation usually lies in the incest barrier. Homosexuality lends itself very well to portraying an experience in a disguised form of something which otherwise is taboo, namely, the incest. In this psychodrama one of the partners, often the patient himself, plays the contrasexual partner.

Under such circumstances, the spiritual relationship with the original heterosexual object remains intact. Nothing has to be changed or replaced. A man loves his sister. If he is homosexual, this love does not have to be replaced. What happens in his relationship with other men is exclusively physical.

Few, if any, homosexuals are really in love with their partners, although many of them claim to be. Contrary to what you may hear from the patients, homosexuality is a purely physical relationship designed to preserve and perpetuate the infantile incestuous fixation.

The next series proves this point and you can see the same thing in most cases of homosexuality you analyze. The heterosexual object remains hidden while a perpetual motion of physical experiences goes on. Often objects are exchanged without interruption. The man goes to a men's room and has contact with other men. He hardly sees the face of his partner. He is not interested in seeing it. What he craves is the contact with the other body, particularly with the genital. But his heart belongs to an unconscious incestuous object.

The next dream is as follows:

[253] *"I was living temporarily in a room that belonged to Jimmy."*

Now, this patient formerly lived with his homosexual partner, Jimmy. They lived as "husband and wife." You would think that this certainly was a spiritual relationship. Nothing indicated this, however. In his dream, he is living "temporarily" with Jimmy.

"I was in bed with Mr. D. (a man from the patient's office) *who also was Joyce* (a girl from the office)."

This again indicates the ambivalence and bisexuality which we always find in cases of homosexuality.

"—We are trying to have intercourse. It is not clear at this point whether it was Mr. D. or the girl, but I didn't feel too much in the mood for it and had difficulty maintaining an erection. I was aware of people in the hall.—"

"People in the hall" means public opinion, the superego, if you will. Homosexuals are always afraid they will be found out and in this way will be exposed to scandals, blackmail, or the like. Some homosexuals remain in exclusively homosexual circles for this reason. They may even consider themselves superior to the "drab" and "dull" normal people.

Our patient is aware of the ever-watchful public and asks himself what people would say if they knew the truth. You will find this and similar symbols in dreams of people who blush, or stammer, or of people who have other types of "social neurosis."

"—I decided to lock the door in case anyone should try to come in."

Of course, the phrase "people in the hall" also refers to the analyst who is outside trying to enter, and so the patient locks the door.

"—The door wouldn't shut properly, and I thought that the hinge had been broken, apparently by a powerful blow from the outside. (Analysis?) I wondered how such a thing could have happened without my waking up. I was in front of a large lilac bush where I played as a child. Mother was there." (Again, reference to mother, again reference to the

fact that the male is really a female. The whole thing harks back to the incest.)

The third dream of the series is the following:

[254] *"I was watching my mother give birth to a child.—"*

The birth of his sister was sufficient to be traumatic because up to that time he was the youngest child, and his sister was his rival in mother's affection.

"—It was graphic, and I could see the baby's head come out, knowing that it couldn't breathe until it was free. I was revolted, and felt I shouldn't be looking, but was fascinated at the same time. It was a boy, and I was delighted, carrying him about and telling everyone this was my son John.—"

The patient's name is also John. What a peculiar coincidence! The child is himself, his mother's child, and also his child. An Oedipus situation! This certainly can give us a clue as to what his homosexuality means.

"—I was telling Bryan (a man in the office), *and he suddenly made me realize that it was my mother's and my own child. I made violent denials, but he said I had slept with her until I was twelve.—"*

At the age of twelve or thirteen, according to his report, he became consciously homosexual. Homosexuals will tell you that up to a certain time they were groping in the dark regarding their sexual make-up, and that at a specific moment they "knew" they were different from others. Such statements, as a rule, have little diagnostic value. The unconscious psychological problems involved in the child's flight from the opposite sex remain the same regardless of what the patient thinks about them. As stated before, it is not his attraction to the same sex but his unconscious resistance to the opposite sex that deserves our medical attention.

The aforementioned dream ends in the following way:

"—The child became a girl, and I felt an overwhelming love for her. I kissed her on the mouth and felt sexually excited. She had some upper and lower front teeth which seemed

remarkable for so young a baby. Mother was up and about right after the birth, and suddenly I realized that now she would have to stop work in order to take care of the baby. My sister Minnie was also involved in the dream."

The end of the dream tells us about some of the dynamic transformations which have taken place in the patient to get him to the stage he was in at the time of the treatment. We see the parallelism between mother and sister Minnie who suddenly appears in the dream. We also notice that the baby may not be a baby after all, but a grownup playing the part of a baby (she has teeth in her mouth); we also see the transformation from a boy to a girl, indicating that shifts of this kind are to be expected also in the patient's neurosis.

Here is another series of dreams. They were collected according to the conflicts they contain and not in order of their appearance.

[255] *"I was cleaning dirt from between my toes. There was quite a deep, ulcerated area from which I removed a mass of pus. This left a cavity. Dr. G. looked on with mild, noncommittal interest. I also was quite detached. I wondered if this ulcer could be syphilitic."*

The patient who is married and has children suffers from an uncontrollable desire to have intercourse with Negro maids. He has deep feelings of guilt about his actions and fears that he might contract syphilis and transfer the disease to his wife and children. In his dream he is removing "dirt." It is as though he were saying, "There is something 'dirty' about me, and I am removing it" (possibly with the analyst's help). The dirt here would symbolize the patient's neurosis. Once it is removed, a cavity, a defect remains. We are impressed by the patient's statement that the doctor looks on noncommittally and that the patient is detached. This is a wish-fulfillment because, in reality, this man is gravely concerned. Here he *annuls* this concern and the whole thing becomes a matter of simple medical attention.

The other dreams lead us to the conclusion that it is the

patient's sister fixation which frustrates him with his wife. The surplus sexual energy is then transferred by him upon the maids. In his desire to get away from his sister image he selects the Negro types as farthest removed from his original desire.

Syphilis has a great deal in common with repressed incestuous and paraphilic (homosexual) desires because (a) it involves a "sexual" problem, and (b) it can remain latent, i.e., an individual can be afflicted with it without knowing of its existence. Thus it lends itself very well as a representative of unconscious sexual trends. Syphilis is also a disease which can be transmitted. It can represent homosexuality inasmuch as homosexual attraction is transmitted to others. Danger lies in both cases in the fact that the disease may become virulent, active, and self-revealing.

Let us consider the next dream of this series:

[256] *"I was in the basement of an apartment house near where I live. I was there with cousin Ruth* (sister's name). *She was unusually pretty and aroused in me more than cousinly feelings. Suddenly, a black cat came stalking out from another room or from the shadows. It was an evil, repulsive, unholy, horrible thing. That is, in a moral sense. Its black, jade-like pelt added a touch of satanic, revolting horror. It was like a sight of abysmal sin of the foulest type. The thing one imagines the religious people of middle ages felt for the 'foul fiend.' (I once had this unique feeling of moral horror when I saw a woman beaten by her husband.)"*

When he was about eight years old he saw a man who apparently was drunk beat his wife in a most ferocious way.

In this dream the cat is the taboo, a thought, which like the bat, represents the foul, repulsive, horrible part of human personality. At the same time it is a mysterious thing.

This dream recalls the famous short story by Edgar Allen Poe, *The Black Cat.* In it, a man killed his wife and walled up the body in the cellar. Sometime prior to this, the man had mutilated a black cat by gouging out one of its eyes.

Then when the man was about to kill the cat, the wife intervened to save the animal's life but lost her own life when the enraged man turned upon her.

Some days later the police thoroughly searched the house, including the cellar, and found nothing suspicious. The murderer, gloating over his triumph, relates the pertinent experience in these words: "I rapped heavily with a cane which I held in my hand, upon that very portion of the brickwork behind which stood the corpse of the wife of my bosom. But may God shield and deliver me from the fangs of the Arch-Fiend! No sooner had the reverberation of my blows sunk into silence, than I was answered by a voice from within the tomb!—by a cry, at first muffled and broken, like the sobbing of a child, and then quickly swelling into one long, loud and continuous scream, utterly anomalous and inhuman—a howl—a wailing shriek, half of horror and half of triumph, such as might have arisen only out of hell, conjointly from the throats of the damned in their agony and of the demons that exult in damnation. . . . Swooning, I staggered to the opposite wall. For one instant the party on the stairs remained motionless through extremity of terror and awe. In the next, a dozen stout arms were toiling at the wall. It fell bodily. The corpse, already greatly decayed and clotted with gore, stood erect before the eyes of the spectators. Upon its head, with red extended mouth and solitary eye of fire, sat the hideous beast whose craft had seduced me into murder, and whose informing voice had consigned me to the hangman."

It is not mere coincidence that our patient had the same feeling when he saw the man beating his wife. And he remembered the story by Poe.

That cat in this dream represents the strivings of the id, the incestuous and homosexual trends which the patient has walled off from his consciousness. Only in dreams of nightmare character as the one above do these trends reappear as the "return of the repressed" (Freud).

(Q) "What about the basement? Has it any significance?"

(A) The basement as the subterranean part of the building often stands for the unconscious. (See page 160.) In some cases it also has special significance as the place where children may engage in forbidden games. In Poe's story it was the scene of a crime.

But the "cat" is not always the representation of the unconscious and the uncanny. In some dreams it is used to represent a woman, particularly if she has "catty" characteristics of being tricky and cunning. It is in general a female sex symbol and is used as such in vulgar references to the female genital. In cat phobias, this connection is particularly obvious. If such phobias occur in women, the underlying homosexual complex can be elicited in analysis.

A forty-two-year-old woman, who was proud of her cleverness in dealing with men, had the following dream:

[257] *"I was sitting on the steps of the house where we lived when I was seventeen.* (I dream of this street very often.) *I was a little girl, and was holding a beautiful Angora cat in my arms. I think its color was blue and its eyes were very beautiful—bluish green. My sister Sylvia was standing a few steps above me, sort of waiting for somebody to pass by and to make a date with her. It was Saturday and she had no date for Saturday night which as you know just didn't happen! I seemed rather pleased that she had no date and as I was holding and caressing the cat, I seemed to be conveying my thoughts to it. The cat seemed pleased, too, and we seemed to be sharing a delightful secret.*

"After a while, two of the boys on the block came along and spoke with Sylvia. They were asking for a date. After a while she said, 'All right.' (The boy who was asking for the date looked very much like my first lover, John. Sylvia and John looked as they did when they were around eighteen.) I still sat on the lower steps, holding and rocking my beautiful cat. Sylvia looked beautiful and immaculate."

A rivalry relationship existed between the patient and her older sister, Sylvia. The latter was more attractive than the patient, and, therefore, more envied. The cat represents the "catty" part in our patient. She says about the cat: "It had the same expression in its eyes that I had when I was young." The patient's identification with her more attractive sister is expressed by introducing her lover John as a suitor of her sister. Here we also see traces of latent homosexuality. ("Triangle situation," i.e., two persons sharing their lover.) In reality, John disliked Sylvia.

The dream ends with her sister's success, but we do not hear anything about the patient's further fate. We do not assume that all the patient wanted to express in her dream was her sister's success with boys, particularly since it is the patient's lover who helps in this success. The reason for this apparent altruism is the patient's identification with her sister. Her arrangement of the successful development in the dream is hypocritical ("catty"), as is her emphasis that she still remained "on the lower steps," while her sister was "standing a few steps above me."

But let us return to the patient whose dream series we were presenting. We have arranged his dreams according to the symptoms they contain. They show the patient's tabooed thoughts of incest and homosexuality. They also show criminal tendencies directed toward his wife. His conflict is "sister versus wife."

In the next dream we see identification with his sister Ruth. The dream presents to us clearly his feminine tendency.

[258] *"I was not well. I went out to the porch. Women were sitting there. One of them was my mother. It seemed I wasn't menstruating properly. My mother was worried. Mother stood me up next to my sister and compared us. She said sister had the same trouble. 'Everything will be well.' "*

I should like to remind you that dreams which contain symptoms, as a rule, show us also the dynamics of the symptoms, a fact which makes them so valuable.

Regarding homosexuality, a few points must be clarified. Homosexuality in a dream does not in itself mean that the dreamer is a homosexual. Since everybody is basically bisexual, the repressed homosexuality may reappear in the dream. We must find the pertinent correlations, the specific details of the contra-sexual identification, the specific "formula" of the patient's homosexuality as it appears in his neurosis.

A series of dreams had in the same night often shows variations of the same theme, usually with the same emotional background. Interesting are the two following dreams of a forty-year-old lawyer dreamed on two consecutive nights. Here is the first dream:

[259] *"I leave home and take a middle-aged Negro prisoner out to the woods, where I knock him down and then burn him to death. On coming home I casually mention to my brother that it would not surprise me if (name of the Negro) were lynched tonight. I am conscious that I am doing this in order to hide my guilt and at the same time I realize that it is a mistake to say anything."*

The "Negro prisoner" is a picture of the patient's own criminal tendencies. It is his dark, antisocial ego kept down by his moral authority as a "prisoner." The dreamer reports his murder to his brother, for, as the analysis uncovered, it was this very brother who was the subject of the dreamer's profound hatred.

A direct continuation of the preceding dream is the following which was dreamed on the night after the one discussed above:

[260] *"I am being tried for the murder of the Negro and deny having killed him. I feel absolutely innocent of the whole affair and tell the court that the only evidence they have is my brother's statement to the effect that on the night of the murder I mentioned that I would not be surprised if it were to happen. I feel some hatred and contempt for him; I feel that he is deliberately lying to hurt me."*

The second dream contains the conscience reaction. In the first dream the patient has a clear feeling of guilt and his dream attempts to solve the guilt conflict (murder) by projecting it (lynching). In dream number 260 we interpret the "brother" as a personification of the patient's moral ego. The court is the dreamer's conscience. But we are faced with the fact that between dream number 259 and dream number 260 something happens which makes the dreamer feel really innocent; the dream 259 apparently has fulfilled its guilt-neutralizing task.

By examining a series of dreams we are often able to reconstruct the patient's specific infantile trauma, which up to that time had remained hidden. Some patients make an attempt to conceal their most important experiences; in other cases, because of mental scotomas, experiences of the patient's past cannot be recalled by the patient himself even after a prolonged analysis. In such cases the active analysis of chains of dreams may reconstruct the forgotten traumatic situations and submit them to the patient's conscious criticism.

The following series of dreams produced by a thirty-five-year-old homosexual man offered an opportunity to find out the relevant traumatic experience of the patient who unconsciously made every possible effort to conceal it. It was a heterosexual experience, to be sure, and a very painful one, indeed—the defloration of the patient's own sister.

[261] *"Taking a walk, I noticed a wagon with a horse but no driver around. The horse wanted to run away. I, therefore, ran after it and seized the reins, which were attached to the back of the car, in order to stop the horse. The reins stretched, however, and finally the horse slipped out of the reins entirely. To my greatest horror, I noticed that the horse was attacking me and trying to bite me. . . . I ran away, the horse ran after me. Then I came to a mill. . . . I entered the building but noticed that the door was made of jute. The*

horse went after me, tore the stuff, stuck its head through the hole, and wanted to bite me."

The analyst sees here the patient's inner struggle in which he loses his self-control (the scene with the reins). The "horse" is a symbol of the patient's animal ego. Through condensation it represents also the object of his strongest attraction. The trauma is revealed by the scene in which the horse is breaking through the door made of jute. The patient shows us also his self-reproaches in the fact that the horse turns against him and wants to bite him. The analyst assumes that a trauma has been inflicted on someone in the past but does not yet know the object. As the associations fail to make it clear and the resistance grows stronger, another dream is taken into consideration.

[262] *"As soldiers, my friend and I are being sent with a report to the commander. We come to an island and lie down. I press my body to my friend's and caress his legs. He says I should not do this. . . . Later a child approaches. I get up and see a group of children playing musketeers. I aim jokingly with an old pistol at the children, but they are not afraid."*

The "island" symbolizes a detached part of the patient's recollections—his main repressed problem.[1] The "report" means the confession in analysis, as well as in the Catholic confession. The "commander" symbolizes the analyst, but also God. The patient does not make the report to his commander; this detail signifies resistance. The trauma is described in the intimate scene with the comrade[2] and in the scene in which he aims with an "old pistol" at children. His first object did not seem to mind his approach ("not afraid"). Associations fail to give any further clues.

---

[1] We see that not all "islands" in dreams are symbols of the "female genital" or of "mother" as some analysts believe.

[2] The patient's homosexuality was the result of his effort to escape the painful heterosexual recollection.

Another dream: [263] *"My sister, another man and I have a quarrel with a gangster. Then I go to bed, while the man and my sister continue having an argument with the gangster. The man gets excited, shoots at the gangster, and misses him; the gangster shoots at the man and kills him. My sister wants to call for help, but the gangster prevents her from calling."*

The patient's sister is married; the man of the dream seems to be her husband. While the patient "goes to bed," the sister's husband is killed by the gangster (the patient's unconscious criminality, active while the patient is asleep). The analyst already recognizes the real object, but no confession follows. The next dream:

[264] *"A man of my acquaintance says: so you know that odd man who lives alone in the old house . . . He fell in love with a gypsy girl who was very attractive but who always used to run away from him. . . . He hurt the girl. As a punishment he was sentenced to walk about in drawers for a whole year. Since that time he lives in the old house."*

The "odd man" is our patient. The "gypsy girl" is his sister, a girl of a very dark complexion. An allusion to the trauma is to be seen in the words, "he hurt the girl." The punishment is the patient's homosexuality (in the dream symbolized by "to walk about in drawers"). The result of his guilt is his neurotic lonesomeness. It is he who punished himself for his crime by withdrawing from normal social life, by renouncing all contacts with girls and thus becoming an "odd man." No confession follows in spite of the discussion of the dream.

The next dream brings the solution: [265] *"I was at home, where I found my older sister and her girl friends. A gypsy girl came in; she was very attractive. I went with her into the adjoining room, where I kissed and touched her. I did not like it that my sister frequently came into the room and looked reproachfully at me. I could not restrain myself, however, and went to bed with the gypsy. She resisted and said*

*that my penis was too big. . . . I already wanted to use force
when my older sister entered the room and said that Mother
would be back very soon."*

At this stage of the analysis the trauma had been reconstructed to the patient who finally confessed all about the
scene, to his own great mental relief. Note the resemblance
between the "old pistol" and the "big penis" in the patient's
description of the traumatic scene. In the dream we see the
homosexual man in a clearly heterosexual, though tabooed,
scene. The "older sister" and the "mother" are also symbols
of the patient's superego.

The following is a rare example of a dream in which the
patient uses experiences which he gained in other dreams.

Who does not know that anxious excitement in a dream
when the train is missed by a hairbreadth, or when the feet
simply won't move just at the moment that the enemy is right
at our heels and we want to escape? Heights of fear and despair are reached unless, through a kindly turn of the dream,
one is lifted into the air, or by simply awakening one gets
out of danger. However, such a way out, as one of my patients
discovered, is a rarity. The dream follows:

[265a] *"I am hurrying to the station. The train is already
there and I fear I shall miss it. I know that I can't rely on
my efforts to catch the train. Every time, in my previous
dreams, that I have attempted to run after a train I have
found my legs made of lead or embedded in a sticky mass. I
could hardly move forward, and I used to miss the train regularly. Therefore, I decided on a short cut to the train. Instead
of relying on reaching the doors on the left side of the train
I simply hang on to the end of a car, contented to reach my
goal, even though I am rather uncomfortable."*

The dreamer, having had some "bad experiences" in previous dreams, attempts to avoid them in this dream. We recognize here a mechanism similar to "dream within the dream."
We know that the difficulties experienced by the dreamer in
trying to escape "danger" are due to the split existing in his

mind. He is also partly a pursuer in this dream; that is, it is really his thoughts and desires which dare not be brought to consciousness and which keep on pursuing him; it is from these that he (his moral ego) seeks to escape. We see, therefore, in this inability to escape a friendly gesture toward his suppressed desires. (Think, for example, of the girl who dreams that a man "pursues" and "threatens her," and who, alas, can't run away!) The dreamer of the above-mentioned dream evidently feels that he has been too "friendly" to his suppressed desires in his previous dreams, that he has always let his "train run out" on him. The wish to be well, at the bottom of this dream, shows itself in the desire of the patient to overcome the past (the previous dream experiences) and to find a "hold on life" (to "hang on to the end of a car").

Yet, as a whole, this dream contains a compromise solution. It was dreamed after a thorough analysis had succeeded in overcoming the paraphilia (fetishism) of the patient. Unfortunately, because of a physical disability, our patient had certain difficulties in establishing normal relations with women, and had to limit himself to intercourse with prostitutes. In the dream he consoles himself by saying: "I will limit my desires" (relative to women); "I will content myself with a shred, a semblance of love, such as is to be gotten for money, in order not to miss this hold on life which my infantile fantasies are keeping from me."

A very interesting dream series is the following, dreamed by a twenty-six-year-old teacher. It is almost self-explanatory.

[266] *"My husband died and I can't remember ever having cried so pitifully."*

[267] *"Train—travelling. Seeing lots of movie stars, one of them making love to me."*

[268] *"Dancing with gentleman friend of my husband. He makes love to me. Everyone pointing at me. Calling me names, etc."*

[269] *"Have dinner appointment with my girlfriend, Sylvia, a frustrated virgin. I read in the paper that a girl in*

the neighborhood had been raped. I think it is Sylvia and I am panicky. She shows up for appointment, I am relieved."

We see here not only that this patient is toying with the idea of becoming a "merry widow" soon, but also that she is suffering from pangs of conscience. ("Everyone pointing at me," "calling me names.") She half-craves, half-dreads what might happen to "frustrated virgins," who do not enjoy the security and protection of a well-providing husband.

THE CENTRAL IDEA

The central idea of the dream is usually also the central problem of the neurosis. We recall the young patient whose dreams were analyzed on pages 82 and 249. The following dream was one of a long series:

[270] *"I dreamed that my father was dying and that when my mother heard the news she was greatly upset and went to see him, for she still loved him. The rest of the family were also upset and, as for me, I was so surprised that I did not know what to think; but I felt very sorry, because I had always wanted to see him again, and one naturally feels sorry for anyone who is dying. I asked if I might see him and finally received the doctor's permission, but there the dream broke off."*

The dream offers to our patient the fulfillment of his deepest wish—that of a reunion between his mother and his father. (His mother had remarried when the patient was eleven years old.) If we compare this dream with the following one, dreamed a short time later, it is very apparent that the patient feels that his welfare is entirely dependent upon the re-establishment of the childhood atmosphere. This is the "central idea" both of his dream and of his life.

[271] *"I dreamed that I was in my house and that I was very glad to be there because I was once more with my mother. I felt the same love for her that I used to feel in my younger days before she remarried. Then I was with my mother in a lonely house. When I came into her room she*

told me she had just had intercourse with Shakespeare. I re-
member that I was very much shocked to hear that she had
committed adultery, but she said that she considered it all
right. I was greatly astonished and could not understand my
mother's actions."

The boy considers the remarriage of his mother as an act
of infidelity committed against his real father. It perplexes
him that one can so easily "change" and love somebody else.
The deprivation of love which the patient experienced after
his mother turned her main attention to her second husband
(Shakespeare) was the propelling power for all of the boy's
compulsion ideas connected with the problem of "change."
His confidence in women is shaken ("she said that she considered it all right" after she was married, whether it was her
husband or not). He lacks reliable moral standards in matters
of love.

A very interesting dream series was examined by W. Bircher. Bircher treated a man who suffered from stammering,
a symptom exhibited particularly in the presence of his relatives. The patient was an illegitimate child whose mother
kept the name of his father a secret. Bircher discovered by
the use of "active analysis" that there was one question the
patient wanted to ask his relatives—the question that consti-
tuted the main problem of his life, namely, "Who is my
father?" But he had to suppress this question, and thus became self-conscious and shy, and stammered whenever he
approached his relatives.

And his dreams? They revealed a wealth of invention.

[272] *He visits a castle* (father is an aristocrat).

[273] *He meets a strange man* (father) *on the street and*
attacks him.

[274] *A notary public opens a will and calls for him* (great
inheritance).

We see here again that the central idea of the dream is
identical with the central problem of the case.

Let us now consider a case we have discussed earlier (page 41). It is the case of a clerk, aged twenty-eight, who complained of an absolute lack of emotion. He felt permanently depressed, for he could not enjoy life and did not know how to get pleasure out of his various social and professional opportunities.

The analysis of his dreams proved that his lack of emotion was merely a superficial one. Behind his "callousness," as he called it, there was one great emotion that had been repressed for several years. It was the patient's hatred of his brother.

Because his brother very often punished him physically, the patient would often exclaim "Wait until I get older, I will have my revenge!"

But he never got "older." He retained his infantile attitude until he was twenty-eight years old; but the thought of revenge became his secret "life plan." He waited for an opportunity to kill his brother and to flee to some other country. The repression of this strong antisocial emotion created an apparent "lack of emotion" in his everyday life and also prevented him from ever committing the contemplated crime.

In his dreams the thought of a belated revenge appears as the central idea.[1] Let us examine some of them:

[275] *"A fellow in jail is being watched by a guard."*

The idea of being in jail means criminality. The patient's "callousness" is the "guard" against his criminal desires.

[276] *"My brother Johnny is 'showing up' my lack of physical strength by keeping me from getting some food."*

Interpretation: "The thought of my brother is holding me back from enjoying life." (Food = pleasure.)

[277] "This dream was of sufficient emotional intensity to cause me to awaken: *I was dancing in a place where after every dance the couples must dash for refuge against the*

---

1 See dreams 7-11 of the same patient on p. 41.

orchestra, which begins to shoot. I dashed for cover behind walls, under tables, and elsewhere, and could hear the bullets just missing me."

Interpretation: The pleasure of dancing (that is, enjoying life) is disturbed by the criminal thoughts (the shooting orchestra). The "orchestra" which would have to be the source of enjoyment becomes the source of deadly hatred. "Orchestra" here is a symbol of the patient's thought polyphony.

[278] *"I see a fellow walking along the street with a little girl. They stop every few minutes, and the fellow lightly beats the girl with a rope. I am walking with other fellows and see him beat her and hear her protests. I go after them to stop him from beating her. He turns toward me, but I pick up a stone and throw it at him."*

Interpretation: The patient recalls being beaten by his older brother when he was a small lad. In the dream the girl is "smaller." The most striking characteristic of our patient is that he cannot forget. He did not overcome his hatred toward his brother (in this dream expressed by "protesting" and "throwing stones.")

[279] *"I saw the Bremen dock in New York . . ."*

Interpretation: Ideas of flight and escape from responsibility after having committed the murder. This is the patient's secret life plan.

The clearest dream, however, is the following:

[280] *"I had killed someone, and the knowledge of this was contained in my autobiography."*

In the active method of treatment we sometimes venture to tell the patient what he had experienced. We collect circumstantial evidence in a great number of dreams, and we reconstruct, for the benefit of the patient, the traumatic experience for which a conscious recollection is not available. Of course, this is done only under exceptional circumstances. Most "unrecallable" experiences concern the sexual sphere. Let us assume that a governess has taken advantage of a child. It may return many years later in the language of the dream. (Cf. page 67.) Since, in the dream material, we do not have any category of time—past, present, and future appear to be fused—early facts can emerge. In our experience, it happened repeatedly that the analysis was blocked at a certain point, and from dream revelations we concluded that some early occurrence in the patient's life was responsible for the block. What the patient experienced in the dream was, to all appearances, not a wish but a recollection. We shall study such dreams later.

The patient's whole pattern of living sometimes appears to be based upon such unrecalled facts. It is in such cases that we feel the need for reconstructing for the patient what *in all probability* had happened. At first, our interpretation has, in the patient's mind, the character of a foreign body. But then the patient begins to work it into his thoughts, his daydreams, he begins to operate with it *as if* this idea were a real recollection. You will realize at this moment, however, *how important it is that we are right, that we are not bringing into the patient's mental life something artificial and frightening, that can only cause new problems and complications.* We must have our material foolproof, and the circumstantial evidence of the case must, under any scrutiny, appear perfectly valid. According to our experience, such interpretations of unrecalled material have a therapeutic value, provided they are correct. A *cathartic effect* is involved here.

The consequences the patient is able to draw from such interpretations may effect changes in his original neurotic pattern, his libidinal forms, and may lead to re-educational adjustments which duplicate those achieved in the regular process of analysis.

Chapter Five

DREAMS AND THE CLINIC

> ... *She was become*
> *The queen of a fantastic realm, her*
> *thoughts*
> *Were combinations of disjointed*
> *things;*
> *And forms, impalpable and*
> *unperceived*
> *Of others' sight, familiar were to hers.*
> *And this the world calls frenzy.*
>
> BYRON
> (*"The Dream"*)

NEUROSIS IN THE DREAM SYMBOL

Before we proceed to the discussion of the various neurotic manifestations in the dream we shall have to inquire how the neurosis as such expresses itself in the dream. The neurosis in the dream appears (a) in the pictures of *persons*: an old lady, a neurotic or an insane person, the "second ego," the "enemy," the "brother," the "sister," and others; sometimes (b) in the pictures of *animals,* which portray the low, brutal instincts displayed in the neurosis; also (c) in the picture of *Christ,* or *saints* as symbols of suffering; (d) all kinds of other than mental *symptoms* may be used for disguising the illness. Very often pictures of neurosis are (e)

294

buildings, such as churches, old edifices, all sorts of structures, factories, gymnasiums, inaccessible fortifications, etc.; or (f) *fenced-in lots,* squares, etc.; (g) *impassable roads,* labyrinths, and the like.

Often the patient sees himself in defensive situations (resistance).

The following was the first dream in the author's own training analysis:

[281] *"I was riding a horse. My task was to guard a fenced-in plot of land. All of a sudden a camel stuck its head across the fence. I rushed toward the animal to chase it away."*

The fenced-in plot expressed the analysand's privacy which was to be invaded by the analyst. He was very anxious that no "camels" stick their noses into his business. The fenced-in lot represents not only private affairs, but may also stand for the neurosis.

The conflict between ego and id may be represented as a conflict between two persons, or a struggle, a battle, a quarrel. (Cf. page 185.)

Another example of symbolic representation of neurosis is found in the dream of a woman patient, aged twenty-four, suffering from a compulsion neurosis. The patient was forced by her compulsion to ask her mother and her husband to repeat again and again certain words used in ordinary conversation.

[282] *"My husband and I bought a church. We want to do business with it in some way. I think we want to rent it."*

The "business" the patient does with her compulsion neurosis ("church") is irritating and annoying to her husband and mother, forcing them to give incessant attention to her. (Freud called compulsion neurosis a personal religion.)

Another patient brought the next dream:

[283] *She saw herself riding on a circular one-way street, while trying to get away from her home.* She was "going around in circles."

The Neurotic Conflict in the Dream

The neurosis is a mental disease based upon a conflict between the instincts (the id) and the morals (the superego). As stated before, the development of our ego is connected with the repression of primitive desires and impulses.

None of us is absolutely free from repression; therefore, nobody is free from more or less distinct neurotic trends. Our culture is based upon repression. Repressions take place without our conscious recognition. More than that, the repressed contents are intolerable to our consciousness. This and the fact that our mental equilibrium is by no means unshakable render repressions a constant menace to our peace of mind. Experiences and impressions of a certain degree and quality may cause our dormant neurotic predisposition to turn into neurotic symptoms.

If, for some reason, repression becomes inadequate, that is, if the banished impulses threaten to break through the barriers, neurotic symptoms come into existence. These symptoms represent, after repressions, the second line of the defensive structure of our minds. They are able to afford the repressed impulses an accessible outlet; they make possible what otherwise must be considered as impossible, the combining of impulse with inhibition, victory with defeat, sin with atonement.

What has been said about symbols is true also of symptoms. They are foci, crossing points, condensation points, for various and often contradictory ideas and emotions. A girl prevented from keeping an appointment by an acute attack of colitis may experience in her symptom at the same time: (a) an increased sexual excitation as an irritation of her intestines; (b) the inhibition of a tabooed gratification in her frustration; and (c) the atonement (for the sinful thoughts) in her pain. (Cf. p. 300.)

As a matter of fact, neurotics are people who are permanently fighting against their physical desires. In their dreams they may openly show these desires or the struggle against them.

Jung and Stekel pay great attention to conflicts of the more recent time (*der aktuelle Konflikt*), although both admit that most of these conflicts are predetermined by infantile experiences. Neurotics are people who again and again experience their past, partly because they want to revive and keep at work the old pleasures of their childhood, partly in order to make up for their failures, to correct their mistakes, and to achieve, at least in their dreams and fantasies, a state as near perfection as possible. An individual who, as a child, vacillated in his affections between father and mother, may as an adult be inclined to "arrange" a "triangle situation" again and again; he may act as an intruder in marriages, may fall in love with the sweethearts of his friends, or the like; the original situation then becomes a pattern for the patient's entire life. The same is true with the eternal Cinderellas, the men who are always deserted by their wives, or individuals who always come too late for their share of happiness. All these neurotic moves have their plastic expressions in dreams, and we are often in the position to distinguish between a reproduction of an infantile situation and the expression of a present-day conflict in the dreamer.

THE PAST IN THE DREAM

"To be healthy means to overcome the past," says Stekel. And indeed, most neurotics display a striking emotional attachment to their "good old days." For many people, childhood compared with adulthood seems to have been the happier period. Many have spent it in a state of almost uninterrupted pleasure. Parents often surround their children with much love and attention; then, when the young people grow older, they are not prepared to realize that life is a rather serious and unsentimental affair. As adults, they are inclined to expect the same attention they received in their childhood environment. In vain, of course! The usual consequence of this mistake is a reaction of disappointment and depression, or obstinacy and the formation of a hostile attitude toward the world and men, in other words, a neurosis.

The greater the difference between childhood and adulthood with regard to the pleasure experienced, the greater the desire for the lost happiness, the stronger the leaning toward the past, the more serious the psychogenic illness.

In cases like these, dreams speak a clear, at times even pathetic language which reflects the patient's tendency. The plots of the dreams are commonly displaced to the localities of the patient's home environment; persons of his early childhood appear as actors in his dreams; the home town, the "former school," the "old country," the "first job," etc., appear in the dreams, showing the patient's infantilism and his desire to relive the past.

For us, dreams of this kind may be important inasmuch as many neuroses are built upon old psychic "traumas," that is, certain emotionally disturbing experiences of the patient's early days. Fantasies and dreams which flow back to these scenes help us reconstruct the pathogenic situation.

The common symbols of the past in the dream are old buildings, museums, old persons, people dressed in old-fashioned clothes, memorials, statues, particular scenes of the patient's past, and so on. Very often, we find the patient in his dream walking through a long suite of apartments (or rooms), each apartment symbolizing a station of his life journey or a period of his past.

Here are some examples of dreams showing regression.

An optometrist aged thirty-four, who was induced by a Negro servant to allow a homosexual act to be performed upon himself when he was ten years of age, reproduces this scene in the following symbolic disguise:

[284] *"I am sitting in an auto in front of a residence which is set back a little distance from the pavement. I am waiting for someone who has gone into the house. I see a servant carrying something (which looks like a number of*

bottles) to be put in the rear of the car in which I am sitting. I recognize the servant, a colored man whom I have not seen for some years. I call out his name which seems to surprise, and perhaps, please him, maybe because I have remembered his name so long. As we drive away we turn and go in the opposite direction from that in which the car was standing, and someone in the car says, 'There is . . .' (Here he mentioned a name that was familiar to me and that fits the old man like a glove, but I have lost it.) Then he added, 'And certainly you want to see him, an old employee.'"

In this dream we see the patient's repressed, hence unconscious wish for the repetition of the old scene. It is this wish, and not the experience itself, that makes the old scene a real "trauma." *An experience itself is never traumatic; the unconscious wish for the repetition of the experience renders it traumatic.*

We interpret in the above dream, the "bottles" (phallic symbols) which are put by the servant in the rear of the patient's car (anus) as the reproduction of the homosexual scene of the patient's childhood. It is a wish-fulfillment idea ("I am waiting for someone"). Many passages of the dream show the regression in a very distinct way: "residence which is set back"; "a colored man whom I have not seen for some years"; "we are going in the opposite direction"; "the old employee," etc.

In investigating experiences of patients, we often make the surprising discovery that *fantasies have the same pathodynamic effect as real experiences.* This may be due to the fact that, to a child's judgment, fantasy and reality are of the same value and are practically identical. Fairy tales are also experience-forming. The "traumatic" character of some fantasies is, therefore, beyond any question.

Regression sometimes goes back not only to the infancy of the individual but to the former stages of our development, to the infancy of mankind. We are often surprised at finding in the dreams of our patients cannibalistic, sadistic, mysophilic, and other atavistic features, like echoes from forgotten times. Repression of atavistic traits leads to neurotic manifestations expressing the defense against these impulses. In connection with this, we find the patient's fear that these impulses might break through the moral barriers. Repression of cannibalism may be responsible for neurotic stomach disturbances. Repression of sadism leads to abnormal reactions such as fainting at the sight of wounds, or the like. Repressed mysophilic tendencies may be the cause of abnormally strong reactions of aversion and disgust.

THE NEUROTIC SYMPTOM IN THE DREAM

We know today that the processes governing sleep and dream are much akin to the processes that go on in the production of neurotic and psychotic symptoms. We know how an emotionally charged idea can be converted into a symptom. Similar mechanisms take place in the conversion of repressed thoughts into dream images.

In the patient's history, the development of the symptom usually shows the following phases (cf. Fig. 57):

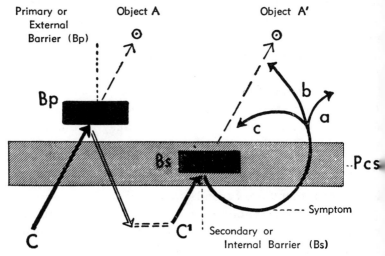

FIGURE 57
Dynamics of the Neurotic Symptom

1. In early childhood an original goal-directed craving (C) has been *frustrated* because the goal was taboo. (*Primary or external barrier—Bp.*)

Example: Mother (Object A) rejects an instinctive sexual approach by the male child.

2. The frustrated craving is *suppressed* because of fear that the repetition of approach might lead to loss of love or another rejection.

3. Meanwhile, the *superego* is established and anchored in the patient's personality of which it becomes an intrinsic part.

4. Preconscious *censorship* is introduced which guards against the resurgence of tabooed desires. (*Secondary or internal barrier—Bs.*)

5. The warded-off craving (C_1) obtains overt expression —in distorted form—as a neurotic *symptom.*

The neurotic symptom shows a three-pronged structure. It represents (a) motor discharge, (b) specific gratification in symbolic form, and (c) self-punishment.

Example: The mother complex in our patient may make him susceptible to all sorts of neurotic reactions. The patient may develop ejaculatio praecox, e.g., in his sexual relations toward women (Object A′). In his symptom then we are able to detect (a) the *motor discharge* (emission), (b) the *symbolic gratification* (the underlying fantasy deals with the tabooed object), and (c) the *self-punishing component* which is expressed in the embarrassing disability (inhibition) toward Object A′.

In a dream, any or all of these three components may be represented.

We may consider it as a rule that *dreams which contain the symptom contain also its psychogenesis.* We shall study this problem in the following chapters in which we see various diseases illustrated by characteristic dreams. The diagnostic importance of the symptom in the dream is relatively small. The picture of the symptom in the dream has to be recognized because the background of the dream shows an important relation to the symptom itself, and thus to the neurotic conflicts of the patient. The correct interpretation of the symptom dream enables us to understand some of the important pathological components of the neurosis or to support suppositions based on other material.

Let us observe the following dream and see how much we can learn from it:

[285] *"I dreamed of being on a large boat—about like an excursion boat. In fact, it seemed as though it were an excursion boat. There was a rowboat with Fred (fiancé) in it. The rowboat was attached to the stern of the large boat. Fred was sitting in the rowboat, holding onto the larger boat so that the small one would not drift away. He held on while I climbed from the large boat into the small boat.*

"Then the whole thing was repeated. I was on the dock, saw the two boats; the small one with Fred in it, holding fast to the larger one. I went to the large boat to climb from there into the smaller boat. It seemed as though someone on the large boat wanted to help me into the small boat. (I think it was a fellow.) I, however, felt that he was intruding, that this was Fred's and my affair and business. Fred did help me into the boat. I noticed a small trickle of water coming into the boat over the gunwhale at the stern of the boat. I was concerned at first, but I climbed into the boat anyway, went to the stern and sat down.

"Then the scene changed again. I had the feeling that I was trying to avoid something, or to get out of doing something. I had some breaking out, probably on my face. I kept looking and looking—I guess in a mirror. Finally, I noticed my face looked funny (in writing this, it reminds me of the time in college that I had measles.) *I tried to think of what it might be, and chicken pox came to my mind. It was then understood that I couldn't make the trip."*

The twenty-five-year-old patient was engaged to marry a young man, Fred, who was living in the patient's home as a boarder. The patient's double fixation to father and mother was responsible for her lack of decisiveness as far as her male partners were concerned. Although very attractive, and courted by many, she was not able to make up her mind about whom she would wed. You will find this symptom (indecision) in the wording of the dream, particularly its first sentences: ". . . about like an excursion boat. In fact, *it seemed* as though it were an excursion boat" (doubt).

It is quite clear that the large boat in this dream represents the patient's family, while the little boat is her anticipated marital life.

The dream gives us the sort of information we want to elicit. The patient is supposed to be in love with her fiancé. But she is a doubter and cannot make up her mind.

In the dream *we see a decision*, and that is what makes this dream so important. She is about to make an "excursion," to transfer, to effect a change from a larger boat, one that is safe and secure like an excursion boat, to a smaller boat, in fact, a flimsy rowboat which is manned by her fiancé. (Antitheses: large—small; secure—insecure.) In the dream the smaller boat holding her fiancé is attached to the larger boat. It is in a state of dependency regarding the larger one. She suspects that Fred is holding on to her family, trying to find security for himself in his marriage to her.

The process of climbing from the large boat to the smaller one is dreamed repeatedly. Repetition is, as usual, caused by frustration. Was the first transfer unsuccessful? Was it annulled and did it have to be repeated? Again a symbol of doubt. In this part of the dream, the patient is on the secure platform of a dock. She observes the whole procedure objectively from a perspective, from the distance. She again notices Fred's boat "holding fast to the larger one." She re-enacts the scene, this time with the aid of a fellow (analyst?), but she feels he is intruding. She accepts only Fred's assistance.

The moment she boards the rowboat, difficulties she had noticed before, ("I was concerned at first but I climbed into the boat anyway"), become more conspicuous. There is danger of getting waterlogged and perhaps of sinking.

And, it is at this point that the dream changes again, the dreamer is not on the boat at all. She is to make a decision, but she is "trying to avoid something or to get out of doing something." Could this be her marriage? In the dream it distinctly seems to refer to the "boat trip." A disease seems to impede her, a facial rash. It reminds her of a time when in college she unexpectedly developed measles. Everybody was making jokes about her infantile disease. She then decides against taking the trip.

If we interpret the skin rash the same way as the patient did, namely, as an infantile disease (attitude) which is not expected to be met with at her age, we shall arrive at the proper solution. The patient tells us that while consciously she hesitates to make a decision, unconsciously she has made her decision: not to join Fred in matrimony. She also provides us with the reasons for her decision: his lack of virility and his dependency on her family. In her dream she conveys to us the idea that she would even welcome a mental or physical disease if this would offer her a plausible way out. A facial rash would also render her ugly and undesirable, while in reality she has an excellent complexion. The antithesis between the wish to remain a child (measles) and the desire to become a grown-up woman is clearly presented in this dream.

(Q) "How do we know that the large boat represents the patient's family?"

(A) We have no specific proof for that; but we have cogent clinical support for what was suspected. The patient comes from a large family in which the members are closely attached to one another. They have fixed family traditions, family rituals, family excursions. The family allegiance is very strong. Mother rules as matriarch over the entire group. And now the time has come for our patient to make a decision as to whether she should abandon the family ties in order to marry. A situation of this kind always provokes ambivalent feelings. The desire to be free from family ties alternates with the desire not to expose oneself to new emotional situations.

Judging from the description of Fred in the dream, our patient does not appear to have absolute confidence in him. As a matter of fact, a subsequent interview with Fred by the analyst confirmed the patient's doubts in the young man's masculinity and resourcefulness.

The closer the patient comes to awakening, the clearer grows the real sentiment of the patient. Here we see what she is trying to conceal—she wants "to get out of doing something." Unconsciously, she has **not** accepted the idea of marrying Fred.

(Q) "Did the patient ever agree to marry Fred?"

(A) She was engaged. It was her indecision that delayed the marriage. When I asked whether she loved him, she replied in the affirmative. And yet she was apparently not ready for marriage. If you had asked her about it directly, she would have replied, "I wish to get away from my family." She had superficial reasons for wanting to get away. The family lived under very crowded conditions. As many as eight or nine members lived in their home.

(Q) "Why did the dream distort her rejection of Fred?"

(A) One reason for hiding her decision was that consciously she behaved as though she wanted to marry Fred. In her dilemma about whether or not she should marry, the dream offered her a third solution: that of withdrawing into disease, and in this way avoiding the real issue. If a conscious "I *want* to do that" is countered by an unconscious "*I don't want* to do that," the neurosis then steps in with an "*I can't* do that."

You find such neurotic "pseudo-solutions" in cases of hysterical paralysis, in persons who cannot walk or write or play an instrument. We always find in these people a clash between two impulses, a desire and a counter-desire; and then the function is suppressed. Functions are likely to be suppressed when tabooed goals are associated with them.

The following dream of the same patient will support our assumptions further:

[286] *"This might be the second part of the first dream— at least the scene changed to this dream. I was walking along in the open, approaching what I thought were trolley tracks. I think Fred was with me, but I wasn't aware of him until*

later. I started to walk along the tracks, and when I looked up, and saw a train coming around the curve, my foot slipped between the grade switching. The train had rounded the curve by then, though it was still a ways off, and was coming closer. Without panic I started to exert a steady pull on my caught foot, to draw it out of the wedge. It started to come out very slowly and only with a great deal of pull. I tried to judge whether it could be pulled out before the train reached me. I remember thinking I must be calm about it— the only way I stood a chance of getting my foot out and saving my life was to be calm. If I became panicky, I most certainly would lose. I kept pulling and Fred and another man came along and tried to help me. They were working more frantically than I. The train approached mighty close but I don't know what happened for I stopped dreaming."

In this dream the patient clearly describes a situation of mortal danger in which she finds herself after getting "stuck." We see here again the motive of emotional fixation and of herself trying to get away. A particular importance lies in the associations which the patient produced:

She had read in the newspaper of a married couple who were walking across the railroad tracks, when the woman's foot was caught in a switch and could not be extricated. Before help arrived, an express train was approaching. The couple made frantic attempts to extricate the foot and when the husband saw that his wife was doomed he did not think of saving himself but threw his arms around her and perished with her under the wheels of the train.

This typical example of marital loyalty must have aroused questions in our patient as to whether Fred were capable of showing such glowing proof of his loyalty, but the fact that she dreamed about the newspaper article bespeaks her fears that marriage might be like going into death together.

Let us look at still another dream by the same patient:

[287] *"It seemed to be the morning of our wedding. I was with Fred. He had on full dress and we were eating*

breakfast. I suddenly realized I wasn't supposed to see him on the wedding day until I joined him at the church. I walked out of the place and went towards my room.

"Then I was in my room. I think I was dressing for the wedding, then it seemed as though the wedding might be over. I left the room, and as I went out the door, I thought that I should call Daddy. I ran out of the house, and I had my long blue housecoat on.

"I saw him among other fellows playing some sort of volley ball. I joined them in their game. I suddenly remembered that this must be my wedding day, and thought that this was a heck of a way to be spending it. So I left to go home."

If we look over the contents of this dream, we recognize that the young lady first was dressing for the wedding and "then it seemed as though the wedding might be over." She did not experience the wedding at all, an unusual situation if we realize how much the ceremony as such means to most girls. First she sees her groom before the wedding which is generally considered bad luck. She risks the possible misfortune. Then she leaves the room to go to her father.

Nor is she dressed for the wedding. ("I had my long blue housecoat on.") She sees her father among other fellows: he is one of her "fellows," viewed as equivalent; but we know that he is preferred. She engages in games, as in the good old days, in her childhood days, when she was carefree and so completely sure of her father's devotion to her.

Toward the end of the dream, the superego takes charge of the situation and the patient becomes more aware of her obligations to Fred.

The contrasting emotions in these dreams concern "family versus marriage," "father versus Fred," "security of childhood versus obligations of maturity." In her dreams we see her indecision, but we also clearly perceive the direction toward which the pendulum oscillates. The prognosis of this engagement appeared dark from the onset.

Although the analyst exerted no direct influence, this engagement was broken after several months. The patient later married another man and her marriage appears to be successful.

PAIN

Like all conversion symptoms, pain phenomena show a complex structure. They are compromise solutions which express both the repressing force and the repressed material. In the service of the superego, they express self-punishing tendencies, but they also serve the opposite purpose, namely, to camouflage forbidden pleasures. This is particularly true of pain which occurs at the so-called *erogenous zones,* such as the breasts, genitals, the rectal zone, or any other part of the body which shows increased libidinous cathexis. Pain in such cases may even substitute for the orgasm. But in all pain neuroses one factor is paramount: the existence of repressed hostility and aggression.

Pain at the erogenous zones may represent, at once, a *memory* of a past pleasurable, though forbidden experience and a *warning* against any attempt to revive the forbidden pleasure.[1]

All these components of psychogenic pain may become clear through dream interpretation; the analyst then is able to evaluate their relative position in the patient's emotional constellation.

In the following we shall study some of the more frequent manifestations of neurotic pain.

NEURALGIA

We shall start with a dream reported by a forty-five-year-old woman who was suffering from pain in her neck, particularly in the lower floor of her mouth. Very often, she also had a stiff neck.

[1] Not only pain, but many other conversion symptoms can precipitate on erogenous zones.

[288] *"Larry was lying on the bed, and I was next to him on the floor. But I was not actually on the floor. I was sort of suspended. What kept me up was this: I was having intercourse with Larry and I was kissing his navel, and that was the thing that kept me suspended. I had to kiss him pretty hard to keep myself up, so hard in fact that his navel became quite rigid, and pulled away."*

This was a woman who in her early married life, or, rather, between one and another marriage, had a number of homosexual experiences to which she was seduced by her aunt, a lesbian. It was unquestionably a recollection of this experience that led to the dream. The breast was the most attractive part on the body of her partner. There was a great deal of mouth-breast contact between the two women, and here we find that in the dream while being intimate with a man she tries to seek out that part of his anatomy that revives recollections of her homosexual past. The heterosexual scene thus proves to be a reproduction of a homosexual act. It is this sexual ambivalence which keeps her "suspended in air." She is engaged in fantasies and does not rest on the solid ground of reality. (Any situation in the dream where the patient finds himself suspended in the air, or on a ladder that leads nowhere, indicates a condition of fantasy that triumphs over reality.)

Trigeminus neuralgia can be recognized in the following dream by a medical student:

[289] *"I am passing through a forest at night; there are many little animals (rats?). I meet three girls* (association: triplets) *of a foreign type."*

The trigeminus nerve is symbolized by the triplets; the gnawing pain by the rats.

Another dream by the same patient:

[290] *"I am driving a streetcar. . . . Three horse heads are in front of me; one of them bites me and prevents me from driving."*

The pictures of the neuralgia described here do not represent the analytical content of the dream; we merely demonstrate the symbolic expression of the symptom and do not go into a more intensive analysis of the case.

MIGRAINE

In cases of migraine which are often connected with nausea' we find dreams containing peculiar cannibalistic, necrophilic, and mysophilic features. A woman patient, aged thirty-eight, dreams:

[291] *"I am eating my mother. . . .* Awake with disgust and headache."

The following dream of a lady suffering from stomach trouble and migraine reveals coprophilic drives:

[292] *"I am talking to a shoemaker. I have a stomach ache and feel suddenly that I am getting diarrhea. A bucket is near by. I use it while talking to the man. Later on I want to leave, but all of a sudden I notice that it was not the bucket I was using but my shopping bag, in which are lying meat, vegetables, fat, etc. I get a headache and feel a strong disgust which lasts a long time after awakening."*

Feces among food—a dream scene which reveals the patient's atavistic desire to devour human feces. The repression of this atavistic desire leads to the symptoms of somatization. They are: aversion, nausea, disturbance of digestion, vomiting spells, etc.

Another patient dreams:

[293] *"I have eaten a living animal. A white mouse or a white rat. When I came to the face, I thought of hurting the animal and felt disgusted."*

The author of the next dream is a forty-four-year-old male:

[294] *"I speak to one of my female neighbors who suggests a trip. I think how awkward it may be to make the trip with two women. I then feel an overwhelming loving feeling for my wife and run upstairs and embrace her. I awaken with a severe headache."*

The dream lends itself to the presentation of an interesting mechanism, namely, that of an "ellipsis." The word comes from the Greek ἐκλείπω, meaning "to leave out." We speak of an ellipsis if a part of a content, usually an important one, is left out.

The patient says here: "I then had a loving feeling for my wife and went upstairs to embrace her. I awakened with a headache." This headache represents a shortcut to what really happened. The patient was thinking how he could take a trip with two women. Apparently he has made his decision because he is anxious to pacify his wife, and it is for this reason that he awakens with a headache.

(Q) "Could we say that the purpose of that dream was to create a headache?"

(A) I don't think so. The headache was the consequence of the dream. Its purpose was to enable the dreamer to experience an act of adultery. The adultery itself was blacked out (ellipsis), but the superego did not stop there. It retaliated for the antimoral act and caused the patient to awaken with a headache. A case of unsuccessful repression, as most psychosomatic symptoms are.

A thirty-two-year-old married woman has been suffering from migraine (hemicrania) since her sixteenth year. The typical attacks occur on the average of every two or three days and last from a few hours to a few days. The attacks are usually preceded by a scintillating scotoma, then nausea and the urge to throw up appear. The most conspicuous symptom of the case is that the attack, as a rule, terminates in a manifest sex orgasm. Hemicrania persists until a spontaneous relaxation through orgasm takes place. In some instances, several orgasms occur in succession before the attack is over.

One of the outstanding traumatic experiences in this case was a terrifying scene which took place when the patient was nine or ten years old. Her father (an alcoholic) came home at night intoxicated and, on his way to his bed, stumbled and fell over the sleeping patient whose bed was standing next to his, and vomited. The girl woke up in panic and pushed away the man who was lying there "like a dead man." Since that time the patient showed some nervous reactions, the foremost of which was fear of vomiting. Later, during her spells of headache, she never permitted herself to throw up. She claimed that she would have rather fainted. But she never fainted.

Her first migraine attack occurred at the age of sixteen, after an exciting scene with her father. He came home drunk, got into an argument with his wife and when the patient tried to interfere he threatened to kill her. She ran away, but a short time after that, she developed attacks of hemicrania.

She married at the age of twenty-five. Her marriage was unhappy and the patient remained frigid until her analysis.

The patient's father fixation was very strong. It was based on her unconscious desire to re-live the early nocturnal experience and to embellish it with a sexual ending.

The following dream shows this distinctly:

[295] *"I was in a theater and saw a play which I have seen once before* (allusion to the past). *But this time the presentation and the actors were different* (the patient refers here to her relations with her husband). *The first time it was a pageant, while this time the performers just walked in on the stage. I was wondering about it. I seem to be in my parents' home.*

"I saw many people and many chickens, the animals were very lively. I had the impression that the animals made dirty." (Reference to the vomiting scene.)

The possibility of an incestuous approach became enhanced by the fact that her girl friend Rose's father once made an attempt to approach her sexually and that her own father displayed a striking interest in young girls.

Her girl friend Rose was suffering from epileptic seizures. Since in childhood there were some sexual games between the two girls, the patient compared herself with Rose and considered Rose's epilepsy and her own migraine as a consequence of these homosexual activities.

The following dream illustrates this:

[296] *"My friend Max has a migraine attack. He takes a walk with me. Suddenly I notice it is not Max I am walking with but Rose. She jumps down from a high step. I say, how can you jump with your headache?*

"Then we go on. Young fellows approach us and I am afraid they will want to start something. But they do nothing of the kind. Instead a big, lean, terrifying woman is there and demands that Rose should kiss her. She refuses and runs away. . . . I awake with headache."

In the above dream the patient's sweetheart Max has migraine (projection). It is important to know that he is an elderly man and a definite "father image." The connection between father and migraine is indicated in this condensed symbol.

In addition, the homosexual threat is portrayed as one of the roots of the patient's migraine spell.

The next dream contains the homosexual root clearly. It is the result of blocked heterosexual outlets through incest fixation and a disappointing marriage. Her infantile libido constellation remained alive and with it her undifferentiated sexual attractions.

In her dream [297] *she saw herself dragged into a club of homosexual women. She saw girls in all sorts of homosexual contacts. One girl seemed to have been forced into this abnormal life, just as she was. It was a young girl who had a*

FIGURE 58

stripe of white hair in the middle of her head. The patient presumed that she became gray from grief, because she had to carry out these horrible things. (Cf. Fig. 58.)

The material of this dream reproduces a scene the patient has experienced with her girl friend Rose in early childhood. The description of the woman's hair is the description of the patient's symptom, hemicrania. The patient herself admits in her dream that homosexuality and the head condition are related to each other.

Her migraine is the curtain behind which the tabooed thoughts and affects can be carried on without responsibility toward her superego.

But the following dream expresses the main problems involved. It runs as follows:

[298] *"I passionately kissed my father . . .* (rest of dream forgotten). *Awoke with headache."*

The analysis proved that the traumatic incident with her father remained in her mind and finally developed into an incest fantasy as a climax of her sexual daydream. Its content remained repressed. The headache appeared as a so-called "conversion symptom" or "somatization" of this repression. A state of clouded consciousness and a scintillating scotoma prevailed until the patient's tabooed fantasy (incest) reached its fulfillment. When the patient had the orgasm, she felt relieved and the headache disappeared.

Other dreams of this patient in which the symptom found its symbolic representation are the following:

[299] *"I was with father alone; father was a widower, and I was not married. It was evening and we were sitting silently. I did not know how I could entertain father.*

"Suddenly the door opened and mother came in. She was dead. She had a bloody band slung around her forehead, showing that she had been slain. I woke up in terror—with a headache."

In this dream all obstacles are removed and the patient is

sharing her father's life. Her headache appears to copy her slain mother's condition.

The head appears in her dreams frequently. One of her dreams brings a picture of a migraine attack, in connection with the head.

[300] *"I was taking a walk. A storm broke out. A bolt of lightning struck my head. I turned around my longitudinal axis several times and then I fell down. Awoke with headache."*

Dreams of this type can be found also in cases of epilepsy. This demonstrates another aspect of the kinship between migraine and epilepsy. The turning around the axis is a symbol of vertigo, which was one of the accompanying symptoms of this case.

Of great interest are the frequent pictures of far-reaching oral regressions and some atavistic trends met with in cases of migraine. In one case cannibalistic and necrophilic tendencies were clearly discernible. The patient (under terror) dreamed of kissing persons who were dead. She displayed an uncontrollable fear of "ghosts" and of staying in apartments where someone had died. In such cases she felt a cold hand or cold lips touching her.

In one of her dreams [301] *she saw food brought in a shopping bag. When she wanted to take it out, the bag grew longer and turned into a coffin. There was a dead body inside.*

Or the following dream, in which quite an unusual combination of food and death is clearly visible:

[302] *"I am in a huge marble hall. I am sitting at a table and am about to eat when a hearse passes by. I dropped everything."*

[303] *"I walked with my aunt Julia who is now dead. I was afraid of her. She wanted to kiss me. I let her do it under resistance and felt her cold lips."*

Here we see a combination of homosexuality and necrophilia. In the patient's equation, "to kiss a dead person" means "to kiss a homosexual object." But apart from this symbolic representation, the necrophilic tendency must be accepted as one of the typical features of the unconscious material hauled to the surface in cases of migraine.

The vomitus which, as a rule, terminates the spell or the nausea which accompanies it may well be due to the undercurrent of atavistic desires which are repulsive and create eliminative defense reactions.

It is interesting to note that in some cases of hemicrania the pain represents the projection of a suicide idea. Graven found this in one of his analyzed cases. The pain in the patient's temple was a symbolization (somatization) of a gunshot idea.[1]

The following two migraine dreams were dreamed by the patient whose colitis is discussed on page 360:

[304] *"I was about to leave on my bicycle when my sister asked me to help her with something. I was dressed to leave and my sister said, 'I declare, you sure are dressed to kill. Where are you going?' I said, 'None of your business.' I was preparing to leave when my sister asked me to go up to the loft of the barn and throw down some pieces of wood. I did. Suddenly I heard a scream. I ran down, and saw my sister's head split open and bloody. I awoke with migraine headache."*

A strong unconscious jealousy exists between brother and sister. It is based on a common sexual experience they once had. The patient's seemingly independent behavior in the dream is sheer hypocrisy. He is his sister's obedient slave. It is this dependency that stirs up in him the idea of destroying her. His motto is, "I hate you because I love you although it is my ruin." Sister's head injury represents the migraine.

At the same time, the dream reproduces the scene of defloration, the fateful experience of the patient's past. When-

---

[1] Suicide ideas of this type can be carried out in a subsequent addiction to analgesics (suicide by poison in fractional dose).

ever his day- or night-dream hits upon this recollection, a migraine attack follows.

The next dream is along the same lines:

[305] *"I am sick with migraine. I am in bed. Our family doctor, and my mother and sister are present. The doctor says to my sister who is about eight years old in the dream: 'You also have hot cheeks. Stay in bed and make cold compresses. It'll pass.'* Awoke with migraine."

The "family doctor" is the analyst. The doctor's observation ("hot cheeks" = "red cheeks") refers to the fact that both brother and sister share in the "sin," and both should share in the pathological consequences.

What arouses the patient's bitterness is that his sister is married and apparently happy, while his own life is wrecked by the repercussions of his past.[1]

ARTHRITIC PAIN

French and Shapiro emphasize the usefulness of dream investigation in the research of disease, alongside of other factors, such as observation and evaluation of the patient's behavior. The authors stress the fact that the patient's personal experiences are woven into the dream and, also, that a close relation between the two exists. Their conclusion regarding the case is that as the patient's submissive sexual impulses become more pronounced, the need to fight them off becomes more desperate, and the aggression generated in this way has to be mastered and subdued. Fear of their discharge augmented by the fear of sexual gratification then leads to motor disability.

Some people wake up in the morning with a symptom. They may tell you, "You say that the thought has created

---

[1] I have made this observation repeatedly: where overt incestuous relations between brother and sister have existed, it is the sister, as a rule, who overcomes her past and adjusts herself to a new sexual situation, while the brother tends to develop a "neurosis of unresolved memories."

my symptom. How is this possible? I woke up in the morning and had my symptom already." You then ask for the dream; it will, as a rule, give you the answer.

(Q) "How does anybody know whether the patient had a pain first, which caused him to awaken and to produce a complex dream, or whether her complexes had caused the pain and the dream?"

(A) For the understanding of the case, it does not matter too much which has come first, because we are interested only in the fact that *pain* and a *specific dream scene* are associated with each other.

French and Shapiro have also made an important contribution to the psychopathology of rheumathoid arthritis and similar conditions. They pointed out the manifold emotional determinations of the organic disease. One of their patients, a young woman, presented the following dream during her analysis:

[307] *"I was being held captive in a large apartment. My arms were bound to my sides like in a strait jacket. I was permitted to roam through the house. But they wouldn't let me out. All they gave me was hard candy. It seemed my mother was holding me captive."*

The dream was closely related to an approaching attack. The patient awoke as though from a nightmare. She reported how her shoulders and arms were stiff and aching.

She continued her associations with a description of how her mother kept her "tied to her apron strings." In the "strait jacket" scene of the dream she could get candy only by bending forward and scooping it up with her mouth.

Apparently, in a case such as this, the arthritic pain sets in and causes the patient to awaken, while a protective reflex stiffens the affected limbs, an act which is experienced in the dream as binding of the arms to her sides. An additional possibility, although in this case there is little substantiative evidence for it, is that her relationship to her mother ("tied to her apron strings") may have influenced the onset of arthritis.

In one of the preceding sessions, she had brought a dream

[308] in which, *while waiting with her mother for a bus, she had started to menstruate. She experienced fear when she saw a woman trying to get into a hole in a balcony three stories above the street. In the same dream the patient danced with an attractive man to the admiration of onlookers, and then entered a streetcar where she had the "nasty and vulgar" experience of seeing the motorman turn and spit into her large shopping bag.*

A young man had tried to kiss her during the evening preceding the dream, but she had felt clumsy as though she had never been kissed before. In her home, anything connected with sex was taboo. In the dream she compensated for her clumsy reaction to the young man's advances by being admired as she danced—but then came the feeling of disgust for having permitted further amorous advance. (The motorman spits into her shopping bag.) Two days later she had the arthritis attack.

During the next session she complained of an inner restlessness that always preceded the onset of an attack. She "could tear" her hair, in other words, use her hands and arms, the parts of her body that are affected by arthritis.

Then came another session with the report of the flare-up and the accompanying dream. . . .

The following day she reported that pain and stiffness had persisted all day. On the following night she dreamed:

[309] *"I was leaving my house to cross the street to go to another house. The streets were very icy. A model T Ford turned the corner and turned over. It fell to pieces. As I started out, mother was in the background and said to be careful. I fell but was able to get up easily. I crossed over and entered the other house. It was my aunt's home. I realized then that I was only partly dressed."*

She added that the arthritis had been bad at night but was "quite better this morning."

In this dream, in which she gets up easily the authors see the subsidence of her somatic symptoms. In being only partly dressed she is free from some of the sexual inhibitions which are so obvious in her other dreams. These features herald the approach of a brief period during which both arthritis and sexual inhibition are considerably eased. And true enough, in a few days she was responsive to the erotic play of another man.

Adequate data for reconstructing the mechanism by which the sexual conflict of this young lady was transferred into bodily musculature is not available, but the material does provide numerous provocative hints. "Dancing" and "walking" in dreams are connected with standing proudly erect, while "falling" means giving way to dangerous, humiliating or disgusting (sexual) relationships. In one dream [310] *a woman appears about to "fall from a high balcony"* and then, after the arthritic attack, a dream shows the patient leaping to her feet with agility. In the "strait jacket" scene she is prevented from reaching for the hard candy. The authors surmise that "as the danger of being overpowered by her submissive sexual impulses becomes more desperate, . . . her more desperate need to master her fear of sexual gratification now takes the form of an impulse to reach out and grab the 'hard candy' that she cannot permit to be forced upon her."

French emphasizes that in many cases of muscular pain analysis he finds an inhibition of strong muscular impulses. The inhibited muscular impulse often turns into visual activity in dreams which involves the inhibited muscle groups and joints.

The activity sometimes is projected to persons other than the dreamer. French makes the interesting observation that in the course of inhibiting activity the patient in his dream may even see completely inactive persons standing like statues but showing an inherent threat. One of his patients saw [311] *a huge, motionless Negro in her dream. He seemed about to attack her.* When discussing this dream with her analyst the patient developed strong headaches. The analyst saw in the picture of the motionless Negro a projection of the patient's impulse to activity plus an energetic denial of it. The activity then appeared "frozen."

MENOPAUSAL PAINS

The following is a typical dream of a forty-four-year-old woman who suffered from anxiety hysteria with psychosomatic symptoms. You will probably discover these symptoms by yourself as you read the plot of the dream:

[312] *"I was riding in a subway—"* To begin, this woman cannot ride in subways because this is one of her phobias. (A dream which contains the symptom must also give us some clue about its dynamics.)

To return to the dream: *"Above the part where the advertisements are, a sliding panel opened and a very big and husky man in a cap and shirt pulled me up to him, and with him, through the opening."*

He must have been very big if he could pull her up that way. Only the relationship of an adult toward a little child could make such an occurrence possible.

"The next thing I remember I was being hustled down a long stairway. When we reached the basement a very homely and ugly woman was standing there. She had dyed red hair and a pancake makeup through which you could see many scars. She looked me over and said, 'All right. Take her up.' I was hustled up another flight of stairs (this seemed to be a twin house, sort of a secret place—the other one must have been a blind for this one)."

In other words, there are two houses; one "front house" and one "back house." The "back house" is a symbol of the unconscious.

"As I was being pushed up the stairs by the big fellow, I knew I was being sold into a house of prostitution."

The "harlot complex" can be found in many women.[1] A

[1] It is, as a rule, based on deep-seated incestuous desires and on an unresolved homosexual complex.

woman of this type may have difficulties in walking on streets because, in her fantasy, "walking on streets" is an equivalent of "street-walking" (prostitution).

There are two main reasons why the subway is a frequent object of anxiety: first, the doors remain closed for some periods of time and this gives the patient a feeling of being trapped; second, the subway is a breeding place of daydreams many of which revolve around sex because people are packed closely together and jostle one another. Many people with abnormal sexual desires use the subway as their favorite hunting ground.

"—When we reached the landing, there was a man who said, 'Take her in.' From the outside I could hear Conga music, and I knew that the girls inside were being trained for sex purposes in time to the music. I was pushed into this room where many girls were lined up such as they would be in a chorus, and they were keeping time to the music. I joined them."

The patient is completely passive and masochistic. She is an innocent victim. She is hustled around. This is what Stekel called "pleasure without guilt." The idea is: "If I am *forced* to do the immoral things I need not have any guilt feelings afterwards."

"—The next I remember we were, all of us, on the stoop of the house, coming down a long flight of stairs going into the street. We were all dressed in flaming-red bird dresses. The kind of dresses the girls wear in the theater, very low cut and very short, with black stockings and high heels. All this time we were shaking and shimmying to the Conga music, all the way down the stairs, and all the way down the street to the corner, where, as usual, there was the elevated train. I imagine this street was between Second and Third Avenue. We were kept in line by two men who watched us very carefully.

"We turned to come back to the house, under orders, of

course. We were still shaking and shimmying, and the shaking got to be very exciting. I could feel my breasts tingling, as also were the other parts of my body, as though they were titillated. It was not entirely pleasant, and yet there was a feeling of doing a good job of it so that I too would be selected. I spoke to one of the girls, she was young and pretty with a very nice, open, clean face. I asked if she had as yet slept with a man, and she said 'No,' but that she hoped she would pass the test and be permitted to do so that night. We had not let up the shaking for one second. I woke up with the drawing and pulling pains in my legs (menopausal pain), feeling shaky and depressed."

In this dream we see the appearance of pain in her legs as a symptom in which masochistic gratification takes place at the moment the patient has engaged in dancing and illicit sexual activities. The general rheumatoid condition of the patient was responsible for her frequent muscular pains which were particularly noticeable after she awakened from prolonged rest. The aching muscles were probably responsible for her awakening. At the same time, the dream showed her in a state of high muscular activity, thus counteracting the existing muscular inadequacy.

A mother's jealousy toward her daughter can be seen in the following dream of the aforementioned patient:

[313] *"I can see Lester standing in back of Lillian. His eyes are very big, with black circles all around them. Lillian is leaning forward in the taxicab, with the same eyes, describing to me how Lester killed her. He stabbed her with a knife and turned it round and round. She was dressed in white, in an old-fashioned dress with a high collar. At the beginning of this dream I was riding in many taxis—changing at different streets. . . ."*

In order to understand this dream fully it is necessary to know that the patient's mother was murdered by her lover when the patient was nine years of age. In her dream it is not her mother but her daughter who has been murdered. This connection between love and death known to the patient from her own childhood is now projected onto the patient's daughter, whose husband the patient covets for herself. In her dream the circles under his eyes bespeak his sexual activity. The patient envies her daughter unconsciously for her love and has secret death wishes toward her. The real murder was committed by shooting. The reference in the dream to a knife and the turning of it round and round bespeaks the symbolic (sexual) character of the scene.

The patient's next dream confirms this interpretation by spinning the ideas further:

[314] *"In a hotel. I am going from room to room and every room I look into (the doors are slightly open) there is a party going on (dancing, drinking and fun). Most of the men had the look in their eyes like Lester in the other dream. (Blue eyes, deeply shaded.) We got into a room—I don't remember whether my husband was with me—and I sat down on the floor, resting my head on the couch. Lester was leaning against me and making love to me. All of a sudden, an elderly gentleman came in from the other room and invited me to dance. We went to the other room where we saw many people in various stages of undressing. I started to giggle because the man whisked me off my feet and started a sort of jumping dance. I was jumping with him, and I saw my-self aloft in his arms, wiggling my legs, keeping time to the music. I enjoyed it tremendously. Woke up with pains in my legs and back."*

We see the patient in a sexual situation first with her son-in-law, later with a stranger. She is in menopause and suffers from various physical discomforts connected with this period. But she has not given up the idea that she should enjoy life, others are doing it (a party in every room). One of the reasons is that throughout her life she remained sexually frustrated. Now, a short time before it is "too late," she wants to take a "last fling" at life. Unfortunately, she has to pay for it with pain and discomfort, which not only remind her that her youth has passed but also offer her an opportunity to atone for her selfish tendencies.

In both dreams the repetitive pattern signifies frustration. The frequent changes may allude directly to the patient's "change of life."

PELVIC PAIN

RECTAL PAIN

A woman patient has been suffering from constipation from childhood. Her father used to give her enemas. She dreamed:

[315] *"I was having intercourse with a guy. I had pain in my rectum while having intercourse. Then I wanted to see why I had the pain and discovered that the man was using my rectum. His organ was funnel-shaped like latex blown up. I had an orgasm and awoke in pain."*

Here the pain masks her orgasm. It is remarkable that the patient, who incidentally suffers from hemorrhoids, experiences her orgasm through manipulations at her rectum, the region conditioned for this type of reaction by the childhood experiences with her father.

Her father was pathologically bowel conscious. He constantly was after his children, demanding to know whether they had proper elimination and gave them enemas at the slightest provocation. This rectal relationship to the patient's father before early puberty, gradually developed into a latent sexual relationship. Her anal zone became neurotically organized, and it might have been this condition which fostered the development of her hemorrhoids.

I should like to point out in this case the connection between orgasm, pain, and the infantile sexual experiences.

If the patient tells us about an "indefinite" pain, dreams of this type help us to uncover the specific etiology of the pain.

VAGINAL PAIN

A dream of the patient, mentioned on page 308, follows: [316] *"I was somewhere in bed with some woman. We touched each other's genitals. Nothing pleasant happened, however. No orgasm. I woke up and had a terrific pain in the vagina."*

Here we have a pain connected with a homosexual fantasy. It is quite possible (and probable) that the physical condition was the primary one; that there was some sensation of pain which caused the patient to awaken, and that in the process of awakening she produced the dream. But what interests us here is the specific concept connected with the sensation, for this shows that there is a link between the two.

ANNULMENT OF PAIN

Sometimes the dream brings a cheerful annulment of pain, and in such cases its wish-fulfillment character can be easily observed. One of my patients who suffered from neuralgia of the radial nerve dreamed that [317] *he screwed off his diseased arm, thus getting rid of the torturing pain.* Another means of removing unpleasant physical conditions is that of "projection." The dreamer behaves as though someone else —not he—suffered the discomfort. Frankl-Hochwart dreamed [318] *about having to pull a soldier's tooth,* and awoke with a toothache. Another time he dreamed [319] *of an ileus operation he had to perform* and awoke with abdominal pains. (Cf. also dream 304 on p. 316.)

The dream can also project bodily discomfort to other parts of the same body. The following dream reported by Freud may serve as an example: A woman patient suffering from toothache dreamed [320] about a *"Mr. Carl Mayer, who complained about headaches."*

SENSORY ORGANS

Eisinger and Schilder proved that *vestibular disturbances* often produce dreams dealing with many little colorful figures such as may be seen in the dreams and hallucinations in cases of delirium tremens.

In the chapter on Dreams of Psychotics (page 464) a case is presented where the *function of seeing* was sacrificed (repressed) by the patient because it was associated with antimoral and antisocial tendencies. An interesting dream is quoted in this connection (q.v.).

It has long been known to psychiatry that hysterical blindness and deafness are due not to an *inability* but to an unconscious refusal of, or resistance to, the act in question, as a defensive measure designed to ward off tabooed cravings.

SLEEP AND DREAM

We are such stuff
As dreams are made on, and our little
life
Is rounded with a sleep.
W. SHAKESPEARE

Sleep is a function of vital importance. It is based upon the inner biological necessity to intercalate periods of pause into our psychophysical existence. Sleep is by no means a passive state; it is the result of an inner central action based upon the wish to sleep (Liebault, Stekel). It is an action in which certain afferent and efferent stimuli are blocked, the central, cerebral irritability is decreased; and consciousness, and with it the contact with the external world, is to a high degree dissolved. The speed of all animal processes is definitely slackened by the functions of the vegetative nervous system, the hormones, and the elements of general decomposition. The restitution of the consumed matter (anabolism) takes place during sleep. But science is still far from a full understanding of this phenomenon.

Freud thought sleep was a psychobiological phenomenon. In his *Interpretation of Dreams* and in his *Introductory Lectures on Psychoanalysis,* he repeatedly stressed the importance of the wish to sleep and defended it as a wish to withdraw from the contact with the outside world.

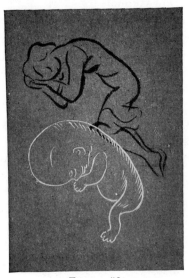

FIGURE 59

According to Freud, sleep is, to a certain extent, an imitation of our fetal existence (see Fig. 59). Since we cannot endure uninterruptedly our relationship to the world, we withdraw from time to time into the primordial state, into an existence similar to that of our intra-uterine period. We create for ourselves an environment of warmth, darkness, and the absence of stimuli. Some of us curl up and assume a position resembling that of an embryo. Freud says that it looks as if the world could lay claim to only two-thirds of us "for one-third of our existence we are yet unborn. Every rising in the morning is thus like a new birth."

Economo, who first gave us insight into the character of lethargic encephalitis, discovered the center in our brain which regulates our sleep. He located it in the rear wall of the third ventricle, in that part of our brain which is phylogenetically one of the oldest.

Sleep is hence older than being awake, and it may be that the philosophers are also right when they state that death is older than life, that our individual life is, so to speak, just an episodic, temporary disturbance of our state of death, the return to which we attempt as long as we live.

The depth of sleep varies. From the moment of falling asleep, in gradual progression, deeper and deeper centers are affected. Sleep proceeds from the higher brain centers to the lower; the lowest centers are never affected, however. It is these layers which are phylogenetically the oldest, and, as stated above, responsible for the inner regulation of sleep.

FIGURE 60

SELENE AND ENDYMION

Roman Sarcophagus from the Second Century, A. D. Courtesy of the Metropolitan Museum of Art, New York.

The bas relief reproduces a scene where the shepherd, Endymion, lover of Selene, goddess of the moon, rests his head on the lap of Somnus, god of sleep and dreams.

Some observers, e.g., Nottenius, maintain that deep sleep is dreamless. Loomis, Harvey, and Hobart confirm this by their investigations. According to them, dreams are associated with the B state of sleep (cf. page 36).

However, all data on the dream-sleep relations are dependent to a large degree on subjective contributions. Either the dreamer observes himself, as Freud did, or research is done by means of a questionnaire. Both methods are highly unreliable.

Sometimes the dream content is dependent on the *position we assume while falling asleep or while asleep*. Adler sees in the sleeping position signs of the patient's general attitude toward life. According to him, discouraged people curl up; people who like isolation cover themselves entirely with the blankets; optimists sleep on their backs.

The sleeping position in turn is often influenced by certain pathological conditions. People suffering from cerebellar disturbances, for example, sleep mostly on the side of the organic process. Also, patients suffering from permanent motor irritation have their distinctive positions (Goldstein).

Bertram D. Lewin has an interesting hypothesis about the development of the dream. He theorizes that sleep, basically, derives from oral gratification. When the infant falls asleep after having been nursed, its sleep is probably dreamless. Lewin speaks of a "blank dream," and believes that the only factor operating in this phase is an after-image of the breast, which persists. Lewin considers this image of the (flattened) breast as the "dream screen" upon which later desires, wishes, and physical reactions are projected as the infant's mind develops. The ego then participates more and more in dream processes, and all the daytime activities color the contents of the dream.

(Q) "What evidence is there in proof of your statement that there is no thought or dream production in the state of sleep?"

(A) I did not maintain that. I said that we have *no proof* that we think or dream while we are asleep. We have proof, however, that we have dreams in the process of awakening. I refer to the body stimulus dreams I have previously quoted (page 26).

I think that the burden of proof lies with those who make a statement. Some workers, even Freud himself, believed that we dream all through the night. I am of the opinion that a proof to this effect has as yet not been delivered. Berger, the inventor of the electro-encephalogram, made some studies on this subject. But brain activity is not identical with thought activity.

The recently discovered "kappa" waves which are observed whenever the individual concentrates, such as is the case, e.g., in solving mathematical problems, do not show during the sleep.

SLEEP DISTURBANCES

Disturbances of the biological function of sleep are caused not only by somatic disfunctions mentioned on page 70, but also by the disturbances of affect homeostasis.

HYPERSOMNIA

The abnormal desire to sleep may be a consequence of organic brain lesion which affects the sleep-regulating centers (narcolepsy), or it may have a purely psychic origin. It is the latter type which arouses our interest.

People who have a strong desire to sleep and to indulge in dreams are in the main not sufficiently satisfied with their life and attempt to escape from the emptiness of their daily existence into the realm of dreams.

In tense and depressive states, sleep, if at all available, represents a welcome haven of refuge and withdrawal from the tasks of life for which the patient feels inadequate. Dreams produced in awakening from such "autotherapeutic" states of sleep are of great psychiatric value.

INSOMNIA

Our flow of energy cannot be maintained constantly on the same level. After being used up, the physical sources of energy must be renewed periodically. If there is an excessive drainage of energy, *fatigue,* a precursor of sleep, sets in.

Fatigue initiates a number of physio-psychological reactions which can be considered as *withdrawal phenomena.* Rest and relaxation come as a result of this withdrawal and bring about a cessation of drainage, and, by inducing sleep, help the body to recuperate. Psychodynamically speaking, fatigue is an orderly retreat of the ego from situations which it cannot master because of the reduced energy available.

If the organism functions normally, recuperation from fatigue is possible by (a) rest and (b) sleep, the first as a preliminary stage of the second. In sleep the adaptive contacts with the outside world are withdrawn; the muscle tone, which always signifies readiness for action, is reduced; and the cortical functions are greatly inhibited. Ferenczi spoke of the "spinal soul" which returns to the individual in such states.

On the basis of his dream research, Freud spoke of a "will to sleep" which can be impeded by powerful emotions such as unfulfilled wishes and other "unfinished business" of our emotional household. Insomnia is caused by an unconscious will to stay awake and alert. (The German word *"wachen"* means "to be awake," but *"Wache"* means "guard.") In addition, insomnia is also caused by the individual's failure to withdraw interest in the outside world.

A person suffering from insomnia is unable in most cases to identify the real causes of his undesirable hyper-alertness. Here, dream analysis can make an important contribution toward an understanding and cure of insomnia.

The dream, however, may be at times responsible for insomnia. There are people who cannot fall asleep because they are afraid that their dreams may put them into a more or less disagreeable state of mind by causing them, e.g., to commit sins against which they have been successfully fighting during the day.

Thus, a man who has repeatedly had dreams of the death of his wife (wish-fulfillment!) may be afraid lest dreams of this kind reappear and charge his conscience with feelings of guilt. A woman who is repressing her sexual desires successfully may be afraid of dreams in which sex is allowed free expression.

Since sleep is based not only upon the blocking of the sensory conduction in the brain stem, but also upon the extinction of consciousness as a function of the cortex, factors which prevent the full dissolution of consciousness must be capable of preventing or disturbing sleep. Such factors include exciting fantasies, tormenting worries, and dreams. The understanding of this part of the brain function may afford us a valuable means of combatting insomnia.

An elderly unmarried woman, suffering from insomnia, reports: "I was very sleepy but I was afraid to fall asleep because when I dozed off I saw [321] *a pair of arms embracing me. I cried, 'No, no!'* "

From this dream we learn that the cause of our patient's sleep disturbance is her inner struggle against unwelcome erotic wishes seeping into her dreams.

SOMNAMBULISM

The overly-strong antimoral or antisocial impulses in the dreamer may turn the *dream thought* into *dream action* (somnambulism). Thought, according to Freud, is action executed with minute energy quantities. Because of an increased pressure of affects, or because the defenses in the ego are defective, the hidden trends of the dream may find their outward expression by way of the motor apparatus. Continued sleep prevents these tabooed impulses from becoming conscious, while, on the other hand, dream censorship renders actions into symbolic equivalents or cuts them to empty gestures. (See also Fig. 3 on p. 26.)

A somnambulic performance is, therefore, not a dream, but a dramatization of a dream, and, insofar as it can be reconstructed, it is amenable to analytic interpretation (Sadger, Stekel, Gutheil, and others).

Analytical experience teaches that in acts of somnambulism it is the dreamer's repressed antimoral and antisocial ego that drives the sleeper out of bed. In his actions he is directed by uncontrolled desires which are now realized although, in most cases, only in rudimentary form.

In many cases the sleepwalker performs a pantomime of

an incestuous act, but other tabooed tendencies can also be detected. A patient who had strong criminal impulses against his brother used to get up at night and walk toward his brother's bed where he stood helplessly clenching his fists as if he wished to choke someone. The patient whose dreams were reported on page 291, and whose main emotion was proved to be hatred against his brother, used to grind his teeth in his dreams. This habit may be related to his repressed hatred.

Here is a dream in which we see the patient's inclination to jealousy and his hatred reaction:

[322] *"Bobby and I were teaching Hedy how to ski. He beat me to the job."*

In the morning, the patient was awakened by a friend calling for him. According to the statement of this friend, the patient's right hand was stretched out, his fists were clenched, and his face expressed extreme hatred. There is no doubt that the patient's jealousy and vindictiveness were enacted dramatically in this way.

Another patient often used to leave his bed at night while in a state of somnambulism, walk toward his mother's bedroom and turn the lights on. The lights would cause him to awaken. Analysis of dreams leading to somnambulism, as well as analysis of other dreams, revealed the patient's unconscious suspicion that his mother, a widow, had relations with a strange man at night. Therefore, the patient, jealously guarding his mother's conduct, would get up and "make sure" that nothing undesirable happened in mother's bedroom.

Here are two of the dreams which led to his somnambulic actions:

[323] *"My employer gets into my room through the window. In order to receive him I have at least to put on my pajamas. (I sleep in the nude in the summer.) I turn the light on, awaken, and see that nobody is in the room. Then I go back to bed."*

[324] *"I have the feeling that someone—an enemy—has*

come to our apartment. I turn the light on and awaken."

Another patient, who, in his neurosis, was repressing homosexual impulses, dreamed:

[325] *"Somebody puts a snake into my bed. I try to kick it out of my bed, so I kick the quilt off. Then I awaken with the feeling that the snake is still in my bed. I put the quilt on the bed again, and realize at last that all that was a dream."*

NIGHTMARES

In children, nightmares (*pavor nocturnus*) are precipitated by disturbances of the respiratory or the digestive apparatus and by psychic overstimulation. The children may perspire during their frightful experience, but as a rule they do not awaken fully. When placed in bed again after being soothed, they usually fall quickly into untroubled sleep and have an amnesia for the experience when they arise in the morning. The material of their dreams can be presumed from their reactions rather than collected from their verbal communications. It is derived from fairy tales and frightening stories about animals. A physician should be consulted when a child has nightmares, for adenoids are often in the background of a respiratory impediment.

Where no organic cause can be found, psychological factors must be assumed. Associating sounds of the parents' sexual relations with animal threats may underly the anxiety, particularly when the sounds are grunts or expressions of pain.

The nightmares of grownups are, however, correlated to the instinctual pressures.[1] The repressed sexual motives (often incestuous) are powerful propellants. A very instructive analysis of nightmares can be found in Jones' book on *The Nightmare*.[2]

[1] "Nightmare" means "Alb*druck*" in German. The suffix "mare," according to Jones, comes from the Anglo-Saxon verb "merran," which means "a crusher."

[2] *The Nightmare* by Ernest Jones, Liveright Publishing Corporation, New York, 1951.

Respiratory System

The exchange of gases taking place in respiration represents one of the fundamental functions of the organism. Life begins and ends with it. Any obstruction in the air passages causes an immediate reaction of anxiety, the endopsychic perception of the threat to life. Very sensitive and efficient mechanisms (cough reflex, sneezing reflex, etc.) guard the respiratory airways from intrusion by foreign bodies. The ancients were so impressed with the importance of respiration for all processes of life that they even suspected that the seat of the soul was the diaphragm, which, in Greek, means Phren (Φρήν). We find this word in "phrenology" and in "schizophrenia."

In investigating respiratory neuroses, dreams serve a double task. First, they initiate awakening whenever the air passages become obstructed during sleep; second, they render some of the unconscious mechanisms underlying respiratory neuroses accessible to investigation.

Mucus in the Throat

A married woman patient, aged forty-two, suffered from nervous laryngeal symptoms. She dreamed:

[326] *"I am in a dance hall. I am wearing a black silk mourning dress. A man asks me to marry him. Then another man asks the same. Finally, my future son-in-law wishes me to marry him. I say, 'Why, you could be my son.' To which he replies, 'All the better.' . . . Then I see a horse which is shedding its skin repeatedly. Somebody says, 'That is very good, for the older it is the more suitable it becomes for horse races.' While talking I notice that the horse has a lasso around its neck which is being tightened by somebody I don't see. I noticed the horse's eyes popping out as if in panic; whereupon I scream and awake with heart palpitations and a strong coughing attack."*

We have to deal here with a so-called "irritative dream"

("*Körperreiz-Traum*"). We may suppose from experience that it was the accumulated mucus in the patient's throat that caused her dyspnea, portrayed in the dream by the scene of the choked horse. The patient's most disturbing symptom, which made her seek treatment, was a permanent mucus irritation in her throat which forced her to expectorate very frequently. Larynx specialists declared the patient "organically healthy."

We do not yet learn anything about the latent dream content. In the strangulation scene we see a part of the dream work, that is, the process of symbolization. The choked horse whose feelings the dreamer experiences so clearly is, according to the above, a picture of herself. As we know, the cause of symbolization is the fact that for several reasons the events to be expressed are painful to the dreamer. Their expression takes place by symbolization.

The above dream may be divided into two parts, which we may call: (A) "the proposal of marriage," and (B) "the choked horse."

In part A, the dreamer is the main person; in part B, the horse is the main figure; but, as we stated before, both dream figures are undoubtedly identical. In part A, several men propose to the *married* patient. Nonsense? There is no nonsense in a dream! What appears as nonsense is the carrier of the main accent in the dream plot. The patient who is in a mourning dress while in a dance hall, undoubtedly sees herself as a widow. (In looking over other dreams of the patient, her death wish against her husband becomes still more evident.) We may analyze this painful thought of the dreamer in the following way: "I wish my husband to die in order that I may plunge into life (dance hall) again and obtain new, better, marital chances." The patient's marriage is unhappy; her sexual relations are unsatisfactory. It is also of importance to know that the patient's husband is eight years younger than she.

The three men who are proposing to the patient in her

dream do not enter the show with equal distinctness. While the picture of the first two men quickly disappears, the figure of the patient's son-in-law keeps its full lucidity to the end. The three men as dream symbols follow the principle of "depicting the general by the special" (see page 160). Instead of saying in the dream, "three men," we may refer to the more general term "men." We then read the sentence: "Men are proposing to me."

We should also take into consideration the change of persons. Again we notice a part of the "dream work" which greatly resembles color printing. Like the three individual colors in the three-color print, the three individual men in the dream portray the same figure in the course of a growing distinctness. More and more clearly the proposer in the dream becomes the patient's son-in-law.

A new alliance would have been possible by the death of the patient's husband, but was rejected by the patient's ethics. This reaction was all the more intensified when, in addition to that, the new suitor was the future husband of the patient's daughter.

The second tabooed wish expressed in this dream (as its latent content) is the patient's sexual desire for her daughter's fiancé. We must theorize that an unconscious jealousy between mother and daughter exists. We let the patient associate at this point at will, and learn that the mother really is jealous of her daughter and, therefore, is charged with a deep feeling of guilt. We learn by exploration that the patient has had her daughter die in her dreams repeatedly. Her conscious reaction is one of a mother who is compensating her feeling of guilt with reference to her daughter by an attitude of "overprotection." Contours of the patient's unconscious life plan become obvious. In order to make a better choice in matters of love she moves both obstacles, husband and daughter, out of her way.

We proceed now to a discussion of the mother-son relationship. Here, too, we first grant the patient full freedom of association and omit no detail. We succeed in deriving the information that the patient adores her son and suffers because the young man does not associate enough with women. (He has a "mother fixation.") As an "enlightened" mother she had already thought of introducing him to a girl for sexual purposes in order to "strengthen his virility." Our supposition thus proves to be correct. There is a real mutual fixation between mother and son.

The patient then reports that she clung passionately to her father, while she adopted a rather cool attitude toward her mother. She had known her mother as a sick woman, always coughing. Her mother died of tuberculosis when she was nineteen years old. The patient took care of her mother, giving herself up completely to her. We think here of the throat symptoms of our patient. This fact leads us to wonder whether the patient herself had not feared the possibility of contracting laryngeal tuberculosis, and then, whether in her symptoms there was any self-punishing identification with her mother's disease.

In the course of the discussion the patient becomes conscious and makes us aware of the fact that in attending her ill mother she often wished her mother's suffering would be ended by death. After the mother died, the patient thought fleetingly that she too might die of tuberculosis of the throat as God's punishment for her death wishes.

We could have supposed the effectiveness of the talion if the symptom had appeared a short time after the mother's death. We could not, however, prove this in the present case. At the time of treatment the symptoms had continued for barely a year. They appeared three months after the engagement of her daughter.

Summarizing, we may say that our patient's father fixation was later changed into a son fixation, owing to a known psychic mechanism. The son-in-law as a son image offered an attainable goal for her repressed incestuous desires and renewed the patient's old conflicts.

Now we proceed to the discussion of part B of the dream which we have entitled "the choked horse." As stated before, the horse symbolizes the dreamer herself. We may say more precisely that it represents the dreamer's animal self, and think of centaurs, unicorns, the Sphinx, and other symbols of the dualistic human nature. The horse is shedding its skin in the dream. An inquiry reveals that a short time before, for cosmetic reasons, the patient submitted to a skin-peeling cure with violet rays.

Part A as well as part B deals with the age problem. The repetition of a motive proves its importance (see page 263). In part B the dreamer advocates the peculiar idea that the older one is, the more valuable he becomes ("the older it is the more suitable it becomes for horse races"). The "wish is father to the thought." While testing her physical values and lulling herself into all kinds of selfish plans she is struck by her Lord's punishment ("somebody whom I don't see"). She sees in the dream, in the picture of the choked horse, her mother dying under dyspnea, and, besides, she sees the ghastly image of her own death as a punishment for her death wishes against so many relatives. In experiencing this she becomes panicky, tears to shreds the thread of her dream, and saves herself from destruction by awakening suddenly.

The dream has probably come into existence because of a physical irritation (mucus in the throat). The stimulus has led to awakening, and the dream has occurred within the awakening process.

As we know, the dream in its original state consists of entangled "thought-feelings," in which there is no succession of events, but only co-existence. It is the *recollection* of the dreamed events that first enables one to arrange the "manifest dream content" according to the laws of logic, a process in which, as we know, various resistances of recollection still need to be overcome. Therefore, both parts of the dream are to be considered as a psychological unity.

The dream succeeding the physical irritation is an independent formation containing the patient's specific conflicts as its "latent content." The patient wishes her relatives to die in order that she may become independent and may be compensated for her lost opportunities in life. However, as a morally firm person she represses these wishes. At the same time she is afraid of God's punishment. In her symptom, which means recollection and warning equally, she anticipates this fate by self-punishment.

BRONCHIAL ASTHMA

Bronchial asthma is a syndrome occurring in persons with the constitutional disposition called by some authors "exudative diathesis." There is a reciprocal influence of respiration and psyche. Even the normal individual's respiratory curve shows distinct fluctuations which correspond to the emotional tensions experienced during the day. The everyday language expresses this clearly. We say, e.g., "he sighed with relief," "his breath stopped," etc. Individuals endowed by nature with an exudative diathesis react more quickly and more severely to various emotional fluctuations, particularly those produced by deep-seated neurotic conflicts.

The outstanding physical features in bronchial asthma are (a) *hypersecretion* and (b) *spasms* in the circulatory bronchial musculature. Patients complain of a pressure on the chest which they cannot "breathe off." This pressure is temporarily alleviated by the attack; it has often the distinct character of a narrowing of the chest and is mostly connected with anxiety. (Compare the Latin *angustia* = narrowness; the German *"Enge"* and *"Angst,"* and the English "anxiety.")

Bronchial asthma is expressed in dreams as obstruction of air passages, in scenes and symbols depicting the patient's dyspneic states, or in dreams showing the general manifestation of anxiety.

A patient suffering from asthma dreamed [327] *"of being in a deep shaft of a garden well, the walls of which were made of smooth metal. His attempts to get out were in vain."*

The "smooth metal" of the walls which makes his coming out impossible betrays his pessimistic outlook. The "deep shaft" symbolizes the respiratory difficulty.

Another dream portraying the patient's dyspnea is the following:

[328] *The patient is sitting on the bed of a deep body of water.*

Among asthmatic patients, Alexander found many water dreams. When investigating the psychological background of these dreams, the Alexander school found in cases of bronchial asthma a preponderance of intrauterine fantasies as an infantile wish to possess mother. Bronchial asthma represents "a cry for the mother," for the security she offers to the child. The patients of this type consider anyone who shares this love as a hated rival.

Franz Alexander examined close to 6,000 dreams of 45 patients and found among them: (1) *intrauterine fantasies* (identification with the fetus); and (2) depictions of *pregnancy, abortion, and birth* (the patient identifies with his pregnant mother). The main conflicts of the patients were the desire to be liberated from the mother and/or the desire to completely regress into the mother.

I can contribute an example of this type from my own collection. The dreamer is a fifty-five-year-old woman.

[329] *"I dreamed that I was so short of breath that I woke up with violent pains in my chest. I fell asleep again and dreamed of having a baby. The baby looked as Helen looked when she was a year old. In the dream I was surprised that I could have a baby because of my age."*

The respiratory congestion and the subsequent expulsion of mucus intimate the state of pregnancy and the expulsion of the child.

However, dreams of asthmatic patients also contain pictures of the patient's bad conscience which is so closely connected with this disease (the "burden on the chest"). The superego reaction may be due to unconscious criminality.

A woman dreamed every night of her child. At the time of the treatment she was trying to obtain a divorce from her husband. Closer investigation revealed that she was constantly repressing death wishes against her child, who was an impediment to her divorce plans. Her main complaints were choking sensations, fear of staying alone with her child, fear of knives, etc. She admitted that she had had thoughts of choking her child when she was caressing it. In one of her oppressing dreams [330] *she saw her child pale and worn out. It folded its hands and implored, "My dear Ma, please come to me."*

As we see, her moral ego was awake at night and in her dreams dramatized her unconscious viciousness.

From other dreams by the same patient we can easily discover the background of the asthmatic anxiety. One of them runs as follows:

[331] *"I killed an animal in the forest."* (This is a confession of her criminality.) *"When I saw the gamekeeper* (moral authority, God, death, and, in connection with the treatment, the doctor), *I was afraid of him* (anxiety reaction). *I quickly skinned the animal and wanted to bury the body but could not dig a trench so fast* (desire to conceal her criminal thoughts). *Then it struck me that I could turn the skin inside out and use the other side. I did that and put on my coat, a beautiful ermine. The gamekeeper did not notice anything."*

In her dream she is fighting against her animal-like instincts. She wants to play the part of an attentive mother (anagogic tendency). Her asthmatic attacks are the expressions of the failure to suppress her criminality.

Another patient of the same type dreams [332] *of fighting against his doctor because the latter wants to hang him.* (Criminal ideas responsible for the choking sensations.)

Stekel also pointed out that the asthmatic spells often symbolize *sexual acts* (masturbation equivalents, intercourse fantasies—"burden on the chest," etc.). The patient may have the feeling that "something is in his throat that must come out," something which may be mucus or an imaginary object.

The "foreign-body sensation" in asthma resembles the phenomenon called "globus hystericus." Some analysts have a fixed interpretation for the globe symptom. It is supposed to represent a "displacement from below upward," the "foreign body" being the phallus. This is true in many cases. It seems, however, of even greater importance to realize that many hysterical patients experience the globus sensation whenever they want to suppress (swallow) a bad thought. An idea obstructs their mind, and they convert this abstract experience into the concrete symptom of throat obstruction. The "bad thought" can be any antimoral or antisocial idea; very often it is the impulse to choke a person.

A patient who had an ambivalent attitude toward her older sister Joan, expressed her asthmatic reactions in her dream as follows:

[333] *"I was in the bath tub and had a strong feeling that I would be strangled by Joan. (I had the feeling of her presence there). I had a bathrobe on and had a Turkish towel over my head, which was slowly suffocating me. I removed it from the area of my nose and mouth with great difficulty —and could vaguely see Joan waiting at the other end of the tub for my passing out. Since I was not dying she seemed to be waiting for the moment when I would. She did not speak, or touch me, but I felt her thoughts. It was like being under her spell.*

"As I was gasping and choking, I bent over the ledge of the tub to help myself. I sensed that Joan was over me and as I was able to breathe in some air, she beat me on the small of my back in fury and frustration.

"I finally awoke with terrific pains in the back."

Joan had suffered from a goiter in her youth and often could not sleep because of respiratory distress. She was operated on and her condition improved. One of the neurotic symptoms in our patient was the feeling that her throat was obstructed and that she might suffocate.

Analysis proved that she identified herself with her sister as self-punishment for the death wishes she had toward her sister when the latter was gasping for air at night and when she later had to undergo a dangerous operation. The self-punishment tendency is clearly reproduced in the scene of being beaten by the sister. (For the psychodynamics of neurotic pain reactions see page 308.)

Important is the passage where the patient admits that she feels her sister's thought (identification). This part of the dream portrays not only the fact that Joan's thoughts in reality are the patient's own, but also her homosexual dependency on her sister, which the patient verified. Joan was not only the object of her rivalry but also that of her admiration. She would have been very happy if her attractive sister had paid more attention to her, instead of being aloof, narcissistic, and engrossed in her own personal problems.

The following dream proves this point:

[334] *"Joan and I were sitting on a bed looking out of the window. Some girl passed by. I looked at her because I knew that she and Joan had had an affair.[1] As she was passing, her buttocks seemed to grow larger and squarer.[2] I looked at Joan in a questioning way and she assured me that although she had had an affair with that girl, she would never look at anyone else again but me."*

The masochistic trend noticeable throughout dream 333 refers to these two factors: sexual dependency and self-punishment.

The head towel may also have some relation to the patient's frequent attacks of headache, a symptom which was found to have expressed the patient's repressed hostility toward her sister. (For more about headache see page 310.)

---

[1] In reality, the patient and her *aunt,* whose name, incidentally, also was Joan, had a homosexual affair when the patient was an adolescent.

[2] Association to her aunt.

STAMMERING

Stammerers also have their particular symbols. In their dreams we see symbols indicating the pressure of their repressed impulses (aggression) or symbols of a general inhibition as characteristics of stammering. The patients see themselves as having gone in the wrong direction, as having slipped upon an icy pavement (impulses). Or they see themselves in all kinds of difficulties: they can not move their feet; they have to climb over fences and jump over trenches; they see people preventing others from traversing certain streets; they see crowds gathering about narrow exits; their breathing stops; their mouth is stuffed (inhibition).

One of my patients, a stammerer, repeatedly saw in his dreams people speaking or dogs barking, without any auditory perception. (It is not certain, however, whether these pictures are typical.)

Another stammerer represented his disturbances by the picture of a dog watching the exit of his house. The dog finally falls to pieces like a load of bricks. His speech difficulties also consisted of having his words "falling to pieces." Thus he pronounced the word "crowd," for instance, as "cr-cr-cr-cr-cr-cr-crowd." The dog watching the exit of his house portrays the inhibiting tendencies. The exit is a symbol of the mouth. Great emotional tension as well as strong inhibitions led in this case to an explosive manner of speaking, similar, in a way, to the staccato explosions of gasoline in an internal-combustion engine. These explosions were the *safe* form into which the dangerous total explosion of ignited gasoline were cut.

Dreams in which stammerers speak are important because they may contain the conditions under which the patient's speech is not disturbed by stammering.

A dream of a stutterer:

[335] *"I am sailing on a boat through a channel, moving straight forward. There are many branches of the channel*

right and left. They are all obstructed. Therefore I am sailing very fast."

Association: boats going through the Panama Canal have to be stopped in their course and to be lifted. In this dream we see the patient's speech represented by sailing. He is avoiding inter-current thoughts (branches) and tries to speak as quickly as possible (a very common ambition of stammerers who attempt to overcome the supposed speech difficulties by speaking quickly.) The patient's association offers a very instructive picture of the disturbance of speaking: the boat has to interrupt its course and has to be lifted on to a higher level. That is, indeed, what the patient does symbolically, when stammering: he interrupts his speech and elevates his thoughts to a higher level, leaving all the oppressing (painful) thoughts below.

One of my patient's dreamed:

[336] *"I was on a horse going over some jumps. The first jumps were ordinary fences with wings, the next jumps were single uprights. The horse had been jumping the ordinary fences well; he also jumped the upright, but not so well. I had an impression that there was an audience."* (Addition: *"There was a certain danger for the horse."*)

In this dream the patient's jumping over fences pictures his stammering ("there was an audience"). The "uprights" symbolize his complexes, which cause him difficulties (the horse jumps them "not so well") which he cannot overcome so easily. Closer examination proved that these complexes were connected with the patient's criminal impulses against his father ("a danger for the horse").

Very often we also find among stammerers, dreams expressing the patient's exaggerated, pathological ambition. *Many stutterers are frustrated orators.* Some have a fantasy of being popular leaders with a tremendous following. Such fantasies, of course, clash with reality. The consequence is that they cannot be big orators—in fact they can not speak coherently. And yet, some of them, if they are given the opportunity to address crowds, particularly if an emotionally exciting subject is to be discussed, are impressive speakers.

All stammerers and people with functional inhibitions suffer from an undue influx of energy, a much greater influx than they can consume. One can see the congestion in their faces, a tremendous concentration of force takes place in their unconscious and it is discharged in small quantities.

Or we find the images of the impulse. All these people have powerful passionate impulses which they have blocked. They harbor aggressive thoughts. You will find in the dreams pictures of hurricanes, and other expressions of abnormally strong impulses. Then, of course, you may find pictures of the symptom itself. The patient may see other people or himself yelling, shouting, cursing. One of the patients treated for stammering harbored in his mind a curse against his father. He started to stutter in front of his father, later he stuttered only in front of his doctor or in front of people of authority. The cause of his speech disturbance was the undischarged curse. What he wanted to say was, "I wish you were dead."

CIRCULATORY SYSTEM

The mutual relations between heart and emotion are well known. Heart palpitations as an expression of emotional excitation, and particularly of anxiety, have led some observers (Ludwig Braun) to the belief that the heart is the specific "organ of anxiety." Guilt feelings, erotic stimulation, love and hate—they all find expression in the rhythm of our heart beat. But disturbed heart rhythms (extrasystoles) also can color the contents of the dream. In the dream we find either the images of the quickening of the heart beat in scenes representing themes of speeding, or expressions of anxiety which normally accompany the change of rhythm.

Braun pointed out that dreams are sometimes the earliest prodromes of *heart diseases,* and mentioned the following very instructive dream of one of his patients:

[337] *"He saw himself followed by someone in a strange country. This someone resembled him to the last detail, was a double of himself."*

According to Braun, this dream contains a wish-fulfillment. The patient who considers himself critically ill, and is right in thinking so, will continue living, which is guaranteed by the doubling of his person.

It is interesting to note that in these serious disturbances of the heart, which originate in grave *anatomic lesions,* the fear of death creeping into the dream is combated by the mechanisms of annulment, projection, transitivism, etc., and is replaced by the cheerful fulfillment of the wish to continue to live.

The phenomenon of arterial *hypertension* was submitted to analytic investigation. It has been the consensus of opinion among the workers in this field that in hypertension a psychogenic component can be detected, and that the emotional factors involved are: passive, impotent rage, ineffective aggression, desire to get rid of the inner tension and inability to find an outlet for it. The lack of "alloplastic" discharge leads to introjection of aggression and to "autoplastic" expression on the level of the circulatory apparatus. Dreams which, as a rule, offer a powerful means of discharging accumulated aggression appear remarkably "tame."

VASOMOTOR DISTURBANCES

QUINCKE EDEMA

A twenty-five-year-old girl was in analysis because of migraine combined with a heart neurosis and psychogenic amenorrhea. In the course of the treatment she reported that from time to time she was suffering from swellings of her eyelids and her lips. The swellings disappeared in most cases spontaneously within five or six hours.

The patient reported about her angio-neurotic condition as follows:

"About four years ago I noticed this symptom when, on a Sunday morning, I was preparing to join a large group of friends on a hike. I was surprised about my condition, as I had hitherto never suffered from skin diseases. I looked into the mirror and I saw a considerable swelling of my lip, which caused me to cancel the appointment with my friends.

"The swellings occurred later again, mostly on Sunday mornings, rarely on weekdays (then after excitement) and showed a relation to migraine. I had my headache usually before or after the appearance of the swellings.

"At the time the symptom appeared, I was undergoing a severe depression. The cause of it was a disappointment in love which made me isolated and introverted. My fiancé had left me. I had too much time on my hands, particularly on Sundays. I hated men and withdrew whenever I had a chance to meet them. I also hated Sundays.

"When my disfiguring symptom appeared, I had an ambivalent feeling toward it; on the one hand, I was glad that I didn't have to be 'sociable'; on the other, I knew that a little diversion would help me and I was sore at my fate that condemned me to lonesomeness. . . ."

Once, during the session, we had the opportunity to discuss the patient's condition again, because she just had her edema. I got up from my seat and approached the patient (who was reclining on the couch). I asked her to shut her eyes, so that I could observe the exact location of the edema. However, the patient refused to close her eyes. I asked for the reason for this reaction and she replied with hesitation that she feared that I might kiss her. I asked her about the connection between kissing and eyes, and learned that the patient's fiancé had the habit of kissing her on her eyelids and on her lips, having discovered in the patient a strong sexual response to this type of approach. Interestingly, the patient was conditioned for this response by her father who often kissed her on her lips and eyelids.

These parts of her body were her erogenous zones.

On the night preceding the swelling the patient had a dream:

[338] *"I get mail. Many letters. I am looking for a particular letter but, to my chagrin, I don't find it."*

The patient associated with the letters a yellow letter which caught her attention. To "yellow" she associated "Autumn," and "death." She then added: "After my love affair was over I wrote a poem called "Burial." The poem, written in the patient's native tongue (Russian), runs as follows (in translation):

> "I'm burying today. Yet I don't cry
> And do not thrust myself upon the earthy mound;
> For 'tis no corpse this hill is hiding shy
> To feed the worms that dwell in humid ground.
> My dead is gliding to a groundless sea,
> The sea I carry in my inmost soul.
> It *swells* from rivers of my tears
> That once broke through the flood-gates of my *eyes.*
> I let him slide into the limpid water
> And strew fresh flowers upon its tranquil *face,*
> Flowers of mourning, I gathered in my heart.
> My *eyes are dry,* my *lips have ceased to tremble:*
> He left me, unmindful of my longing,
> Left me alone, in sorrow and despair.
> Now toll you fun'ral bells, bells of my anguished soul,
> And when the last tone's gone—I'll be alone."

The patient wrote this poem after her fiancé gave in to the pressure of his family and canceled their engagement. She was waiting a full year for him to change his mind and return to her. It was in vain. Then she decided to put him out of her mind.

Guided by her dream about letters, her analyst asked her whether she used to receive letters from her fiancé regularly. She confirmed this and added that now she realized that the dream letters had the shape he had always used. She preserved his letters and put them away wrapped in a paper on which she wrote, "Letters from a man I loved."

When the patient was told that, unconsciously, she was

still waiting for a letter from him, and for his return, she denied this vehemently at first. She stated that, on the contrary, she was always afraid of meeting him on the street. Some men she saw on the street gave her a shock and caused heart palpitation because they resembled her former lover.

But all these symptoms confirmed one fact: that her fiancé was still very much alive in her daydreams. She craved him and his kisses and defended herself against these unrealistic cravings. As a result, she experienced a symptom in which the excitement of anticipation caused a bulging and swelling of her erogenous zones, while the resistance to the anticipated pleasure caused all the negative manifestations, such as disfigurement, itching and functional impairment. We must also not forget the "archaic" level of this symptom which is the omnipresent incestuous wish.

The patient's unconscious desire to revive infantile incestuous experiences which took place at the erogenous zones supplied the matrix for the current conflict. By her ultimate disfigurement (occurring, incidentally, on Sundays, the only day when she could think of replacing her fiancé), the patient succeeded in maintaining a *pathological loyalty* to the estranged lover, thus helping to perpetuate her unrealistic daydream of a reunion.

The angio-neurotic condition disappeared under analysis and had not recurred two years after the treatment, when the patient was seen for the last time.

Gastro-Intestinal Disorders

In investigating psychosomatic conditions affecting the gastro-intestinal tract we often make the observation that the patient's conception of his body does not correspond to the established anatomic norms. Naïve and infantile, or even archaic ideas about the relative position of the organs may be encountered with the subsequent confused symptomatology.

One of the most interesting observations we make in some

cases of gastro-intestinal neuroses is that the patient unconsciously imagines that his digestive apparatus is a sort of a tube reaching from his mouth straight down to his anus. The upper opening, which we could call "stoma," comprises the entrances to both the gastro-intestinal and the respiratory apparatus, while the lower opening, the "cloaka," comprises the eliminative openings of both the ano-rectal and the genito-urinary tracts. It is a reflection of the embyronic entodermal structure, Fig. 61.

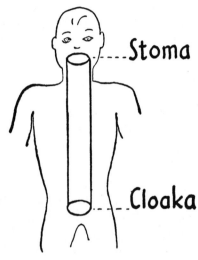

FIGURE 61

Shifts of cathexis along the imaginary tube are customary. They explain the somatization of pregnancy or of a sexual fantasy at the region of the throat or the expression of sexual disgust through the act of vomiting. As a reflex (vector), vomiting is designed to eliminate from the body substances which are harmful. It is anchored securely in our system by reactions of disgust which make us eject objects which are not useful for the building up of our body. If we vomit food on occasions when objects other than food are the cause of our disgust, then we can assume that we act toward food as though it were something else: "displacement from below upward." The concomitant shift of cathexis takes place along the imaginary internal tube.

Fear of the female organ or the idea that this organ may be endowed with teeth like a mouth (*vagina dentata*) is also based on a shift along the imaginary tube, this time from above downward. Some cases of impotence are based on this fear.

On the other hand, the desire to get rid of an unwanted pregnancy may be expressed by an uncontrollable vomiting (*hyperemesis*), as though this eliminative process of the gastro-intestinal system could affect the genital apparatus in a direct way.

The following dream projects the pregnancy idea upon the gastro-intestinal tract.

[339] *"I saw my sister Ethel. She had a big stomach as though she were pregnant. Her haircut was just as mine. I wake up with nausea and desire to throw up."*

The patient suffers from many phobias. One of them is that she might be forced to vomit in a public place. The connection in the dream between her sister's pregnancy and the patient's desire to vomit bespeaks the patient's identification with her sister. The patient is in her late forties and beyond the possibility of a pregnancy, but in her unconscious she sees herself young again and capable of being pregnant. Her symptom takes only one feature out of the fancied condition: the malaise, so often found in pregnancy. The suffering expresses the patient's need for self-punishment because of her repressed jealousy toward her sister.

Infantile pregnancy fantasies are responsible for such shifts of cathexis. We find among children particularly often the idea that pregnancy is the result of eating, with a subsequent appearance of a "big stomach." Children in whom feelings of sibling rivalry are awake, often watch their mother's emesis as a welcome opportunity for throwing off the baby.

There is also a tendency, particularly in hysterical patients, to consider the repressed thought material as swallowed food.

Reactions of globus character—in dreams or symptoms—may refer to the problem of incorporating acceptable or ejecting "indigestible" thoughts. Vomitus or defecation in such cases "cleanses" the psyche (symbolically) of all "impure" matter. Voluntary refusal of food, anorexia, food "fadism" and other syndromes may be based on such symbolic evaluations of the function of eating.

One of the infant's animistic forms of mastery over the outside world is that of incorporation. On this primitive level objects of the outside world are tested orally regarding their pleasure value. The pleasure-bearing objects are accepted and incorporated, while the unpleasant, and hence unwelcome, objects are rejected and spit out. In this process lies the basic pattern of assimilation of the acceptable and projection of the unacceptable.

In children this animistic way of thinking may be traumatized at an early stage of development. It then expresses itself in fantasies and *dreams of being eaten*. This represents the idea of being overwhelmed by the outside world; an "end-of-the-world" fantasy in childhood fashion. Kimmins reports several dreams of this type.

One of his patients, a nine-year-old-boy, produced an anxiety dream [340] in which *he was about to be eaten by the chief of cannibals. He "was just going to bite me when I woke up."*

Another of his little patients dreamed [340a] that *a tiger ate his mother, father, brother and him,* "and then I woke up and cried and said, 'It isn't true.' "

Pavlov's study on conditioned reflexes in dogs has given impetus to the closer investigation of mental influences upon the gastro-intestinal tract. In the history of a psychosomatic symptom, we find a stimulating experience leading to certain organic reactions; then we find associations which achieve the same effect by eliciting a chain reaction for which the organ has been conditioned by the original experience. An intestinal grip may cause a patient to suffer repeated diarrheas; while in this state, he may, by coincidence, experience an emotional rejection. A pattern may thus be set and he may show the tendency to respond to any other rejection with diarrheas.

Organic predisposition may play a part. One patient who suffered from the fear of a possible diarrhea when contemplating a date with a girl or a trip by train happened to have an enlarged sigmoid. The two conditions, *per se,* have nothing to do with each other, except that the anatomic anomaly lends itself well for the precipitation of a neurosis.

The close relations between the gastro-intestinal tract and the mind have been investigated more recently by men like Cannon, Cushing, and others. The role of the subcortex as the intermediary and of the autonomous nervous system as the conduction link of psychosomatic stimulation has been established. The psychology and metapsychology of the nutritional processes has been studied and elucidated in their symbolic meaning for the individual.

Anorexia, (pathological lack of appetite), *bulimia,* (pathologically increased appetite), and other food neuroses have been related to the individual's affect metabolism as a part of the general energy metabolism. The tissue changes in peptic ulcers, e.g., were found to have a definite psychogenic component which lies in an unresolved infantile conflict. The conflict is that of "dependency versus independence." While the conscious behavior in ulcer patients is independent, ambitious and aggressive, unconsciously these individuals have a great need for emotional support which they have either failed to obtain in their childhood or have received in over-abundance. In the first case, they crave what they have missed, in the second, they wish to perpetuate a protective pattern of their childhood. Rest cures (protection) and milk cures (mother influence) have often spectacular effects—and not only because of organic considerations.

In dreams of such patients, particularly those in which the

patient's relation to his mother is portrayed, we often find the characteristic motive of a frustrating mother.

Just as *eating* in the symbolic language may represent the wish to incorporate, to take possession of or to assimilate, the *elimination*, on the same level, represents the proud act of giving. Antisocial tendencies may affect either of these functions in the sense of a reversal. Eating then turns to anorexia or vomiting, while eliminating turns to constipation, drying out of secretions, and similar functional disorders. The period of toilet training offers many opportunities for the establishment or perpetuation of such reversal reactions.

The products of secretion (urine, feces) may easily become weapons of attack when sadistic and antisocial tendencies are dammed up in search for adequate expression. We then find enuresis (see page 367), diarrheas, colitis, spastic constipations, and the appearance of various neurotic pain phenomena.

We shall now take a look at a few dreams produced by patients suffering from gastro-intestinal disorders.

An instructive dream of a patient who suffered from a peptic ulcer is the following:

[341] "*I was at my mother's house. She had guests. They were eating. I participated. My parents talked confidentially. I resented this. They invited other people for the next day, but not me.*"

The patient's resentment and feeling of being slighted by his mother serves as a general expression of the patient's attitude toward life, for which the gastric symptom is an organic equivalent. (This patient's case is described on page 441.)

The following series of dreams belong to a twenty-one-year-old university student whose very neurotic parents were divorced when the patient was a small child. His mother was cold and undemonstrative; but, at the same time, irritable and given to spells of ill temper. His father was an obsessive-compulsive perfectionist who very often aroused the patient's impotent rage.

The immediate reason for the patient to seek treatment was a depression following a disappointment with his fiancée, Carol, who broke off their engagement.

[342] *"In this dream I was a father of a newly born child and in a way I was very happy about it, feeling a sort of wonder at having produced something. Margaret, my girlfriend, was the mother but she was not around. That was the queer part of the situation . . . we seemed to be living separately, yet as man and wife."*

The "separated" condition of the married couple reproduces the parental situation. The patient compensates here for his "caloric deficiency," the lack of warmth which his parents displayed toward him, by being a far better parent toward *his* child than his father had been toward him. His own comment on the dream is as follows:

"In trying to describe the feeling tone of this dream the best way to express it seems to be to say that I was proud to be married and to have a child. At the same time there was a strange feeling that Margaret should be separated from me. I kept thinking of her down at her house and feeling that it was silly that she should not be at my home with the baby."

The patient thus confirms our supposition that he finds his father especially ill-equipped to take care of a child and that he thinks a loving mother should be around to do the job.

As though this was not clear enough, the next dream pushes this topic further:

[343] *"I was at home and all my family were there. I can't make out whether I was preparing for a trip or whether I was taking the baby down to see Margaret. The action took place in a room in the northeast corner of our house, a room that was the scene of many battles between my parents in my childhood."*

The fusion between this dream-born "little family" (the

patient is unmarried) and his own family (parents and siblings) is thus established.

The next dream belongs to the same category:

[344] *"I was with Carol* (former fiancée). *We had a very friendly relationship and were sitting in a breakfast nook of her home* (which reminds me of the breakfast nook in our home). *I believe that we were drinking coffee.*

"Carol's son came in. The child was about eight or nine. I was very affectionate with the child and made a great deal of him, compliments and such."

The feelings of frustration were a frequent motive in the patient's dreams. Here are a few dreams of this type:

[345] *"I was driving home in my new Chevrolet with Margaret. We were returning from a party. We were holding hands and yet I felt that it was I who was making advances and that she was not responding."*

[346] *"My father called me a 'problem child.' When I asked him why, he said because I arrive at my meals late. I explained this to him but he wouldn't see my point. Then I started crying and beating my hands together, feeling terribly frustrated."*

[347] *"I was on a motor trip and was out of money. I felt miserable because I didn't believe my signature would be honored at a local bank.*

"Then the dream shifted to my home town. I was ordering traveler's checks and the teller, a woman, passed me some checks to sign. The checks seemed unusual in form and appearance. I decided to call the teller's attention to this fact, but I had trouble getting her attention. When I finally succeeded in telling her what was the matter, she did something very odd, which is hard to report. She produced, out of a drawer, a set of silver dishes and a roll of money and, I think, gave them to me. Queerly enough, all objects seemed to be connected to one another by a string.

"I still wanted my traveler's checks. By this time I was in misery of frustration, especially as at this time the bank was

so crowded that I couldn't get the teller's services at all."

To facilitate the understanding of this dream, may we refer to what was said on page 203 regarding the symbolic value of money. The patient is in need of the independence which traveler's checks can offer to their bearer. He is ill-equipped to be on his own. The dream, therefore, transfers him to his home town (home) where the pattern was set for this type of reaction. The dreamer then tells us about his tragedy of not getting enough "attention." He gets "dishes" and "money," i.e., home cooking and financial support; but on both there are "strings attached." He has to conform with the routines (meal time) of his despotic father and, as time goes on, he sees himself farther and farther from his independence (crowded bank).

The following are dreams in which the psychological background of *mucous colitis* is reflected. To dispel any misunderstanding, it must be emphasized here that not all dreams of organ-neurotic patients have a "typical" character. Dreams presented here are selected for didactic purposes.

The patient is a thirty-four-year-old government employee suffering from migraine spells (see page 316) and the fear of a sudden loss of bowel control. The latter symptom was particularly annoying. The patient was unable to maintain his position, unable to go out with girls and to think of marriage. As a matter of fact, the patient had been engaged twice and had to cancel the engagement each time because he anticipated an "accident" that might occur in church in front of the altar and the assembled guests.

The analysis of this case revealed as pathogenic factors a strong *sister fixation* (based on sexual experiences in childhood), *sadomasochistic traits* associated with a marked anal eroticism, and a goodly measure of a general *psychosexual infantilism*.

His infantilism, sadomasochism, and his sister fixation stood guard against any attempt at finding a mature solution to his sexual needs. Let us look at his dreams:

[348] *"I was shooting at a terrific speed down a perpendicular road on a scooter. Girls were standing on the side and made admiring remarks. When I arrived at the bottom of the hill my neighbor said, 'Aren't you ashamed of yourself: Such a big fellow using a child's toy for driving?'"*

The speed in the dream indicates the strength of the dreamer's id drives. He is engaged in "driving" an infantile kind of vehicle (scooter). We find here an expression of his superego control ("Aren't you ashamed?"), a feeling which plays a paramount role in the patient's interpersonal relations.[1] But above all, we notice that in his infantile pursuits (driving downhill is also a symbol of masturbation) he is passing girls by, although they are full of admiration for him (narcissism, exhibitionism).

Loss of sphincter control, the patient's constant spectre of a "catastrophe" can be seen in the following dream:

[349] *"I am in charge of a platoon in the Army. I report to my C. O.: 'Platoon X ready!' I hear laughter behind me, and when I turn around, the entire platoon appears to disperse and to dissolve. I feel terribly embarrassed."*

In his dream the patient has *lost* the troop he was supposed to *command*. Something in him strives for expression. He tries to hold it back—but he fails. What could this be?

[350] *"I was in a dance hall. I wanted to dance. Somebody said, 'Don't do that. It's just pushing and being pushed.' In the back of the room I saw my sister. I had a glass of wine in my hand. I joked with the girls and was in good spirits. My sister waved to me, indicated that I should join her. She smiled and said, 'You seem to be all out of control tonight.'"*

In the background of the entertainment hall is the patient's sister. She seems to warn him *not to let himself go* when he is having a good time with other girls. Does she want him to be faithful to her only, although she herself is married?

The problem of losing control is so paramount with our

[1] This reaction is common to individuals who, in their neurosis, repress exhibitionist tendencies.

patient that it appears in many of his dreams. In any case, the question, "Will my id overwhelm my ego?" seems to express itself in the question, "Will I be able to control my bowels?" A break-through of the id is identified with the dreaded involuntary defecation. We see that the patient uses the "stool language" to express his intrapsychic problems.

Let us see a few of the so-called self-control dreams. Such dreams are to be found in all individuals who are exposed to an overstrong pressure by their antisocial drives (see page 160).

[351] *"I am driving a hansom. The horses get skittish and out of control. I am afraid we'll land in a pit. We come to the edge of a precipice. Under greatest difficulties I get the horses under control."*

[352] *"I see a train coming. Workers are repairing the tracks. Then I am the engineer. The train moves at a terrific speed along a curved road. Suddenly, I see that the tracks are dividing in two. One track ends in an abyss, while the other goes on. I steer the engine with strong, desperate effort onto the safe track. The train stops then and I am saved."*

[353] *"In my home town. I was racing on a bicycle down a hill, and I almost ran over a child. I passed her by the skin of my teeth. A man was standing nearby and made a threatening gesture with his fist."* P.S.: *"I was on my way to a party."*

The last two dreams indicate the presence of sadistic and criminal tendencies which the patient has difficulty in controlling. He is living on the edge of a precipice. He must control his drives. What are they? The "child" the patient has almost run down in his last dream indicates the presence of antimoral (sexual) or antisocial (criminal) impulses regarding a child. (We shall see later that they refer to a past experience when the patient's object was a child.)

The next dream portrays the child as a kitten:

[354] *"Shoveling coal with my sister. Suddenly my sister*

remarks, 'Why are these cats screaming so much?' We walk over and see father. He pulls a half-dead kitten out from under a heap of coal. The kitten's body is covered with blood. My sister says, 'Kill it!' I take the shovel and strike the injured animal. It becomes a lifeless, bloody mass. Awake with a colicky feeling."

P.S.: "Every time I hear of an act of cruelty I get this colicky feeling."

It becomes clear that the patient's real sexual object is his sister. The "bloody mass" refers to an act of defloration.

[355] *"I was lying next to a blonde girl* (sister is blonde). *I couldn't see her face.* Wake up with emission and terrible colics. Had four bowel movements during the morning."

The next dream is more distinct:

[356] *"I am with my sister in bed. I press my body against her.* (Emission.)"

We see here the sexual act reduced to a superficial contact.

Under the impact of these dreams, the patient confessed that he seduced his sister who was five years younger than he to various sexual games. This occurred when she was eight or nine years old. In the course of these games he deflorated her. (Allusions to this experience are contained in many dreams which refer to blood.) He wishes now to continue this relationship and has to fight his tendency to reveal it (confessing compulsion). Many dreams carry this motive, particularly those connected with the affect of embarrassment. The next dream also deals with this and, in addition, refers to the patient's colonic history. As a child he was suffering from a bad constipation. His father applied frequent enemas. The prolonged rectal treatments have conditioned the lower parts of his intestinal tract for the subsequent organ neurosis. Homosexual tendencies also play a part here.

An important dream:

[357] *"I was lying in bed. There was a young girl (about eight years old). A young boy had intercourse with this girl.*

Her body was hairless. Suddenly I saw that the boy crawled upon my back and started to make the same kind of movements as he did with the girl. His penis looked like the nozzle of an enema. Awoke with colic pains and diarrhea. (Nine bowel movements during the day.)"

The secret between the patient and his sister has led him to the unconscious fantasy of murdering the girl. He could thus remove her from her husband and his rival and also remove the cause of all his troubles. These antisocial ideas also had to be suppressed. He assumed a rigid and compulsive style of living, deprived himself of all joys of life and kept his colic-ridden body more in bed than outside of it.[1]

The next dream shows these circumstances:

[358] *"Was in the Army. My rifle was out of order and I asked for another. I also filled my leather ammunition case with live ammunition."*

The "Army" represents his self-imposed discipline. Many of his dreams regress to the time of his Army service, a time when everything was "under control." The "rifle" which in his dream is "out of order" represents his sex life. For years he craved a physical contact with a woman, but he was unable to establish it either with his fiancée or any other woman. Every sexual excitement shifts to his intestinal apparatus. Colics and diarrhea stop his erotic undertakings in their tracks. "Ammunition" symbolizes feces. The words "live ammunition" indicate their close relations to the criminal ideas directed against his sister.

The next dream is very instructive in this respect:

[359] *"At the entrance to our home town. A farmer leads two cows which suddenly get wild. He calls to me for help. I hit the animals with a stick. The cows turn against me. They change into my father and sister. My father shoots at me but fails. My sister runs to our dog house to sik our dog*

---

[1] The original experience with his sister also took place in bed. The patient's neurosis reproduced a part of the scene for the purpose of atonement.

against me. However, the dog turns against father and sister. They run into the house and keep on shooting. I take cover behind the outhouse. Then I shout, 'If you want to kill me, go on, I don't care.' "

This dream proves that the patient seeks protection from his criminality by his colitis. (He takes "cover behind the outhouse.") In the dream we see again the elemental breakthrough of animal instincts and their objects (wild cows turn into father and sister). Father represents the superego. His role in the application of enemas was mentioned. He also warned him of "women who make a man weak." (Castration fears.) We see here the self-punishing tendency expressed in the patient's appeal to his father and sister (both sexual objects of a kind) to kill him.

It was clear in the analysis that the patient was "sister-sick." His attitude toward his sister (whom he had "soiled") was symbolically expressed in his neurotic attitude toward the toilet. In a great number of dreams we see him in a futile search for a place where he could have his bowel movement without being disturbed (punished).

Let us look at the next dream:

[360] *"I had to go to the toilet. At first I could find none and kept opening many doors until I opened a door which led to a garden restaurant. There were several toilets. I saw a man who said, 'You can't do this here.' I walked away and defecated behind a bush. Nobody saw me do this."*

"Opening doors" represents the defloration of his sister. The dream expresses distinctly the forbidden character of his desire. ("You can't do this here.")

[361] *"In the Army. I must move my bowels and cannot find a men's room. I jump behind a bush but there I see an officer. Then I run into a room, two girls walk out. I let them pass and storm inside. Then I find a toilet at last."*

In his quest for a specific (incestuous) gratification, he lets many a girl "pass" who might be interested in him. His life passes in a continuous attempt to revive a past experience.

His jealousy of his brother-in-law is found in the next dream:

[362] *"I am attending a wedding at the home of my grandparents. I must step out (urge to move bowels). I am looking for a toilet. See that I am watched. I go back to the wedding.*

"Then I am in the house of the newlyweds. There is a large group of people. When I want to get in the room, I see a barbed wire around it. I squeeze through under difficulty. My sister smiles ironically. I feel embarrassed."

The "barbed wire" is called "incest barrier" in our language. He has "squeezed through." His sister smiles knowingly. Her smile cuts his heart. He complains about it in a dream:

[363] *"I see an airplane crash. I rush forward and see a pilot and a young woman dead. The woman's head is cut off. I start crying, but my sister laughs at me. I say to her: 'This is the way all women are today. They have no heart.'"*

The airplane tragedy represents his own downfall. His illness is keeping him a bachelor since his sister has betrayed him. He describes his feelings in his next dream:

[364] *"There is some celebration. My cousin and sister are here. Everybody seems to have a good time. I sit alone in a depressed mood. I leave the room and go to the cemetery. On the street I meet Mrs. W. I try to hide from her, but am discovered. She asks, 'What are you doing in a cemetery?' I say, 'I can't be happy. Why should I celebrate?' She wants to take me back to the celebration but I refuse. A girl comes along and asks me to go with her, but I say, 'No. I'm going home.'"*

This dream speaks for itself.

Summarizing, we may say that in our patient elimination is a vector of a sexual and criminal aggression. The symptom of colitis is an expression of the impulse to relive an old incestuous experience and, at the same time, to commit an act of murder on the "faithless" object. In the patient's symbolic parallelism the act of defecation represents both the antimoral act of incest and the antisocial criminal act ("live ammunition"). The repetitive pattern (several eliminations a day) is due to the fact that the discharge of energy is taking place on a symbolic (unrealistic) level. It is a sign of futility. (See page 227.) Pain and suffering contain the self-punishing tendency. Simultaneously, however, the illness secures the patient's infantile setup by preventing him from replacing the original incestuous object.

GENITO-URINARY TRACT

ENURESIS

Nocturnal enuresis shows a number of more or less typical dreams accompanying or preceding the act of urination. We find dreams about sliding down hills, often in connection with anxiety. One of my patients, a boy of five, had the following enuretic dreams:

[365] *He was extinguishing fire.*

[366] *He was pursued by dogs.*

Such scenes were charged with anxiety to which he reacted with urination.

Another boy, aged thirteen, dreamed [367] *of war. He did not know a war had started, and he was taken prisoner by the enemy. He was to be shot.* Anxiety and micturition.

The same patient dreamed:

[368] *"War time. Mother was to go to the well to fetch water. I yelled to her not to go because the enemy could see her."* Anxiety and micturition.

The patient's mother was divorced. The boy suspected her of having relations with other men and was jealous. Often when she left the house the boy would follow her to find out if she had an assignation with a man. In his dream the patient portrays his inner conflict by a scene of "war." The phrase "one did not know" refers to his own doubt as to his mother's means "to have relations with other men." The boy is worried about his mother's reputation in case she should "fetch water" from some other place. "What would people say if they knew about it?" ("The enemy could see her") is his problem. He considers himself the defender of the honor of his family. In his distress about all these problems he passes water, as if to show that he would like to be an infant again, to revive the "good old days" when father and mother lived together and concentrated their love on him.

Enuretic children express most of their emotional excitement by micturition. In many cases the process of urination is sexualized and is a kind of infantile emission. Other cases show urination as an instrument of the patient's pathological ambition, defiance, desire to attract pity and attention, identification with infants, or the like.

In many cases the act of micturition represents a special form of aggression. The urinary stream in such cases is an equivalent of a projectile discharged from a gun.

A girl, aged ten, dreams:

[369] *"I feel the urge to pass water. I am in a park; apparently I am a soldier. I step out of the rank and file, go to a corner of the park, open the fly of my trousers and urinate."* (Micturition.)

This dream contains the fulfillment of the patient's unconscious wish to become a man as the root of her neurosis.

SEXUAL DISORDERS

THE SPECIFIC MASTURBATION FANTASY

The specific masturbation fantasy must be obtained from the patient when we are considering his masturbatory practices. The patient often fails to give us this information. He may even claim that no fantasy has been experienced. Our experience teaches, however, that the masturbation fantasy is very often unconscious, a fact which renders the patient's statements unreliable. We are always anxious to obtain information about the masturbation fantasy, because nothing can give us a better insight into the patient's conflict situation and his specific (neurotic) libido constellation than the scene he, consciously or unconsciously, visualizes when masturbating. The more "infantile" a fantasy is, the more likely it is that it will be unconscious; but a dream can reveal it, and it is from dreams that we learn all about the patient's incestuous, paraphilic, criminal, and other cravings, while the patient's conscious sex life appears pure, bland, and innocent.

The following dream brought by a thirty-year-old actor suffering from anxiety states and various sexual disturbances reveals the specific love object very clearly:

[370] *"I was at home with some boys with whom I used to play. It seemed that we were on an auto truck and were prepared to fight fires. I carried a very fantastic fire extinguisher. With this I ran into a house and went into the bedrooms. There was no fire here, so I went to the front rooms and there found a group of girls, among them my sister Mary. I took this fancy fire extinguisher and jokingly squirted some of the water into her face."*

The patient learned masturbation from his boy friends. In the above dream we also find the verification of this fact in the words "boys with whom I used to play." "To fight fires" means here "to calm down the inner passion," fire being a symbol of excitement and lust. The passion is calmed by masturbation, which is represented here by the picture of a "very fantastic fire extinguisher" (a phallic symbol) held by the patient in his hands. The next question to be answered in this dream is, Who is the dreamer's love object? The answer is given by the patient himself. In his dream he "jokingly" squirts the contents of his "fire extinguisher" into his sister Mary's face. Thus the above dream reveals the dreamer's specific masturbation fantasy as being the incestuous relationship with his sister.

Another illuminating example of a masturbation fantasy can be seen in the following dream by a young man:

[371] *"I kissed the hands of several ladies. When I did so to the mother of my friend William, her hand turned into a handle bar of my bicycle."*

Interpreting the "mother of my friend William," as the patient's mother (displacement), we find clear reference to masturbation in the picture of the "handle bar of the bicycle," a phallic symbol. The specific masturbation fantasy of our patient is incest with his mother. In this case, as in the preceding one, the patient maintained (with full right) that he never had a conscious fantasy accompanying his masturbation. The analysis brought the repressed fantasy to the surface.

[372] *"I am masturbating in the dream, and while doing this I fancy a coitus scene with a beautiful lady. I experience an emission. At this moment a young man enters the room and I talk to him in a friendly manner."*

The patient experiences his emission at the moment a young man enters the room. This young man is the patient's brother, and the dream reveals the patient's unconscious homosexual fantasy in masturbation. The fancied scene with a lady corresponds to the patient's wish to become normal. Conscious masturbation occurred apparently without being accompanied by fantasies. This dream permits us to substitute the object of the masturbation fantasy as being homosexual and therefore repressed.

IMPOTENCE IN THE MALE

Impotent men and frigid women often dream of love affairs being interrupted by persons peeping or entering or by other disturbances; of journeys in the course of which they must leave the trains (premature emission!); of climbing mountains, and being stopped by intervening difficulties. As stated before, dreams containing the patient's disturbance often portray not only the disturbance itself but the specific pathogenic situation as well.

[373] *"I see myself in a room with my father and my wife. I want to get into bed with my wife and have sexual intercourse. I am highly disturbed because I have to look after my father. I finally get into bed. I seem to be sick from my neurotic condition. I wonder if my father, who meanwhile has gone into the bathroom, can see me while I am in bed with my wife."*

In this dream the patient is disturbed by his father in his sexual affairs. According to our previous statements, we have every reason to consider the patient's attitude toward his father as the main pathogenic factor. In this case the father fixation was verified as the basis of the patient's impotence.

[374] *"I was following my father on some path. He told me to be careful not to step on the little ducks that were along my way. I seemed, however, to have stepped on one of them. I picked it up and saw that it was injured. I therefore put it into a pool where it could recover. It did recover finally. Suddenly, I saw a long yellow snake come out of a bush near by and kill the little animal by one stroke of its poison-charged fangs. I heard the words: 'It was better before, indeed.'"*

"Following my father" means here having a normal sexual life. The patient's father frequently advised him to be careful in his relations with the opposite sex. The patient was too cautious, one might say; he was impotent. The dream shows us the danger of venereal diseases (the poisonous snake) and demonstrates the opinion that it is better to be impotent than to be sick. The patient suffered from a strong "syphilophobia," which, of course, played a great part in his sexual inhibitions. But the dream shows us also his sadistic personality in the scene "killed the animal" (that is, woman) and in that of the snake killing the animal. "Hurting" and "killing" here are on the same level; the patient thus does not differ from the "snake" in his attitude toward the "little duck."

The inner cause of the patient's impotence is his unconscious sadistic impulses. The dream contains also allusions to the patient's fear of castration, which, however, will not be discussed here.

Another interesting example (patient aged thirty-one, suffering from impotence):

[375] *"I am in a bathtub with Lillian R. I want to kiss her. At this moment my sister wants to enter the room. I keep the door shut. I try to prevent her from entering the bathroom. She is stronger than I. Finally she leaves, but there is no intimacy between Lillian and me afterwards. I have a strong feeling of guilt."*

This dream displays the patient's sister fixation (particularly in the words "She is stronger than I") and shows us why the patient cannot succeed with other girls.

The patient's feeling of guilt as expressed in the dream requires a closer examination. The patient reported that when he made his acquaintance with this girl he had the thought in his mind that while he was enjoying life his sister was lonesome and sad. He thought the same also about his mother, who had been a widow for ten years. He, therefore, used to take both mother and sister out to theaters and concerts in order to "make up" to them for his enjoyment of life.

A closer investigation revealed that the patient did not want his sister (to whom he was so closely attached) to mix with other people. He was extremely jealous of anyone who approached her. He established a so-called "chastity complex," a chastity junction between his life and his mother's and sister's. His unconscious idea was: "I shall secure their chastity if I remain chaste myself." He therefore unconsciously did not want to be potent with other girls.

The same patient dreams:

[376] *"I am in my room. My sister Irene lives with me. I wonder what I shall do if a girl calls on me. Irene will interfere with my freedom. I light the stove in my room. The heat of the stove threatens to destroy the wallpaper. I therefore extinguish the fire in the stove."*

The dream fulfills the life plan of our patient. He lives with his sister in one room. The fire in the stove symbolizes his unconscious love toward his sister, a love that is dangerous (prohibited, tabooed). The patient therefore decides to extinguish it (that is, to become impotent).

Another example: An orthodox Jew from Poland, aged forty-eight, wishes to be treated for impotence of one year's duration. He has been married for twenty years, has two daughters, one eighteen years of age. The patient complains of a lack of sexual interest for his aging wife. It became obvious that his "dullness" started, not gradually, but remarkably sudden. Asked for the more detailed circumstances, the patient answered that a short time before, having lost his potency, a quarrel in the family brought him into a state of great excitement. He discovered his younger daughter's diary, in which she expressed her passionate love for a young man. In connection with this the patient made a tremendous scene with his daughter. This excited him so much that he cried for the first time in his life. Finally, he forced his daughter to promise him that she would break off with her friend, which she did. It was strange enough that, according to his report, on this occasion he "exhausted" his "nervous" powers so much that he became impotent. During treatment he dreamed:

[377] *"I got a very young pig to eat. I cut its head off and pushed it away, lest I see that it was pork meat I was going to eat. Then I cut off a piece of that. It tasted very good. Suddenly I felt disgusted and awoke."*

No great skill of interpretation is necessary to convince us that the "very young pig" which this orthodox Jew is going to eat is the "prohibited thing," the patient's young daughter, as taboo for him as the pig. The dream deals with the prohibited pleasure. The patient has to cut off the head of the "very young pig" in order to enjoy his meal—the head because just that reminds him most of the tabooed object. He admits that on the street he admires young girls of his daughter's age. Of course he can do that, he can look after them, because they have another "head" on their body. But we also see his moral reaction in his feelings of disgust and his anxiety which drive him out of his bed.

The analysis discovered here a strong fixation of the patient's libido toward his daughter. We were not surprised to hear that he had to forbid her to sit down on his lap, because he often was aroused this way. We now understand his lack of interest in his wife. We further discovered here also the "chastity complex." The patient verifies the fact that he had the idea of saving his daughter's virtue by sacrificing his own sexuality to God. Hence his impotence.

The man was cured in about four weeks.

Another patient dreamed:

[378] *"I am in the catacombs. There I see the body of a saint lying on a bier. The body is in the state of advanced decomposition. In spite of my repulsion I feel compelled to touch the body with my hands, if I am not mistaken, with the wish that the powers of the saint should pass over to me."*

The dream becomes intelligible when we realize that there is indeed a saint with whom similar procedures are practiced; it is St. Anthony of Padua, Italy. Pious people visit his sarcophagus and touch it with their hands, wishing that this apostle of innocence and chastity guard them against evil temptations. Our patient had visited this tomb a few years before and knew this custom well. The "powers" of the saint which he is craving in his dream are powers of chastity, and it is clear that the patient's impotence has the "chastity" clause as one of its roots. (We omit here other meanings.)

The *chastity clause* plays an important part in the psychogenesis of impotence. The unconscious "will to impotence" (Stekel) is often based upon unconscious asceticism. Dreams help us to uncover this inner antisexual factor.

In cases of impotence the patient often has dreams expressing frustration. Then there are dreams expressing fear of women. And dreams expressing inhibitory clauses, particularly the chastity clause. Some men are impotent, not because they have a castration complex or fear of punishment for indulging in sex activities, but because they have made a vow of chastity and have forgotten the vow. A good example is that of a man who while under fire during the war said to himself: "I swear that I will give up sex if I get out of this danger." He got out of danger, but some time later he discovered that he was impotent. He didn't realize that unconsciously the clause was still active.

An interesting dream depicting the symptoms of *ejaculatio praecox* is one reported by McDowell. It was dreamed under hypnosis. The patient was an unsophisticated person and unaware of the meaning of symbols. In this dream [379] the patient saw *long, white stairs going up into the sky as far as he could see. Women were lined up on both sides of the staircase. They were all "reaching out" for him as he was running up the stairs as fast as he could run. He saw a beautiful girl at the top, lying on a soft bed. He went to bed with her and had a quick emission. After that he started to run up the stairs again, leaving the girl behind him. Her arms were raised toward him and she looked disappointed. . . .*

The patient knew nothing about the fact that walking up stairs was a symbol of intercourse (page 154). The dream also portrays the fact so often found in analysis that behind the multitude of women the patient is attracted to, there is often the image of one woman hidden. She represents the secret sexual goal, in most cases a forbidden one (incestuous). The above dream seems to indicate this, and the analysis would have to focus upon the "girl at the top of the staircase."

FRIGIDITY IN WOMEN

We see frigidity often expressed by pictures of general frustration. A lady once asked about the meaning of the stereotyped dream she had for several years:

[380] *"I was climbing up a mountain under great difficulty. When I was almost at the top I suddenly lost my equilibrium and fell down. Here I awoke with heart palpitation."*

The dream symbolizes difficulties in life and the patient's pessimistic feeling that her efforts are in vain. The sexual meaning is more interesting. We see here a frustration. Frigidity or coitus interruptus? That is the only question. The lady was then asked: "Are you married?"

She said: "Yes."

"Does your husband practice coitus interruptus?"

"No."

"Then the dream is the expression of your frigidity. Your passion reaches a certain height, but you do not succeed in getting full satisfaction. (Orgasm = top of the mountain.) Moreover, you are suffering from anxiety states and heart palpitation as a result of the 'free floating' libido."

The patient corroborated this diagnosis.

A similar dream representing a frustration is the following very instructive dream of a thirty-three-year-old lady:

[381] *"I am dead, but I feel and hear everything. I hear the wonderful song of a bird but not clearly enough. I concentrate all my senses in order to perceive it better. The tone seems to come nearer and nearer, and within the next moment I expect to hear it fully. But the tension will not relax. I cannot move, as I am dead. I can only hear the bird coming closer and then going farther away again. I feel extremely sad."*

The above dream was reported by Wengraf. It gives a beautiful picture of the emotional stages during the intimate act of a frigid ("dead") woman—the yearning for relaxation and the depression because it is in vain.

Let us now examine other dreams of frigid women and summarize our results.

[382] *"I am cleaning my refrigerator and have difficulty. I believe that I finally washed it satisfactorily."*

[383] *"I went to some house and locked all the doors. I was told to leave one door open so that Dan (brother) should have a warm place to sleep."*

[384] *"I went to a country market. I seemed to be in search of dill pickles. I found the pickles but discovered that I didn't have the money to pay for them. I therefore borrowed a dollar from Minnie and brought the pickles home and placed them in a jar."*

In the first dream there is a distinct reference to the patient's frigidity in the word "refrigerator" (a symbol of the female organ). The patient has "difficulty" in making it fit for use. In the second dream we not only see the symbol of the patient's erotic inhibition ("I locked all doors"), but also the reason back of this mental mechanism. There is "one door open" in her heart, but it is open only to her brother, to "have a warm (!) place to sleep." The dream reveals an unconscious brother fixation as the background of the patient's frigidity.

The "pickles" of the third dream are well-known phallic symbols. The patient has made an effort to get "pickles" (she had had difficulty in getting married), but after she got them at the "country market place," she discovered her frigidity. The words "I borrowed a dollar from Minnie" are of importance. Minnie was a friend who used to boast of her passion and of her success with men. Our patient wishes to "borrow money" from her, to get a part of her passion and success. At the same time this passage of the dream reveals the inner cause of the patient's frigidity. It is her latent homosexual tendency, seen in the fact that the dreamer, not being able to develop love for men, seeks love from women. "Placing pickles into a jar" is a clear sexual picture.

Summarizing, we may say that frigidity in dreams is expressed in signs of general inhibition, difficulty, and emotional defect ("I have not enough money," "I cannot see or hear clearly," etc.); also in terms of "warm-cold," "dead-alive," "open-closed," and the like.

Impotent and frigid people often dream of difficult problems they must solve and important examinations they have to pass. The dream is usually accompanied by the fear of failure. An analyst once brought a dream of a patient in which [385] *the dreamer was to pass an "examination in physics" and was anxious as to the result.*

His report was interrupted at this point, and he was asked whether the patient was impotent. The astonished doctor acknowledged that this was the case. The guess was in no way arbitrary. The meaning of the words "examination" and "in physics" conveyed this. One could surmise that the patient in his dream was to be examined as to his physical abilities. His lack of confidence indicated a feeling of impotence.

According to Benedek and Rubenstein, the sexual cycle in women is a psychosomatic unit which manifests definite correlations between the hormone production and the quality of the sexual drive. According to these authors, predominantly pre-genital (dependent, oral, and anal) tendencies are expressed by the patient whenever the hormonal level is low, which can also be observed in dreams. At a high level of hormone production dreams express sex affects or their solution on the genital level.

During the post-ovulatory (progesteron) phase the ego is charged with passive, receptive qualities of libido; it diminishes in activity and its capacity to control outer-world stimulation (hypersensitiveness of the premenstrual period). In the estrogen phase, the ego is strong and its power of integration is intact. The highest level of estrogen production coincides with the onset of the progesteron phase. Genital demands are still strong, but passive receptive tendencies come more to the fore and narcissistic and retentive trends prepare the individual for motherhood. Mother identification dreams occur in this phase more frequently. At the low ebb stage of progesteron production a generally low libido tone prevails, eliminative trends get the upper hand and are often accompanied by feelings of aggression and anxiety (premenstruum).

The investigations of Benedek and Rubenstein are very interesting and should be continued. If they prove correct we can conclude that a direct connection exists between processes which take place on the endocrine and vegetative level and the manifestations of the unconscious.

Freud had suspected that such a connection existed, and Ferenczi offered the explanation for it. He believed that in inflammatory and other pathologic processes not only leucocytes were attracted to the afflicted organ but that also libido was drawn to it, and that thus its libido cathexis was raised.

HOMOSEXUALITY

In the analysis of homosexuality, those dreams in which a heterosexual situation is depicted are of much importance, for what establishes the homosexual neurosis in the patient's mind is not so much the patient's attraction to his own sex as the fear, hate, and resistance that he feels toward the opposite sex.

The following dream of a forty-four-year-old male homosexual is a good example of this constellation.

[386] *"I was on a road near my childhood home. Suddenly, I ran across the road and was heartily welcomed by a woman. I kissed her* (no erection). *I thought I play-acted a bit. I saw no cars on the road and thought of a car accident."*

The dream takes the patient back into his childhood. There is a woman who "welcomes" him. It was one of the tragic factors in the patient's life that his mother never paid any attention to him. She displayed irritability and impatience and, most of the time, left him in the care of servants.

The woman of the dream is a mother image. Ever since he was a child he had trained himself not to invest any feelings into a relation with a woman, for he was afraid of being rejected and humiliated. Later, he thought, by way of a "rationalization" that he would not be able to have an erection anyway (castration fear). Using this hypothesis, he never put himself to a test in this direction and usually withdrew before he was able to establish an interpersonal relationship with a woman.

In his homosexual relations this fear played no part. He was interested in the other person's penis and rarely permitted any manipulation of his own body. Playing the part of a "good mother" he "welcomed," he "accepted" the other fellow, representative of himself, and particularly, his undamaged penis.

The dream shows that in his neurosis the patient made the attempt to reconstruct a warm and loving mother-son relationship. He wanted to demonstrate on his partner what he wished his mother had done to him. By establishing this pattern he perpetuated unconsciously a heterosexual, incestuous relationship.

His lack of erection was a protective feature in two ways: on the one hand, he was afraid his love (erection) would be frustrated by the woman (mother), and on the other, he had to neutralize incestuous feelings by paralyzing his erection.

The "car accident" also points to repressed sadistic feelings toward women. Stekel proved that the main reason for the homosexual's fear of the opposite sex lies in his dormant sadism. By abandoning the heterosexual relation, he exerts a socially protective influence as a concession to his superego.

Our patient was a heterosexual with a tabooed, hence repressed, contrasexual object (mother).

The words "I play-acted a bit" refer to the psychodramatic representation of a basically heterosexual scene by a homosexual arrangement. The statement regarding a "car accident" contains the patient's constant fear that he might suffer the accident of rejection (or outright castration) if he "lets himself go" and follows the heterosexual desire.

The fact that in his homosexual neurosis the patient plays the part of an (idealized) mother can be seen in the following dream which also discloses the patient's sadistic component.

[387] "*I was a woman. I was kneeling alongside a bed. Another woman was lying in it. A red scar was visible on her abdomen between her vagina and her navel. I seemed to want to fondle this red scar.*

"Woke up thinking this was an unimportant dream; forgot about it."

Whenever a patient makes such a deprecatory remark about a dream we take it for granted that the dream contains a very important detail. And so does the dream quoted here. It shows the patient in the feminine role, which tallies with what was said before. The scar refers to a remark the patient's mother was thoughtless enough to make when he was still a child. She often said, "When you were born you ripped me open." (Caesarian section? Perineal tear?) The dream uses this experience as material for its plot. The patient always thought that his mother held him responsible for this "cruel act" and that she disliked him for this reason. Throughout his youth he made attempts to please his mother only to meet with her impatience and rejection.

The material of this and other dreams distinctly reveals the existence of sadistic ideas regarding his mother and other women, as a reaction to the early rejection. We can detect them in this dream, too, but here the patient is in a submissive (masochistic) attitude, represented by the kneeling position. Fondling the scar which runs from vagina to navel would also indicate the fusion of sexual and sadistic tendencies. If, in reality, the patient goes on fondling a man's genital, he is sure that he will not find any scars there that would remind him of his tragic, unintentional guilt. The dream indicates that the patient may have seen his mother's abdomen early in his life and, possibly, also a scar from an operation; however, conscious confirmation of this hypothesis was unobtainable.

How much the patient tried to get into his mother's good graces and to obtain her attention is shown in the following dream.

[388] *"Lots of motherly-looking, middle-aged women, waiting to go into a movie house. I come out of a show and dance by, all alone. I am a clownish figure in Victorian costume."*

The reference to the past is contained in the "Victorian costume" the patient is wearing here. "Victorian" also means asexual. The dream again shows that the patient is performing a psychodrama, that he plays a role in front of women.

It shows, furthermore, that the women are mother substitutes, and that in order to attract their attention, the patient is ready to assume the masochistic self-emasculating attitude of a clown (a frequent pattern in masochism). As stated before, the masochism displayed by this patient is the substitute of an unconscious sadistic attitude towards women as the most important dynamic factor in his homosexual paraphilia.

Nervous System

CEREBRAL HEMORRHAGE

Some pathological *changes in the brain* are accompanied or preceded by characteristic dreams. A woman who, during menstruation, suffered a *cerebral hemorrhage* had the following dream a night prior to her apoplexy:

[389] *"She went to a forest to work. She could not move her hand and got scared."*

She awoke with a scream, called her husband, and told him that there was a foreign hand lying on her blanket. The man said that she was crazy. She seemed a little confused indeed and her speech was disturbed. Finally, a doctor was called in. The patient asked the doctor to remove the foreign hand from her blanket. Before awakening she had another dream:

[390] *"She saw herself in the forest lying in a coffin next to a dead woman. Somebody took an arm away from this woman and gave it to the patient. She could not move it."*

In this patient the apoplectic insult stimulated a dream in which she perceived the paralysis and, for reasons of self-defense of the ego, projected this perception to another person. This projection (or transitivism) is due to the disturbance of the cerebral body image by the hemorrhage. In her dreams the patient saw herself as a healthy person and her double as dead or foreign.

FACIAL PALSY

Pollak of Sussex (G. B.) reports the following interesting case. One of his patients dreamed [391] *that she saw her grandfather, who had the same "wry face" as she had on one of her photos.*

In the morning the patient awoke with a "wry face" herself. It was a facial palsy which had recurred in this family for three generations.

EPILEPSY

The epileptic attack may be symbolized by falling, losing equilibrium, thunderstorms, drowning, curtains falling, etc. One of Stekel's patients dreamed:

[392] *"A flier makes a daring loop and cries: 'Long live Horthy!' He falls down. I think, 'That is the punishment for his crying.'"*

In this dream the patient's criminal ideas against his father ("Horthy") appear as the repressed pathogenic material.

384 THE HANDBOOK OF DREAM ANALYSIS

The words "Long live Horthy!" are hypocritical. The patient's "falling" is due to an identification with his father (whom he wishes to die) and symbolizes the epileptic attack.

Another patient dreams:

[393] *"I am leaning out of a window in order to see Max on the street. I am afraid of losing my equilibrium."*

Here we see another picture of the attack. We omit further interpretation of this dream.

Some patients have a particular stereotyped dream leading to an attack. This dream represents the aura. The content of the aura can generally be accepted and interpreted as a dream. In the aura we very often see the preliminaries of the attack and, besides, the deeper psychological causes of the particular fit.

According to Stekel, the patient's strong atavistic (criminal and sadistic) instincts, insufficiently repressed, break through in the epileptic attack. The attack sometimes represents a criminal action crippled and reduced to spasmodic jerks and punches. Careful observations and analyses (Stekel, Jung, Pierce Clark, and others) have proved that in the attack the patients experience death, rebirth, and the mother's womb fantasy, possibly as a wish for a mental and physical rebirth, a renewal of their diseased lives under normal and healthy conditions.

One of Stekel's patients dreamed:

[394] *"I am swimming in a pool which becomes narrower and narrower and finally turns into a channel. I come to a narrow spot where I press my body through a lattice window. I come onto a meadow where I see many naked persons."*

In this dream the patient experiences his birth in the picture of pressing his body through a lattice window. He comes to a new country, to paradise. Every fit of this patient is such a "rebirth," the paradise to which he retires when his dramatic inner life confronts him with insoluble problems. In his fits, the patient succeeds in annihilating his own real existence. He withdraws from this gruesome world in order to be reborn into a new and better one.

Dreams of epileptics are often overtly criminal. Very often, however, their criminal character is disguised, the strongest emotions mitigated in a way similar to that in which the patients themselves cover their boundless inner brutality under a polish of overpoliteness and servility.

A patient had an attack early in the morning. Under great difficulties he recalled the dream he had had the night before. The dream was very "innocent":

[395] *"I was walking in a forest and saw there a young girl picking flowers."*

No associations were available. The post-epileptic amnesia hindered the patient in concentrating, but he could recall that he had been reading a book (Maupassant's short stories) before going to bed. He mentioned that the author was his favorite writer. When he was asked which short stories he had read before falling asleep he, at first, could not say. Maupassant's book was then handed to him and he found the story; it dealt with the lust murder committed by a teacher on a little girl. The patient confessed that in former years he read this story several times because he liked it so much.

The dream leading to the epileptic attack was undoubtedly a fragment. The continuation of the scene (meeting a girl in the forest) was repressed because it contained a lust-murder situation. It could be verified by other material that the patient experiences this scene in his epileptic attack.

The following is a complete series of dreams produced within twenty-five sessions by an epileptic woman aged forty-four:

[396] *"I was a school teacher and unable to control my class. The children were running about. I could not get them to work and was very nervous."*

This is a typical dream of a person who stands under high

pressure of inner instincts and is afraid of not being able to control them. Whenever they accumulate, an explosion seems to be imminent. The epileptic attack stands for such an explosion.

[397] *"I put on water to boil and as I turned the gas on a frog jumped into the pot. I was frightened and dropped the pot onto the floor."*

The boiling water symbolizes the patient's soul. The frog which jumps into the pot is a tabooed thought that pops into the patient's mind and frightens her. Dropping the pot is another symbol of the seizure.

[398] *"Somebody choked me. I wanted to shout but I couldn't. I was paralyzed from my neck down."*

In this dream we learn something about the character of the above-mentioned tabooed thought. It is a criminal idea. The patient identifies herself with her victim. But who is the victim? We can expect that the next dreams will offer more information. "Paralysis" in this dream prevents the patient from engaging in dangerous activity. This is a mechanism often seen in cases of hysteric paralyses.

[399] *"As I was walking on the street a fire broke out. The houses in front of me and those behind me were ablaze. I was looking for an escape and could not find any. Awoke with a scream."*

Fire symbolizes the emotional tension in the patient's mind. She is standing between her moral and her antimoral impulses as if between two fires.

The next dreams contain the following scenes:

[400] *"I fell out of the window."*

[401] *"My car fell to pieces."*

[402] *"I found my bathroom flooded with water."*

All these dreams symbolize the seizure or the emotional tension under which the patient's mind operates. The next dream finally brings the solution:

[403] *"I was walking on a boardwalk with my sister. She was a little ahead of me, and as she turned around the corner*

I lost sight of her. When I arrived at that place I saw a steep incline there. My sister was not there. I looked around and found her lying on the water. She was apparently drowned. Nobody seemed to care. I took a long board and pushed her body closer to me so that I could pull her out of the water. Then I started first aid. . . . After that I awoke without knowing if my efforts were successful."

The patient reveals here her hostile attitude toward her sister. The patient reported that her sister, being younger, used to attract much of her parents' attention, a fact which caused our patient to feel jealous and resentful in her younger days. It also annoyed her greatly that her sister was more successful in her social life, that she was able to live an easier life than our patient who was always forced to carry the responsibilities of her home. We see an allusion to this fact in the words "She was a little ahead of me." She envies her sister and wishes her to die. More than that, she fights against an impulse to kill her sister. Whenever this antimoral drive threatens to break through, the patient drowns it in her epileptic attack.

In the above dream the patient's sister is drowned. We have good reason to believe that the original impulse aims at choking, drowning, and suffocation.

Stekel reports numerous dreams in which the atavistic root of the epileptic attack becomes very evident. Missriegler described analogous mechanisms in narcolepsy. Similar mechanisms can be found in cases of chronic migraine, as is shown on page 310.

Using dreams in the psychology of epilepsy is very helpful because we have no other way of looking behind the curtain, behind the screen of the seizure. The patient cannot tell us anything about it because during the spell he is unconscious and afterward he has a retrograde amnesia. In the dreams we can observe some of the mechanisms of epilepsy, particularly in those dreams which portray the attack.

The following are a few typical dreams of an epileptic:

[404] *"I saw a little man at the window of my bedroom on the fourth floor. He was holding onto the iron bars and beckoning with one finger to me to come closer. I became anxious and angry at the same time."*

When he says "angry" he is speaking euphemistically. This type of patient is extreme in his aggressive impulses. Once this writer visited such a patient in his summer home. It was a hot day and the analyst had to climb a hill. When he came to the patient's house, he asked the patient for a glass of water. At that moment the patient had an attack. It was obvious that he resented being asked for a service. You may consider this as far-fetched, but if you know how touchy epileptics are, you will see that this was no exaggeration.

Let us continue with the reaction to the dream:

"I jumped out of bed (he really did) *and rushed to the window to repel the man. I fell down and lay unconscious for half-an-hour."*

We see in this dream that the patient is in an exposed position, is in danger of falling. The bars represent protection: we protect ourselves in this way against intruders and society protects itself in the same way against its trespassers. This "protection" thus carries a double meaning. The "little man" represents the patient's criminal idea. It is in the struggle against this thought that the patient "falls." (If he succeeded in repelling the menace, the "little man" would fall.)

Another dream:

[405] *"I was slaughtering a calf. Blood streamed copiously. There was so much blood that I thought there was no meat there."*

The atavistic trends are clear. "Calf" may stand for "child."

Next dream:

[406] *"A man, devil, was threatening me with a knife. I said, 'You can't do anything to me, I am a free man. Your knife will drop to the floor.' He made a thrust at me, and his knife really dropped to the floor."*

You see here in the "devil" a religious motive. Religious trends are common in epileptics. They help the patient maintain his emotional equilibrium in the face of strong sadistic impulses. In the knife which the devil (the patient's "alter ego") wields we see his criminal tendencies, in the dropping of the knife the protective epileptic seizure, which enables him to remain a "free man."

Of course, in every one of these cases, the specific affective constellation must be found. The mere discovery of criminal or sexual impulses is unspecific and insufficient.

These were random dreams that indicate the possibility of finding out something about the otherwise hidden material of epilepsy.

DREAMS UNDER STRESS

"TRAUMATIC NEUROSIS"

An individual may experience what we call a "psychic trauma" when he is involved with forces which are too new to him to be parried by the already established defenses, or forces which overcome the existing defenses because the latter are inadequately developed. In his attempt to regain mastery of his environment, the stricken individual may employ infantile or archaic forms of reaction. One primitive form thus used is the *repetitive pattern* of his dreams which can turn the shocking experience into a routine occurrence.

In traumatic neurosis ("battle fatigue," e.g.) dreams are fraught with anxiety. The motif of being annihilated is common. Some of these dreams resemble those found in cases of epilepsy.

The content of such dreams is usually a specific frightening experience. In many instances dreams of violent situations, such as drowning or burning, occur which reproduce some real experiences encountered on the battle field. In such dreams it is important to evaluate the strength of the ego. Is the dreamer able to gain the upper hand? Does he feel destroyed and defeated? How does dream anxiety compare to conscious anxiety? All these questions contain important references to the patient's capacity of adaptation to stress.

Kardiner emphasizes the stereotyped character of dreams in traumatic neurosis. He also finds that many of these dreams appear broken up—they begin "to say something," but they never complete it. Redundance and perseveration are rampant. Kardiner quotes many dreams, of which the following are a few examples:

[407] One of his patients *saw himself coming down the elevated stairs. Suddenly he dropped dead and rolled down the stairs.* The patient awoke with fear.

[408] *The patient sees himself on the Woolworth tower looking down. Suddenly he slips and falls to the ground. His body makes a hole in the ground as it is smashed to pieces.*

[409] *The patient is shot at and is hit "right through the head."*

All these dreams were narrated by the patient eight years after the original trauma. We know now that the psychodynamic purpose of such dreams is to abreact the effect of the trauma. All kinds of threats of annihilation are hallucinated in the patient's dreams and each awakening enhances his feeling of triumph over death and destruction.

The perseveration of death images in the dreams deprives them of their shocking character and lowers their surprise effect (law of diminishing returns). Repetitions of the traumatic experience in dreams are typical for all post-traumatic repetitions of the shocking experience. This recuperative work may require years. Its objective is the restoration of an intact and well-functioning ego, an ego that is again capable of adaptation to and mastery of the outside world as a prerequisite of survival.

Birth dreams, "end-of-the-world" dreams, separation from mother, and frustration dreams are among the most frequently encountered dreams under battle-fatigue conditions.

The world around appears unfriendly, the patient himself is helpless, unable to cope with it, unable to escape the threat by an orderly withdrawal.

Some dreams reveal compensatory aggressive traits with subsequent or accompanying anxiety (guilt). Insensible, destructive aggression in dreams may disgorge a part of the dammed up anxiety, which is due to repressed sexual (heterosexual and homosexual) or non-sexual cravings. In such dreams similar actions may occur that characterize the overt "amuck" reactions of the epileptics.

DREAMS UNDER ANESTHESIA

We are fortunate to have obtained some insight into dreams produced under anesthesia. One excellently analyzed dream has been reported by Federn in 1944. It was his own dream and was produced while he was under a nitrous oxide anesthesia applied for a tooth extraction.

[410] In his dream *the dreamer sees himself as the chief military commander and the chief statesman of great territories and organizes the affairs of one province after the other. He knew in the dream which country it was. But after awakening he did not know whether it was China or Greece. He noticed, however, that the frontiers of these provinces were straight lines like the borders of many of the states in the U.S.A.*

The dreamer was aware of the time it took to accomplish his task, it was very long, maybe half-a-year. He was able to accomplish his work under strain and tension and his decisions were made in a great hurry and carried out equally fast, but with perfection. The dreamer was satisfied with the way he was performing his duties. In doing so, he was pervaded by a feeling of happiness and satisfaction. It appeared necessary to have all the actions in the dream executed with utmost speed. The dreamer's glorious and victorious fight was carried out without conceit or desire to show off, but simply as action dictated by the sense of duty.

Federn emphasizes the motion in the dream, as a contrast to his position, strapped in a dentist's chair. Instead of the complying and obedient attitude he displayed at the anesthesia, the dream showed him a "masculine superman." He had visions of strength compensating for the feebleness and defenselessness of the anesthesized individual.

Federn later compared the contents of his dream with a poem written by the Polish bard Mickiewicz in which the hero, while in a post-epileptic dream state, saw himself arguing with God, asking God for omnipotence. This appearance of religious motives in dreams under anesthesia (proximity of death) appears to be rather frequent.

Federn's analysis of his dream is very stimulating. It is in line with his ideas about the ego cathexis. In one point, however, we disagree with Federn's deductions. It is when he says that his dream occurred "in deepest sleep and not in awakening."

We believe that this anesthesia dream was just as much a product of an awakening ego as the dreams of people awakening under normal circumstances. Federn's conclusions, therefore, concerning the difference between the two types of dreams are bound to be erroneous.

Federn associated the straight lines of the boundaries with the lines of illuminated X-ray pictures of his teeth, which he saw before he lost consciousness. They were the objects to be changed by the operation. The dream offered the dreamer a hallucination of activity, efficiency, and success, thus counteracting the breakdown of his ego. It presented a continuity of living which appears undisrupted by the temporary loss of the ego. The whole plot of the dream is pervaded by the idea that something is to be put in order and straightened out.

Federn emphasizes the high speed of the dream; he explains it with the fact that in the anesthesia-sleep, contrary to the physiological sleep, it is not fatigue that leads the individual into the state of unconsciousness but the toxic agent. Fatigue and some forms of fever usually account for slow-paced dreams. In our opinion, the high speed of Federn's dream and the efficiency of the dream performances are due to the dreamer's identification with the surgeon and his wish to have the operation over with dispatch and efficiency.

We shall now present an anesthesia dream from our own collection. It was dreamed by a thirty-four-year-old chemist who was placed by his dentist under nitrous oxide general anesthesia. When he was gradually regaining consciousness, he had what he called a vision:

[411] *"I saw myself in a room. The floor was covered with Persian rugs (father has always been interested in them). I saw father's mahogany desk covered with a glass top. Everything is red: the rug, the desk, and the walls. Both parents are standing behind the desk and I am some distance before it. It is like a tribunal* (see dream [577] on page 571). *On the left side (extracted tooth was on left side) I see a telephone and hear a shrill ringing. (The telephone rang at the moment of my awakening.) It rings louder and louder; it hurts my ears. Father's eyes are wide open, terrifying. He raises his finger and yells at me just as he does in reality. He yells louder and louder and the telephone rings louder and louder.*

"My mother stands there—big, cold, motionless. It is as though she were a judge, a statue of justice, or a goddess— her name is Diana in reality—and father were the district attorney. (In reality she is taller than father.) I have no feeling of anxiety, but it hurts.

"Suddenly something terrible happens. I am aware of a strong light and of noise like singing—Hosannah—as though angels were singing—I know I am dead and in the other world. I know that this Goddess of Justice (superego?) has now thrown away her veil and is showing me the 'meaning of life,' her genital. As though she wanted to convey the idea that Woman, the female sex, is the ultimate law of life. I

open my eyes, raise my arms, and yell, 'This is impossible!'
(Meaning: 'Impossible that this should be the solution of the
riddle of life.')

"*It is impossible that we human beings struggle, study,*
strive for ideals, and that all this should mean nothing, while
sex should mean everything. The goddess answered, 'Many
people have been thinking the same way.'

"*Then I saw legions of dead men, women, and children,*
all with open, amazed eyes, with their arms opened. I knew
they were dead as I was. And it was then that I understood
that the expression of their eyes was not fear of death but
desperate astonishment. At this moment I shouted, 'If only
I could get back to life, even for one moment, to tell this to
the human race, to give them the message about what the
struggle for life really means.'

"*The Goddess answered coldly, 'Many wanted to do the*
same.'

"*I knew then that I shall remain for all eternity in this*
amazement, unable to share my knowledge with other
humans.

"*The light grew brighter, more glaring, and I recognized*
in it the dentist's light showing in my face.

"*I awoke with the words, 'If after this I ever return to*
sanity, it will be the greatest miracle.'"

We see here what could almost be called an "archetype."
The patient said, "I always hated my father. He looked
down upon women. He was the embodiment of an ossified
conservatism. My whole life was spoiled by his emotionalism.
He had me circumcised without necessity. I saw in women
the salvation of humanity. I had the feeling that only women
can rebuild society. I met wonderful women in my lifetime.
I wanted to have a daughter who would be the savior of
humanity. I wanted to show father what a woman can accomplish. I wanted to write a drama under the title 'Between
Father and Son.'

"I have always been fascinated by big, cold, and beautiful

women. Mother was beautiful. We lived in crowded quarters and I often had opportunity to see mother in various stages of undressing. As a child I used to bathe with mother and sister in one bathtub. I was always impressed by my mother's breasts."

Freud was criticized because he attempted to explain man's problems of living in all their ramifications from the perspective of the Oedipus complex. We see, however, that, when in the moment of danger (succumbing to anesthesia), man thinks of the possibility of dying, the most powerful affect, the strongest libido-cathected desire of life pushes forward: the *incest* desire.

It makes its appearance while the superego gives in. We see its function at the onset of the dream (the Goddess of Justice and the district attorney) but soon the "veil is lifted."[1] At the moment of impending death, the tortured human mind turns back to the font of its existence.

DREAM AFTER OPERATION

A postoperative dream (after cholecystectomy):

[412] *"I was desperately trying to adhere to a given framework of thought or occupation (maybe poem reciting) and was constantly forced to be preoccupied with unimportant details, to concentrate on insignificant words, such as 'and' or 'better be' or the like. I tried to convince myself (or someone else) that the general framework is more important than the detail it contains. I was constantly frustrated, however, by an obsessive, nay frantic, interest in irrelevant detail."*

This dream represents a consolation for the patient. We still see in it signs of prostration and fatigue caused by the surgical encroachment (the obsessive-repetitive pattern), but the dream has already begun to make the dreamer reconciled to the fact that certain parts of his anatomy (gall blad-

[1] Cf. F. Schiller's poem "Das verschleierte Bild zu Sais" (the Veiled Statue at Sais). *Schillers sämtliche Werke*, Ph. Reclam jun. Lipsia, 1917.

der) are not at all important, that they are "insignificant details" of "the general framework" of reference, and that their loss is unessential, as long as the body as a whole (the "framework") was preserved.

Neuromuscular Disabilities

OCCUPATIONAL NEUROSIS

The individual's adjustment to the outside world includes, according to Alfred Adler, three spheres: *Work, Sex* and *Community*. If a person is well-integrated regarding these three relations, the probability is that he or she is in a mental equilibrium.

Working capacity is an important category, inasmuch as it indicates, to a high degree, the patient's capacity for independence. It is one of the side effects of immaturity, psychopathy, and emotional dependency to fail in emancipating oneself from the protective and nutritional influence of the parental home and establishing oneself in the community as earner of a livelihood.

In many cases of neurosis, rebellion affects just this sphere. The patient becomes pathologically disabled and inferiority feelings as well as guilt reactions help to perpetuate the patient's dependent attitude.

We find in such conditions all sorts of muscular neuroses, spasms, hyperalgesias or paralyses, in which we can see all the characteristics of a neurotic organ disorder.

Some of the neuromuscular disabilities are in the service of the superego and show a defensive character. They are designed to prevent antisocial and antimoral acts.

One female patient found her right arm paralyzed when she awakened in the morning. She had dreamed [413] that *she was hitting (killing) her daughter.*

Other neuromuscular disorders are due to repressed masturbation and can be rightly considered masturbation equivalents, as e.g., some of the hysterical paralyses accompanied by an increased tonus. Tabooed action and inhibition, illicit gratification and self-punishment find a simultaneous expression in most of these nervous disorders.

Of special significance are conditions of *chronic fatigue* which result from a constant clash between the reality principle and the pleasure principle. Inactivity caused by this type of fatigue consumes a considerable amount of energy, for the patient's intrapsychic conflicts go on despite the inactivity.

Many *occupational inhibitions* are due to inhibition of aggressions.

Cristina M., a married woman of forty, a Rumanian concert pianist, entered analysis because of pain, weakness, and stiffness in both thumbs, a condition which seriously interfered with her piano playing. The symptoms first appeared during her convalescence from an appendectomy two years prior to her analysis. After this, they usually manifested themselves shortly after she began playing and became more intense as she continued. Sometimes the pain came on suddenly, radiating upwards along her arms; occasionally, the mere intention of playing the piano caused a paralyzing feeling of disability. As repeated physical examinations were negative, psychotherapy was recommended and accepted.

Her father was a meek and quiet man. Her parents' marriage was unhappy; they did not get along well, and soon drew apart from each other. The mother was a cold, undemonstrative woman from whom, all through her life, Cristina sought in vain for a sign of affection.

The patient had always loved to listen to fairy tales, and her nurse and other elders indulged her; many of the stories were gruesome and aroused fear and morbid excitement. She was greatly impressed by Cinderella with whom she completely identified herself.

When she was eighteen, Lupescu, an assistant music teacher

at the academy, began to court her. At first, he tried to impress her with his playing. The relationship then became physical.

His influence on Cristina was truly diabolical. He was a manifest sadist; their relationship degenerated swiftly into a wild course of ill-treatment and humiliation. She hated him but could not resist him. He discovered her hidden masochism and took advantage of it to the fullest extent. Soon her few remaining sexual tendencies disintegrated completely; she was systematically conditioned to a purely masochistic paraphilia.

In her naïve sexual dependency she believed him utterly; on the other hand, through the lure of his competent piano playing he succeeded in keeping a firm hold on her romantic mind. She once said, "He played a piece—Schumann's *Symphonic Études*—that has haunted me throughout my life. I have never heard it played more beautifully. I was in love with Lupescu's playing while I hated him as a person. Many girls fell in love with him because of his playing."

How ruthless her paraphilic relationship with Lupescu was can be seen in the fact that during its three years' duration, Cristina underwent at least twelve abortions. Lupescu liked the idea of making her pregnant. He also enjoyed thinking about the operation she had to endure.

Not until she was twenty-two was she able to escape from Lupescu. By then, however, the sado-masochistic pattern was established so solidly that it persisted until her treatment.

One of Lupescu's ruthless ideas was to force Cristina to introduce him to her sister Rita, so that he could extend his sadistic practices to her. She gave in although she anticipated the misery that her sister would endure. Possibly an unconscious factor involved here was latent hostility (sibling rivalry) dating back to the time when Rita's birth seemed an intrusion.

After she left Lupescu, she had several shortlived affairs, experimenting to discover if she could enjoy normal rela tions with men. She found them thoroughly unsatisfactory. When she was twenty-four she met a man who was to become her husband. She craved peace and security and he seemed to offer it. She grasped the chance without any consideration of love, and married him.

The following dream casts some light on her relation toward her husband:

[414] *"My mother sings as if she had two voices. Then her figure changes into that of a man (my husband's?)."*

Association: "He is so motherly to me that I feel guilty when I am not nice to him." This dream is of great significance. We see here that, in the symbolic language of her neurosis, her husband represents her mother, a dominating and overprotective person.

Because the patient was married to a man she did not love, she could not overcome her paraphilic inclinations. Only a real love could have offered her an emotional outlet strong enough to destroy her infantile fixations and the resultant abnormal sexual tendencies. The patient's choice represented a typical "neurotic arrangement" (Adler), a system unconsciously designed to perpetuate pathological conditions. The situation became even more involved when, in the course of time, more specifically since the age of twenty-nine, the sexually disappointed patient began to reject her husband's physical attentions. By the time she was thirty-seven, they no longer had any relations, and this continued until the time of her treatment.

At the age of thirty-five she began to study with an Italian teacher, Sartori, to whom she was strongly attracted. Because of emotional and cultural isolation, she was ready to fall in love at the slightest provocation, and this was offered by her association with Sartori. Furthermore, the student-teacher relationship fitted well with the sado-masochistic pattern established by Lupescu in her youth. Sartori lived in an unhappy marriage, and so he represented a welcome attraction. Although he never encouraged her, she kept on spinning her sexual fantasies in which he played the main role. In her real behavior, she first tried to please him and to gain his love by her pianistic achievements. Later she often attempted to get his attention in a masochistic fashion by behaving like a naughty child which deserves to be reprimanded.

It was at this time that Cristina's sexual relations with her husband stopped altogether. The factor of reality in her sexual life sank to its lowest level, while the musical atmosphere in which she lived stimulated her fantasy to a maximum. Her masochistic personality became more and more outspoken; she began to crave more and more humiliation. Thus she often manufactured disappointments, used her frustrations for masturbatory purposes, and prearranged most of the subsequent personal and professional defeats which were soon to follow.

The next dream is interesting in this respect:

[413] *"My mother sits in a room. I am with her. Suddenly I notice something on the table that looks like a little glimmer. It glows like a big phosphorescent bug. It is something ominous—like a disease. The thing grows and grows—I am terrified. Suddenly it begins to fly, and it turns into a gruesome, ugly bird. It swallows a little bird that was flying about. I hear the poor little thing screech in fear and pain, the sounds coming from the big bird's stomach."*

This dream betrays the patient's moloch fantasy. In it we recognize traces of fairy tales to which the patient was exposed in early childhood. The picture of the big and ugly bird swallowing the helpless little bird represents an identification. Identification here is portrayed as incorporation. The swallowing scene also represents a reunion with the protective and omnipotent power. the patient's mother. In her neurosis the patient replaced her mother by Lupescu, who, by his fateful influence, "swallowed" completely the patient's personality.

The phosphorescent bug was associated with the sacred

beetle of the Egyptians, the Holy Scarab, which, according to Egyptian belief, represents "the cause of things, the soul of things, the fertility and the resurrection." In the patient's mind—all these things symbolized an omnipotent (phallic) mother.

The motif of a female persecutor turning into a male appeared in her dreams again and again.

An example follows:

[414] *"A big animal was following me. I was running away from it. The animal wanted to destroy me. The animal then turned into Mr. Sartori. When I saw him I was not afraid any more."* (The big animal = the phallic mother.)

Another important dream:

[415] *"My mother died. I am told that mother was "laid out" in a sitting position, wearing a snow-white dress. I don't want to see her dead. I am afraid to look at her. People are constantly taking me to her—but I refuse to look at her."* (Association: "She was sitting as if at the piano.")

This dream expresses the important junction between playing the piano and death. In it the patient identifies herself with her dead mother, the reason for this identification is her feeling of guilt.

[416] *"A young man is dancing. I tell him that this will kill his mother."*

In this dream we see the connection between enjoyment and death. Since the pleasure the patient experienced was based upon death wishes, both had to be suppressed. Thus the patient condemned herself to a life of suffering and privation in consequence of which piano playing as the greatest source of pleasure became impossible.

The next dream belongs to the same category. It runs as follows:

[417] *"I am an inmate of a woman's penitentiary or a house of prostitution. I am supposed to give a concert and am preparing for it. Other women are around. I have the feeling of being different, an exception."*

In this dream, penitentiary is associated with the house of prostitution: penitence with sex. Both with piano playing. The patient wishes to be different—one of the strongest cravings of her childhood. It promised her a chance of being noticed and loved—by a mother who favored the patient's younger sister, Rita. "Playing" here also represents "playing with the genitals," an activity which was severely reprimanded by her mother in childhood.

When, at thirty-eight, Cristina had her appendix removed, her illness offered her an opportunity for extensive erotic daydreaming. In the hospital, she relished the idea that Sartori might visit her and display a more personal interest, or at least sympathy. For a long time he did not appear, however; and when he did—a short time before her discharge—he was brief though friendly, and spoke no more than the usual words of encouragement. Cristina felt hurt and dejected. In this reaction she repeated a pattern of her childhood, namely the fear of loss of her mother's love.

When after several weeks she was up again, she noticed pain and weakness in her thumbs which prevented her from practicing on the piano.

At the time she experienced her first attack of appendicitis, she was preparing for a concert under Sartori's supervision. Ominously, she was to play Schumann's *Symphonic Études,* the same work Lupescu had used as a vehicle for his romantic pursuits. In the opinion of concert pianists, Schumann's *Études* offers no unusual technical difficulties, and makes no demands on the musician for a particular muscular exertion. Factors which predisposed Cristina to the outbreak of her occupational disability were, according to her own confession, strong emotional upsets during her lessons with Sartori. She was always sexually excited when she took her lessons; she expected scolding and reprimanding, and enjoyed the thrill of this anticipation.

She said, "I was never satisfied with my playing. Everything looked hopeless. I thought I would never amount to anything. I almost wished to have an illness as an excuse. Even the appendix operation was welcome."

Cristina's sexual activity was in inverse proportion to her musical activity: the more she played, the less sexual desire she felt; the more she practiced, the more intense became her feeling toward her teacher, for whom she played, and the less intense her interest in her husband. Playing stimulated her antimoral and antisocial impulses and thus became a function suitable for a neurotic conversion. She once said, "Ever since Lupescu, musical art and sexual purity have been synonymous to me." (In a typical fashion, she only considered intercourse impurity, not masturbation.) She went on, "I have a queer feeling that Sartori is inwardly in love with me and is faithful to me by keeping himself pure. I know that this is nonsense, but I hold on to this belief."

This motif also appears in the following dream:

[418] *"I am going uphill—I do not know where. I hold a bunch of flowers in my hand, wrapped in white paper. I hold on to it very tightly. I know that someone wants to take it away from me. Suddenly, I feel a force coming from above, like a terrific wind, and the flowers are torn away from me. I stay there, like a dead person, unhappy, and cry."*

The flowers represent her craving for a pure and innocent love. She has dissociated love from sex. She could indulge in the latter without violating the former. The "someone" who wants to take away her vow of chastity is the man. The man (also the analyst) deprives her of her childhood dreams of chastity. What remains is her neurotic restitutive complex: her sado-masochistic paraphilia which can offer her the transcendental feeling of satisfaction at having preserved her infantile chastity, regardless of her adult life.

Here we must also mention the peculiar relation between playing piano and paraphilia. Cristina had noticed the resemblance of Lupescu's technique on the keyboard and his sadistic conduct. She said, "I often compared in my mind the playing of a concert pianist with the act of whipping. Once I said to a friend of a well-known concert pianist and former teacher: 'This Q. handles the keyboard as if he were beating his children.' I know he frequently spanked his children. This upset me terribly. I wished he would do the same to me. I even behaved toward him in a provocative manner."

She dreamed:

[419] *"I was waiting for Mr. Sartori. A colored maid was around. I asked her how long I would have to wait. The maid replied, 'He is in your inside.'"*

The dream means that the patient tries to identify herself with her teacher when she plays the piano. We are here reminded of the little bird who is inside the big bird and of the cannibalistic concept of identification. In this dream the patient has incorporated her teacher. Analysis also revealed a well-defined masculinity complex. Dreams presenting a phallic woman dealt also with her own wish to be one. Music denoted that addition of importance and power that would otherwise be rendered by masculinity. An idea that she had once had a penis which had been taken away could not be ascertained without doubt. But it was clear that she wanted to play the part of a male, since, as she later stated, her father always wanted to have a boy. Besides, she had a sadistic conception of the man-woman relationship and began early to hate the woman's part. In her neurosis, because of repression and overcompensation of her hatred against men, she was submissive, and showed masochistic delight at being ill-treated. Music, which offered her power and superiority she thought lacking, had phallic importance to her. It offered an unchallengeable form of masculinity; no one could deprive her of it. As a polar contrast to it, music represented to her also a child, which officially she pretended not to want. She said, "I thought of children. They are just a mass of flesh. I was not sorry that I had none. I have music. This is something nobody can take away from me. Music is imperishable, music is life itself."

In the following, we shall study several incidents which show how the symptoms occurred.

Cristina said: "Once I played a Beethoven sonata for Sartori. I let myself go and played according to my deepest feelings. I was happy that some of the difficult passages rolled off smoothly. But Sartori did not like my conception of the composition. He said I should play the Sonata the way Beethoven would play it. When I wanted to play the work again, he declined to hear it. I felt despondent. After that hour I had pain in my hands and could not sleep at night." (He acted like her mother; he was indifferent.) The patient then continued: "The summer before I developed my hand trouble, I was preparing the Brahms *sonata* in F minor and the *Symphonic Études* by Schumann. Sartori said suddenly, 'Let us stop Brahms, we shall play it in the fall. It is too hot to study it now.' I felt dejected. I knew we should not be able to play anything in the fall. I felt that something was going to happen to me. I felt too deeply hurt by Sartori's interest in Jean (another student) and his taking the part of his wife who always treated him so badly. I was convinced he had enough of me and that matters could not go on. A few days later I was an invalid."

On another occasion she related: "At the Academy I was praised repeatedly for the brilliant execution of rapid passages. Now this is where my fingers fail me most. My hand is like a diminished copy of myself. When I feel well physically, my body has a good muscle tone and is elastic. So is my hand. Depressions affect my whole body and my hands. The other day when I went to the Red Cross office to investigate what happened to my family in Rumania, I was very much excited. I did not want to think that they might not be alive. In that moment my arms felt paralyzed. I react to all worries with my symptoms."

She had suffered a slight injury to her finger in childhood; it had to be bandaged. Her nurse took the opportunity to tell her the story of "Little Tom Thumb." She called the injured finger "little baby." As far as could be ascertained, this was the first identification of the finger with a human being.

Analysis showed that an associative connection existed between (1) the tale of "Little Tom Thumb,"[1] (2) the patient's thumbs which were neurotically afflicted, (3) her sister Rita, "the baby," (4) the embryo she once saw after an abortion, and (5) the missing penis.

Cristina once said, "I loved Rita fanatically. I wanted to protect her from all dangers as a mother would protect a child. That is why I am so desperate about having brought her and Lupescu together. I always called her 'my little baby.' She was an excellent piano player and I often envied her the ease and brilliance of her technique. Father loved her more than any other child."

The competitive motif in her relation to Rita echoes again: "Three months ago I was invited to give a concert for refugees—I thought of my sisters in Europe and my arms became totally lame. I recalled that once Rita called me selfish because I devoted my whole life to playing the piano and did not share the responsibilities of the household. This remark stuck in my mind and I often thought it was selfish to be occupied exclusively with music. Whenever I enjoy music, I think of Rita, of what she had said about me and also of the fact that she may not be alive any more. I feel guilty for enjoying music. I have the feeling that my success is Rita's failure, that when I am fine, she is miserable, all because she once made this remark. I think she always knew I had a more genuine musical talent than she had, although she was technically better than I."

Cristina's feelings of guilt led her to be superstitious: "I think my illness has something to do with Rita. I deeply regret that I left her in Europe. Sometimes I feel relaxed, and in the next moment a thought flashes through my mind. Now, you are at the peak of your success but look at the

[1] In Cristina's native tongue "Little Tom Thumb" is called "Little Baby."

others, what they have to suffer! Presently I lose the feeling of exhilaration, I say to myself, 'You must not be happy'— and all is over."

We see here the effect of an important neurotic clause which locks the symptom rendering it virtually unremovable: The patient's happiness brings misery to her family; she, therefore, must never be happy. The discussion of this problem brought the most impressive emotional and symptomatic relief.

She said: "I must admit that prior to the operation I wanted to be ill. I am very imaginative. If I would strongly imagine that I have a headache, I would get it. I did not know how I could help myself. Illness was always a way out. During my convalescence (after my operation) I practiced a great deal. Everybody warned me not to overdo. But I was in such tension that I had to do it. Besides, I was bitter towards Sartori because I had the feeling that through my illness I had lost too much time. I also wanted to give vent to my hatred toward Mrs. Sartori and playing the piano offered me a way of abreacting. In addition I was bitter toward Sartori, because at that time I was convinced I meant nothing to him."

At one time the patient made a significant statement about this point: "When I look at this woman (Mrs. Sartori) my fingers become a hundred percent worse. She is the cause of Sartori's unhappiness. I could strangle her. Her hands are big, ugly, and repulsive. She has some masculine and sadistic features. She often reminds me of Lupescu." (In her dreams, Cristina repeatedly saw women choked to death, whose identity it was not difficult to establish.)

Music represented an important vehicle for Cristina's daydreams. Once she said, "Mrs. Sartori always hated what I played. She never approved of my conception of the work, even if her husband was satisfied."

The patient who had rejected her adult feminine role, established through her music a vicarious gratification. Music thus received the symbolic character of a sexual act; as a consequence, conflicts involving the patient's sexual sphere affected also her musical expression. In her neurosis, playing piano became an equivalent of masturbation, an act which was always accompanied by sado-masochistic fantasy. In this fantasy, through a process of fleeting identifications and projections, such as are typical for sado-masochism, she played simultaneously an active and a passive role: pianist and musical instrument; punisher and victim; father and child; teacher and pupil; mother and daughter; the sister who was jealous and the sister who was the object of this jealousy; husband and wife; etc.

In her neurosis, the function of her hands was rendered painful as a defense against criminal and tabooed sexual cravings. Hands that were bent on committing criminal acts (strangling of the husband and the rival) and other moral and social transgressions by means of music, had to be immobilized. Inasmuch as the hand had a phallic significance, the patient's disability equalled self-castration. Of importance also is the symbolification of her fingers, particularly the thumbs; they were the most severely affected parts.

The analysis was also able to reveal that in our case the thumb at times, and in the context of various daydreams, represented a child the patient had wished would die (sister Rita) and at other times a child that had been killed before it was born (reference to her many abortions). The thumb thus became the point of somatization of various, and often contradictory, emotions. The patient's strong need for self-punishment which drew considerable power from religious sources ("If thy right hand offend thee cut it off." . . . Matt. 5:30) led to an almost complete blocking of her artistic ambitions. Her symptoms became manifest at a time when she studied a work of Schumann which in her mind linked Sartori with Lupescu. It mobilized acutely her dormant feelings of guilt concerning her sister Rita, and rendered her musical pursuits impossible. As a result, the patient established in her mind the formula that she must never be happy. By this neurotic proviso she attempted to deadlock any restorative effort.

TIC

In a psychoanalytic investigation of the tic, Stekel demonstrated that this disorder represents a rudimentary form of an antimoral or antisocial act. The full act which has been denied an overt expression can be reconstructed by the use of dreams.

One of Stekel's patients suffering from an eye tic—spastic closing of the eyelid—had the following dream:

[419] *"I fought a duel with my father. We shot at each other with guns. When my ammunition gave out, I ran away. Father kept shooting at me. I shouted, 'This is no duelling any more, this is murder.'"*

The eye tic represented the initial stage of aiming and shooting. The target (father) is clearly indicated in the patient's dream.

A twenty-two-year-old pianist had the tic of moving his shoulders and neck as though he wanted to loosen a tight collar. The ultimate solution of this tic was possible through the help of dreams. We were able to reconstruct the repressed experience which had contributed to the development of the pathological muscle reaction. During their sojourn in Florida, the patient's sister, an exceedingly attractive girl, sat on his neck while he walked into the surf. He was at that time fourteen or fifteen years old, while his sister was thirteen. He remembered having felt the pressure and warmth of the girl's genital region. The recollection then was lost. But, it remained alive as a wish for a repetition. The patient's movement with neck and shoulder was designed to establish a closer contact with the imaginary body.

These were the dreams in which the leading idea was detected.

[420] *"My friend B. and I are taking a walk. Our sisters are following at a distance. We pass a peculiar-looking fellow,*

apparently insane. He urges his little boy, who rides a scooter, to go faster and faster. At breakneck speed the boy shoots down a steep road, falls, and is killed. The insane roars with wild laughter.

"When we pass him we get frightened about our sisters who are walking behind us and could be at his mercy once he turned against them.

"I decide to go back and stop the insane. A short struggle ensues. It ends when I knock him down with a quick blow on the neck."

In this dream we see the element of "walking," (into the surf), the "sisters" (duplication) are "following" him (i.e., the *thought* of his sister obtrudes upon him). The "insane" man is the patient's own "insane" thought of an incestuous relation with his sister. The scene with the "insane" man's son indicates that if one should let himself go and not consider the consequences, a tragedy would result. (The "little boy" has phallic significance.) The laughter of the insane signifies the patient's perception of the repressed idea (cf. page 60). He hits his sister's oppressor on the *neck* to subdue him. In our language this means, "my neck (and shoulder) enables me to discharge my antimoral incestuous desire without having to resort to acts endangering my sister."

[421] *"In a pullman sleeper on my way to Florida. A lady of our acquaintance, whose berth is above mine, gives me a special type of chocolate and says, 'If you cannot sleep well, this will help you.' We talk for a while about music. She then writes me her hotel address in Miami Beach so that I can call on her when I arrive. While she writes, my shoulder or elbow touches her genital region. She is very much excited. I awake with an emission."*

This dream takes the patient to Florida, the scene of the fateful experience. The "acquaintance" is a substitute for the patient's sister. The "special chocolate" which she offers him as a hypnotic makes us conclude that we are dealing here with the expression of the patient's "specific masturbation fantasy" ("this will help you"). We also see in this dream the reference to the future, i.e., to his daydream wishes for a reunion, a repetition of the past experiences. The "finale" of the dream is self-explanatory.

In his tic the patient is able to re-experience the traumatic event, to discharge the tabooed emotions and through the fact of his disability he can punish himself for the moral transgression.

The tic "announces," as it were, to the world at large—if the world could only understand its symbolic language—the secret that oppresses the tiqueur. It is one of those exhibitionistic neuroses in which we find what Theodor Reik called "a confessing compulsion."

NEUROSIS IN DREAMS

HYSTERIA

Of the two common forms of hysteria, the *conversion hysteria* and *anxiety hysteria,* the first has been discussed among the individual psychosomatic disorders. Here we may add that "conversion" represents a special manifestation of repressed complexes (emotionally charged ideas). The repressed energy is transformed (converted) onto the two nervous systems, the *cerebrospinal* and the *vegetative nervous system.* The latter encompasses a large part of the so-called psychosomatic disorders.

We mentioned on page 308 the importance of erogenous zones for the precipitation of conversion symptoms. We can find in this connection that some anatomic regions have been "genitalized," that is, that they carry a libido cathexis commensurate to the genital region, under normal circumstances. Tissues which are thus affected show swelling and hyperemia (cf. Quincke edema, page 349) which confirms this shift of cathexis.

In the following we shall deal with anxiety hysteria and a few of the more common phobias, also with some other hysterical manifestations, such as Amnesia, Fugue, and Depersonalization.

ANXIETY HYSTERIA

AGORAPHOBIA

In dreams of persons suffering from agoraphobia we find the symbols of general inhibition, but instead of the particular fear of walking, riding, or passing certain places, there is an encompassing fear of the patient's own impulses breaking through inhibitions. (Pictures of wild animals, skittish horses, and so on.)

An example: [423] *"I am walking in the street. Suddenly I am stopped by a horse and carriage crossing the street. There are two pairs of horses; the pair in the back attack the front pair with their hoofs. The reins of the front pair are broken and the freed horses run wildly toward the spot where I am standing. I run away, but the horses follow me into my house and even upstairs. I awake with strong heart palpitation."*

We see the patient's symptom in the words "I am stopped." The "carriage" which is crossing the patient's path is a thought coming into his mind. The "front horses" symbolize the "conscious," the rear ones the "unconscious thoughts." The unconscious impulses are pressing against the patient's consciousness, his immoral against his moral and social feelings. It is this pressure which causes the patient's phobia. We can also interpret the "first pair of horses" as "the present," and the second as "the past." The latter interpretation is as follows: The patient's recollections are disturbing his present state of mind.

The patient has to endure a grave conflict between his parents and his wife. He dare not admit that his marriage has been a failure. In the dream the "back horses" symbolize his parents, while the "front couple" represent his unhappy marriage. He represses ideas of betraying and even of killing his wife and fleeing to another country ("the carriage"). He cannot forget that he had to give up the girl he loved for his wife whom his parents suggested to him as a mate. Hence his conflict between the "past" and the "present." His agoraphobia is in the service of his superego. So long as he cannot even cross a street without feeling the agony of fear there will be no killing, no unfaithfulness, and no escaping. The symptoms serve as protection against his own antisocial impulses.

The next dream of the same patient is very informative:

[424] *"There is an excavation in an old city."* (Symbol of analysis. Reference to the patient's past. We may expect important revelations about the conflict "past versus present.") *"We come to a huge square stone in the center of a large room."* (Memorial. Symbol of an unforgettable recollection.) *"On the pedestal there is a big cup. I wonder what is inside, but an old man resembling a priest approaches and warns me not to open it."* (Resistance against uncovering the last secrets of his unconscious. The resistance shows the weakest spot of his neurosis, however, and betrays just as much as it is supposed to conceal.) *"He says, 'There are bones; whoever touches them cannot move.'"* (We notice the reference of the secret to the phobia.) *"Nevertheless I open the cup, and see bones, parts of a spinal column, and parts of a chest. I put it back quickly and want to leave, but the walls of the room come nearer and nearer. I can barely press one part of my body through a narrow slit between two walls, but there I get stuck and cannot move forward or backward. An invisible force keeps me back."*

The patient does not want to see his criminal ideas against his wife expressed in the dream by the parts of the skeleton. The walls coming nearer and finally arresting him represent the patient's phobia as well as the prison which he anticipates in his dream. The dream contains the patient's love problem. The "bones" symbolize his past experience with his ·first sweetheart. He does not want to face the truth that his thoughts are constantly impelled toward her and that he considers his marriage a prison which prevents him from any personal development, from getting out, or improving his condition. In the above dream, there are also allusions to an infantile problem, namely, to the masturbation complex. The warning voice is the paternal imperative concerning the patient's genitals (cup) which are not to be touched. The bones, particularly the spinal column, in this cross-section symbolize the idea of damages as a consequence of masturbation.

You will recall dream number 20 in which the woman saw a soldier shoot through a window into her room. She awoke in fear. She was suffering from agoraphobia and was unable to walk on the street alone. She wished to relive an experience in which the soldier, her cousin, had seduced her.

A woman of this type would have difficulty in walking on the street, because, in her fantasy, this means becoming a streetwalker (prostitute). It was mentioned that the subway is a breeding place of sexual daydreams. There is a peculiar sexual atmosphere. There is often an opportunity for a physical contact. In some anxiety hysterias we see defenses against such thoughts. The defenses in such cases do not seem strong enough, and additional defenses must be constructed; "streetwalking" must be stopped completely, and riding in the subway must be discontinued.

As stated on page 79, dreams preceding and following the neurotic reactions such as anxiety states, fits, depressions, or other symptoms, are of special importance. The specific pathogenic situation which is responsible for the outbreak of symptoms is usually revealed in such dreams. *Dreams can sometimes be the cause of symptoms* exhibited by the patient on the day following the dream night. (But dreams can never cause a neurosis.)

Let us study a few examples: a woman aged thirty-four had the following dream five weeks after the difficult delivery of her third child:

[425] *"I was traveling in a train, and apparently my two little boys had run out to play. After some time the train started, leaving my two boys outside. I grew quite frantic and implored everyone to stop the train, but no one seemed to understand me."*

After this dream the patient awoke with a strong heart palpitation which persisted during the whole morning. The interpretation of this dream enables us to understand the patient's anxiety. The dream contains a wish-fulfillment. The patient had very difficult childbirths. She suffered from hyperemesis during her pregnancy, and the delivery was both very painful and very dangerous, because her uterus was displaced. The children were unwanted, yet all efforts to remove the fetus were in vain. The patient was never able to experience complete sexual enjoyment because of her constant fear of becoming pregnant. The dream shows the patient's lack of sexual satisfaction in the incident of the train stopping, and contains the reason for this disturbance—the problem of "children." In this dream, the patient gets rid of her children, an antimoral thought which immediately causes a neurotic anxiety reaction. The patient has hostile feelings toward her children and is afraid lest these feelings become known. In her neurosis she exhibited the well-known accompanying symptoms of repressed criminality, such as fear of knives and fear of insanity, in which state she might kill her children (that is, fulfill her unconscious wishes).

The following dream was contributed by a thirty-four-year-old woman suffering from *agoraphobia*. Because of her anxiety she was unable to walk on streets for four years and was forced to stay in her apartment. The dream runs as follows:

[426] *"My aunt Fanny with whom I live had an accident and injured her back. Somehow it was my fault. My aunt Polly tells me that she won't live long on account of this injury, and that we will have to move to another, cheaper place to reduce the rent."*

The patient toys with the idea of her aunt's death. Her

criminal thoughts meet with strong guilt reactions, however, which force the patient to punish herself by imprisoning herself in her apartment and depriving herself of all the happiness and opportunity that a free social intercourse entails.

EREUTHOPHOBIA

Patients suffering from the fear of blushing (ereuthophobia) dream very often of fire, explosions, red colors, effervescent liquids, of getting the face wet, and other pictures portraying the congestion of blood in the face. A twenty-four-year-old patient suffering from ereuthophobia dreams as follows:

[427] *"I went into a store to get a battery filler for my car. The shopkeeper seemed to object to something. He took a syringe filled with water and sprayed it into my face. I don't know why."*

We recognize the syringe spraying water, a symbol of the male genitals. The latent homosexuality and other infantile features played a great part in this case. The analysis proved that the patient's blushing tendency (in his dream portrayed by the picture of the syringe spraying water into his face) was based on his inner perception of this infantile attitude. He was ashamed of his homosexual desires and blushed whenever he faced other people.

One of my patients dreamed [428] *of having been attacked by a woman who sprayed blood into his face.*

In this case, latent sadistic impulses against women caused the patient's blushing. The patient used to experience this symptom most frequently in the presence of women.

Sometimes we find blushing in symbols of the direct opposite (extreme pallor) as in the case of a lady [429] *who saw herself holding lilies* (symbol of chastity) *in her hand.*

This demonstration of chastity has the same psychological mechanism as that of the "chaste" blushing, namely a displacement of the sexual excitement upward to the face and, at the same time, an expression of self-consciousness and feeling of guilt.

(Examples of dreams referring to other types of phobias are presented in other chapters of this book.)

AMNESIA AND FUGUE

We should like to mention a few dreams which may help to cast some light upon amnesia and fugue, two conditions which sometimes appear in hysterical and other psychopathological disturbances. *Amnesia* is characterized by a loss of memory during a specific time. It is sometimes punctuated by single memory traces (memory islands) and may be definite in its inception and end abruptly (epilepsy, hysteria, intoxication), or show a chronic course with remissions (Korsakoff, senile dementia, brain lesions). It can also be retrograde and extend over hours, days, or months (after brain concussions, hanging attempts, and in epileptic equivalents). The memory loss may refer to one's own self or to the outside world.

A *fugue* is often associated with amnesia. The hysterical patient may disappear from his home and wander about, having lost his sense of identity. After a time ranging from hours to months the patient may recover but show a retrograde amnesia. The causes of both hyponoic conditions are life situations which the patient finds unbearable. Instead of dealing with them maturely he runs away from them. Patients of this type show the phenomenon of multiple (or dissociated) personality. Hypnosis may produce such conditions artificially, and may also help the patient to return to normalcy.

However, dreams can offer insight and guidance in such conditions. One of my patients, a thirty-two-year-old woman, married, described a fugue in which she left her husband and went to her father who was divorced and lived in a neighboring town. She appeared confused, dazed, and disoriented. The father called in a physician who brought her out of this condition. During analysis she had the following dream:

[430] *"I am in a sort of penthouse garden. Many people around. A glass window opens and a dwarflike creature comes up on a ladder. Offers a tumbler with a drink on a platter. I am disgusted by his looks and refuse the drink—I know it is poison. I am surprised that nobody pays attention to this intrusion. A fascination emanates from the person and it makes me drink. I am about to fall into unconsciousness when I awaken with a start."*

This dream portrays the symptom and, as such, is capable of enlightening us about the inner mechanisms of the symptom.

(Q) "Is the dwarf a phallic symbol?"

(A) Yes. But if we start to decipher symbols without getting first the dynamics of the dream, we shall not get far. This is a typical mistake of the less experienced interpreters; they try to decode the symbols first.

We must start by simplifying the manifest dream content. We ask: "What happens here?" Our answer is that in the dream out of the lower recesses of the house, a sinister creature comes up, a dwarf. It offers the dreamer a drink, i.e., enjoyment, which she refuses at first, knowing it to be harmful, and then, fascinated by the creature, she accepts. It makes her lose consciousness.

We assume that similar circumstances made her lose consciousness when she developed the state of fugue.

The dream conveys to us a scene in which her father, on whose lap she was once sitting as a small child, had pressed his genital against her body. The dream clearly indicates the approach of the dwarf from below (the creature comes up on a ladder) after a window in the roof had been opened. And then repulsion turns into acceptance. Since the approach in the dream is oral there is reason to believe that a fellatio has occurred. The patient, however, denied that such an act had taken place. We can, therefore, assume that it was a part of a subsequent wish fantasy, for the dream is quite outspoken in this respect. The "poison," of course, can be considered to be the incestuous wish. The unconscious state into which the patient is about to succumb, indicates her desire to withdraw her defenses and to surrender to her id.

There is also reason to believe that the experience to which the dream alludes is one that has taken place while the patient's power of judgment was inadequate, for instance, because she was very young, one to two years of age. Experience teaches that those patients who were exposed to traumatic impressions while in a state of lowered lucidity (half-sleep, infancy, etc.) later are particularly inclined to develop hyponoic conditions.

"Many people around" means secrecy.

Other motives can also be seen in dreams of such patients. A forty-year-old woman had fugue attacks with amnesia twice. The first attack occurred when her mother had a heart attack and the patient was to go to call the family physician. She reports: "I left home at 10 a.m. I thought I was at my father's shop. He later said I was never there. Instead, I found myself at night, at about twelve, at the doctor's home with father and my husband who, apparently, were summoned there. I was told that I was found hammering at the doctor's door calling, 'Mother, mother, mother!' "

When the patient left her home with the intention of going to the doctor, something happened to her which is submerged in amnesia. You can easily see that the patient's unconscious drove her to a criminal neglect of her ailing mother. The Oedipus situation is clearly depicted in her suppressed impulse: The patient brought about the death of her mother and hurried to her father rather than to the doctor who might have helped. Fortunately for the patient, the mother did not die; otherwise the patient might have suffered a strong conscience reaction.

Narcosynthesis or hypnosis in many cases helps to elucidate the dark interval of amnesia. But dreams may be of just as much help and carry even deeper. However, neither hypnosis nor narcosynthesis are entirely free from the danger of being misused by the patient. The patient's fantasy may distort the findings, even when he is under narcosis or hypnosis. Interesting in this respect is the digest of "The Lost 15 Minutes" which appeared in the *Reader's Digest* of May, 1949. This article presents a case in point.[1]

It is a story of a man who was accused of having killed his wife with a butcher knife. The defendant was an Air Force sergeant who was married for three years and had two children. He was living in California when he received orders to go to Alaska. He wanted his wife to join him there and wrote repeatedly to her begging her to come out. She refused. In one of his letters he even threatened to come back home and to kill her. He gave her an ultimatum which expired at the end of June.

After the ultimatum had expired, he purchased a few gifts for his wife, bought return tickets for himself, his wife, and his children, and flew to California.

When he arrived at home he found his wife very cool to him. She told him—according to his report—that he could not stay at home as he had planned because she was in love with some other man—an ex-sailor. The flier went down on his knees and pleaded with his wife to stay with him. He wanted her to have a priest from a nearby parish arbitrate their dispute. His wife agreed. The curate reconciled the couple and advised them to go to Alaska together.

When they came home, the wife confessed that she had fooled him, that she did not love him, and what's more, that their second child was not his but the other man's. It was then, according to the defendant, that he got into a peculiar state of mind. He remembered having prayed and having had a vision of a long, sharp knife.

What followed was completely erased from the patient's consciousness. He came to after about fifteen minutes and

[1] "The Lost 15 Minutes" originally appeared in *Argosy*, May 1949, Popular Publications, Inc., New York.

"knew" that he had killed his wife, "because my wife and I were the only ones there."

The defendant was submitted to an experiment designed to elucidate the period of amnesia. An intravenous injection of sodium pentothal was used. During the experiment the defendant reported an entirely different story. While under narcosis, he stated that there was another man, his rival, present when his wife was killed. His wife and the man were living together in another apartment as "husband and wife" and they told him that they were going to take the children away from him. His wife supposedly told him at that point that her lover would kill him "so we can have happiness." And then the ex-sailor allegedly killed the defendant's wife. In his narcosynthetic confession the prisoner was not at all surprised how little logic the confession contained; but justice took its peculiar course.

The ex-sailor was asked to testify. He admitted that he and the defendant's wife had had relations with each other and that they had rented an apartment under his name. However, he denied having been near the scene of the crime at the specified time and was able to present a perfect alibi. He was dismissed. The jury acquitted the defendant but had no further evidence to institute action against the other suspect.

Not having direct material on which to base an opinion, all our conclusions will be of limited value. But it is a fact that the murder of the adultress wife ultimately remained unsolved.

If we compare the two confessions of the defendant, the one he offered voluntarily and the one he brought out under narcosis, we are impressed by the fact that the first one has much more credibility than the second. It is psychologically understandable that a husband who learns of the infidelity of his wife, who is told cynically that the child he has been bringing up is not his own, and that his wife is sharing the life of another man while pretending to be married to him—

that such a husband may develop an impulse to avenge his humiliation. In this case, the marital relation seems to have been strained for a long time, since a previous threat to kill his wife was admitted freely by the defendant. It is also known that some individuals develop amnesia after having committed crimes of passion. Amnesia substitutes for the flight from the scene of the crime, it follows the flight reflex pattern, except that it is primarily a flight from the ego instead of from the intolerable situation.

On the other hand, it is rather difficult to assume that a man who "has gotten what he was after," so to speak, who has far-reaching plans with a woman, and who knows that this woman is willing to go with him—that such a man should want to kill this woman.

In this respect, dreams may have provided a more objective material for the study of an amnesic episode than a confession that has been forced out of the deep repositories of the mind by narcosis.

DEPERSONALIZATION

Depersonalization is a state in which the patient feels either himself, or the world, or both, as strange and dreamlike. A strong resistance directed against the patient's emotional experience makes itself obvious. The patient then turns away, so to speak, from his unwelcome experiences. He watches himself as though he were another person while he is having the experience. He also withdraws his emotionally charged interest from the outside world. His own world then becomes dull, "unreal," and offers no personal value to the patient.

In the case of a twenty-four-year-old woman suffering from states of depersonalization and derealization, the following dreams proved highly informative:

[431] *"I am in a hospital. The nurse assigns me to a bed which belongs to another patient and is very dirty. I do not want to lie down in it.*

"During the dream I had a constant feeling of unreality."

The "other patient" whose bed is dirty represents the dreamer's "alter ego," which is full of "dirty thoughts." The endopsychic perception of this province of the ego leads to feelings of unreality.

[432] *"My friend Sina was somehow identical with my friend Xenia."*

In shifting affects from one object to another, the changed cathexis leads to a confusion of identities. The confused identity then leads to the feeling of strangeness.

[433] *"I enter the room and sit down at the table. Suddenly I see myself sitting opposite of me. I get terribly frightened. A fight ensues between myself and my other ego. I make some promises and run out."*

In this dream the "promises" represent the concessions the patient makes to the id. She allows herself to depress the level of consciousness to such an extent that her antimoral and antisocial tendencies can obtain a partial outlet. (Compare at this point what was said about the "mirror dreams" on page 130 and the "splitting of the ego" on page 185.)

[434] *"I am on a boat alone. I am afraid I will always be alone. Suddenly I see my father who at the same time is my husband."*

The patient's affect oscillates between father and husband. She is not sure which is her real object. Such mixed cathexes may lead to depersonalization.

[435] *"I come to a strange city. It is dark. All of a sudden a crazy woman runs out of a house. I am terrified. An elderly gentleman passes me and I am relieved. He tells me, however, that Dimitri (husband) has died. I am desperate. Then I say— 'Well, then I'll go to Dr. Gutheil to work as a housekeeper.'"*

The feeling of unreality is expressed by the patient's coming to a "strange city." This phrase refers to the fact that she is about to embark upon a train of thoughts which appear "strange" to her, because they are antimoral. While the lights of her consciousness are dimmed ("It is dark") the suppressed thought breaks through ("a crazy woman runs out of a house"). Anxiety accompanies this release of energy ("I am terrified"). The dream then reveals the tabooed idea (death wish toward husband) and also suggests a practical solution for the merry widow.

[436] *"I am traveling to N. with Dimitri. Suddenly the picture changes and I see Dimitri being carried home. He is badly injured. I become insane.*

The main anxiety-provoking idea in cases of depersonalization is that the condition may be a symptom or a prodromal manifestation of insanity. The above dream shows the reason for both the symptoms of depersonalization and the subsequent anxiety. In the words, "the picture changes," the patient expresses the change of her attitude toward her husband. Whenever such change takes place, the patient develops her feelings of unreality. These feelings are always the result of a dissociation of the emotional object cathexes or a dissociation of affect between ego and id.

[437] *"I visit Vassilissa at her home. She is in bed. I lie down next to her. She puts her arms around me and touches my breasts. Speaks affectionately. I want to free myself from her, but I feel paralyzed. Then I run away. On the stairs an insane woman is sitting, with a silly grin on her face."*

The strange woman is the symbolization of the patient's own crazy (homosexual) ideas.

Doubts usually accompany the feeling of estrangement. The patient may ask (by way of her symptom):

(1) "Am I what my superego wants me to be or am I what my id induces me to be?"

(2) "Are you the way my ego knows you (e.g., beloved), or the way my id perceives you (e.g., hated)?"

(3) "Do I live in the present or in the past?"

(4) "Am I married to Dimitri (realistic object) or to my father (infantile object)?"

(5) "Am I heterosexual or homosexual?"

(6) "Am I myself or somebody else?"

The psychosexual infantilism of the patient makes the preservation of her bisexuality understandable. Her failure to find gratification on a realistic level brings infantile cravings to the foreground. We shall not go deeper into this matter at this point.

COMPULSIONS AND DREAMS

A compulsion neurosis is a *system* of obsessions and compulsions. It is built around a secret nucleus. An obsession is an obtruding *idea*. A compulsion is an *act* which has to be carried out. It is locked by anxiety; if it is resisted, anxiety is liberated.

In dreams of patients suffering from compulsions we often find various expressions of doubt. This doubt, as is well-known, is the basis of every neurotic compulsion. Also various compulsive states may indicate the compulsion neurosis in the dream. The patients see themselves in uniform, or trapped, locked up, nailed on crosses, tied to posts, deprived of freedom, and so forth.

A very instructive dream which distinctly shows a painful "compulsion state" is the following dream by a twenty-nine-year-old clerk suffering from a counting compulsion. We see here distinctly the high degree of sado-masochism which accompanies most compulsions:

[438] *"I am in a room entirely naked. The floor of this room consists of sharp steel upright plates which are about two inches apart. In order to avoid being cut to pieces I try to take a position in which I can lean upon the knives with as little weight as possible. After many attempts I finally get into the following position: I clutch two plates with my fingers and lean on my knees. Thus, although I become injured and suffer great pain, I maintain the best possible position while waiting for help."*

The doubt in compulsion neurosis originates in the patient's attempt to "annul," to negate, an experience of his past. He behaves as though the experience had not taken place. Dreams lead us to the critical, doubt-producing experience.

Doubt in itself may represent a compulsion. Pathological doubters often use the "either-or" situation in their dreams. A typical dream of such a doubter, a man aged thirty-nine, suffering from compulsory ideas, is the following:

[439] *"I am with—or meet—a number of young people. They learn from something said by me—or by someone else —that I must offer an apartment for rent. We are driving. I am at the wheel and collide with a machine driven by a girl going in the opposite direction. I see her arguing with the driver of another car about her being in the right—or wrong. While I contended—or argued to myself that I would contend—that she caused the accident by first turning to the left, I felt I had seen her first turn to the right."*

The entire dream is a drastic expression of doubt. Nothing is certain, everything is questionable. Who is speaking, the dreamer or someone else? Is he with, or does he meet, the young people? Who is the cause of the accident, the dreamer or the girl coming from the opposite direction (like the dreamer's thoughts, which always contradict themselves)? Did the girl turn to the left or to the right? Questions, questions —nothing is certain. We notice in this dream also the patient's feeling of guilt ("arguing," "self-reproaches") which, as we know, plays the most important part in the psychology of compulsion neuroses.

A young lady of twenty-four who was in doubt about her feelings toward one of her friends (Paul) had the following peculiar dream:

[440] *"I refused Paul's invitation to come to H. (place where he lives). I went to Professor B's lecture instead. When it was over I looked at my watch to see if I still had time to go to H. I had my knapsack, which I usually take with me when I go to H. At first it seemed that I had enough time, but later I realized that it was not half-past three but quarter-past six; hence it was too late. I decided to go to the*

station anyway in the hope of getting another train to H. All of a sudden the scene changed and I was discussing my intended trip to H."

The doubt scenes emphasized in the dream report are so obvious that they need no further interpretation.

The roots of the pathological doubt are found in.

(a) The "annulment" of certain real experiences because of their tabooed character; the dream analysis then helps us to reconstruct the pathogenic experiences with or without the patient's cooperation.

(b) A disturbed superego identification connected with a wavering between masculine and feminine tendencies; extreme cases of this disturbance are described on page 422 as depersonalization. Interesting material concerning this disturbance can also be found in Oberndorf's "Feeling of Unreality" and "Depersonalization in Relation to Erotization of Thought." Dreams serve us for establishing facts and transforming the libidinous fixations.

(c) A contrast between conscious and unconscious drives; here again dreams offer us insight into the inner dynamics and afford us means to settle the emotional conflicts.

The following dream is another typical dream of a doubter:

[441] *"Went on a long trip on foot. I think it was on foot. (Can't be sure of the purpose of the trip.) On the way I was going over a long bridge or up a long hill (I'm not sure which). Then I had to ask a man to do a complicated errand for me. On part of it I followed him to see that he got on his way. He was most distrustful. I told him (which was true) that the request had come from someone he would have to trust and obviously could trust—someone like David B. perhaps, whose honesty was above reproach. He still distrusted me. He knew one of the people we met en route who was concerned in the errand. I said that there were now two people whose word he couldn't help but accept. He went on, still distrustful."*

No particular skill is necessary to diagnose this dreamer's personality.

One of the roots of the pathological doubt in compulsion neurosis is the character of the patient's ego structure. Stekel has pointed out that in schizophrenia the patient's dual personality expresses itself in a simultaneous, peaceful co-existence of the two parts, the "ego" and the "alter ego"; in compulsions, however, we find an "ego" and a "counter-ego," each denying the other its place and interlocked in an indecisive struggle.

An example of such a dream is the following product of a doubter:[1]

[442] *"I dreamt I was traveling on a train which was in the nature of a shuttle service to some main line. As I was riding on this train I was conscious of another train running parallel to my train in the same direction. I asked someone if he knew where this other train went and he said it was going to the same point of destination as our train. I couldn't seem to understand why there were two trains traveling to the same destination on two separate tracks. I was conscious of traveling to and fro with these shuttle trains. I went from one train to the other and kept asking people where each train was going. I was confused and apprehensive trying to determine the correct train to travel on."*

We notice that the patient is on a shuttle train. It is not a train that gets him any place, for it does not run on a main line. Another train, apparently just as fast as his train, follows it side by side.

The patient notices this but does not understand it. He asks questions but he does not get proper information. He is "traveling to and fro" on both trains. By this statement he proves that both trains represent parts of himself, different parts, but put into operation simultaneously. It is an "as well as" or an "either-or," representing a picture of the "point-counterpoint" thinking mechanism so characteristic

[1] Contributed by Dr. J. O. S. Jaeger of New York.

for the compulsives. It is a sterile motion, a "perpetuum mobile" that fills his time and thought with non-essential occupation which is designed to keep him from thinking what he is not supposed to be thinking. This thinking automatism also keeps him from committing antisocial acts.

The following dream is typical:

[443] *"I was in uniform among people who were in uniform. We had guns and were shooting high in order not to hit anybody."*

The uniform represents the patient's neurosis. The dream shows patient's aggressive tendencies which are displaced and rendered ineffective. What are the aggressive tendencies of this thirty-eight-year-old bank clerk? The next three dreams are more conclusive:

[444] *"I walked upstairs. Cats were following me. Among them was a dog."*

[445] *"I saw the motion picture 'Blue Bird.' A fairy changes a cat into a woman who personifies the evil. The same fairy changed a dog (bulldog) into a man. Dogs are enemies of cats."*

The patient, himself, recognizes that "cat" represents the woman. We find that he has sadistic tendencies toward women. He is the bulldog. He has fantasies of attacking women orally and of tearing them to pieces with his teeth.

[446] *"I carry a woman in my mouth, like a wolf, blood dripping from my jaws."*

We see that he is oppressed by wild, atavistic urges which are hard to control. They are directed primarily against his mother and sister, the objects of his sinister love. He suffers from a gazing compulsion. Is it a coincidence that the patient's sister has a disfigured face? (Cf. also p. 215.)

Such reactions are based on repressed sadistic impulses. The disfigurement is *the result* of a sadistic disfiguring act, which is blacked out, so that only the end phase remains conscious. It attracts, however, all the cathexis originally designated to the entire process.

The connection between staring and the sadistic tendencies ("eyes that kill") can be seen in many of the patient's dreams. The following is an example:

[447] *"Walking in the park with my mother. We pass some terrifying animals (dragons?) in cages. I stare at them defiantly. As we walk along, I see a man whose leg is crippled. I try not to look at him.*

"Later, my mother is replaced by my sister. A machine (like airplane) with swaying arms strikes my sister on the top of her head and knocks her to the ground. I am very angry."

The animals represent the patient's antisocial urges. Their effect is shown in the crippled man and the attack on the patient's sister. The patient is anxiously trying to suppress these tendencies by a complicated system of self-punishment and various ascetic procedures. When going to bed, he spends some time in a purposely uncomfortable position—raised left leg, right arm, and head—as a sleeping ceremonial. Experienced analysts recognize in such a sleeping ceremonial, the religious complex. The patient's position is a rudiment of a prayer and a caricature of a sacrificial act. This idea is expressed in the following dream:

[448] *"My sister and I flee through a jungle. Suddenly, I feel something dripping along my spine—it is blood.*

"I thought I was bleeding for my family. I am the sacrificial lamb of the family. Sometimes, I think I could kill all of them in a mass murder."

ACTIVE ANALYSIS OF AN OBSESSIVE IDEA BY THE USE OF DREAMS

The following is a brief report of the successful analysis of a compulsion idea by the use of active dream interpretation:

Judge Maurice B., thirty-four years old, suffered since the age of fifteen from the compulsory idea that he must give his superior a box on the ear. The compulsion was at times so strong that in order to become calm he had to leave the room.

It happened very often that in such a state he would begin a quarrel with his superior and commit the intended act at least with words. It was a characteristic of the compulsion that there was no undertone of hatred in it. The patient's situation was very painful because he was always in fear of an early end of his career.

Relying on the experiences of analysis, that the relation toward superiors is usually determined by the father complex, we proceeded to discuss the patient's attitude toward his father. Analysis revealed a pathological fixation. The patient remembered that it was his father whom he felt like boxing on the ear.

We were originally inclined to consider the intended impulse of slapping the face only as the symbol of another impulse, a prohibited one, such as tenderness, touching of the genitals, or the like. However, we were very soon obliged to change our point of view. The first dream brought by the patient gave us a hint that the sources of the compulsory idea were in another sphere. The dream was as follows:

[449] *"I enter the house of the Court of Justice. From a room Usher C. greets me, 'How do you do, Herr Hauptmann* (that is "captain"; literally, "chief man"), *if you really are one.' I explain that I did serve in the army but that I do not wish him to address me as an officer, at least not as 'Herr Hauptmann.'"*

Our attention is arrested by the sentence: "Herr Hauptmann, if you really are one," which is to be considered an expression of doubt. In this connection the following dream was found to be pertinent:

[450] *"I am lying on the table in such a way that only my feet touch the edge of the table; the rest of me is hanging in the air. Someone wants to make me conscious of it, but another warns him against telling me. He should consider it a secret; otherwise something might happen to me. But I tell them, 'It only depends on belief!'"*

A superficial examination of this dream allows us to put

our preliminary interpretation into the following words: the patient is dominated by a secret; he fights his distrust toward the world ("it only depends on belief").

And the secret? We inquire for other states of doubt and learn the following: the patient suffered for a long time, during his sixteenth and seventeenth years, from spells of doubt, so much so that he was compelled to touch individual objects to be sure that they were "real" and not imaginary.

Mostly, however, he was troubled by a doubt as to whether or not he was really himself. Once, during a lesson in religion, the catechist was talking about doubt in confession. The boy conquered his timidity and asked the priest's advice regarding his doubt in his identity. The priest suggested the use of a drastic measure in order to cure the boy of his "stupidity," as he called it. He said: "Whenever you don't know exactly whether or not you are really yourself, have someone slap you in the face and you will then find out."

The remark of the priest at first did not seem to make an impression on the boy. His comrades and he laughed at the good joke. Later he forgot this incident entirely, and it was only during the treatment that the recollection of this occasion came back to him. It proved to be exceedingly important for us. In the following dream we see (considering the displacement common in dreams) the doubt in the patient's family origin.

[451] *"I see several groups of children who are apparently my aunt's children. I investigate the likenesses among the individual groups and find one group which does not resemble the other groups. I find, besides, that this group of children belongs to another mother and not to my aunt."*

We must give attention here to the matter of the resemblance of the children to each other. We shall soon see that dissimilarity is caused not by "another mother" but by "another father."

The preceding dream is to be understood in the same way. The patient is "hanging in the air"; he has no connection with the family of his forefathers. This is the "secret" spoken of in his dream. He tries to get over it by stating that "everything depends on belief," but his neurosis shows that he has not succeeded in doing so.

After some time there is another dream [452] which advances our analysis:

"In a restaurant in my home town several fellows are sitting, my brother Frank among them. The fellows maintain that Frank is a Jew. Frank bets large sums with the fellows that he is not. The outcome must be decided by the certificate of baptism."

Interpretation: If the patient's brother is a Jew, our patient is also a Jew. How can the fellows in the dream maintain that? In fact, those who maintain that are not the fellows but the patient himself, the author of the dream. Here we have again a clear expression of the patient's doubt as to his origin.

Has the patient a Jewish complex? Referring to the patient's big nose, his analyst asked him: "Have you ever had any criticism regarding your nose?"

"Yes!" he answered promptly. "It has always seemed to me to be Semitic. We have, however, been definitely Gentile for ages."

This analytical material made clear the patient's unconscious idea that he was not the son of his father, that his father was not the "Hauptmann" (chief man) of his mother. We, therefore, began the investigation of this complex. The patient remembered that when he was about thirteen or fourteen he asked his mother why he had such a Semitic-sounding name as "Maurice." The mother answered that in her youth she had had a Jewish friend, a veterinary surgeon in her home town, who was named "Maurice." After his death she and her husband agreed to give their son the name Maurice, in memory of this good friend. Even in those days this information made a deep impression upon the boy. The doubt entered his mind as to whether his mother had had a liaison with the veterinary surgeon and whether or not he was the son of this man.

With this communication the compulsory idea was clarified. The boy's doubt as to his origin was soon repressed and remained unconscious. It became the basis of his neurosis, primarily because it concerned his attitude toward his mother. This gnawing doubt was well capable of shattering his exalted mother ideal. In this connection we must also consider the strengthening of the homosexual component of our patient. In his compulsion he tried to get rid of his tormenting doubt. He attempted again and again to take the advice of the priest (box on the ear), not in order to identify his own ego, which was never doubtful to him, but to answer the chief question of his life, without which there was no possibility of his becoming a well-adjusted member of society, no trust in the world or in mankind. He tried to solve the problem with regard to his father, later to his father's images. Behind all his doubts there was one great doubt: *Is my father really my father?*

Success in this case, after this solution of the compulsory idea, was made possible by active dream interpretation. By keeping the trend of the analysis at all times in our hands, by preventing a too abundant stream of communications, and by inducing the patient to utter relevant recollections almost continually we succeeded in a relatively short time in removing the obsessive idea.

DREAMS OF PSYCHOTICS

> *The dreamer is a madman quiescent,*
> *the madman is a dreamer in action.*
> F. H. HEDGE

INTRODUCTION

In his dream book Freud examines the etiological and clinical relations between dreams and psychoses, and points out the striking similarities between them. This resemblance has been noticed before. Wundt says: "Indeed, in the dream we can live through almost all phenomena met with in asylums." And Hughlings Jackson says: "Find out all about dreams and you have found out all about insanity."

Among psychoanalysts, theoretical studies on the subject of psychoses have been made by Freud, Ferenczi, Hartmann, Schilder, Staercke, and others. Ever since we have attempted to "understand" psychoses we find in psychoses all the mechanisms we know from our study of dreams, namely, symbolization, projection, introjection, condensation, distortion, and so on. We find the psychotic's attitude toward reality (including the reality of the patient's own ego) disturbed. We say that the patient's reality testing "is deficient."[1] The centers of his interest are pathologically displaced; he may withdraw interest from the ego or the environment. Then a permanent or temporary feeling of *depersonalization*, a feeling that the end of the world has come, or some other pathological manifestation, becomes visible in dreams, delusions, and hallucinations.

Other mechanisms occur in delusions which are commonly observed in dreams; for instance, a relapse to a primitive way of perceiving reality, or a far-reaching regression which the inner and the outer world may be seen confluent. The patient may then feel his ego as a part of the world, or the world as a part of his ego. In some states (stupor) recognition of the external world is entirely lacking. After awakening from this state some patients report that they have been in a kind of daze and do not remember anything; others report that they have had daydreams or have seen daydream-like pictures.

Schilder reports the following confession of a patient after the latter recovered from a stupor. The patient had the feeling that [453] *he was on a long journey. At one time he was swimming in azure crevasses, at another time he was*

---

[1] Before the child is capable of testing reality, its "reality" represents hallucinatory wish-fulfillment. The psychotic mind relapses onto this stage.

*lying in the hot engine room of a steamer which seemed
sunk in the water. A tall blond sailor drank the sinking drops.
Over the patient there was a continuous roaring like the
roaring of the ship's guns. He believed himself to be in the
Mediterranean Sea. It seemed to him as if he had been kidnaped.* "*Then I saw phosphorescent spots on the water
which came closer to us. Maybe they were divers. Then again
I was situated on the airy top of a lighthouse; the wind was
shaking the windows. Then I was lying tied in a cellar of
the same lighthouse. There some people pricked my head
with long needles. I heard the peeping of baby chickens over
my body.*"

The patient lives in a magic world. The fact of his lying
in bed in the hospital has been perceived and experienced in
spite of his state of stupor. He experiences movements
(swimming), skin sensations (airy top, hot engine room,
pricking), visual sensations (phosphorescent spots, azure
crevasses), auditory sensations (guns, chickens, shaking of the
windows), and even the sensation of taste (drinking the
"sinking drops"). However, he displaces and disfigures his
subjective, visual, auditory, tactual, and gustatory experiences and projects them. Externally, there is nothing to
indicate that the patient has had these experiences; he is
in a state of motionlessness and stiffness which is probably
due to his mental split (impulse and counter-impulse experienced at the same time); the absolute lack of activity
is the result of this split. He is lying in bed in a state of
complete rigidity. In his dream the patient symbolizes this
rigidity by the scene of being tied. He feels overpowered by
something (tied) or somebody (kidnaped). The "hot engine
room" indicates the high tension of impulses hidden under
the patient's stuporous apathy. Some day this "hot engine"
may burst and drive the patient into a state of frenzy.

It is a fact that in cases of insanity, delusions and hallucinations, to a great extent, transpire into the dream pictures.
It is then difficult to distinguish between the original dream

plot and the "secondary elaboration" made by the morbid ego. Fortunately, these distorted dreams do not lose much of their psychological validity.

Sometimes particular dreams initiate a psychotic attack, for instance, dreams of earthquakes, catastrophes, the end of the world, the Last Judgment, or the like. They portray the patient's ego experiences which fuse with those of the outer world. Thus the patient's experience of his own mental breakdown may be experienced as the breakdown of the whole world.

There is no causal connection between the dream and the psychosis; dream experiences may lead to certain reactions in real life, to hysterical symptoms, etc., but never to a psychosis.

Dreams of psychotics follow the same rules of interpretation as all other dreams. They are often more colorful, the situations may change more frequently, the logical thread may become interrupted more easily, but interpretation follows generally in the established manner. Many patients cannot separate dreams from hallucinations and report dreams interwoven with hallucinated pictures.

THE MANIC-DEPRESSIVE PSYCHOSIS

The melancholic phase of this disease was subjected to psychological investigation by Freud and his pupils years ago. We shall set down the most important results of the psychological research on this psychosis.

The patient shows a remarkable weakening of interest in the outer world. In his dreams we often miss the expression of the patient's depressive state of mind. They are often dull and poor in emotion, corresponding to the patient's apathetic state, but then we also find similar dreams in neurotics. Subjective difficulties are often portrayed as objective obstacles. The most important contribution the dream of the melancholic patient has produced is that we often see in it the introjected object of the patient's hatred (Freud) and pictures in which the patient identifies himself with his abnormally strong superego. His introjected hatred causes an increase of sadistic feelings which are employed by his superego to punish himself. The introjection of persons against whom the patient has diverted his hatred may be portrayed in his dreams (or delusions) in a symbolic way as a physical incorporation (cannibalism). This is the reason why we so often find cannibalistic features in the dreams and delusions of such patients (Freud).

Schilder gives an instructive example of a case where the delusions contain open cannibalistic ideas. The patient is a woman aged twenty-six:

[454] *"I wish to be hanged. (Why?) . . . It can also be burned. (?) Because I burned all people. . . . I have torn them to pieces, have drunk out their blood. . . . (Why?) Because I was irresponsible. . . . You have to erect a big stake and to burn me; then all will become alive again, all babies and all women will have their men, and all mothers will have their children. . . . I have opened all hearts and eaten them up.*

". . . I am a funnel, I have devoured all men, but you can tear me to pieces, prick me with needles—I shall not defend myself. . . . I have broken all men. . . . There are strange bones in my body; in the dream I see myself breaking strange people to pieces and taking the bones into my body. . . . There is no dead nature; I have ruined all people, and they cannot be repaired; they are rotten and in these rotten bodies poisonous plants are growing. What we eat is human meat of people I have killed. . . . I have swallowed many people. . . . I did not know my mother; perhaps, if I knew my mother, I would have obeyed her. . . . (But you lived with your parents?) *They were not my parents; I only thought they were. I was always with my aunts and uncles. One mustn't do that."*

In this chain of delusions in which we also have a short report of a dream (breaking people to pieces) we see the patient's desire to be punished for what she did in her sadistic fantasies. According to the "poena talionis" this patient has to be torn to pieces and burned to death. Her guilt which, in reality, consists of death wishes and hatred against her mother (she did not "know" her mother, although she grew up with her) is expressed in an exaggerated way in her delusion. She has killed all people, she is responsible for all the misfortune of the world. This exaggerated feeling of guilt can be only a product of an elevated and sadistic superego which is supposed to make the patient pay in accordance with the extent of her guilt. The self-reproach is visible in the patient's words: "Perhaps, if I knew my mother, I would have obeyed her," and in the words: "One mustn't do that." Of course, she knew her mother; but she not only did not "obey" her, she hated her. That is what her delusions say, and that is the main idea around which her psychosis is constructed. Schilder reports that the patient's psychosis started with the hypochondriac idea of being unable to cook. She used to live in her mother's home, although she had been married for a long time. She was very fond of eating. In her childhood she used to like candy very much. After her psychosis appeared, her delusions were centered about eating. The problem of eating was the connecting link between her and her mother. It must have led to that unconscious cannibalistic hatred reaction which later became the background of her psychosis.

Hypochondriac melancholics produce their symptoms or, at least, their desire to have symptoms, in their dreams. They are made miserable by their dreams. They often complain more about their dreams than about their symptoms. The deeper reasons for these complaints are also to be found mostly in the dreams.

In the following we see an example of a dream of a melancholic patient with the hypochondriacal idea of being impotent. (Not true in reality.)

[455] *"I see myself at the home of my sweetheart. Her*

sister enters the room. I have the feeling that I have just finished the treatment and say: 'Imagine, dear, I am all right now, so far. . . . But only my sex is not yet in order!'"

The patient's imagined "impotence" was caused by his mental fixation to his sister. He was *unable* to love any other woman. The inner psychic perception of this "inability" led to his opinion (delusion) that he was "impotent." His unconscious desire to be impotent was the result of his tendency to punish himself for his sinful ideas concerning his sister.

Recovery from a melancholic state is often preceded by a marked cheering-up of the dream content.

A thirty-three-year-old patient dreamed at the beginning of his melancholic phase in a typical way by expressing his profound feeling of guilt and his desire to punish himself:

[456] *"Somebody insulted the girl friend of my business partner. I started to fight him and finally I killed him."*

The patient's partner has no girl friend; our patient, however, has one, although he is married and has two children. In his melancholic state his superego becomes violent, accuses him of doing injustice toward his wife, and requires punishment. In this dream he kills the evil-doer in himself (suicide idea). Note the phrase "insulted the girl friend." We interpret: the patient feels that he insulted his wife by his relationship with his girl friend.

Toward the end of his melancholic phase he had the following dream:

[457] *"I am with a friendly man who wants to sell me new eyeglasses. At first the price seems to be too high, but finally we come to an agreement."*

This dream was dreamt after I had explained to the patient that he had been looking upon the world as if through dark eyeglasses which made life appear dark. The patient exchanges his glasses in his dream, and by this he indicates the dawning of recovery. And indeed, the above dream inaugurated the period of improvement and return to normalcy.

In *manic states* the patient's superego is fond of the ego. A complete amalgamation of both ego and superego we find in the symptom of megalomania (delusion of grandeur) which often accompanies the manic states. Freud believes that these states are the consequence of the patient's desire to overcome certain unbearably sad experiences. Manic states often do not create an echo in the patient's dreams. We find then "indifferent" dreams. The majority of dreams, however, correspond to the patient's elated emotional state.

In observing dreams of patients who suffer from manic-depressive conditions we can obtain valuable information as to how strong the patient's ego is and what is the position of the ego in the struggle against the pressure of the patient's antisocial and antimoral tendencies. We can also see to what extent the patient lacks insight into his condition under the impact of the disease. Also, how well he manages his affairs and how well he adjusts to reality.

The following is a series of dreams which a patient who suffered from manic-depressive psychosis produced. This patient was not amenable to shock therapy. He showed undesirable physical reactions to electric convulsions. So the only means we had left was symptomatic treatment and psychotherapy. We have carried the patient through several manic and several depressive phases. The dreams reported here occurred before and after depressions, and before and after his manic conditions. You will see how the depressions and the manic states represent themselves in his dreams, and how they cast their shadows in advance.

The patient dreamed as follows at the beginning of a depressive phase:

[458] *"Mac W. is at the club. He talks to a club member about business. The member starts yelling at Mac. Mac backs away and calls the deal off."*

We see here a withdrawal reaction in the face of a threat. The patient's adaptive pattern at this time is not to tackle the problem but to retreat. (Mac W. stands for the patient.)

Another dream of the same period:

[459] *"I was driving with Blanche. We had to pick up different members of her family (brother, sister, mother, etc.). My dog was along. He jumped out of the car. I went after him. He was run over. I was holding him in my arms and walking with him. I was disconsolate."*

In the dream, the whole family of Blanche meets the patient; in reality, this had not happened. The family lives in California, the patient is in New York. But the dream shows us that he feels that many people are imposing on him. He is resentful. He was asked how he would react if Blanche did have her parents and family here and they would come to see him. He confirmed that he would consider this an intrusion.

Then he sees the dog run over by the cars. The little creature smashed by the "big things" of this world. He is unable to cope with the dangers of the world.

(Q) "Is this a suicide idea?"

(A) Yes, it is. One feels that way looking upon this dream. We are not surprised if we read about a person who jumped out of a window following a dog or a cat which accidentally fell to its death. In the great devotion of human beings to animals we often see such transfers to animals of affects originally directed to people. The dog or cat represents to the owner (unconsciously) a human being. In this dream the dog is the dreamer himself.

After a short normal interval following the depression, the patient had the following dream:

[460] *"Robert (a friend of mine) is out of work and comes to work for me. Someone asks Robert how much business he did with his former boss. He wouldn't tell."*

This dream shows an active and enterprising ego. He is giving other people opportunity to work for him. His aggressiveness is growing.

But the rallying ego is unable to cope with the depression. The next dream again shows decline in the patient's ego strength.

[461] *"I went to visit my cousin. He was a woman. He was on the verge of breaking down or getting insane. One of his men tried to sell me tickets for something. I refused to buy. I was told that the tax collector was looking for me."*

A new depression is coming. Someone is breaking down. Again the patient is imposed upon ("tried to sell me tickets") and has a growing feeling of guilt ("tax collector was looking for me").

The next dream is even more pronounced:

[462] *"Our driver takes his hands off the wheel and our car heads for the curb. I grab the wheel and stop the car from going into the curb. I bawl the driver out but he doesn't care. In a few minutes another car stops, overheats and burns. We all gather for a police investigation. A fellow in a doorman's uniform pushes me slightly. I resent it. Another man is asked his address, he refuses. The fellow who had asked him gets tough and claims to be a detective."*

We see here a growing agitation and apprehension. He still is capable of control ("stop the car from going into the curb"), but there is police investigation (guilt) and there are threats of aggression.

Throughout his life the patient was exposed to a great deal of aggression. Playmates taunted him because he was a thin and scrawny youngster. He grew up with a strong feeling of insecurity and inadequacy. His parents never paid attention to him and he was completely dependent on servants who brought him up. He never was able to meet aggression in an effective way. His depression accentuated this inadequacy.

DREAMS AND SUICIDE

One of the most serious concerns of the practicing psychiatrist is that of preventing desperate patients from committing suicide. In many cases such intention is only a passing one, a result of a transient mood, but it may lead to irreversible decisions. It is, therefore, with great interest that the psychiatrist watches the patient's reactions during the treatment. Many of our patients are potential suicides; most of them have, at one time or another, toyed with the thought of self-destruction. Some come to analysis after having made one or more unsuccessful attempts in this direction. In countless cases psychotherapy is able to dispel the patient's gloom and to save his life. Sometimes it loses the race. Unfortunately, we have no absolutely reliable means of preventing suicide, except for our clinical experience and psychological acumen. Not all patients who commit suicide are insane; those who are sane cannot be kept under constant supervision, and the decision to place a non-psychotic patient in a hospital for reasons of a possible attempt is not always easy. As a rule, positive transference and the average skill of a trained psychotherapist are sufficient to deliver the patient from extreme despair and to give him hope for recovery.

Better general psychiatric training has made the individual physician able to diagnose depressive conditions more accurately and to differentiate between "harmless" and "dangerous" suicide threats. But, of course, mistakes in this respect do occur, and some of them are fatal.

Dreams can be of great assistance in evaluating prognostically a given therapeutic situation. For the impulse to commit suicide, like any other impulse of the patient, manifests itself in dreams. The psychiatrist then has an opportunity to observe it *in statu nascendi* and, if necessary, to intervene effectively to prevent its perpetration. And, indeed, since dream interpretation made its decisive progress, the number of suicides committed in the course of treatment has decreased considerably. The chief value of dreams is that they not only indicate the patient's intentions but also usually contain hints as to the deeper mental mechanisms involved.

The whole complex carries such import that it deserves to be studied in detail. Dreams immediately preceding a suicide attempt appear most suitable for an investigation of the dynamics of the case.

The following is a dream of a patient who made a suicide attempt but was rescued. She drank eight ounces of a bromide solution and cut her wrists. She is a forty-nine-year-old, unmarried woman suffering from menopausal depression.

[463] *"With a childhood friend, Mary, now dead, I make a trip to the mountains. It is winter. We are walking together for some time. The landscape is in snow and ice. For some reason our ways separate. She stops while I walk on. But soon I see, there is nothing ahead.* (The patient reported this dream in German. She said *'Es geht nicht weiter. . . .'* This sentence can be translated also as 'It's no use. . . .') *I must go back. The road is very difficult. I can't go on. . . . Suddenly, I see on the other side of a ravine something like a peaceful summer landscape. I grow weaker and weaker. I hold on to my pointed cane which I am using as a crutch, but then I let myself go . . . and awaken."*

If we attempt to condense the contents of this dream (dreamed one night prior to the suicide attempt), we come by simplification to the following formulations:

1. The patient is in company of a person now dead.

2. The friend's trip ends (she dies) while the patient goes on.

3. The patient encounters insurmountable difficulties. ("There is nothing ahead." Or, "It's no use. . . .") The patient's development (road) is blocked in both directions.

This is the most revealing part of the dream. It is at this point of complete frustration that the patient experiences the vision of peace—"on the other side." The antithesis here is between "this side" and "the other side." This side is cold, wintry—fraught with dangers (picture of the patient's emotional impoverishment caused by withdrawal of object cathexes), while the other side appears promising.

4. She grows weaker and lets herself go—she gives up the struggle.

Psychologically interesting are a few additional details obtained through the patient's association. Her friend, Mary, was a gay and popular girl. During her lifetime, even after marriage, she had many boyfriends. Our patient, who spent a rather frustrated life, always secretly envied her friend for her ability to enjoy life without scruples. Entering the change of life she is now reminded in a most definite manner that her own past life was but a series of missed opportunities and unfulfilled hopes (the road back is blocked). Her dream tells her that it is now too late (there is nothing ahead).

The association to the "pointed cane" is also important. The dreamer uses it as a crutch. When asked what came to her mind in connection with this detail of the dream, the patient replied that it reminded her of a shepherd's staff. Then she recalled having seen a picture of Jesus carrying a similar staff. At this point the supposition was expressed that the patient was using her faith as a crutch to surmount her difficulty. She immediately agreed, saying that her religion (Catholic) expressly prohibits the commission of suicide, and that when she decided to take her own life she first prayed for forgiveness.

One of the reasons for the patient's identification with Christ was the fact that her mother, like His, was named Mary. Hidden behind the figure of her friend Mary stood the figure of the patient's mother who, incidentally, had also died prematurely. After her mother's death, the patient shared the apartment with her father and took care of his household. During the treatment, after a period of extolling her mother's virtues and blaming herself for not having been a good daughter, she admitted that her relations with her mother had always been strained. There were quarrels and disagreements, particularly because her mother was strict about her contacts with men. When her mother died—the patient was about twenty-eight at that time—she hoped that the main obstacle to her social life had been removed; however, she found herself withdrawing from company, self-conscious, oversensitive (as a result of her feeling of guilt), and so her situation did not improve. Later she appeared to abandon hope for a realistic sexual adjustment and to devote herself exclusively to the care of her father. Analysis established that she hated her mother in particular, because once, when she was about nineteen, she overheard her parents having intercourse. Her first thought was: "This woman enjoys her life, but she wants to stop me from enjoying mine." There is reason to believe that in the condensation of the figures of girl-friend and mother, joy of life was the common denominator.

Looking over this dream we can say that its poor prognosis is based upon the complete pessimism pervading its content. The apotheosis of peace appears to the dreamer as a distant view. But no way leads to it (the ravine). The vision occurs simultaneously with expressions of weariness and lack of combative spirit.

But where is the wish-fulfillment? Undoubtedly it lies in a distant promise the dream offers. The patient is tired of the struggle; she wants peace at any price—even if it can be obtained "on the other side" only. . . .

If this interpretation is true can we assume that the dream, known to us as a guardian of our mental equilibrium, a warner, and avenger, a fulfiller of our wishes and a bolsterer of our ego, is also capable of easing us into destruction of ourselves? If we do not accept the idea that the summer scene in the dream has the purpose of conjuring for the dreamer (as a last and desperate attempt to save her life) the potential beauty of life, the warmth and joy of summer that may follow the winter snows—then we must accept the proposition that dreams are indeed capable of easing the individual into accepting death as a solution. Two factors speak against the former of the two possibilities; first, in the dream the peaceful landscape is in fact inaccessible, and second, that the patient *did* make a self-destructive attempt despite the dream.

Thus we may assume that under certain pathological circumstances, for instances, in melancholia, in which a so far unknown, probably somatic (toxic) factor affects the structure of the patient's personality, the life-saving function of the dream may fail, and the dream may place itself, as it were, in the service of the death instinct. As an expression of wish-fulfillment under the new circumstances, we now find the dream's concern with the elimination of displeasure and suffering. The dream facilitates the re-establishment of perfect peace and harmony, a Nirvana of passivity and wishlessness as maintained in death or before birth. In this way the dream prevents a disorganization of the ego which may be caused by a persistent and insoluble mental conflict. The dream unifies the ego in its customary way, this time by focusing its conative tendencies on the idea of death. It is then a homogeneous ego that perishes in self-destruction.

We know, of course, from the studies of Abraham and Freud that in melancholia the ego (which has become the target of aggression and/or destruction) is not a normal one. It is an ego into which an object of primary aggression has been incorporated by narcissistic identification.

In explaining the patient's capacity for suicide, Freud points out that a strong self-love of the ego is the primary state from which instinctual life originates. Whenever life is threatened, anxiety appears as a sign that narcissistic libido has been liberated. Under such circumstances, how can the ego agree to self-destruction? Freud then goes on to say that the analysis of melancholia has taught him that the ego can destroy itself only if it begins to treat itself as an *object*, and if hostility originally designated for an object falls back upon the ego.

Taking the above factors into consideration, we may assume that, in our case, it is the hated object of the mother that has been introjected into the patient's ego. (Mother's untimely death increased the patient's impulse for identification.) The thought of destroying this object-laden ego carried with it as a premium the promise of an ultimate union with father. This secret unconscious wish—projected into a distant future, the hereafter, appears fulfilled in the patient's dream as a vision of warmth (libido gratification) in contrast to the cold (loss of libido) maintained in the patient's conscious state. (It is interesting in this connection that Christ was also promised a union with Father after death.)

Summarizing we may say: the interpretation of the above dream enables us not only to reconstruct the pessimistic thought which led the patient onto the path of self-destruction but also to evaluate the specific role of the suicide idea in the dynamics of the depression.

A forty-two-year-old married woman, a physician, suffered from manic-depressive psychosis. In the depressive phase she produced the following dream, the last she reported before committing suicide:

[464] *"I was accused of having committed ritual murder. The authorities behave as though they exculpated me, but I know this is only a trick. Ultimately they want to put me in jail. I see myself running away, rushing frantically through a maze of rooms and corridors, like a labyrinth."*

If we simplify this dream, we arrive at the following formulations:

1. The patient feels accused of a crime. Since the dreamer is also the author of her dream, it is safe to assume that the accusation represents a self-accusation, such as we commonly see in melancholic conditions.

2. The patient feels that the authorities will ultimately punish her.

3. The dreamer wants to escape punishment by running away, and finds herself in a labyrinth-like maze.

After having thus fixed the skeleton of the dream plot, we may now proceed to the discussion of the details.

Ritual murder is the crime of killing a person for ritualistic purposes. At various times and in various places, followers of various religions accused one another falsely of having perpetrated this crime. The crime consisted in using the blood of the victim for the preparation of ritual meals. Psychoanalytic investigation has thrown light upon this problem. We know now that in this superstition we are dealing with projections of long repressed atavistic drives, particularly of the sadistic and cannibalistic tendencies inherent in man.

It is no coincidence that our patient in her bout of self-accusations happened to select this crime. The oral-cannibalistic root of the manic-depressive psychosis which has been investigated by psychoanalysis may account for this detail of our patient's dream. In her case, it is the incorporated figure of a dominating (phallic) mother and the aggression directed against this object which is responsible for the choice of symbolism. In her dream the patient distrusts her self-criticism, she feels the sadistic and destructive character of the super-ego and tries to evade it, by flight into confusion, insanity, death. (Cf. the self-accusation in dream 454 on p. 438.)

At first glance this dream resembles the *nightmare dreams* seen so frequently in other individuals who picture themselves as being pursued and fleeing through a maze of rooms. Sometimes it is the awakening that puts an end to the panic experienced in the dream. A closer inspection of this dream, however, makes its special character clear: the dreamer is trapped. The persecutor is not the "villain" we find in dreams of hysterics, but the authority, which calmly awaits the victim's surrender while the latter is still frantically struggling in a sort of mousetrap. The basic emotion in this dream is hopelessness.[1]

Our next dream is that of a forty-year-old clergyman suffering from depression. He has a history of one suicide at-

[1] For the benefit of those who wish to see in the picture of the labyrinth an intra-uterine symbol, we can interpret the patient's suicide idea as a desire to retreat from life's difficulties into the Nirvana of intra-uterine existence.

tempt which he made a few years prior to treatment. This dream is "dangerous" from the standpoint of its suicidal potential:

[465] *"I come to mother (who died six years ago) and, crying bitterly, say to her: 'Since you died I have not been successful. I wish you were here.' And as an echo—or did my mother answer?—I hear: 'I wish you were here.' Then it seems as if I fall into a deep pit or down a precipice and I awake feeling queer.* It is some time before I become oriented to reality."

The task for the psychotherapist in this case is to counter-act the patient's tendency to "join" his dead mother.

I will present two cases for the sake of comparison and differential diagnosis. The first is that of a patient, a forty-three-year-old insurance broker, suffering from reactive depression. He dreams:

[466] *"Pearl is in the car with me and we are going to Bud's house. I find that I am headed the wrong way and I want to turn in the opposite direction. A sign in the road reads 'No U-Turn.' I am about to turn anyway, but I see a policeman standing in the roadway, and so I make a right turn into a side street. I am still ahead in the wrong direction, so I turn down another narrow side street. I come to the end of the block and find my way barred by a tall building. I honk the horn and the building disappears. I turn again and I am standing on the edge of a cliff overlooking a river. Suddenly I am entering Bud's apartment. (It seems to be an apartment I had occupied many years ago.) The radio is on very loud and I tell him to turn it down. He says, 'No, I don't want the cops to hear it. . . .' Now I am driving down the Parkway, headed toward Bud's house (as though I had not been there yet). A huge pile of sand appears in front of the car, and I swerve sharply to avoid running into it. I straighten out the car and apply the brakes and, as I do so, I see a large tree lying on the ground to my right. I just miss the bare branches as I pass and then come to a full stop. Two cars have been in*

collision and the one on my side has apparently knocked down the tree. A man is leaning across the hood of the car bleeding profusely. Some other people seem to have been injured. . . ."

If we simplify the contents of this dream we find that the dreamer's circuitous route ends with a scene of disaster. We see him frustrated (wrong way, blocked roads), handicapped by his conscience (policemen); we see an expression of mental conflict (collision of cars) with subsequent injury, indicating the possibility of self-injury since it is the dreamer's own thought that gives the specific color to the dream. And yet—we find here no unequivocal expression of hopelessness or gloom.

Interesting, indeed, are some of the details. In his dream the patient had been to see Bud, his friend, who—significantly —lives in one of the patient's own previous apartments. The patient then behaves as though he had not been there, as though he were trying to get there. . . . He wants to undo something, he wishes he had not done it. And then comes the peculiar statement of the friend; he is playing the radio so loud because he does not want the cops to hear it. Some data of the patient's history may help us understand these obscure passages.

The patient had left his wife and child to follow the lure of a young woman, Pearl, who was at that time his secretary. He soon discovered that she had been having affairs with other men, and among them was his friend, Bud, to whom he had introduced the girl socially. The meeting took place in the apartment mentioned in the dream. When he discovered that the girl had betrayed his confidence, he was at first very much upset and wanted to kill her; later, he wanted to take revenge on his friend (vision of people bleeding profusely following a crash). He was in a desperate mood and so depressed that he had to be placed temporarily in a sanitarium. After his release he underwent psychotherapy. During his analysis it became clear that the patient regretted having broken up his home in favor of an unworthy woman. He wanted to go back home—but he did not know how to bring about reconciliation. (Analysis helped him to solve the problem.) As stated above, at no place in this dream do we find pessimism or despair. The patient wishes he had never introduced Pearl to his friend; or that he had never left his family. But in his dream he is constantly preoccupied with the idea of getting back on the right road, of readjusting his life. At one place he is even able to employ magic (omnipotence) to remove obstacles. He honks his horn and a building disappears. The patient's associations reveal that the building is the one where his wife and child are living. Whenever he passes it, he is plagued by feelings of remorse. In the dream he erases this painful memory by wishful thinking. The radio which plays so loud reminds him of a scene in the movies. A murder was committed, while the loud sound of the radio muffled the noise of the pistol shot. The patient is fighting against an impulse to commit murder—not suicide; but his superego is sufficiently strong to dissipate it.

The repetition of motives, such as we see it in the dream ("headed the wrong way," "no U-turn," "headed in the wrong direction," "my way barred," "standing on the edge of a cliff," "a pile of sand in front of my car," etc.), indicates, generally speaking, a futile effort. This holds true for a dream as well as for a repetition compulsion. The futile effort here is the patient's attempt to reconcile his fateful sexual dependency on the young woman with his sense of loyalty and responsibility.

The following dream which may be called "harmless" was dreamed by a forty-five-year-old woman suffering from a gastric neurosis:

[467] *"After another scene with my husband I decided to commit suicide by taking poison. I see a white powder on the table and prepare myself for the last act. Then I see myself in a coffin carried by four men toward the graveyard. My parents* (now dead) *walk behind the coffin. I commence to weep*

and awake weeping bitterly because of my own misfortune."

We find a similar mechanism in suicide ideas of children. These ideas are aggressions directed toward other persons (parents). We detect here no identification of the type seen in melancholia. Self-pity expressed in the dream shows that the patient's ego is strong and fully charged with narcissistic libido.

The analysis of this case proved that the patient had repressed criminal feelings toward her husband. She toyed with the thought of killing him by poison, after she had read about a similar case in the newspaper. Her stomach trouble was found to be a result of self-punishment (identification with the victim).

Her symptom offers her desire for talionic self-punishment an adequate outlet. A real suicide attempt would duplicate this tendency, a fact which is not in keeping with the law of symbol economy according to which mental processes operate.

Dying in the dream does not necessarily represent the dreamer's wish to die. As a matter of fact, this is hardly ever the case. The wish to die in the dream usually appears in a disguise, as we have seen it in the dreams 463 (p. 445), 464 (p. 449), and 465 (p. 451). The reason for a symbolic expression of death in the dream is not entirely clear; it may be due to the fact that the thought of dying, at first, is resisted by the ego. Experience teaches that most dreams where dying appears in an overt form are dreams following traumatic incidents rather than dreams forecasting suicide. The war with its plethora of traumatic incidents has produced a great variety of death dreams of the type mentioned. (See page 390.)

Of special interest are dreams of the following type: the patient is a married physician, aged thirty-two, suffering from impotence. In the course of his treatment he had a dream which caused him to awaken with a start:

[473] *"I see myself dead and laid out in a hall of a funeral chapel. There are many people around, but I recognize no one. I know that I have died from a bite of a poisonous snake.*

I feel very sad about it and consider the consequences this may have for my wife. The rabbi is speaking with a matter-of-fact voice, rather bored. However, he extols my virtues and finishes his sermon by saying, '. . . and he never cut classes. . . .' The whole audience cries."

Simplifying the dream we may say:

1. The dreamer died following an insidious accident.

2. His virtues are extolled (posthumously) and his previous achievements as a law-abiding individual are praised.

3. The dream carries a strong emotion. The patient considers the consequences of his ill fortune for his wife and notices a strong general reaction to it by others. ("The whole audience cries. . . .")

Asked for associations to the snake, the dreamer produced very important information. When he was twenty-four, he acquired a syphilitic infection from a fellow-student who was very promiscuous. He often spoke of her as a "snake in the grass." The spirochetae he observed in the microscopic specimen also came to his mind in this connection. The traumatic effect of the venereal disease on the patient was exceedingly strong. For a long time he played with the idea of suicide. But the trauma had also another unexpected effect: the patient developed a general sexual inhibition which persisted even after the infection was cured, and most annoying of all was his impotence which had prevented him from consummating his marriage for more than a year prior to his treatment.

Now we understand the dream. It is not the patient's death the dream is portraying so dramatically; it is the death of his penis, i.e., his impotence. The emotion of the dream gives us a reliable clue: "I feel very sad," "I consider the consequences for my wife," "The whole audience cries." His diminished self-confidence is restored in the dream by the dream's secret recuperative effort: The dreamer may be suspected of being immoral—today—but once, in his past, he used to be a good boy, ". . . and he never cut classes. . . ."

In our attempt to assay which dreams may be considered "harmless" and which "dangerous" as far as the dreamer's suicide plans are concerned, we come to the following conclusions:

Exact rules cannot be established as yet. We are inclined to consider as dangerous those dream situations in which the patient's pessimism becomes absolute, i.e., where his ego becomes extremely passive and ready to "give up." As Freud put it: "The ego sees itself deserted by its superego and lets itself die." In the dreams I have cited, we noted such statements as: "I let myself go . . . ," "Ultimately they want to put me in jail."

Frustrating experiences as such do not indicate hopelessness. Much depends on the conduct of the ego in the dream. If the dream portrays an actively functioning ego which is capable of mastery, the frustrating dream may be considered "harmless" as far as its suicide potential is concerned.

As stated on page 454, overt, i.e., undisguised expressions of death are to be found in dreams of healthy individuals whose ego has not been properly conditioned to traumatizations, and lead to a subsequent development of compensatory dream hallucination of death, followed by recovery (through awakening). This development affords the dreamer a triumphant and uplifting experience of indestructibility. Such dreams, according to Kardiner, are usually rather fragmentary. Other cases of dreams containing undisguised death expressions can be seen in those "harmless" dreams in which the infantile idea of dying is associated with the idea of punishing members of the patient's environment or of gaining sympathy; and finally, in dreams where the dreamer's death is portrayed as a symbol of another condition, e.g., of his impotence. In dreams of this type the dreamer identifies himself with his ineffectual (=dead) genital (*totum pro parte*).

The next two dreams are those of a physician aged thirty-two who complained of a lack of interest in life, in his profession, and in women. His general emotional dullness was accompanied by a strong feeling of depression.

[474] *"George S. committed suicide because of his poverty. I saw him going up in the elevator that is in the 'Dianabad' and then disappear down the corridor. I suddenly realized what he might be up to. The next moment I saw a crowd of people gathering around the sidewalk below the roof of the building."*

[475] *"I see Amory B., the favorite child of his family, playing with a hammer and driving nails into something. I feel afraid that he might hit his fingers with his hammer. Then he dies of some unknown disease, and his parents grieve over his death and go about in a sort of daze. With other physicians I attend the funeral and afterwards, with the other doctors, try to determine the cause of his death. . . . I am also determined to be free from restraint and the supervision of my mother in my sexual life. My sister decides likewise, and she and I are going out with one another to have sexual intercourse and a good time."*

The two preceding dreams tell us not only that the patient has ideas of suicide but also the reasons for his pessimism. This gives us the opportunity to save the man from suicide by destroying his pathological fixations.

The first of these two dreams becomes clear when we learn that George S. is a man who almost married the patient's sister years before. However, she feared he could not make an adequate living and said so. His "poverty" corresponds to the patient's dullness and shows that "George S." is in reality the patient himself. ("Dianabad" is a Viennese bathing establishment frequented by our patient but never by George S. who lives in the United States.)

Concluding our comment on the first dream, we may say that our patient's "dullness," which causes his depression, is due to the fact that his sexual desires are directed toward his sister. This is a hopeless situation. His sister fixation has monopolized his emotions, making him indifferent to all other pleasures and activities of life.

The second dream repeats this motive even more clearly. The patient, "Amory B.," tells us about his masturbation fantasy (playing with hammer). The fact that he "hurts" himself while "playing with the hammer" shows that he believes masturbation to be harmful. In his childhood he had reason to complain of a lack of attention from his parents. In his dream he is "the favorite son of his parents," and his death caused by an "unknown disease" (suicide) causes the parents much grief (wish-fulfillment).

The succeeding part of the dream tells us not only the contents of the patient's masturbation fantasy, but also his secret life plan. The idea is to get rid of the "supervision" (that is, the moral considerations) and to live with his sister. The hopeless sex situation of our patient thus causes his depression and gives rise to suicide ideas. It is clear that if we succeed in destroying these ideas, we suppress the patient's impulses for suicide.

SCHIZOPHRENIA (PARANOID STATES)

In dreams of schizophrenics we find the well-known dissociation of affects which is so typical of this psychosis. The emotional level in the dreams of schizophrenics, in general, is rather shallow. This finding coincides with clinical observation as well as the findings obtained through projective techniques (Rorschach, T.A.T., etc.). The symbols are very clear and easily discernible. As a rule, we do not give any interpretation to the patient, and consider disfigurations of dreams caused by hallucinations which find their way into the dream as a form of association. An example of the dream of a schizophrenic patient follows:

[476] *"A Persian carried me in his arms. He had a long black beard. I felt a volcano in my chest."*

The patient, who was unhappily married, used as dream material in this little strange dream, a story her father once told her. She learned from her father that in Persia there are more men than women. In her dream she fancies that, contrary to her unhappy marriage, she is being carried by a Persian in his arms. By the "volcano" in her chest she expresses her warm gratitude for this attention.

The Persian symbolizes the patient's father. The dream situation is based on the patient's father fixation. We see here the mechanism of (a) condensation and (b) regression. It was her father who once told her the story about the Persians, and it was he who used to carry her in his arms when she was a child. In her dream her regression goes as far back as this period of her life.

The same patient had another dream in which the psychotic content prevails. It is difficult to say whether or not, and to what extent, this dream was influenced by hallucinations:

[477] *"I hear the voice: 'They need you for the re-establishment of the world's regime.'"* (The delusion of the patient was the paranoid idea of being used by hostile powers for international political affairs.)

We undoubtedly owe the increase of our knowledge about the background of paranoia to Freud's ingenious discoveries. Freud proved by very convincing analyses that the persecution delusion is due to a projected latent homosexual idea, even in those cases in which persons of the opposite sex are virtual pursuers. Dreams offer good evidence for these statements. They are, above all, able to present the latent homosexual goal. But not only the homosexual; every idea which has an obsessive character can be perceived by the psychotic in the form of persecution. Instead of saying, "The thought of Mr. X does not leave me," the patient may say in his psychosis, "Mr. X pursues me."

An example: [478] *"A number of people moving about me, and I am bewildered and want to go somewhere but the people keep pushing me away from the direction in which I start to go."*

The paranoic idea "people keep pushing me away" may be interpreted in our case as "the thought of my sisters interferes with my development." The patient, a thirty-three-year-old man, lives with his five sisters in an apartment. The mental dependence on his sisters is so great that he cannot adjust himself to life. He lives on his sisters' income, has never had a contact with a woman, although he has always desired it ("direction in which I start to go"). In his dream he projects this fixation in a typical way ("people keep pushing me away").

The *poison delusion* can be interpreted in a similar way. A patient's delusion [478a] *"I have been, (or I am being) poisoned by Dr. X,"* corresponds to the idea that his sexual preoccupation with the person of Dr. X is poisoning his mind. This is particularly true in cases where the patient suspects the doctor of poisoning him by an injection.

Not infrequently, patients whose paranoid system is predicated upon repressed homosexual ideas, dream about poisonous snakes attacking them. One of these patients, in a dream [478b], in which he *saw himself attacked by a poisonous snake, decided to accept the bite, since "it didn't matter any more."*

The split in the patient's personality confuses his attitude toward his environment and toward his own ego. The subjective becomes objective; the patient's personal life often appears projected and is experienced as if it were a part of the environment. Many schizophrenics experience their split personality very plastically, as, for example, one of my patients who saw in his dream [479] *himself being dead, and while some other people (colored?) tried to let him down into a grave, he (his living ego) tried to lift the dead.*

A schizophrenic woman aged thirty-five dreams:

[480] *"I am carrying Mother in my arms as though she were a little child. She is very sick and small. I don't know whether she is dead or alive, but I feel very sad and grieved. Suddenly I am in a locked room without Mother. There are*

many women. They want to bathe me. I am defending myself and afraid of their contagious diseases. Finally they take me into the hospital."

The dream expresses the patient's latent homosexuality. She identifies herself with her mother (carrying mother in her arms) and looks for other women as images of herself. The "contagious diseases" she fears in the dream are the sexual "infection," the attraction transferred by women. In defending herself against the influence of women (struggle against her latent homosexuality) she gets sick (as her mother was in the dream) and is taken into a hospital (asylum).

It is striking in schizophrenia how easily symbols are created and understood by the patient. One of Schilder's patients complains about her enemies who consider rubbing her hands or brushing her teeth as sexual acts. In her dream [481] *she saw a drop running out of a nut.* She supposed that it was the uterus. She claimed that a "mental guide" gave her a cigarette case and said that she must not touch the cigarettes because that would be a sexual act.

Another of his patients reported the following dream:

[482] *His mother was running after him with a knife. . . . His father was mad at him because he was flirting with an English lady; his father pulled his sword and pierced the woman's genitals, killing her in this way.*

We see his sexual tendencies directed toward his father. This trend is connected with a strong undercurrent of sadism, which is undoubtedly based upon his hatred of his mother. In this case we see the picture of his mother running after him as a portrayal of his obsessive ideas (knife) directed against his mother. In reality it is not his mother who threatens him, but his own criminality which endangers his peace of mind.

In schizophrenia it happens mostly that one part of the split personality creates the symbolic language and the other understands it (often perceived as "voices" which explain everything).

The schizophrenic identification reminds us of the dream identification. The male patient may consider himself as his own brother or as the son of somebody else ("family novel"), the female patient may consider herself as her sister, etc. Because of the primitivity of the mental processes in schizophrenia we also find identifications with lifeless matter.

The following dream of a thirty-five-year-old female schizophrenic patient[1] shows many interesting details in this respect. It runs as follows:

[482a] *"I take a walk through the woods. They are dense, and the buds are ready to open. A late spring holds them back. The weather is like a clock that had stopped to wait for a sign. At the same time I know I cannot get the right time unless the watchmaker repairs my clock—"*

Here the word "clock" which the patient used poetically for comparison suddenly becomes a real clock, her personal property. She received a clock as a gift from a woman who later died from cancer. To her the clock signifies disease. She toyed with the idea of destroying it. The watchmaker thus refers to the psychiatrist. The shift from the abstract "clock" which the patient uses for purposes of comparison to the concrete and specific clock she has at home, is a typical sign of the schizophrenic impairment of the normal capacity of operating consistently with abstracts; it is a part of the primitivisms we observe in the schizophrenic psyche.

"—He is a very wise old man. When I first called him, he said: 'I will make your clock go again, but you must give me the pass word. If you give me the right combination, your clock will be as good as new.'—"

The "old wise man"—cf. page 127—symbolizes her father, but also the spiritual guidance she needs and expects her therapist to offer her. She expects to be helped in a magic way. We are anxious to hear more about the combination.

"—The man had a kindly smile and I knew I had to pass a test. It was the Cage Test. I picked up some sticks and made

a cage of them. Into the cage I put two unrelated sentences—" (again an interference between abstract and concrete) *"—one of them was: 'He is only a man' and the other: 'A peach of a girl.' I shook these sentences (which I put into the cage) well, and before I knew it, I had the answer for my nice old watchmaker. He gave me a peach—"* (again confusion between the object and its predicate—the "peach of a girl" becomes a specific peach) *"—and I took the skin off. Underneath I found a bad-tasting black core. So I threw it away. That was the beginning of a real spring.—"*

In this part of her dream the patient describes her withdrawal. She was rejected by her family and tried to find peace and acceptance in marriage. However, her husband was intellectually her inferior and so, after many fruitless attempts to establish a community of interest with him, she withdrew into the confines of her own self. An ear affection leading to deafness helped her in this job of introversion. Whenever her husband annoyed her with his inane remarks, she shut the hearing aid off and isolated herself from him. Once, when she inquired about their financial status, he flared up and told her that he was doing all he could but, after all, "I am only a man." The *sentence* in the dream stands for a *person,* her husband; a typical prelogical mechanism. It is clear, of course, who is the "peach of a girl." The patient's narcissistic overevaluation of herself is designed to counteract feelings of inadequacy generated by the rejection she suffered from her family. However, she feels that the "peach" she thinks she is has a "bad-tasting black core." She is aware of her inner weaknesses and wants to improve. This is what we call the "anagogic tendency of the dream." Getting rid of the "black core" leads to the advent of the "real spring." She continues:

"—It was a spring the way I had never known it before. I felt as though I had been in the cage all the time, together with the two sentences. As though we were three in bed instead of two. When I looked again, the man was in the cage and all my covers had slipped off the bed. The spring sun

shone into my room and I felt as if I had just woken up from a hundred years' sleep. I got up and found the sun on my face and that was enough to make me happy."

The patient finds her salvation through the splitting off of that part of her personality which is dissatisfied with her life. She casts it off like the dark core of the peach. The price she pays for this purification of her soul is the dissociation of her personality. There are three now in bed, instead of two. The spring represents her spiritual resurrection—unfortunately by means of her psychosis. Her hatred toward her husband is annihilated, her despair about her hopeless marital life turns into a blissful acceptance of whatever the spring means to her, and the sun shines on her face as though God were giving her a sign that he has accepted her sacrifice. In her treatment the psychiatrist represents this God-father figure. She flirted with the psychiatrist and was jealous of his wife. She felt herself persecuted by her.

Some psychotic (schizophrenic) patients complain that some of their organs are missing, that they have no eyes or no stomach and such bizarre ideas also appear in their dreams.

One of my patients, a thirty-two-year-old woman complained that she had no eyes. Her illness developed generally. It followed a "successful" suppression of a compulsion, namely, the urge to gaze at the genital region of men. Being religious, she made a desperate effort to get rid of the "sinful" compulsion until she finally succeeded. She did not have to look at men, she did not see anything,—she did not have eyes.

In her dreams, this simple, unsophisticated woman saw the connection between sex and eye of which she was not aware.

In one of her dreams [483] *she saw a frankfurter stand. She bought three frankfurters and ate them. "While I am writing this," she said, "the frankfurters turn into male genitals."*

Such a recognition of symbolism is frequent among schizophrenics. Therefore, interpretation cannot be considered as a very valuable factor in promoting insight. It serves only as basis and background for our therapeutic strategy.

A schizophrenic patient[1] claimed that he disliked wearing coats because they never fitted him well. They cut him under the arms and were tight around his chest. He showed characteristic dreams:

[484] *"I am looking at my teeth in the mirror and actually see cavities, but no other portion of my face."*

[485] *"I was walking down the street and my jacket kept falling off because I had no shoulders."*

The lack of an organ in dream or delusion bespeaks the patient's perception of withdrawal or displacement of the customary organ cathexis. The organ which has been deprived of emotional charge ceases to exist. Specific complexes account for such shifts. In the above case, the "shoulders" represented "masculinity," and their loss was a symbol of castration.

"Loss of face" has a similar symbolic value.

We often find in dreams of schizophrenics an indication as to the possible cause of the outbreak of the psychosis.

According to modern investigation (Schilder, Hartmann, and others), there exists an immediate cause for an acute schizophrenic outbreak, no matter what we think of the pathogenesis of this psychosis. Even an organically based psychosis may show a psychogenesis, at least, in its acute outbreak.

In one of this author's cases the schizophrenic patient complained that he was dead. He "died of a heart collapse as a consequence of a sunstroke." The patient was twenty-three years old and became ill shortly before he graduated from college. He tried to convince his physician that his heart was not beating, and that a man whose heart was dead had, of course, to be considered dead. One of his dreams gave us the key to his case. The dream ran as follows:

[1] Treated by Dr. Kona Simon of New York.

[486] *"I am in the company of young fellows. They drink wine and sing gay songs. I cannot join them. I am dead."*

The patient at first could not recall the gay songs his colleagues were singing. He was then asked to name a few of the songs he knew. He mentioned the names of three folk songs, and, strangely, all of them had the motive of unfaithfulness and desertion. The analyst's next question referred to this. He learned that the patient had been in love with a girl for years and wanted to marry her as soon as he was through with his studies. His parents objected, however, and forced him to give up the relationship. He apparently succeeded in overcoming his love, but he used to stand in front of his sweetheart's house waiting for her, merely to look at her from a distance. He thought of her day and night. His sacrifice was only superficial; his love was not dead. Then he had to leave town for a certain time. When he came back he learned that his former fiancée had married another man, one of his colleagues. It was then that his love (heart) died. He was a living corpse. The time of his disappointing discovery and of the first outbreak of his psychosis were closely connected.

Other conditions under which acute psychotic attacks may occur are: death of close relatives, marriage of sisters or brothers to whom the patients are closely attached, disappointments in love, business, and work. These experiences mobilize the endogenous components of the psychosis, thus leading to an outbreak. As in the above dream, we can find these factors in other products of the patient's mind, as delusions and hallucinations, and use our findings for our therapy.

Conclusions

We have tried to show that dreams are built along the same principles as the delusional systems in psychoses. To understand the meaning of dreams, particularly those dreamt by psychotics, therefore, is to understand the meaning of psychoses. Freud considered the dream as a psychosis of short duration. He said: "A dream is a psychosis, with all the absurdities, delusions, and illusions of a psychosis. No doubt, it is a psychosis which has only a short duration, which is harmless and even performs a useful function, which is brought about with the subject's consent and is ended by an act of his will. Nevertheless it is a psychosis, and we learn from it that even so deep-going a modification of mental life as this can be undone and can give place to normal functioning. Is it too bold, then, to hope that it must also be possible to submit the dreaded spontaneous illnesses of the mind to our control and bring about their cure?"

Freud has given us powerful impulses toward the realization of this goal. His last sentence has an almost visionary character.

IMPULSIONS

Dream analysis can be of help in unraveling those pathological conditions in which the patient is driven by uncontrollable forces to commit acts opposed by his conscience. We are referring here to *cleptomania, pyromania, dromomania,* (pathological wanderlust), *dipsomania,* and *drug addiction.* The modern psychiatrist who believes that the impulsive behavior is predicated upon specific unconscious patterns and motivations, appreciates the guidance dream interpretation is able to furnish in his search for the psychodynamics of pathological behavior.

CLEPTOMANIA

The sexual root of this impulsion has been established by psychoanalysts very early. The act of stealing substitutes for another forbidden act, often the incest.

We shall present here a few characteristic dreams of cleptomaniacs. Not all of these dreams contain relevant information; a selection has been made of those which are most instructive for our purpose.

The following dreams were produced by a young man who was arrested for theft in a department store. This case has been described in detail elsewhere:

[487] *"A celebration is given in honor of our proprietress. A man begs alms at the corner. The proprietress passes by and first addresses him in a friendly manner. The man says that he has been in her service for a long time and asks her for assistance. But the woman turns away from him and I see by her face that she is angry. Then the man goes into a few stores asking for leather, while I wait outside. His request is turned down everywhere."*

The "celebration" is the fulfillment of an unconscious desire. The "beggar" is the patient himself. He refers to the time when the "proprietress" (= mother) was very friendly, i.e., his childhood. Later, his mother, whose husband had died, had to work hard to provide a livelihood for herself and her only son, the patient. What she refuses ("she turns away from him") he wants to "take" for himself.

We see him then in "a few (department) stores" asking for "leather." This point will be clear when we hear that the patient is interested in a young girl and that he recently stole a leather pocketbook to offer it to her as a gift. His idea of courting is to buy gifts for his girl. He does not display too much affection otherwise and is not attracted sexually to any of his objects. He prefers masturbation.

The real object of his attraction becomes evident in the next dream:

[488] *"With my mother in Court. I am accused of theft. The plaintiff is about my age. Many persons in the courtroom. I was not guilty. The one caught was a man with reddish hair. Without a verdict I leave.*

"I wait for mother in another room. Next to me sits a young girl. The plaintiff is also there, but he leaves right away. I remain alone with the girl, kiss her, and get very excited. . . ."

The "plaintiff" ("about my own age") is the patient's own

conscience; the entire court scene is the representation of his intrapsychic conflicts.

The "man with reddish hair" is a sensual individual, the antimoral, antisocial part of the patient's ego. Of interest in this dream is the passage "I wait for my mother." It is noticeable that the interest in the girl sitting next to him is derived from that in his mother.

Many of the patient's daydreams deal with the theft of jewelry. The next dream reveals the deeper motive of this craving.

[489] *"Evening, bad weather. On the way to the office. Passed by a jewelry store. A disorderly display: rings and stones galore, but the most precious stone was missing. Continued on my way, while an acquaintance walked behind, swearing at me. Then I looked into a brightly lit coffee-house. My acquaintance stepped in while I walked on down the street."*

"The most precious stone" is the patient's incestuous object. The man behind him who keeps "swearing" represents his conscience. This is an important detail. The "plaintiff" of the former dream as well as the critic of this dream represent the patient's well-functioning superego. This is a decisive criterion for differentiation of cleptomania from common larceny. We see the play of contrasting forces in the patient's unconscious, the antisocial and the moral force, and we may even see the yielding of the antimoral component, as in the aforementioned dream: The acquaintance is the one that steps into the jewelry store—while the patient walks on.

It is not sufficiently known that behind cleptomania often a much more serious impulse may be hidden than that of sexual aggression: the impulse of murder. The act of stealing then is a highly diluted and attenuated performance which reproduces the whole gamut of emotional excitement, the "crime-and-punishment" mood which masks the underlying experience.

The following dreams of a cleptomaniac [1] bear witness to such a psychological connection:

[490] *"A colleague came to me with a girl and said: 'See, old boy, a girl may be slain this way.' He then stuck a knife into her body."*

[491] *"I saw myself on a stage playing the part of Mortimer in 'Maria Stuart.' I professed love to Maria which she did not accept. I thrust a knife into her breast with the words, 'If thou lovest me not, neither shalt thou love another.' Whereupon I collapsed and awoke."*

The basis for cleptomania in this case was the patient's ambivalent attitude toward his cold and undemonstrative mother. He wanted to get (= steal) her love, and at the same time, he wanted to kill her for her lack of response. This "stabbing" may be taken both as a sexual and a criminal symbol. The dream number [491] refers clearly to the unresponsive "incest object."

The following dream was dreamed by a thirty-six-year-old teacher who was struggling against an impulse to steal little objects in "Five-and-Ten" stores.

[492] *"I was walking a herd of animals—each animal a mixture of tiger and elephant. There were two groups among them; those who kept back and those who went along. This time the slow group kept on pushing ahead, until they got out of hand and crashed into a store front."*

"Walking a herd of animals"—like a shepherd—refers to the patient's occupation (teacher). He is to control animals —which are half-tigers and half-elephants. It is a combination of wild and subdued, cruel and mild—in other words, it represents the patient's dual personality. The group that was "kept back" suddenly pushes ahead: his impulses get out of hand and crash into a store—a "Five-and-Ten" store.

The fact that the dreamer introduces the tiger as a symbol of his impulse indicates the presence of sadistic tendencies in his neurosis which analysis was able to discover. To dis-

1 Analyzed by W. Stekel.

cuss their specific constellation and dynamic importance would lead us too far afield, however.

PYROMANIA

What was said about the unconscious motivation of cleptomania applies also to pyromania. The sexual meaning of fire was mentioned before (page 212). In pyromania both actions, the setting of fire and the extinguishing of fire by the use of water, must be considered as symbolic.

One of Stekel's patients, a thirty-nine-year-old commercial clerk who was preoccupied with fantasies of arson dreamed:

[493] *"I am in an ancient building which, however, seems familiar to me. I hear voices from the corner of the room. I am fearfully excited. Suddenly I hear fire signals on the street. Everybody shouts 'Fire! Fire!' I run into the street dressed only in my underwear. At a distance I perceive the red glow. My father's mill is on fire. People begin to throw water. I, too, take hold of an enormous hose and direct it forcefully upon the burning building. The thought comes to me that my parents might be inside the mill. I shout, 'Save my father and mother!' I wake up with palpitation and emission."*

Since early childhood the patient had regular opportunity to witness parental intimacies. He was sleeping in their bedroom. These experiences left indelible traces in the patient's mind. In his neurosis the patient identified himself with his father.

"The ancient building" refers to his past. The "voices" reproduce the fateful nocturnal impressions mentioned before, which left him "fearfully excited." "Fire" and "red glow" represent the condition of being aroused. The "enormous hose" is the child's conception of the paternal organ. "Saving" and "rescuing" as symbols were mentioned before (page 103). The emission attests to the sexual character of the entire scene.

DROMOMANIA

This is a neurotic disturbance consisting of an uncontrollable impulse to travel, move about, climb mountains, and the like. It is usually based upon a "flight reflex," which can be "centrifugal," i.e., leading *away* from the patient's childhood patterns, or "centripetal," i.e., leading *back* to the past and the unforgettable joys of childhood. As all other neurotic reactions the flight is usually unsuccessful.

The following stereotyped dream was reported by a young man suffering from a respiratory neurosis and dromomania:

[494] *"I walk along a narrow, smutty passageway and meet uncanny, mummyfied figures. Through a small window with the aid of a ladder, I reach down into a bright corridor (like the one in my home town). The yard is surrounded on all sides by high walls over which tree branches are hanging. In the center of the yard there is a basin and a kind of fountain. I reach the open space with a sense of relief. (Sometimes in the dream I go through the scenery in the reverse direction.)"*

The walk through the "narrow, smutty passageway" is a duplication of the birth process. Of much interest are the "small window" through which the dreamer hopes to get out and the "fountain" (cf. page 128, figures 32 and 33) at the "center of the yard." The "home town" refers to his mother. The patient's trip in the "reverse direction" is taken whenever he has an increased desire to relinquish the struggles of reality and to regress to the sheltered intrauterine existence, to be reborn and start a new, better life again.

The patient suffered from an uncontrollable urge for mountain climbing. Many factors (which we shall omit at this time) made him realize that this was not a customary sport for him, but an impulsion like dipsomania or drug addiction.

While on his tour, the patient was in a changed mental state and resembled a person who was running away from something or running toward something. The analysis showed the close connection between the patient's intrauterine fantasy which was crowned by a vision of rebirth and the patient's relation to the mountain, a symbolic representation of his mother. "Inside versus outside," "homeward versus toward far and distant places" were the two poles between which his mind oscillated.

INTOXICATIONS

The dreams seen in most cases of acute intoxications are more or less similar to those found in schizophrenics. The *mescaline* intoxication is best known in this respect. Here we often find dreams and hallucinations in which time moves at a tremendous speed (Berringer); also symptoms of micropsia and macropsia. The patients have a peculiar impression of being part of their environment (disturbances of ego perception).

Intoxication with *marijuana* offers dreams and hallucinations in which time is perceived as passing exceedingly slowly. *Cocaine* and *alcohol* mobilize repressed instincts, mostly homosexual and criminal, apparently by unleashing inhibitions. In *alcohol hallucinations* the patients often hear voices which are projections of their own conscience pangs.

Time perceptions seem to be affected also by *opium*. While in an opium daze, De Quincey dreamed a story which extended over seventy years.

CHRONIC ALCOHOLISM

In the following I should like to present the case of a fifty-one-year-old writer who was subjected to an uncontrollable urge to drink.

His personality analysis revealed a high degree of oral dependency, passivity, and insecurity. As a child he suffered a great deal from sibling rivalry. His mother died when he was five, and his stepmother preferred his younger brother.

He showed unconscious hatred against women in general, yet deep in his mind he also preserved an ideal of womanhood, of warmth and acceptance, represented by the memory of his mother. It was at the "breast" of his "mother" that he "drank" when the bartender generously offered him oral gratification.

Simultaneously with the decline of the patient's heterosexual adjustment—his marriage collapsed because of his drinking—the homosexual tendencies increased. This is a frequent finding in alcoholism. These tendencies expressed themselves in the patient's desire for pluralistic sexual practices (several objects at the same time), in the "triangle complex" (interest in partners who belong to someone else), and in pathological jealousy. Strong masochistic tendencies also were detectable.

A characteristic dream is the following:

[495] *"With a number of neighbors I was sleeping on the sidewalk on lower Broadway to protect some fundamental right that someone was trying to take away from me.*

"We went to a drinking fountain which kept revolving, but we caught up with it. Others tried to push ahead of us, but I insisted on going in proper order of arrival.

"Cops came and wanted to take me away (charge: misdemeanor), but the others saved me. They flashed lights on us and I remember hating them and being afraid of them."

The patient is in protest against the analyst (policeman) who wants to elevate him from his degrading position of a "Bowery Bum." The "lower Broadway" represents the Bowery, the place where derelicts hang out. It is his "fundamental right" to manage his affairs his own way, ever since his "birth right" had been taken away from him in his childhood. He was pushed aside by his stepmother in favor of his brother. In this respect the patient is very sensitive. "Others tried to push ahead of us, but I insisted on going in proper order of arrivals," so that everyone can get his share at the "drinking fountain" which keeps revolving.[1] But he finally "caught up with it."

Just as he rebels against the analyst as a representative of orderly society, so he rebels against this society itself. He has a "chip on his shoulder." "Society owes him a living." (Oral dependency, a phenomenon frequently found in the "oral neurosis," alcoholism). Alcohol immobilizes him, makes him helpless and dependent so that others (the society=mother) must take care of him.

The "triangle situation" is expressed in this transference dream:

[496] *"I was dining at the home of Dr. S. In the course of our conversation I remarked that I was going to make love to my wife soon.*

"Then his wife came in and I made love to her."

In the dream in which "Dr. S." stands for the analyst, the patient establishes a homosexual relation with the latter via his wife; the woman is the object of the common enjoyment.

Dwindling potency increases his feminine trends and the tendency to be a sexual co-partner rather than a conqueror through his own merits.

The following is a "pluralistic" dream in which oral erotic features predominate:

[497] *"I was in a room with a woman who resembled my stepmother as she appeared about twenty years ago (when she was still a lush and appetizing[2] woman); there was also Marylin, my present girl friend, and a third woman whom I cannot identify. We were making love orally. None of us was undressed.*

"Suddenly I felt my father was about to enter the room, just as I was at the point of emission."

---

[1] The picture of the revolving fountain reminds one of the ataxia of the intoxicated individual.

[2] Note the oral-erotic element in this characterization.

Here the "father" represents the superego, as did the "cops" in the first dream.

The paranoid jealousy reaction in *chronic alcoholism is* due to the increased latent homosexuality and the impaired potency. In dreams of these patients we find abundant homosexual material. The patients fight with other men, with devils; they are stabbed by criminals, etc.—all these are signs of repressed homosexuality and criminality. One of Schilder's patients in his delirium tremens [498] *saw himself in bed, his scrotum and penis cut off. He was crying about it. He felt that he looked like a woman and even thought that he had an opening which looked like a vagina in place of his penis.*

The "little animals" seen in dreams and hallucinations of alcoholics are symbols of self-reproaches and feelings of guilt. (See page 171.)

Poe, who indulged heavily in alcohol, experienced the pangs of his conscience in hallucinations [499] about *animals like rats and pigs.*

The most impressive portrayal of his conscience reaction is his poem "The Raven." Taken as a daydream, it offers us not only a picture of the dreamer's pangs of conscience but also indicates the circumstances of his "guilt," a guilt which "never more" shall be extinguished. One may consider the person of "Lenore" as a never-vanishing recollection of one of the poet's intimate experiences. To discuss all allusions to the character of the "guilt" which are to be found in the poem would lead us too far.

In most cases of intoxication we find these features: *increased pressure of antisocial and antimoral drives, psychosexual infantilism* (including bisexuality, exhibitionism, and sadomasochism) and an ever-present *oral-dependent attitude.* (We should also add that in the backgrounds of these patients as well as those of drug addicts we find a remarkably high frequency of *actual incestuous relationships.*)

Drug Addiction

The background of drug addiction has been investigated by analysts for a long time. In many cases a definite psychogenesis of the addiction can be reconstructed. What was said about the various impulsions holds true also for the uncontrollable urge to use drugs, namely, that the urge has the task of replacing an urge of much more prohibited character.

A good example for this is the following dream produced by *a hypnotic addict:*

[500] *"In front of a public school a young man is standing. His penis is exposed. He is waiting for a girl to pass. A policeman arrests him. P.S. The policeman appeared to be drunk."*

The dream reveals the patient as fighting against an unconscious urge to expose himself to a school girl. The addiction is represented by the policeman who is "drunk."[1] It is an "arresting" force, as far as the roughly antimoral tendency is concerned, but, at the same time, it is an "intoxicating" force.

The *injection* by which drugs often are introduced also has a symbolic value in many cases. In dreams we can find its explanation. Thus a woman morphinist aged thirty-four, unhappily married, dreamed [501] *of her teacher writing with chalk on a blackboard and the white letters turning to gold.*

This teacher had seduced her when she was eight years old. Since that time she was masochistic and craved for tall and strong men. If "chalk" in this dream is substituted for "syringe" and both are taken as phallic symbols, "writing" can then be understood as an intimate act, the recollection of which is lasting and precious ("white" turning to "gold"). The patient's injection puts her into a dreamlike state of joy in which, unconsciously, she can indulge in memories.

---

[1] He has been overwhelmed by a toxic agent which eliminates him as a representative of law and order.

(If we consider this dream from the "anagogic" point of view we find that it expresses the patient's desire for improvement, very much as the attempts by alchemists to turn inferior metals into precious ones.)

It is worth mentioning that some cases of *addiction to analgesics* develop on the basis of chronic pain conditions, e.g., headache.

The following is a dream of a pyramidon addict. In his case the constant therapeutic and prophylactic (!) use of the drug represented a form of "suicide on the installment plan." The patient tried thus to evade a severe conflict he had between his feelings toward his wife and his pathological tendency toward promiscuity. His dream was as follows:

[502] *"I am in bed, seriously ill. My wife sits at my bedside and says that she is sorry to see me leave her. I say: 'It is too late now; I have taken the pill. I think it is veronal.'"*

Veronal is a potent hypnotic which has been frequently used for the purpose of suicide.

The following are dreams of a *morphine addict* treated by Graven. The case is that of a physician whose analysis uncovered a strong father fixation.

[503] *"I was absent from school for a long time. I met the principal and knew I couldn't tell him I was ill because I looked healthy. I told him that my morphinism was the cause of my absence. We walked to our home and talked with father. The principal said that I should stay in psychiatric treatment or I will end in an asylum."*

The dream bespeaks strong conflicts because of the addiction. The "principal" is the patient's conscience and, at the same time, the analyst. The patient here introduces his father as the main actor of his drama. He has always discussed his affairs with his father. He did not change even when he found out (early in his life) that his father was a man of weak character who was spending a great deal of his time and money with dissolute women. The next dream bears witness to this attitude.

[504] *"I enter a coffee-house with my sister. She turns into my father and I turn into a little boy. My father is the owner of the coffee-house and I am a waiter. Someone criticizes the coffee cake which my father had made. I take the blame upon myself to protect father."*

We notice the self-denying attitude the patient assumes to defend his father. The passage in which his sister turns into his father is, at first, uninterpretable. But the next dream sheds light on this detail:

[505] *"My sister in bed. The lower part of her body is uncovered. I bite her genital. She is very depressed."*

An oral aggression against the sister's genital. The dream refers to a traumatization which has taken place in bed.

This and the following dream [506] in which *the patient sees himself in a room with a young girl,* offer a hint that a defloration had taken place in the past. For the dream ends with the sentences:

"A young man enters and throws her down on the floor. I see a dead bird on the spot where she fell down."

The patient finally admits this. It is the memory of this incident and the struggle against it which have led him to his addiction and are causing his social and moral deterioration. He says in his dream:

[507] *"I was in a hospital. My sister is a nurse there. There is no place for me and I have to lay on the wet floor of the hallway until a room is free.*

"Then large water masses stream along the hallway and carry me down to the toilets. I am afraid to fall into a hole on the floor. A little man promised to help me."

His moral degradation through addiction is hinted at by the "water masses" (drives) which sweep him "down to the toilets," down to the gutter.

Interesting is the next dream in which the injection needle is symbolized as a "bee or wasp."

[508] *"Taking part in a banquet. Difficulties with admission. Instead of tickets they gave us bees (or wasps). I had*

two of them. One flew away, but I caught the other. To my greatest annoyance it kept humming. The tone aroused a feeling of pain which I had when I awoke."

The "banquet" here has a sexual meaning and refers to the incestuous scene. The bee keeps humming; it is a constant reminder (obsessive memory) and disturber of his peace of mind (conscience reaction). There is only one way to stop the "bee" from "humming" says the patient to himself: the "sting" (injection). The subsequent euphoric fantasies and sensations help him over the constant "pain" he has when he is awake.

The next dream brings another determination of the symbol "injection":

[509] *"I am in church with a companion. We are looking at pictures."*

The patient associates Saint Sebastian, the martyr, with the picture in church. The symbol of the injection needle is represented by the arrows piercing the Saint's body. It also includes the patient's idea of unconscious gratification following the piercing with the needle, very much as salvation follows the Saint's martyrdom. Thus, in the patient's unconscious, religious and sexual motives appear condensed.

The English poet Coleridge, who was known for his opium addiction, once fell asleep while reading the book "Purchas' Pilgrimage." He had a dream in which he visualized his most impressive poem, "Kubla Khan."

DREAMS OF CHILDREN

Unfulfilled wishes, among them "day residues," are the most frequent motives of children's dreams. The environment is responsible for some of the child's anxiety dreams. Unwisely selected fairy tales, ghost stories, and other anxiety producing material which adults sometimes present to a child may reappear in dreams and frighten the youngster out of his sleep.

The first dreams of a child usually occur between the ages

of two and five, that is, when the ego begins to acquire an integrated form. C. W. Kimmins suggests that the character of the dreams undergoes changes as the child's personality develops. According to this author, kinesthetic dreams (falling, flying, floating), for example, do not appear before the age of nine.

The young child does not completely differentiate the dream from reality. Later, he has a tendency to confabulate whenever the dream impression is indistinctly remembered.

In the child's anxiety dreams, the threatening animals in most cases represent the parents in their fear-inspiring attitudes. Devil, God, the angels represent punitive and rewarding forces in harmony with their accepted meanings. It is clear that the fewer "devils" and "Hells" the child has to contend with during the day, the less likely will these images reappear in the child's anxiety dream.

If the child sleeps in or near the bedroom of his parents some impressions of sexual activity taking place between the parents may enter the dream plot.

The creaking bed, the movements of the bodies, half-suppressed expressions of pain or enjoyment may find their reproduction in the child's dream. The little dreamer may see railroad engines approaching dangerously close or may witness a threat to the mother or to himself. The accompanying affect is invariably anxiety.

In communities and nations where attendance at school is associated with strict disciplinarianism, the child's daily school experiences may color his dreams. The general absence, in American children, of fearful dreams about school and teachers is a tribute to our advanced school system.

Only those children who are inadequately nourished have dreams and nightmares about food. The night terrors invariably disappear once the situation has been corrected.

During fever states the child is prone to have kinesthetic dreams, particularly those of flying and floating in which slowness of movement is characteristic.

Death dreams usually make their first appearance during early adolescence. In them, the child may attend his own funeral cognizant of the grievous effect his demise has on his parents (narcissistic and hypochondriacal motives).

The child of four or five may have dreams about sibling rivalry, but evidences of jealousy, the most destructive of human intra-psychic forces, do not appear in his dreams until puberty.

A six-year-old boy showed signs of sibling rivalry toward his little brother, a two-months-old baby. He once attacked the infant with scissors, and on several occasions he openly expressed his hostility toward his rival.

One night he was driven from his bed by a dream, and he fled to his mother who asked why he was so excited. He then related his dream:

[510] *"A man had a dog, and the dog hurt a cat, and the cat's head was cut off, and it was our baby's head, and the head was alive, and the head kept crying."*

The boy refused to return to his bed, expressed a desperate fear of the baby's crying head, and could not be calmed by his mother when she tried to convince him that the whole episode was "only a dream."

The boy used to laugh with glee at the baby's crying which he compared to the mewing of a cat. In the dream, we see his hostile attitude toward his brother.

We can discern here the outlines of symbolization. The little brother became a cat because his voice reminded the dreamer of a cat's meow. The dreamer's own hostility was expressed in the dog's attack on the cat.

The intelligent mother understood her son's attitude and succeeded in altering it. Moral reactions begin at an early age. The case of this boy should not be passed without noting that the boy's fear was a distinct conscience reaction.

Grotjahn pointed out that the sleep of children shows a flowing transition from the wake state and that the dream contents show the tendency to be carried over into the wake life.

DAYDREAMS

> *My eyes make pictures when they are*
> *shut.*
>
> COLERIDGE
> (*"A Day Dream"*)

INTRODUCTION

The dream is not only produced during sleep. On the contrary! *We dream much more during the day than during the night.*

Freud considers daydreams as the first steps toward hysterical symptoms. He emphasizes the fact that hysterical symptoms are not a direct result of recollections which rise to consciousness, but are connected with fantasies built around recollections. Besides conscious fantasies, the daydream also contains unconscious fantasies, which must remain unconscious because they are derived from repressed material. Daydreams contain wish-fulfillments (like dreams) and are based (like dreams) to a great extent on the individual's infantile experiences. Like dreams, they enjoy a certain lessening of censorship for their production.

Careful observation has proved to a great extent that we all are daydreamers. This observation has also taught us that we are constantly indulging in dreams, no matter what we may be doing or thinking. Only when our conscious attention in its entirety is attracted by external stimuli do we possibly fully detach our thoughts from our dreams. Here we touch upon the problems of attention, memory, and ability to concentrate.[1]

In dreams, deliriums, or fantasies reality is forgotten and we are taken with the creations of our own unconscious. Nobody is entirely free from daydreams. Complete contact with reality is an ideal of perfection which mankind has not yet attained. Our power of concentration depends upon the emotional value of daydreams.

[1] R. W. Emerson: "We remember what we understand, and we understand best what we like; for this doubles our power of attention, and makes it our own."

Many neurotics complain of a "loss of ability to concentrate" and of a "loss of memory." It sometimes appears as if the patients were right, but an exact test as used in a psychiatric examination would prove that the memory of these patients is entirely intact. Why then the patients' complaints? The answer is not hard to find. In reality the patients complain about their daydreams. These so engross the attention that the patients' available energies seem insufficient to permit concentration.

Another factor plays a great role in this condition. Our daydreams are, as a rule, emotionally charged. On the other hand, reality with its relatively low emotional charge is often unable to attract a great amount of attention. The patient, therefore, prefers to indulge in dreams. This poor economy of attention makes him believe that he has a poor memory. Such disturbances of memory can be completely removed by psychotherapy which endeavors to solve the patient's problems by subjecting his daydreams as well as his night dreams to careful examination. It is necessary, of course, to train the patient to recall his daydreams, a task which is sometimes rather difficult.

If we, the so-called normal persons, were to make a record of our daydreams, we should be highly astonished at the great number of strange ideas we harbor in our minds. It is true that we cannot follow our daydreams to their full extent. What we are able to record are flashes, fragments of daydreams, particularly vivid before we yield to the arms of Morpheus. We call these fragments *hypnagogic thoughts.* Also, after awakening, we sometimes catch a flash, half night-dream and half daydream, which we call *hypnopompic thought.* Both hypnagogic and hypnopompic thoughts are considered as messages from the unconscious. They are suitable for analysis.

The analysis of daydreams is another important propelling power of our treatment. Analytical resistance can be discovered and combated far more quickly and easily by extending our therapeutic influence to the problem of daydreams.

Daydream reports are not to be confused with "free associations" as reported in the analytical sessions. Daydreams are dreams and meet all the requirements of dreams. Kehrer says of daydreams: "They occur in an apparently wake state, which, however, is peculiarly changed; they consist of vivid ideas passing before the dreamer's mental eye or ear, ideas concerning some agitated fancied reality. The daydreamer invariably plays the role of an onlooker and passive listener of the fancied scenes, even if, as it mostly happens, he is the center of the drama. . . ."

In recollection, daydreams often appear fragmentary as the following example reported by a thirty-two-year-old lady suffering from anxiety testifies:

[511] *"The three brown girls looked like three apes. . . . I would make a fine mistress. . . . My baby's crib looks like a little rat cage. . . . My husband pulls his eyebrow as if he were trying to pull some bad thoughts out of his mind. . . . The drooping rose suggests dying embers. . . . My mate does not do his duty. . . . Flowers have mates. . . . My husband is generous with me in everything but in his love expressions, with which he is very stingy. . . . The constant lover is punished; it is better to be false. . . . The pillow on the edge of my bed looks like the dead body I saw in one of my last dreams."*

The language of these daydreams is clear. The patient suffers from feelings of inferiority because she believes she is being neglected by her husband. She compares herself with other women and depreciates them ("apes"). She suspects her husband of unfaithfulness ("bad thoughts") and plays with the thought of revenge ("mistress"). She thinks of her merits as a mother ("baby's crib") and considers her husband ungrateful. Death wishes against her husband and her child ("dead body") come to the surface and, along with her repressed sexual desires, bring about her anxiety states in the form of conscience reactions.

A series of daydreams of a young medical student who complained about absent-mindedness and lack of concentration follows:

[512] *"I cannot study . . . the stuff is too difficult. . . . Unless I get through I can't become a doctor. . . . The girl I met last night. . . . I want tenderness and attention. . . . I will never be able to get married. . . . My sister Grace is happily married. . . . Again the girl of last night. Whether she loves me. . . . My brother Dave is at home now. . . . What are they doing at home right now?"*

Glancing over the series of thoughts the patient had while sitting over his books, we see distinctly that in his dreams he lives at home and not in the city where he attends medical school. He is constantly comparing himself with his two brothers. We also notice the high degree of jealousy which the young man, closely attached to his sister, Grace, develops. He envies his brother-in-law for having married his sister. He envies his brother for his success in life. These emotions and thoughts divert his mind so thoroughly that he appears to be absent-minded.

Analysis of thought processes teach that thinking either *prepares* the individual for action or *substitutes* for action. The first represents the blueprint for the innervations which are necessary for the active function of mastery. Daydreams belong to the second type of thinking. They completely replace action and proceed along magic lines of omnipotent wish-fulfillment and narcissistic self-gratification.

It is for this reason also that they represent an important matrix for neurotic symptoms. A clash of an antimoral or antisocial thought with the ever watchful superego leads to acute display of anxiety, depression, confusion, headaches, dizziness, conversion.

The daydream is also the main vehicle for unconscious (mental) masturbation. As such it bears the roots for fleeting or persistent guilt feelings with subsequent acute depressions. The character of the masturbation daydreams is determined predominantly by the Oedipus complex.

The conversions which follow intensive daydreaming are "autoplastic" functions which *overt action* would have turned into external innervations and adaptations ("alloplastic" function of personality).

(Q) "Are daydreams just as short as 'night' dreams?"

(A) The short duration of the "night" dream is determined by the duration of the awakening act. Contrary to the dream, the daydream continues almost uninterruptedly while we are awake. It accompanies conscious thought, like the counterpoint movement in a musical composition. Daydreams show a definite relation to the individual's adaptation to reality and to the degree of his alertness. There are ups and downs, pulse waves, if you will, in daydreaming. As the contact with reality recedes, the daydream becomes more pronounced. As our consciousness becomes dimmed, all the mechanisms known about the dream come to the fore. Symbolization occurs, emotional accents are displaced, the primitive soul expresses what verbalization has failed to express.

Many of these daydreams originate in current perceptions. Beyond that, many unsolved complexes attach themselves to daydreams in a cathartic attempt; they jump on the bandwagon, so to speak, in quest for fulfillment.

If, during normal sleep, parts of the ego were awake and concerned with maintaining contact with and adapting to the outside and inside world, those parts of unconscious thoughts which then would push forward would have to be kept down by the still functioning parts of the ego. These "repressed" thoughts would then use the "night" dream as a vehicle for expression. This would be taking place as long as and to the extent that parts of the ego were available for the adaptive task. Such dreams then would be prolonged, and all mechanisms of the dream as we know them would be discernible for an indefinite time.

ARTISTIC PRODUCTION AND DAYDREAMS

Stekel has shown to what extent artistic production resembles a confessional. Freud, Rank, Sachs, Landquist, and others proved that the daydream has a close connection with the work of art. This connection can be overlooked only by a superficial observer such as Eckart von Sydow. Rank is certainly right when he considers the forming of the unconscious fantasy essential to artistic creation. We proceed on the supposition that the artist attempts to solve his deepest problems by the means of his artistic productions. Since none of his problems can be fully solved by the use of symbols (color, tone), the artist repeats his attempt again and again. Here are perhaps the roots of his inexhaustible productivity. Again and again he attempts to liberate, to exempt, to unburden himself, and to discharge the powerful inner forces through his work.

Heine speaks of the "great sufferings" from which his "little Lieder" arose, and Beethoven confesses: "What I feel in my heart must come out, and that's why I compose."

MUSICAL DAYDREAMS

How is one to understand a musical confession? Of all the arts, music is one which has the least literary content. The composer communicates his mental experiences by a practically direct method. It is feeling which vibrates toward the hearer, and it is feeling again which is set into sympathetic vibration in the hearer. But feelings have no form. They are "wordless," they cannot be "understood," because they have nothing to do with logic. Confessions expressed in this way, whether they arise from the gentle plucking of a string or from the thunderstorm of a symphony, can be heard only by ears attuned to the speech of poets. And only the ears of favored artists are capable of this. With ordinary hearers the situation is different. The "feeling" which the composer communicates to the hearer, the "tune" of his daydreams transferred to the hearer through his work, are used by the latter for building up his own daydreams. The composer wreathes about the hearer the euphony of his melodies. The listener follows willingly, carried away by the stream of music. Yet he has his own canoe of daydreams too, in which, comfortably seated, he lets himself drift along with the current. Thus daydream speaks to daydream, and a composer whose musical daydream comes close to the age-old dreams of humanity is a master indeed.

Daydreams and music have much in common. The similarity is based on the fact that the daydream, like music, for the most part, has no literary content. It runs its course in a series of "sensations," in that embryonic form of thought which, finally, through a complicated cerebral mechanism is to be changed into conscious thoughts. For this reason we hear songs so often on the lips of those whose dreary, monotonous work forces them to do without many of life's pleasures, for example, needleworkers, day laborers, servants. They sing, and it seems as if their longings, rising from damp spiritual dungeons, go out into the world on the wings of dreams.

Of course, there are musical compositions whose melodies are voluntarily subordinated to a "program" (*Programmusik*). In others, melodies accompany the literary content and lend color to it as in many songs and operatic works. Here the sound and the word are more or less connected. They build mutually associative connections. For the same reason those fiery marching rhythms when the toreadors make their appearance and the song "On to the Fray, Toreador!" seem inseparable to our ears.

It may happen that this associative combination is "lost" for a time. You sing a song and have "forgotten" the words. Closer examination may reveal that the content of the song was suppressed because it happened to be "complex-tainted." Many people hum a melody, apparently without thinking of the text, yet if necessary they can easily recall the words. Very often familiar tunes apparently hummed without a "text" in reality have words, whether we are conscious of them or not. Stekel has repeatedly pointed out this fact, and in several cases he analytically examined melodies which were hummed apparently "thoughtlessly." I call attention particularly to the tune dream of a patient which began with "I am a little widow" and contained the secret desire of the patient to be a widow soon.

I have treated several patients whose night dreams or day-dreams contained fragments of melodies. Following Stekel's example, I analyzed them. I should like to quote a case which, in my opinion, is not very frequently seen. It concerns an eighteen-year-old student who suffered from a head tic. Once he dreamed [513] *of a certain melody and actually sang it in his sleep*. His own singing woke him up, but very soon after awakening, the melody slipped from his mind. During the morning it struck him again, but he was not able to bring it into any known relation.

I jotted down the notes corresponding to what the patient sang. This is approximately what it sounded like:

FIGURE 62

As the patient and I tried to remember where the melody came from, we finally discovered that it was a fragment from *Don Juan*, Act III. And the words? It is almost unbelievable that such a text and such a melody just "happened" to strike a patient suffering from a head tic. This is the correct music and text of the opera:

FIGURE 63

The patient, an enthusiastic music lover, identified it at once, having heard *Don Juan* several times. Evidently, in the melody sung in his sleep, the patient experienced his head tic symbolically as a sort of conclusion to some unpleasant thoughts.

The following dream in which a melody was sung is of the same order. The underlying words were invented by the schizophrenic patient herself. The dream runs as follows:

[514] *"I am somewhere. I suddenly see a snake which is striped in black and white. The snake is a man who is disguised as a snake. He sings:*

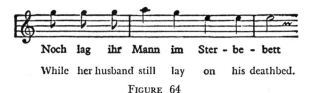

Noch lag ihr Mann im Ster - be - bett

While her husband still lay on his deathbed.

FIGURE 64

The rest was forgotten."

The patient was occupied with the care of her husband, who was slowly dying of general paresis. They had a boarder, a Russian count, whom she secretly loved. The situation at home was such that, while in one room her husband lay dying, in the next the count, a healthy young man, received women visitors. The patient, who came from a very religious family, was able to resist all temptations consciously, but not in her dreams, night as well as day. She was considerably shaken up psychically by this continuous discord. It was certainly understandable that in her delusional states she saw herself for the most part cross-eyed, looking with one eye to the left and with the other eye to the right. Her psychosis came on with a condition of acute confusion just before her husband died. In this condition, as she later explained in a lucid interval, she had a desire to put her husband, who in the meantime had died, in vinegar and oil "in order to preserve him" for herself. It was a clear expression of her guilty conscience.

The words "while her husband still lay on his deathbed" can be supplemented by the words "she was already thinking of another marriage." This supposition finds confirmation in the fact that one of the most frequent auditory hallucinations of this patient was this: "You'd like to become the wife of the

Czar, wouldn't you?" This voice she always ascribed to hostile, bolshevistic groups.

The next case we are presenting should prove of great help in investigating musical daydreams. It is that of a sixteen-year-old high school student from the South who was being treated for fetishism and a series of compulsion symptoms. Among other things he had the compulsion to sing certain songs or fragments of all sorts of compositions, to whistle them, or to play them on the piano countless times. The patient was distinguished by an exceptional musical ability and had a remarkable memory for musical compositions.

Though his relatives greeted the boy's diligent application to music with great satisfaction, the patient confessed to me that his industry had nothing to do with a particular love for this art but was the result of a remarkable quality he possessed. With the aid of musical motives he was able to relive in spirit pleasant events and experiences of his past. He connected particular daydreams with particular songs or compositions. Whenever he heard these, he lived over his corresponding daydreams. When asked to play, he played those pieces which enabled him to relive particular experiences.

The following are the most important items of his life history:

Shortly after his birth his parents were divorced, and his mother returned to her parents. Until he was two years of age he did not see his father. At that age he had only a fleeting view of him when, for some reason, the father visited his divorced wife. The child never saw him again. His mother strove to destroy all curiosity about his father which the boy later showed, by painting a very black picture of him.

The life of this boy, who was surrounded by those who loved him, was apparently one of uninterrupted joy, until his mother's second marriage threw it into such a state of confusion that medical assistance had to be called in. The lad refused to have anything to do with his stepfather. In spite of the fact that this cultured and intelligent man did all in his power to become friends with the boy, he failed completely up to the time of the treatment.

Later another complication set in. Shortly after this second marriage, as if to spite his parents, the lad began to display a lively interest in his real father and to use his shadowy remembrance as a basis for a series of fantasies. The school catalogue contained, besides the students' names and addresses, also their fathers' names. The boy felt himself compelled to learn by heart the names of the fathers of all his friends. He carried this to such a degree that he could instantly name the father of any of his friends when the friend's name was mentioned.

In addition, he invented another game with names in which he used music. It quite often happened that while he was playing a certain piece he experienced a certain daydream. As explained above, he experienced the same dream each time he played this piece. The opposite also held. When he desired to experience this particular daydream he played the corresponding piece. Gradually the musical piece and the daydream merged into an inseparable associative combination. For the most part he composed mentally the words to the piece which he happened to be playing. The words were—and this was especially characteristic in this case—the combination of two names, that of a school friend and that of the latter's father.

The following examples, selected from a large choice at my disposal are from Beethoven's Fifth Symphony, with the patient's own words:

[515] *Daydream about his friend Bill D. Butler and his father Arthur G. Butler* (hummed):

Bill   D.   But - ler   Ar - thur   G.   usw.

FIGURE 65

(The names in these examples are not those given by the patient.)

[516] *Daydream about his schoolmate James J. Gordon and his father Dr. P. D. Gordon* (hummed):

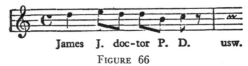

James   J.   doc-tor   P.   D.   usw.

FIGURE 66

Looking over these fragments of daydreams we see, impressively depicted in them, a part of this boy's tragedy. What he is trying to effect by means of his dreams is not the union of a son and his father, a union in which the melody is the bond of sentiment bringing the two together; it is a symbolic attempt on the part of the patient to unite his own destiny with that of his own father. In doing so he displaces the names and uses the language of music as a means. The youngster disclosed that he used to run around the streets aimlessly for hours hoping to run into his father. He knew that he would not be able to recognize him, but he admitted that he felt an inner voice would tell him who his father was and that he would then run into his arms. In thousands of dream situations he went back to the time when he was alone with his mother and could then luxuriate in her love. He used to whistle, for example, the following motive from Beethoven's Sixth Symphony softly to himself:

FIGURE 67

In the dream accompanying this tune [517] *he and his mother sat at the piano and played the symphony four-handed. In spirit, he inhaled the fragrance of her body; he drank in the sweetness of her voice; he whistled and whistled, and poured his entire being into the song.* A sort of intoxication came over him, until finally he was able to compose himself.

He was in the habit of keeping an old library card in his pocket. The card dated back to the time before his mother's second marriage. For him there was no present, only a past, and this ended when he was eight years old. The following motive (Mozart, First Sonata, Adagio) was the basis of the following fantasy:

[518] *"I studied this with my mother before she lived with stepfather. . . . At that time I read the book 'Westward Ho!' The hero of this book made a deep impression on me. I identified myself with him. The Mozart motive reminds me of this hero."*

The boy's stepfather—let us call him Dr. H. B. Parker—once said that he liked Beethoven's Ninth Symphony so much that he would like to have it played at his grave. This remark caused our patient to repeat the following motive many times in singsong fantasies. I wish to call attention to the fact that the lad had absolutely no idea of this open death wish concerning his stepfather. Daydream [519]:

— doc - tor H. B. Par - ker

FIGURE 69

Daydream [520] (Beethoven's Fifth Symphony):

FIGURE 70

"Stepfather tarries in Mexico and the patient is alone with his mother. . . ."

We see here that in his musical fantasies the patient nullifies his mother's second marriage and continues to weave the fairy tale of her first. Even the death wishes concerning his stepfather found their way into song, which was the patient's highly original method of expressing his conflicts. But the fact must not be overlooked that the experiences which the patient relived through his music showed for the most part a lust-colored character. This lust, in return, was used as a stimulus for further dreams. In this case art was more than a mere "sublimation" of eroticism. It was a clear equivalent for masturbation.

The relations between daydreams and music are not always so clear. In an ideal case we should be able to "interpret" every artistic production; but, in reality, the "tools" for musical expression are very delicate. In the musical production the artist's unconscious uses the "kinetic" energy of the melody as only one part of its expression. There is another part also which is the "potential" energy—the retarded movement, the tension lying in chords. This tension conceals impulses which drive toward movement—a basic phenomenon of harmony in general.

The expert observes various dynamic effects not only in the sounds of single chords but also in the transition of chords, in the relation between the "masculine," hard, "major," and the "feminine," soft, "minor," triad; the artist's unconscious energies transferred into sounds rendering the inaudible into audible; the psychic tension into the musical. The expert should study the individual temperament of the composer which often directs his choice of instruments, time, rhythm, and structure of the composition. The better our musical education, the better shall we understand the symbolic language of that daydream which expresses itself through musical composition.

Many composers have called their compositions "dreams"

or have expressed their dreams musically. Tartini is said to have composed his "Devil's Trill," according to a dream he had (Cf. page 33), Liszt wrote "Love Dreams." We find dreams in E. D'Albert's "Tiefland" (Pedro's dream), in Beethoven's "Fidelio" (Florestan's delusions). We know Mendelssohn's music to "Midsummer Night's Dream," etc. Perhaps some day we shall be able to look at the composition, even if it is not a musical representation of a dream, for the signs of a composer's personality and for his specific conflicts.

DRAWING AND PAINTING DAYDREAMS

It is not only painted dreams as, for instance, Murillo's "Angel Kitchen," the pictures of the younger Breughel, Schwind's "The Dream of the Knight," etc., Max Klinger's "Dream Pictures," or Kubin's "Dreamed Landscape" that can be used as a means for interpreting the artist's unconscious. Proceeding from the supposition that in his works of art the painter produces nothing but dreams, we may also interpret other pictures, though with far greater difficulty. The spacing of the figures, the contrasts of light and shade, the facial and bodily expressions of single figures, the symmetry, the relation between foreground and background, symbolic features, etc., all must be taken into consideration. In order to be able to interpret paintings, not only artistic training but also intuition and great experience in dream interpretation are necessary.

Freud's genius accomplished a pioneer work also in this field. We quote here a few passages from his highly interesting contribution "Eine Kindheitserinnerung des Leonardo da Vinci," which appears in Volume IX of his *Gesammelte Shriften*. Freud analyzes there Leonardo's picture (Fig. 71) which portrays Maria seated on the lap of her mother Anne, bent toward the Christ-child, who plays with a lamb.

The two women have the same blissful smile on their lips, that unearthly tender smile we know so well from the picture "Mona Lisa." (Fig. 72.)

FIGURE 71
After da Vinci's ST. ANNE, VIRGIN AND CHILD JESUS
(Original in Louvre, Paris)

A few biographic facts (which Freud relates) will illustrate
the interpretations. Leonardo was an illegitimate child of
Ser Pedro da Vinci and a peasant girl Catarina. He spent the
first few years with his mother and came to his father when
he was about five years of age. Ser Pedro da Vinci married a
noblewoman, Donna Albiera, shortly before the boy was
born. His marriage was childless, however, and this seems to
be the reason why finally he had the boy brought to his or
rather his father's home. The boy found there not only the

FIGURE 72
After Da Vinci's MONA LISA

good stepmother, Mona Lucia, who, we assume, was not less affectionate toward him than any other grandmother is toward her grandson. This must have stimulated Leonardo to portray a child well-protected by a mother and a grandmother. Freud points out that Anna and Maria on Leonardo's picture show only a slight difference in age. Although the picture shows grandmother, mother, and son, the two women in reality look like two mothers—one who stretches her arms toward him, Albiera, the other in the background, as if farther away from the boy (Jesus—Leonardo), Catarina, both endowed with the blissful smile of motherly happiness. Leonardo's childhood was just as peculiar as this picture. He had two mothers—one real, from whom he was taken away, and one young and affectionate stepmother, his father's wife. The composition of the picture is the result of the artist's desire for condensing both figures. And, indeed, mother and grandmother, or rather the two mothers, constitute a unity in the composition. If we attempt to define both figures, Anne and Maria, in the picture, we find it not at all easy. One might say that both are merged into one, in the same way as are poorly condensed dream figures (Freud). "With the unearthly smile of St. Anne the artist also denied and concealed the jealousy which the unfortunate woman felt when she had to surrender to the nobler rival, her son, just as she had surrendered her husband before."

In the following presentation we shall discuss the relationship between drawing and daydream, using a case in which drawing was a precipitation of the patient's pathological fantasies. A thirty-four-year-old clerk had a brother two years younger who was stronger and taller than he and, most significant, more successful in life. The patient envied him and tried to differentiate himself as far as possible from his brother. The main reason for his envy was the fact that the patient's parents favored their other son.

In the course of the years the patient developed a peculiar system of mental masturbation. He produced fantasies in which a smaller, thinner, and weaker woman conquered a taller and stouter woman. This motive had been repeated in thousands of fantasies, dreamed in lots of dreams, and visual-

FIGURE 73

ized in many drawings and sketches for the sake of obtaining sexual gratification.

A dream of this kind is Fig. 73 on p. 501.

[521] *"A small Negro woman tussling with a big one and conquering her. Emission."*

The sketch was done by the patient for sexual arousement.

In the course of years another type of picture daydream

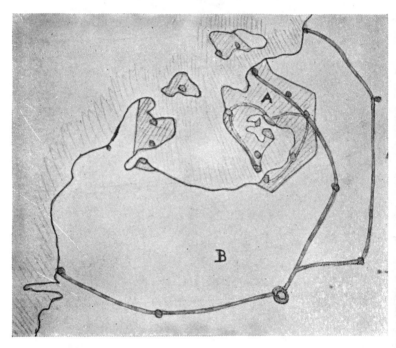

FIGURE 74

came up: the geographical dreams [522]. The underlying idea is the same as in the sexual daydreams (Fig. 74):

"A small but very progressive civilized country, A, having many traffic lines, railroads, large cities, rich in trade and science, is a neighbor to country B, which is large but impoverished, in a low state of civilization, and therefore dependent on the other." (Example: Japan and China.)

Here also the contrast between "small and strong" and

"big and weak" can be seen. Fantasies of this kind were drawn in great quantities to express the patient's desire for success, to overcompensate his feeling of inferiority. They were his only means of obtaining an elevated feeling of power and influence, and hence for a long time they could not be substituted. In our interpretation we omit the homosexual-masochistic root responsible for the patient's arousement.

Next we present a case in which personal conflicts obtained a specific expression in art. Siegmund K., aged thirty, an orthodox Jew, an illustrator, has suffered from stammering

FIGURE 75

since he was nine years old. Among his childhood experiences there are two which have great importance. The first is a circumcision ceremony witnessed when he was about four years old. The impression of this ceremony was so strong that the boy envied girls because they are spared from it. The second is a dream or a fantasy which is illustrated (Fig. 75.) and described by the patient in the following way:

[523] *"I was the only child at that time. My mother was at home. It was evening; my mother and my cousin Eva were seated at the table; mother was knitting and Eva was reading a book. I was playing on the floor. It was extraordinarily quiet—one could only hear the movement of the needles. All of a sudden the door opened silently and in came, soundlessly, an imp-like little man. The women did not notice him. I was deathly frightened and expected something terrible to happen. . . . A mysterious matter. . . . Perhaps something of an erotic character. . . . I was paralyzed with fear and was not able to utter a word."*

While the patient was the only child, he slept in the same bed with his father. Then twin sisters arrived. The patient reports that he was decidedly against any increase in the family and often cried because he felt neglected. The birth of his sisters caused also a great deal of thinking about the problem of procreation, and one of his own explanations at this time was that it is an imp who delivers babies into a mother's house. This delivery, he thought, was connected with some kind of injury to the mother.

Unfortunately the patient had to endure the arrival of a new child almost every year—three sisters between the ages of six and ten, a brother at eleven, and a sister at twelve. He hated his brothers and sisters. When he was six he almost threw his baby sister out of the window as a joke. Later he often dreamed that his brothers and sisters had died, preferably by suffocation.

The symptom of stammering at first was shown exclusively in the presence of his father. This was probably because his father criticized him severely for his speech difficulties. Later the "danger zone" grew. The patient began to fear that he might get stuck while leading prayer in the synagogue, or that he might get out of breath while addressing somebody, etc. He suffered all the more as he used to imagine that one day he would become a famous speaker worthy of his noble first name "Siegmund," which means "victorious mouth."

The patient's sex life was awakened very early. When he was five he happened to surprise his parents in an intimate scene, the real meaning of which he comprehended only several years later. And just as in his fantasy [523] a sinister imp enters his room amidst a hushed silence—something new, sinister and unknown, so sex enters the boy's mind with the experience in his parents' bedroom. How profound this experience was can be seen in the following dream:

[524] *"A little baby lies in a crib. A young man and a girl sit on a bench. The child turns into an imp and spies out the couple as if it begrudged them something."*

The dream presented in the course of the treatment undoubtedly was stimulated by the boy's experience. (Here he sees himself as an imp.) The better he understood the real character of the experience, the more he felt driven into opposition to his father, particularly when after the birth of his siblings he noticed a distinct shifting of general attention toward his younger brothers and sisters. At fifteen, he was a veritable "revolutionary," an atheist, ridiculing people who went to the synagogue, etc. This state did not last, however. The patient changed again radically one year later. While his opposition to his father remained unchanged until the time of his treatment, he once more began to develop strong religiosity and to adhere zealously to all the requirements of tradition.

When he was sixteen the patient was persuaded by his father to enter a Yeshivah (a college for Talmudic studies). The patient at first objected to it, but he gave in sooner than was expected. Even while on his way to the Yeshivah town he cried and thought of suicide. But the very moment he stepped into the Yeshivah his mind changed completely, he was permeated with his mission, and very soon acquired the exterior and the habits of the Talmud disciples to the smallest detail. He applied himself with a zeal characteristic of people who, inwardly wavering, try to get the necessary objective intellectual explanation for their subjective emotional attitude. For the patient's inner faith was never absolutely free of doubts. In order to meet this inner conflict he became involved in various theological meditations.

Like other doubters, he showed a distinct inclination for obsessions and compulsions. Thus, he often suffered from spells of blaspheming which troubled him most while he was at prayer. When he was twenty-four he had the compulsion to throw away things he was holding in his hands; instead, he held them more tightly. One thinks here of the "joke" the patient made when he was six years old, that is, almost throwing his baby sister out of the window. Furthermore, he was often in doubt as to whether he did not talk nonsense in conversation. Very often, he had to fight the compulsion to talk nonsense. We see that, while on one hand the patient was consciously striving toward ideals, on the other hand he felt

FIGURE 76
Jacob fights with the Angel.

clearly the pressure of his animal ego. He tried to fight it and at the same time feared that he might be defeated by his drives. This inner psychic struggle is illustrated by a drawing portraying Jacob's nocturnal fight with the Angel (Fig. 76).

In the Bible this scene is described as a struggle in which the Angel hurts Jacob in the "groin." (Connection with the patient's castration complex.)

As with most patients suffering from obsessive ideas, our patient believed in the "omnipotence of thoughts." This belief was highly strengthened by his study of the Kabbala, a Jewish secret science which was in practice particularly in the Middle Ages. He became superstitious, knew nothing "positively," and began to feel that even the dogmas of his religion were not sufficient to guarantee mental imperturbability. He wanted them to be much more dogmatic. He said: "I must be moral *because God orders me* to be moral, not because it is 'better' or 'wiser' to be moral. God must be a dictator. His laws must be beyond my understanding: otherwise He is no God for me. . . ."

If we put "father" instead of "God," we can see in the patient's absolute subordination to the divine law how much the former atheist and rebel has changed in his relation to his father. But the change exists only in the symbol of the father—"God"; for, in reality, his conscious attitude toward his father remained openly hostile. He observed his father's conduct with rare accuracy. He wanted to find out if his father liked him as he used to or if he preferred the other children. He interpreted whatever his father did as directed against himself. He could get excited, for instance, when his father yawned while our patient was drawing (lack of interest in his work!); when, in his presence, his father playfully knocked with his fingertips on the dinner plate (sign of being bored); when he clicked his tongue while eating; when he took advice on business matters from one of his daughters, etc. After a casual argument he did not speak to his father for more than a year. On another occasion he accused his father of making him sick and imagined with great satisfaction what would happen if he went insane and his father were responsible for that.

Taking the complete material into consideration, we arrive

without difficulty at the conclusion that our patient unconsciously loves his father with all his heart. In his neurosis he shifts this love to another object—Religion; he renders it "impersonal," while the component of hate supplied by the old Oedipus situation remains conscious. We can see this hatred in numerous dreams, but we can also perceive that this attitude is bipolar (ambivalent). The patient oscillates, like Balaam of the Bible, between cursing and blessing. And indeed, Balaam's lot fertilized the patient's artistic imagination so highly that he depicted it in a great many sketches.

Figure 77 portrays a biblical scene and is called *"Balaam's Ride."* Balaam, we know, was to go to Moab and curse the Israelites. On his way, an angel blocked a ravine he was to pass and persuaded him to bless the Israelites. In the sketch we see the ravine and the angel, in the peculiar shape

FIGURE 77

of a human mouth (the walls mean teeth). "Passing of Balaam" would mean "passing of hostile words"; the blockade symbolizes the mental inhibition tne patient suffers whenever he wants to express his hostility. "Cursing" becomes "blessing"; antisocial drives turn into social ones. But the inhibition leads to the disturbance of speech, which manifests itself, as stated before, mainly in the presence of the patient's father. The drawing shows the patient's identification with Balaam, an important structure in the patient's neurosis. The patient was never able to reveal to his father what he really wished to tell him, what was on the tip of his tongue whenever he faced him, namely, that *his father was the center of his life,* that his life was empty and shallow without his father's love. He had to strengthen the guards of his consciousness to restrain the breaking through of this confession. But in his dreams and in his artistic fantasy (Fig. 78) this love attained a sublime expression:

FIGURE 78
Prophet Elisha calls to his father Elijah who rides to Heaven:
"My Father, my Father, the chariot of Israel!"

We must discuss the patient's castration ideas in connection with his attitude toward his father. The castration complex plays a great part in this case. It has been repeatedly stimulated by the patient's frequent experiences with circumcision. As stated before, one of the earliest exciting experiences of his life, in his fourth or fifth year, was the witnessing of a circumcision ceremony. Later he showed strong defense reactions toward any kind of cruelty. Thus he fainted at a circumcision ceremony when he was seventeen, and he once fainted while watching the extraction of a tooth. As the closer investigation could prove, the first active manifestation of the castration idea was directed against the patient's father. The following dream was used as an example of castration dreams [87] on page 147. We repeat it here: [525]

"I am fighting with J. (an orthodox old gentleman, father image), *grab his necktie and tear it to pieces. The single parts are bleeding."*

Castration ideas are directed also against the patient's brother, whose arrival stopped the patient from considering himself as the "only male" among the children. We find this reaction in his dreams:

[526] *"My brother was lying in bed. I did something to his penis. A red fluid like blood came out. I wanted to wipe it out, but it did not disappear. My brother slept all the time. I thought I would tell him that the fluid came from his tooth. He woke up soon after that and touched his tooth."*

"Castration" is put into an equation with "pulling teeth," which reminds us of the patient's fainting experiences. We disregard here the connection between "castration" and "mouth" which is important for the psychology of stammering.

FIGURE 79

The active castration idea had also its ambivalent counterpart in the patient's fear of castration, probably due to a reaction of his superego. There were two regions on the patient's body where he experienced peculiar neurotic reactions: the genitals and the eyes, both organs having close relation to the castration complex. The thought of "blinding," or the word itself, caused a severe drawing pain in his scrotum. The patient also suffered from the obsessive idea that he might push some pointed object (pencil) into his eyes, thus blinding himself. His neurotic ideas found their way into artistic creation. The two drawings (Figs. 79 and 80) are samples from a large number.

In the sketch *"Blinding of Samson"* (Fig. 79), we find the same reference to the castration as in the biblical passage itself. The giant becomes weak and helpless after his hair has been cut (castration) and after he has been blinded (another picture of castration). Our patient had several nightmare dreams dealing with the scene of being blinded. We are also reminded of the patient's compulsion to push pointed objects into his eyes.

FIGURE 80

FIGURE 81

FIGURE 82

A closer inspection of the drawing *"Abraham and Isaac,"* as seen in figure 80, reveals by the "defensive" way Isaac (the patient) holds his hands, the pathogenic character of the circumcision and castration in the patient's emotional life.

The passive castration idea stimulates tendencies of asceticism and self-castigation. We found these tendencies in our patient. Thus he thought of circumcision, which to him meant castration, as a means to further "female qualities" which, in the light of the Kabbala, are designed by God for the Jewish people. According to this source, God represents the creative, masculine principle. The religious ecstasy of the Jew thus represents a kind of suprasensual communion with God. It is this kind of ecstasy which can be seen clearly in the drawing in figure 80, in which the son is expecting the death stroke by the knife of his father.

It is not easy to discover in the following picture dream [526], the unconscious *self-portrait of the patient,* a thirty-seven-year-old man suffering from impotence. It shows the two parts of his neurotic ego, the infantile religiosity and his crippled, blindfolded ego. The figure of the crippled man symbolizes the patient's impotence (Fig. 81).

The drawing in figure 82 by the same patient [527] signifies again the patient's *profound religiosity and his devilish, criminal drives.* Now the cripple of the preceding drawing can be understood as a symbol of sadism, one of the causes of the patient's impotence.

In the fight of the two men we see the patient's emotional split. Both figures are parts of the patient's ego. The figure of the devil and the church seen in the background offer sufficient evidence for the supposition that the patient's main conflict is between criminality and morality. We are right in suspecting here also a pathological brother complex (Cain complex) based on envy.

The patient suffers also from anxiety states with breathing disturbances (see choking in the picture!).

Let us now observe the following picture (Fig. 83). Ac-

FIGURE 83
GIORGIONE'S DREAM
(Also called THE DREAM OF RAPHAEL.)
Engraved by Marcantonio Raimondi (1480-1530). Courtesy of the Metropolitan Museum of Art, New York.

cording to Born, Marcantonio Raimondi made this drawing after a picture by Giorgione which was lost. We find here the motif of the two nude women—front and back—which characterizes so many paintings by Giorgione, but the illustration, otherwise, seems to represent a real dream.

What impresses us most is the contrast between the serene sleep of the women and the excitement that goes on across the water. The female figures (both undoubtedly representing two sides of the same woman) appear to be lying on a dry rock a relatively safe distance away from the water.

Out of the troubled waters four fantastic creatures emerge and seem to be approaching the sleeping women. They have phallic characteristics. However, with the exception of the creature closest to the women, all seem to be preoccupied with themselves and their own needs. The last one resembles a frog croaking his mating call. The next one seems to have found satisfaction of its hunger in an oval dish, while the second from the front directs its attention to its posteriorily located genital parts and the oval tail-like formation growing therefrom.

The background of the drawing consists of two main parts. The right side shows a conflagration. There a towerlike structure is on fire. The left side appears to be a castle or fortified town. Its doors and windows are lit by the nearby fire, but otherwise, with its many towers and ramparts it appears to be a haven of safety. To this haven, victims of the conflagration are striving in boats. On the right side they are seen jumping from windows and walls, carrying one another out of the reaches of the fire. They are all nude and, judging from their silhouettes, seem to be males. On the uppermost part of the burning tower, a covered terrace-like structure, one can see a wheel with two figures apparently tied to its circumference. Such wheels were known as instruments of torture. The tower thus may be suspected of being a torture tower, the fire having —in some respects—brought liberation to its prisoners.

The left side of the picture is taken up by a stone wall,

which is flanked by a column. The sleeping women recline at the foot of this wall. The background of the drawing is gloomy and grotesque.

If we accept the supposition that this drawing is the reproduction of a real dream, we may attempt to interpret it. In the opinion of this writer, the painter's composition represents his sexual frustration. The painter is tortured by the pressure of his physiological drives (the tower of torture) devoured by the flames of his passions (the fire) from which there is only one escape: religion. Luther's hymn "A mighty fortress is our God" comes to mind. The castle-like structure with towers and ramparts which apepars as a haven to those who flee from the conflagration as well as the strong wall on the left of the drawing suggest this interpretation.

The sleeping women are the objects of the dreamer's unfulfillable (incestuous) desires. Phallic figures surround them. But these animals are too much preoccupied with their own needs to be a real threat to the women. Autoerotism is suggested here. The atmosphere is, accordingly, gloomy and fraught with guilt and anxiety.

Since Freud's first pulication on psychoanalysis of art, many books and articles appeared by various analytic and non-analytic writers who stressed the diagnostic and therapeutic value of artistic production. However, as impressive and keen the deductions may be, they all suffer from a lack of a uniform frame of reference and a scientific system of appraising the subjects' productions unless we wish to rely too much on free associations. We are still very much dependent on intuition and perspicacity of the individual interpreter, a factor which lowers to a certain degree the reliability of our findings. I am happy to say, however, that more recently efforts are made to establish a more tangible frame of reference regarding the psychological evaluation of artistic production.

Chapter Six

DREAMS IN PSYCHOTHERAPY

The Dream as a Mirror of the Psychotherapeutic Situation

THE TREATMENT IN THE DREAM

It is always important that the analyst be well-informed about the patient's attitude toward the treatment. Sometimes this attitude appears in the dream in a disguised form, as the following dream of a thirty-four-year-old Hungarian physician demonstrates:

[528] *"A friend of mine named Dr. B. was to perform an autopsy at the City Hospital. I was to assist in it because I was perhaps better qualified to discern any possible pathology. During the autopsy evidence of a subclavicular abscess was found, and during the examination of the brain, I insisted that it showed evidence of syphilis. Dr. B. and another physician stated that there was no disease present. It seems that one-half of the brain was attached to an electric device for the purpose of shocking it. This device was some distance from the autopsy table, and it appeared that a second half of the brain was placed by the side of the first by trickery. As the current was turned on, the second half gave shrieks as if it were alive. Some women standing by uttered 'Oh!' as if a crime had been committed."*

This dream was reported after the patient had been informed that his cooperation in the treatment was indispensable. In his dream, an "autopsy" is to be made and the patient is to cooperate ("to assist") because of his "better knowledge" of pathology. (We are both physicians.) These facts, as well as the problem of the intended "shocking" of the brain, lead us to the conception that "autopsy" here means "analysis." Every autopsy is to a certain degree also an analysis. The two parts of the brain signify the two parts of the patient's personality spoken of in our analysis.

The interesting parts of this dream are found in the little details. First the "subclavicular abscess." "Subclavicular" here means "subconscious"; "abscess" means "something rotten"; both together signify "something rotten in the subconscious sphere," that is, neurosis. "Syphilis" means a "sexual disease"; there "is something wrong with sex." "Crime" means "unconscious criminality." Toward women? "Some women uttered 'Oh!' "

The dreamer sets up a picture of the treatment (by the picture of a post-mortem) giving us important insight into his conflict situation. After analysis of this dream we break his neurosis on a broad front, bringing the problems of his sex and his other instincts into the discussion.

The dream shows here the aspect of resistance. That is the reason why the treatment appears in a disguised form. In the dream the patient expresses his opinion that he is a "better doctor" than the doctor who is treating him (a very frequent depreciation). In his displacement of the examination from "mind" to "body," the patient voices his deeply seated doubt as to whether his disturbance really has a mental root.

The analysis in the dream is often represented as "examination," "leading," "teaching," "guiding," "repairing," etc. Very often we see in dreams containing symbols of the treatment important hints as to the particular problems (the complexes) of the patient. The dream about autopsy is a good example.

The next dream illustrates the symbol "leading." (Woman patient aged forty-eight):

[529] *"I was being led by a man from one large wire-*

*inclosed passage to another, through an almost endless num-
ber of passages, until we came to one which was supposed to
be our destination. We passed people behind bars."*

"People behind bars" are, according to the patient's association, "criminals" or "insane." The patient suffered from
the fear of insanity, and the analysis proved that this fear
was based on her antimoral, mostly criminal, impulses against
her husband and her children. (She always feared that she
would kill her family while in a state of frenzy.) She always
saw the picture of an asylum before her eyes.

In her dream she is guided by her doctor through the passages of her mental life, and she realizes her as yet controlled
criminal impulses ("people behind bars"). Her fear of insanity is the fear that her impulses may win their ways
through her inhibitions and that she may commit deeds
which she will regret.

Another picture of the treatment as an examination is illustrated by the following dream, in which we again recognize the dreamer's specific love condition:

[530] *"A doctor is examining a wound, or a detached
wounded part, that he has treated. It looks like two layers of
gelatine put together (round like cakes of soap). He pulls at
it, opening it at different places, and removes white specks
which look like corns (foot corns). He says that they should
be removed or that he always removes them to prevent cancer.
I recall, with a feeling of satisfaction it seems, that I have
been in the habit of picking away such things.* (Picking the
nose comes to my mind as I write, but I am not sure that this
thought about the nose occurs in the dream.)"

We see here the "two layers" as symbols of the two layers of
the patient's mind, the conscious and the unconscious. (Compare the two parts of the brain in dream 528.) The "soap"
and the "picking" of the corns show a close relation to the
patient's masturbation complex. It does not surprise at all to
learn that our dreamer very often indulges in a lustful rubbing of his big toes against each other, a practice which is

known to be a mask of masturbation. He speaks of a "wound" the doctor is examining. As the dream deals with the problem of masturbation, the latter must have been traumatic (trauma = wound) to the patient. And really his masturbation fantasy, as revealed in the other material, was incest with his sister. The dream has a very optimistic tinge— the patient feels a satisfaction in "removing" the single layers of his "corn"[1] by which he hopes to prevent "cancer" (that is, his destructive illness will not remain incurable).

Another example of the treatment expressed symbolically is given in the dream on page 209. There "water" signifies "analysis."

If the patient tries to analyze his own dream within his dream, the analysis, in most cases, proves to be wrong and serves only the unconscious purpose of the patient to mislead the analyst into a desired direction. The patient's interpretation should be accepted with extreme skepticism. Only in exceptional cases does the patient present a right view, as the following dream illustrates:

[531] *"I am traveling in a railroad car. After getting out of the car I notice that I take an old and shabby hat instead of my own, which was renovated a short time ago and which has a nice broad brim. I am thinking how I can get my hat again and (at the same time) analyze the mistake in my dream. I say: 'Apparently there is a resistance against the renovated hat and a tendency toward self-punishment in my taking the old hat.'"*

We interpret the "renovated hat" as the patient's life, "renovated," improved by the treatment. In his dream, the patient interprets his desire to get back his "old and shabby hat" and his giving-up of the "renovated hat" (normal life) correctly as an expression of his wish to punish himself. This dream was one of the last produced in his treatment (see also, "the last dreams," page 529) and demonstrates that the

---

[1] Compare the phrase "To know where the shoe pinches" with the symbol "corn."

pathological impulses making desperate attempts to become victorious again are being criticized and analyzed by the patient even in his dream.

It is astonishing that the direct influence of the analyst's interpretations upon the patient's individual symbolism proves to be relatively meager. Patients who have learned the meaning of a symbol, or psychoanalysts who know the symbolic significance of dream pictures, continue, nevertheless, to dream in the symbolic language whenever antisocial or antimoral ideas are to be expressed. It seems that this primitive language is an adequate means of expressing our unconscious personality, and that between this region and consciousness there is an almost insurmountable gap.

Of course, we very often find that our suggestions and interpretations are being used by the patient in his own way for the construction of new dream situations.

Some analysts, S. Lowy, for example, consider the ability of the unconscious to "digest" the analyst's interpretation as highly important. Another analyst (Tremmel) uses the so-called *Komplex-Reiz*, (Complex stimulus), the method of stirring up the suspected complex by proper questioning and conversation. Both Lowy and Tremmel proceed on the theory that questions and discussions directed toward the suspected complex become "digested" by the patient's unconscious and may stimulate the production of recollections although the complex itself has not been mentioned.

The First Dream

The first dream in the treatment often turns out to be of supreme importance. We see in it, as a prelude to the treatment, the patient's attitude toward his disease and toward the doctor, his readiness to be cured and, at the same time, his main conflicts. We do not usually interpret the first dreams to the patient. At what stage of the analysis and to what extent we make our revelations to the patient is a question of circumstances and technique. In general, we interpret as late as possible, giving the patient the opportunity to report the history of his case without our influence.

We shall now describe the therapeutic situation and the prognosis of a patient's case according to his first dream.

A twenty-seven-year-old man suffering from a sadomasochistic paraphilia brings the following dream:

[532] *"I am a married woman and am going to sue my husband for a divorce. I want to see a lawyer. Apparently I am a person of very high social position. In this dream I am of the opinion that lawyers are of low social caste. I am therefore worried as to whether it would not be preferable to disguise myself and go to see one in his office."*

The patient, a bachelor, sees himself in this dream as a married woman. His first dream presents him as a female. The patient, asked for a reason for this "divorce," is not able to find any, save his opinion that marriage is usually an unsuccessful venture. His attitude toward the "lawyer" is very significant. The patient considers the procedure of consulting a lawyer a kind of degradation. He has an idea of disguising himself while making use of the lawyer's service.

The simplification of this dream is: "I am in trouble and look for help. I consider this action as degrading and want to disguise myself."

It is not difficult to recognize his neurosis in his trouble, and his doctor in the "lawyer." With regard to the patient's disguising tendency we interpret this dream as an expression of his inner resistance to treatment. We see, however, that this resistance dream reveals the weakest spots of the patient's neurosis—his feminine attitude, his pessimism with reference to marriage (which can be based only on experiences of his home life), the relationship between the patient's paraphilia and his criminal ideas (hence the person of the lawyer instead of the physician); the fact that in his neurotic state he considers himself as superior ("I am a person of very high social position"); and finally his depreciation of his doctor. The patient has strong resistance and must be watched and prevented from discontinuing the treatment.

The following first dream sounds quite different:

[533] *"I am in a dark room. Somebody pulls up the shades and light comes into the room. In the corner of this room is a large trunk. I open it and begin to pull out one piece after another; first books, then suits, then laundry."*

A beautiful example of the patient's cooperation! The analysis revealed in the picture of light falling into the dark room the patient's confession—symbolized as unpacking his trunk.

In the following first dream the main conflicts of the patient (woman, aged thirty-one) are to be seen very clearly:

[534] *"I am on the way to your office. I board a bus going south on —nth Street. I find myself in a very strange vehicle indeed, but seem to feel that there is nothing unusual about it. A series of roller-coaster cars are hitched together and are pulled by some power at the front. Between the last car and the others is a child's wagon. With a forgotten female companion I am sitting half in the last roller-coaster car and half in the wagon. In front of me, in the wagon, is a slim adolescent Negro boy."*

The patient interpolates here the following association: her husband sleeps soundly. When she wants him to get up early she calls him "a little colored boy." The man then gets angry and leaves the bed. (The patient's brother has dark, kinky hair and a dark complexion. He uses much brilliantine to keep his hair smooth, as some Negroes do.) The patient then continues: *"The only thing I remember about his (the Negro's) appearance is that his long slender feet are white. He wears a patent-leather dress, oxfords, and handsome expensive-looking silk hose.[1] I inspect them closely. They have black and white stripes three-quarters of an inch wide. As the vehicle increases in speed the wagon rides upon the car*

---

[1] Usually the patient buys the hose for her brother and her husband. Those seen in the dream are similar to the ones she has recently purchased.

in front. Whenever we are making good progress the Negro drags his foot on the street and slows us up. Several times the conductor (a girl) comes back to see what is the matter, but the boy pulls in his foot. She places the blame on all three of us and tells us to get out of the wagon."

And now let us analyze this informative first dream. The "strange vehicle" in which the patient is sitting ("half in the last roller-coaster car and half in the wagon") is a functional symbol of the patient's mentality; half adult (the last car) and half child (the child's wagon). She did not succeed in detaching herself from her infantile emotional world, and the outer sign of this emotional split is her neurosis (in the dream symbolized by the accompanying woman).

In the child's wagon is a Negro boy. The patient's associations point in the direction of her husband and her brother. And indeed, the analysis proved that the patient treated her husband as a brother. In her childhood she had had sexual experiences with her brother, and her husband later took her brother's place. In many dreams and fancies the patient's unconscious desire to nullify her marriage and to "marry" her brother was clearly seen. The associations to "brother and husband" came almost simultaneously to the patient in this dream. (Condensation.) The situation became clearer when the patient informed us that she usually buys the footwear for her brother as well as for her husband.

Riding in a car with someone has an erotic significance. It is necessary to know that the patient suffered from frigidity. The increase of the speed of the train here means the increase of the excitement which should lead to full satisfaction and the overcoming of her frigidity. However, "each time we are making good progress the Negro drags his foot on the street and slows us up." We see here the absolutely convincing fact that the patient's inhibition ("slowing up") is due to the influence of her brother (the Negro). His sitting in the child's wagon shows that his influence dates from the patient's childhood.

Later on in the dream we see that the patient sees a female representing the analyst (the "conductor"). The homosexual component of this patient will be the most important problem of her analysis. The patient has a deep feeling of guilt ("she places the blame on all three of us") because of her brother fixation.

Looking over the results attained in the analysis of this dream, we may say that this treatment starts with a good prognosis. The patient has made up her mind to leave her infantile manner of "traveling" through life. She has told us much about her neurosis. A multitude of problems is brought to the surface—brother fixation, frigidity complex, her attitude toward the doctor, her willingness to be cured, her feeling of guilt. The doctor sees himself in the midst of "the case," with many doors opening into the labyrinth of the patient's soul, and he enters this labyrinth equipped with a technique of dream analysis, much as Theseus was equipped with the thread of Ariadne.

The following first dream leads us right into the center of the case:

[535] *"I was talking to someone. When I looked down at my Persian-lamb coat it was rubbed out in several spots. It had turned a pinkish red. (The red was the same color as the one my art director had used on an advertising layout this afternoon.) I was horrified and asked, 'Do all Persian coats get this way?' The other person answered, 'Yes, usually.' I felt better about it. I thought that I had received an expert opinion."*

The twenty-eight-year-old patient came for treatment because of intense anxiety states.

We see here her illness, her inferiority feelings, her "rubbed out" coat. The reference to "rubbing" referred to her masturbation complex which rendered the "coat" inferior. She feared that masturbation had made her face aged and unattractive in appearance. The experienced interpreter also suspects at this point that the guilt feelings may also refer to a defloration which at this time (first dream) the patient attempts to conceal. (The "pinkish-red" color points in this direction.) The concern that people might notice the history of her sexual activities on her face is expressed in the word "advertising" which she associates to the red color. The patient then reports in her dream that she felt consoled by her analyst when she had consulted him prior to this dream (the "expert opinion"). She tells us that she felt better. The patient finds herself in a prognostically hopeful disposition.

The connection between "coat" and "analysis" was also established. The patient was about to have her Persian lamb coat repaired when she visited the analyst for the first time. The question of budgeting the analysis was discussed at this occasion. After having returned home from the doctor's office, the patient discussed this question with her mother who suggested that it might be a good idea to postpone the fixing of the coat so that funds would be available for therapy. To "repair the fur coat," thus became a symbol of and a substitute for the patient's mental condition.

[536] *"I was going to practice boxing, and asked for adhesive tape to put over my eyebrows. A friend who saw me putting on white tape suggested that I put on the new 'skin-colored tape.'"*

This was the patient's first dream in analysis. He associated with it that recently he noticed that an actor on stage was wearing an adhesive over his eyebrows, apparently a consequence of an accident. He was covering (hiding) an injury. The friend in the dream suggests an even better "covering up," a skin-colored type.

This first dream thus indicates the patient's drive to appear normal and to camouflage any possible pathological manifestations. He is identifying himself with an actor.

Another first dream brings as an important "leit-motif," the patient's mother complex.

The patient, a thirty-five-year-old army officer, reported:

[537] "I dreamed this after having seen you. *I was going through all kinds of tests, mental and physical, and doing well, until my mother came along and said to the examiner: 'Don't bother with him, he is just a little boy.' I fought against it and managed to get along pretty well. . . ."*

A short time later the same patient confirmed his mother fixation by the following dream:

[538] *"I am in a new apartment. I think I live there with a woman—my mother. Dr. Gutheil comes there to analyze me, or to teach me."*

"Living with mother" is the patient's secret desire. He leads the analyst there, as though he wanted to demonstrate to him where his trouble lies.

The Progress of the Treatment as Revealed in the Dream

Dream analysis gives us reliable information about the progress of the treatment. Thus, for example, we see with great satisfaction the following dream. Up to the time of this dream the patient had been very much attached to his family and very dependent on their advice:

[539] *"I took my wife on a trip to my home town. We had been there a couple of days, but I realized that soon we should have to leave for Washington. My wife did not seem to be very much interested in seeing my childhood scenes. My father left our house and went to play pinochle at our neighbors'. I decided to take the next train and return to Washington."*

In the dream we see the patient making a trip back to his parents' home. We see his estrangement and the decision to return to Washington, the place of his occupation, from the past to the present, from infantile fantasy to reality.

An optimistic sign can be seen in the following dream of a patient who has just overcome the depressive phase of his neurosis:

[540] *"I am playing cards. In my hand are six aces."*
Since four aces is the highest possible number of aces in a
deck, the patient's exaggeration (six aces) shows his tendency
to overestimate the "trump" in his game of life.[1]

Another optimistic dream is the following:[2]

[541] *"The doctor pulls an infected nail out of my hand
and puts iodine on the wound."*

The nail is the emotionally charged complex the doctor
removes from the patient's brain.

THE LAST DREAMS

Toward the end of the treatment the patient often brings
dreams portraying the collapse of his fantasy world. Here is
an example:

[542] *"With another person* (the second ego) *I am in a
city* (neurosis) *in which all the buildings in sight, some of
which are seen at a considerable distance, have been partly
torn down. I think of some of them as about to fall. I notice
the weak, bulging walls of one in particular. On this one the
roof is off, and I suggest to the person with me that we leave
in order to avoid the danger of injury from a falling building."*

Very often we see in the last dreams the doctor dying,
leaving, etc., pictures which symbolize the patient's inner
detachment from his physician. A rather frequently occurring involuntary joke in the dreams of cured patients is the
doctor taking over their disease.

TRANSFERENCE AND RESISTANCE IN THE DREAM

TRANSFERENCE

Transference as a psychological phenomenon is a primitive
psychic process which is utilized in the psychoanalytic tech-

[1] Improvement dreams are often simply "comfort" dreams containing the
patient's wish to get cured without doing anything to support the analyst in
his curative efforts. Sometimes they are results of the patient's wish to please
the analyst in the state of transference.

[2] This case was reported by Dr. Catherine Siegel-Fürst of New York.

nique. Most people, particularly neurotics, are inclined unconsciously to endow persons of their environment with attributes of persons of earlier days (parents, close relatives, etc.) who played important parts in their lives. With Freud, we call these persons who usually attract a large amount of the patient's emotions, "images." Thus the patient reacts to teachers, employers, etc., as if they were his parents and he was still a child. Transference intrudes permanently into the patient's life and biases many of his reactions and relationships. In the analytical treatment the patient, who in his everyday life has been making "transferences" to all kinds of persons, such as officials, superiors, etc., will establish another transference to his physician. We are then able to observe this phenomenon, and it is in the dream that it sometimes reveals itself with startling clarity.

Up to the time of Freud the question of transference in the treatment of neurotics had never been given due weight. Now we know that transference is indispensable in the treatment, and that correct interpretation of transference dreams opens the door to the unconscious, because "transference" dreams portray the picture of the patient's secret attitude toward his life. Stekel adds that *within the transference situation the patient also tries to settle his most important life conflicts,* regardless of whether they are infantile or concerned with present-day complications.

A woman patient, aged twenty-eight, suffering from masochistic disturbances, dreamed [543] *that her child was sick, and a "specialist" advised an expensive hat, i.e., a "specially careful treatment," for the youngster.*

The "specialist" is a symbol of the analyst. The dream idea of a "specially careful treatment" should be explained. The patient's main conflict was that in her youth her father did not pay enough attention to her, preferring other children. Thus she had reason to complain about the "treatment" as not being "especially careful." It was not difficult to see that behind the patient's desire for being ill-treated by the male partner, behind her masochistic tendency in her relationship toward men, was hidden an old idea of attracting her father's attention, at least in its negative expression. She transferred this attitude to her doctor and one day interrupted the treatment by complaining of the physician's "impoliteness."

Beginning of transference and fear of ensuing emotional entanglement can be seen in the next dream:

[544] *"I was driving along and encountered a friend going the same way. I engaged my hand somehow on the doorknob of his car to keep us close as we rode along. I soon realized with fright that I was unable to disengage myself, and that my safety depended on the absolute equality of our speed. I couldn't separate myself unless we stopped."*

The meaning of this dream is predicated on the patient's idea that it might be too difficult for him to "disengage" himself from the close relationship with the analyst. This fear is the fear of homosexuality. If the above dream does not make this complex completely clear, the next one presents it more clearly:

[545] *"I was invited aboard a boat by a man who was rather stout. He was affable, forceful and persuasive. He resembled a lawyer. There was something toad-like and repulsive about him. I realized he was probably a homosexual and refused to go aboard."*

The toad-like face of the man reminded the patient of a well-known psychiatrist. The boat is also associated with psychiatry. A friend of the patient, a psychiatrist, has one. It is evident that the "persuasive lawyer" stands here for the analyst; the dream expresses the patient's feeling toward him.

A woman patient whose analyst was suffering from a cardiac condition transferred upon him the affection of a mother. She dreamed:

[546] *"I am on a boat. There is going to be a party. I ask my analyst if I will see him there."* (The patient attempts here to establish a non-professional relationship with her

physician.) *"He tells me sadly that he will not be there, but that I should have a good time. I ask him why he will not come, but before he can explain I realize that he must rest. We both know he means his heart. I want to cry and I run downstairs. . . ."*

The exaggerated reaction of sympathy also compensates for the patient's wish that her analyst should die. This would prevent him from penetrating too deep into the patient's unconscious and would, simultaneously, terminate her transference which, at the time of the dream, was beginning to cause some concern to the patient.

A thirty-four-year-old teacher dreams:

[547] *"I am riding on a bus. It is speeding. We smash into another car. I shout at the driver. The others listen.*

"My sister meets me at the bus station. She is near tears. She tries to tell me something about her marriage—that she is dissatisfied.

"We visit a doctor. My sister is suddenly in a bathtub with him, talking to him about something she is lacking in her marriage. She asks him to kiss her as a medical experiment. When this is over, she says, 'see what I mean?' He avoids her eyes, lights a cigarette, obviously moved by the kiss.

"She and I leave. We are both nude."

Simplifying this dream, we see in the first of its three parts a conflict (crash) in which she has found herself because of one of her hasty decisions (speed in driving). The second part (in which she is disguised as her sister) identifies this conflict as a marital one. It is she (and not her sister) who goes to see the analyst because of this difficulty. Soon she finds herself in a bathtub with her physician, "as a medical experiment." She thus conveys to the analyst her specific erotic fantasy. From her life story it becomes clear that, in her transference, she wishes to repeat with her analyst experiences she had had with her brother when she was a child: they bathed together. Her brother fixation thus comes to light. (Her being in the nude is not only a sign of her exhibitionistic tendencies, but also a symbol of analysis.)

The patient has strong narcissistic and omnipotent feelings and believes that the reason why she does not respond sexually to her husband's attentions is because he does not appreciate properly her sexual potentialities. In her transference dream she demonstrates practically how irresistible she is in reality.

How easily patients repeat childhood patterns while in the state of transference can be seen in the following dream of a woman physician. It was dreamed a short time after her analyst had to undergo a cholecystectomy. The patient was very solicitous during the time her analyst was hospitalized and reiterated how much "we need you." One of the first dreams she produced after her analyst resumed practice expresses a childish dissatisfaction with the interruption of her analysis. The dream runs as follows:

[548] *"I am in Dr. Gutheil's office. It resembles the living room in our parents' home. Dr. Gutheil comes into the room briskly and begins to exercise Yoga. He does this in a whirlwind fashion, very skillfully. I just stand there, being unable to utter a word. Dr. Gutheil says, 'I have to do that every day as a post-operative exercise.' I feel extremely frustrated and offended."*

The patient here unconsciously resents the fact that the analyst was taking care of himself instead of taking care of her. The fact that she places the scene of action in her parents' home proves that the analyst represents her father. She courts his attention as she did her father's when she was a child. Her desire for exclusive attention in analysis and her unconscious intolerance to any lessening of it betrays this important basic infantile pattern. (Of course, the overt attitude of the patient was above reproach.)

A very informative transference dream is that dreamed by a nineteen-year-old girl suffering from homosexuality:

[549] *"I arrive at your office for my first session. You tell me to take off my clothes. I take off some of them. You then*

tell me to take off more and I remove the rest of them. You are sitting in a chair beyond a wash basin resembling a dentist's bowl, but are not facing me. Shortly after I have removed my clothes, two women enter and stand before you. One is about thirty-five years old; the other gives the impression of being her mother. The younger woman laughs and coyly holds her skirt in front of her. You turn to me, fill the basin with water, and tell me to dip my head in it. I submerge my head and notice in the water a number of large horse chestnuts which discolor somewhat. You take one of the chestnuts and place it in my left ear. I immediately experience a strong cutaneous reflex."[1]

This dream was the second in the analysis. It contains fragmentary recollections of the first session in which the patient learned the chief rule of the therapy: absolute frankness in the report. Frankness is symbolized in the dream as undressing. The patient first takes off "some of her clothes"; she has still some resistance in her report, but finally she becomes convinced of the necessity of telling the whole truth and "removes the rest of her clothes." It is a good sign, this readiness to display herself mentally nude in front of the doctor!

And now this transference dream brings flashes of the significant complexes of the patient—two women enter the room, one of them the mother of the other. Both mother and daughter serve one purpose only—to represent the "mother complex." The patient demonstrates in her dream the mother complex and makes the doctor examine this problem first. At the same time she shows here something which explains to us her latent homosexuality; it is the so-called "triangle situation" as a specific libidinal constellation. Here we see one man (the doctor) and two women (mother and daughter). This is the situation she is constantly attempting

[1] The patient had some erogenous zones on her body and, when they were kissed or otherwise stimulated, a cutaneous reflex resulted on her thigh and hip.

to establish. Her sweetheart, for instance, is in love with another girl, and the patient feels best only when the third one is in their company. The root of this peculiarity was later traced back to an experience of the patient's early childhood when she listened to an intimate scene between her parents. The last scene of the dream, in which the doctor places chestnuts into her ear, portrays, according to the "material" interpretation ("displacement from below to above"), an intimate act. What makes this scene of particular interest is the fact that the irritation of her ear was never capable of creating the "cutaneous reaction" as an erogenous act. The ear has here another significance. In the patient's childhood, she often played with her brother, and he was the one who used to put chestnuts and other fruits into her ear.[1]

A twenty-two-year-old student suffering from masochism expresses his specific morbid idea, the wish to be ill-treated by a woman, in the following dream:

[550] *"A woman analyst offered to treat me for half of the amount I am to pay you."*

The patient's basic idea in this dream is: "If you want to cure me, give me the pleasure I am missing." In this case the satisfaction of masochistic desires is sought. The patient prefers a woman doctor to whom he can submit in a treatment which in his eyes is a sort of humiliation.

The following is a very instructive dream (the patient is a thirty-year-old ex-sailor):

[551] *"Last night I dreamed that I go with a woman to Dr. G.'s office. My mother and others ask who she is; I do not know and am so anxious to go there to the office that I am interested in her mainly as a guide. She shows me the door. I enter, although I trip on the threshold which is high. Dr. G. is just finishing with another patient and comes out of his office. G. (and others) give me a stern, angry look when I*

trip. The woman points out, 'No. Today is special, so you use the special office.' I remember this and go past the regular office to the special office rooms.

"As I start to enter his office the door opens and a tall man (I am now much smaller) is standing in the office. He makes a motion to demonstrate posture as a rebuke, and he looks accusingly at me. I am frightened by this and by something else.

"Then, suddenly, the whole place is full of all the things that have always frightened me, though I didn't know it. There are many boys and girls, aged thirteen to eighteen, all in party dress, tuxedos. I recognize them all and know they all mean the same thing. Everyone I ever knew is there —adults, also. The tall man is most prominent at first, then they all are whirling about me. By this time I am in terror beyond belief. A beast or something is slowly settling on my bed to strangle me or to overpower me. Daring the chance of making it worse I wake up with no idea of where I am. . . ."

The patient, whose nightmare you have just heard, has a family problem. The man comes from a very strict New England family. Not that they punished him much; but they had very rigid rules and regulations about living. They wanted the patient to comply with these rules and to live a conforming life as a part of their community. In the patient's mind there gradually developed a strong, rebellious spirit, and the desire to detach himself from his family by force, particularly from his father. This rebellious desire was accompanied by its polar counterpart, a masochistic desire to comply with his father's pattern of life. It was a clash between the rebellious, masculine, and the conforming, feminine attitude.

The patient really had a poor posture and throughout his life was constantly reminded by his parents to "straighten up." In his dream, we see a group that is whirling around him, a group of people who are in tuxedos, who, according to him, are conservative conformists. We said before that his family did not punish him physically; they imbued him with the belief that a person who does not conform is "no good," is worthless. Anything he did by himself, of his own initiative, and as an expression of his own individuality, was deprecated. Thus he finally developed the idea that any person who was independent was "no good." If he wanted to be independent he had to be a rebel.

When he became interested in a woman of his own choice, he saw himself guided to the doctor's office. You can see here the essence of his neurosis. When he trips over the threshold he really demonstrates that he is not going to conform, that he is protesting. At this point, his father (and also the analyst) gives him a stern, angry look. This detail betrays his masochistic, complying, conforming attitude. What this man does not know is that, while he thinks that by rebelling against authority he is detaching himself from his family, his neurosis forces him to adopt a complying attitude.

At the same time, his sibling rivalry comes to the fore. The neurotic idea is to become the family's favorite by compliance. His submissive attitude leads him to various manifestations of servility, among which is his poor posture. The purpose of the symptom is to give the parents an opportunity, just as they did in his childhood, to step in, to pay attention to him, to correct him, to look at him accusingly. He wants to perpetuate a childhood situation, and has apparently found a way of gaining favoritism in this neurotic way. In his dream a "special office" and a "special treatment" are given to him.

What we want to show in this dream is that, in transference situations, we obtain a reflection of a basic pattern of the patient's life. The transference dream answers not only the question of whether we play the part of the father or the mother to the patient. In this patient's dream, the analyst plays the part of the father distinctly, but that is not the main point; we also find *the pattern the dreamer has established for his life.* In our case, the answer is that, while he apparently demonstrates his independence, he secretly has decided to conform. This internal split accounts for his difficulties.

The following short transference dream is one of the first which the dreamer brought to his analytic sessions:

[552] *"I am listening to Dr. G. He demonstrates my chest X-rays, pointing out the lesion in my left chest. I look around to see who is present."*

The man had had a lesion in his lung when he was a young student, but it had been in the right chest. In the dream it appeared in the left chest. You may remember what we said about the symbolic meaning of "left." The patient looks around to see who is present. Apparently he is afraid that people might find out that he has tuberculosis, in other words that he has something to hide.

This man is suffering from a "social neurosis." He cannot speak in public. He stutters, blushes, sweats, gets all kinds of anxiety conditions when he has to appear before an audience. In the dream he is with Dr. G. and the doctor demonstrates his pulmonary lesion to others. What is the doctor doing in this manner? He is *betraying a secret* which the patient strives to hide.

The man's main difficulty is that he leads a double life. He is married and leads a respectable life in his community. At the same time, he has relations with other women. His marriage, which he wants to preserve, and his social position, would be jeopardized if his double life should be exposed. Some of the women are married. He despises himself for leading this sort of life, but he cannot help it. An uncontrollable impulse drives him on. His wife is frigid and although essentially courteous and cooperative, is sexually not satisfactory. Besides, having been brought up in a strictly religious home, in his mind sex has always been associated with something sinful. He thus began to desire sex more intensely when it was associated with sin.

In his dream, he fears the analyst may betray him. But,

still, he has no reason to believe this, because he knows about the ethical code of the medical profession. However, once his mother had betrayed his confidence. His father usually took care of all disciplinary matters when he came home from work. When he was seven or eight the boy misbehaved and asked his mother not to tell his father about it. He knelt down and begged her. She promised to comply, but when the father came home she did tell him, and the boy was punished. At that time he was profoundly disappointed by his mother's deception.

This may not be the deepest root of his neurosis, but it certainly is one of the deepest roots of his distrust toward the analyst. Throughout his life he has definitely repeated the pattern. It is, therefore, not a mere coincidence that, while he presents his problem to the analyst, and while he sees himself X-rayed, so to speak, he is afraid that he might be betrayed.

A statement which this writer received from a patient, after a clash with her, demonstrates clearly that transference, in reality, means resistance. The patient, who had been in treatment with another analyst before, brought a dream and started to analyze it.

"I think that instead of analyzing the dream, you ought to associate and leave the analysis to me," her analyst said smilingly. She flared up, insulted, and left in a huff. When she came back, this is what she said:

"I am afraid of dreaming now. It is as though I don't trust what you are going to do with the dreams. It often happened that I told Daddy silly little things, and he would laugh at me." The analyst has inadvertently copied her father's behavior, she believes. "I wanted to interpret my first dream and you didn't want to hear it. I wanted to show you what a good girl I was, how nicely I could interpret. I got frightened. I thought you didn't love me. Only a person who loves me can be on my side of the fence." (At this point the patient, a grown person, a married woman, uses almost baby

talk.) "I can confide in him. When I first saw you, I remarked that you looked like my uncle Charlie. He treated
his children as cruelly as my mother treated us." (The patient begins to sob.) "I always wanted to please people. I
am terribly unhappy when I see a person is not pleased. I
want to be a good girl. I was hurt when at college the teacher
gave me a B. It was not fair of him, not fair to fail to notice
how I felt about his course. I see how I treated him like my
father. I wanted to be his model girl."

This is an expression of resistance while, at the same time,
it teaches us something about a basic pattern. The patient's
specific pattern of life is to please father images by being a
"model girl." Imagine the hardships a person must encounter
who goes through her life trying again and again to recap-
ture a feeling that had meaning to her when she was a child.

(Q) "Can an analyst successfully analyze his own dreams?"

(A) Analysts are, in most cases, able to analyze their own dreams.
Freud gave us a glowing example of this ability. But occasionally,
particularly when the analyst is confronted with some neurotic reaction
of his own, his subjective interpretation may prove to be insufficient.
It is proper in such cases to ask the opinion of another analyst. In
general, however, analysts, having been analyzed themselves, are free
from strong neurotic influences.

RESISTANCE

"Resistance" is the name given to that phenomenon which
occurs in the course of every analytical treatment and in
which the patient temporarily or permanently not only does
not cooperate with the analyst but even creates difficulties
in revealing his life history. One might suppose that the
patient would welcome the doctor's attempts to discover
and dispel his conflicts. This is by no means the case, however.
Instead of gladly relinquishing his conflicts, the patient,
without consciously wishing it, makes every effort to hinder
his doctor.

This results from the fact that neurosis is a defensive construction of the patient's own ego. It is built, among other reasons, for the purpose of simulating a solution of his inner conflicts without really sacrificing the infantile position. As has been mentioned, neurotics repress antisocial impulses and construct all kinds of defense mechanisms against any lifting of the repression. One of these constructions is anxiety. The patient is afraid to deliver himself up fully; he is even afraid to admit the existence of the repressed impulses which his whole illness was designed to keep out of sight. The psychotherapist attempts to eliminate these impulses and to deprive the patient of all neurotic, though pleasurable, fantasies before he is able to offer the patient other means of attaining satisfaction. Resistance is, therefore, understandable. Its extent is commensurate to the pressure of the unconscious complex.

A twenty-five-year-old man dreams:

[553] *"I walk on the street pushing a perambulator. Suddenly I notice a suspicious-looking man who immediately begins to follow me. I feel very uneasy and hasten my footsteps. So does the man. I make all sorts of detours. But the man, apparently a gangster, is always just behind me. Finally, I run and so does the gangster. My fear turns into panic when I see that my persecutor suddenly appears in front of me and forces me, by looking strangely into my eyes, to stand still. I feel like a rabbit hypnotized by the eyes of a snake and feel that something terrible will happen without my being able to resist."*

The persecutor in this dream is a symbol of the analyst, who persistently follows the patient in all the bypaths of his neurosis. In addition to illustrating the tendency to escape, other details of the dream reveal to us at the same time the patient's main conflicts, that is to say, his homosexual and his criminal tendencies. The first can be seen in the perambulator scene which shows the patient's identification with a woman. And indeed, persecution dreams like these are very often dreamed by women. Homosexual is the scene in which the patient submits to the hypnotic influence of the man, who symbolizes the physician. The picture of the "gangster" signifies, according to our statements in the preceding chapters, a projection of the patient's criminal ideas. The patient suffers from various symptoms of a well-developed anxiety neurosis. One of his most aggravating symptoms is the fear of being stabbed from behind, a scene of a clearly homosexual character.

The next dream gives an example of the struggle against the physician. It is a dream of a forty-year-old lady whose analysis revealed a strong father fixation:

[554] *"I was walking alone in the dark toward the house where a doctor lived. Just before I approached the house I became entangled in a rope held or dangled by a queer-looking little man. He kept laughing at me and at my poor efforts to become free of the rope. Each time I got up to walk on I fell down again."*

The "little man" resembles the father of one of the patient's friends. It is a distinct "father image." The dream shows the patient's efforts to get out of the mental "darkness," out of the neurotic fixation (rope, a common symbol of fixation). We see in this dream the sign of resistance (the patient is unable to reach the doctor's house) and the hint toward the weakest spot of the neurosis, the father fixation.

The following resistance dream also not only reveals the patient's resistance but shows, besides, important points for analytical attack:

[555] *"I was treated by Dr. Gutheil or Dr. Stekel. Stekel said that the analyst must be of Gutheil's build. One of the doctors took out the spinal column (mine?) to examine it while I was gone. . . . Then I was talking to some fellow in my room, perhaps a brother of George S., as he was in my room packing his belongings preparatory to leaving."*

The dream is apparently flattering the doctor. However, this flattery is hypocritical. The patient wants to "leave" and to have the analyst examine his "spinal column" during his absence. (Allusion to autopsy and suicide idea. The second allusion to suicide may be seen in the scene of George S. "packing his belongings preparatory to leaving.")

The patient has the doctor examine his "spinal column" while he is absent, which means, first, that he is not convinced of the mental origin of the disease and is of the opinion that he should be treated organically ("spinal column" instead of "psyche"); second, that he does not want to cooperate—he leaves the whole job to the doctor. George S. has a close connection with the patient's sister.

Thus the sister fixation and the acute suicide ideas were at the time the dream was produced the most important problems for the patient—and for his doctor.

[556] *"I was to unscrew iron bars. There were new bars above and old ones below. I wanted to unscrew only the new bars and to leave the old ones as they were."*

The patient draws a sketch:

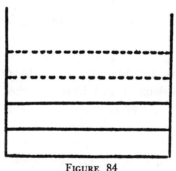

FIGURE 84

We see here the upper and the lower layers of the patient's mind. He is willing to "unscrew" (to give up in the treatment) the superficial material of his neurosis, but he wants to keep back the deeper problems.

The main complex in this case was the patient's pathologically increased ambition. In this resistance dream we see this problem expressed by the contrast of the "above" and "below."

[557] *"My sister Ruth was to see you because of some personal troubles. I ask you afterwards whether she was here and you say 'Yes.' I am glad that you at least see how nasty she is and how much she interferes with my welfare."*

The patient wants me to treat his sister (who is in good health) instead of himself. In this wish we see his resistance. At the same time, he offers here his important conflict concerning his sister.

Here is another interesting resistance dream: [558] *Franz and I discussed a scientific project which should be carried out in the depths of the earth. Franz suggested that the digging had to be done parallel to the earth because the earth is round.*

"Digging" is a symbol of analysis. The dreamer is a physician who used to be a general practitioner and who now is training to be a psychoanalyst. However, when it comes to *being* analyzed, he wishes that the digging should be done *parallel to the surface* instead of into the depths. He does not want to reveal the deepest layers of his mind. Franz, who offers the suggestion, is a physician who also wanted to be a psychoanalyst; he thus represents the dreamer himself.

A forty-year-old woman physician dreamed:

[559] *"I am in the receiving ward of a hospital. An ambulance arrives with a body. Dr. E. and I are to do the autopsy. He plunges a trocar into the left hypochondrium and a stream of fluid under pressure spurts out. I tell Dr. E., 'This is no way of doing things.' I take an instrument combining scissors and knife and I proceed to dissect the head. I start with the eyelids. I cut the eyelids off and suddenly the body comes to life. The eyes become alive. I thought at first that the body was that of a man, but the face was that of a beautiful woman.*

"I look on, she becomes more and more beautiful. I start

to yell, and call, 'Dr. Carrelly! Dr. Carrelly!' (I don't know any doctor of this name) *to help me, but no one comes. I am conscious of a tremendous tragedy that I have caused, a wave of regret and pity overcomes me. 'How is she going to live?'*

"*As she grew more beautiful, her skin at first dead, ash-grey, and ugly was revived and turned smooth and pink. Her eyes, at first blue, became darker until they were black and luminous. The woman was very big and impressive.*"

The dreamer, who is of a rather short stature, reports in this dream about her own analysis (autopsy). Dr. E. is a psychiatrist who is also trained in pathology, and who performs autopsies, if necessary. He represents the patient's "alter ego" and also her analyst. She accuses him of being clumsy and she shows him "how things ought to be done." The main problem is the patient's outlook on life—her eyes. Behind the image of the eyelids lies a story. The patient recalls having read an ancient legend about a Chinese scholar who wanted to be able to study the wisdom of the sages all his life, uninterruptedly. He was irked by the fact that at night his eyelids would close against his will and prevent him from studying. He therefore cut off his eyelids in the hope that he would be able to study without interruption. The legend says that, later, on the spot where the cut-off eyelids were buried, a tea bush grew and offered the scholars a stimulating drink which helped them overcome their drowsiness.

In this association the patient blames her analyst for having mentioned her masculine identification which she expressed in one of her dreams. (Compare here this patient's dream presented on page 139.) The dream related here was a product of the subsequent night, after the patient had responded to the analyst's casual remark about the masculine identification with an unusually strong protest. At first, she did not want to see this complex, but the dream showed her a vision of femininity and demonstrated its power to her. (The big beautiful woman.) "She is not ineffective (dead)," her dream protests, "she is alive and active." The discomfort caused by the "masculine identification" is over, the patient has warded off an unpleasant discovery (resistance).

Of course, her masculine complex finds also its expression in the dream, in the trocar that is plunged into the abdomen, in the knife wielded by the patient, and in the body which is that of a man with a woman's face.

Interesting is the name of Dr. Carrelly. It is condensed from two other names: *Dr. (Alexis) Carrel,* who made the well-known experiments with reviving hearts, and *Dr. Kelly,* whom the patient twice assisted in operations on the eye. She fainted on both occasions and had to be replaced during the operation.

(The close connection between eye operations and castration was described on pages 215 and 510.)

We must realize that resistance does not entirely disappear throughout the treatment. Even after the solution of most of his conflicts, the patient still tries, with more or less success, to reconstruct his neurosis from fragments of symptoms, but fortunately we are able to recognize these tendencies in time to fight them.

The following dream was reported at the end of the treatment which was given by various physicians who employed various methods:

[560] *"There was a storm at sea and many people lost their lives. I was on a rescue ship that was picking up the dead bodies and skulls. Most of the bodies were already skeletons, although it was only a short time after the storm and the wreck."*

Our treatment (in the dream symbolized as a storm) removed the patient's symptoms after a short time (three months). In his dream the patient is surprised that he finds "skeletons" after so short a time. We see our patient making an attempt to rescue the destroyed complexes (the "dead bodies"), but we can also see that his efforts are in vain—a good sign, a dream which is able to give the doctor optimism and satisfaction.

The patient's failure to abandon his infantile fixations may be expressed in the dream dramatically. Rarely, however, can one find this problem presented so eloquently as in the following dream reported at a later stage of analysis by a patient suffering from obsessions.

[561] *"My brother and I are at a party with many friends; a 'coming-of-age' party. Each young boy or girl must step forward and then he goes through a ritual in which he is given a gift and then he changes and his parents become invisible.*

"Then came our turn. First I went through with it. My mother tried to stop it, but I succeeded fairly well, although we had to move and start over again because of her interference.

"Then came my brother. I thought, 'He is so small that he will be ashamed, especially of his small genital. (This was part of the ritual; we were naked.) I cheered him and backed him up one hundred per cent as he came forward.

"Father was confused but tried and did become invisible. The great difficulty was with mother. She would not permit it. She became frantic—she begged and pleaded to be allowed to run things. Then she made an hysterical scene. My brother wanted to quit, but I told him to go through with it. Anxiety and fear, and hate arise. I push her angrily back. She throws herself helplessly on the ground, making a humiliating public spectacle. We berate her. She is furious and says, 'I interfere, eh?—like this?—' and makes copulatory motions with her pelvis. I feel sexual desire for her—as once long ago—but mostly a terrific rage and resentment against being interfered with, just as I do today. I think we can do nothing with her; I will have to see Dr. Gutheil. . . .

"Then, some way or another, I think I carry mother's dead body away in my car (as I saw it in a movie) with the intention of destroying it, I guess.

"Then I see Dr. and Mrs. Gutheil looking very fine and friendly. I wave politely and I wait for them to cross the street. Many soldiers are about and Dr. Gutheil has, at times, a uniform and medals.

" 'They are beginning to swell up for the parade,' I say, meaning that the soldiers are collecting. So although Dr. and Mrs. G. could have made it across the street, they are now detained, talking and waiting.

" 'Tomorrow at three,' I say, and Dr. G. finally realizes I am not talking about the parade. The above experience of coming of age is by now a dream I will bring him. We part."

This dream shows an impressive dramatization of the patient's futile attempts at overcoming his incestuous fixation.

The "coming-of-age" ritual reminds us of the puberty rites and initiation ceremonies of the primitive tribes. (Roheim, Freud, Frazer.) The coming-of-age ceremony means, in the patient's dream, just as in the rituals of the Australian aborigines, the overcoming of incestuous fixations. Our patient's dream portrays the difficulty he encounters in rendering his mother "invisible." (It is a simpler matter with his father who soon becomes "invisible.") Being the author of his dream, the patient shows clearly his resistance to the giving up of his infantile love object. The sexual attraction his mother used to have for him at that time (which the dream betrays) is the obvious cause of his difficulty. The dream ends with a display of rage and—apparently—of murder. To destroy a love object is easier than to overcome it. We mentioned before (page 57) that this is also the mechanism found in many a case of matricide.

The patient's brother plays here the same part of a "double" as Lieutenant Brown does in one of his previous dreams (page 140). The patient's real brother has not complained about having a small genital; but our patient has a definite feeling of inadequacy as far as his masculinity is concerned.

Interesting is the relation to the analyst and his wife who represent both the patient's parents and—by identification with the analyst—his own bisexuality.

"Crossing" here means getting well. Analysis has at this point seriously shaken his mother fixation.

He could cross, but, at this time, "soldiers" gather and force him to be "detained." "Talking and waiting" is a symbol of his analysis. "Soldiers" represent the patient's obsessions (cf. page 425). The development of his obsessions is as follows:

Incestuous desire → repression and hatred toward the incest object → anxiety (fear of the overwhelming impulse) → compulsive behavior (to stave off anxiety and arrest action).

The very moment the patient's fixations decline (through analytic insight and transference) anxiety reappears, making it necessary for him to counteract it again by means of compulsive behavior ("soldiers"). In this way his activity is checked ("talking and waiting").

Towards the end of the dream, the patient has a strong desire to turn the experience of the dream into a dream, a mechanism we described on page 229. He wants to undo the cathartic and analytic effect of the incestuous dream because insight confronts him with the necessity to deal again with his anxiety.

Conclusions

In the preceding cases we have learned to appreciate the dream as the pilot of the treatment. The dream informs us at the beginning about the "therapeutic situation" and the prognosis of our treatment. The dream is a reliable control for our work, showing us always anew the patient's attitude toward his physician and toward his disease. It is as though we were holding his pulse throughout the treatment, registering every change of reactions. By using our dream interpretation we can observe our patient's responses and adapt our approach to his current attitude. In many cases, dreams are the *only* key to the locked doors of the patient's unconscious. It would take us months and years were we to expect the patient himself to open these doors. This is particularly true in those cases in which a secret plays a part in the patient's illness as, for example, in some cases of compulsion neurosis, in amnesia, fugues, and in various hyponoic conditions.

PRACTICAL SUGGESTIONS

Before we go on, here are a few practical suggestions as to how we can best handle our patients regarding dreams.

This is what we call "dream discipline":

(1) We have to make our patients remember this: The very moment we agree that the dream is a form of thinking, we disqualify all arguments as to whether or not we dream. You will find patients who will come to you and tell you, "Doctor, I never dream." In such a case, you will calmly explain to the patient that every human being dreams. When? Every single night. As a rule, we forget dreams because we are not interested in them. Our memory is a function of our attention. And as a rule, we pay little or no attention to our dreams. Most of our patients make the startling discovery that after we have informed them of the fact that everybody dreams every night, or rather, every time they are awakening, they are able to remember their dreams.

(2) It does not help to make a resolution at bedtime: "In the morning I am going to have a dream for the doctor." In the morning, before the patient has awakened completely, he must concentrate for a while. He must try to render a connection between the flickering out dream world and the flickering up day consciousness. If he can penetrate the twilight of this state, he has shown the best physical and mental approach to obtaining dreams.

It is a fragment of a dream that we get under all circumstances. What we get is a tail end of a dream, and we must be satisfied with it. In reality we dream much more. At the same time a constant drain of emotions is taking place. These emotions are discharged in very uncoordinated form, as a complete jumble of feelings and thoughts. And they all occur almost simultaneously. Our mind, controlled by the superego, is in favor of order and thus a certain system of thoughts finally evolves in the images of the dream, according to grammar, syntax, and logic.

(3) We insist that the patient write his dreams down immediately on awakening. Later, parts of the dream or even the entire dream may be forgotten.

We draw our conclusions regarding the patient's cooperation from the fact that he brings his dreams written. A patient who fails to bring a written record of his dream usually shows other signs of resistance. Lack of dreams is one of the first signs of resistance. The patient must show determination to cooperate with us in our work throughout the treatment. By facilitating our efforts he is contributing his share to his recovery. If he wanted to dictate the dream to me during our session and we then had to discuss it, unnecessary time would be lost in technicalities. We must operate economically.

(4) The patient must also know that when he wakes up and says to himself, "I had a very important dream. I am quite sure that I will remember it when I come to the doctor," this is the same as discarding the dream. There are very few cases where such a dream survives the early morning hours. It usually disappears as a result of various inner resistances. It is in order to placate his own feeling of responsibility that the patient tells himself he will remember. It is really a declaration that he is now through with the dream and is ready to abandon it to oblivion. Dreams in general are volatile and because they are fraught with tabooed material they have no interest in being preserved.

There is one type of patient, however, who floods us with dreams, bringing, for example, five dreams every session. This usually represents a form of resistance. The patient wants us to be kept engaged in the analysis of his dreams so that he does not have to cooperate actively and make spontaneous revelations. It is as though he were saying: "Here you are; you are welcome to pick out what you please as long as you keep me out of this." Cases of this kind require special handling.

(Q) "You say that if you don't record the dream in the morning you may lose it. I had a patient tell me last night that he got up in the morning and had no dream. I was wondering whether he hadn't remembered it and then purposely had forgotten it."

(A) That is quite possible. However, in such cases, the dream is usually repressed before its details are fully remembered.

(Q) "How do you handle lack of associations to a dream?"

(A) Apart from the fact that this is a sign of resistance which may later be reduced by analytical means, we find it very helpful to demonstrate to the patient what association means. Many of our patients, at first, do not understand what it means to associate. In such cases it is helpful to produce one's own associations to a given passage of the dream. Naturally, one has to be careful not to reveal too personal matters, so as not to disturb the transference. Misconceptions regarding associations are numerous. Some patients labor under the misapprehension that to associate means to produce word associations as Jung introduced them some time ago, chair-table, road-church, and so on. We must insist that a condition be reproduced of free floating thought and a patient should tell whatever comes to his mind.

(Q) "What effect, if any, have drugs on dreams?"

(A) Some of them affect the mode of our thinking and may bring about changes of the ego in its provinces. A scientific study of the unconscious by the use of drugs is constricted by the fact that drugs do not permit the unconscious to express itself freely and in an unadulterated form. Material brought forward by narcosynthesis is to the greatest extent conscious material that was held back by resistance.

(Q) "With regard to the writing down of dreams, the following questions occur to me. If by writing down the dream early in the morning the patient brings in material that ordinarily he would forget during the day, are you not insisting that he present material for the interpretation for which he is not as yet prepared? Shouldn't we rather wait until such material comes up during the day with his normal associations?"

(A) We can only repeat what was stated before: whatever the patient brings out is but a fragment of what he has really dreamed; a fragment which is already prefabricated and elaborated on. What concerns us here is to find first the raw material for the associations, as much of it as is possible and as soon as possible, because during the day a number of secondary elaborations occur under influence of daydreams, and further distortion of the dream takes place. Our work then is more difficult. The time necessary for unraveling the deeper meaning of the dream is prolonged. Your point is well-taken, but it is dictated primarily by your customary awe for "free" associations. In the course of our discussions you may have come to feel that you may wish to change this all too conservative attitude.

And now a few words about a *practical way of surveying the dream material.* Dreams which have been interpreted are organized according to the complexes they contain. That does not necessarily mean that it must be done in this manner. We found it valuable and helpful, particularly for the active type of dream interpretation. For instance, you have a dream in which the patient's symptom is expressed. You have a sheet of paper on which you make a note: "Symptom" and in the same line you make your notations. You put the number of the dreams and the page of your book where the dream is noted. The dreams are numbered consecutively. Let us assume that dream 3 on page 35 is one that contains the patient's symptoms. If some time later you find another dream in which the symptom occurs, you note it next to the first one. In this way you gradually obtain a mirror of the patient's main problems while the analysis is going on.

By applying this method, a series of dreams is formed around the leading complexes, allowing us to review them in the light of our growing knowledge of the dynamics of the case.

You see, therefore, that we distinguish between two kinds of dream series: a *chronological series* of dreams recorded in successive nights, and a *psychological series* based on the latent content of the dreams. Each has its own practical value in analysis. The first gives dream plots in the manner of installments of a novel (Stekel), the second offers an ever-increasing insight into the main issues of the case.

(Q) "Are long dreams more informative than short ones?"

(A) Not necessarily. Sometimes a very short dream leads us to the center of the problem.[1] Much depends on the additional information (associations) we can elicit in connection with the short dream.

Maintaining a proper routine in our attitude toward the patient's analysis, we also impress upon him the necessity to report dreams as often as possible, since, in our view, the patient produces them every single time he awakens. All he has to contribute is the recalling of them in the morning. It requires his conscious effort to do so and his cooperation in this respect is an indication of his will to recover.

Reminding the patient again and again that we expect him to deliver dreams, we exert indirect pressure on him and place upon him a part of the responsibility which ultimately he will have to shoulder by himself when he has adopted the mature standards of living.

In the active analysis, a situation hardly ever develops which is like that described by Lorand in his book on *Technique of Psychoanalytic Therapy* (page 167). He mentions that dreams did not occur until the *second year* of analysis because until then the patient "did not take the trouble" to remember dreams.

In our technique, it is the analyst's duty to convince the patient of the significance of dreams, to encourage cooperation. A passively conducted analysis is an expectant procedure which completely relies on the patient's revelations. In the case quoted by Lorand, a full year had elapsed before he was able to obtain what is called "objective material" of the unconscious, namely dreams.

(Q) "What are we to do with patients who do not report dreams?"

(A) We must explain to the patient in the first few sessions that everyone dreams every time he awakens, and, in general, only the *lack of attention* to the dreams is the cause of forgetting them.

Patients should know that dreams are important and necessary and that they shorten the duration of analysis. By telling this to the patient

[1] See dream 24 on page 51.

we often create in him such an ambition to deliver dreams that he feels sorry and disappointed if he misses a dream for a single night.

(Q) "Some patients say that they have had a dream, but that they have forgotten it after awakening. What can be done about this?"

(A) The patient should keep a pencil and paper near his bed in order to jot down his dreams immediately upon awakening. Dreams are often vague and vanish easily. Therefore, the patient should not procrastinate in putting them down by thinking: "I recall the dream so clearly now that I shall certainly recall it in the morning"—a very erroneous opinion, indeed. Under such circumstances dreams usually vanish.

The first question of the patient after awakening should be: "Did I dream anything?"

(Q) "Some patients say that they have not recorded their dream because they found it obviously unimportant."

(A) There are no unimportant dreams! At least the patient is never able to discern which dream has importance and which has not. Therefore, no censorship of dreams by the patient! As a matter of fact, we usually find that the relevant dreams are deprecated by the patient with the remark: "This is a very unimportant dream."

(Q) "Can we do something to foster the patient's dream production?"

(A) No external means are necessary for coaxing the patient's dream production. Most important is the solution of the resistance shown in the patient's lack of material. It is useful to examine daydreams whenever the production of night dreams declines.

It does not matter very much if the patient does not bring dreams for three or four days. But we very rarely see a case in which the patient has never brought a dream. Skillful questions during the sessions stimulate the stream of associations and dreams as well, driving them up to the surface of consciousness. Exceptions are abnormal conditions of the brain such as are found in certain cases of psychosis and of acute or chronic intoxication.

And now a few words about the *interpreter*. A successful dream interpreter is one who, in addition to the skill and experience necessary for this field of research, also possesses all the qualifications for a successful psychotherapist. The interpretations presented in this book will prove to you how important it is that the dream analyst be well-informed and well-read. Fairy tales, folklore, the Bible, and literature in general are indispensable.

The following dream offers such an example:

The twenty-two-year-old patient dreamt [562] that *she was lost in an old city and that a fox gave her directions. The bushy tail of the fox aroused the patient's attention in the dream.*

Her associations failed to identify the fox. She was asked whether she knew Grimm's fairy tales. She replied that she did, but she gave no further information. She was then asked whether she knew the story about the "Golden Bird." At first she could not recall it, but with the analyst's help she was able to reconstruct it as she had heard it in her childhood. In the Grimm story, a prince goes out to find a golden bird, a golden horse, and a princess of the golden castle. A fox advises him, just as is the case in the dream. The fox of the fairy tale was the princess' brother who was changed into an animal.

The dream suddenly became transparent. It explained why the patient felt confused ("lost in an old city"); it showed that the cause of her neurosis was to be sought in her past ("old city") and that it had something to do with the patient's brother.

The fact that the "bushy tail" of the fox was emphasized gave rise to a discussion of possible physical contact. Whereupon the patient was able to offer valuable analytic material to substantiate this supposition.

The interpretation of this dream would have been difficult if it were not for the fact that the content of the fairy tale was known to the analyst.

Experiences of this kind are so frequent in the practice of the analyst that we cannot be emphatic enough in recommending the study of the great works of literature, the Bible, mythology, and folklore.

Other examples of interpretations which were guided by the analyst's knowledge of the background of the dream rather than by the patient's co-operation can be found in numerous places in this book.

We stated on page 553 that apart from considering dreams in the chronological order as one would a novel printed in installments, it is desirable to organize the dream material according to the complexes it contains. The advantage is obvious. It allows us to evaluate the relative importance of individual relations and attitudes within the general psychodynamic picture. It also offers a cumulative picture of the various aspects of the patient's neurosis.

In the following is a sample of such an arrangement. The first figure represents the consecutive number of the dream, the other represents the page in the case folder. The chart belongs to a patient suffering from claustrophobia.

NAME

Symptom:	4/15, 15/62, 26/110, 34, 125, 35/126, etc.
Relation to Analysis:	3/13, 4/15, 8/40, 9/42, 17/65, etc.
Father:	2/9, 6/18, 8/40, etc.
Mother:	1/4, 5/16, 7/20, 24/106, 25/108, etc.
Relation to Women:	10/44, 12/50, 14/62, 15/63, 16/64, 25/108 etc.
Relation to Men:	2/9, 11/45, 13/61, etc.
Superego (Morals):	6/18, 17/65, etc.
Wife:	10/44, 16/64, 18/67, 21/73, 25/108, etc.
Ambition:	11/45, etc.
Narcissism:	32/121, etc.
Id Drives (Impulses):	30/119, 33/123, etc.
Oral Eroticism:	25/108, 26/110, etc.
Anal Eroticism:	11/45, etc.
Etc.	

DREAM INTERPRETATION AND THE PSYCHOLOGICAL SCHOOLS (CRITICAL SURVEY)

DOGMATISM IN PSYCHOANALYSIS

Freud's fundamental work, *Interpretation of Dreams,* was a milestone in the development of modern psychology. It not only revealed to the psychotherapist the deeper layers of the patient's mind but also made possible the establishment of a general "Depth Psychology." Freud and his disciples put stone upon stone until the formerly frail structure of dream interpretation became a stately edifice. However, the imagination of some analysts has played havoc with the scientific nature of dream interpretation. The use of a fixed symbolism belongs here. According to Abraham, the *spider* in the dream represents the "phallic mother" of whom one is afraid. The fear of spiders, in his view, expresses the fear of mother-incest.

It would be just as plausible to consider the spider as a symbol of something mysterious, sinister, in ourselves, a symbol of the unconscious, or of insanity.[1]

One of my patients (a woman aged thirty-four) had a spider dream which does not fit into this scheme at all. The dream runs as follows:

[563] *"I lose my bag and am worried because it is a very precious one. My husband helps me to look for it, but we can't find it. Then we go to bed and to my surprise, I become aware of an enormous cobweb which looks like a wall between my husband's bed and mine. In the center of the cobweb I notice a terribly big spider. I scream and implore my husband to remove the spider. He takes the fleshly body of the spider and throws it out of the window. At this moment I see the cobweb changing into a real wall between our beds. Though my thoughts are longing for something to happen and to give me satisfaction, my longing is in vain."*

The patient complained that her husband had the habit of embracing her tightly, "like a spider," with his arms and legs, while being intimate with her. She felt repelled by that, especially because her husband was not very potent.

The "precious bag" is the patient's libido (also, genitals). She expects her husband to "find" it; but, alas, he fails to satisfy her. Between her mind (bed) and that of her husband

[1] A popular expression in Vienna for a person who hallucinates is "er spinnt" (he spins). "Fantastic nonsense" is often expressed by the word "Hirngespinst" (brain cobwebs).

there is a "wall," an insurmountable impediment. Her hatred for her husband's physical approach is the "spider." She expects him to remove this impediment.

No "phallic mother" was to be found in our attempt to trace back the spider symbol to ideas and experiences of the patient's past. The patient had very little of what we call "latent homosexuality." Her attitude toward her mother did not show any infantile abnormality. The mother was a kindly and unassuming woman. The patient's association with reference to the spider, therefore, has its full value. All other generalizing interpretations are at the stage of guesswork.

Also in the following dream the spider has no connection with a "phallic mother." The dreamer's mother is not "phallic," but a meek and indulging person, who throughout her life had to suffer abuse from her husband.

The dream is as follows:

[564] *"I was reading a very old book. As I opened it, big spiders, about two inches long, spread out from it. I wanted to kill them, but was too touchy about it."*

The patient associated with this dream the memory of the sexual experiences of his early childhood (the "old book"). As a farmer's son, and, living in a remote part of the country, he engaged freely in all sorts of sexual activities, among them incest, homosexuality, and intercourse with animals. When he grew up he felt burdened by his past experiences and wished he could forget them. The dream shows them still very active (the size of the insects) and himself still unable to control them ("too touchy" to kill them).

We see, therefore, that the spider has no fixed meaning and that we must consider the whole dream in order to decipher its symbolism.

What applies to the symbol "spider" also applies to the symbol *dragon*. Winterstein interprets dreams of the famous Swedish scientist Swedenborg in an equally schematic way. Here is one of Swedenborg's dreams:

[565] *"I saw many animals following one another. When they stretched their wings they proved to be dragons. I flew over their heads, but I brushed one of them. . . ."*

Swedenborg himself believes that these dragons signify deceitful love which hides its dragon-like character until you see its dragon's wings. While this interpretation seems logical and shows "common sense," Winterstein's statement leaves us not at all satisfied. He says: "The dragon symbolizes, I dare say, the deceitful mother as castrator."

Winterstein sees in the following dream a picture of Swedenborg's "mother with castration wound." The dream runs as follows:

[566] *"I dreamed that I passed water. A woman was lying in bed looking on. She was red and stout. I grasped at her breasts; she did not object. She showed me her genital; it was ugly. I did not want to have anything to do with her."*

In the above-mentioned dreams we can see the dreamer's religious conflicts (dragon = sin); and a homosexual complex (dragon = devil = homosexual obsession) which is based upon his fear of women (dragon = woman, as the dreamer interprets correctly). Swedenborg suffered from paranoia, in which the homosexual complex plays a great part. It is possible that Swedenborg's fear of women was based on disgusting experiences; but there is no evidence offered by the dream that an "ugly genital" means a "castrated genital," nor is such a supposition of any psychological use. It is also possible that the dreamer had bad experiences with his mother, disappointment, even a breakdown of his mother ideal; the dream shows a distinctly infantile situation in the micturition scene; but we do not further our psychological insight into the patient's personality by introducing such vague constructions as "the deceitful mother as castrator," or "mother with the castration wound."

Freud's interpretation of the *labyrinth* shows a similar dogmatism. Everyone is familiar with the comparison of the labyrinth to the human mind; we can interpret "entering the labyrinth" as "getting mixed up," or the like. But Freud gives us a fixed formula for the interpretation of the labyrinth. He says: "Thus, e.g., the myth of the labyrinth can be recognized as the representation of an anal birth; the twisted ways are the intestines, the thread of Ariadne, the umbilical cord."

Another dogmatic dream interpretation can be demonstrated in the following dream of a young girl reported by Freud:

[567] *She enters a large hall and sees a person seated on a chair six times, eight times and more, who, each time, is her father.*

Freud interprets the hall as the uterus, and considers the dream as an equivalent to the dreamer's fantasy of "meeting" her father while in her mother's womb. Freud also maintains that the multiplicity of the father's person in the dream expresses the fact that the "process in question" (father approaching mother during pregnancy) has occurred repeatedly.

Contrary to this interpretation we may say after simplifying the dream content: the dream shows the girl's father fixation. Wherever she is, whatever man she meets, she sees her father everywhere, in every man.

The person of the father may also signify an "experience with her father" which comes to her mind as a recollection whenever she is to meet another man. The "six" may represent the number of sessions per week with Freud. We could also see a reference to Freud as a father-image. "Six" ultimately may mean "sex."

In her book, *Dream Analysis,* Ellen F. Sharpe demonstrates clearly the circumstantial primitivity in interpretation. The book contains dreams analyzed in an orthodox manner with the assistance of copious associations.

In one of her dreams [568] *the patient sees the combination of letters K.O.H. which have a chemical reference.*

According to the analyst, the formula finally "yielded" the meaning of "Ka. Ka.," which, in some parts of Europe, represents a child's expression for feces. The patient first inadvertently said *"S.O.S."* instead of *K.O.H.* *S.O.S.*, therefore, was analyzed by the author. *S* "proved to be" the hissing sound created by the act of urinating, and *O* a sound of distress made by the child that is subject to an "accident."

Let us assume that the interpretation of this dream does not represent a series of platitudes but the patient's deepest thoughts and feelings, mediated by her unbiased associations. Let us further assume that the excretory character of these associations justifies the analyst's deductions. According to the author, we are dealing here with the symbolic reproduction of a well-known, commonly experienced unpleasant situation. The reader asks vainly for the clinical purpose of such an interpretation.

Individual Psychology (Adler)

In accordance with his general outlook, Adler does not pay much attention to dreams. Thus we find only a few short dream reports in his contribution, "How I Read a Case History." He sees in the dreams, as in the patient's symptoms, only the patient's "arrangements," which are in accordance with his unconscious "will to rule," as the exclusive propelling power. Adler says that dream interpretation as used by him has for its aim the demonstration of the patient's inner preparations to live up to his life plans and to unmask him to himself as an arranger of his sufferings.

The patient's complaints are, according to Adler, expressions of his attitude toward his environment and are very often used by the patient as a means to dominate relatives and other persons with whom he comes in contact. Dreams show preparatory functions oriented according to the so-called "leading life line" of the patient. The whole neurosis is, according to Adler, a struggle with the final tendency to improve one's position in life.

We, therefore, are not surprised at finding the following dream interpretations in Adler's book:

[569] "I often had a disturbing dream," a patient reports. "I dreamed that *father or mother was very ill. Crying, and with pangs of conscience, I used to awake then and could not fall asleep for a long time. And while I was tossing in bed, I would make up my mind to get changed, to unburden my parents of their work, to make ways for father and to help mother in her housekeeping.*"

Adler comments on this stereotyped dream by emphasizing the fact that most children dream occasionally about the death or serious illness of their parents. "To interpret this hastily as a 'death wish' is the privilege of a schematic and insinuating psychology. Occasionally it comes true. We shall accept this interpretation only if the accompanying mood of the dream makes it possible, if the other attitude of the dreamer justifies such an interpretation. In the majority of cases, however, the dream points purely in the direction of the patient's foreseeing the future. What will happen when my parents are dead?

"In our case it is absolutely manifest that the girl is apprehensive of her future. She needs her parents in order to dominate them."

Adler is right in maintaining that not all dreams of parents being dead are fulfillments of "death wishes." Dreams may prevent shocks by anticipating the shocking experience of death (cf. page 29). A statement that patients need their parents only "in order to dominate them" is too narrow, however.

In the above dream, the patient's "accompanying mood," her obvious feeling of guilt which causes the sudden change in her attitude toward her parents, points, of course, in the direction of death wishes.

In his *The Practice and Theory of Individual Psychology*, we also find few dream interpretations. It is interesting, however, to follow Adler's ideas and to see how little he makes use of dreams, relying completely on his supposition that dreams have only an "anticipatory, prescient function," and are nothing but another way of expressing the patient's power-craving tendencies.

He describes a business woman, suffering from agoraphobia and confined to bed with an organic illness. She dreamed [570] *that she entered a shop and saw girls playing cards.*

Adler says that in cases of agoraphobia he observed, the symptom was used by the patients as a means of forcing their will upon their environment. The dream of this patient had the following interpretation: she sees herself in a future situation in which she will be out of bed and able to detect transgressions of rules. She is convinced that in her absence everything must go wrong. She anticipates transgressions by her employees. Instead of working, they play cards. She thinks that as soon as she regains her health she will take charge and demonstrate her importance once more. The dream, according to Adler, is prearranged in accordance with the dreamer's designs and purposes.

Adler does not think that dream interpretation is very important. To him the dream is but a synchronous movement of thought, running parallel to the personality demands. Its language, although it is difficult to understand, indicates the patient's emotional trends. Intelligibility, important for thinking and speaking, becomes superfluous in the dream which, contrary to the thought, does not prepare us for action.

The following is another dream of a woman patient interpreted by Adler. In her dream [571], the patient *saw herself in a ballroom, wearing a pretty blue dress. She danced with Napoleon."*

Adler interprets Napoleon in this dream as a substitute for the patient's brother-in-law. His patient gives the characteristic explanation for it. In her dream, she has raised her brother-in-law to the role of Napoleon so that taking him away from her sister will be worthwhile.

We see the one-sidedness of this type of interpretation. The question of the patient's sexual interest in her brother-in-law has not been investigated at all by Adler. Knowing the sexual meaning of "dancing" in the dream, the unprejudiced examiner would at least investigate the patient's attitude toward her brother-in-law, in addition to discussing the superiority and inferiority problems. It seems very possible that a conflict based on this unconscious attitude might have been uncovered if the dream had been analyzed by an independent method.

Adler's way of interpreting sexual dreams is seen in the following example taken from his book *Ueber den nervösen Charakter*:

[572] *The patient in the dream is lying at Adler's feet and reaching with her hand upwards in order to touch the material of his silk dress. Adler makes a lascivious gesture. Then the patient says smilingly: "You aren't better than other men." To which he nods affirmatively.*

Adler tells us that the patient experienced a similar situation with her father when she was a child. At the time of treatment she had a relationship with a married man. Adler sees in this dream the "male protest" of the patient. She is below, to be sure, but she reaches upward. She degrades her physician by changing him into a woman (silk dress) and by stating that he is not better than other men.

This interpretation may be correct as far as the problem of the patient's ambition is concerned; but the whole question, the problem of transference, homosexuality (man wearing woman's dress), etc., remains unsolved. Adler does not see the patient's irony in her words "you aren't better than other men"; these words are directed to a man who makes all possible efforts to overlook her sex.

According to Adler, the dream represents a sketch-like reflection of psychic attitudes. It shows the way the dreamer reacts to forthcoming tasks. This reaction may be normal or neurotic, but the dream is always a fiction showing the patient's attempts to control future situations. This attempt, of course, is due to his will to dominate.

Stereotyped dreams and recalled childhood dreams show the "fictitious leading line" (*Leitlinie*) most distinctly. Repeated dreams during the same night show a feeling of insecurity and the increased desire to tackle certain important problems.

Adler's patients seem to be very tractable students. They dream in an individual-psychology way. Let us look, for instance, at the following dream by one of them:

[573] *The patient has informed his aunt that he was through with Mrs. P. He pointed out the woman's good and bad traits to his aunt who, thereupon, remarked that he had forgotten one trait, namely, Mrs. P.'s desire to dominate.*

In his interpretation, Adler sees himself identified with the aunt by the dreamer. The patient's brother is identified with Mrs. P. Both women were superior to the patient. In this transformation of men into women, Adler sees the patient's tendency toward depreciation. The dream warns the patient in the words of his aunt which are the words of Adler.

We notice that Adler recognizes the depreciating tendency of his patient; the patient really ridicules Adler's method which pays so much attention to the "lust for domination." Indeed, Adler's interpretation touches only those motives which are able to verify his ideas about the patient's ambitions. It leaves a large number of problems open to investigation.

Psychosynthesis (Jung)

Carl Gustav Jung, creator of the psychosynthetic method of psychotherapy, distinguishes between an "interpretation on the subjective plane" and an "interpretation on the objective plane." The freudian interpretation, in which the dreamer's relation toward his environment is considered, is, in Jung's nomenclature, an "interpretation on the objective plane."

According to Jung, an interpretation in which dream symbols are treated as representations of real objects is an interpretation on the objective plane. An interpretation in which every part of the dream, and all persons who appear in it, are taken as representations of the dreamer himself is an interpretation on the subjective plane. This form of interpretation stresses the tendencies or parts of the patient's personality.

Jung states, furthermore, that the psychoanalytic method fails at the point where the dream symbols cease to be connected with personal attitudes and begin to represent the images of the collective unconscious. Images of the collective unconscious become meaningful only when subjected to a psychosynthetic approach. Psychoanalysis reduces symbols into causal components, while psychosynthesis "integrates the symbol" into a higher, more general expression.

In the dream [574], *"I am in bed with my mother,"* the Freudian may see the so-called Oedipus complex. The Jungian will interpret this dream on the subjective plane as being an expression of the patient's tendency "to bring motherly instincts up to the surface" (Schindler). Jung's therapy attempts to aid the patient in developing and increasing his leading instincts, as exhibited by his dreams. We call this tendency of interpretation "the final, or *anagogic,* tendency."

Jung describes the case of a patient who saw him in her dreams [575] *as a kind of father and admired him greatly.* Although he made clear to her the "transference situation" emphasizing her relation toward him as "daughter-father-godfather relationship," the patient continued dreaming in this manner.

Jung demonstrates that these dreams could not disappear because the patient's relation toward him in the interpretation (on the subjective plane) had to be considered as a symbol of the patient's Ethos striving for God. The person of Jung in the dream means the Ethos within the "subject," patient. It does not mean Jung as another person, a love "object." The patient's striving for God (Ethos) was a desire which, of course, was not satisfied; hence the repetition of the dream.

It seems superfluous to emphasize that Jung's interpretation "on the subjective plane" is also one-sided. A more intensive analytical examination would probably prove that the reason for the patient's continuing to produce transference dreams, despite all interpretations, was the fact that she did not stop loving her physician, which he apparently did not realize, perhaps because of his own counter-transference.

Another example of Jung's dream interpretations which he uses in order to demonstrate the superiority of his method to the freudian is as follows:

[576] *About to cross a broad stream. There is no bridge, but she finds a ford where she can cross. Just as she is on the point of doing so, a big crab that lay hidden in the water seizes her by the foot and will not let go. She wakes in terror.*

Before we report Jung's analysis we wish to say what we are able to read in this dream after simplification of its content. The patient is about to cross some boundary line (inhibition, moral restriction, etc.) and to make some decision; something (crab) prevents her from action, even after she has learned that it is possible to carry it through. The crab is a backward-walking animal. It must symbolize the retrograde, regressive tendency. It is some past experience that prevents the patient from going the way she has found to be right (= the heterosexual love?).

We make use of the patient's associations reported by Jung. The patient associates in her dream: (1) her fear of cancer; the German word "Krebs" means both crab and cancer; (2) Mrs. X died of cancer; (3) crabs walk backward; (4) her friend, the sentimental attachment to her which was obviously of homosexual character; (5) the frequent quarrels with her friend in spite of all "ideal" friendship (both girls very irritable); (6) she had long since realized that this friendship had outlived its function; (7) the patient had formerly an exaggerated, fantastic relation to her mother, and after her death transferred her feelings to her friend, etc.

We are now able to say more about the dream. The patient's homosexuality and other infantile (animal-like) drives which she considers as malicious and destructive, as is cancer, are the remainders of the past (crab walking backward = past); they drag her down and prevent her from making a proper love adjustment. Some impressive experiences of her past (traumas, etc.) which have to be found by the use of the patient's associations, experiences of a highly destructive character, must be taken into consideration as life's obstacles. Furthermore, it has to be verified by questioning whether the patient believed that cancer had something to do with a sinful life (religious component) and was God's just punishment for overstepping moral restrictions (stream). The other side of the stream is to be also considered as the "other world," where one has to stand trial for his good and bad deeds. Being bitten by an animal is another symbol of pangs of conscience.

Objects for a further active analysis offered by this dream are: (1) the patient's homosexuality, (2) the shocking experiences of her past, and (3) her religious conflicts.

And now let us see the way Jung approaches this dream. The obstacle that is to be overcome and the boundary that is to be crossed lie in the patient herself. When she is about to pass this barrier she encounters an unexpected danger. It is an animal that moves backwards. It threatens to drag down into the depths the whole personality of the dreamer. Jung thinks here of a deadly disease that begins insidiously and proves to be incurable. Making use of the patient's associations, Jung brings out the patient's belief that it is her friend who stands in her way and tries to drag her down. She does not recognize that the obstacle is in her own mind.

As a consequence of her error, she strives in an impractical manner toward idealism, with the sole purpose of preventing her friend from dragging her down.

Jung's interpretation of this dream (on the subjective plane) helps to remove the patient's mistake.

The crab which appears in relation to the patient's friend also appeared in relation to her mother. It represents the patient's exaggerated need for love. One of her acquaintances, a Mrs. X., died from cancer (crab) when she was the patient's present age. Mrs. X. was known to have had relations with many men. The patient is afraid of such tendencies in herself, and by clinging to her friend, she achieves a certain degree of protection against the excessive heterosexual demands. In her mind, Mrs. X's disease (cancer) represented a punishment by fate for her heterosexual activities; her case serves as a warning against promiscuity.

Jung realizes that this synthetic interpretation offers much that is of purely analytical character. He therefore feels compelled to state that while his interpretation represents a form of analysis on the objective plane, he has come to his conclusions by making use of the subjective type of interpretation.

We leave it to the reader to decide which of the demonstrated methods is the most economical and the least speculative. Our interpretation included both the subjective and the objective planes. Proceeding from the basic dream situation ("hindered crossing"), making occasional use of the patient's associations, we tried to disclose the symbolic meaning of the dream as generously as possible.

In the following we present another example of the psychosynthetic dream interpretation, a case analyzed by one of Jung's prominent pupils, Kranefeldt. The author quotes the case of a girl and the experiences she had under anesthesia. It was a case of abortion. The girl did not take the mishap of her pregnancy too seriously, but during the anesthesia she had a peculiar experience which caused her to shudder whenever she was thinking about it.

While under anesthesia, [577] *she saw herself in a large building which appeared to be in the open air. Everything was permeated with solemn silence. Round about the hall there was a crowded audience seated in a semicircle which ascended like an amphitheatre. In the center of the hall there stood a pair of scales. The dreamer saw a number of people being called upon to deposit their good and bad deeds on the scales and to justify themselves. Many assistants appeared to be working at the scales. When a bad deed was placed on the scale, the scale descended and a deep voice, coming from an invisible being, spoke judgment.*

The patient's deeds were weighed. The voice then announced: "She is purged from sin." Thereupon the "good" scale moved downward. The patient felt that she had been approved.

Kranefeldt's comment on this dream is interesting. He is reminded of the "Egyptian Tribunal of Death" (Fig. 13), in which the god Anubis weighs the hearts of men before a court of forty-two judges of the dead. Kranefeldt also thinks here of a scene in *Faust* and the words "Condemned! Condemned!" The "Last Judgment" and God's voice finally come to the analyst's mind.

He sees in this image a good example of an archetypal picture, a product of the collective unconscious.

It is clear that a person undergoing an operation may have the idea of possible death; the experience of anesthesia itself may cause this association (anesthesia = loss of consciousness = falling asleep = death). The scene of the Last Judgment experienced in the dream shows us the patient as a profoundly religious person who has a bad conscience (abortion). The dream offers her a victory of her good deeds as a consolation. (See Chapter V, "Dreams under Stress," page 389.)

It may be a fruitful attempt to investigate the parallels between the pictures of the dream and the rites of ancient and modern peoples. It is beyond any doubt that we may find parallels between the unconscious reactions of all civilized people. What does it mean to the individual? What value has it for the understanding or the treatment of the sick? It is a part of comparative psychology and has its ethnological, philosophical, but hardly any psychotherapeutic importance.

Jung's synthetic and anagogic ideas, however, will remain as lasting contributions to the science of oneirology.

Jung criticizes Freud's and Adler's concepts as one-sided. He particularly emphasizes the fact that "causality," which plays so great a part in freudian concepts is but a part of psychology, and that, e.g., the "creative element" of the psyche cannot be explained or dealt with on that basis. Contrary to Freud, who looks for the cause of the subsequent disturbance in the patient and to Adler, who examines the initial situation with regard to its final purposes, Jung claims to consider all these factors and to add to them the *causae formales,* the formative forces in the patient's psyche.

Needless to say that Jung's patients are also tractable students of his psychology, and dream all sorts of "archetypes" for his benefit.

[578] One of them *sees himself surrounded by many feminine figures and a voice within him says, "I must first get away from father."*

Jung interprets "father" as the embodiment of the traditional spirit, as it shows itself in religion, which seems to stand in the patient's way. "He holds the dreamer a prisoner to consciousness and its values" and prevents him from becoming aware of his unconscious tendencies.

Then the dreamer sees a [579] *snake drawing a circle about him, while he, like a tree, stands in the center "grown fast to the earth."*

The snake being one of the ancient archetypes (cf. page

103) interests Jung very much, and he sees in the dream a reproduction of the magic circle, "the mandala." The snake biting its own tail is an old symbol of the wholeness of life. (See page 127, Fig. 31.)

Then the patient sees in a "visual impression" [579a] *a veiled woman.* Jung interprets this vision as the dreamer's anima, i.e., the projection of his unconscious femininity, also a symbol of his unconscious.

When the next "visual impression" [579b] shows this *veiled woman with her face uncovered,* the interpreter sees in it a good prognosis.

Some time later (visual impression) [580] *this unknown woman stands in the land of sheep and points the way.*

Jung recognizes in the "land of sheep" the "land of childhood," and maintains that "in order to reach the next peak we must first go down into that land where the roads just begin to part from each other."

In one of his next dreams [581] the patient *hears his father call anxiously: "That is the seventh!"*

As though Jung did not know the mystical importance of this number! "The seventh" is "the highest stage before enlightenment." ". . . After that, the disclosure of the collective unconscious would begin, and that would sufficiently explain the anxiety of the father as the embodiment of the traditional mind," i.e., the conservative mind that has no understanding for the trends of the collective unconscious.

In his next dream, [582] *the man sees his mother pouring water from one bowl into another, an act which is performed with great solemnity, "as if it is of the utmost importance to the surrounding world. Then the dreamer is cast out by the father."*

"The father" is the "collective consciousness," while "the mother" represents the "collective unconscious." Water is the water of life. Jung sees in his dream again a good prognosticon. "The unconscious transposes the location of the life forces, and thus a change of standpoint is indicated."

The patient's next dream is that of [583] *two playing cards, an ace of clubs and a seven.*

In commenting on this dream, Jung emphasizes the fact that the "ace" is "one" (the lowest card) and, at the same time, it is an "ace" (the highest card). "The ace of clubs,

FIGURE 85

with its cross form, points to the basic Christian symbol. . . ." Jung points out that in Swiss-German the club is also called "Chruz," which means "cross." (See Fig. 85.) The three-leaf character of the symbol is "an allusion to the threefold nature of the one God. . . ." "Lowest and highest is the beginning and the end, the alpha and omega."

The seven changes symbolize the transformation which would culminate in the *solification.*

Jung then discusses the transition from the cross symbol to the rose symbol (*per crucem ad rosam*) which is condensed to the "rose-cross" (Rosicrucian) of the Middle Ages, the "golden flower" of the Chinese, and the "blue flower" of the romantics.

And as though the patient wanted to prove him right, he dreamed [584] of *a long wandering on which he found a blue flower.*

In the following we quote a few more random samples:

[585] *The patient has a visual impression in which a skull changes into a red ball, then into a woman's head which emits light.*

[586] In another vision the patient sees *a globe. An unknown woman stands upon it and prays to the sun.*

[587] Another of the patient's visual impressions shows him *surrounded by nymphs. A voice says, "But we were always there. Only you did not notice us."*

[588] . . . *The voice says, "Everything must be ruled by the light."*

Dreams: [589] *An unknown woman follows him. He keeps running in a circle.*

[590] *The anima accuses him of being too little concerned about her.*

[591] . . . *There is a map on which is drawn a circle with the centre.*

[592] *A treasure lies in the sea. One must dive through a narrow opening. . . . The dreamer ventures the leap in the dark and finds down there a beautiful garden . . . with a fountain in the centre.*

If Jung's impression that the unconscious dream content cannot be tampered with is correct, the problems presented by his patients appear to be very much Jung-specific.

SUMMARY

Dream interpretation does not mean successful application of a certain preconceived theory of the physician, but rather the discovery of mechanisms which give us a sufficient insight into the patient's specific and individual mental situation. The more we bring out of an individual dream, the more quickly and completely we can attain our aim: that of curing the patient.

Freud emphasizes the fact that in some cases apparently insignificant features of a dream may prove indispensable for the interpretation, and the solution of the patient's immediate problem may be delayed when the analyst fails to turn his full attention to these features in time.

This is an important statement. It exhorts us to make a serious and painstaking study of the technique of dream interpretation.

The real art is to find among several possible interpretations of the dream the only relevant one which enables us to understand the therapeutic situation of the moment and gives useful hints as to the direction of our further research. The dream is, in reality, a stereometric body. The different interpretations of the various schools of psychotherapy are similar to cross sections through this body.

Careful supervision of the patient's communications is indicated. Patients who have to report dreams daily for months and years, as is customary in the orthodox analysis, are often highly pleased if they can serve their analyst with constructed symbols. The analysts' overanxiousness to decipher sexual symbols is not only a source of their inner enjoyment, but also means to them an inner triumph over their analyst.

"There is often as much skill required to discover the moral behind the immoral as the immoral behind the moral," says Stekel. Since we know how often paraphilias with all their sexual symbolism substitute for unconscious morality (for example, fetishism), we have learned to distrust somewhat the generous presentation of sexual associations by our patients. The same applies, of course, to the "above and below" symbols served in opulence to Adler followers by their overzealous patients, and to symbols of the "collective unconscious" produced by patients of Jung.

Dream interpretation will assert itself successfully as a

science worth teaching and studying only after we have become independent in the technique of our interpretation. We must interpret less, but all the more reliably. Our interpretations must be correct even if they do not bear the stamp of the "school" (à la Jung or à la Adler). The abundance of single interpretations and their depth, however, will depend only upon the interpreter's ingenuity, experience, and intuition. They will distinguish the real artist among the dream interpreters and will give testimony of those qualities which are beyond teaching and study.

DREAM INTERPRETATION IN ACTIVE ANALYSIS

Freud opened for us the "royal road to the unconscious" by showing us a way of understanding the hitherto obscure language of the dream. He once stated that a psychology which cannot explain the dream is useless even for the understanding of the normal mental life. This is very true indeed. Dream interpretation offers us a basis for many other types of interpretation, of the normal and abnormal life, of symptom formations, of character, and of neurosis in general. But above all, dream analysis is one of our most potent psychotherapeutic weapons.

The technique of interpretation has developed from a more or less naive method of symbol decoding to a complex dynamic system of reconstructing and comprehending thought processes of a primitive order as they are found in the latent dream content. As these processes correspond to the thought mechanisms involved in the psychogenetics of nervous and mental disease, we may expect that by getting insight into the dynamics of the dream we may also, automatically, enhance our understanding of the dynamics of the disease under investigation. For, to a high degree, dream images represent a mirror of our thought processes.

While a full knowledge of the intrinsic processes of displacement, distortion, and symbolization is, and always will be, indispensable for the management of the neurotic symptom, we now apply our interpretative skill towards the disclosure of psychodynamics rather than hunt for the meaning of individual symbols.

This approach in dream interpretation is conducted in the direction from the manifest content of the dream to its latent content, from the reconstruction of the dream situation to the reconstruction of the patient's problem constellation. Only after this has been accomplished is the individual symbolism analyzed.

As is well known, the average psychoanalytic treatment conducted on the basis of daily sessions consumes between one and three years; but treatments of five and even more years' duration are by no means exceptional. Although shortening the treatment appears desirable from more than one standpoint, many psychoanalysts still insist that only the "orthodox," long-term psychoanalysis is practicable. To them, long treatments represent the only kind of therapy conforming to the rules, and they are inclined to consider abbreviated methods as incomplete, superficial, or simply non-analytical. This is regrettable for two reasons: first, psychoanalysis, which for a long time developed along investigative lines rather than therapeutic, left a good deal to be desired with regard to its curative results, and second, public reaction to failures following short treatments is not so strong as to those following treatments which have consumed years of prodigious effort and expense.

Some analysts attempted to improve this situation by developing new theories in the hope that a better *theoretical* understanding of the mechanisms involved would increase the *therapeutic* success. Ferenczi tried to render the psychoanalytical method more "active" by a daring speculation on transference and regression; and Rado speaking about results stated as follows: "The somewhat capricious therapeutic results of psychoanalysis have forced us to revise our views on the pathology of neuroses." Hardly any attempt was made to effect changes in the original technique of psychoanalysis so as to improve the results.

Years ago, a great deal of emotional antagonism usually arose when the question of changing the psychoanalytical technique was raised. It appeared as if psychoanalysis had reached the peak of its perfection. When patients who were rehabilitated or improved by a reformed psychoanalytical technique were cited or demonstrated, critics would invariably say that the results were due to the personality of the therapist or to transference, but that the procedure in question had nothing to do with psychoanalysis. For a "psychoanalysis" that does not follow the rules of the standard technique and does not last a few years, is not a psychoanalysis.

Although the length of the psychoanalytic procedure and the rigidity of its technique were considered a major handicap by many psychoanalysts in the early days of the psychoanalytic movement, as well as today, attempts toward a reform of the cumbersome orthodox technique came only from "renegades" and "outsiders." We may mention here the works of Stekel, W. Reich, Horney, and Rank. Also the experiments with narcoanalysis, hypnoanalysis, and group analysis.

Stekel demanded that every new case should be considered as a psychiatric and therapeutic *novum* capable of overthrowing all existing views. And many years later, at a meeting devoted to the discussion of brief psychotherapy, Franz Alexander complained that many psychotherapists use the same technique in all their cases, selecting the cases on the basis of their technique rather than attempting to modify the technique to fit their cases. According to him, the detrimental results of this attitude are to be found in the fact that many cases are treated by a prolonged technique of psychoanalysis although they might be helped by briefer methods, and that the rigidity of technique and thinking hampers the free development of psychotherapy. Alexander believes that if the principle of flexibility in technique were generally adopted, psychoanalysts would not continue the treatment uninterruptedly over long periods.

In the past years several factors have been advanced to explain the drawbacks of the orthodox analytical procedure. Masserman, for example, maintains that psychoanalysts who use a special technique to study human behavior apply the same technique also as a therapeutic procedure. He calls this approach time-consuming, expensive, and, in many cases, unnecessary. According to Alexander, cases in which the therapeutic and investigative aims fully coincide represent a minority: "In the majority there is a varying discrepancy between these two objectives." He goes so far as to say that the application of the classical technique may even prove dangerous; it may be a psychic onus to which a patient may react not only with transitory, but even with permanent deterioration. Similarly, Oberndorf states that in some cases too persistent and too thorough a preoccupation with the unconscious may keep alive the inner strife in the patient's personality and may retard "those synthetic processes which make for ego integrity."

The views presented here, particularly the newer currents emanating from the group around Alexander, come very close to those expounded many years ago by Stekel and his school. It was Stekel who first warned that an *artificial psychoanalytical introversion* lasting for several years may lead to undesirable complications of the existing neurosis, and that it may even replace it by a "psychoanalytical" neurosis which may be harder to manage than the original one.

While in his days Stekel's views met with a unanimous rebuff by the orthodox school, today the trends toward relaxation of the orthodox routine can no longer be overlooked. A change is gradually taking place which deserves attention. This change is by no means unopposed. As matters stand, the new movement will have to do away with much resistance from the dogmatists of psychoanalysis before it will find a general recognition. Many terminological as well as technical differences will have to be clarified. One of the criticisms of the new trends is the same that was mentioned at the beginning: the method that uses a different technique is no psychoanalysis. In conformity with this view, the majority of the speakers at the "Brief Psychotherapy Council" (held in Chicago in 1942) in a tenacious adherence to the old standards, refused to identify any briefer method with the classical psychoanalysis and did not even deem it advisable to bestow upon the brief approach the name, Psychoanalysis.

What is psychoanalysis? To answer this question, we can use Freud's own definition in which the master stipulates that "any method of research acknowledging both transference and resistance, and proceeding from them, may consider itself as psychoanalysis, even if it reaches conclusions different from those of my method." Alexander is inclined to extend the definition of psychoanalysis "to all uncovering procedures which are based on the combination of emotional discharge, insight, and integration of the newly uncovered material." Psychoanalytic therapy, according to him, includes "all the uncovering types of procedure which aim at inviting unconscious material into consciousness and then helping the patient through interpretative work to bring these newly won psychodynamic quantities into harmony with the rest of his personality." The standard psychoanalytic technique is *only one* of the various procedures capable of achieving this aim.

We see that Freud and Alexander take a broader view in this matter than Kubie, e.g., who defines a psychoanalyst as "one who is a member in good standing of any Psychoanalytic Society which is in turn a member of the international body." In this question, we subscribe fully to the views expressed by Freud and Alexander. Neither the adherence to a particular society nor the application of a particular technique can be considered as the decisive criterion as to who is and who is not an analyst. Some psychiatrists even wonder if the much advertised uniformity of training in psychoanalysis is not one of the roots of the inbreeding and orthodoxy that has isolated psychoanalysis from the rest of medicine for so many decades.

Participants of the Brief Psychotherapy Council made an attempt to formulate the indications for a brief psychotherapy. The result of this endeavor is interesting, inasmuch as brief psychotherapy was acclaimed as a most useful and versatile method. Indeed, in glancing over the scope of indications for brief psychotherapy, one finds it so large that one wonders what conditions, if any, remain to be treated by the prolonged method.

Although the breadth of indications for brief psychotherapy as stipulated by the Brief Psychotherapy Council impresses us as being rather large, we are surprised to see that, on the other hand, the general opinion of the Council as to the therapeutic results of brief psychotherapy is well on the conservative side. Judging from the official report, most participants were inclined to believe that brief psychotherapy cannot effect complete and lasting cures.

As far as the "temporary results" of brief psychotherapy are concerned, those who apply the active, i.e., abbreviated form of psychoanalysis know that their rate of relapses after a successful treatment compares well with that of analysts who practice the orthodox method.

In his thirty years of experience with analysis, the author has had the opportunity to treat a great number of patients who developed "relapses" after having gone through one or more orthodox analyses. A complete absence of relapses cannot be claimed by any method of psychotherapy. Grotjahn reports that, of a small group of nine patients suffering from psychosomatic disorders, three were seen after a long psychoanalysis. Likewise, Oberndorf in one of his papers states that a patient first seen by him in consultation in 1929, "returned after having been psychoanalyzed for longer or shorter periods by four recognized analysts—all of whom had

had the benefit of organized psychoanalytical education."

It is known that some of our cases are chronically "relapsing." They concern individuals whose egos are poorly integrated and whose neurotic manifestations show recurring patterns. These people require medical aid and moral support as often as their symptoms reappear. We do well, therefore, in such cases if we suppress our narcissistic desire for "perfect cures" and offer our assistance whenever it is needed.

During the past decades, we have witnessed a great number of "brief psychotherapies" in their rise and fall: mesmerism, couéism, hypnotism, persuasion, suggestion, etc. It is not another brief psychotherapy that we need, but a *brief psychoanalysis*, a reformed, abbreviated psychoanalysis that is free of its ballast, and brought to an optimum of efficiency. The reform in question will also have an important social implication. It will render Freud's epochal discovery, which up to the present day has been a psychotherapy for the few, accessible to a majority of the people.

In evaluating the results of briefer forms of psychotherapy, a great deal of misunderstanding arises from the fact that brief psychotherapy is often confused with a psychotherapy which consists of a few sessions at long intervals. The latter form is practiced—by necessity—in mental hygiene clinics. Indeed, the psychotherapy most orthodox analysts use in clinics is not a "minor psychoanalysis," but genuine freudian psychoanalysis arbitrarily abbreviated by the individual psychoanalyst to suit the situation. We must bear in mind that the average analyst never has been really trained for an abbreviated form of psychoanalysis. If in the clinic he uses the method he has been trained to apply, he is soon likely to get into difficulties with the patient's transference and resistance, and then, discouraged and disillusioned, he may be ready to give up most of the accepted rules and to practice his own individual brand of psychotherapy. Just as it is impossible to adapt father's suit to fit the young son by merely cutting down the length of the sleeves and the pants, so it is impossible to apply the complicated freudian technique to hospital work. As a matter of fact, the Brief Psychotherapy Council was arranged principally for the purpose of discussing the most effective therapeutic application of psychoanalytical knowledge to clinics and hospitals. Unfortunately, instead of changing the technique so that the standards of individual psychology would be maintained, and—at the same time—the difficulties of the hospital routine overcome, the Council made another attempt to select cases that would suit a brief psychotherapy. However, the Council was neither able to establish an exact technique of, nor to recommend uniformly an exact indication for the brief psychotherapy. Therefore let us repeat: *brief psychoanalysis* and not a vague "brief psychotherapy" is the answer to our problem.

We attempted to demonstrate how *a reform of the technique of interpretation* of the analytical material may improve the current psychoanalytic procedure. By virtue of this reform, some of the limitations of the method may be reduced or eliminated. Our method offers a way in which the individual treatment can be shortened while the theoretical criteria of the classical psychoanalysis, such as the management of transference, resistance, etc., as well as practical arrangements, such as the five-sessions-a-week system, etc., are maintained.

We have shown that the interpretation of dreams is the most suitable example of how analytical material can be utilized in an economic way. Today a decline in the use of dream interpretation by psychoanalysis is clearly noticeable.

One of the causes of this decline seems to lie in the fact that, of all theories advanced by Freud, that of dream interpretation has undergone the fewest improvements and that the technique of dream analysis remained old-fashioned in many respects. Today, as in bygone days, the most time-consuming element in psychoanalysis is the system of "free associations." On the other hand, some analysts in interpreting analytical material tend toward over-simplification and the use of old and well-worn clichés. Fenichel, for instance, states apodictically: "Anxiety aroused by going out onto the streets is a defense against exhibitionism." (Always?) And R. Fliess interprets the superstition of knocking on wood three times as follows: "Wood = mother; finger = penis; and three = male genitalia." Bertram Lewin's interpretation of "nothing" as meaning "the female genital" was mentioned on page 150. Such an interpretation of symptoms and symbols, based on generalizations and portraying the analyst's own associations rather than those of the patient, cannot contribute a great deal to the progress in the science of psychoanalysis. It leads to a demand for a more clinical, inductive approach to analytical problems and for less arm-chair speculation.

This demand can be met by a change in our system of interpretation. In order to comprehend the deeper meaning of a dream, the analyst must first expose himself passively to its manifest content. He must detach himself spiritually from all he has learned about symbolism and concentrate exclusively upon the reproduced drama of the dream. If he keeps his mind flexible, he will soon obtain a suitable point of "entry" into the hidden content of the dream.

"Free Associations"

In the technique of analysis as used by Freud, the analyst is dependent upon the associations of the patient to a very high degree. The collection of the material in this way consumes a great part of the time devoted to the treatment. After the patient has given associations hour after hour and week after week, the analyst has to pick out the relevant data and the "common motives" of this material for use in his interpretation and deeper research. He does it to the best of his knowledge, skill, and belief, but here is the point where he already is acting deliberately and opens the door to all kinds of preconceived ideas.

Another difficulty lies in the fact that patients often prepare their associations in advance, particularly in cases which do not yield to short treatment.

One may maintain that any association, even an arbitrarily constructed one, is a part of the patient's personality and hence represents a valid analytic material. Indeed, this cannot be denied. However, insofar as this uncooperative way of associating represents a form of resistance and interferes with the progress of the treatment, it must be rejected. While the doctor may be pleased by the apparent abundance of the "material," the analysis revolves for weeks and months and years around well-known problems and well-worn phrases. This is all the more true in cases of patients who have been under analysis for a long time, who are familiar with the analytical terminology and problems, or who, as often happens, have studied analytic literature, books on dream interpretation, etc. In these books they obtain the weapons which they use cleverly in their everyday battle against their doctor. Only a very inexperienced or a very passive analyst can consider this kind of cooperation helpful.

The active method, which enables us to dispose of the patient's associations at times, must, therefore, shorten the duration of the treatment, a fact of important economic and psychological significance.

It should not be understood that we always decline to hear the patient's associations. On the contrary, we often make use of them. What we are attempting, however, is to render our work as independent and unprejudiced as possible.

We also realize that knowledge of the dream content has no value for the patient unless it is combined with emotional reactions. Merely being told or merely accepting intellectually what one is told counts for very little. It is not the knowledge or belief which matters. In the buried material of the patient's unconscious we find ideas which are charged with emotion and yet are not accessible to consciousness. It is this emotion that has to be discharged by the patient. In the standard form of psychoanalysis much comes to the analyst's attention over a long period of time. But transference is also at work all the time and much is resolved without being detected. Lowy states correctly, therefore, that "in the shortened, so-called active forms of psychotherapy, such neglect of important psychic contents is not permissible."

We always attempt to get our interpretation as far as possible without the help of the patient. We try to find out the relevant unconscious connections of the dream by the application of experience and intuition. And indeed, despite the rules dream research was able to establish, interpretation of dreams will always remain an artistic task requiring a high degree of intuition and depending upon the skill of the individual interpreter. Our technique endeavors to overcome the circumstantial method of examining the chains of "free associations." We ask the patient to produce associations with those passages which cannot be understood in any other way.

It has been pointed out that if the analyst succeeded in making his interpretations more independent of the patient's associations, without sacrificing the scientific basis of his work and without engaging in a mechanistic "reading" of symbols, he would undoubtedly shorten the duration of the average treatment. As stated above, he would not have to renounce associations altogether; but associations would be restricted to those points only where an independent analysis is impossible. This applies to the psychoanalytical material in general as well as to the dream material in particular.

The argument that only the use of free associations makes an interpretation scientific is not valid. It would be justified if we were dealing with patients who cooperate and not, as is well known and expressed in the theory of "analytical resistance," with patients who are guarding their secrets and their neurotic positions which guarantee them a relative mental equilibrium *within* their neurosis. They are always ready, if given the chance, to sabotage the therapeutic efforts of their analyst, and the easiest and commonly accepted way to do this is to offer the analyst non-essential or pre-censored information. While collecting the patient's "free associations" (which are supposed to be the ultimate authority for the analytical work), we find that the patients soon become aware of the problems in which the analyst is particularly interested, and that, consciously or unconsciously, they adjust their tactics to those of their analyst. They select from the vast reservoir of their recollections those which they deem important for the analyst, and they are particularly clever at applying this technique of associating when they notice that the analyst is on a wrong track. Indeed, patients who have undergone treatments, or who have read analytical literature previously, are excellently equipped for leading the analyst astray. The constant struggle with the physician for the precious possession of the neurosis affords the patient an ultimate triumph which is all the more impressive the more time and means have been consumed for the treatment. Judging from reports of patients, there is nothing so absurd that it cannot be presented as an "association," or cannot be accepted as an "interpretation" by the patient, particularly when the latter is in a state of transference.

It cannot be denied that every association, even a constructed one, may have its value, since it is a part of the patient's mind under investigation. It is equally true, however, that it may also be used as "analytical material," just as dreams and other mental phenomena studied during analysis. This characteristic of the associations, namely, that they, too, can be analyzed, opens for the patient the possibility of driving the analysis consciously or unconsciously onto sidetracks and developing a kind of geometrical progression of associations—a situation which, in reality, occurs not infrequently. All we have to do is to analyze the patient's associations by the use of additional associations, and to repeat the same procedure with the additional associations. It is indeed doubtful whether this way of analyzing secures a thorough scientific study of the case, but it is not doubtful that it leads to a tremendous consumption of time and effort.

What value have associations even if they are free? In the general analytic production, associations are the matrix from which useful material can be drawn. Let us take an ideal case. The patient is cooperative and offers associations in abundance. Do they represent the pathogenic complexes we desire to discover? No. The analyst's effort is directed towards the discovering of common motives and intermediate thoughts, in other words, he attempts to elucidate the occult relations between the unconscious material and the associations produced. The analyst operates with the working hypothesis that the associated ideas point toward the unconscious problems of the patient, that they have an underground connection with the latent material of the neurosis. At this point any analyst may be subject to arbitrary judgment, because there is no authority outside of his knowledge of the case, his experience, and his intuition that would tell him which parts of the reports he may accept and which he may reject.

Unfortunately, the average analyst is rarely free from bias. Glover speaks of "residual training transferences," of "traditions," and of a "moralistic satisfaction" to be obtained by the analyst from having expressed orthodox views which may hamper the doctor's usual clinical acumen in evaluating the patient's material.

Many analysts allow for occasional exceptions in the conduct of the analysis. Oberndorf, for example, mentions two cases he treated with "heretic" brevity. Some doctors (Abraham) tend to relax the free association rule. Others do not mind asking questions or selecting analogies in order to foster the production of material. But a large group still favors a more perfectionistic, passive attitude and refuses to be more spontaneous in the conduct of the analysis. To use Glover's term, they often "feel guilty" in having been too spontaneous. On the other hand, they may also feel guilty if the analysis lasts too long. Glover says, "Analysts no doubt feel that lengthy analyses reflect on their technique."

In his *Supplements*, Freud admits that the interpretation of symbolic elements of the dream often remains independent of the dreamer's associations and that they are to be explained by "auxiliary" methods of dream interpretation. He further emphasizes the fact that the so-called "typical dreams" offer very meager material for associations. The analyst is forced to use other ways of investigation in order to gain insight into their latent contents.

Freud himself often made use of an active method, and it is he who quotes a dream analysis of one of his disciples, Rank, who also refused to pay attention to associations. Freud says, "This emission-dream allowed for an interpretation going into the last details after a generous renunciation of the dreamer's contribution. . . ."

In his *Interpretation of Dreams*, Freud mentions, in one instance, that he did not ask the patient for associations to the dream because he knew the dreamer's personal relations. He thus succeeded in interpreting parts of the dream "independently."

We see that even the master himself sometimes refuses to pay attention to associations and relies solely upon his intuition and knowledge of the case. He realizes the difficulties of scientific dream interpretation and tries to face them. He states: "It is nothing miraculous when, in associating, one arrives at a certain point, proceeding from a single dream element. It is possible to associate something to any idea; however, using this aimless and arbitrary chain of thoughts, one might easily become a prey of self-deception. In all that there is arbitrariness and making use of chance and one can, in this way, breed out any interpretation to any dream."

Freud then defends his theory against the above objections. He believes that it cannot be a mere chance that the amazing connections of the single dream elements with others offer such clear explanations for the dream; or that the explanation of symptoms by the use of dream interpretation can remove them. He claims that there is no "aimless" thinking, etc.

The objections show, however, that there are many very important points of attack, even in that "orthodox" method of dream interpretation which relies on the patient's associations to such great extent. In reality the orthodox psychoanalysts are unable to leave the patient's associations "free." They are continually influencing them by involuntarily putting in suggestions. An association which is supposed to be the sole and ultimate authority and the touchstone of interpretation often proves to be a deliberate construction, intended to oblige the physician. That is why the patients of Adler often associate social problems, those of Jung, archaic patterns, and the patients of Freud, castration ideas.

Sadger, one of the oldest disciples of Freud, offers good evidence of this. He keeps shorthand records of his case histories. He reports a case in which the patient repeatedly dreams [593] of *a woman with an emaciated thorax who held a shawl or a curtain in front of her chest. In his dream the patient wanted to pull it aside in order to find out where her nice bosom was.*

The patient interprets this emaciated woman as being "naturally" his mother, who used to be like that before her breast was amputated—the patient interprets "castrated"—as a consequence of cancer. "Perhaps" when he was a baby his mother held a shawl to her nude breast, and then left it a bit open. . . . He then fancies that "probably" he has acquired a certain technique of using his lips or his tongue by sucking, and concludes psychoanalytically that his habit later led to his stuttering. . . . In a similar way he confesses that when he sucked a woman's mammilla he used to "break her bosom," so to speak, by lifting the lower part of it in order to put it into his mouth. This is, according to the patient, also a kind of castration.

We must not forget that this report is based upon a shorthand record of the patient's "free associations." The unprejudiced observer will conclude that the patient in his "free associations" undoubtedly reported what he believed to be a verification of his analyst's wild theories. He did his analyst "a favor" by associating all the stuff and nonsense his analyst wanted him to bring out.

And now let us raise the following questions: How deeply can we penetrate the unconscious unaided by the patient's free associations? Aren't we forced to remain within the sphere of the conscious material if we apply a more active technique?

In order to answer these questions we must bear in mind that we have no reliable standards to judge which analytical findings are "profound" and which are "superficial." The opinions concerning this matter vary, primarily for terminological reasons. It may be claimed that our interpretations will deserve the name of being deep only if we succeed in connecting the symbolisms with an early stage of the patient's psychosexual development; or if we descend to the lowest level of the unconscious and to the most primordial impulses; or if we establish a relation with the earliest analogous childhood situation. (Descending to a deep level then would mean going as far back as possible in the patient's life history in order to discover the earliest infantile pattern for the present-day reaction.) In Glover's questionnaire "the answers to the questions about 'depth' were the least satisfactory of all returned."

Stekel repeatedly pointed out that although it appears to be true that most neurotic situations of the present seem to be founded on infantile patterns, we may doubt whether it is right to consider neurotic manifestations always *sub specie* of early infantile experiences, as if our present life derived its emotional character exclusively from the past. But even if our present life were an exact replica of the past, experience teaches that we can arrest the patient's neurotic development on whatever level (infantile or adult) we liberate the patient's pathogenic complexes from their neurotic encapsulment. Today, we realize that a reconstruction of an analogous childhood situation does not exclude the possibility that a great number of problems of the latent material, and perhaps *the basic pathogenic conflict* (which is the real "deepest root"), remain undisclosed. We should, therefore, be more exact with regard to the interpretation if we changed the question "deep or superficial" into the question "correct or incorrect" depending on whether or not, in the interpretation, the pathogenic problems contained in the symptom or symbol had been disclosed. Since we do not know what element of our analytical work deserves the merit of being *the* curative weapon, we cannot even claim that it is the depth of our interpretation. It seems, therefore, that all we need is to discover the disturbing complexes, to establish the relative role they play in the patient's neurosis, and to contribute passively and actively to their solution, regardless of whether or not we have followed them as far back as the mother's womb.

We believe that a reform of dream analysis will greatly contribute to the shortening of the average psychoanalytical treatment and will, among other things, render the method much more suitable to the use in the hospital practice.

In the following we shall demonstrate how one-sided an analyst can be even if he uses the method of free associations, and how difficult the objective evaluation of the analytical material may become. Let us select Sharpe's dream book for our purpose. Her book is based on lectures on dream interpretation which she delivered at the London Institute of Psychoanalysis from 1934 to 1936. It is one of the latest textbooks on the subject. Her method reflects the approach to dreams as it is used and taught by the freudian school, and that is why it is quoted here.

Sharpe's patient is an American girl who was *three years* in analysis with her. We are not informed about her diagnosis. From the description of the case, however, we assume that the patient suffered from periodical depressions connected with agitation. According to Sharpe, the patient's "major neurotic breakdown" (the first attack?) occurred in early womanhood. At the time when she first came for treatment with the analyst, and for months thereafter, she was not able to go out alone.

The analysis, the author says, was "very incomplete" (after three years!) but the depressions passed and her anxiety was alleviated. (Remission?) The patient married. She came for treatment again after eight years (recurrent attack?). She was depressed and agitated and showed again her old agoraphobia; but this time she motivated it by her urge to keep on urinating.

The analyst tells us a few facts from the patient's life. She was the daughter of a medical officer in residence at an asylum. There were serious disagreements between her parents. Her mother was absent from home most of the time, and the patient was left in the care of a nurse.

At the time of the second analysis, we learn from the patient's associations that her mother was about to return home. Then, without transition and apparently following the patient's swerving associations, the analyst talks about the patient's sister who had been away for years and has now returned home with a child born abroad. Then again, the patient's associations and the analyst's report switch, and the problem of urination is discussed. The patient recalls a cat which urinated "all over the house" because of a bladder disease. She also remembers having seen in her husband's waiting room (patient's husband was a doctor) a lady who urinated on the floor. The patient is able "at this point" to recognize that her fear of passing water is "the same" as she had experienced when a child. At that time, she used to call her nurse, "Quick, Nannie, quick!"

In one of the first few hours of the second analysis the patient brings the following dream:

[594] *"I was in a bedroom and a man was giving a woman some wine and I wanted some. He didn't give me any but he came over to my bed and kissed me. I woke up feeling happier."*

The patient, in associating, reports that when her sister arrived with the little baby, she did not want to see her at all and felt "like breaking down and crying my eyes out." We do not get any information as to why the patient did not want to see her sister, why—strangely enough—she was near a breakdown upon seeing her. The reader feels that apparently some important conflict about which we know nothing had existed between the sisters. Instead of elaborating on the topic introduced by the patient, the analyst turns unexpectedly to the aforementioned cat. The cat was a nuisance. It occupied the patient's entire attention. She tells of how little attention her sister's child actually required (again, the trend of the associations is directed toward the patient's sister, but it passes unheeded!) and emphasizes that despite this fact, she seemed to feel at that time "as though the whole family had descended upon her." She wished to be alone with her husband.

Then we hear that about the same time her mother had returned. She invited the patient repeatedly to parties, etc., not knowing that because of her phobia she was unable to attend. At last the patient told her mother about her trouble and was "amazed that she was kind and understanding." She even gave the patient money for the analysis. "Poor mother. I feel sorry for her. Why, instead of being sorry for myself, should I feel sorry for her? She is well and independent and has a gay life."

After this detail, two more or less incoherent episodes were

reported: one was about the patient's excitement when she
had to wait in a store; the other was about her last holiday
when a storm broke out and the rain flooded her room. At this
point a childhood recollection was reported. She would go to
her parents' bed in the morning frequently. "That's strange
to think of—as strange as thinking that mother once fed me
as a baby. I shouldn't think my sister will have more babies."
Again, the sudden association of her sister which is disregarded by the analyst. Instead of following this path, the
author dwells on the patient's casual remark about her father
being very fond of her.

This was the material comprising several sessions before
the dream occurred and the session after the dream. Sharpe
then proceeded to the interpretation. She made the patient
realize that her panic had its early setting in childhood; that
her urinating phobia was due to an "aggressive fantasy of
destroying by water." She pointed out "the rivalry with the
mother for the father's wine, and the correlation of this
rivalry with her impatience at the store." (?) The phrase "be
quick, I'm going to urinate" was identical with her "rage at
not being given what she wanted when she was a baby," and
the act of micturition "was a hostile act against her mother."
The author showed the patient why she felt sorry for her
mother; it was because of her having caused her mother—
omnipotently—to stay away when the patient was little, and
to have no more children after she was born.

In looking over the material of the dream and the results
obtained through this interpretation, the reader cannot help
feeling that this analysis, despite the apparent abundance of
associations delivered and discussed, was not free from bias
and was incomplete. Even if the author's interpretation was
right and micturition was a substitute for destroying, the
material presented in the associations (a cat and a woman
urinating) is not sufficient evidence for such an interpretation. Above all, it is by no means clear in what way, if any,
the problem of micturition is connected with the dream re-

ported by the patient. We hear that the bedroom scene means a jealousy scene and the bedroom, in reality, is that of the patient's parents. This interpretation may be correct; but we have hardly any material on which to base it. We must, therefore, assume that the analyst interpreted the dream scene by connecting with it—arbitrarily—the patient's remark about going to her parents' bed frequently when she was a baby.

We know that the patient was with her father most of the time, while her mother was absent, and that her parents did not care very much for each other. Therefore, in Sharpe's analysis, the patient's jealousy of her mother does not seem to be sufficiently motivated. No part of the patient's associations indicates it. Besides, in the dream, she does not get father's "wine," to be sure, but she gets a kiss from him and feels "happier." Nothing in the dream shows destructive hostility. We see only a desire for whatever the wine may symbolize and a kiss as a happy ending.

However, let us for a moment accept Sharpe's interpretation. What is its essence? What were the ultimate pathogenic findings of the dream? The Oedipus situation. Her sister complex was persistently neglected, although the patient brought important information in this direction.

If we take the patient's material into consideration, especially the association of her sister to the woman in the bedroom, the patient's reaction toward her sister's baby, her feeling that the whole family was descending upon her when her sister arrived, and her desire to be alone "with no one to interfere,"—we may surmise that the dream dramatizes the patient's envy of her sister. Of course, a further investigation would have to be directed toward ascertaining this conjecture through a careful study of further communications. The analyst would necessarily also have to clarify the role the sister's husband was playing in the patient's life (the kissing scene is suspicious in this respect). It seems that the patient was envying her sister her peaceful life, her happy marriage and her child, while her own life was miserable, frustrated, and filled with the silly desire to urinate, an impulse, which, incidentally, may with equal right be considered as a symbol of the repressed sexual impulse. Perhaps the envy she felt toward her sister was a new edition of the envy she once felt toward her mother. (We heard her say about her mother, "She is well and independent and has a gay life.") It would have only meant that some of her life situations followed infantile patterns.

We do not maintain that the analysis attempted here is "better" than that presented by Sharpe. What we wish to demonstrate is merely that, in interpretations, even an analyst who uses associations profusely cannot avoid *selecting* the material. Sharpe incorporates revelations made on previous occasions into her material; on the other hand, she disregards associations which, to her, apparently do not seem sufficiently important. Whatever the reason for her doing so may be, a dream analysis such as that shown here helps us to correct our opinion about the ultimate authority of associations.

We must free ourselves from the influences of our psychological schools.

An example of such a biased dream interpretation is that published by Richard Sterba under the title, "Dream and Acting-out."

The circumstances of the dream: one evening a man fell and fractured his right elbow while he was on the way to his appointment with the analyst. He came to the doctor's office in severe pain and without having had his arm x-rayed or treated. He described how, while carefully making his way over the slippery sidewalk, he had stumbled over a step with which he was quite familiar. He then narrated a dream from the preceding night. Sterba wants to prove that certain dreams occurring during the night influence the patient's behavior during the day, that the dreamer acts out what he has experienced in the dream. Usually we hear about experiences which were transformed into dreams. Sterba describes (a point which is well taken) that sometimes dreams affect our actions.

But look at his interpretation! It is biased by preconceived ideas. Not only does he give preference and accentuation to unimportant material, but he overlooks important material by concentrating on the unessential. The dream is as follows:

[596] *A little boy damaged the right front fender of a car. A little girl stood in front of a building, a house or a hospital. Two men carried the seemingly injured or ill girl into the building.*

There are three pictures here: (a) a boy damages the right front fender of a car; (b) a little girl stands in front of a building; and (c) two men carry the seemingly injured girl into the building.

The following interpretation is offered by Sterba. You know what importance orthodox Freudians attribute to castration. When the analyst heard the "front" fender of the car was injured, the fate of the case was sealed. Castration wishes and retaliation in kind were "immediately revealed."

What does this mean? The patient may have been a student of Freud, for he "immediately revealed" what he knew his analyst would immediately accept. Some of us may not realize immediately that the "damaged front fender of the car" means castrating father. The patient recognized *himself* (correctly) in the little boy, and he also recognized the damaged car as his father's property. That means automatically that his father's penis was castrated. By stumbling and falling next day he acts out the retaliation for his oedipal wishes. A very interesting thought, but the question is still open as to whether or not the retaliation is really due to castration wishes.

A girl is carried into the hospital. The analyst interprets this girl as the patient, because she was injured. The patient becomes a girl, i.e., castrated.

And now let us look closer at this dream. Simplifying the manifest content of the dream we may say that the patient (the little boy) *has done something forbidden* (he has damaged a car). Putting it in a more general way, we may say that he has *committed an injury* to something (*a*).

In the next part of the dream we see a *girl injured*. We must ask ourselves if the car may not represent the girl (*b*).

Our formula *a + b* indicates a succession of two seemingly unrelated incidents. According to page 253 ("Succession and Coexistence"), we must examine the dream also in view of the possibility that *a + b* indicates *b because of a,* in other words, that the two events are related to each other by way of a causality.

Is the interpretation of the "car" as "father" self-evident? We speak of a car as a "she." The fact that the car "belongs to the father" could make it a symbol of the mother, because the mother belongs, so to speak, to the father. And, certainly, a car is something into which you put things and into which you put yourself. It is well-suited for a female symbol.

The car as a driving force may, of course, represent the penis, power, and aggression.

We do not say that our interpretation is right and Sterba's wrong. We are submitting to you a number of equally valid ways of interpreting this dream. For this interpretation makes sense, too. At this point we may suppose that the patient has aggressive ideas about women, possibly about little girls. Because of these aggressive ideas he has a feeling of guilt and he punishes himself by breaking his extremity. This fracture may, of course, represent an equivalent of self-castration. If we can prove this through other analytic material, our interpretation will stand up against any forced clichés such as the idea of castrating father. Suppose this boy suffered from impotence as a protection against his aggressive impulses directed toward little girls. We see, in fact, a girl injured; we see her carried into the hospital.

Experienced interpreters will consider a dream in which the dreamer sees himself as a little boy, a retrospective dream.

Dreams of this type usually refer to events which have taken place in the dreamer's past. In our case one can say that in the dream the patient makes the following confession: "As a little boy I have done injury to the front organ of a little girl (sister?). I have guilt feelings and a wish for self-punishment." (Self-castration?)

This probable latent dream content remains unrevealed. Instead, the patient reveals immediately the old cliché of the Oedipus complex which we all have had at one time or another to a higher or lower degree. The patient comes under the influence of transference and becomes the teacher's little apple polisher. He does him favors and associates active castration wishes.

He will also accept his analyst's views not because they are true, but because he wants to please him. And if the man falls into this trap, this can only happen at the expense of the therapeutic result. Time will be wasted with trivial generalities. Contrary to this, our own interpretation refers to a specific event with a specific guilt which may have been triggered off by analysis. The dream reveals it to the analyst; but it remains unheeded.

Suppose the patient really has a castration complex. The analyst did not investigate the possibility that guilt other than the oedipal may be hidden behind the castration complex. He saw in the next part of the dream that the little girl who was standing in front of the building was carried into the hospital; he interpreted this part as meaning that the patient saw himself as a victim of castration. For it was he and not the girl who was injured and carried into the hospital. Emasculation (castration) makes the boy change into a girl.

In the orthodox interpretation, this dream seems to represent only one of the psychic dynamisms. We wish to emphasize that we do not doubt that the dream has a connection with the patient's injury, and it is quite possible (and probable) that a castration wish toward the patient's father really existed. But if we accept an interpretation on such a general level we take the risk of overlooking other important material.

We should, therefore, propose the following interpretation of the aforementioned dream: The patient sees himself as a little boy, i.e., at *a time of his life* when he was a little boy. We shall call this part of the dream the "reference to the past." We then continue: "While a little boy, he did something 'wrong'."

And now, instead of assuming that a transformation of the boy into a girl has taken place—which is rather artificial—we can assume that, as in the dream, this forbidden act committed by the boy, and the injury which, according to the dream, was sustained by the girl, occurred simultaneously. To us the dreamer confesses that, as a consequence of the boy's action, a little girl was injured. We then look for details, one of which is the reference to the fact that the injury has affected a "front part" of the "car."

At this point we could stop and ask for associations, but only if the patient is not too far indoctrinated with analysis. He ought to give us some information—regarding his sister, for instance, if he has one. Under all circumstances we would make, at this point, a mental note with regard to the experience we suspect, namely, defloration of a girl, probably his own sister. We must remember that in the dream the right front fender was not broken off (castration) but "damaged." This may be of value for the interpretation of the symbol.

(Q) "Can both interpretations be correct?"

(A) Yes. I have mentioned (page 31) that a dream always fulfills several concurrent wishes and represents several trends simultaneously. We called it the principle of functional economy. You can imagine how economically we are operating if by making several cross sections through a dream we raise to consciousness several trends in the patient.

As stated before, even in the most passive approach to the dream, we are forced to select from the associations the patient produces those which we consider important. Without having a special technique at our disposal which enables us to select the right associations, we are floating on a sea of possibilities.

It is important for the active treatment that we proceed in analysis according to the dream material. The active analyst knows what he is going to discuss with his patient during the session because the dream will tell it to him. If he notices that the patient's report deviates from the topic expressed in the dream, the analyst will censor his association and ask him to go back to the particular factors of the dream. The patient's associations will not be completely free, but, to a certain extent, supervised. Of course, the patient's attempt to switch onto a sidetrack and to bring us away from the main problem has in itself diagnostic importance.

Analytic literature abounds in interpretations which reflect the indoctrination of the patients with psychoanalytic theories. Associations of patients who have this kind of education are often worthless. They do not prove anything except the tractability of the neurotic patients. Numerous examples of such forced interpretations can be found in the recently published book by Charles Berg, *Deep Analysis*.

Take for example the following dream [597], in which the patient *saw himself having a tooth out.*

What does it mean to have a tooth out? Berg quotes the patient as saying that in his dream it did not matter whether he would keep the tooth and endure the pain or have it out. He felt that in either case he would have to face a tough situation. And then, after referring to his emotional tie with his father, the patient abruptly says in effect that he has been masturbating because he wants to re-experience his love for his father. This, "of course," is responsible for his lack of love for women.

Everything here is so natural and—by mere coincidence—Freud's statement that dreams of losing teeth mean masturbation is confirmed by the patient himself.

But even Freud declared that he found it exceedingly hard to analyze typical dreams. Berg offers further examples of his "deep analysis" of dreams. One night the patient had two dreams.

In one of them [597] *he saw himself standing next to a dry dock. A man approached him, then turned away and then jumped into the dock. The patient followed him because he felt he was obligated to do so. He had a passing thought that he should catch the man in mid-air and pull him aboard. However, he was terrified by the thought of falling to the bottom, and he woke up.*

Then the patient went to sleep again and dreamed [598] *that he was back in college with his friend, Ian. He remarked how nice it was to be back in the old college. Later they went into Ian's room. There Ian fell ill and became unconscious. A doctor came in and examined him. The patient saw a "funny little pig or piglet" which kept running about and trying to squeeze under the door. Then Ian regained consciousness and the patient became overjoyed. Ian came to while lying on top of the patient; the latter tried to insert his organ, at which time he had an emission.*

The analyst then asks the patient to associate to the "dry dock." The patient thinks of "graving dock" and connects "graving" with "grave," his own grave, into which he might have fallen had he not awakened. And then, "of course," he recognizes the hole in the ground as a female symbol. He also is able to identify the man who jumped into the dock. It "must have been my organ."

Regarding his second dream, the patient meditates that Ian, with whom he entered the room and who later became ill, must have been "my damned organ again." He did not know the meaning of the piglet and suspected that it represented his "pre-pubertal virility," i.e., that form of sexual activity which has not yet been curtailed by castration.

In another dream [599] the patient *sees himself in a large hall. A great all-day organ recital is to take place there, and all people are looking forward to it with interest.*

Of the "great hall," the patient says that it represents the interior of his mother. At the thought of the "great organ recital," he bursts into laughter and says significantly that it was his father who was to perform. The patient obtained sexual gratification in this way and succeeded in avoiding anxiety. These are his own observations. Listening to this type of association you may think that an analyst and not a patient is talking.

Such a production of material can be used as proof for anything, any success and any failure. The truth is that it is biased, that it is in the best case presented by a patient who is biased; but this is not scientific material.

One more dream and we will be done with it. Berg narrates that after having obtained material which suggested the "primal scene," the patient, in his dream [600] *is in a taxi with a woman whom he soon approaches sexually. However, he does not find excitement. He is so bored, in fact, that he is not sorry to find himself in an upstairs room in a house in Poland.*

This he immediately interprets as the land of the Po.[1] He insists, however, that it is an "independent Poland," where everybody can use his po independently, i.e., without interference.

The doctor interprets this as a good sign which indicates that the patient is about to become independent of his anal childhood fixations. The narration then goes on.

Above the door the patient sees an inscription welcoming him and wishing him a good time inside.

This is observed as a regression from the "frustrated" Oedipus level to the relatively "unfrustrated" anal erotic level. The interpretation infers that the patient, whose regression into his mother's womb has apparently been frustrated, is expressing a desire to regress into the relatively more receptive rectum.

We could go on in this way, but these examples of applica-

[1] "Po" or "popo" is an expression used in some parts of Europe for "buttocks."

tion of "free associations," the "basic rule" of freudian analysis, should suffice.

A scientifically applied dream analysis will enable you to avoid these pitfalls. You will then probably interpret much less; but what you will interpret will show more realism and will be more closely connected with the case, with life, and with the problems with which the patient is struggling. You may be called "superficial" by the "profound" ones, because you will not go as far back as the mother's womb or the father's rectum, but you will get insight into the main conflicts of the patient so that they can be solved analytically. If you are of the opinion that the neurosis is the result of mental conflicts, and if your goal is to discover the relevant conflicts, to expose them, and to help the patient solve them, your aim is clear, your endeavor to the point, and it has all the earmarks of a clinical procedure.

(Q) "May I ask you a question? How can you give insight to a patient without indoctrinating him to a certain degree?"

(A) The answer to this important question is that we make all efforts *not* to indoctrinate the patient. All we do is to instruct him gradually in the art of clinical thinking in order to form a common platform for the therapeutic teamwork. In other words, what we wish for is: cooperation and teamwork, but not indoctrination with preconceived ideas.

It is wrong to work with clichés, even when dealing with so-called "typical dreams," such as those about loss of teeth, or the like. In the specific case we must find the specific meaning. We must learn to evaluate the patient's associations in such a way that we do not become guilty of influencing the results or of permitting ourselves to be fed commonplaces dressed in psychoanalytic jargon.

(Q) "I should still insist on my original question. I am sure that you frequently have had patients, particularly intelligent patients, who have done a great deal of reading about psychoanalysis. Following the standard procedure, you ask them to associate and then you get their associations which are influenced by analytic knowledge. Now, how do you proceed from there?"

(A) One of the understandable side-effects of the current psychoanalytic mass indoctrination of the American public is that many of our patients are psychoanalytically well-informed. As stated before, associations based on reading are as good as worthless. Sometimes we must interpret *despite* associations. This is not merely a matter of theory. This is a policy based on experience. You all know how difficult it is to analyze a person who has had some training before or who has read a great deal. Some time ago we went through quite an ordeal in treating an analyst who was unable to produce spontaneous associations. He offered interpretations exclusively. He was treating his own condition as though he were treating another person's; and yet he constantly overlooked his main problems. In addition, he neutralized all his emotional responses encountered in analysis, and over-intellectualized the interpretations. It is in this type of case that an independent dream analysis is of such great help since it allows us to check the patient's veracity before his associations are accepted as clinical material. One of our patients developed a special phobia on the basis of his psychoanalytic information. He read somewhere that psychotics dream about incest openly. He reacted with severe anxiety whenever he had a more transparent incestuous dream.

(Q) "Some analysts claim that interpretations at first just peel off and are not accepted and, therefore, no harm can be done by them even if they are incorrect. Is this true?"

(A) That depends on circumstances. The problem of timing interpretations is very important. The general rule is that to interpret anything you must first know the dynamics. Our interpretations, as a rule, are done in a very casual way. We drop a word here or there. We don't give lectures. Proceeding in this way, the harm cannot be too great even if our interpretation happens to be wrong. But we must strive toward a complete understanding of the case, or of a given mechanism, before we venture an opinion or an interpretation. The circumstantial evidence must be unequivocal in any case, and our opinion must be based on knowledge and not on guesses.

Applying as we do an improved technique of interpretation, we are able to understand some of the patient's problems at a very early time. However, in active psychoanalysis we must be cautious not to let the patient surmise what we know; that requires restraint on our part. We all are, as a rule, so proud of what we know that we would like to tell it to the patient right away. But we must use good judgment and time our interpretations properly.

To know when and what to interpret is one of the most difficult skills in analysis. It can be acquired only through prolonged training. All of us are likely to make mistakes in this respect in the beginning, and to offer our interpretations too soon. This may cause undesirable reactions in the patient. Those of us who practice the short-term psychotherapy must be doubly careful not to provoke any undesirable situations.

(Q) "For an interpretation to be of therapeutic value, is it necessary that it be absolutely correct?"

(A) It depends on what you call correct. In our opinion, to be correct means to reveal a part of the patient's real problem. Of course, an "absolutely correct" interpretation is just as much an ideal as an absolutely correct idea or theory. We are using a scientific approach to explore the patient's unconscious. We confront the patient with the evidence offered by his own revelations. In our interpretation we may not have covered the entire area, but we may still be "right." If you and I are looking at New York Harbor, you may notice a Dutch ship at anchor while I may see the Statue of Liberty. We are both right. But a master is he who sees the essential, the genuine motive hidden behind the images and distortions of the dream.

Although we use the active method of psychoanalysis, we, too, interpret as late as possible. The fact that we know an interpretation soon does not entitle us to use it, unless the therapeutic situation warrants it. One of the requirements of the trained psychotherapist is to be able to control his own emotions, particularly his narcissism and sadism. Narcissism is displayed when the analyst, in order to show how "good" he is, reveals his knowledge too soon. Sadism may be seen when the analyst in his premature interpretations desires to demonstrate how "bad" the patient is. The latter view is not justified even theoretically, because in analysis we must also be able to reveal to the patient not only his catagogic, base instincts, but also his anagogic, uplifting tendencies which are in the service of his superego.

(Q) "Can all dreams be interpreted?"

(A) Unfortunately, they cannot. We must admit that sometimes we cannot find the proper interpretation despite all our effort. At other times, interpretations do not seem to be "complete." Then the patient's information, and material obtained through other dreams are useful in completing and confirming our findings. All of our interpretations, however, remain to some extent incomplete. We, therefore, take as many cross sections through the dream as possible. In difficult cases we analyze only those revelations which enable us to further our work for the moment.

Outside of the difficulties lying in the matter itself, the limits of our interpretation depend on: (a) the patient, and (b) the doctor. The patient's inner resistance varies many times during the analysis, and may appear and disappear even in the course of a single session. The patient may recall an additional part of the dream or give an association that may serve as a key to the solution of another part of the dream.

On the other hand, the doctor also may find himself in a temporary neurotic condition. For this reason, psychoanalysts customarily undergo a training analysis before starting with their psychoanalytic practice. The physician's specific conflicts cause him to overlook similar conflicts in the patient or to overemphasize and misinterpret particular dream details.

The simplification, first introduced by Stekel, is the most important principle of the active approach. (See page 248.) After the manifest dream content has been reduced to a kind of précis or a headline, we attempt to ascertain the main emotion of the dream. From both we usually derive some information about the latent dream content, at least in its bare outline. Time and again we come back to the old dreams. We analyze them in series, looking for repeated motives, for the central idea, for antithetic emotions. We try to secure insight into the patient's instinctive cravings and his defense mechanisms; his anagogic and catagogic trends; his gratifications and his anxieties; in short, we lay as many cross sections through the dream as possible in order to do justice to the polymorphous structure of the dream.

Active dream interpretation requires special study. To the uninformed, many interpretations arrived at in an active way may appear as a sort of "hit-or-miss game," whereby the hits admittedly are prevalent. What the outsider does not realize is the underlying skill in forming simplifications, in reducing complicated dream structures to simple equations—a skill that is a product of training and experience; a skill, however, that can be transmitted and acquired.

The question as to whether the patient can discharge the emotions connected with the latent dream content in this active analysis just as well as in the orthodox analysis can be answered in the affirmative. The patient is afforded enough opportunity for discharging his complexes. Of course, he does it mostly at a time when the analytical situation favors it. It is the analyst's knowledge of the case, his experience and his intuition which tell him when this opportunity has arrived.

The effect of this abreaction is exactly the same as that achieved in the orthodox way in a passive analysis. It appears that, as far as the emotional discharge and the shift of cathexes is concerned, it does not make any difference whether the patient is gently guided into confessions or whether he retains the unchallenged lead. Alexander is right when he is of the opinion that it is of secondary importance which technical devices are used to bring about emotional discharge. According to him, the individual nature of the case determines whether this abreaction should take place on the couch, by the use of free associations, by a face-to-face conversation, suddenly or gradually, through the analytical interview, or through real life situations while the patient is under the influence of analysis.

The advantages of the active approach are evident. The most important is that, without jeopardizing any rule of a causal therapy and without encroaching upon the management of the analytical situation, we are able to reach our psychological objectives in a considerably shorter time. Such a procedure deserves the name of a "brief psychoanalysis."

There are dreams which cannot be interpreted without the patient's aid. The following dream by a forty-five-year-old spinster offers a typical example of this kind:

[595] *"We had a party at our home. I suggested that we start to recite poems."*

No association was available, particularly none that would

elucidate the character of the poems. The patient was asked to name at random any poem she knew. Her resistance grew stronger—she claimed that her "mind went blank." She was coaxed slightly and reminded to relax, not to hurry—and after a few minutes the following lines of a poem she used to know as a child came to her mind:

> Turn back again,
> Time in thy flight,
> Make me a child again
> Just for tonight."[1]

This poem shows better than any report the patient's infantilism. The middle-aged woman is emotionally still a child. Her unconscious desires are directed toward the bright and sunny days of her childhood. Our conversation, stimulated by this dream, revealed a strong family fixation which was responsible for the fact that this fairly attractive woman failed to find a proper partner.

It is a fact of the greatest importance that the patient is not capable of revealing the main conflict unaided by the analyst, even were his analysis to continue for years. The patient has a blind spot, a mental scotoma, for the problem before his eyes and it is absolutely futile to expect the analyst to secure insight into the conflict situation by relying solely upon free associations. We, therefore, desire to develop the dream interpretation to a degree in which the skeleton, at least, of the latent dream plot and the emotional content can be reconstructed in a fixed manner. In this way we build up our working hypotheses for a better utilization of the material presented by the patient. It is clear that a working hypothesis must remain labile so that it may be replaced or supplemented at any time by new findings. Every analyst, however orthodox, makes use of working hypotheses based upon previously acquired experience. Dream interpretation itself is a kind of working hypothesis. It is, therefore, a fallacy to believe that the application of a working hypothesis as such jeopardizes

---

1 These lines are not worded exactly as the patient gave them.

the scientific objectivism of the research. On the contrary, the application of the active method makes the therapeutic work more concise and constructive and diminishes the factor of waste. By having the patient discover and discuss his main problems we make him revive and discharge his complexes. We do it, of course, not as one of our critics said, "by hurling the complexes at the patient's head," but by displaying all the necessary psychotherapeutic tact and by meeting all the requirements of individual psychology, at a time which we consider suitable. Our experience teaches that this "provoked" emotional discharge has the same therapeutic value as the discharge experienced in the passive analysis at any other stage of the treatment.

The associations may or may not give us insight. The association is the most fickle part of dream interpretation. We must consider the associations with a critical eye and must always think of the total material. Out of the associations the relevant material must be culled. If you rely on a patient's associations as *the* relevant material, you may arrive at wrong conclusions. However, if you apply the active dream analysis, you can evaluate which part of the association material is valuable and which is irrelevant. Sometimes, we have to stop the patient from associating because we notice that the trend of his associations is leading us nowhere.

We must also keep in mind that we are dealing today with different material from that with which Freud was confronted in his time. The patient of today comes to us "well-prepared," with some knowledge of psychoanalytic literature and terminology. He is, in general, less inclined to be shocked by analytic revelations. He may even introduce himself with the words, "I have an Oedipus complex," or "I have a mother fixation," or "My main problem lies in the disturbance of my inter-personal relations. Where do we go from here?"

The more patients know about psychoanalysis and matters in which we are interested, the less reliable are their "free associations."

EPILOGUE

And so we have come to an end. I trust we have had good times together while retracing the intricate pathways of the dreaming mind. We have become acquainted with many ways of penetrating to the core of the dream. What we need now is experience for which, as the old saying goes, there is no substitute. A great deal of supervised work with experienced analysts and a large variety of cases are necessary to develop and increase the skill of grasping the inner dynamics of the individual dream; for the dream is but one of the manifold manifestations of the enigmatic human mind. As there are no two individuals exactly alike, so also are no two dreams really alike. They reflect the dreamer's unique personality and derive their meaning from the individual's specific past and present conflict situation. They show us what is different in us, although in their deepest recesses they also show what all humanity has in common, in what we all are alike. The acquired skill in interpreting dreams will always have to be augmented by the analyst's capacity for loving empathy with his patient and his unfettered intuition; two qualities which are beyond the scope of any instruction.

The adage of old Heraclitus that "everything flows," applies also to the methods of psychotherapy. Recent congresses, symposia, and council meetings have shown not only that we are in need of improvements in our efforts to cure mental disease, but also that progressive ideas are already on the march.

GLOSSARY AND BIOGRAPHICAL INDEX

INTRODUCTORY NOTE
This Glossary is designed to provide useful definitions and the specific frames of reference in which various words are used in this book.

A

Abasia: Inability to walk.

Aberration: Morbid deviation from normal functioning.

Abraham, Karl: 1877-1925. A German psychoanalyst, who, through his associations with Bleuler and Jung in Switzerland, became acquainted with Freud and subsequently became the first psychoanalyst in Germany. His many writings were characterized by their conciseness and the didactic manner in which they dealt with complex problems. His studies of manic-depressive states and the pre-genital levels of libido are regarded as classics of psychoanalytic literature, as are many of his papers on childhood sexuality.

Abreaction: Term introduced by Freud. From *abreagieren* (German) "to discharge." Removal of emotional blocks, complexes, and symptoms by re-experiencing the repressed causative situation through action or talk in a therapeutic setting.

Absence: Transient loss of consciousness. Seen in hysteria and in epilepsy.

Abstraction: Isolation of a part, qualitative or quantitative, from a whole. Forming of general concepts from isolated parts.

Abulia: An impairment or a loss of will-power.

Active Analysis: A method introduced by Stekel in which the analyst deliberately influences the type and quantity of material to be analyzed and gives the patient direct guidance.

Acute: Having a short and severe course. (Antonym: *Chronic.*)

Adaptation: The patient's adjustment to his environment.

Adler, Alfred: 1870-1937. A Viennese psychiatrist who was among the first pupils of Freud. He later formed his own school, that of *Individual Psychology.* He based his theory of neurosis on the concept of a congenital organ inferiority and the compensatory mechanisms the patient employed to overcome it. He was a pioneer in organizing child guidance centers, particularly in connection with public schools. Among the many concepts which he developed and which have been utilized by psychotherapists the world over are those of *over-compensation, masculine protest, family constellation,* and *goal-directed behavior.*

Aerophagia: Swallowing of air in an excessive, spasmodic way.

Aetiology: (See *Etiology.*)

Affect: Feeling which blends with thoughts and actions, influences them, and in some conditions rules them.

Affinity: Attraction.

Aggression: Forcefully executed unprovoked action against another person or against one's self.

Agitation (Agitated State) : Restlessness and overactivity.

Agoraphobia: Morbid fear of open spaces, e.g., streets.

Alcoholism: Morbid addiction to the use of alcohol, and the symptom of disease in which excessive drinking of alcohol is involved.

Alexander, Franz: 1891——. A Hungarian-born psychiatrist. Author of many books and articles on psychoanalysis. Introduced important reforms in the psychoanalytic technique designed to render the method more flexible and efficient. At present Director of the Institute for Psychoanalysis in Chicago.

Alimentary Tract: The tubular system carrying food from its ingestion (by mouth) to its excretion (by the anus) .

Allusion: Reference by a symbolic or metaphoric representation.

Alter Ego: The "second ego," the counterpart. Usually synonymous with the repressed antisocial and antimoral parts of personality.

Altruism: Actions or thoughts concerned with the benefit of others.

Ambivalence: Term introduced by E. Bleuler. See *Bipolarity.*

Amenorrhea: Abnormal absence or stoppage of menstrual flow.

Amnesia: A morbid inability to remember experiences that occurred within a limited period of time.

Amnesia, Retrograde: Includes inability to remember experiences extending backward in time from the onset of amnesia.

Anabolism: The biochemical process of changing food into living intracellular material.

Anagogic: Trend leading "upward," toward lofty ideals. Term used frequently by C. G. Jung. (Antonym: *Catagogic.*)

Anal: Pertaining to the anus, its functions and symbolic significance.

Anal Erotism: Sexuality associated with the anal zone. Stage in the libido development.

Analgesia: Absence of sensibility to pain.

Analysand: One who is being psychoanalyzed.

Analysis: Process or result of solving. (See *Psychoanalysis.*)

Anesthesia: Absence of feeling; may be local or general, total or partial.

Angioneurotic Edema: See *Quincke.*

Anilingus: Paraphilia in which an oral approach is made to the anus of the sexual partner.

Animism: Belief that all things, animate and inanimate, have a soul.

Annulment: See *Negation.*

Anorexia Nervosa: A nervous disorder in which are manifested a loss of appetite for food and a deliberate limitation of amount of food consumed.

Anthropology: The study of mankind, its history, and its social development.

Antimoral: Pertaining to thought or action which is against the conscious or unconscious moral standards of the individual practicing it.

Antisocial: Pertaining to thought or action directed against the rules of society.

Antithesis: Active opposition. In dreams: contrasting forces.

Anus: The opening at the end of the alimentary tract through which the feces are eliminated.

Anxiety: An affect distinguished from fear; an apprehension about something that is not present in objective reality, while fear is associated with a real threat. There is a tendency to use the two terms interchangeably.

Anxiety Hysteria: Hysteria in which anxiety is the chief symptom.

Apathy: Absence of feeling, indifference.

Aphasia: Impairment or loss of the ability to speak or communicate one's thoughts in other coherent expressions of language, and/or impairment or loss of ability to comprehend language communications.

Aphonia: Loss of voice from neurological or psychic causes. Sometimes in hysteria.

Apoplexy: Hemorrhage of the brain caused by rupture or blocking of an artery.

Apperception: Thought process in which knowledge that is being acquired is related to previously obtained knowledge.

Apprehensiveness: Anticipation of harm or danger.

Archaic: Pertaining to primitive psychic forms.

Archeology: The study of objects used by prehistoric man.

Archetype: The original type. Synonymous with Jung's term: *primordial image.*

Arteriosclerosis: Hardening of the arteries.

Arthritis: A disease of the joints.

Artificial Dream: A voluntarily invented plot imitating the contents of a dream.

Asceticism: Renunciation of the pleasures of the flesh in favor of a life of strict self-discipline which is expected to bring spiritual and intellectual reward.

Asexuality: Absence of sexual interest.

Asocial: Not social.

Assimilation: The fusion of new intrapsychic content with previously existing content.

Association: Expressing ideas or words of which one thinks in connection with an experience. This is also one of the methods of uncovering unconscious material. (See also: *Free Association.*)

Asthenia: Absence of strength and energy.

Atavism: Reversion to the characteristics of a remote ancestor.

Ataxia: Improper co-ordination.

Atonement: Reparation for a crime or sin.

Atony (Atonia): Decrease of tone or strength.

Attachment: Emotional connecting or binding to an object.

Attention: Direction of consciousness towards an object.

Attitude: A psychological readiness to act or react in a particular manner.

Aura: Physical and mental sensations preceding an epileptic attack.

Aureole: Halo.

Autism: A primitive form of thinking in which subjective or subjectivized material is used, much of it from the unconscious. Observed usually in schizophrenia.

Auto-analysis: Self-analysis.

Auto-eroticism: Term introduced by Havelock Ellis. Conscious stimulation, by action or thought, of one's own sexual organs in order to obtain sexual pleasure without the participation of a partner. (Synonym: *Masturbation.*)

Auto-immunization: Self-immunization against a physical or psychic disorder.

Automatism: An action that one performs automatically, i.e., without conscious intent.

Autonomic Nervous System: A part of the nervous system which is to a great extent independent of the central nervous system and thus is largely self-controlling. It exists throughout the body and conducts also psychic stimuli.

Autopsy: Literally: personal observation. Medical examination of a dead body by dissection. (Synonym: *Post-mortem examination.*)

B

Bacteriology: Science of the study of bacteria.

Baptism: Initiating into the Christian Church by applying water to the person or persons in the name of the Father, the Son, and the Holy Ghost.

"Basic Rule": Rule in analytic procedure which requires that the patient tell, without selection, all that comes to his mind at a given moment. (Synonym: *Rule of Free Association.*)

Battle Fatigue: Nervous syndrome due to physical, emotional, and mental stresses of combat.

Behavior: Manner of action.

Benign: Mild. In medicine: not dangerous, or not prone to get worse. Antonym: *Malignant.*

Bipolarity: Term used by Stekel for *Ambivalence.* The simultaneous existence of two contrasting affects in one individual: love-hate, pleasure-pain, confidence-suspicion.

Birth Trauma: A psychic and physical shock which disturbs the infant as he is born.

Bisexuality: Undifferentiated stage in the development of an individual's sexuality. Sexual desire directed toward both sexes.

Bleuler, Eugen: 1857-1939. A Swiss psychiatrist who coined the term *schizophrenia* to replace the then accepted term of *dementia praecox.* Chiefly noted for his studies of schizophrenia, he was active in building the psychoanalytic movement in Switzerland and was the teacher of Abraham, Jones and other prominent psychoanalysts.

Body Image: Cerebral (cortical) localization of all body sensations. Anatomic basis of the physical ego-feeling.

Breuer, Joseph: 1841-1925. A Viennese neurologist. Collaborated with Freud in a study of hysteria.

Brill, Abraham A.: 1874-1948. Austrian-born American psychoanalyst who was the pioneer of freudian psychoanalysis in the United States. He translated Freud's major writings into English, and through lectures, organizational work, his own writings, and practice did much to familiarize the American public and physicians with the basic theories of Freud.

Bulimia: Ravenous appetite, often from psychic causes.

C

Cannibalism: The eating of human flesh. In neurotic patients, cannibalistic impulses, if present, are usually expressed symbolically; in some psychoses they are expressed literally.

Cardiac: Pertaining to the heart.

Castration: Removal of sexual organs. In psychoanalytic sense: particularly of the penis.

Castration Complex: Complex involving fears of or wishes for castration.

Catabolism: The process of breaking down complex tissue material into simpler forms. Destructive metabolism.

Catalepsy: A nervous condition, occurring in hysteria and schizophrenia, in which all voluntary motion is halted and sensibility is absent. This condition is accompanied by muscular rigidity, paleness and coldness of body, as well as by slowness of pulse and respiration.

Catatonia: A schizophrenic condition characterized by changes of muscular tension and stupor.

Catharsis: Emotional discharge. The removal of a complex by bringing it to consciousness and fully expressing it.

Cathexis: Emotional charge. The concentration of affect (libido) on an idea or object.

Centrifugal: Away from the center.

Centripetal: Toward the center.

Cerebral: Pertaining to the brain (cerebrum)`.

Cervical: Pertaining to the neck (cervix).

Character: A sign of the nature of anything. Ways in which an individual deals with conventional situations.

Chastity Clause: Repressed specific clause in which the patient has vowed to remain sexually or morally pure.

Chorea: A convulsive nervous disorder. (Synonym: *St. Vitus Dance.*)

Chronic: Pertaining to a disorder of long duration.

Circumcision: Removal of the foreskin of the male organ, for hygienic or religious reasons.

Clause: A binding statement in an agreement. (See also *Chastity Clause* and *Death Clause.*)

Claustrophobia: Morbid fear which arises with the thought of going into closed spaces such as locked rooms, subways, and elevators.

Cleptomania: Compulsion to steal.

Climacterium: The "change of life" which occurs usually between the ages of forty and fifty.

Clinical: Pertaining to bedside operation. *Kliné* (Greek) = "bed." Used in reference to actual observation of the patient, contrary to speculative approaches.

Clitoris: Small, erectile part of the female organ which corresponds to the penis in the male.

Cloaca: A cavity on the rear of the embryonic body into which urinary, reproductive, and intestinal ducts open.

Clonic: Pertaining to a spasmodic contraction and relaxation of the muscles.

Clouded Consciousness or *Clouded Sensorium:* Disorientation and unclear perception due to sensory disturbance.

Coitus: Sexual intercourse. *Coitus Interruptus:* Coitus which is terminated voluntarily before emission occurs.

Collective Unconscious: The contents of the unconscious which, according to Jung, are distinct from the personal unconscious in that they are physically inherited by a group or by mankind in general, as, e.g., symbols which have generally accepted meanings.

Coma: A stupor of such depth that all consciousness is gone.

Complex: Term introduced by C. G. Jung. A repressed set of ideas grouped about emotionally charged contents which may appear in the consciousness in disguise to exert an important and sometimes dominant influence on the individual's thought and behavior. (See also *Castration Complex, Oedipus Complex.*)

Compulsion: Morbid urge to execute acts, even absurd ones, against the conscious desire to do so.

Conation: The tendency or ability to strive toward a goal which may be conscious or unconscious.

Concomitant: Accompanying.

Condensation: A process which transfers the affect from a group of ideas to one idea.

Conditioned Reflex: Habit pattern induced and developed in animals or persons.

Conditioning: Shaping. Particularly of habit patterns.

Confabulation: Filling in memory gaps with fantasies which the patient believes are real. Often in organic brain disorders.'

Confusion: A state of being mixed or disordered. Frequently refers to disorientation.

Congenital: Existing at birth.

Conscience: A part of the psyche which regulates, suppresses, and modifies instinctual expression in accordance with the individual's sense of moral and social values. Part of the *superego*.

Consciousness: That part of the mind which is aware of phenomena taking place inside and outside of the personality *now*.

Constellation: A pattern of associations charged with affect and active in the consciousness as influences on behavior. (Cf. *Complex*.)

Constitution: The fairly constant inherited composition of the organism, methods, and capacities of the body.

Conversion: Transfer of psychic energy into physical symptoms. *C. Hysteria:* Form of hysteria in which neurotic complexes find their manifestations in physical symptoms, e.g., hysterical vomiting.

Convulsion: A violent, involuntary muscular contraction.

Coprophilia: Morbid fondness of filth, especially feces.

Cortex: External layer of the brain. (Adj.: *Cortical*.)

Cunnilingus: Form of intercourse consisting of an oral approach to the female genital.

D

Death Clause: Repressed specific clause in which thoughts of the patient involve the death of himself or another person.

Death Instinct: An instinct striving to transform living organisms into their original pre-organic, i.e., inorganic state.

Defecation: Act of discharging feces.

Defense Mechanisms: Devices which are consciously or unconsciously constructed and utilized by an individual for the purpose of warding off antimoral and antisocial trends in his personality.

Defloration: Deflowering, i.e., depriving of virginity.

Déjà vu: A mistaken feeling one has that what he is experiencing now, he has experienced before.

Delirium: Confused or clouded state of consciousness; most frequently encountered in a state of intoxication.

Delusion: A false belief which cannot be revised even if the facts are made known to the afflicted individual.

Dementia: Mental deterioration.

Dementia praecox: See *Schizophrenia.*

Depersonalization: Loss of ego identity.

Depression: Dejection. Downcast. A component of manic-depressive psychoses.

Depth Psychology: Pertaining to investigation of the unconscious.

Derealization: Feeling that one's self or the outer world is unreal.

Desensitization: Removing or rendering a complex less disturbing.

Desexualization: Removing psychic energy from the sexual region as in sublimation.

Deterioration: The gradual impairment of the personality structure and functions.

Detumescence: The subsidence of excitement. Softening of the erectile, firm genital organs.

Diabetes: A disease characterized by excessive discharge of urine. Usually connected with a high content of blood sugar. (*D. mellitus.*)

Diagnosis: The recognition and identification of a disease.

Diarrhea: A morbid discharge of loose material from the intestines.

Diathesis, Exudative: Morbid disposition to react to certain nervous injuries by producing edemas.

Dichotomy: A division into two separate parts.

Didactic: Instructive.

Dipsomania: A periodic and uncontrollable urge to consume intoxicating liquids (alcohol). Often associated with an underlying depression.

Disorientation: Confusion about one's own identity, or about relations of objects or ideas to each other, to time and/or space.

Dissociation: A splitting of part of the personality, e.g., a group of complexes, from the whole. The removed part functions as another whole, as though it represented another person.

Don Juan Complex: A complex indicating that the male patient, because of childhood disappointments in relationship to his mother, or because of latent homosexuality, practices promiscuity.

Dramatization: The appearance in dreams of underlying conflicts in exaggerated, dramatic form.

Dromomania: Literally, running mania. A morbid urge to travel.

Dualism: Two mutually irreducible elements composing a single unit. The state of being twofold.

Dynamic: Pertaining to a specific activity within a process; often used in relation to the underlying force which brings about changes in emotional reactions.

Dynamisms: Agencies which supply energy to anything and cause action to take place. (See *Dynamic.*)

Dysfunction: Impaired function.

Dysmenorrhea: Painful and difficult menstruation.

Dyspareunia: Painful and difficult coitus.

Dysphagia: Difficulty in swallowing.

Dyspnea: Difficulty in breathing; short or labored breathing.

E

Echolalia: The echo-like repetition of another's speech.

Echopraxia: Echo-like repetition of the actions of other people.

Ecstasy: Mental exaltation.

Edema: Swelling caused by abnormally large quantities of fluid accumulated in the tissue spaces between the cells of the body.

Ego: That part of the total personality which consciously tests reality and adjusts one's functioning and goals.

Egocentric: Self-centered. Considering everything in relation to one's self.

Ejaculatio Praecox: Premature ejaculation during intercourse.

Electra Complex: The female Oedipus Complex. Often ignored in favor of the latter which is generally used to include both the male's and the female's complex. From the Greek legend in which Electra persuades her brother, Orestes, to take vengeance on their mother and her new husband for having slain their father. Electra never married and throughout her life brooded about the fate of her father.

Electro-convulsive Treatment (ECT): A measured amount of electricity sent through the frontal lobes of the patient's brain in certain cases of mental disease.

Electro-encephalograph: An apparatus which makes a graphic recording of electrical currents in the cortex. (Electro-encephalogram, E.E.G.)

Ellipsis: Omission of words or facts.

Ellis, Havelock: 1859-1939. An English, psychoanalytically oriented, man of letters who devoted much of his scholarship to his seven volume work entitled *Studies in the Psychology of Sex* which was written with devotion to scientific authenticity and in a literary style that was appealing to a wide audience.

Empathy: Intellectual understanding of another person coupled with an ability to feel with him.

Encephalitis, Epidemic (Sleeping Sickness): An infectious disease manifesting languor, drowsiness, muscular weakness, cranial nerve palsies.

Endocrine: Pertaining to inner secretion. Material discharged by the glands directly into the circulation.

Endocrinology: The science which is concerned with internal secretions.

Endogenous: Originating internally.

Endopsychic: Within the psyche.

Engram: A lasting trace of a psychic experience. Also, a lasting trace left in the protoplasm of the tissue by any stimulus. Term introduced by R. Semon.

Entity: A distinct thing.

Enuresis: Involuntary urination; bed-wetting.

Enzymes: Bodies of ferment produced by cells. Pertains to metabolism.

Epilepsy: A chronic nervous disease in which the patient is seized by convulsions and falls down in a coma.

Epileptic Equivalent: Reaction which takes place instead of an epileptic seizure, e.g., a *Fugue.*

Erection: Swelling and rigidity of the male organ in sexual activity.

Ereuthophobia (Erythrophobia): A morbid fear of blushing.

Erogenous: A thing tending to arouse erotic desire.

Erogenous Zones: Areas of the body which can arouse or intensify sexual desire when they are stimulated.

Eros: Love; the Greek god of love.

Erotic: Pertaining to love.

Erotism (Eroticism): A sexual manifestation, usually refers to a specific zone, as *Anal Erotism.*

Ethnology: Science which studies the divisions of mankind into races.

Etiology: Science which describes causes; in medicine: a study of the causes of diseases.

Euphoria: Feeling of buoyancy and fine health.

Exacerbation: Intensification of an illness or its symptoms.

Exhibitionism: Morbid desire to expose to others one's genitals or other parts of the body which are normally concealed.

Exogenous: Of external origin.

Expiate: Appease; atone.

Extramarital: Outside of marriage.

Extrovert: One whose interests are in the world outside of himself.

Exudative, Diathesis: See *Diathesis.*

F

Falsification of Memory: Changing a memory so that it is no longer true.

Fantasy (Phantasy) : Forming mental images of scenes, often in sequences, of experiences which have not actually happened or have happened in a way considerably different from that fantasied.

Fear: A feeling of alarm inspired by the presence of a real danger. Sometimes mixed with anxiety, and often used interchangeably with the latter.

Fecal: Pertaining to or containing feces.

Feces: The bowel discharges of waste matter from the intestines.

Fellatio: Oral contact with the male organ.

Fenichel, Otto: 1897-1946. A Viennese-born theoretician of psychoanalysis who taught, organized, and directed psychoanalytic groups in several European countries before establishing himself in the United States in 1937. Author of *The Psychoanalytic Theory of the Neuroses* and many other contributions aimed at synthesizing psychoanalytic knowledge.

Ferenczi, Sandor: 1874-1933. A pioneer Hungarian psychoanalyst who had first been a neurologist. He stressed the importance of uncovering the earliest traumas of childhood. The International Psychoanalytic Society was founded in 1910 upon his initiative.

Fertilization: Impregnation. The joining of a male germ cell to a female germ cell to form one fertilized cell.

Fetish: The object of *Fetishism.*

Fetishism: Sexual fixation on an object, often an article of clothing which substitutes for a tabooed, unconsciously desired sexual partner.

Fistula: An ulceration leading to an internal hollow organ. *Vestibular fistula:* A pathological communication between the *vestibular apparatus* and the external surface of the skull.

Fit: A violent precipitation of an illness, sometimes including convulsions and even unconsciousness.

Fixation: A rigid formation and maintenance of a desire for a particular object, used as a rule in reference to a tabooed love object, with a consequent inability to love another, socially acceptable object.

Flaccid: Flabby and, therefore, easily giving way to pressure.

Flatulence: Presence of an abnormal quantity of gas in the intestinal tract.

Flatus: Gas rectally expelled from the body.

Focus of Infection: The area on which the disease centers, i.e., the focal point.

Folklore: Traditional stories and customs of a people which have been preserved for many generations and have usually been accepted as marked with wisdom and learning.

Forced Fantasy: Refers to a method developed by Ferenczi to produce fantasies.

Free Association: Saying whatever comes to mind; e.g., in connection with a dream or a dream passage. Required in freudian psychoanalysis as a "basic rule."

Freud, Sigmund: 1856-1939. Founder of the psychoanalytic method of investigating and treating nervous and mental disease. He was born in Freiberg, Moravia, then in Austria, now a part of Czechoslovakia. He studied medicine at the University of Vienna where he later was professor of neuropathology, a position which he held from 1902 until 1938 when he went to London as a refugee from the Nazis. Out of his early studies under Charcot in Paris and his work with Breuer in Vienna he developed a system of treating nervous disorders in which he used free association rather than the hypnosis employed by his teachers, Charcot and Bernheim. His thought-provoking writings in which he formulated a new terminology for a large number of psychic phenomena gradually spread throughout the world.

At first an object of lively controversy, they later were accepted by the leading schools of psychiatry the world over.

His books—*Interpretation of Dreams, Totem and Taboo, Psychopathology of Everyday Life,* etc., were milestones of psychiatric thought, and were widely read and discussed by medical men and the lay public alike and thus had an important direct and indirect effect on medicine, education, and the social sciences of our time.

Frigidity: A woman's coldness toward sexual stimulation, and her inability to have orgasm.

Fugue: An epileptic equivalent or a symptom of hysteria. The patient moves about or travels in a dream-like state, and, afterwards, has no memory of what occurred while he was in this condition.

Functional: Pertaining to the actual process of working or doing.

Functional Disturbance: A disturbance of a physical or mental function which may be of psychic or psychosomatic origin, i.e., without definite anatomic changes in the organ.

G

General Paresis: A general paralysis caused by syphilis of the central nervous system.

Generative Organs: The organs immediately involved in reproduction of the species.

Genital (ia) : Organ (s) of reproduction.

Gerontophilia: Sexual attraction directed toward old people.

Globus Hystericus: A sensation, not infrequent among hysterical patients, of a lump arising from the chest to the throat.

Goldstein, Kurt: 1878——. American neuropsychiatrist born in Kattowitz, Germany. Formerly director of Neurological Institute of Frankfort-on-the-Main, Germany; professor and director of neurology and psychiatry departments at various German and American universities and hospitals. Co-editor of the *Journal of Nervous and Mental Diseases.* Author of numerous scholarly articles and books in his field. Most important are those on *Aphasia* and *The Organism.*

Gyne(co)phobia: Morbid dread of women.

H

Habit: An acquired and settled method of repeating a specific reaction to a specific stimulus.

Hallucination: Sensory perception of things which do not actually exist.

Hemicrania: Pain confined to one side of the head.

Hemorrhage: Bleeding.

Heredity: The transmission of physical or mental traits from parents to offspring.

Heresy: An opinion which is contrary to established and accepted beliefs or doctrines and tends to inspire dissension.

Heterogeneous: Of different kind. Composed of elements which are dissimilar.

Heterosexuality: Sexual attraction to a person of the opposite sex.

Homogeneous: Of the same kind.

Homosexuality: Sexual attraction to a person of the same sex.

Hormone: A chemical agent developed by an organ in the body (usually a gland) carried by the body fluid to another organ in which it has stimulating effect.

Horney, Karen: 1885——. An American psychiatrist born in Germany of Norwegian and Irish parents. At first a Freudian, she now has her own psychoanalytic system and school.

Hyperalgesia: Exaggerated sensitiveness to pain.

Hypersomnia: A morbid condition in which the patient sleeps for an excessively long time and is given to drowsiness.

Hypertension: Abnormally high tension; high blood pressure.

Hypertrophy: An abnormal overgrowth or overdevelopment of a part of the body.

Hypnagogic Thought: Flash of thought perceived in the semiconscious state leading into the state of sleep.

Hypnopompic Thought: Flash of thought perceived in the semiconscious state leading from sleep into wakefulness.

Hypnosis: A sleep-like state induced in the patient by psychological means employed by the therapist.

Hypnotherapy: Treatment by hypnotism.

Hypnotism: Induction or study of hypnosis.

Hypochondria (Hypochondriasis): An individual's morbid concern about his health and fear of disease.

Hypoglycemia: Deficiency of sugar in the blood.

Hyponoic State: State of decreased consciousness.

Hysteria: A neurotic condition characterized by various functional disturbances, e.g., nausea, loss of motor control, or simulation of organic disease.

Hystero-Epilepsy: Hysterical convulsions similar to those in an epileptic attack.

I

Id: The fundamental life tendencies, the instincts from which the ego develops. (See also *Ego* and *Superego*.)

Idealization: The process of mentally giving qualities of perfection to anything.

Identification: Attributing to one's self, usually unconsciously characteristics or the identity of another person, group, or object.

Ideogram: A picture or a symbol of a picture which conveys an idea. Some writings, e.g., Chinese, consist of ideograms.

Illusion: A false interpretation of an actual perception.

Image: Likeness, substitute. (See *Imago.*)

Imagination: Mentally shaping and synthesizing objects or ideas into pictures or patterns different from any involved in one's previous experience.

Imago: This word is used in psychoanalysis to describe the parental image formed during the infantile period and later repressed and associated with the affect of infancy.

Impotence: A male's inability to perform a satisfying sexual intercourse.

Impulse: A thought or act which results from a psychological driving force.

Incest: Sexual relation between persons so nearly related by blood that marriage between them would be unlawful.

Incest Barrier: Any force which prevents the fulfillment of incestuous desires, particularly the moral and social restrictions directed against incestuous activity.

Incubus: A male demon said to have intercourse with women during their sleep. Normal position of men in intercourse. (Antonym: *Succubus.*)

Individual Psychology: The system of psychology founded by Alfred Adler.

Infantile Trauma: An injury to the psyche sustained in infancy.

Infantilism, Psychosexual: A manifestation of psychic sexual activity which emanates from infantile stages of sexual development. Term used by Stekel in connection with *Paraphilias.*

Inferiority Complex: Term coined by Alfred Adler. Feeling of limitations or weaknesses of one's ego acquired, as a rule in early childhood.

Insanity: Sometimes loosely used to mean psychosis or any mental disease, but chiefly as a legal term denoting an individual's mental and, consequently, legal irresponsibility.

Insight Therapy: Treatment which strives to show the patient his underlying conflicts with the purpose of effecting a change in his personality or his reactions.

Instinct: Innate primal urge, e.g., Freud's "life instinct."

Integrate: To make into a whole.

Intoxication: A poisoning. Usually associated with the drinking of alcoholic beverages.

Intrapsychic: Within the psyche.

Intrauterine: Within the womb. Hence, pertaining to any tendency, expressed in symbol, fantasy, delusion, action, or posture, to return to the womb.

Introjection: A process in which an individual's interest is withdrawn from the environment and directed toward intrapsychic images of an object, e.g., the image of a girl who has been unsuccessfully wooed or who has died. (Antonym: *Projection.*)

Introspection: Looking into one's self. Preoccupation with one's thoughts and feelings.

Introvert: A term used by Jung to describe a personality type which turns most of its attention inward upon itself. Often used to describe morbid concentration of interest upon ones self. (Antonym: *Extrovert.*)

Involutional Melancholia: A psychosis, with symptoms of self-depreciation, suicide tendencies, and despondency, occurring in later middle years or old age and associated with senile involution, i.e., a reversal of biological development.

J

Jackson, John Hughling: 1834-1911. British neurologist. Wrote pioneering books on brain tumors, aphasia, epilepsy, and other disorders of the nervous system.

Jelliffe, Smith Ely: 1866-1945. American neuropsychiatrist, editor of psychiatric literature. He and William A. White in 1913 published "The Psychoanalytic Review," the first psychoanalytic journal in the United States.

Jones, Ernest: 1879——. British psychiatrist and psychoanalyst. Was among the first followers of Freud. Made important contributions to the theory and practice of psychoanalysis. Founder and Honorary President of the British Psychoanalytic Society and Founder of the "International Journal of Psychoanalysis."

Jung, Carl Gustav: 1875——. Swiss psychoanalyst, early associate of Freud from whom he parted in 1912 after a series of differences extending over several years. His main deviations from the freudian view are the following: libido represents the will to live rather than a sex instinct; the understanding of a neurosis should be sought in the present problem rather than in early childhood traumas. His classification of people as "extroverts" or "introverts," his studies on word associations, and on the unconscious, particularly his conception of a "collective unconscious" have attracted much attention. His work emphasized the ultimate necessity of accepting a religiously meaningful life.

K

Kinesthetic: The sense pertaining to muscular movement.

Kinetic: Pertaining to motion.

Korsakoff Psychosis: A psychosis characterized mainly by disorders of attention and memory. Sometimes caused by alcoholism. Named for the Russian neurologist, Sergey S. Korsakoff.

Korzybski, Alfred H. S.: 1879-1950. Born in Warsaw, Poland; came to the United States in 1916. General Editor of International Non-Aristotelian Library and Director of the Institute of General Semantics. Author of *Science and Sanity* and other works concerned with general semantics.

L

Labyrinth (of the ear): A system of communicating canals in the interior of the ear.

Latent: Concealed, unconscious.

"Law of Series": Law, established by Paul Kammerer, of Vienna, according to which human experiences show a tendency to appear in series.

Leitmotif: The dominant motive.

Lesbian: Female homosexual.

Lesion: Organic injury leading to destruction of tissue.

Libido: The term is used on different levels, e.g., by Freud as the energy of the sexual desire, and by Jung, in the broad sense of being the driving force of life.

Libido (or Libidinal) Fixation: Fixation of libido, usually at an early period of psychic development on an erogenous zone, parent, sibling, or other object.

Life Plan, Secret: An unconscious plan which the patient strives to fulfill through his neurosis. Term introduced by A. Adler.

Lingam: A symbol under which one of the Hindu Trimurti, *Siva,* a representative of destructiveness and creativity, is worshipped; hence, *Lingam* is a symbol of male and female creativity, or of *Bisexuality.*

Lorand, Sandor: 1893——. American psychoanalyst, born in Hungary. Author of several technical books and many articles on psychoanalysis.

Lucid Interval: An interval between two attacks of mental illness when the psychotic is sufficiently aware of his real surroundings and able to react to them in the manner of a normal person.

M

Macropsia: Disturbance of vision in which the external world is seen as through a magnifying glass.

Magical Thought and Action: The patient's attempt to achieve something in reality by the mere thought of doing it or by an action which has no reasonable relation to it; e.g., the belief that by assuming a certain posture one can kill or save from death a person who is thousands of miles away. ("Belief in the omnipotence of thought.")

Malfunction: Defective function.

Malignant: A morbid condition which tends to worsen. The term often implies a threat of death. Cancer is a *malignant* disease. (Antonym: *Benign.*)

Mandala: Term used by Jung. Magic circle. In ancient religions a tool of concentration.

Mania: The excited stage of manic-depressive psychosis; hence, popularly, any excessive display of excitement or interest. Also used to characterize specific *compulsions,* e.g., *cleptomania, dromomania,* and any exaggerated desire or obsession.

Manic-depressive Psychosis: A psychosis in which excitement, and/or exaltation, *mania,* and *depression* alternate.

Mannerisms: Persistent use of bizarre, peculiar and non-conforming ways of dressing, bearing, talking, or conducting one's self.

Marihuana (or *Marijuana):* A narcotic made from a plant, *cannabis sativa,* grown chiefly in Mexico and smoked in cigarettes. Use is habit-forming.

Masochism: Morbid desire to be ill-treated as a condition for sexual gratification. The word derives from the name of the Austrian Count Leopold Sacher von Masoch (1836-95) who wrote several novels in which the heroes had the aforementioned morbid desires.

Masturbation: Stimulation of one's own sexual organ or eroge-nous areas with sexual gratification as the goal. (Synonym: *Auto-erotism.*)

Mechanism, Mental: A combination of mental processes which have been conditioned so that they occur automatically when appropriately stimulated.

Megalomania (Delusion of Grandeur) : The delusion of being a person of great importance, such as a king, a millionaire, or a specific prominent person.

Melancholia: Mental depression. A phase of manic-depressive psychosis.

Memory: The recalling and recognizing of impressions of a former experience.

Menorrhagia: Excessive or prolonged menstrual flow.

Menses: Menstrual period.

Metabolism: The sum total of all body processes involved in building up and destroying protoplasm.

Metamorphosis: Transformation.

Metapsychology: Beyond psychology. Hence, speculative and di-rectly unverifiable consideration of the mind.

Micropsia: Disturbance of vision in which the external world is seen as through a microscope.

Micturition: Urination.

Migraine: A violent ache, usually confined to one side of the head, often psychogenic. (Synonym: *Hemicrania.*)

Mind: That part of the personality which formulates thought from the material comprising all the individual's experiences.

Mneme: Memory contained in the body cells—according to Rich-ard Semon.

Monosexuality: Trend directed toward only one sex. Can be of a *heterosexual* or *homosexual* character.

Morbid: Diseased. (Synonym: *Pathologic.*)

Motor discharge: Discharge of an unconscious impulse by muscu-lar action.

Mucous Membrane (Mucosa): A thin layer of tissue which lines all body canals and all hollow organs, e.g., genito-urinary tract.

Mutism: A state of being silent and dumb from psychic causes.

Mysophilia: Morbid craving for filth.

N

Narci(ssi)sm: Self-love. Libido fixation onto one's own ego.

Narco-analysis: A method in which information, normally inaccessible, is elicited from the patient while he is under the influence of a drug.

Narco-hypnosis: Use of narcotics inducing hypnosis.

Narcolepsy: Disease characterized by sudden attacks of loss of muscle tone and of sleep.

Narcosis: Deep unconsciousness induced by narcotics.

Narco-synthesis: Treatment technique in which hypnotic drugs are used for releasing the patient's inhibitions to reveal intimate information. The discharged emotional material is collected and synthesized by doctor and patient.

Narcotomania: A morbid desire to avoid painful experiences through a habitual use of drugs.

Necrophilia: Morbid attraction to dead bodies.

Negation: Denial. Usually used with reference to a denial of reality. (Synonym: *Annulment.* Term introduced by W. Stekel.)

Neologism: A new word, an old word used in a new sense, or a condensation of several words.

Neurasthenia: Physical prostration resulting from a functional disturbance of the nervous system.

Neuritis: The inflammation of a nerve.

Neurosis: A disorder of the psychic functions which in its severest expressions may render the patient incapable of performing his work or participating in social life. Based on a conflict between the id cravings and the inhibiting force of the superego.

Neurotic Arrangement: Adler's term for an unconscious pattern of behavior for the purpose of keeping the neurotic elements active within the patient's specific life performance.

Nightmare: A frightful dream, often accompanied by sensations of unbearable physical oppression.

O

Obedience, Belated: Unconscious obedience to a command which earlier had been rejected and/or repressed.

Oberndorf, Clarence P.: 1882——. American psychiatrist and psychoanalyst. Professor of psychiatry, College of Physicians and Surgeons, Columbia University Medical School. Author of *The Psychiatric Novels of Oliver Wendell Holmes, Which Way Out?*, etc.

Obsessions: Morbid ideas, melodies, or words obtruding upon the patient's mind against his will.

Obsessional Neurosis: A neurosis characterized by a morbid system of obsessions and compulsions.

Occupational Neurosis: A neurosis which impairs a specific occupational skill. The occupation itself is not the cause of the neurosis.

Oedipus Complex: The desire to possess the parent of the opposite sex. From the Greek myth in which Oedipus, saved in infancy from the death which his father sought for him, later slays his father whose identity he does not know, and marries the queen, who, unknown to him, is his mother. When he learns that the two important figures in his dramatic actions were his parents, he blinds himself.

Oneirology: The science concerned with the study of dreams.

Ontogenesis: The development of an individual organism.

Oral Erotism: Pleasurable sensations derived from stimulation of the mouth.

Orgasm: The acme of sexual excitement.

Overcompensation: Exaggerated compensation for a congenital organic inferiority. Term coined by A. Adler.

P

Paleologic: Pertaining to primitive man and his manner of thinking.

Palsy: Paralysis.

Paralysis: Loss of function of a muscle due to an injury or disease of its motor nerve.

Paranoia: Chronic mental disease characterized by delusions of reference and persecution. Adj: *Paranoic.*

Paranoid: Resembling paranoia.

Paraphilia: Sexual perversion. Term used by the Stekel school.

Paresthesia: Feelings of numbness, tingling, or pricking on the skin.

Paroxysm: A sudden and uncontrollable attack such as a violent emotional outburst, a fit, or a sudden intensification of symptoms.

Parturition: Process of giving birth.

Pathogenic: Causing disease.

Pathognomonic: Characteristic for a specific disease.

Pathologic: Morbid, diseased.

Pathology: Branch of medicine which studies the nature of disease.

Pattern: A model or form; e.g., pattern of behavior.

Pedophilia: An adult's morbid attraction toward children.

Penis Envy: An unconscious envy of the male, particularly of his possession of a male organ. Found by Freud to be an important factor in the psychology of women.

Perception: Awareness of a stimulus.

Peripheral Neuritis: Inflammation of nerve endings or terminal nerves.

Peristalsis: Wave-like movements of the alimentary canal as it conveys its contents.

Personality: The totality of a person's physical and mental qualities.

Petit Mal: Its literal meaning is "little illness"; used to describe the milder form of epilepsy. (Antonym: *Grand Mal.*)

Phallic: Pertaining to the male organ.

Phallic Woman: A woman who derives pleasure from playing the male role.

Phantasy: See *Fantasy.*

Phobia: An irrational fear associated with a particular thing or a group of things. See also *Claustrophobia.*

Phylogenesis: Development of a race or a species.

Pleasure Principle: A mechanism of the id which seeks immediate release from pain and immediate attainment of pleasure. Is opposed by the *Reality Principle.*

Poena Talionis: An ancient Roman law according to which the culprit was punished by the same injury as he had inflicted upon his victim.

Poison Complex: A group of ideas in which concern about being poisoned or poisoning others is expressed.

Polymorphous: Having many forms.

Polyuria: Excessive urination.

Postepileptic: Pertaining to the period which follows an epileptic attack.

Posthypnotic Suggestion: A suggestion which is made while the subject is in a hypnotic state, but is to be followed after he has been returned to the normal state.

Post Partum: After childbirth.

Postulate: An assumed and indemonstrable prerequisite.

Potency: Male sexual ability.

Power Complex: A complex of tendencies to subordinate both the intrapsychic and the external environment to the ego.

Pr(a)ecox: Precocious, premature. (See *Ejaculatio P.* and *Dementia P.*)

Preconscious: Material immediately available to the conscious, though at a given time not actually conscious. Borderland between Unconscious and Conscious. Jung's concept of a "personal unconscious" (in contradistinction to a "collective unconscious") comprises "Unconscious" and "Preconscious."

Precordial: The area in front of the heart.

Pregenital Sexuality: An immature stage of sexual development.

Prenatal: Before birth.

Presbyophrenia: Insanity of old age, characterized by disorientation of memory although there is mental alertness.

Primal Scene: The scene in which a child for the first time sees or hears an intimate act between his parents.

Primordial: Primary; in the original state.

Prodrome: A symptom which is a forerunner of a disease.

Prognosis: A forecast of the future course of a disease.

Projection: Throwing a subjective perception into the objective world or giving apparent objective reality to a subjective perception.

Prophylaxis: Prevention of disease.

Prototype: The original model from which later models were made.

Pruritis: Itching.

Psyche: Mind.

Psychiatry: Science dealing with the diagnosis and treatment of nervous and mental disorders.

Psychoanalysis: A psychological method introduced by Freud of investigating and treating nervous and mental conditions, particularly the neuroses.

Psychodynamics: The dynamics of the mind.

Psychogenic: Of mental origin.

Psychogenesis: The psychic origin of disease.

Psychology: The study of the human mind.

Psychoneurosis: Neurosis which is diagnosed as being purely psychogenic. (Synonym: *Neurosis.*)

Psychopath: An individual who has various character and personality disturbances, but who is not psychotic and does not come within the classifications of any particular neurosis.

Psychosexual: Psychic elements associated with sexuality.

Psychosis: A serious disorder of the mind, often characterized by delusions and hallucinations.

Psychotherapy: A term which refers to all psychological methods of treating diseases. One of them is *Psychoanalysis.*

Psychotic: Pertaining to a psychosis.

Puberty: That stage of a person's life during which his procreative organs attain maturity.

Pyromania: Morbid compulsion to set fires.

Q

Quincke Edema (Angioneurotic Edema): Swelling of the skin and/or mucous membranes, often occurring under neurotic conditions.

R

Rado, Sandor: 1898——. Hungarian-born psychoanalyst. In U. S. A. since 1932. At present clinical professor of psychiatry and director of the Psychoanalytic Clinic for Training and Research, Department of Psychiatry, Columbia University.

Rank, Otto: 1884-1939. An early Viennese lay-analyst (Ph.D.) who separated from Freud and set up his own school of "Will Therapy." In his early psychoanalytic work he attempted to correlate the analytic findings with philosophy and literature.

Rationalization: Forming reasons to support an invalid proposition which is often unconscious.

Reaction Formation: A method of opposing an unconscious tendency that would be objectionable to the conscious by developing an opposite tendency. *Example:* Exaggerated cleanliness hiding mysophilic preoccupation.

Reactivate: To cause to become active again.

Reasoning: Attaining a conclusion by applying thought to the process of forming relationships between various data.

Reality Principle: The modification of the pleasure principle in terms of adjustment to the demands of the external world.

Rebirth: Pertaining to desires to be born again, or delusional thoughts that one is born again, often as God.

Reference Idea: An individual's idea that other people think or act as they do exclusively to indicate something to him. Usually a projection of the individual's own thoughts. A man with unconscious homosexual desires may think that the actions and words of other people "refer" to him as a homosexual.

Reflex: An inherited or conditioned specific response to specific stimuli.

Regression: Return to earlier stages of development.

Regurgitation: The return to the mouth of food which has entered the stomach.

Reich, Wilhelm: 1897——. Originally a freudian psychoanalyst, he later seceded and formed his own school. In his theoretical approach, he ascribed an important role to the sociological structure in the development of the psyche. He opposed Freud's postulate that a *death instinct* was one of the two basic instincts, the other being the *life instinct.* In 1939, he announced that he had discovered the *orgone,* a radiating energy. According to Reich, biologic energy is atmospheric (cosmic) orgone energy. His most important analytic work is *Character Analysis.*

Reik, Theodor: 1888——. A lay psychoanalyst (Ph.D.), born in Vienna, came to the United States in 1938. Was closely associated with Freud for many years. Author of numerous books and articles on psychoanalysis and its borderlands.

Remission: An abatement of symptoms.

Repression: The process of removing emotionally charged material from consciousness into the unconscious.

Resistance: A mental struggle, often unconscious, against recalling, recognizing, or revealing material pertinent to the treatment of the disorder; also, the struggle against the analyst who threatens to uncover the hidden material.

Resurrection: The act of arising from the dead, often of an emotion or an idea which has been buried in the unconscious.

Ritual: Pertaining to obsessive-compulsive systems which are structured along the lines of religious rites or ceremonies.

Romance, Family: Belief in being born of some very influential parents, a royal family, etc. (Synonym: *Family novel.*)

Rorschach Test: A personality test developed by Hermann Rorschach, a Swiss psychiatrist. A series of inkblots of various shapes are viewed by the subject who then gives his associations. This test is often employed as an aid in differential psychiatric diagnosis and prognosis.

S

Sachs, Hanns: 1881-1947. A Viennese who gave up his practice of law in favor of a career as a psychoanalyst and educator. He was one of Freud's first pupils, editor of the psychoanalytic journal, *Imago,* and author of *The Creative Unconscious* and other books. In 1932 he came to the United States where he taught at Harvard University and at Simmonds College.

Sadism (Sado-masochism): Morbid practice of ill-treating a person. Sadistic tendencies are also expressed in fantasy life. The word is taken from *Marquis de Sade* (1740-1814) who in his novels described this practice. (See *Masochism.*)

Scatology: The study of the feces.

Schematic: Pertaining to a systematic plan.

Schilder, Paul: 1886-1940. A Viennese neuropsychiatrist who came to the United States in 1928. Author of some two hundred and fifty papers, pamphlets, and books on psychiatric and psychoanalytic questions. Internationally famous at the age of twenty-seven for his description of encephalitis periaxialis diffusa ("Schilder's Disease"). He wrote the first work on psychiatry which was based on psychoanalytic findings. His *Goals and Desires of Man* and *Mind: Perception and Thought in Their Constructive Aspects* are among his better known works.

Schizoid: Bearing a surface resemblance to schizophrenia.

Schizophrenia: In its literal and popular meaning—a split mind. The term was coined by E. Bleuler and was an improvement literally and factually on the old term, *dementia praecox,* which meant a mental disintegration in adolescence. In schizophrenia there is a pronounced loss of contact with and comprehension of reality, severe disruption and disintegration of personality, and occurrence of any one or several of such symptoms as catatonia, paranoia, delusions, hallucinations, and unpredictable and bizarre behavior.

Scop(t)ophilia: Sexual pleasure obtained by looking at intimate scenes.

Scotoma: "Blind spot." A circumscribed defect in the field of vision.

Screen Memory: A true memory which is used to hide another memory of a related experience.

Scrotum: The skin sac which contains the testicles.

Semantics: Pertaining to the meanings of words.

Sensation: An immediate result of a present stimulus of a sense organ. It is distinguished from perception which implies use of a group of sensations and material from past experiences.

Shadow: A jungian term for the *alter ego.*

Sibling: A brother or sister.

Simulate: Feign (illness).

Sleep, Partial: Sleep in which part of the psyche is awake, e.g., in hypnosis.

Sodium Pentothal: A drug used for sedative or hypnotic purposes.

Somatic: Pertaining to the body; from Greek *soma.*

Somatization: Conversion of mental experiences into physical symptoms. (Synonym: *Conversion.*)

Somnambulism: Sleepwalking.

Sphincter: Ring-like muscle which regulates the opening and closing of a hollow organ.

Stammering: A jerky and halting manner of speech.

Stekel, Wilhelm: 1868-1940. Viennese psychoanalyst. One of Freud's first pupils and assistants. Founded his own school based on a more active technique of psychoanalysis. Author of an encyclopedic work, *Disorders of Instincts and Emotions.* He held that all neuroses emanate from mental conflicts. His "active method of psychoanalysis" enabled him to obtain therapeutic results in a relatively brief period of analysis. He was a leader in sex education, and a foremost authority on dream interpreation, compulsions, and obsessions. He died in London where he had lived after the nazification of Austria.

Stigma: A mark or impression.

Stoma: (Greek) Mouth.

Strabismus: Commonly called "cross-eye." A squint deviation of an eye from a normal direction.

Stupor: A state of extreme lack of responsiveness, sometimes almost amounting to unconsciousness.

Stuttering: See *Stammering.*

Sublimation: A process, mainly unconscious, in which energy derived from antimoral and antisocial drives is transformed into morally and socially accepted actions.

Subliminal: Under the threshold (of consciousness).

Succubus: A female demon said to have intercourse with men during their sleep. Normal position of women in intercourse. (Antonym: *Incubus.*)

Superego: A part of the psychic structure which correlates and controls the activities of the id and the ego.

Suppression: The conscious exclusion of ideas and the emotions with which they are associated from the mind.

Sympathetic Nervous System: See *Vegetative Nervous System.*

Symptomatology: The study of symptoms.

Syndrome: A group of symptoms or signs which are related to each other.

T

Taboo: A religious rite by which certain persons, animals, or things are rendered sacred, inviolable, and prohibited.

Tachycardia: Abnormally fast beating of heart.

Talion: See *Poena Talionis.*

T. A. T. (Thematic Apperception Test): Test (developed by Murray) to evaluate the subject's personality. A series of pictures is submitted to the subject who is asked to make up stories about them.

Telepathy: Transference of thought and emotion from person to person without the use of the known senses.

Temperament: The manner in which one is disposed to react to stimuli.

Tenet: Any belief which an individual or a group holds to be true.

Terminology: The technical words, or the special ways in which words are used by a particular group or individual, especially by a branch of science or a representative of the branch, e.g., *psychoanalytic terminology, Freud's terminology, Adlerian terminology.*

Tertium Compariationis: The common quality of two things in comparison to each other; e.g., the *shape* of an electric bulb, which is like that of a pear.

Thalamus: A mass of gray matter situated at the base of the brain and believed to be the center for crude perception of pain and the effective qualities of sensations.

Therapy: Treatment.

Thinking: Mentally formulating.

Tic: Involuntary twitching, often psychogenic.

Totem: Animal, living or dead, or any object or plant, believed to have blood relationship to the clan or tribe which it symbolizes.

Training Analysis: A psychoanalysis which the analysand undergoes as part of his training to become an analyst.

Transference: The unconscious shifting of affect from one person to another; e.g., in analysis the patient may unconsciously attribute characteristics of his mother, father, siblings, or other persons to the physician, and the physician may represent any of these persons to the patient.

Transformation: Changing into the opposite.

Transitory: Temporary, transient.

Transmigration: The shifting of the soul from the body of a dead being into the body of another being.

Trauma: An injury. In psychoanalysis, a *psychic trauma,* i.e., an injury sustained to the psyche during an experience which in itself may have been pleasant or unpleasant. (See also *Infantile Trauma.*)

Tumescence: Swelling, often used to describe expansion of male organ as it attains erection.

Typical: Pertaining to a type, an example, or a characteristic.

U

Umbilicus: The navel.

Unconscious: A deep and undefined area which includes material from the personal unconscious and the collective unconscious.

Urethra: The canal through which urine passes as it is eliminated.

Urticaria: A skin condition, "hives," in which welts, itching, and burning are manifested.

V

Vaginism: A painful spasm of the vagina, often psychogenic.

Vasomotor: The nerve system which controls contraction and expansion of blood vessels.

Vegetative Nervous System: A part of the autonomic nervous system.

Vertigo: Dizziness; a disorder of sense of equilibration.

Vestibular Apparatus (of the ear): A part of the interior of the ear.

Voyeur: Person who has the paraphilia of peeping at intimate scenes in order to obtain sexual gratification. (See *Scopophilia.*)

Vulva: The female's external sexual organs.

W

Wagner von Jauregg, Julius: 1857-1940. Viennese neurologist and psychiatrist. Successor to Krafft-Ebing as director of the neuropsychiatric clinic of the University of Vienna. Nobel Prize winner in 1927 for his discovery that fever can be utilized to cure syphilis of the central nervous system.

Wet Dream: Popular expression for *Nocturnal Emission.*

Will: The power of making a choice.

Will to Power: A term of Nietzche's used by Adler to describe the neurotic's drive away from inferiority and toward superiority.

X

Xenophobia: Morbid fear of strangers.

BIBLIOGRAPHY

For the benefit of the reader and researcher, this bibliography contains not only books and articles quoted in the text but also over 800 references to the more important works on the subject written in the last fifty years in eight languages (English, French, German, Italian, Spanish, Russian, Portuguese and Dutch).

ABBREVIATIONS

Abn. = Abnormal; **Am.** = American; **An.** = *Anais (Port.), Anales (Span.)*, Annals; **Angew.** = *Angewandt (Germ.)*, Applied; **Ann.** = *Annales (French)*, Annals; **Arch.** = Archives; **Aerztl.** = *Aerztlich (Germ.)*, Medical (Lit.: Physician's); **Beih.** = *Beiheft (Germ.)*, Supplement; **Beitr.** = *Beitrag (Germ.)*, Contribution; **Ber.** = *Bericht (Germ.)*, Report; **Bl.** = *Bladen (Dutch)*, Journal; **Bol.** = *Boletin (Span.)*, Bulletin; **Brit.** = British; **D.** = *Deutsch (Germ.)*, German; **Forsch.** = *Forschung (Germ.)*, Research; **Fortschr.** = *Fortschritte (Germ.)*, Progress; **Gaz.** = *Gazette (French), Gazyeta (Russ.)*, Journal; **Gen.** = Genetic; **Geneesk.** = *Geneeskunde (Dutch)*, Medicin; **Ges.** = *Gesamte (Germ.)*, General; **J.** = Journal; **J.A.M.A.** = Journal of the American Medical Association; **M.H.** = Mental Hygiene; **Mschr.** = *Monatsschrift (Germ.)*, Monthly; **Ned.** = *Nederlandsch (Dutch)*, Dutch; **Päd.** = *Pädagogik (Germ.)*, Pedagogy; **Proc.** = Proceedings; **Psa.** = *Psychoanalyse (Germ.), Psicoanálisis (Span.)*, Psychoanalysis; **Psychol.** = Psychology; **Psychother.** = *Psychotherapie (Germ.)*, Psychotherapy; **Quad.** = *Quaderno (Ital.)*, Note Book; **Quart.** = Quarterly; **Rev.** = *Revue (French), Revista (Span.)*, Review; **Riv.** = *Rivista (Ital.)*, Review; **Sachv.** = *Sachverständiger (Germ.)*, Expert; **Schw.** = *Schweizer (Germ.)*, Swiss; **Sexualw.** = *Sexualwissenschaft (Germ.)*, Sexology; **Soc.** = Social; **Tijdschr.** = *Tijdschrift (Dutch)*, Journal; **Vrach.** = *Vrachebnaya (Russ.)*, Medical (Lit.: Physician's); **Wien.** = *Wiener (Germ.)*, Viennese; **Wschr.** = *Wochenschrift (Germ.)*, Weekly; **Zbl.** = *Zentralblatt (Germ.)*, Central Organ; **Ztschr.** = *Zeitschrift (Germ.)*, Journal; **Ztg.** = *Zeitung (Germ.)*, Newspaper.

A

Abel, Karl, Der Gegensinn der Worte. *Sprachwissenschaftliche Abhandlungen*, 1889.

Abraham, Karl, *Dreams and Myths*. Nerv. and Ment. Dis. Publ., 1913.

—— Sollen wir die Pat. ihre Träume aufschreiben lassen? *Int. Ztschr. f. Psa.,* I, 1913.

—— *Selected Papers.* Hogarth Press, London, 1942.

—— Die Spinne als Traumsymbol. *Int. Ztsch. f. Psa.,* VIII, 1922.

Achelis, W., *Das Problem d. Traumes.* Püttman, Stuttgart, 1928.

Adler, Alfred, *The Practice and Theory of Individual Psychology.* Harcourt, Brace and Company, New York, 1929.

—— *The Neurotic Constitution.* Moffat, Yard, and Co., New York, 1917.

—— *Individual Psychology.* Kegan, Trench, Trubner, & Co., Ltd., London, 1924.

—— On the Interpretation of Dreams. *Int. J. Indiv. Psychol.,* II, 1936.

—— Ein verlogener Traum. *Zbl. f. Psa.,* I, 1911.

Adler, G., Study of a Dream: Contribution to Concept of Collective Unconscious and to Technic of Analytic Psychology. *Brit. J. Med. Psychol.,* XXVI, 1941.

Aeppli, E., *Der Traum u. seine Deutung.* Rentsch, Zurich, 1943.

Aichele, J., Animals in Dreams and Imagination of Children and Adolescents (German). *Zbl. f. Psychother.,* 1940.

Alexander, Franz, *Proceedings of the Brief Psychotherapy Council.* Institute for Psychoanalysis, Chicago, 1942, 1944.

—— Ueber Traumpaare und Traumreihen. *Int. Ztschr. f. Psa.,* XI, 1925.

—— About Dreams with Unpleasant Content. *Psychiat. Quart.,* IV, 1930.

—— Indications for Psychoanalytical Therapy. *Bulletin of the New York Academy of Medicine,* June, 1944.

—— and French, T. M., *Psychoanalytic Therapy.* Ronald Press, New York, 1944.

—— and Wilson, G. W., Quantitative Dream Studies: A Methodological Attempt at a Quantitative Evaluation of a Psychoanalytic Material. *Psa. Quart.,* IV, 1935.

Allers, Rudolf, Zur Pathologie d. Labyrinthtonus. *Mschr. f. Psychiat. u. Neurol.,* XXVI, 1909.

Anderson, J. E., Dreams as a Reconditioning Process. *J. Abnorm. & Soc. Psychol.,* XXII, 1926.

Aristotle, *De Somno et Vigilia.* Ed. by G. A. Becker. Lipsia, 1823.

—— *Parva naturalia.* Clarendon Press, Oxford, 1908.

Arnold-Foster, M., *Studies in Dreams.* Macmillan Co., New York, 1921.

Arieti, Silvano, Primitive Intellectual Mechanisms in Psychopathological Conditions. *Am. J. Psychotherapy,* IV, 1, 1950.

Artemidoros of Daldis (contemporary of Marcus Aurelius), *Oneirocritica.* Germ. by F. S. Krauss, Hartleben, Vienna, 1881.

Astvazaturov, M. I., A Survey of Modern Doctrines of Dream Symbolism and their Diagnostic Value (Russian). *Sovetskaya Vrach. Gaz.,* I, 1935.

B

Baege, M. H., *Naturgeschichte d. Traumes*. Hesse & Becker, Lipsia, 1928.

Bagby, E., Dreams during Emotional Stress. *J. Abnorm. & Soc. Psychol.*, Vol. XXV, 1930.

Barahal, H. S., Dream Structure and Intellect. *Psychiat. Quart.*, X, 1936.

Baudouin, C., *Introduction à l'analyse des rêves*. Collection Action et Pensée, Geneva, 1945.

Bayley, H., *The Lost Language of Symbolism*. Williams & Norgate, London, 1912.

Baynes, H. G., The Importance of Dream Analysis for Psychological Development. *Brit. J. Med. Psychol.*, XVI, 1936.

—— *Mythology of the Soul*. A Research into the Unconscious from Schizophrenic Dreams and Drawings. Bailliere, Tindall & Cox, London, 1939.

Becker, W. H., Nervenärztliche Erfahrungen zum Traumproblem. *Psychiat. Neur. Wschr.*, p. 300, 1937.

Bellamy, R., An Act of Everyday Life Treated as a Pretended Dream and Interpreted by Psychoanalysis. *J. Abn. & Soc. Psychol.*, X, 1915.

Benedek, Therese and Rubenstein, Boris B., *The Sexual Cycle in Women*. Psychosom. Med. Monogr. III, 1 and 2, 1942.

Benedict, A. L., Dreams. *N. Y. Med. J.*, April, 1919.

Bennet, E. A., The Use of Dreams in Psychotherapy. *Ment. Hyg.*, London, IV, 1938.

Benon, R., Confusion mentale et Onirisme. *Gaz. med. de Nantes*, XLIV, 1931.

Berg, Charles, *Deep Analysis*. W. W. Norton & Co., New York, 1947.

Berger, H., Ueber das Elektroenkephalogramm des Menschen. *J. f. Psychiat. u. Neurol.*, Vol. XL, 1930.

Bergler, Edmund, Third Function of "Day-residue" in Dreams. *Psa. Quart.*, July, 1943.

Bergmann, Gustav von, Ulcus duodeni u. veget. Nervensystem. *Berl. klin. Wschr.*, LI, 1913.

Beringer, N., Exper. Psychosen durch Meskalin. *Ztschr. f. d. ges. Neurol. u. Psychiat.*, LXXXIV, 1923.

Berkely-Hill, O., A Note on the Symbolic Use of Figures, *Int. J. Psa.*, II, 1921.

Bernfeld, Siegfried, Zwei Träume von "Maschinen." *Int. Ztschr. f. Psa.*, VI, 1920.

Berrien, F. K., Recall of Dreams during Periods of Sleep. *J. Abn. & Soc. Psychol.*, XXV, 1930.

—— A Statistical Study of Dreams in Relation to Emotional Stability. *J. Abn. & Soc. Psychol.*, XXVIII, 1933.

Bettelheim und Hartmann, Ueber Fehlleistungen des Gedächtnisses bei der Korsakoff Psychose. *Arch. f. Psychiat.*, LXXII, 1924.

Bien, Ernst, Dreifache Deutung eines Traumes. *Zbl. f. Psychother.*, IV, 1931.

—— Aktivanalyt. Traumdeutung. *Ber. üb. d. VI. Allg. ärztl. Kongress*, Dresden, May, 1931.

—— Die latente Homo- und Heterosexualität im Traume. *Psa. Praxis.*, III, 1933.

—— *Die Angst von dem Erröten.* Enke, Stuttgart, 1930.

Binger, Carl, et al, *Personality in Arterial Hypertension.* Psychosom. Med. Monogr., 1945.

Binswanger, L., Psychoanalyse und klin. Psychiatrie. *Int. Ztschr. f. Psa.*, VII, 1921.

—— *Wandlungen in d. Auffassung und Deutung des Traumes.* Springer, Berlin, 1928.

Bircher, W., Ein geheilter Fall von Epilepsie. *Fortschr. d. Sexualw. u. Psa.*, Deuticke, Vienna, 1931.

Birnbaum, K., *Selbstbekenntnisse.* Springer, Berlin, 1920.

Bjerre, P., *Das Träumen als Heilungsweg d. Seele.* Rascher, Lipsia, 1931.

Blanton, S., Dreams Have Meaning. *Hygeia*, Feb., 1941.

Bleuler, Eugen, *Dementia Praecox.* Deuticke, Vienna, 1911.

—— Träume mit auf der Hand liegender Deutung. *Münch. Med. Wschr.*, LX, 1913.

Blum, E., Zur Symbolik des Raben. *Psa. Bewegung.*, III, 1931.

Bodkin, M., The Representation in Dream and Fantasy of Instinctive and Repressing Forces. *Brit. J. Med. Psychol.*, VII, 1927.

Bonaparte, Marie, A Lion Hunter's Dream. *Psa. Quart.*, XVI, 1947.

Bond, N. B., The Psychology of Waking. *J. Abn. & Soc. Psychol.*, XXIV, 1929.

Bonjour, *Les Rêves.* Bibliotheque Universelle, Lausanne, 1920.

Born, Wolfgang, *The Dream.* Ciba Symposia, X, 2, 1948.

Bornsztajn, M., Zur Frage: "Die Spinne als Traumsymbol." *Int. Ztschr. f. Psa.*, IX, 1923.

Bosch, G., Ensueño y realidad. *Bol. d. Instit. Psiquiat.*, II, 1930.

Bose, G., Dreams. *Indian J. of Psychol.*, V, 1930.

Boss, M., Psychopathologie d. Traumes bei schizophrenen u. organ. Psychosen. *Ztschr. f. d. ges. Neur. u. Psychiat.*, CLXII, 1938.

Bostwick, A. S., Spatial and Time Relations in Dreams. *Nature*, London, 118, 1926.

Boulder, G. P., The Parallel between Dreams and Psychoses. *Med. Record*, August, 1920.

Braun, Ludwig, *Herz u. Angst.* Deuticke, Vienna, 1932.

Brenman, Margaret, Dreams and Hypnosis. *Psa. Quart.*, XVIII, 1949.

Bresler, J., *Das Träumen als geistig-seelische Nachtarbeit.* Marhold, Halle A. S., 1938.

Brill, Abraham, Artificial Dreams and Lying. *J. Abn. & Soc. Psychol.*, IX, 1914.

—— Fairy Tales as a Determinant of Dreams and Neurotic Symptoms. *N. Y. Med. J.*, 1914.

—— The Universality of Symbols. *Psa. Review*, XXX, 1943.

Brink, L. and Jelliffe, S. E., Compulsion and Freedom: The Fantasy of the Willow Tree. *Psa. Review*, V, 1918.

Brody, Matthew, The Biological Purpose of the Dream. *Psychiat. Quart.*, XXII, 1, 1948.

Brown, A. E., Dreams in Which the Dreamer Knows He Is Asleep. *J. Abn. & Soc. Psychol.*, X, 1915.

Brown, S., Sex Worship and Symbolism of Primitive Races. *J. Abn. & Soc. Psychol.*, X, 1915.

Bruce, H. A., *Sleep and Sleeplessness*. Little, Brown & Co., Boston, 1915.

Bryan, D., The Pearl and Castration Symbolism. *Int. J. of Psa.*, VI, 1925.

Burdach, K. F., *Physiologie als Erfahrungswissenschaft*. 1830.

Bürklen, K., Eine Untersuchung d. Blindenträume. *Ztschr. f. das österr. Blindenwesen.*, XIV, 1927.

Burr, C. B., Two Very Definite Wish-fulfillment Dreams. *Psa. Review*, III, 1916.

Burridge, W., On Dreams and Theories. *J. Ment. Sciences*, LXXVII, 1931.

Burrow, Trigant, The Physiolol. Basis of Neurosis and Dreams. *J. Soc. Psychol.*, I, 1930.

Burstin, J., Le symbole en psychiatrie. *Ann. Med. Psychol.*, CIV, 1946.

Burt, C., The Dream and Daydreams of a Delinquent Girl. *J. Exper. Pedag.*, VI, 1921.

Byrne, J. G., *Studies on the Physiol. of the Eye: Still Reaction, Sleep, Dreams, Hibernation, Repression*, etc. Lewis & Co., London, 1933.

Byron, George Gordon, *Complete Poetical Works of Byron*. Houghton Mifflin Co., Boston, 1933.

C

Cannon, A., Hypnotism and Dreamland. *M. Press*, CCXII, 1944.

Cannon, W. B., *Bodily Changes in Pain, Hunger, Fear and Rage*. Appleton-Century, New York, 1934.

Carrer, C., Notes on Analysis of a Case of Melancholia. *J. Neurol. and Psychiat.*, 1921.

Casey, R. P., Dreams and Decision. *Psychiatry*, VI, 1943.

Cason, H., The Nightmare Dream. *Psychol. Monogr.* XlVI, 1935.

Cassierer, E., *Philosophie d. symbolischen Formen*. Berlin, 1923.

Christoffel, Hans, Farbensymbolik. *Imago*, XII, 1926.

—— Beschäftigungstraum (Sisyphustraum) und Beschäftigungsdelir. *Ztschr. f. Neurol.*, CXVIII, 1928.

Chrysanthis, K., Length and Depth of Sleep. *Acta Med. Orient.*, May, 1946.

Cicero, *De Divinatione.*

Claparède, E., Rêve satisfaisant un désir. *Arch. de Psychol.,* XVI, 1917.

Clark, Pierce, Clinical Studies in Epilepsy. *Psychiat. Bul.,* IX, 1916.

Cohen, B., Ueber Traumdeutung in d. jüd. Tradition. *Imago,* XVIII, 1932.

Coleridge, S. T., *Poetical Works.* London, 1877.

Combes, M., *Le rêve et la personalité.* Boivin, Paris, 1932.

Coriat, I. H., *Stammering.* Nerv. & Ment. Dis. Publ., New York, 1928.

—— The Nature of Sleep. *J. Abn. Psychol.,* VI, 1912.

—— *The Meaning of Dreams.* Little Brown & Co., Boston, 1920.

Crenshaw, H., Dream Interpretation. *N. Y. Medical J.,* XCIX, 15, 1919.

Cubberley, A. J., The Effects of Tensions of the Body Surface upon the Normal Dream. *Brit. J. Med. Psychol.,* XIII, 1923.

Cushing, Harvey, The Possible Relation of the Central (Veget.) Nerv. System to Pept. Ulcers. *New Engl. J. Med.,* CCV, 1931.

Cutting, M. S., *What Dreaming Means to You.* Dodd, Mead, and Co., New York, 1927.

D

Daly, D. D., Numbers in Dreams. *Int. J. Psa.,* II, 1921.

Daly, King C., Dream and the Problem of Consciousness. *J. Gen. Psychol.,* XXXVII, 15.

Dangel, Richard, Ein Siamesisches Werk über den Traum. *Imago,* XVII, 1931.

Darlington, H. S., Tooth-losing Dream. *Psa. Review,* XXIX, 1942.

Dattner, Bernhard, Gold und Kot. *Int. Ztschr. f. Psa.,* I, 1913.

—— Die Stadt als Mutter. *Int. Ztschr. f. Psa.,* II, 1914.

Delage, Y., Quelques points de la psychologie du rêveur. *Bull. Instit. gen. psychol.,* XIX, 1919.

Despert, J. Louise, Dreams in Children of Pre-school Age. From *The Psychoanalytic Study of the Child,* Vol. III/IV, International Universities Press, Inc., New York, 1949.

Deutsch, E., The Dream Imagery of the Blind. *Psa. Review,* XV, 1928.

Dostoevsky, Fedor, *Der Idiot.* German by R. Herzog. Gutenberg Verl., Vienna.

Drenfold and Hirschberg, Dreaming and Dreams. *N. Y. Med. J.,* 1913.

Dugas, L., Reflexions sur un rêve. *J. de psychol. norm. et pathol.,* XXXI, 1934.

Dulaure, I. A., *Die Zeugung in Glauben, Sitten und Bräuchen.* Lipsia, 1909.

Dunbar, Flanders H., *Emotions and Bodily Changes.* Columbia Univ. Press, New York, 1938.

Dunlap, K., Sleep and Dreams. *J. Abn. & Soc. Psychol.,* XVI, 1921.

E

Eble, E., Beispiele zur Traumdeutung. *Int. Ztschr. f. Psa.,* XIII, 1927.

Economo, C. von, Encephalitis lethargica. *Wien. Med. Wschr.,* LXXIII, 1926.

—— Studien über den Schlaf. *Wien. Med. Wschr.*, LXXVI, 1926.

Eder, M. D., Augenträume. *Int. Ztschr. f. Psa.*, I, 1913.

—— A Camera as a Phallic Symbol. *Int. J. Psa.*, V, 1924.

—— Dreams as Resistance. *Int. J. Psa.*, 1930.

Ehrenwald, Jan, Telepathy in Dreams, *Brit. J. Med. Psychol.*, Vol. XIX, 1942.

—— Psychotherapy and the Telepathy Hypothesis. *Am. J. Psychotherapy*, IV, January, 1950.

Eichenberger, E., Somatisch bedingte Angstträume. *Arch. Psychiat. u. Nerv.*, LXXXVII, 1929.

Eisenbud, Jule, The Dreams of Two Patients in Analysis Interpreted as a Telepathic Rêve à Deux. *Psa. Quart.*, XVI, 1947.

Eisinger, K. and Schilder, P., *Träume b. Labyrinthläsionen. Mschr. Psychiat. Neurol.*, LXXIII, 1929.

Eisenstein, Victor W., Dreams Following Intercourse. *Psa. Quart.*, XVIII, 2, 1949.

Eisler, R., Der Fisch als Sexualsymbol. *Imago*, III, 1914.

—— Ueber einen bes. Traumtyp. Beitrag zur Analyse d. Landschaftsempfindung. *Imago*, VI, 1920.

—— A New Point of View in Dream Interpretation. *Psa. Review*, XV, 1928.

—— Mutterleibs- und Geburtsrettungs-Phantasien im Traum. *Int. Ztschr. f. Psa.*, VII, 1921.

—— Geburtstraum eines fünfjährigen Knaben. *Int. Ztschr. f. Psa.*, VIII, 1922.

Eitingon, Max, Bericht über die Berliner psychoanalytische Klinik (1920-1922). *Int. Ztschr. f. Psa.*, XIII, 1922.

Ellis, Albert, Re-analysis of an Alleged Telepathic Dream *Psychiat. Quart.*, January, 1949.

Ellis, Havelock, The Relation of Erotic Dreams to Vesical Dreams. *J. Abn. & Soc. Psychol.*, August, 1913.

—— *The World of Dreams*, 1911.

—— The Synthesis of Dreams. *Psa. Review*, XII, 1926.

Elwyn, Verrier, A Note on the Theory and Symbolism of Dreams among the Baiga. *Brit. J. Med. Psychol.*, XVI, 1937.

Emerson, R. W., *Complete Writings*. Wise & Co., New York.

Endtz, A., Ueber Träume d. Schizophrenen. *Int. Ztschr. f. Psa.*, X, 1924.

Epstein, D., Zur Differentialdiagnose org. u. psych. Erkrankungen, zugl. Beitr. z. Symbolik von rechts u. links. *Zbl. f. Psa.*, I, p. 411.

Erickson, M. H., On the Possible Occurrence of Dreams in an 8-month-old Infant, *Psa. Quart.*, X, 1941.

Euripides, *Hekuba.*

Ewarts, A. B., Color Symbolism. *Psa. Review*, VI, 1919.

Ewen, J. H., Sleep and its Relation to Schizophrenia. *J. Neurol. & Psychiat.*, XIV, 1934.

F

Farber, L. H. and Fisher, C., Experimental Approach to Dream Psychology through Use of Hypnosis. *Psa. Quart.*, XII, April, 1943.

—— and Hill, Lewis B., Unconscious Mental Activity in Hypnosis. *Psa. Quart.*, XIII, 1944.

Fechner, W., *Elemente der Psychophysik*, 1889.

Federn, Paul, Das Erwachen des Ich im Traume. *Int. Ztschr. f. Psa.*, XX, 1934.

—— Die Geschichte einer Melancholie. *Int. Ztschr. f. Psa.*, 1923.

—— Dream under General Anesthesia. *Psychiat. Quart.*, XVIII, 1944.

—— Ego Feelings in Dreams, *Psa. Quart.*, I, 1922.

—— Ueber zwei typische Traumsensationen. *Jb. f. psa. Forsch.*, VI, 1914.

—— Zur Frage des Hemmungstraumes. *Int. Ztschr. f. Psa.*, VI, 1920.

Feldman, Sandor, Interpretation of a Typical Dream: Finding Money. *Psychiat. Quart.*, XVII, July, 1943.

—— Interpretation of a Typical and Stereotyped Dream Met with Only during Psychoanalysis. *Psa. Quart.*, Oct., 1945.

—— Physik in d. Traumsymbolik. *Int. Ztschr. f. Psa.*, XV, 1929.

Fenichel, Otto, *Psychoanalytic Theory of Neurosis*. W. W. Norton & Co., New York, 1947.

—— Eine Traumanalyse. *Int. Ztschr. f. Psa.*, XV, 1929.

—— (and others), Symposium on Neurotic Disturbances of Sleep. *Int. J. Psa.*, XXIII, 1942.

—— Two Dream Analyses. *Bull. Menning. Clin.*, III, 1939.

—— Bewusstseinsfremdes Erinnerungsmaterial im Traume. *Int. Ztschr. f. Psa.*, XI, 1925.

—— Beispiele zur Traumdeutung. *Int. Ztschr. f. Psa.*, XIII, 1927.

Ferenczi, Sandor, Die Rolle der Homosexualität in der Pathogenese der Paranoia. *Jb. f. Psa.*, III, 1912.

—— *Further Contributions to the Theory and Technique of Psychoanalysis*. Boni & Liveright, New York, 1927.

—— Gulliver Phantasies. *Int. J. Psa.*, 1928.

—— Die psychol. Analyse d. Träume. *Psych. Neur. Wschr.*, XII, 1910.

—— Ueber lenkbare Träume. *Zbl. f. Psa.*, II, 1912.

—— Wem erzählt man seine Träume? *Zbl. f. Psa.*, III, 1913.

—— Zur Augensymbolik. *Int. Ztschr. f. Psa.*, I, 1913.

—— Zur Ontogenese d. Symbole. *Int. Ztschr. f. Psa.*, I, 1913.

—— Ungeziefer als Symbol der Schwangerschaft. *Int. Ztschr. f. Psa.*, II, 1914.

—— Affektvertauschung in Träumen. *Int. Ztschr. f. Psa.*, IV, 1916.

—— Träume der Ahnungslosen. *Int. Ztschr. f. Psa.*, IV, 1916.

—— Die Nacktheit als Schreckmittel. *Int. Ztschr. f. Psa.*, V, 1919.

—— The Symbolism of the Bridge. *Int. J. Psa.*, III, 1922.

—— und Hollos, Imre, Zur Psychoanalyse der paralytischen Geistesstörung. *Beih. z. Int. Ztschr. f. Psa.*, Vol. 5.

Finckh, J., Schlaf und Traum in gesunden und kranken Tagen. *Münch. ärztl. Rundsch.*, 1924.

Fischer, E. *Der religiöse Komplex im Kindertraum.* J. Püttmann, Stuttgart, 1929.

Fischer-Defoy, *Schlafen und Träumen.* Kosmos, Stuttgart, 1929.

Fliess, Robert, Knocking on Wood. *Psa. Quart.*, XIII, 3, 1944.

Flournoy, H., Symbolisme de la clef. *Int. Ztschr. f. Psa.*, VI, 1920.

—— Quelques rêves au sujet de la signification symbolique de l'eau et du feu. *Int. Ztschr. f. Psa.*, VI, 1920.

Flugel, J. O., Polyphallic Symbolism and the Castration Complex. *Int. J. Psa.*, V, 1924.

—— A Note on the Phallic Significance of the Tongue and of Speech. *Int. J. Psa.*, VII, 1925.

—— A Dress Reform Dream. *Int. J. Psa.*, XI, 4, 1930.

Fodor, Nandor, The Negative in Dreams. *Psa. Quart.*, Oct., 1945.

—— Nightmares of Suffocation. *J. Nerv. & Ment. Dis.*, XI, 1945.

—— Telepathic Dreams. *Am. Imago*, III, 1942.

—— The Psychology of Numbers, *J. Clin. Psychopath.*, VIII, 1947.

—— *The Search for the Beloved.* Hermitage Press, New York, 1949.

Foerster, R. H., Ein Traum mit kannibalistischer Tendenz. *Int. Ztschr. f. Psa.*, 1921.

Fokschaner, W., Ein Geburtstraum im d. Form. eines Flug- u Falltraumes. *Int. Ztschr. f. Psa.*, VIII, 1922.

Fortune, R. F., Symbolism of the Serpent. *Int. J. Psa.*, VII, 1926.

Foxe, A. N., Five as a Symbol. *Psa. Review*, XXXI, 1944.

Frankhauser, K., Ueber Traummystik. *Psych.-neur. Wschr.*, I, 1930.

—— Traumdeutung. *Zbl. f. Neurol.*, 124, 1930.

Frazer, Sir James G., *The Golden Bough.* Macmillan, New York, 1927.

French, T. M., Reality Testing in Dreams. *Psa. Quart.*, VII, 1927.

—— Insight and Distortion in Dreams. *Int. J. Psa.*, XX, 1939.

—— and Shapiro, Louis B., Dream Analysis in Psychosomatic Research. *Psychosomatic Medicine*, XI, 2, March-April, 1949.

—— and Alexander, Franz, *Psychogenic Factors in Bronchial Asthma.* Psychosomatic Med. Monogr., IV, 1941.

Freud, Anna, Schlagephantasie im Tagtraum. *Imago*, VIII, 1922.

Freud, Sigmund, *Gesammelte Schriften.* I-XI. Internat. Psychoanalyt. Verlag, Zurich, 1925.

—— *New Introductory Lectures on Psychoanalysis.* W. W. Norton & Co., New York, 1933.

—— *An Outline of Psychoanalysis,* W. W. Norton & Co., 1949.

—— Theory and Practice of Dream Interpretation; Additional Notes. *Int. J. of Psa.*, XXIV, 1943.

—— *Der Wahn u. die Träume in W. Jensen's "Gradiva."* Deuticke, Vienna, 1912.

—— *The Interpretation of Dreams.* Transl. by A. A. Brill. The Modern Library, 1950.

—— Märchenstoffe in Träumen. *Int. Ztschr. f. Psa.*, I, 1913.

—— Ein Traum als Beweismittel. *Int. Ztschr. f. Psa.*, I, 1913.

—— Das Motiv d. Kästchenwahl. *Imago*, II, 1913.

—— Darstellung d. "grossen Leistung" im Traum. *Int. Ztschr. f. Psa.*, II, 1914.

—— Metapsych. Ergänzungen z. Traumlehre. *Int. Ztschr. f. Psa.*, IV, 1916.

—— Traum u. Telepathie. *Imago*, VIII, 1922.

—— Bemerkungen z. Theorie u. Praxis d. Traumdeutung. *Int. Ztschr. f. Psa.*, IX, 1923.

—— Die okkulte Bedeutung d. Traumes. *Imago*, XI, 1925.

—— Delusion and Dream. *New Republic*, New York, 1927.

—— Eine erfüllte Traummahnung. *Imago*, 1941.

Frey, E., Zur Biologie d. Gefühlsdynamik u. Symbolbildung. *Schw. Arch. f. Neur. u. Psych.*, L, 1942.

Friedemann, Max, Anagoge Uebertragungsträume. *Psychother. Praxis*, II, 1935.

Friedjung, J. K., Weckträume. *Int. Ztschr. f. Psa.*, VI, 1920.

—— A Dream of a Child of Six. *Int. J. Psa.*, V, 1924.

—— Der Oedipus-Komplex im Fieberdelirium eines 9-jährigen Mädchens. *Imago*, XII, 1926.

Frink, H. W., Dreams and their Analysis in Reference to Psychotherapy. *Med. Record*, 1911.

—— Dream and Neurosis. *Interst. Med. J.*, 1915.

Froeschels, Emil, A Peculiar Intermediary State Between Waking and Sleeping. *Am. J. Psychotherapy*, III, 1949.

Frohman, Bertrand, Analyse eines Schlüsseltraumes. *Psa. Praxis*, I, 1931.

Frosch, J. S., Ueber die experim. Erzeugung v. Träumen in d. Hypnose. *Nervenarzt*, IX, 1936.

Furrer, A. Tagphantasie eines 6½-jährigen Mädchens. *Imago*, VIII, 1922.

Furtado, D. and Valente Pulido, A Case of Narcolepsy with Oneiric Manifestations. *J. Ment. Sci.*, XC, 1944.

G

Gahagan, L., The Form and Function of a Series of Dreams. *J. Abn. & Soc. Psychol.*, XXIX, 1935.

—— Sex Differences in Recall of Stereot. Dreams, Sleep-talking and Sleep-walking. *J. Genet. Psychol.*, XLVIII, 1936.

Galant, J. S., Ueber d. Traumleben d. Onanisten. *Ztschr. psa. Päd.*, III, 1929.

Garma, Angel, *Psicoanálisis de los Sueños.* Associacion Pscicoanalitica, Buenos Aires, Argentina, 1948.

—— Vicissitudes de los simbolos. *Rev. de Psicoanalisis*, IV, 1946.

—— La Proyeccion y la vuelta de los instinctos contra el yo en el sueño. *Pscicoterapia*, III, 1936.

—— Conflictos genitales en los sueños. *Rev. de Psicoanálisis*, IV, 1947.

—— The Traumatic Situation in the Genesis of Dreams. *Int. J. Psa.* XXVII, 1946.

—— La genesis del juicio de realidad. (Una teoría general de la alucinación.) *Rev. de Psicoanálisis*, II, 1945.

—— El método psicoanal. de interpretación de los sueños. *Rev. de Psicoanálisis*, I, 1943.

Gifford, E. W., Yuma Dreams and Omens. *J. Am. Folklore*, XXXIX, 1926.

Gill, M. M. and Berman, M., Treatment of a Rare Case of Anxiety Hysteria by a Hypnotic Technique. *Bull. Menninger Clin.*, VII, 1943.

Glover, Edward (Editor), *An Investigation of the Technique of Psychoanalysis*. Williams & Wilkins Co., Baltimore, 1940.

Goethe, J. W.: Faust.

Goitein, Lionel P., Footnote to an Allegory of Bellini. *Psa. Review*, January, 1942.

Goja, H., Hallucinationen eines Sterbenden. *Int. Ztschr. f. Psa.*, VI, 1920.

—— Nacktheit und Aberglaube, *Int. Ztschr. f. Psa. VII*, 1921.

Goldschmidt, Lazarus, *Der Babylonische Talmud,* Der. jüd. Verlag, Berlin, 1936.

Goldstein, Kurt, *Language and Language Disturbances*. Grune & Stratton, New York, 1948.

Gomes, M., Le rêve et la selection des idées. *Arch. Braz. Med.*, XVIII, 1928.

Gregory, J. D., Visual Images, Words and Dreams. *Mind*, XXXI, 1922.

—— The Dream of Frustrated Effort. *Psyche*. IV, 1923.

—— Dreams of Fear. *Psyche*. II, 1922.

Göttke, L., Ueber d. Traumleben d. Epileptiker. *Arch. Psych. u. Nervkr.*, CI, 1934.

Graber, G. H., Ueber Regression und Dreizahl, *Imago*, IX, 1923.

—— Die schwarze Spinne, *Imago*, XI, 1925.

—— Ein Paradies-Traum, *Ztschr. psa. Päd.*, IV, 1930.

Graven, Philip: Ein Fall von Morphinismus in Stekel's "Polyphonie d. Denkens." *Fortschr. d. Sexualw., u. Psa.*, Deuticke, Vienna, 1926.

Green, G. H., *The Day-dream. A Study in Development.* University of London Press, London, 1923.

—— The Problem of the Terror Dream. *Psyche*, V, 1924.

—— *The Terror Dream*. Kagan Paul, London, 1927.

Groddeck, George, *Das Buch vom Es*. Int. Psa., Verl., Vienna 1926.

Gross, Alfred, Zeitsinn u. Traum. *Int. Ztschr. Psa.* XIX, 1933.

Grosschopf, E. V., Schlaf u. Traum, *Ps.-neur. Wschr.*, XXXIX, 1937.

Grotjahn, Martin, Laughter in Dreams. *Psa. Quart.*, April, 1945.

—— Dream Observation in a two-year-four-month-old Baby. *Psa. Quart.*, VII, 1938.

—— George Groddeck and his Teaching about Man's Innate Need for Symbolization. *Psa. Review*, XXXII, 1945.

—— The Process of Awakening; Contribution to Ego Psychology and Problem of Sleep and Dream. *Psa. Review*, XXIX, 1942.

—— Some Clinical Illustrations of Freud's Analysis of the Uncanny. *Bull. of the Menninger Clin.*, XII, 2, 1948.

Gruhle, H. W., Die Traumdeutung d. Antike, *Arch. f. Ps. & Nervkr.* LXXXVI, 1929.

Grünebaum, G. E. von, A Note on Arabic Dream Interpretation. *Psa. Review*, XXX, 1943.

Grünberger, F., Beobachtungen über das Sprechen aus dem Schlaf. *Int. Ztschr. f. Indiv. Psychol.*, Vol. V, 1927.

Gutheil, Emil A., *Psychotherapie des prakt. Arztes*, Verl. f. Medizin, Vienna, 1934.

—— Two Cases of Enuresis, in Stekel's *Peculiarities of Behavior.* Liveright, New York, 1924.

—— Traumdeutung im Talmud, *Psa. Praxis*, III, 1933.

—— Basic Outline of the Active Analytic Technique. *Psa. Review*, 1933.

—— *The Language of the Dream.* Macmillan, New York, 1939.

H

Hacker, F., Systemat. Traumbeobachtung m. bes. Berücks. der Gedanken. *Arch. f. d. ges. Psychol.*, XXI, 1911.

Hafter, C., La evolusión de la moderna interpretación de los sueños. *Actas Ciba*, 1946.

Hagentorn, A., Narkose, Hypnose, Traum, Wachtraum. *Wien. Med. Wschr.* 1934.

Halbwachs, M., Le rêve et les images souvenirs. *Rev. Philos.*, XLVIII, 1923.

—— L'interpretation du rêve chez les primitifs. *J. de Psychol.*, XIX, 1922.

Hall, C. S., The Validation of Dream-Analysis as a Method for Appraising Personality. *Am. Psychologist*, 1946.

—— Diagnosing Personality by the Analysis of Dreams. *J. Abn. & Soc. Psychol.* XLII, 1947.

Hardcastle, D. N., Sleep, Dreams and Terrors. *Lancet*, 1943.

Harnik, J., Die Magd als Symbol der Mutter. *Zbl. f. Psa.*, II, 1912.

—— Beiträge z. Symbolik des "ausgelöschten Lichtes." *Int. Ztschr. f. Psa.*, V, 1919.

—— Resistance to Interpr. of Dreams in Analysis. *Int. J. Psa.*, XI, 1930.

Harriman, P. L., The Dream of Falling. *J. gen. Psychol.* XX, 1939.

Hart, Henry Harper, The Eye in Symbol and Symptom. *Psa. Review*, XXVI, 1949.

Hartmann, Eduard von, *Philosophy of the Unconscious*. Harcourt, Brace & Co., New York.

Hartmann, Heinz, Vorstudien über Manie. *Ztschr. f. d. ges. Neur. u. Psych.* LXVIII, 1921.

—— und Schilder: Zur Psychologie epilept. Ausnahmszustände. *Allg. Ztschr. f. Ps.*, LXXX.

Hassall, J. C., The Serpent as a Symbol. *Psa. Review*, VI, 1919.

Hastings, H.: *Encyclopedia of Religion and Ethics*. Edinburgh, 1910.

Hattingberg, Hans v., Ueber d. seel. Ursachen d. Schlaflosigkeit. *D. med. Wschr.*, LXI, 1935.

Hawthorne, W. C., Some Dream Experiences. *Psa. Review*, XII, 1925.

Heine, H., *Buch der Lieder*, Wolf Verlag, Lipsia, 1919.

Helpach, Willy, Traumdeutung oder Traumforschung? *Neuzeitl. Forsch.* Bad Wörishofen II, 1948.

Herbert, S., Drei Träume. *Int. Ztschr. f. Psa.*, III, 1922.

Herma, H., *et al*: Freud's Theory of the Dream in American Textbooks. *J. Abn. & Soc. Psychol.*, XXXVIII, 1943.

Hermann, Imre, Angstraum u. Oedipusphantasie. *Int. Ztschr. f. Psa.* VII, 1921.

Herschmann, H. und Schilder, P., Träume der Melancholiker. *Ztschr. f. d. ges. Neur. u. Psych.* 1920.

Herzberg, A., Dreams and Character. *Character & Personal.* VIII, 1940.

Heyer, G. B., *Das körperlich-seelische Zusammenwirken in den Lebensvorgängen*. Munich, 1925.

Heymann, G. und Brugmans, J., Eine Enquete über die spezielle Psychologie der Träume. *Ztschr. f. angew. Psychol.*, XVIII, 1921.

Hildebrandt, F., *Der Traum u. seine Verwertung*, 1875.

Hill, J. C., *Dreams and Education*. Methuen & Co., London, 1926.

Hinrichsen, O., Traum als Arbeit. *Ps.-neur. Wschr.*, 1937.

Hitschmann, Edward, Beiträge zur Sexualsymbolik des Traumes. *Zbl. f. Psa.*, 1, 1911.

—— Goethe als Vatersymbol. *Int. Ztschr. f. Psa.*, I, 1913.

—— Zum Thema Enuresis, Harnreiztraum, psychische Hemmung. *Zbl. f. Psa.*, III, 1913.

—— Ueber Träume Gottfried Kellers. *Int. Ztschr. f. Psa.* II, 1914.

—— Zu Tagträumen d. Dichter. *Imago*, IX, 1923.

—— Wandlungen d. Traumsymbolik b. Fortschr. d. Behandlung. *Int. Ztschr. f. Psa.* XVII, 1931.

—— Beiträge zu einer Psychopathologie d. Traumes. *Int. Ztschr. f. Psa.*, XX, 1934 and XXI, 1935.

Hoche, August, *Der Traum*, Ullstein, Berlin, 1924.

—— *Das träumende Ich*, Fischer, Jena, 1927.

—— *Schlaf u. Traum.* Ullstein, Berlin, 1928.

Hoff, Hans. Zusammenhang v. Vestibularfunktion, Schlafstellung und Traumleben. *Mschr. f. Psychiatr. u. Neurol.,* XCVII, 1937.

—— and Pötzl, Otto, Zeitrafferwirkung. *Ztschr. f. ges. Neur. u. Psych.,* CLI, 1934.

Hoke, E., Träume d. Lungenkranken. *Med. Klinik,* 1930.

Hooper, S. E., Controlled Dreams. *Psyche,* IV, 1923.

Horney, Karen, *New Ways in Psychoanalysis.* W. W. Norton & Co., New York, 1939.

Horsely, J. Stephan, *Narcoanalysis.* Oxford University Press, 1943.

Horton, L. H., Inventorial Record Forms of Use in the Analysis of Dreams. *J. Abn. & Soc. Psychol.* VIII, 1914.

—— What Drives the Dream Mechanism? *J. Abn. & Soc. Psychol.* XV, 1920.

—— The Mechanic Features in the Dream Process. *J. Abn. & Soc. Psychol.,* XVI, 1921.

Hubbart, L. D., A Dream Study. *Psa. Review,* VIII, 1921.

Hug-Hellmuth, H., Analyse eines Traumes eines 5½-jährigen Knaben. *Zbl. f. Psa.* II, 1911.

—— Kinderträume. *Int. Ztschr. f. Psa.* I, 1913.

—— Ein Traum, der sich selber deutet. *Int. Ztschr. f. Psa.* III, 1915.

I

I, Ging. *Buch d. Wandlungen.* Trans. fr. the Chinese into German by R. Wilhelm. Diedrichs, Jena, 1924.

Ikin, A. G. et al., The Psycho-galvanic Phenomenon in Dream Analysis. *Brit. J. Psychol.,* XV, 1924.

Isakower, Otto, A Contribution to the Psychopathology of Phenomena Associated with Falling Asleep. *Int. J. Psa.* XIX, 1938.

J

Jacobi, Jolan, *The Psychology of Jung.* Yale University Press, New Haven, 1943.

Jackson, John Hughlings, On the Evolution and Dissolution of the Nervous System. *Brit. Med. J.,* 1884.

Jaensch, E. R., Zur Methodik experim. Untersuchungen an opt. Anschauungsbildern. *Zbl. f. Psych. u. Physiol. d. Sinnesorgane.* LXXXV, 1920.

—— *Grundzüge d. Physiologie u. Klinik d. psycho-phys. Persönlichkeit.* Berlin 1926.

—— Die Wahrnehmung des Raumes. *Ibid,* Suppl., VI, 1911.

—— *Ueber d. Aufbau d. Bewusstseins.* Lipsia, 1930.

Jameison and McNeil, Some Unsuccessful Results with Psychoanalytic Therapy. *Am. J. of Psychiat.* XCV, 1933.

Janet, Pierre, Les obsessions et la psychasthenie. II, 1903.

Janzen, E. K., Ueber Tiersymbolik in Symptom u. Traum. *Ps.-neur. Bl., Amstd.,* XXXVI, 1932.

Jekels, Ludwig, A Bioanalytical Contribution to the Problem of Sleep and Wakefulness. *Psa. Quart.,* XIV, 2, 1945.

—— and Bergler, Edmund, Instinct Dualism in Dreams. *Psa. Quart.* IX, 1940.

Jelliffe, Smith Ely, Two Morphine Color Dreams, with Note on Etiology of Opium Habit. *Psa. Review,* XXXI, April, 1944.

—— Daydreams and Thinking. *Proc. M. H. Congress,* November 1912.

—— and Brink, L., The Role of Some Animals in the Unconscious. *Psa. Review,* IV, 1917.

—— The Symbol as an Energy Container. *J. Nerv. & Ment. Dis.* LVIII, 1919.

—— and White, William Alanson, *Diseases of the Nervous System.* Lee & Febiger, Philadelphia, 1935.

Jendrassik, E., Ueber d. Entstehung d. Halluzinationen u. d. Wahnes. *Neurol. Zbl.,* XXIII, 1905.

Jensen, W., *Gradiva,* 1913.

Jesover, J., *Das Buch der Träume.* E. Rowohlt, Berlin, 1928.

Jewell, J. R., The Psychology of Dreams. *Am. J. of Psychol.,* XVI, 1905.

Jolowicz, Ernst, Consciousness in Dream and in Hypnotic State. *Am. J. Psychother.,* 1, 2, 1947.

Jones, Ernest, Zur Psychoanalyse d. christl. Religion. *Imago,* XII, 1923.

—— Psychoanalytic Notes on a Case of Hypomania. *Am. J. of Insanity,* October, 1909.

—— *On the Nightmare.* Hogarth Press, Ltd., London, 1949.

—— *Papers on Psychoanalysis.* (Fifth Edition) Williams & Wilkins, Baltimore, 1948.

—— The Relationship between Dreams and Psychoneurotic Symptoms. *Am. J. of Insanity,* LXVIII, 1911.

—— A Forgotten Dream. *J. Abn. & Soc. Psych.* VII, 1912.

—— Frau u. Zimmer. *Int. Ztschr. f. Psa.* II, 1914.

—— A Peculiar Dream. *Int. J. Psa.* VII, 1925.

—— Snake Symbolism in Dreams. *Nature,* London, CXVIII, 1926.

—— Der Mantel als Symbol. *Int. Ztschr. f. Psa.,* VIII, 1927.

Jung, Carl Gustav, *Two Essays on Analytic Psychology.* Bailiere, Tindal & Cox, London, 1928.

—— Kryptomnesie. *Die Zukunft,* XIII, 1905.

—— *Psychology of the Unconscious.* Kegan Paul, London, 1921.

—— The Mechanism and Interpretation of Dreams. *Jb. f. psa. Forsch.,* III, 1912.

—— *Wandlungen u. Symbole d. Libido.* Deuticke, Vienna, 1925.

—— *Archetypen d. kollektiven Unbewussten.* Rhein-Verlag, Munich, 1935.

—— *Traumsymbole d. Individuationsprozesses.* Rhein-Verlag. Zurich, 1936.

—— Bewusstsein, Unbewusstes u. Individuation. *Zbl. f. Psa.* II, 1939.

—— Ein Beitrag z. Kenntnis d. Zahlentraumes. *Zbl. f. Psa.,* I, 1911.

—— *Modern Man in Search of a Soul.* Harcourt Brace & Co., New York, 1933.

—— The Dreamlike World of India. *Asia,* New York, 1939.

—— *The Interpretation of the Personality.* Kegan Paul, London, 1940.

—— *Seelenprobleme d. Gegenwart.* Rascher, Zurich, 1931.

—— *Studies in Word Association.* Heineman, London, 1918.

—— *Die psychol. Aspekte d. Mutter-Archetypus.* Eranos Year Book, 1938.

—— and Kerenyi: *Das göttliche Kind in mytholog. u. psycholog. Beleuchtung.* Pantheon, 1940.

—— *Zur Psychologie d. Trinitätsidee.* Eranos Yearbook, 1940.

—— *Collected Papers on Analytical Psychology.* Bailiere, Tindall & Cox, London, 1916.

K

Kafka, G., Notiz über einen im Traum angestellten Versuch d. Traum selbst zu analysieren. *Ztschr. f. angew. Psychol.* VIII, 1914.

Kant, O., Technique of Dream Analysis. *J. Abn. & Soc. Psychol.* XXXVII, 1942.

—— Dreams of Schizophrenic Patients. *J. Nerv. and Ment. Dis.,* Mar., 1942.

Kanzer, Mark G., The Therapeutic Use of Dreams Induced by Hypnotic Suggestion. *Psa. Quart.,* XIV, 2, 1945.

Kaplan, L., Ueber wiederkehrende Traumsymbole. *Zbl. f. Psa.,* IV, 1914.

Kardiner, A., *Traumatic Neuroses of War,* Paul Hoeber, Inc., New York, 1941.

Kardos, M. I., Zur Traumsymbolik. *Int. Ztschr. f. Psa.,* IV, 1916.

—— Aus einer Traumanalyse. *Int. Ztschr. f. Psa.,* IV, 1916.

—— Zur Traumdeutung. *Int. Ztschr. f. Psa.,* II, 1919.

Karpinska, L. v., Ein Beitrag z. Analyse "sinnloser" Worte im Traume. *Int. Ztschr. f. Psa.,* II, 1914.

Karpman, Benjamin, Dream Analysis of a Constitutional Psychopath. *Psa. Review,* XXXIII, 1946.

Kazowsky, A. D., Zur Frage nach d. Zusammenhange v. Träumen u. Wahnvorstellungen. *Neurol. Zbl.* X, 1901.

Keller, H. I., Neuerscheinungen über Schlaf u. Traum. *Ztschr. f. angew. Psychol.* XLI, 1932.

Kenneth, J. H., Spatial Relation in Dreams. *Nature,* London, XCVIII, 1926.

Kessel and Hyman, Value of Psychoanalysis as a Therapeutic Procedure. *J.A.M.A.,* 101, 1933.

Kielholz, A., Von den Träumen einer Blinden. *Mschr. f. Psychiat. u. Neurol.* CIV, 1941.

Kiewiet de Jonge, A. J., Der Traum als Erscheinung erniedr. Bewusstseins. *J. f. Psychiat. u. Neur.* XXVII, 1922.

Kimmins, C. W., *Children's Dreams.* George Allen and Unwin, Ltd., London, 1937.

Klages, Ludwig, Vom Traumbewusstsein. *Ztschr. f. Psychopath.* III, 1914.

Klatt, G., Träume eines Abstinenten. *Int. Ztschr. f. Indiv. Psychol.* 1929.

Klein, D. B., The Experim. Production of Dreams During Hypnosis. *Univ. Texas Bull.,* 3009, 1930.

Kleitman, Nathaniel, *Sleep and Wakefulness.* University of Chicago Press, Chicago, 1939.

Klimes, K., Waking Dreams during Altered State of Consciousness. *Arch. f. Psychiat.* CXIV, 1941.

Knight, Robert P., Evaluation of the Results of Psychoanalytic Therapy. *Am. J. Psychiat.* XCVIII, 3, 1942.

Knopf, Olga, Drei Träume. *Int. Ztschr. f. Indiv. Psychol.* VI, 1928.

Kogerer, H., Ueber d. Phantomglied. *Wien. Med. Wchschr.,* 1932.

Köhler, P., Beiträge z. systemat. Traumbeobachtung. *Arch. f. d. ges. Psychol.* XXIII, 1912.

—— Ein Beitrag z. Traumpsychologie. *Arch. f. d. ges. Psychol.* XXIV, 1913.

Kolisch, E., Ein böser Traum. *Ztschr. f. Psychother.,* VI, 1914.

Korzybski, A., *Science and Sanity.* The International Non-Aristotelian Library Publishing Co., Lancaster, Pa., 1941.

Krainsky, N., Energetische Theorie d. Traumes. *Neurol. Bote.* XIX, 1912.

Kranefeldt, W. N., Die Bedeutung d. Jungschen Psychol. f. d. Neurosentherapie. *Biolog. Heilkunst,* XLIX, 1932.

—— Die Psychoanalyse. Göschen, 1930.

—— Continuous Analysis. *Brit. J. Med. Psychol.,* XV, 1935.

Kratter, Otto, Das Erröten in d. Träumen eines Ereutophoben. *Psa. Praxis,* II, 1932.

Krauss, F. S., Der Vogel. Sexualsymbolische Studie. *Int. Ztschr. f. Psa.* I, 1913.

—— Ein Traum König Karls. *Int. Ztschr. f. Psa.* VI, 1920.

Kretschmer, Ernst, Das Ressentiment im Traum. *Ztschr. f. d. ges. Neur. u. Psych.* CXXXVI, 1931.

Kristianpoller, Alexander, *Traumdeutung im Talmud.* Monumenta Talmudica, Harz Verl., Vienna, 1923.

Kroll, S., Der Wille z. Krankheit. *Zbl. f. Psychother.,* V, 1932.

Kronfeld, Arthur, *Perspektiven d. Seelenheilkunde.* Springer, Berlin, 1930.

Kruger-Theimer, O. F., Das Traumerlebnis, ein Beitr. z. "Kindesaussage." *Kriminalistik*, XII, 1938.

Kubie, Lawrence S., *Practical Aspects of Psychoanalysis*. W. W. Norton, New York, 1936.

Kulovesi, Y., Der Raumfaktor in d. Traumdeutung. *Int. Ztschr. f. Psa.*, XIII, 1927.

L

Laforgue, René, Ein Traum Baudelaires. *Psa. Bewegung*, II, 1930.

Laignel-Lavastine, Valeur sémiologiue des reves. *J. med. franc.*, XV, 1926.

Laird, D. A., Smoking as a Symbol in a Woman's Dream. *Psa. Review*, XII, 1925.

Lalkaka, K. A. J., Evolution of Common Sex Symbol as Revealed in Dream. *Indian Physician*, Nov. 1944.

Landauer, K., Handlungen des Schlafenden. *Ztschr. f. d. ges. Neur. u. Psych.*, XXXIX, 1918.

—— Unentstellte Träume. *Ztschr. psa. Päd.*, II, 1927.

—— Freud's Lehre vom Traum. *Psych.-Neur. Bl., Amstd.*, XLI, 1937.

Landquist, J., Das künstlerische Symbol. *Imago*, VI, 1920.

Lanier, S., The Harlequin of Dreams. *Psa. Review*, II, 1915.

Landry, L., La notion de la mort dans les rêves. *J. de Psychol.*, XXX, 1933.

Laszlo, V. de, Versuch einer Traumdeutung auf Grundlage d. analyt Psychologie. *Zbl. f. Psychother.*, VIII, 1935.

Lauer, Ch., Das Wesen d. Traumes in d. Beurteilung d. talmud. u. rabbin. Literatur. *Int. Ztschr. f. Psa.*, I, 1913.

Lawrence, W. J., The Phallus on the Early English Stage. *Psyche & Eros*, II, 1921.

Lazarsfeld, R., Zur individualpsych. Traumlehre. *Int. Ztschr. f. Indiv. Psych.*, VIII, 1930.

Lenzberg, K., Traumform u. Traumsinn. *Int. Ztschr. f. Indiv. Psych.*, VI, 1928.

Leonhard, K., *Die Gesetze d. norm. Träumens. Thieme*, Lipsia, 1939.

Levin, M., Reconstruction Dreams. *Am. J. of Psychiat.*, XCVI, 1939.

Levy, L., Die Sexualsymbolik d. Bibel u. d. Talmud. *Ztschr. f. Sexualw.*, I, 1913.

—— Sexualsymbolik in d. bibl. Paradiesgeschichte. *Imago*, V., 1917.

Lewin, Bertram D., The Nature of Reality, the Meaning of Nothing, with an Addendum on Concentration. *Psa. Quart.*, XVII, 4, 1948.

—— Mania and Sleep. *Psa. Quart.*, XVIII, 1949.

Lidz, T., Nightmares and Combat Neuroses. *Psychiat.*, I, 1946.

Liebeault, A. A., *Le Sommeil provoqué et les états analogues*. Paris, 1889.

Liertz, R., Ueber das Traumleben. *Ztschr. f. Psa. Päd.*, I, 1926.

Lincoln, J. S., *The Dream in the Primitive Cultures*. Grosset Press, London, 1935.

Lind, J. E., The Dream as a Simple Wish-fulfillment in the Negro. *Psa. Review,* I, 1914.

Linde, B. D., Zwei interessante Träume. *Zbl. f. Psa.,* III, 1913.

Lindner, Robert, *Rebel Without Cause,* Grune & Stratton, New York, 1944.

Loar, L., An Adventure in Musical Psychoanalysis, *J. Musicol.,* II, 1940.

Loewenstein, Rudolph, A Posttraumatic Dream. *Psa. Quart.,* XVIII, 1949.

London, L. S., The Meaning of the Dream. *J. Nerv. & Ment. Dis.,* LXXV, 1932.

Loomis, A. L., Harvey, E. N., and Hobart, G. A., Electrical Potentials of the Human Brain. *J. Exper. Psychol.,* XIX, 1936.

Lorand, Sandor, Fairy Tales, Lilliputian Dreams and Neurosis. *Am. J. Orthopsychiat.,* VII, 1937.

—— On the Meaning of Losing Teeth in Dreams. *Psa. Quart.,* XVII, 1948.

—— *Technique of Psychoanalytic Therapy.* International Universities Press, New York, 1946.

—— Crime in Fantasy and Dreams of the Neurotic Criminal. *Psa. Review,* XVII, 1930.

Lorenz, E., Die Träume des Pharao. *Psa. Bewegung.,* II, 1930.

Lowson, J. D., The Interpretation of Dreams, *Psyche,* II, 1921.

Lowy, Samuel, *Biological Foundations of Dream Interpretation.* Kegan Paul, London, 1943.

—— Die biolog. Stellung d. Traumes. *Ned. Tijdschr. Psychol.,* VI, 1938.

—— Das Problem d. Tagesreste. *Zbl. Psychother.,* IV, 1931.

Lungwitz, H., *Das Träumen als geistig-seelische Nachtarbeit.* Marhold, Halle A. S., 1938.

Lynkeus, Joseph Popper, Dreaming like Waking. *Psa. Review.,* XXXIV, 1947.

M

Mack, Ruth J., A Dream from an Eleventh Century Japanese Novel. *Int. J. Psa.,* VIII, 1927.

Maeder, J., Sex u. Epilepsie. *Jb. f. psa. Forsch.,* I, 1909.

—— Symbolik im d. Legenden, Märchen, Gebräuchen u. Träumen. *Psychiat. Neur. Wschr.,* X, 1909.

—— Zur Entstehung d. Symbolik im Traum in d. Dem. Praecox, *Zbl. f. Psa.,* I, 1911.

—— Ueber d. Funktion d. Traumes. *Jb. f. psa. Forsch.,* IV, 1912.

—— Zur Frage d. teleolog. Traumfunktion. *Jb. f. psa. Forsch.,* V, 1913.

—— Ueber d. Traumproblem. *Jb. f. psa. Forsch.,* III, 1913.

Malinowski, B., *Magic, Science and Religion.* Beacon Press, Boston, 1948.

Marcinowski, J., Gezeichnete Träume. *Zbl. f. Psa.,* 11, 1912.

—— A Detailed Dream Analysis. *Psyche & Eros,* I, 1920.

—— Zwei Entbindungsträume einer Schwangeren. *Int. Ztsch. f. Psa.,* VII, 1921.

—— Dreams, Superstitions and Neuroses. *Psyche & Eros,* II, 1921.

—— Eine Traumanalyse. *Fortschr. d. Sexualw.,* II, 1926.

Makhdum, M. M., Symbolic Representation of the Dreamer's Body in Dreams. *Indian J. Psychol.,* XIII, 1938.

—— On the Stimulus-Response Relationship in Dreams. *Indian J. Psychol.,* XIV, 1939.

Malumud, W. and Linder, F. E., Dreams and Their Relationship to Recent Impressions. *Arch. Neur & Psych.,* XXV, 1931.

—— Dream Analysis. *Arch. Neur. & Psych.,* XXXI, 1934.

Marshall, C. R., A Factor in Hypnagogic Images. *Mind,* XLV, 1936.

Maupassant, Guy de, *Little Louise Roqué. Collected Works.* The World Syndicate Publishing Co., New York, N. Y.

Maury, I. J. A., *Le sommeil et les rêves.* Didier & Cie, Paris, 1878.

Mayer, A., Bemerkungen über d. Bedeutung d. Traumes in d. Gynäkologie. *Münchn. Med. Wschr.,* LXXIX, 1932.

Mayer, F., La structure de la rêve. *Arch. Psychol.,* XXV, 1935.

McConnel, V. H., The Significance of the Snake in Dreams. *Psyche,* XXIII, 1926.

McCurdy, J. T., The Embryology of Dreams. *Psa. Review,* III, 1916.

—— *The Metamorphosis of Dreams.* Harcourt, Brace & Co., New York, 1925.

—— The History of a Dream Theory. *Psa. Review,* LIII, 1946.

McGlade, H. B., Relationship between Gastric Motility, Muscular Twitching during Sleep and Dreaming. *Am. J. Digest. Dis.,* April, 1942.

Meerlo, A. M., Telepathy as a Form of Archaic Communication. *Psychiat. Quart.,* XXIII, 1949.

Menninger-Lerchenfeld, Der eigene Doppelgänger. *Psychother. Praxis,* II, 1937.

Merejkowski, Dmitri, *Leonardo da Vinci.* Lipsia, 1903.

Mette, A., *Der Weg Zum Traum.* Dion Verlag, Berlin, 1939.

Meunier, Rand Masselon R., *Les rêves et leur interprétation.* Blend et Cie, Paris, 1910.

Meyer, Ch., Zur Psychologie d. Traumbewusstseins. *Psychol. u. Med.,* III, 1929.

Meyer, S., Zum Traumproblem. *Ztschr. f. Psychol.,* LIII, 1909.

—— Die Traumform als Inhaltsdarstellung. *Int. Ztschr. f. Psa.,* VIII, 1922.

—— Träume von Morphinkranken. *Psychother. Praxis,* II, 1935.

—— The Analysis and Interpr. of Dreams Based on Various Motives. *J. Abn. & Soc. Psychol,* II, 1913.

—— Die Traumfolge eines Alkoholkranken. *Psych. Neur. Wschr.,* 1936.

Meyerson, I., Remarques pour une théorie du rêve; observations sur le cauchemar. *J. de Psychol.*, XXXIV, 1937.

Missriegler, Anton, Ueber Narkolepsie. *Fortschr, d. Sexualw. u. Psa.*, Vienna, 1924.

—— Der Traum als Barometer d. analyt. Situation. *Psa. Praxis*, I, 1931.

—— Vierzig Lebensjahre in einem Traum. *Psa. Praxis*, II, 1932.

Mitchell, E. G., The Physiolog. Diagnostic Dream. *N. Y. Med. J.*, CXVIII, 1923.

Mittelmann, Bela, Psychoanalytic Observations on Dreams and Psychosomatic Reactions in Response to Hypnotics and Anaesthetics. *Psa. Quart.*, XIV, 1945.

—— Ego Functions and Dreams. *Psa. Quart.*, XVIII, 1949.

Moers-Messmer, H. v., Träume u. d. gleichzeitige Erkenntnis d. Traumzustandes. *Arch. d. ges. Psychol.*, CII, 1938.

Moore, M., Recurrent Nightmares: Simple Procedure for Psychotherapy. *Mil. Surg.*, XCVII, Oct., 1945.

Morgan, W., Navajo Dreams. *Am. Anthrop.*, XXXIV, 1932.

Morgenstern, S., Ueber d. Traum-u. Phantasieleben d. Kindes. *Ztschr. f. psa. Päd.*, XI, 1937.

Moxon, C., Mystical Ecstasy and Hysterical Dream States. *J. Abn. & Soc. Psychol.*, 1921.

Müllendorf, *Die Schwänke des Nasr-ed-Din und Buadem.* Reklam Bibliothek, No. 2735, Lipsia.

Müller, Erwin, Traum u. Märchenphantasie. *Ztschr. f. päd. Psychol.*, XXXI, 1930.

—— Zur Kotsymbolik von Wertgegenständen. *Int. Ztschr. f. Psa.*, IX, 1923.

Müller, F. P., Traum u. Delirium. *Psych. Neur. Bl. Amst.*, 1928.

Müller, L. R., Waking Consciousness and Psychology with Special Reference to Mechanism of Dreams. *D. med. Wschr.*, Feb., 1941.

Muralt, A. v., Zur Frage d. Traumdeutung. *Schw. Arch. f. Neur. & Psych.* XI, 1922.

Murray, H. A. and Wheeler, D. R., A Note on the Possible Prophet. Nature of Dreams. *J. Psychol.*, III, 1937.

Musatti, C. L., Simbolismo onirico e sogni ricorrenti. *Riv. Ital. Psicoanal.*, II, 1933.

N

Nachmansohn, M., Ueber experim. erzeugte Träume. *Ztschr. f. d. ges. Neur. u. Psych.*, XCVIII, 1925.

—— Traumanalyse in Hypnose. *Nervenarzt*, I, 1928.

—— Zur Biologie d. Traumes. *Allg. Ztschr. f. Psych.*, XCV, 1931.

Nacht, S., La pensée magique dans le rêve. *Rev. Fr. de Psa.*, VII, 1934.

Nacke, P., Die forensische Bedeutung d. Träume. *Arch. Kriminol.*, V, 114, 1900.

—— Der Traum als feinstes Reagenz f. d. Art d. sex. Empfindens. *Mschr. f. Krim. Psychol.*, November, 1905.

—— Ueber Kontrastträume. *Arch. Kriminol.* XXVIII, 1907.
—— Die diagn. u. progn. Brauchbarkeit d. sex. Träume. *Aerztl Sachverst. Ztg.,* XVII, 1911.
Neuer, Alexander, Das Training im Traum. *Int. Ztschr. f. Indiv. Psychol.,* VI, 1928.
Nicoll, M., *Dream Psychology.* Oxford Univ. Press, 1917.
—— An Outline of the Idea of Rebirth in Dreams. *Brit. J. Psychol.,* I, 1921.
Nunberg, Hermann, Ein Traum eines 6-jähr. Mädchens. *Ztschr. f. psa. Päd.,* I, 1928.

O

Oberndorf, Clarence P., Considerations of Results with Psychoanalytic Therapy. *Am. J. of Psychiat.,* XCIX, 3, 1942.
—— *The Psychiatric Novels of Oliver Wendell Holmes.* Columbia Univ. Press, 1946.
—— Feeling of Unreality. *Arch. Neur. and Psych.,* XXXVI, 1936.
—— Depersonalization in Relation to Erotization of Thought. *Int. J. Psa.,* XV, 1934.
Ogden and Richards, *Meaning of Meaning.* Kegan Paul, London, 1923.
O'Neill, Eugene, *Mourning Becomes Electra.* Liveright, New York, 1931.
Orlow, J. E., Das Problem d. Traumes vom Standpunkt d. Reflexologie. *Arch. f. d. ges. Psychol.,* LXX, 1929.

P

Pailhas, Rêve periodique. *Arch. int. neurol.,* LII, 1933.
Pascoe, W. J., The Eye in Connection with Dreams. *Brit. J. Physiol. Opt.,* XIII, 1939.
Pear, T. H., The Analysis of Some Personal Dreams. *Brit. J. Psychol.,* VI, 1914.
Pederson-Krag, G., Telepathy and Repression, *Psa. Quart.,* XVI, 1947.
Peerbolte, M. L., Die Wiederholungstendenz in Träumen. *Psych. Neur. Bl. Amstd.,* XL, 1936.
Paine, S., Kleine Beiträge z. Traumforschung. *Zbl. f. Psa.,* III, 1913.
Peterson, M., Eine Bestätigung der "symbolischen Gleichungen." *Zb. f. Psa.,* IV, 1913.
—— Ein telepathischer Traum. *Zbl. f. Psa.,* IV, 1913.
Pfeifer, S., Der Traum als Hüter d. Schlafes. *Int. Ztschr. f. Psa.,* IX, 1923.
Pfister, Oscar, Experimental Dreams Concern. Theoretical Subjects. *Psyche & Eros,* II, 1921.
Pichon, E., Un court document d'oniro-critique. *Rev. Fr. de psa.,* III, 1929.
—— Rêve d'une femme frigide. *Rev. Fr. de Psa.,* V, 1932.
Pierce, F., *Dreams and Personality.* Appleton, New York, 1931.

Pilcz, A., *Ueber Hypnotismus, okkulte phänomene, Traumleben, etc.* Deuticke, Vienna, 1926.

Pipal, K., Der Lehrer im Traum d. Kinder. *Ztschr. f. psa. Päd.,* IV, 1930.

Pitsch, F. W., Psychose, Traum u. Krankheitsverlauf. *Zbl. Psychother.,* X, 1938.

Poe, E. A., *The Best Known Works.* Blue Ribbon Books. New York, 1941.

Pollak, Franz, Ueber eine eigenartige Form v. Traum u. Wahnentwicklung. *Ztschr. f. d. ges. Neur. u. Psych.,* XCV, 1925.

Porosz, M., Die Bedeutung u. Eklärung d. sex. Träume. *Arch. f. Dermatol.* CXI, 1912.

Pötzl, Otto, Ueber einige Wechselw. hysteriformer u. organ. zerebr. Störungsmech. *Jb. f. Psychiat. u. Neur.,* 1917.

—— Experim. erzeugte. Traumbilder in ihren Beziehungen z. indirekten Sehen. *Ztschr. f. d. ges. Neur. u. Psych.,* XXXVII, 1917.

—— Schlafzentrum u. Träume. *Med. Klinik,* XXII, 1926.

—— Analyse eines Traumes mit Zoopsie. *Psych. Neur. Wschr.,* XXIX, 1927.

—— Ueber richtende Momente im Traum. *Wien. Med. Wschr.,* LXXVII, 1927.

—— Tachystoskopisch provozierte opt. Halluzinationen. *Jb. f. Neur. u. Psych.,* XXXV, 1914.

Prescott, F. C., Poetry and Dreams. *J. Abn. & Soc. Psychol.,* VII, 1912.

Prince, Morton, The Mechanism and Interpretation of Dreams. *J. Abn. & Soc. Psychol.,* 1910.

Prinzhorn, Hans, *Die Krise d. Psychoanalyse.* Der neuz. Verl., Lipsia, 1928.

—— Schlafzentrum und Träume. *Med. Klinik.* XXII, 1926.

Protze, H., Der Baum als totemist. Symbol in d. Dichtung. *Imago,* V, 1917.

Putnam, J. J., Ein charakteristischer Kindertraum. *Zbl. f. Psa.,* II, 1912.

—— Dream Interpretation and the Theory of Psychoanalysis. *J. Abn. & Soc. Psychol.,* IX, 1914.

—— A Study of Symbolism Occurring in a Patient's Dreams. *Psa. Review,* V, 1917.

—— The Interpretation of Certain Symbolisms. *Psa. Review,* VI, 1918.

R

Raalte, F. van, Kinderträume u. Pavor nocturnus. *Int. Ztschr. f. Psa.,* I, 1913.

Rado, Sandor, Eine Traumanalyse. *Int. Ztschr. f. Psa.,* IX, 1923.

Rahmet, H., The Causation of Dreams. *Med. Record,* LXXXV, 1914.

Rank, Otto, Beispiel eines verkappten Oedipustraumes. *Zbl. f. Psa.,* I, 1911.

—— *Eine Neurosenanalyse in Träumen.* Int. Psa. Verl., Vienna, 1924.

—— *Art and Artist.* Knopf, New York, 1932.

—— Symbolschichtung im Wecktraum. *Jb. f. psa. Forsch.*, IV, 1912.

—— Zum Thema d. Zahnreizträume. *Zbl. f. Psa.*, I, 1911.

—— *Der Doppelgänger.* Int. Psa. Verl., Vienna, 1925.

—— *Psychoanalyt. Beiträge. z. Mythenforschung.* Int. Psa. Verl., Vienna, 1919.

—— Ein Traum, der sich selbst deutet. *Jb. f. psa. Forsch.*, II, 1910.

—— Zur symb. Deutung d. Ziffern. *Imago*, I, 1912.

—— Aktuelle Sexualregungen als Träume. *Zbl. f. Psa.*, II, 1912.

—— Eine noch nicht beschriebene Form d. Oedipustraumes. *Int. Ztschr. f. Psa.*, I, 1913.

—— Der Fisch als Sexualsymbol in modernen Bildwerken. *Imago.* III, 1914.

—— Traumdeutung, *Jb. f. psa. Forsch.*, VI, 1914.

—— Die "Geburts-Rettungsphantasie" in Traum u. Dichtung. *Int. Ztschr. f. Psa.*, II, 1914.

—— Fehlhandlung u. Traum. *Int. Ztschr. f. Psa.*, III, 1915.

—— Ein gedichteter Traum. *Int. Ztschr. f. Psa.*, III, 1915.

Rascovsky, Luis, Sueños adecuados para la divulgación del conocimiento onírico. *Rev. de Psa.*, III, 1946.

Raspe, C., Untersuchungen ueber Kinderträume. *Ztschr. f. Päd. Psychol.*, XXV, 1924.

Ratcliff, A. J. J., *Traum und Schicksal.* Sibyllen-Verl. Dresden, 1925.

Rausche, H., *Unsere Träume u. Traumzustände.* Enke, Stuttgart, 1926.

Reed, R., Serpent as a Phallic Symbol. *Psa. Review*, IX, 1922.

Reik, Theodor, *Probleme d. Religionspsychologie.* Int. Psa. Verl., Vienna, 1919.

—— Zur Rettungssymbolik. *Zbl. f. Psa.*, I, 1911.

—— Kriemhild's Traum. *Zbl. f. Psa.*, II, 1911.

—— Beruf u. Traumsymbolik. *Zbl. f. Psa.*, II, 1912.

—— Symbolisierung d. Frauenleibes. *Int. Ztschr. f. Psa.*, II, 1914.

—— Der Nacktheitstraum d. Forschungsreisenden. *Int. Ztschr. f. Psa.*, II, 1914.

—— Zur Sexualsymbolik. *Int. Ztschr. f. Psa.*, III, 1915.

—— Gold u. Kot. *Int. Ztschr. f. Psa.*, III, 1915.

—— Völkerpsycholog. Parallelen z. Traumsymbol d. Mantels. *Int. Ztschr. f. Psa.*, VI, 1920.

—— Zum Thema "Traum u. Nachtwandel." *Int. Ztschr. f. Psa.*, VI, 1920.

—— *Der eigene und der fremde Gott.* Int. Psa. Verl., Vienna, 1923.

Reitler, Rudolf, Zur Genital u. Sekretsymbolik. *Int. Ztschr. f. Psa.*, I, 1913.

—— Augensymbolik. *Int. Ztschr. f. Psa.*, I, 1913.

Renz, B., Schlange u. Baum als Sexualsymbole in d. Völkerpsychologie. *Arch. f. Sex. Forsch.*, I, 1916.

Rhan, A., Erklärungsversuch des Zahnreiztraumes. *Int. Ztschr. f. Psa.,* XVIII, 1932.

Ribot, T., La pensée symbolique. *Rev. Phil.,* LXXIX, 1915.

Riklin, F., *Wunscherfüllung u. Symbolik im Märchen.* Schr. z. angew. Seelenkunde, Deuticke, Vienna, 1908.

Rignano, E., A New Theory of Sleep and Dreams. *Mind,* XXIX, 1920.

Ritter, O., Von den Rätseln d. Traumwelt. *Ztschr. f. Psychol.,* CXIV, 1930.

Rivers, W. H. R., *Dreams and Primitive Culture.* Longmans, Green and Co., London, 1918.

—— Affect in Dreams. *Brit. J. Psychol.,* XII, 1921.

—— Methods of Dream Analysis. *Brit. J. Psychol.,* II, 1922.

—— *Conflict and Dream.* Harcourt, Brace & Co., New York, 1923.

Rivière, Joan, Phallic Symbolism. *Int. J. Psa.,* V, 1924.

Robitsek, A., Die Analyse von Egmont's Traum. *Jb. f. psa. Forsch.,* II, 1910.

—— Die Stiege u. Leiter als sex. Symbole in d. Antike. *Zbl. f. Psa.,* I, 1911.

—— Zur Frage d. Symbolik in d. Träumen Gesunder. *Zbl. f. Psa.,* II, 1912.

Roffenstein, Gaston, Experimentelle Symbolträume. *Ztschr. f. d. ges. Neur. u. Psych.,* LXXXVI, 1923.

Rogers, G., Dreams. *Rev. de med.,* LX, Nov.-Dec., 1945.

Róheim, Géza, Animism and Dreams. *Psa. Review,* Jan., 1945.

—— Technique of Dream Analysis and Field Work in Anthropology. *Psa. Quart.,* XVIII, 1949.

—— *The Eternal Ones of the Dream. A Psychoanalytic Interpretation of Australian Myth and Ritual.* Int. Univ. Press, New York, 1945.

—— Die Urszene im Traum. *Int. Ztschr. f. Psa.,* VI, 1920.

—— Telepathy in a Dream. *Psa. Quart.,* I, 1932.

—— Dreams of a Somali Prostitute. *J. Crim. Psychopath.,* II, 1940.

—— Myth and Legend. *Am. Imago,* II, 1941.

Roos, Allen, A Dream of the Prodrom. Phase of Acute Appendicitis. *Psychosom. Med.,* IV, 1942.

Rorschach, Herman, Reflexhalluzinationen u. Symbolik. *Zbl. f. Psa.,* III, 1911.

Rosenbaum, Ernst, Zur "aktiven" Traumdeutung. *Fortschr. d. Sexualw. u. Psa.,* 1931.

Rosenstein, G., Beziehungen v. Traum u. Witz. *Zbl. f. Psa.,* I, 1911.

S

Sachs, Hanns, *Gemeinsame Tagträume.* Int. Psa. Verl., Vienna, 1924.

—— Traumdeutung u. Menschenkenntnis. *Jb. f. psa. Forsch.,* III, 1911.

—— Ein Fall intens. Traumentstellung. *Zbl. f. Psa.,* I, 1911.

—— Ein Traum Bismarcks. *Int. Ztschr. f. Psa.,* I, 1913.

—— Traumdarstellung analer Weckreize. *Int. Ztschr. f. Psa.,* I, 1913.

—— Das Zimmer als Traumdarstellung d. Weibes. *Int. Ztschr. f. Psa.,* II, 1914.

—— Ein absurder Traum. *Int. Ztschr. f. Psa.,* III, 1915.

Sadger, Isidor, Ein Fall v. pseudoepil. Hysterie psa. erklärt. *Wien. Klin. Rundschau,* 1909.

—— *Die Lehre v. d. Geschlechtsverirrungen auf psa. Grundlage.* Deuticke, Vienna, 1921.

—— Ueber Pollutionen u. Pollutionsträume. *Fortschr. d. Med.,* XXXVI, 1918.

—— Ueber Prüfungsangst u. Prüfungsträume. *Int. Ztschr. f. Psa.,* VI, 1920.

Salmon, A., I sogni nella teoria psicoanal. di Freud. *Quad. psichiat.,* XI, 1924.

Sanctis, S. de, L'interpretazione dei sogni. *Riv. di psicol.,* X, 1914.

—— Cos'è il sogno? *La coltura med. moderna,* I, 1922.

—— La conscienza onirica. *Scientia,* XLIII, 1928.

—— Nuovi contrib. alla psicofisiologia del Sogno. *Riv. di psicol.,* XXIX, 1933.

Sarason, S. B., Dreams and T. A. T. Stories. *J. Abn. & Soc. Psychol.,* XXXIX, 1944.

Sarkar, S. L., A Study of the Psychol. of Sex. Abstinence from the Dreams of an Ascetic. *Int. J. Psa.,* XXIV, 1943.

Sarma, R. N., New Light on Dream Psychology from Upanishad Sources. *The Hindu,* Oct., 1932.

Saul, L. J., Utilization of Early Current Dreams in Formulating Psychoanal. Cases. *Psa. Quart.,* IX, 1940.

—— Psychologic Factors in Combat Fatigue: Special Reference to Nightmares. *Psychosom. Med.,* Sept., 1945.

Saussure, R. de, L'aphasie onirique. *Rev. med. de la Suisse Rom.,* XLIII, 1923.

—— Note sur un rêve d'un claustrophobe. *Arch. de psychol.,* 1925.

Savage, G. H., Some Dreams and Their Significance. *J. Ment. Sci.,* LVIII, 1912.

Scarpatetti, W. v., Alarmierende Traumsymbolik b. Depressiven. *Psa. Praxis,* III, 1933.

Schaeffer, A., Geschichte eines Traumes. *Imago,* XIV, 1928.

—— Der Mensch u. des Feuer. *Psa. Bewegung,* II, 1930.

Scheersohn, F., Traum u. Spiel. *Schw. Arch. f. Neur. u. Psych.,* XXXVII, 1936.

Schenk, P., Ueber d. Schlaferleben. *Mschr. f. Psychiat. u. Neurol.,* LXXII, 1929.

Scherner, R. A., *Das Leben d. Traumes.* Berlin, 1861.

Schilder, Paul, *Psychotherapy.* W. W. Norton & Co., New York, 1939.

—— *Psychiatrie auf psa. Grundlage.* Int. psa. Verl., Vienna, 1925.

—— *Selbstbewusstsein u. Persönlichkeitsbewusstsein.* Monogr, a. d. Gesamtgeleit d. Neur, u, Psych., Berlin, 1914.

—— *Wahn und Erkenntnis.* Monogr. aus d. Gesamtgebeit d. Neur. u. Psych., Springer, Berlin, 1918.

—— Body Image in Dreams. *Psa. Review,* April, 1942.

—— *Mind: Perception and Thought.* Columbia University Press, New York, 1942.

—— *Goals and Desires of Man.* Columbia University Press, New York, 1942.

—— u. Herschmann, H., Träume d. Melancholischen, *Ztschr. f. d. ges. Neur. u. Psych.,* LIII, 1919.

Schindler, Walter, Die Traumdeutung im Lichte d. versch. tiefen-psychol. Schulen u. ihre klin. Bedeutung. *Ber. über d. IV. Allg. ärztl. Kongress f. Psychother. in Bad Nauheim,* April, 1929.

Schmeing, K., Flugträume u. "Exkursion des Ich." *Arch. f. d. ges. Psychol.,* C, 1938.

Schmid, G., Die Gesetzmässigkeiten d. Traumlebens. *Ztschr. f. Psychol.,* CXXXV, 1935.

Schmideberg, Melitta, Ein Prüfungtraum. *Int. Ztschr. f. Psa.,* XIX, 1933.

Schmidt, W., Magische Traumerlebnisse. *Arch. f. Psych. u. Nerv.,* LXXXVI, 1929.

Schmitz, A., Wahrträume u. Erinnerungsfälschungen. *Psych. Neur. Wschr.,* XXIII, 1922.

Schneider, Daniel E., Time-Space and the Growth of the Sense of Reality: A Contribution to the Psychophysiology of the Dream. *Psa. Review,* XXXV, 3, 1948.

Schneider, Kurt, *Die abnormen seelischen Reaktionen.* Deuticke, Vienna, 1927.

Schönberger, S., A Dream of Descartes. *Int. J. Psa.,* XX, 1939.

—— Clinical Contribution to Analysis of Nightmare Syndrome. *Psa. Review,* XXX, Jan., 1946.

Schreiner, W., Einige Traumbeobachtungen. *Ztschr. f. Psychol.,* CXXXIV, 1935.

Schroetter, K., Experim. Träume. *Zbl. f. Psa.,* II, 1912.

Schulte-Vaerting, H., Die rezess. Erbmassen werden im Traum zu dominanten. *Psychol. u. Med.,* IV, 1930.

Schulze, H., Ein Spermatozoentraum im Zusammenh. m. Todeswünschen. *Int. Ztschr. f. Psa.,* II, 1914.

Schwab, G., Das Träumen als psychophysische Funktion u. pathol. Erscheinung. *Psych. Neur. Woschr.,* XXXIX, 1937.

Seashore, C. E., The Frequency of Dreams. *Scient. Monthly,* II, 1916.

Seelert, I, Zur psa. Traumdeutung. *D. Med. Wschr.,* XLVII, 1921.

Seidler, R., Kinderträume. *Int. Ztschr. f. Indiv. Psychol.,* XI, 1933.

Selling, L. S., Effect of Conscious Wish upon Dream Content. *J. Abn. & Soc. Psychol.,* XXVII, 1932.

Sharpe, Ellen, *Dream Analysis.* W. W. Norton & Co., 1938.

Short, Ernest H., *The Painter in History.* Hollis & Carter, London, 1948.

Siebert, K., *Fehlleistung u. Traum*. Braumüller, Vienna, 1932.

—— Die Gestaltbildung im Traum. *Arch. f. d. ges. Psychol.*, XC, 1934.

Sigg-Boeddinghaus, M., Die prakt. Verwend. d. Traumanalyse von C. G. Jung. *Psychol. Rundsch.*, III, 1931.

Silberer, Herbert, Bericht über eine Methode gewisse symb. Halluzinationserscheinungen hervorzurufen u. zu beobachten. *Jb. f. psa. Forsch.* I, 1909.

—— Märchensymbolik. *Imago*, I, 1912.

—— Von d. Kategorien d. Symbolik. *Zbl. f. Psa.*, 11, 1912.

—— Spermatozoenträume. *Jb. f. psa. Forsch.*, IV, 1912.

—— Zur Symbolbildung. *Jb. f. psa. Forsch.*, IV, 1912.

—— *Problems of Mysticism and Symbolism*. Moffat, Yard & Co., 1917.

—— *Der Traum*. Enke, Stuttgart, 1919.

—— Zur Verdichtungtechnik. *Int. Ztschr. f. Psa.*, VIII, 1922.

Silverberg, William, Notes on the Mechanism of Reaction-Formation. Dream Material. *Psa. Review*, XIX, 1932.

Simonson, E., Ueber d. Verh. v. Raum u. Zeit zur Traumarbeit. *Imago*, XIV, 1928.

Sinclair, M., Symbolism and Sublimation. *Med. Press*, August, 1916.

Sirna, A. A., An Electroencephalograph: Study of the Hypnot. Dream. *Am. J. Psychol.*, XX, 1945.

Skliar, N., The Origin of the Sleep. (Russian) *J. nevropath. i psichiat.*, XXI, 1928.

Slight, D., Hypnagogic Phenomena. *J. Abn. & Soc. Psychol.*, XIX, 1924.

Smith, M. H., An Interesting Dream. *Int. J. Psa.*, V, 1924.

Soesman, F. J., Organreizträume. *Ned. Tijdschr. Geneesk.*, LXXII, 1928.

Sokolow, A., Dreams of Alcoholics during the Treatment (Russian). *Sovetsk. Nevropatol.*, IV, 1935.

Sollier, P. et Courbon P., De l'imagination au delire et au rêve. *J. de psychol. norm. et path.*, XX, 1923.

Solomon, M., On the Analysis and Interpretation of Dreams. *J. Abn. & Soc. Psychol.* IX, 1914.

—— A Few Dream Analyses. *J. Abn. & Soc. Psychol.* IX, 1914.

—— Some Remarks on the Meaning of Dreams. *Med. Record*, LXXXV, 1914.

—— A Contrib. to the Analysis and Interpr. of Dreams. *Am. J. of Insan.*, LXXI, 1914.

—— Meaning and Interpr. of Dreams. *Arch. Neur. & Psych.*, XLVI, 1941.

Soulie de Morant, G., Les rêves étudies par les chinois. *Rev. fr. de psa.*, I, 1927.

Sperber, Alice, Ueber d. Auftreten v. Hemmungen bei Tagträumen. *Imago*, XVI, 1930.

Sperber, M., Zur Technik d. Traumdeutung. *Int. Ztschr. f. Indiv. Psychol.*, VI, 1928.

Spielrein, S., Selbstbefriedigung u. Fussymbolik. *Zbl. f. Psa.*, III, 1913.

—— Zwei Mensesträume. *Int. Ztschr. f. Psa.*, II, 1914.

—— Tiersymbolik u Phobie b. einem Kinde. *Int. Ztschr. f. Psa.*, II, 1914.

—— Briefmarkentraum. *Int. Ztschr. f. Psa.*, VIII, 1922.

Spiller, G., *A Contribution towards a Science of Dreams.* Farleigh Press, London, 1914.

Staerke, J., Der Hammer als männl. Potenzsymbol. *Int. Ztschr. f. Psa.*, II, 1914.

—— Sensation d. gemeins. Traumes. *Int. Ztschr. f. Psa.*, II, 1914.

—— Psychoanalyse u. Psychiatrie. Beiheft, *Int. Ztschr. f. Psa.*, IV, 1921.

—— Gross u. klein kann im Traume wichtig u. unwichtig bedeuten. *Int. Ztschr. f. Psa.*, II, 1914.

—— Zur Drachenfliegersymbolik. *Int. Ztschr. f. Psa.*, II, 1914.

—— Neue Traumexperimente im Zusammenhang m. älteren u. neueren Traumtheorien. *Ps.-neur. Bl., Amst.*, XVI, 1912.

Stegmann, M., Ein Vexiertraum. *Int. Ztschr. f. Psa.*, I, 1913.

—— Darstellung epilept. Anfälle im Traum. *Int. Ztschr. f. Psa.*, I, 1913.

Steiner, Maximilian, Die Traumsymbolik d. analyt. Situation. *Int. Ztschr. f. Psa.*, XXI, 1935.

Stekel, Wilhelm, *Disorders of Instincts and Emotions.* Liveright, New York.

—— *Autobiography. ibid*, 1950.

—— *Die Sprache des Traumes.* Bergmann, Munich, 1911.

—— Der epil. Sympt.-Komplex u. seine analyt. Behandlung. *Fortschr. d. Sexualw. u. Psa.*, 1924.

—— *Träume d. Dichter.* Bergmann, Wiesbaden, 1912.

—— *Sex and Dreams.* Badger, Boston, 1922.

—— Die Uhr als Symbol. d. Lebens. *Zbl. f. Psa.*, II, 1912.

—— Der Traum eines Sterbenden. *Zbl. f. Psa.*, III, 1913.

—— Individuelle Traumsymbole. *Zbl. f. Psa.*, IV, 1914.

—— Analyse einer Dyspareunie an Hand einer Traumdeutung. *Psa. Praxis*, I, 1931.

—— *The Interpretation of Dreams.* Liveright, New York, 1943.

—— *Die Technik d. analyt. Psychotherapie.* Med. Verl. Huber, Bern, 1938.

Sterba, Richard. Dreams and Acting Out. *Psa. Quart.*, XV, 2, 1946.

—— Ein Prüfungstraum. *Int Ztschr. f. Psa.*, XIII, 1927.

Stern, A., Night Terrors. *N. Y. Med. J.*, CI, 1915.

—— Day Fantasies in a Child. *N. Y. Med. J.*, CVIII, 1918.

—— Sexualsymbol. Wunschphantasien in einen frei erfundenen Kinderspiel. *Ztschr. f. psa. Päd.*, VI, 1932.

Stiles, P. G., *Dreams.* Harvard Univ. Press, Cambridge, 1927.

Still, G. F., Day Terrors. (Pavor Diurnus) in Children. *Lancet*, Feb. 1900.

Stocker, A., Oedipustraum eines Schizophrenen. *Int. Ztschr. f. Psa.* VIII, 1922.

—— *Les rêves et les songes.* Ed. Oevres de St. Augustin, St. Maurice, 1945.

Storch, A. and Heichelheim, F., Zum Traumglauben in d. Antike. *Zbl. f. Psychother.*, IV, 1931

Storfer, A. J., *Marias jungfräul. Mutterschaft.* Barsdorf, Berlin, 1914.

—— Eine Traumtheorie vor 150 Jahren. *Psa. Bewegung.*, I, 1929.

Strachey, A. S., Analysis of a Dream of Doubt and Conflict. *Int. J. Psa.*, III, 1922.

Stragnell, G., The Dream in Russian Literature. *Psa. Review*, VIII, 1921.

—— Condensation and Resymbolization in Dream Interpretation. *Psa. Review,* IX, 1922.

—— The Golden Phallus. *Psa. Review*, XI, 1924.

Streiff, J., Ueber d. Sehen im Traum. *Ztschr. f. Sinnesphysiol.*, LVI, 1925.

Struempell, E. v., *Die Natur u. d. Entstehung d. Träume.* Lipsia, 1899.

Sturt, M., A Note on Some Dreams of a Normal Person. *Brit. J. Psychol.*, XIII, 1922.

Sumner, F. C., Core and Context in the Drowsy State. *Am. J. Psychol.*, XXXV, 1924.

Sun, J. T., Symbolism in the Sumerian Written Language. *Psa. Review*, XI, 1924.

Sussmann, L., Beitrag z. Problem d. Träume d. Schizophrenen. *Nervenarzt*, IX, 1936.

Swoboda, Herman, *Die Perioden d. menschl. Organismus in ihrer psych. u. biol. Bedeutung.* Deuticke, Vienna, 1904.

Sydow, Eckert V., Träume u. Visionen in d. Religion d. Indianer Nordamerikas. *Imago*, XXI, 1935.

—— in Prinzhorn's *Die Krise d. Psychoanalyse.* Der neugeistige Verl., Lipsia, 1928.

Symons, N. J., A Note on the Formation of Symbols. *Int. J. Psa.*, VI, 1925.

—— Two Dreams. *Int. J. Psa.*, X, 1929.

Szekely, S., Beiträge z. indiv. psychol. Traumtheorie. *Int. Ztschr. f. Indiv. Psychol.*, XII, 1934.

T

Tait, W. D., Motor Speech Functions in Dreams. *J. Abn. & Soc. Psychol.*, 1923.

Tannenbaum, S. A., The Art of Dream Interpretation. *J. Urol. and Sexol.*, 1919.

Tarachow, Sidney, The Analysis of a Dream Occurring During a Migraine Attack. *Psa. Review*, XXXIII, 1946.

Tausk, Viktor, Darstellung der Lage d. Träumers im Traume. *Int. Ztschr. f. Psa.*, I, 1913.

—— Zwei homosex. Träume. *Int. Ztschr. f. Psa.* II, 1914.

—— Ein Zahlentraum. *Int. Ztschr. f. Psa.* II, 1914.

—— Kleine Beiträge z. Traumdeutung. *Int. Ztschr. f. Psa.*, II, 1914.

Teilard, Anna, *Traumsymbolik*. Rascher Verl., Zurich, 1944.

Thenon, J., El estudio psicoanalítico de los sueños en las neurosis. *Rev. Crim. Psiquiat Y Med.*, XVII, 1930.

Thompson, S. R., An Inquiry into Some Questions Connected with Imagery in Dreams. *Brit. J. Psychol.*, October 1914.

Tieresias, P. N., *Il libro dei Sogni*. Hoepli, Milan, 1933.

Toffelmeier, G. and Luomala, K., Dreams and Dream Interpretation of the Diegueño Indians of Southern California. *Psa. Quart.*, V, 1936.

Trachtenberg, Joshua, *Jewish Magic and Superstitution*. Behrman's Jewish Book House, New York, 1939.

Trapp, C. E. and Lyons, R. H., Dream Studies in Hallucinating Patients. *Psa. Quart.* XI, 1937.

Travis, L. E., Suggestibility and Negativism as Measured by Auditory Threshold During Reverie. *J. Abn. & Soc. Psychol.* XVIII, 1924.

Tremmel, E., Komplexreiz-Methode. *Fortschr. d. Sexualw. u. Psa.* 1, 1924.

Tridon, A., *Psychoanalysis, Sleep and Dreams*. Kegan Paul & Co., London, 1925.

Turel, A., Sexualsymbolik. *Ztschr. f. Sexualw.*, IV, 1918.

V

Valentine, C. W., *Dreams and the Unconscious*. Macmillan Co., New York, 1921.

Varendonck, J., *The Psychology of Daydreams*. Allen and Unwin Ltd., London, 1921.

Vaschide, N., *Le sommeil et les rêves*. Flammarion, Paris, 1911.

Velikovski, Emmanuel, Dreams Freud Dreamed. *Psa. Review*, XXVIII, 1941.

—— Psychoanalyt. Ahnungen in d. Traumdeutungskunst d. alten Hebräer. *Psa. Bewegung.*, V, 1933.

—— Can a Newly Acquired Language Become the Speech of the Unconscious? *Psa. Review*, XXI, 1934.

Vierordt, H., *Das Büchlein d. Träume*. Reuss & Itta, Konstanz, 1922.

Vindron, J., Essai d'interprétation des phénomènes de l'incubat. *J. de Psychol.* XXIV, 1927.

W

Wälder, Robert, Sexualsymbolik b. Naturvölkern. *Psa. Bewegung.* I, 1929.

Walleczek, F., Warum träumt man? *Arch. f. d. ges. Psychol.* LXVI, 1928.

Walker, D. F., Record of a Remarkable Dream. *J. Soc. Psych. Res.*, No. 450, 1928.

Walsh, W. S., Dreams of the Feebleminded. *Med. Review*, 1920.

—— *The Psychology of Dreams*. Dodd, Mead & Co., New York, 1920.

Waterman, G. A., Dream as a Cause of Symptoms. *J. Abn. Psychol.* V, 1910.

Watson, J., An Analysis of Some Personal Dreams. *Proc. Am. Soc. f. Psych. Res.*, VIII, 1914.

Watt, H. J., *The Common Sense of Dreams.* Clark Univ. Press, Worcester, Mass.

Weber, F. P., Thoughts about Thinking and Dreaming. *J. Neurol. & Psychopath.*, I, 1920.

Weber, R., Rêveries et images. *Int. Ztschr. f. Psa.*, I, 1913.

Wechsler, I. S., *The Neurologist's Point of View.* L. B. Fischer, New York, 1945.

Weinberg, A. K., The Dream of Jean Christophe. *J. Abn. & Soc. Psych.* XIII, 1918.

Weiss, E., Totemmaterial in einem Traume. *Int. Ztschr. Psa.*, II, 1914.
—— Ueber Symbolik. *Psa. Bewegung.* III, 1931.

Weiss, H. B., Oneirocritica Americana. *Bull. N. Y. Pub. Library*, XLVIII, 1944.

Weiss, K., Ein Pollutionstraum. *Int. Ztschr. f. Psa.*, VI, 1920.

White, William A., Symbolism. *Psa. Review*, III, 1916.
—— *Foundations of Psychiatry.* Nerv. and Ment. Dis. Publ., Washington, D. C., 1921.

Wiersma, E. D., Untersuchungen u. Erfahrungen über Träume. *Ned. Tijdsch. Geneesk.*, 1934.

Wilder, Joseph, Facts and Figures on Psychotherapy., *J. Clin. Psychopath.*

Wile, I. S., Autosuggested Dreams as a Factor in Therapy. *Am. J. Orthopsych.*, IV, 1934.

Wilhelm, R., and Jung, C. G., *The Secret of the Golden Flower.* Harcourt, Brace & Co., New York.

Willoughby, R. R., An Adaptive Aspect of Dreams. *J. Abn. & Soc. Psychol.*, XXIV, 1929.
—— A Note on a Child's Dream. *J. Genet. Psychol.*, XLII, 1933.

Wilson, G. W., A Prophetic Dream Reported by Abraham Lincoln. *Imago*, 1, 1940.

Winterstein, A. v., *Schlaf u. Traum.* Springer Verl., Berlin, 1932.
—— Swedenborg's relig. Krise u. sein Traumtagebuch. *Imago*, XXII, 1936.

Wisdom, J. C., Three Dreams of Descartes. *Int. J. Psa.*, XXVIII, 1947.

Wittels, F., *Sigmund Freud.* George Allen and Unwin, Ltd., London, 1924.

Weissenberg, S., Ueber das Bettnässen u. d. Rolle d. Träume in seinem Bilde. *Ztschr. f. Kinderh.*, XL, 1925.

Weiszäcker, V. v., Ueber Träume b. sogen. endogener Magersucht. *D. med. Wschr.*, LXIII, 1937.

Welch, Livingston, The Space and Time of Induced Hypnotic Dreams. *J. Psychol.*, I, 1936.

Wenckebach, H. v., Ueber d. Neurosen d. Herzens. *Wien. med. Wschr.,* XVI, 1919.

Wengraf, Fritz, *Psychotherapie des Frauenarztes.* Verl. f. Medizin, Vienna, 1934.

Wertham, Fredric, *Dark Legend.* Duell, Sloan and Pearce, New York, 1941.

Westerfield, J. S., *The Scientific Dream Book.* Brewer, Warren and Putnam, New York, 1932.

Westphal und Katsch, Das neurotische Ulcus duodeni. *Mitteil. aus d. Grenzg. d. Med. u. Chir.,* XXVI, 1913.

Wexberg, Erwin, Zur Verwertung d. Traumdeutung in d. Psychotherapie. *Int. Ztschr. f. Indiv. Psychol.,* I, 1914.

Witty, P. A., and Kopel, D., The Dreams and Wishes of Elementary School Children. *J. Educ. Psychol.,* XXX, 1939.

Wolberg, Lewis R., *Hypnoanalysis.* Grunne & Stratton, New York, 1945.

—— *Medical Hypnosis.* Grunne & Stratton, New York, 1948.

Woodward, J. W., Analysis of a Dream. *Brit. J. Med. Psychol.,* X, 1930.

Woods, Ralph, *The World of Dreams.* Random House, New York, 1947.

Wortis, S. B. and Kennedy, F., Narcolepsy. *Am. J. Psychiat.,* XII, 1933.

Wundt, Wilhelm, *Grundzüge d. physiolog. Psychologie,* Lipsia, 1880.

Wynaendts-Francken, C. J., Träume b. Männern u. Frauen. *Neurol. Zbl.,* XIX, 1907.

Z

Zenker, G., *Traumdeutung u. Traumforschung.* Astra Verl., Lipsia, 1928.

Zude, W., Der Kuckuck in d. Sexualsymbolik. *Ztschr. f. Sexualw.,* IV, 1917.

Zulliger, H., Neue Erscheinungen über Schlaf, Traum, u. Grenzgebiete. *Ztschr. f. angew. Psychol.,* XV, 1919.

—— *Der Traum.* Fränkische Verlagshandlung, Stuttgart, 1926.

INDEX

Identification, 91, 94, 132, 156, 174, 265, 267, 269, 274, 282, 345, 393, 400, 401, 438, 495, 527, 549; contra-sexual, 283; female, 523, 541; masculine, 545
Identity, confusion (loss of), 423
Ideo-grams, 100, 102; -symbolism, 100
Ides of March, 251
Ileus, 326
Illegitimate child, 133, 290
Illicit act, 90, 706, 107, 112
Illness, 50, 166, 241, 406, 478, 563, 604, *see also* Disease; of child, 530; desire for, 403
Image, (Imago), 22, 26, 132, 530; body, 88; father, 85, 132; mother, 52, 132
Imaginary organ, *see* Phantom limb
Immaculate, 281; Conception, 102, 103
Immaturity, 396
Immorality, 48, 576
Immortality, 132
Imp, 504, 505
Impatience, 81, 83
Impersonation, 265
Implanting, 68, 69
Importance, 85, 86, 263
Impotence, 60, 90, 97, 370, 372, 373, 375, 439, 440, 558; will to, 375
Impression (s), visual, 573, 575
Improvement dream (s), 528
Impulse, *see* Instinct; and counter-impulse, 436; tabooed, 245; unconscious, 412; *see also* Force
Impulsions, 467
"In front," 47, 254, 276
Inanimate objects, 136, 149
Incarnation, 166
Incest, 42, 183, 244, 245, 269, 276, 282, 367, 370, 395, 410, 517, 548, 549, 558, 559; barrier, 275, 366; fixation, 120, 265, 275, 279, 548; wish, 274, 280, 369, 375, 419, 517
Incline, steep, 187
Incorporation, 400; *see also* Cannibalism
Incubation, 66
Indecision, neurotic, 134
Independence, capacity for, 396; emotional, 88
Indian, 148; head (s), 141; writing, *see* Writing
Indifference, 270
Indignation, 181
Individual Psychology, 562
Infantile, attitude, 56; experience (s), 299; fantasy, 528; fixation, 53, 275; material, 18; position, 141; pregnancy fantasies, 354; trauma, 284

Infantilism, 298, 537, 540, 541, 548, 560; psychosexual, 272, 425
Infectious disease, 78, 130, 154
Inferiority feeling (s), 20, 44, 82, 157, 160
Infidelity, 45, 49, 112, 172, 269, 290, 421; thoughts of, 245; *see also* Adultery
Influence (s), diabolic, 398; distortive, 154
Inheritance, 191, 196, 204, 290
Inhibition, 42, 106, 133, 160, 182, 300, 375, 378, 397, 543, 568; sexual, 243, 377
Initiative, lack of, 56
Injection, 477; intravenous, 421
Injury, 74, 371, 415, 424, 425, 452; fear of, 77, 415
Inmate, 186
Innocence, 374
Insanity, 52, 410, 424, 434, 436, 443, 520; fear of, 156, 415; picture of, 52; symbol of, 558
Insect (s), 172, 260; *see also* Bug (s)
Insertion, 235
Inside, 254, 404
Insight, 118, 261, 270, 581
Insomnia, 331, 405
Installment, 167
Instinct (s), 160; antimoral, *see* Antimoral; antisocial, *see* Antisocial; of self-preservation, 135
Instrument, 72, 139, 544; choice of, 496
Insult, 440
Insurance, fire, 270
Integration, of ego, 581
Integrity, of ego, 34; of mental function, 110
Intellect, 39, 44; level of in dream, 39; material, 21
Intellectual women, 257
Intelligibility, 121
Intensity of emotion, 41
Intercourse (coitus), 49, 52, 90, 110, 124, 140, 145, 154, 155, 174, 182, 245, 246, 276, 278, 290, 325, 370, 371, 547; symbol (s) of, 375; with animals, 559
Interest in life, 456
Interference, 120
Interpretation, 93, 123, 124, 202, 293, 570, 577, 607; active, 248, 577; biased, 522; by the opposite, 194; economic factor in, 576, 578, 580, 612; final, 567; of paintings, 497; "orthodox," 557; primitivity in, 585, 591, 595, 603, 605; subjective, 521; technique of, 248, 523, 576, 584